STATE OF ILLINOIS
Dwight H. Green, *Governor*
DEPARTMENT OF REGISTRATION AND EDUCATION
Frank G. Thompson, *Director*

NATURAL HISTORY SURVEY DIVISION
Theodore H. Frison, *Chief*

Volume 23	BULLETIN	Article 1

The Caddis Flies, or Trichoptera, of Illinois

HERBERT H. ROSS

Printed by Authority of the State of Illinois

URBANA, ILLINOIS

August 1944

Reprinted by Arrangement

ENTOMOLOGICAL REPRINT SPECIALISTS
P.O. Box 77971, Dockweiler Station
Los Angeles, California 90007

First reprinting, 1972

ISBN: 0-911836-04-7

PREFACE TO THE REPRINT EDITION

The original publication of this report coincided with a great upsurge of interest in the Trichoptera, triggered mainly by the publication of *The Caddis Flies or Trichoptera of New York State* by Cornelius Betten in 1934 and the excellent series of well-illustrated caddisfly papers begun by Martin E. Mosely in 1924. In North America, many students returning to academic life in 1945 after World War II became interested in these fascinating insects and have contributed enormous amounts of information, especially concerning the North American fauna. As a result, literally hundreds of articles have been written since those cited in the *Trichoptera of Illinois,* several hundred new species have been added to the known fauna, great strides have been made in rearing or associating larval and adult forms, and a considerable number of changes have been made in the generic and family placement of a large number of species and genera.

References to these many additional points of information can be found by consulting papers of the following list of authors in *Zoological Record* and *Biological Abstracts.* The list does not include general entomological treatises or ecological and physiological papers, but is relatively complete from the standpoint of literature dealing with systematic material concerning the species of Trichoptera in North America.

Norman H. Anderson
Nathan Banks
Cornelius Betten
Robert L. Blickle
Caroline Brickstein
A. Brindle
Kenneth W. Cummins
Jared J. Davis
Donald G. Denning
J. M. Edington
Sidney W. Edwards
David A. Etnier
Oliver S. Flint, Jr.
Ann Elizabeth Gordon
Hilmy M. Hanna
Norman E. Hickin
William L. Hilsenhoff
D. E. Kimmins
Edwin W. King
John M. Kingsolver
Justin W. Leonard

Fannie A. Leonard
I. M. Levanidova
Donald M. Merkley
John C. Morse
Wallace J. Morse
Martin E. Mosely
Andrew P. Nimmo
Alvah Peterson
Robert W. Pennak
David W. Root
Herbert H. Ross
Fernand Schmid
Fred F. Sherberger
Stamford D. Smith
G. J. Spencer
James E. Sublette
Jan Sykora
John D. Unzicker
J. Bruce Wallace
Glenn B. Wiggins
Toshio Yamamoto

F.C.J. Fischer's *Trichopterorum Catalogus* (1960 +) will prove indispensible as a guide to this order of insects.

Herbert H. Ross
Athens, Georgia
March 1972

FOREWORD

THE caddis flies, comprising the insect order Trichoptera, are one of the most abundant groups of aquatic insects in Illinois. In both lakes and streams they constitute an important factor in the food economy of our Illinois fishes. For this reason, and because the fauna of the order in the entire Middle West was virtually unstudied, a survey of the caddis flies of Illinois was undertaken in 1931.

In the summer of that year Dr. Cornelius Betten of Cornell University, Ithaca, New York, was employed by the Illinois Natural History Survey to initiate the extensive field work and acquaint the systematic entomological staff of the Survey with the characters used in the classification of caddis flies, and, insofar as possible at that time, with the identity of the various species inhabiting the waters of our state. Since 1931, Dr. Herbert H. Ross, Systematic Entomologist of the Survey, has been responsible for the continuation and completion of the project.

This final report is the culmination of 12 years of field work and study. Most of the field work was carried on in conjunction with other Survey projects, especially those on the Miridae and Cicadellidae, and has followed in general plan and organization our other projects summarized in preceding reports. Caddis flies were collected from all parts of the state and at various seasons, both the adult and immature stages being included in the study. As the work progressed it became apparent that a study of the entire North American fauna was necessary to identify properly the Illinois species, and much of the information so obtained has been invaluable in interpreting material from this state.

We are indebted to several institutions and persons outside the Survey for great help in these studies. In addition to Dr. Betten, who has given constant help and cooperation, we are especially indebted to Dr. Nathan Banks of the Museum of Comparative Zoology, Cambridge, Massachusetts, for making available for detailed study and lectotypic designation the types of Banks and Hagen species in that institution. Persons too numerous to mention have contributed a tremendous amount of information, especially distributional data, in the form of material submitted for identification; although these cooperators are not listed, we wish to draw attention to the significant data their efforts have brought to light.

Several members of our staff in the Insect Survey Section also have contributed greatly to the final manuscript. The full illustrations of adult and larval forms, and also of the cases, are with few exceptions the work of Dr. C. O. Mohr, Associate Entomologist and Artist. Dr. Mohr and Miss Kathryn M. Sommerman, Artist and Entomological Assistant, also added many figures used to illustrate the keys and aid in the diagnosis of genitalic characters. Dr. B. D. Burks, Assistant Entomologist, and Dr. Mohr were responsible for much of the field work, especially the rearing work done at field stations. Finally, the manuscript was read and styled by the Survey Technical Editor, Mr. James S. Ayars.

T. H. FRISON, *Chief*
Illinois Natural History Survey

CONTENTS

Page

INTRODUCTION... 1

BIOLOGY.. 1
    Life Cycle.—Eggs and Oviposition.—Larval Habits.—Adult Habits.—Parasitism.

HABITAT PREFERENCE.. 5
    Typical Large Rivers.—Unusual Large Rivers.—Tributary Streams.—Ozark Hills
    Streams.—Unusual Small Streams.—Lake Michigan.—Smaller Glacial Lakes.—
    Dead River Marsh.

DISTRIBUTION... 12
    Ranges Centered in Illinois.—Ranges Projecting Into Illinois.—Summary.

COLLECTING AND PRESERVING.. 15
    Adult Collecting.—Collecting Larvae and Pupae.—Rearing Methods.—Preservation.—
    Clearing Technique.

CLASSIFICATION... 18
    Family Groupings.—Generic and Specific Characters.—Terminology.—Material Stud-
    ied.—Disposition of Material.—Records Outside Illinois.

    KEY TO FAMILIES.. 22
        RHYACOPHILIDAE.. 30
        PHILOPOTAMIDAE.. 44
        PSYCHOMYIIDAE... 51
        HYDROPSYCHIDAE.. 76
        HYDROPTILIDAE... 117
        PHRYGANEIDAE.. 161
        LIMNEPHILIDAE... 176
        MOLANNIDAE.. 205
        BERAEIDAE... 208
        ODONTOCERIDAE.. 209
        CALAMOCERATIDAE.. 209
        LEPTOCERIDAE.. 209
        GOERIDAE.. 256
        LEPIDOSTOMATIDAE... 258
        BRACHYCENTRIDAE.. 260
        SERICOSTOMATIDAE... 266
        HELICOPSYCHIDAE.. 266

EXTRALIMITAL TRICHOPTERA... 268

CHECK LIST OF NEARCTIC TRICHOPTERA................................... 291

LITERATURE CITED... 305

INDEX... 313

Connecting Channels of Fox Lake, Illinois

Caddis flies abound in connecting channels and bays of our northern Illinois lakes, which have added many species to our Illinois fauna. Most of the species found in these lakes do not occur in rivers and streams.

The Caddis Flies, or Trichoptera, of Illinois

HERBERT H. ROSS

INTRODUCTION

THE caddis flies, or Trichoptera, are for the most part medium-sized to small insects resembling moths in general appearance. Their larvae are aquatic in habit and caterpillar-like in appearance. The order Trichoptera contains over 750 species, ranking about seventh among the insect orders. For Illinois, we have now recorded 184 species, the largest known list for any state. It must be remembered, however, that Illinois does not have the same wealth of diverse aquatic situations as some other states, the lists of which will be greatly increased with intensive collecting.

In 1931, when this project was started, the only available listing of Illinois species was contained in Dr. Cornelius Betten's then unpublished manuscript of the Trichoptera of New York. In this, Dr. Betten listed not only published records but also the results of his own collecting in the vicinity of Lake Forest, Illinois. This list enumer-ated 37 species for Illinois. Since that time we have added 146 species to the list, showing how poorly the caddis fly fauna of the entire midwestern and central states was then known.

There is no doubt that additional species will be discovered in the state with continued collecting. For this reason, species known from nearby points have been included in the keys. In addition, as an added precaution to anticipate future discoveries, all genera known to occur in the Great Plains area and eastward have been included in the keys to genera.

Immature stages are known for 120 species treated in this report. There are so many additional species and genera, especially in the western states, for which the immature stages are unknown that the treatment given here will have to be considered as only provisional in certain families for the continent as a whole.

BIOLOGY

The bundle of sticks crawling about in the water, green worms under stones in the stream, swarms of "flies" around the lights along river and lake—these are forms of caddis flies familiar to the general insect collector. They are but a few isolated phenomena, however, in a picture of life histories and interrelationships varied in pattern and interesting in detail.

Life Cycle

In general the life history of caddis flies follows this pattern: The eggs are laid near or in the water, each soon hatching into a worm called a *larva*, which lives in the water and may build a case of sticks, sand grains and other small objects. When full grown, this larva makes a cocoon in which it changes into a transformation stage called a pupa. The adult structures (e.g., wings and genitalia) develop within the pupa. When the adult structures are fully developed within it, the pupa cuts its way out of the cocoon, swims to the surface, crawls out of the water and attaches itself firmly to a stick, stone or other object. The adult then bursts the pupal skin, wriggles and crawls out of it and flies away free. Mating flights follow; a period ensues for

[1]

maturity of the eggs within the body of the female, which then lays the eggs in the water, beginning the cycle again.

Detailed accounts of various phases of caddis fly life histories have been written by many authors and constitute an extensive literature. This was summarized by Betten in 1934 and again, very extensively and completely, by Balduf in 1939. Consequently, only a brief résumé of the biology is given here. In our Illinois studies, we have stressed the taxonomic aspects; so the following information concerning oviposition is drawn almost entirely from the two sources mentioned above.

Eggs and Oviposition

Caddis flies lay many eggs, the number probably ranging from 300 to 1,000 per female. Considerable information is known regarding the manner and place in which these eggs are deposited, but a tremendous amount remains to be observed.

The adult females of Rhyacophilidae, Philopotamidae, Psychomyiidae, Hydropsychidae and Hydroptilidae enter the water and there lay strings of eggs, fig. 1B, on stones or other objects. These strings are usually grouped to form irregular masses, each containing from a few to 800 eggs. The eggs are surrounded by a thin, cement-like matrix.

Females of other caddis fly families usually extrude the eggs and form them into a mass at the end of the abdomen before depositing them. These masses are usually irregular or ovoid, but in some genera are very definite in form, as, for example, the genus *Triaenodes*, in which the eggs are arranged in a flat oval, fig. 1A. In all egg masses the matrix surrounding the egg is gelatinous and swells upon absorbing moisture.

The Leptoceridae, Phryganeidae, Molannidae and Brachycentridae usually attach the egg masses to submerged stones, logs or vegetation. The females of some of these have been observed entering the water or putting the abdomen into it for this purpose. Other families, such as Helicopsychidae, Goeridae, Lepidostomatidae and Sericostomatidae, deposit the egg masses in or near the water, apparently as frequently one way as the other. When not laid in the water, the masses are usually placed near it.

The family Limnephilidae has been the subject of interesting observations and speculations. The egg masses are deposited above the water on plants or stones which protrude above it, on objects along the shore or sometimes on twigs high in trees. In this last case the gelatinous mass may liquefy with rain, and the drops so formed run down the twigs and drop into the water, carrying young larvae with them. Evidence of actual migration to water of young larvae hatched from egg masses far from the water's edge has not been demonstrated. Rain probably plays an important part in this phenomenon.

Larval Habits

Mode of Living.—Possibly the most interesting, and certainly the most startling, aspect of caddis fly biologies is the construction, by many species, of houses in which they live. Not all species have these houses, and many of the houses are of different types. Much has been written regarding possible classifications of these habits, including the formulation of complex systems and explanations. I believe, however, that the following brief synopsis will present most of the pertinent data.

Free-Living Forms.—The larvae of the genus *Rhyacophila* are completely free living, having no case or shelter; they lay a thread trail and have many modifications for free life in flowing water, including widely spaced, strong legs and large, strong anal hooks, fig. 133. For pupation they form a stone case or cocoon.

Also free living are the early instars of many Hydroptilidae (see p. 160).

Net-Spinning Forms.—Larvae of Hydropsychidae, Philopotamidae and Psychomy-

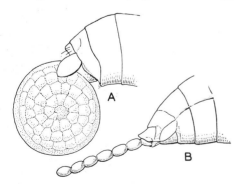

Fig. 1.—Eggs of caddis flies. *A, Triaenodes tarda; B, Cyrnellus marginalis.*

iidae spin a fixed abode which is fastened to plants or other supports in the water, sometimes in still water but more frequently in running water. Three common types of these structures are found, all of them spun from silk and forming some sort of net; when taken out of water they collapse into a shapeless string. There is always an escape exit at the end of the tube.

1.—Finger nets, fig. 2. These are long, narrow pockets of fine mesh, with the front end anchored upstream, the remainder trailing behind with the current. They are built by the Philopotamidae.

2.—Trumpet nets, fig. 3. In this type the opening of the net is funnel shaped, and the end is fastened in such a way that the water movement distends the net into a trumpet-shaped structure. This type of net is used extensively by the Psychomyiidae.

3.—Hydropsychid net, fig. 4. Peculiar to the family Hydropsychidae is the habit of erecting a net directly in front of a tubelike

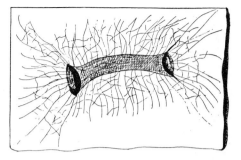

Fig. 3.—Trumpet net of *Polycentropus* sp. (After Noyes.)

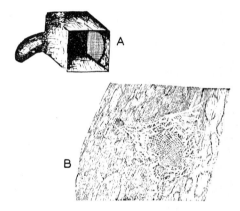

Fig. 2.—Finger nets of *Chimarra aterrima*. (After Noyes.)

Fig. 4.—Nets of *Hydropsyche*. *A*, diagrammatic figure of house; at the left is the tube in which the larva lives; in front of it is a vestibule having a catching surface with a fine mesh in the side wall; near this net is the opening of the larval tube. (After Wesenberg-Lund.) *B*, net spun over a crevice of a submerged stick which houses the larva. (After Comstock.)

retreat concealed in a crevice or camouflaged by bits of wood, leaves or similar material. These nets may be erected between two supports in the open, as in the case of *Potamyia*, or the net may be constructed as one side of an antechamber, as in the case of many species of *Hydropsyche*, fig. 4.

In all these types the caddis fly larva cleans the food and debris off the net, ingesting anything edible swept into it by the current. Normally the larva spends most of its time with its head near the net ready to pounce on any prey. When disturbed, it backs out of the net or retreats with great agility. The flexible body structure enables the larva to move backward rapidly, but it can move forward only slowly.

Tube-Making Forms.—Some psychomyiid larvae, notably of the genus *Phylocentropus*, burrow into sand at the bottom of streams, cementing the walls of the burrow into a fairly rigid structure which may be dug out intact. The mechanics of food gathering in this group are not well understood.

In both the net-spinning and tube-making forms, pupation takes place in the end of the tube or retreat. The larva constructs a cocoon of leaf fragments, stones or whatever other material is available, lining it with silk. The pupa is formed here.

Saddle-Case Makers.—Larvae of the rhyacophilid subfamily Glossosomatinae make a portable case which consists of an oval top made of stones and a ventral strap made of the same material, fig. 136. The larva proceeds with its head and legs projecting down in front of the strap and the anal hooks projecting down at the back of the strap. For pupation, the strap is cut away and the oval dome is cemented to a support, the pupa being formed in the stone cell thus made.

Purse-Case Makers.—Following exactly the same principle as the above are many cases of the Hydroptilidae. In general appearance they resemble a purse, fig. 465. The larva occupies the case with the head and legs projecting out of a slit in the front margin while the anal hooks project out of a slit in the posterior margin. For pupation, however, the case is cemented along one side to a support and the slits are cemented shut to form the pupal chamber. Not all Hydroptilidae have cases of this type, some of them having true cases (see p. 160).

Case Makers.—All caddis fly larvae except those listed above make portable cases which the larvae drag with them in their daily movements. These cases are usually made of pieces of leaves, bits of twigs, sand grains or stones which are cemented or tied together with silk. Rarely the case is made entirely of silk. Case construction varies a great deal from one group to another, from one species to another within the same genus, and frequently within the same species. In general, cases subject to greatest stream current are the most solidly constructed, whereas those in small ponds where there is scarcely any water movement are the most loosely constructed.

For pupation the case is anchored to a support and a top added to the case; the pupa is formed inside this shelter and no additional cocoon is made.

Feeding Habits.—Most caddis fly larvae are practically omnivorous, eating whatever comes to hand. Such forms as the Hydropsychidae and Limnephilidae eat a preponderance of plankton, sessile diatom growths and other small organisms, but if opportunity affords they will eat insect larvae and often each other. When their populations become crowded, caddis fly larvae are cannibalistic to a high degree.

Certain genera are primarily predaceous, the most notable ones being *Rhyacophila* and *Oecetis*. Examination of stomach contents shows that both of these are voracious eaters; we have found 40 to 60 Chironomidae larvae in single individuals of *Rhyacophila*, the alimentary tract being crowded with these midge larvae from one end to the other. In these two genera the mandibles are long and narrow, apparently fitted for grasping prey of this type. Such mandibles do not occur in phytophagous forms which may be cannibalistic.

The order Trichoptera as a whole, however, may be characterized as one in which the minute aquatic life is assimilated and converted to units of larger size which are in turn usable by a variety of larger organisms.

Respiration.—This function in the Trichoptera is accomplished by cutaneous exchange or by gills. It varies greatly within families and genera. Usually the larvae of greater size have the larger or more abundant gills, and the small larvae have no gills at all. This is by no means a general rule throughout the order. In those species having gills, gill pattern and type is almost uniform throughout the entire period of larval growth, from the youngest to the full-grown stage.

Adult Habits

Caddis flies include many strong fliers, such as *Macronemum*, but they also include other genera that fly only short distances. A few species have brachypterous or apterous females which cannot fly but which run with great agility.

In daytime most of the caddis flies rest in concealed crevices or on foliage in moist, shaded glens bordering streams. At dusk the adults fly quite freely, often skimming back and forth across a body of water just above the surface. These flights are probably mating flights, since males are frequently involved; observations indicate that these flights are not correlated directly with oviposition.

The adults have mouthparts that are adapted for the ingestion of liquid foods and have no hard grinding parts for mastication of hard foods. In some families such as the Phryganeidae the end of the labium forms a large, terminal membranous lobe similar in general appearance to the proboscis of higher Diptera. Records indicate that in spite of having no other means of getting food, adults of many species normally live 1 or 2 months, and probably in all species nearly a month.

Oviposition is discussed in connection with the eggs.

Parasitism

The only record of parasites of caddis flies in North America was reported by Mickel & Milliron (1939). They reared a hymenopterous parasite, *Hemiteles biannulatus* Gravenhorst, from cases of *Limnephilus indivisus* from Itasca Park, Minnesota. In Europe the hymenopterous parasite *Agriotypus* has been reared from caddis fly larvae.

HABITAT PREFERENCE

Over most of Illinois, caddis fly habitats are streams and rivers with medium to slow current, with fairly warm water and frequently with a heavy silt deposit. This statement applies not only to the main water arteries but also to most of the small creeks and branches which feed them. These streams run through the highly developed agricultural area which includes most of the state. Markedly different types of streams are either restricted to small areas such as the Ozark Hills, or very locally distributed, as for example, the spring-fed brooks at Elgin.

In Illinois, natural lakes are restricted to the northeastern corner of the state and are all of glacial origin. Here are found a few typical lake species but they do not form a large proportion of our caddis fly fauna. Artificial lakes are common over most of the state but have few caddis flies.

Typical Large Rivers

The Mississippi, Illinois and Wabash are in some respects typical not only of our large rivers but also of the more sluggish lower portions of smaller ones such as the Fox and Kaskaskia. These have enormous numbers of the net-spinning caddis flies, especially *Potamyia flava, Cheumatopsyche campyla* and *Hydropsyche orris, bidens* and *simulans.* The case-making species are confined almost entirely to the Leptoceridae, and those taken in abundance include *Oecetis inconspicua* and *avara, Athripsodes cancellatus* and *transversus,* and *Leptocella candida, exquisita* and *diarina.* Abundant web-spinning forms include *Neureclipsis crepuscularis* and *Cyrnellus marginalis.*

In these situations there are generally few or no very early season species. Most of the species occur in the adult stage throughout the late spring and summer months with continuous generations.

Unusual Large Rivers

Kankakee River.—Of all the rivers in Illinois, the Kankakee, fig. 5, is the most unusual from the standpoint of the caddis fly fauna. Here we have taken 12 species found nowhere else in the state. Several other species are common here but rarities

Fig. 5.—Kankakee River at Wilmington, Illinois. This is one of three rapids on the lower portion of this river, in all of which caddis flies of unusual interest are found.

in other localities. The stream originates in the swamps and lakes of northern and western Indiana, flows through the lower portion of the northeastern eighth of Illinois and empties into the Illinois River a few miles west of Joliet. The water is always colder than in our other rivers, almost always clear and in Illinois passes over three swift rapids. The first rapids are at Momence and are caused by a limestone outcrop over which the river flows; below the outcrop the river gradually slows and in this portion are luxurious beds of eel grass which extend almost the full width of the river bottom. The second rapids are at Kankakee, extending from the foot of a power dam about one-third of a mile downstream; here the river is wider and shallower, and the bottom more gravelly, than at Momence. The third rapids are at Wilmington, also below a power dam, but nearly a mile long; here the bottom has the swiftest portion strewn with boulders and the steepest gradient of all three rapids.

There is a remarkable difference in the taxonomic composition of the caddis flies found in each rapids. Certain species unique to the river are common to all three rapids, but others may be very abundant at one and rare or entirely lacking in the other two. For instance, *Brachycentrus numerosus* and *lateralis* and *Micrasema rusticum* are all very abundant at Momence but have never been taken at Kankakee or Wilmington. *Hydropsyche cuanis* occurs in countless swarms at Wilmington but is a rarity at the other two rapids. *Hydropsyche aerata* is very common at Kankakee but is rare at the other two. *Hydroptila albicornis* is common to all three rapids but is found nowhere else in Illinois. There is no doubt that the physiological attributes of the water are quite different at the three points described, and these differences are likely due to the effect of the power dams and the sewage affluent which goes into the river below each city.

Rock River.—This river, running diagonally across the northwestern eighth of the state, is essentially a clear, swift, cold-water stream with a rock or gravel bottom. In the early 1900's it was an unusually rich stream from the standpoint of large variety and numbers of fish, but affluent from factories, city sewage and silt-laden drainage ditches have altered the stream considerably. The caddis flies found there today, however, show distinctive features in contrast to those of other streams. This is the only river in which *Hydropsyche bifida* occurs in large numbers; it is one of the few streams in which we have taken *Athripsodes mentieus*, *Chimarra obscura* and *Hydropsyche valanis*; and it is the only stream where we have taken the northern *Limnephilus moestus*.

Tributary Streams

Collecting in the smaller rivers and creeks soon shows that as the size of the stream decreases the potentialities for a varied fauna increase. The species mentioned as abundant in the large rivers are found also in these smaller streams but in smaller numbers; conversely, we find here in numbers species which are usually rare in river collections. These include, among the net- and web-spinning groups, *Cheumatopsyche analis*, *oxa* and *aphanta*, *Hydropsyche bronta* and *arinale*, *Nyctiophylax vestitus* and *Polycentropus cinereus*. The case makers are represented by a great variety of the "micros," or Hydroptilidae, such Limnephilidae as *Pycnopsyche* and *Caborius*, and a great variety of Leptoceridae, especially species of *Athripsodes*, *Triaenodes* and *Oecetis*.

Most of these small streams, as stated above, are similar in general characteristics to the large rivers. They are sluggish, silt laden for much of the year and have fairly warm water. Most of the species have continuous generations from late spring to early autumn and few of them are early seasonal forms. The chief exceptions to this are the Limnephilidae mentioned above, which aestivate during the summer and transform only in autumn, and our only common species of Rhyacophilidae, *Rhyacophila lobifera*, which has only one generation, maturing early in spring.

Ozark Hills Streams

In the southern tip of Illinois there is a small range of hills reaching an elevation of about a thousand feet. These are one of the eastern remnants of the Ozark Mountains. In these hills are numerous streams quite different from the usual type found in the northern part of the state. They have rocky beds, and in winter and spring they are swift and clear. Green moss grows in the streams, and they are muddied only temporarily after rain. The banks are wooded with dense stands of trees which form a canopy over the water when the leaves are out. In early spring, beginning in March, these streams abound in a variety of caddis flies; case makers crawl over the rocks, and others crawl in the moss or under the stones.

The taxonomic composition of all these Ozark streams is virtually the same and it is remarkably distinct from all other streams in the state. Species confined to this area include *Rhyacophila fenestra, Agapetus illini, Dolophilus shawnee* and a number of Hydroptilidae, among them *Ochrotrichia shawnee, eliaga, anisca* and *unio, Hydroptila virgata, vala* and *amoena* and *Neotrichia riegeli* and *collata*. Species of *Hydropsyche, Cheumatopsyche* and other genera which are common in other streams of the state are a rarity here.

Of unusual interest in this area are four other caddis flies. *Chimarra feria* is very common in these streams but has been taken nowhere else in the state; *C. obscura*, which we find in several other parts of Illinois, has not been taken in our recent collecting in the Ozark Hills but was apparently fairly common in them around 1900, judging by collections made at that time by C. A. Hart. Taken at the same time and place by Hart were several collections of a species of *Athripsodes* believed to be *flavus* (see p. 228); this species has not been taken in the area in our recent survey. The fourth species is *Neophylax autumnus*. These limnephilid larvae make a hard stone case and are exceedingly common in most of the Ozarkian streams. They occur sparingly in other parts of the state.

Early in summer these streams tend to dry up, often going beyond even a pool stage to the point at which no water can be seen along the entire course of the stream. This dry period frequently extends into November and December before water again flows; yet by spring the life in the water is invariably present in great abundance. The manner in which many of the caddis flies survive through this dry period is unknown. Examination of the dry bed has given information on three species which pass through this period in the larval or pupal stage; it is likely that some of the others pass it in the egg stage.

Where the stream bed is shaded and the ground contour provides some subsurface drainage into it, stones and shelflike outcrops may remain damp underneath indefinitely. In these damp situations we found large numbers of *Neophylax autumnus* larvae aestivating; later in the autumn while the stream was still dry these larvae transformed to pupae, and we watched actual emergence of adults from these nearly dry cases. Digging a few inches into the stream bed, we discovered active larvae of *Chimarra feria* and a healthy pupa of *Rhyacophila glaberrima* under stones at a level where stones and sand were moist. In no case did we find signs of active forms along portions of the stream bed which were not shaded.

Unusual Small Streams

Scattered around the state are a number of streams quite different in character and fauna from the usual stream running through most of the agricultural land. Ex-

Fig. 6.—Brook in Botanical Gardens at Elgin, Illinois. This and three parallel sister brooks are fed by seepage and are cold and clear throughout the year. Here live several northern caddis flies found nowhere else in the state.

cept for those in the Ozark Hills, these streams are isolated and local, probably mere relics of habitat types which may have been extensive and numerous before the forests were cleared and the swamps drained in advance of the plow. Some of the caddis fly species occurring in these relic areas are a rarity in this entire Central States area but fairly common in streams of some of the northeastern states. These individual localities have unusual species, many of them not the same as those found in similar Illinois localities. In Indiana and southern Michigan this same type of relic area is found.

Elgin.—Just north of the city of Elgin are the unique Botanical Gardens situated along the low, east bluff of the Fox River. The park is an undisturbed remnant of the original woods of the region and contains a great variety of interesting herbs, shrubs and trees. Out of the sides and base of the bluff run many seepage rivulets which merge to form five small brooks, each from 1 to 3 feet wide and a few inches deep, with a stony bottom and a fairly rapid flow, fig. 6. The water is cold and clear at all times. In all of these streams the caddis flies are extremely numerous, their cases literally paving the bottom of the streams. Here we have taken seven species found nowhere else in the state: *Glossosoma intermedium, Dolophilus moestus, Rhyacophila vibox, Hesperophylax designatus, Molanna tryphena, Limnephilus rhombicus* and *Drusinus uniformis.* The first four are common, especially the *Glossosoma* and *Hesperophylax,* the cases of which may be found by the thousands in these streams.

Not only are these species peculiar to these streams, but other species found in neighboring streams are practically absent. Other species which occur include chiefly *Lepidostoma liba* and *Diplectrona modesta,* both found only locally elsewhere in Illinois. These conditions mark this Elgin group as the most unusual and interesting of our relic streams.

Somewhat similar in nature are two other spring-fed brooks near the Botanical Gardens. In one we discovered a large colony of *Hydropsyche slossonae* and in the other a colony of *Chimarra aterrima,* both rare and local in the state.

Split Rock Brook at Utica.—This small stream originates, fig. 7, in a spring near the head of a short, wooded ravine and flows along a channel 2 or 3 feet wide through

a rich growth of herbs and shrubs. The water is clear and cold and uniform in volume except after hard rains.

This stream has two distinct parts to its course. In the upper, shaded portion we have taken *Diplectrona modesta,* our only Illinois record of *Polycentropus pentus* and great numbers of the case maker *Neophylax*

Fig. 7.—Brook at Split Rock, near Utica, Illinois. Another spring-fed stream which is clear and cold throughout the year. Unusual species found here include *Polycentropus pentus* and *Ochrotrichia riesi* and *spinosa.* (Photo by Donald T. Ries.)

autumnus. It was in this locality that we found individuals of this last species emerging as adults in February and early spring, the only such record for the entire genus (see p. 203).

In the lower portion, which flows through a cleared area along the railroad right-of-way, we found *Ochrotrichia riesi* and *spinosa,* to give us the only Illinois records of these species. In this portion of the stream the species mentioned in the preceding paragraph were extremely scarce.

Apple River Canyon State Park.—The Apple River flows out of southern Wisconsin and cuts across the extreme northwestern corner of Illinois. Above and below Apple River Canyon State Park the river is sluggish, silty and nearly devoid of caddis flies except for some of the tolerant species, such as *Oecetis inconspicua.* Through the park, however, it traverses a few miles of rocky land, and has here a rock bottom, faster current, shaded banks and practically clear water, fig. 8. In this stretch we have taken several species rare in the state, such as *Psychomyia flavida*, *Hydropsyche bronta* and *Neotrichia okopa*.

Of greatest interest at the park is a very swift point in the river where the "leech-egg" cases of the hydroptilid *Leucotrichia pictipes* are found. These are attached at the sides of 30- to 50-pound boulders in the very center of the current. This is the only place in the state where this species has been found, and our only other nearby records are considerably to the north, in Wisconsin and Michigan.

Cave Streams.—There are few caves in the state which discharge a permanent flow of water, and most of these have few or no caddis flies of interest in the resultant stream. There are two, however, which produce cold, permanent streams with interesting species: (1) At Union Spring, near Alto Pass, is a small cave out of which flows a stream about a foot wide; in the few feet from the cave to the bottom of the hill a colony of larvae belonging to *Hydropsychid Genus A* occurs under the stones (see p. 83). (2) Near Quincy is a cave from which flows a small stream in which

there is a large colony of *Lepidostoma liba*; while we have found the species in two other small, spring-fed streams in the state, this is the only locality in which the species is numerous.

Seepage Area.—At Matanzas Lake, near Havana, there is a sharp valley cut through the sand ridges by a small stream. At the side of this little valley, right at the base of the hill, we found a seepage area a few feet in diameter and not as deep as the thickness of a caddis fly case. Cases of *Frenesia missa* literally covered this small area, many of the larvae crawling up on the leaves until the case was almost completely out of the water.

In the summer of 1941 this little spring apparently dried up, for no cases were found in it in October, the month in which pupation occurs. A few scattered individuals were found in the adjacent stream, and these likely represent a small reservoir of population for the rehabilitation of the seepage areas after drought conditions.

Other Peculiar Streams.—There are several other streams which have caddis

Fig. 8.—Apple River in Apple River Canyon State Park, Illinois. Outside the park this stream is sluggish, muddy and has little aquatic life. The rapids inside the park, however, afford a varied caddis fly fauna, including our only record of *Leucotrichia pictipes*. (Photo by Donald T. Ries.)

flies unusual for Illinois but which differ only slightly in general characteristics from average streams in the vicinity. Prominent among these is Quiver Creek, a fairly clear, cold, rapid stream flowing through the sand region just north of Havana, where

cies. The larvae of these probably occur on stones in the lake beyond the wading line.

Unique to our state fauna was a colony of *Hydropsyche recurvata*, found at the south edge of Evanston. The larvae were

Fig. 9.—Lake Michigan, at Zion, Illinois. Collecting within wading distance of shore nets only scattered caddis fly records. Presumably more of the species live at a depth beyond the grinding action of the undertow. Several species of Leptoceridae and *Hydropsyche recurvata* have been taken in Illinois only in or along Lake Michigan.

we have taken a variety of interesting species, the collection here including our only record of *Lype diversa*; also the Salt Fork and Middle Fork rivers, near Oakwood and Danville, fairly large streams with many riffles, rocky rapids and less silt than usual in Illinois, streams in which rare species such as *Helicopsyche borealis, Hydropsyche frisoni* and *cheilonis*, and many Hydroptilidae occur.

Lake Michigan

Our information concerning Lake Michigan, fig. 9, is based chiefly on light collections along the shore. We have made shore collections along the entire Illinois beach but have been unable to take more than scattered larvae in most places.

Several species of the case-making genus *Athripsodes* have been taken at lights along the shore of the lake; these include *dilutus, erullus* and *resurgens*, the last two constituting our only Illinois records of the spe-

fairly common on the larger stones in 3 to 4 feet of water. This species is northern in distribution and usually lives in rivers. Apparently in this situation the wave action and coldness of water were a sufficient substitute for its usual conditions.

Smaller Glacial Lakes

In a few counties in the northeastern corner of Illinois are a large number of glacial lakes, fig. 10, similar in general character to the northern lakes of Wisconsin, Michigan and Minnesota. They vary in depth, the shallower ones having extensive marsh areas; their size varies from a few to several hundred acres. The water is clear, and the bottom is clean stones, a mass of reed and sedge roots, or a bed of peaty organic matter. Large beds of aquatic plants abound in the little bays or the short, sluggish connecting waterways; the predominant plants are *Elodea, Ceratophyllum, Utricularia* and *Potamogeton*.

These lakes have a caddis fly fauna quite different from that of the river systems. Conspicuous to a high degree are the Leptoceridae, whose cases may be found under almost every stone and on every weed. The Hydroptilidae, Molannidae and Psychomyiidae are the only other families represented in numbers; the Limnephilidae and Phryganeidae are almost entirely confined to marsh situations.

The commoner Leptoceridae include *Oecetis inconspicua, cinerascens, immobilis* and *osteni, Triaenodes tarda* and *injusta, Leptocella albida* and *exquisita, Leptocerus americanus, Athripsodes dilutus* and *tarsipunctatus* and *Mystacides longicornis* and *sepulchralis.* Some of these, such as *Oecetis osteni, Mystacides longicornis* and *Leptocella albida,* are confined to lakes; most of the others may be found in rivers, artificial ponds or canals. The combination of all these together, however, along with the absence of Hydropsychidae and other stream dwellers, is a phenomenon unique to these lakes.

The curious case of *Molanna uniophila* (see p. 206) occurs on sand bars in these lakes; the minute cases of *Orthotrichia* and *Oxyethira* abound on the stones and plant stems; and the transparent, small, green cases of *Leptocerus americanus* cluster in the tips of the *Ceratophyllum.*

Dead River Marsh

At Zion, just north of Waukegan, there is a large marsh area through the center of which runs the Dead River, fig. 11, so named because Lake Michigan, by backing up into it, prevents its flow except at times of heavy rain. This ribbon-like river is therefore more like a marshy lake than a stream; its banks are crowded with extensive beds of cyperaceous growth and its channel is choked with mats of *Ceratophyllum* and *Polygonum.*

Living in this mass of plant stems is one of the most extraordinary communities of caddis flies in Illinois. Large, case-building Phryganeidae are common, including *Phryganea cinerea* and *sayi, Banksiola selina, Fabria inornata* and *Agrypnia vestita;* the

Fig. 10.—Grass Lake near Fox Lake, Illinois. Certain of the lake species, in particular the Leptoceridae, are found in the lake proper rather than in the connecting channels.

Fig. 11.—Dead River, in Dunes Park near Zion, Illinois.   This river is more marsh than stream.   It is the only situation in the state in which large numbers of both individuals and species of the large Phryganeidae have been found.

leptocerid *Triaenodes aba* is common; *Polycentropus interruptus* is also common. Except for *Phryganea sayi*, these are known only from similar nearby situations. Restricted in Illinois to this locality are *Fabria inornata*, *Triaenodes baris* and *Polycentropus remotus*.

A somewhat similar marsh area is located along the edges of the Des Plaines River near Rosecrans, just a few miles south of the Wisconsin line. In this area we have taken *Triaenodes aba* in considerable numbers, but only a few of the other species common in the Dead River.

DISTRIBUTION

In the preceding pages an analysis is given of the manner in which the various species of Illinois caddis flies are distributed in relation to habitats within the state. To understand the faunal characteristics, however, this should be correlated with the geographic distribution of the species in relation to the entire continent.

We have found that the geographic distribution of caddis fly species within Illinois may give an erroneous impression of their continental distribution. For instance, the fact that *Cheumatopsyche lasia* occurs principally in the central and northern parts of Illinois might indicate that the species is primarily northern; such is not the case, most of the records for the species being southwest of Illinois, and a few northwest, with no records yet known from northeast of Illinois, fig. 12. Similarly our Illinois records of *Phylocentropus placidus* are from

the extreme southern portion of the state, whereas the main range of the species is to the northeast.

These circumstances have led to a study of the continental range of as many species as possible. The results are of considerable interest because of the scarcity of caddis fly records in past literature and because of the demonstration that many caddis flies have an extensive range. Since many species are known from few records, the following remarks apply to the better known. It is difficult to determine accurately the center of distribution of any caddis fly species on the bases of existing records, because in many areas in North America collecting for this order has been very inadequate. The present analysis attempts to give a picture gleaned from available records.

The Illinois species may be divided roughly into two general categories. The first

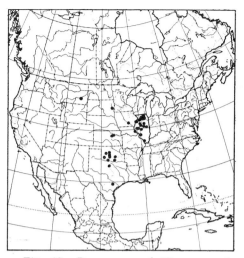

Fig. 12.—Range map of *Cheumatopsyche lasia.*

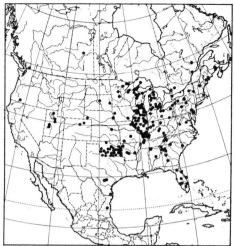

Fig. 13.—Range map of *Oecetis inconspicua,* the commonest North American caddis fly.

includes those whose range centers roughly in or near Illinois; the second those touching Illinois on the outskirts of their range.

Ranges Centered in Illinois

Widespread Species.—Some of the common Illinois species of caddis flies have a range which occupies almost the entire continent. Examples include *Oecetis inconspicua*, fig. 13, and *avara, Cheumatopsyche*

campyla and *analis* and *Hydroptila hamata.* The first four of these are exceedingly common in the central and eastern states and occur in scattered collections westward to the Pacific Coast.

Central States Species.—Conspicuous examples of this set are some of the caddis flies inhabiting the large rivers typical of this part of the country. *Hydropsyche simulans* and *orris* are two such species; they have overlapping ranges, fig. 14, and the

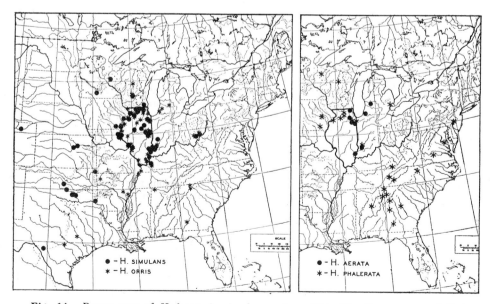

Fig. 14.—Range map of *Hydropsyche simulans* and *orris.*

Fig. 15.—Range map of *Hydropsyche aerata* and *phalerata.*

area of overlap coincides very closely with the Corn Belt. Another type of range in this class is illustrated by *Hydropsyche aerata*, which appears to have a very restricted range, fig. 15. Among the Hydroptilidae are several species which, on the basis of present records, appear to be restricted to the Corn Belt and its immediate vicinity; these include *Hydroptila angusta, grandiosa* and *ajax* and *Neotrichia falca*.

Ranges Projecting Into Illinois

Northern-Northeastern Species. — Of the caddis flies having a range that just touches Illinois, or nearly touches this state, the most numerous are northern and northeastern species. Examples include representatives of many families: *Hydropsyche slossonae* and *recurvata*, fig. 16, *Chimarra aterrima*, fig. 17, *Oecetis osteni, Limnephilus moestus, rhombicus* and *argenteus*, and many others. These include both lake and stream species. Each of these species has a slightly different range, some extending south just into Illinois, others deeper into the state and still others not reaching it at all. A number of these species, such as *Mystacides longicornis* and *Neureclipsis bimaculatus*, are Holarctic and many more will undoubtedly prove to range extensively northwestward through the northern coniferous for-

est. This group, as would be expected, embraces a large number of species which have been found in Illinois in isolated and local colonies and an additional number which have been taken in southern Wisconsin and Michigan but not yet in Illinois.

Northeastern-Ozark Species.—One of the most surprising discoveries in this investigation was the unexpected number of species common to both the northeastern states and the Ozark series of mountains, including various areas in Oklahoma and, to some extent, the "cross-timbers" which extend diagonally across Texas. Most of the species exhibiting this type of range occur in Illinois, especially along its northern, eastern and southern margins. Present collections indicate that the Illinois Ozarks are one of the few existing connecting links between the northeastern and southwestern parts of the range. This is well shown in the case of *Chimarra obscura*, fig. 18.

Some species, such as *Cheumatopsyche sordida*, have a range of the same type but highly discontinuous, so that the Ozark records are at a great distance from any others known at present.

Ozark Species.—A few caddis flies occur only in the Ozarks, extending throughout their course from Illinois to Oklahoma and into the neighboring hills and ranges. Examples include *Agapetus illini, Dolophilus*

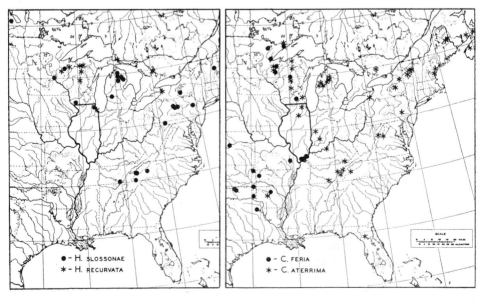

Fig. 16.—Range map of *Hydropsyche slossonae* and *recurvata.*

Fig. 17.—Range map of *Chimarra aterrima* and *feria.*

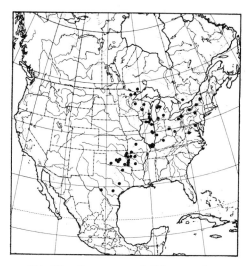

Fig. 18.—Range map of *Chimarra obscura.*

shawnee and *Ochrotrichia anisca.* These species and others of similar faunistic habits occur in the Ozark Hills of southern Illinois.

Southwestern Species.—Another group of Illinois caddis flies is southern or southwestern in general distribution. This includes such forms as *Cheumatopsyche lasia,* fig. 12, and *Chimarra feria,* fig. 17. The range of each centers around Oklahoma, with extensions eastward to Illinois and as far northward as Montana or Minnesota. It is interesting to note that the former extends throughout the northern portion of Illinois; the latter has been found in Illinois only in the Ozark Hills of the southern part of the state.

Certain other southern or southwestern species have a range extending into southern Mexico. This is true especially of many Hydroptilidae, of which *Mayatrichia ayama* ranges from southern Mexico to New York, following closely the pattern of *Chimarra obscura* in fig. 18.

Southeastern Species.—A few members of the Illinois fauna have been collected in other states only to the south and east. This group includes *Hydropsyche incommoda, Cheumatopsyche burksi* and *Hydropsychid Genus A,* extending from Illinois to Georgia or Florida. A small number of species not yet taken in Illinois are known to range from Georgia to Indiana; these include *Macronemum transversum* and *Hydropsyche depravata,* which have essentially the same range as the three just mentioned. *Hydropsyche phalerata* has a range which centers in the southeast but differs from the above examples by extending considerably north of Illinois, fig. 15.

Summary

A review of the above data shows that in North America the caddis flies form several fairly distinct geographic groups. One of these, embracing the states of the Corn Belt, centers roughly in Illinois. Throughout the northern and northeastern states is one large group of species; to the southwest, extending through the Ozarks into Mexico, is a second large group; and to the southeast is a third smaller group. All three of these contain fairly distinctive species that range into Illinois, which is approximately at the meeting point of these "avenues" of distribution. This axial position has been demonstrated with several other groups of insects studied for the state, including the Miridae, Orthoptera and Plecoptera, although in each the details are different.

COLLECTING AND PRESERVING

Caddis flies have such diverse habits and habitat preferences that several kinds of collecting are necessary to get representative samples from a given area. In most cases these same methods are equally effective with other aquatic groups, including stoneflies, mayflies and midges. The adults are aerial and the larvae aquatic; further, it is more the rule than the exception that at any one place the adults in the air and the larvae in the stream belong to different sets of species. Collecting for one phase must not be stressed to the exclusion of the other.

With one exception, caddis flies, both immature stages and adults, should be collected in liquid, preferably 80 per cent grain alcohol. The exception is adults of the genus *Leptocella,* readily distinguished in the field by a long, narrow shape, extremely long antennae and white ground color (see p. 213). In this genus it is necessary for specific diagnosis to use color patterns formed by the delicate wing hairs, which rub off with remarkable ease. Specimens of this genus should be killed in a cyanide or other dry bottle, a few at a time, and carefully handled to avoid rubbing in transit and in pinning.

Adult Collecting

Adults of most caddis flies come to lights readily on warm nights having neither wind nor a bright moon. Collecting at lights is thus a profitable source of material. In towns, illuminated store windows and signs attract many of these insects and provide convenient collecting points.

Vapor Glow-Tubes.—Adult Trichoptera are attracted very strongly to blue light and hence are to be found most abundantly around blue "neon" lights, or glow-tubes. Fortunately for the entomologist many of these blue lights can be found in towns and these will serve as good concentration points for caddis flies. At points where such lights are not available we have had very good success with a portable mercury glow-tube which emits a strong blue light and is very attractive to Trichoptera and many other insects. This is described in detail by Burks, Ross & Frison (1938).

Automobile Headlights.—Another type of night collecting we have found effective at points away from towns is as follows. Drive an automobile to a spot overlooking a stream or lake and turn on the bright lights. Into a shallow pan, such as a pie pan, pour enough alcohol to cover the bottom with from one-eighth to one-fourth inch of liquid. Hold the pan directly under a headlight. If aquatic insects are on the wing, they will come to the light and eventually drop into the liquid, which traps them. With a small piece of wet cardboard, scrape the entire insect contents of the pan into a small bottle of alcohol, which should then be labeled, location, name of collector and place being given.

If few insects fly to the car lights, it is convenient to dispense with the pan. In this case the caddis flies may be picked off the light easily by dipping an index finger in alcohol, "scooping up" the insect rapidly but gently on the wet surface and then dipping it in the bottle. An aspirator, or sucker, also can be used with success.

Sweeping.—For daylight collecting, sweeping often proves effective. Resting places differ widely with the species, but most caddis flies prefer shaded, humid places. For these, sweep vegetation overhanging the water, whether it is herbage nearly trailing

in the water or boughs which hang above it. I have noticed that many times the flies seem to prefer (for resting places) coniferous trees near the stream, and heavy beating of these is usually profitable. Sometimes the flies are numerous in bark crevices of large tree trunks along stream banks; here they are extremely difficult to detect, for they mimic bark to a remarkable degree when their wings are folded. Be sure to have your net ready when you examine a tree trunk, because the flies dodge and fly with surprising speed when alarmed.

Bridges.—One of the favorite resting places of adult Trichoptera is the shaded, damp, underside of a concrete bridge. When other collecting fails it is sometimes possible to pick up from a few to many caddis flies resting under a highway bridge. Here again the flies are wary, and must be approached with caution and a ready net.

Along the Water's Edge.—Frequently the adults may be captured on stones, sticks and vegetation in the water. This is true especially of the Rhyacophilidae. A method which sometimes gives good results is to press floating vegetation, such as water cress, until it is slightly submerged. Any adults resting in this foliage will swim to the surface in a moment or two.

Collecting Larvae and Pupae

All Nearctic caddis flies are aquatic in the developmental stages. For this reason almost any water habitat has possibilities for the collection of larvae and pupae. These should be preserved in liquid, preferably 80 per cent grain alcohol, as with the adults. If vials are filled with larvae, the liquid should be changed a few hours after collection.

The easiest way to start a search for these immature stages is to turn over stones and logs in riffles and rapids; if present, larvae and cases may be found without difficulty in these situations. Handfuls of drift, weeds from the stream or river bottom, and debris may be laid on the bank, and the caddis fly larvae may be picked out as they begin to move, at which time they are easily detected.

Cocoons of caddis flies may generally be identified because they are securely fastened to some object. These should be removed very carefully, in order to avoid breaking the silk membranes more than necessary.

Where conveniently situated they may be cut away from both sides with the sharp ends of a pair of forceps.

Rearing Methods

Association by Pupal Dissection.—In almost all caddis fly groups the larval sclerites are packed into the posterior end of the pupal chamber after the pupa is formed. Later in the pupal life the adult structures take definite form within the pupal skin, and, just before actual escape of the pupa, the complete adult may be teased out of the pupal skin. Such pre-adult specimens show all adult characters except those of wing venation, which does not develop until the wings have expanded and dried by natural emergence. Of greatest importance is the fact that the genitalia of both sexes become completely formed, hardened and colored before emergence of the adult.

If, then, a cocoon or case is collected which has a mature pupa in it, the larval sclerites and fully formed genitalia are associated, and it is possible thus to link the adult and larval forms of the species. This type of association was fully explained by Vorhies (1909) in his report on the Wisconsin caddis flies. It was described again by M. Milne (1938). We have used this method for many years as a means of linking the various developmental stages. It is frequently necessary to collect in the same locality several times before certain species can be associated, but we have found it more satisfactory than cage rearing because of extreme cannibalism developed by caged larvae.

Cage Rearing.—A few caddis fly groups have pupal cases with a slit at one end, instead of the conventional mesh used by most groups. In these species the larval sclerites are kicked out of the case by the respiratory movements of the pupa. This is true throughout the family Leptoceridae and to a limited extent in the genus *Parapsyche*. For these species we used cages for rearing numbers of specimens. The type of cage used was square and suspended by side flanges from a raft constructed to form square openings, as described and used for stonefly rearing by Frison (1935, p. 303). The caddis fly adults were so fast in their movements, however, that a layer of muslin had to be tied over the cage and the lid placed over this; such an arrangement allowed the operator to take off the lid, see what adults had emerged and grasp them with fingers or forceps through the muslin.

Preservation

As mentioned before, for study purposes it is most practical to preserve all stages of caddis flies in liquid, preferably 80 per cent grain alcohol. This allows study of different structures from various angles, since the material is flexible. Furthermore, the muscle tissue of caddis flies does not become coagulated as in some other insect groups and can be cleared readily in caustic soda or potash solution.

One genus, *Leptocella*, must be collected dry, as mentioned on p. 213. Specimens of this genus should be killed a few at a time in a strong cyanide bottle and handled and pinned with great care to avoid rubbing the delicate hair which makes up the pattern.

For display purposes or for color study, it is sometimes necessary to pin material of other genera. The pin should be inserted with care to avoid piercing the scutellum and middle line. These areas may be diagnostic for family or genus.

Clearing Technique

Accurate identification for almost every caddis fly species must be based on characters of the genitalia, not only in the males but also in the females of those groups in which specific characters are known for this sex. It is usually necessary to clear the genitalia to see the diagnostic characters, and for this operation we have found the following procedure entirely satisfactory.

Remove the apical half or third of the abdomen from the specimen and place this portion in cold 10 to 15 per cent caustic potash or caustic soda solution. Allow it to soak 6 to 12 hours, depending on its size and color; then remove it to a dish of distilled water. If the specimen softens up in a minute or two, gently squeeze, prod and press until the dissolved mass of viscera has been worked out of the shell. If the specimen does not soften, resoak it in hot 5 per cent caustic solution for 5 or 10 minutes; then squeeze out the viscera. The following procedure is recommended for hot treatment: Put the caustic solution in a vial, which should be placed in a beaker of water; a little twisted wire should be placed in the beaker so that the vial will not actually touch the bottom; heat the beaker until the water boils; the caustic solution will not boil. This water bath treatment guards against overclearing of the specimen. After the viscera are more or less extracted, transfer the specimen through at least three baths of distilled water, leaving it at least 1 hour in each, and then place it in a dish of alcohol to which a few drops of 1 per cent acetic acid solution have been added. Remove the preparation to neutral alcohol. It is now ready to study.

For liquid preservation, the cleared genital capsule and the specimen to which it belongs can be placed together in a small shell vial 74 by 4 mm.; this vial can then be filled and stopped with a cotton plug and inverted in a ring-neck, 3-dram vial. Hard red rubber stoppers are desirable for these vials; to insert stopper, wet it with alcohol, place a long pin alongside it and insert both together into the neck of the vial as far as desired; then hold stopper in place and pull out pin. This technique allows air to escape from the vial as the stopper is inserted and prevents air pressure from being built up inside the vial below the stopper.

For pinned specimens the genital capsule, if not too large, may be placed in a minute shell vial with a small amount of glycerine in the bottom. The vial can be corked and mounted under the specimen by simply running the specimen's pin through the cork. The genitalia can be removed from this container with a pin which has a minute hook at the end. For further details, see article about this procedure by DeLong & Davidson (1937).

For study under a compound microscope, these cleared genitalia may be placed in pure glycerine. Very convenient for such study is a slide with a ground-out place or well in which the glycerine may be placed. Minute angles may be made from fine wire or pins and these used in the glycerine to keep the preparation in place while it is being studied or drawn. The glycerine keeps the preparation perfectly flexible and it also has a fine refraction, even when a cover slip is not used. Glycerine and alcohol are readily miscible so that preparations may be transferred from one to the other without harm.

For the family Hydroptilidae it is desirable to clear the entire specimen without detaching the abdomen. The procedure is the same as above except that in this case it is necessary to tear a slit in the base of the abdomen through which the dissolved viscera may be expelled. This technique destroys a clear view of the wing venation, but this is seldom decipherable even in an uncleared specimen and does not appear essential now for either family or generic diagnosis. On the other hand, characters of the ocelli, legs, thoracic structure and genitalia, which are all essential for identification, are not plainly visible without clearing.

CLASSIFICATION

Adults of the order Trichoptera are distinguished by the following combination of characters: head with long antennae; mouthparts with vestigial mandibles, well-developed maxillary and labial palpi, their parent sclerites more or less fused to form a flabby, proboscis-like structure; thorax with tergites and pleurae normally divided; two pairs of wings present (abortive in the females of several genera), covered with setae which may be hairlike or modified into

Fig. 19.—Lepidoptera. A typical moth showing the scales on wings and body and the sucking tube, which is coiled up under the head when not in use. Species in which the tube is poorly developed or entirely lacking always have the wings with a very dense and uniform covering of scales.

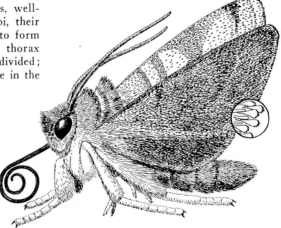

scales, with simple venation and only the hypothetical number of crossveins.

The Trichoptera belong to the holometabolous group of orders. The reduced crossveins will distinguish them from the Neuroptera, Megaloptera, Mecoptera and their allies; the two pairs of wings will distinguish them from the Diptera; and the narrow ventral portion of the meso-episternum will distinguish them from the Hymenoptera.

Members of this order are most closely related to the Lepidoptera, many forms of the two groups being quite similar in general morphology and wing venation. Almost all Lepidoptera differ from Trichoptera by having a coiled sucking tube which may be very long, fig. 19, or quite short. All those Lepidoptera occurring in this region which have no sucking tube or only a short one have the wings entirely covered with closely packed scales, as in fig. 19. The Trichoptera of this continent do not have a coiled sucking tube; most of them have no scales on the wings, but a few species either have patches of scales which do not cover the entire wing or have scales which are scattered and interspersed with hair.

The Trichoptera larvae have a distinct head capsule, full complement of mouthparts, single-segmented antennae which are often difficult to see, a pair of distinct, single-facet eyes, sclerotized pronotum (mesonotum and metanotum sometimes sclerotized also), three pairs of distinctly segmented legs, all provided with claws, and a pair of anal hooks. Tracheal gills of various sizes and shapes are sometimes present. The end of the abdomen never has a long mesal process as in some Megaloptera and Coleoptera.

Family Groupings

The Trichoptera are represented in North America by 17 families. This division departs in certain respects from the traditional plan of dividing the order but has been necessary because of the following circumstances.

1. In attempting to formulate a key to the larvae it was noticed that some subfamilies of the Sericostomatidae appeared more closely related to other families than to each other. A tentative key was made up in which the various groups of this nature were treated as separate families.

2. One difficulty with past keys was the uncertainty of diagnosing a female specimen to family, especially when the specimen was slightly teneral and the venation difficult to determine. A search for other characters which would circumvent the use of wing venation in the key brought to light differences in thoracic sclerites, tarsal claws and arrangement of spines and spurs on the middle legs. Using these in the family key, it was possible to key out both males and females together, and the resultant grouping agreed almost perfectly with the independent grouping suggested by the larvae.

3. The pupae offered only little evidence on the question, but what there was decidedly favored the new family segregations.

It appears, therefore, that the old family Sericostomatidae represented a heterogeneous assemblage of diverse groups such as the Helicopsychidae, Goeridae and Brachycentridae; these had been considered as one family solely on the basis of a secondary sexual similarity, namely, the three-segmented and curved or modified maxillary palpi of the males. Certain other groups, such as the Beraeidae, have been treated as separate families; and the opinion of Betten and others that the Odontoceridae and Calamoceratidae are distinct is substantiated by characters of all stages. There are many points to be cleared up in the placement to family of several genera from western states. In addition, many immature stages need to be discovered. These points, however, do not preclude an analysis of the present material.

The Rhyacophilidae, in particular the genus *Rhyacophila*, appear to be the most generalized family in the order. The simple wing venation, fig. 21, well developed ocelli, unmodified mouthparts and other characters of the adults, together with the simple type of larvae with either no case or a simple one, seem to represent basic characters from which developed other specializations of the order.

Three families, Philopotamidae, Psychomyiidae and Hydropsychidae, are a natural group differentiated by the annuliform maxillary palpi of the adults and the net-building habits of the larvae. Of these families the Philopotamidae appear the most primitive, having diverged relatively little in adult structure from the Rhyacophilidae. The sclerotized larval mesonotum and metanotum, and larval gills mark the Hydro-

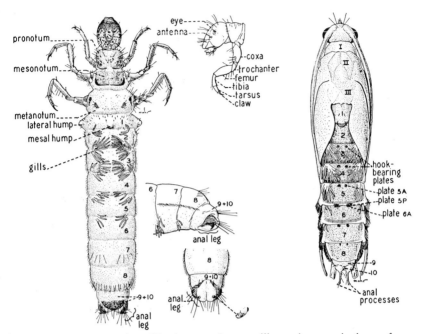

Fig. 20.—*Limnephilus submonilifer* larva and pupa, illustrating terminology of parts.

psychidae as the most specialized members of this group.

The Hydroptilidae comprise an isolated group combining certain primitive adult characters with a great variety of larval and biological specialization. The larvae are peculiar among the entire order, apparently, in having a sort of hypermetamorphosis in which the young larvae are active and free living, later building cases. The more primitive of these cases are simple adaptations of the saddle cases of some Rhyacophilidae, but the more specialized are similar in construction to the true cases of the Leptoceridae and other families.

The remainder of the families form the large complex of true case-makers, including the large families Leptoceridae and Limnephilidae. This group presents a real problem in determining the phylogenetic arrangement of the families. It may be divided into two or three series on the basis of certain characters as outlined below, but whether or not these segregations are artificial or natural will 'rest on further evidence and investigation:

A. Ocellate series (ocelli well developed).
    1. Phryganeidae—probably the most primitive member of the case-making group.
    2. Limnephilidae—this family may not be closely related to the Phryganeidae but

is certainly one of the more generalized members of the case makers.

B. Nonocellate series (ocelli absent).

Many families of this group have been regarded as very primitive. It is certain, however, that having no ocelli they could not have given rise to groups that have, such as the Phryganeidae. The Molannidae are probably the most primitive members of this series. It seems impractical, however, to attempt a phylogenetic analysis of the series at the present time. Also included in it are the Odontoceridae, Calamoceratidae, Goeridae, Lepidostomatidae, Leptoceridae, Beraeidae, Helicopsychidae, Sericostomatidae and Brachycentridae.

Generic and Specific Characters

For the diagnosis of genera and species an effort has been made to use such characters as could be seen easily on specimens preserved in liquid and, insofar as possible, on preadults dissected from pupae. This has led to the substitution of head, thoracic and leg characters for wing venation in many places in the keys. In certain families, such as the Hydroptilidae, these new characters have proved to be the first satisfactory basis for generic separation, at least in key form.

In almost all groups the adults have been separated to species on the basis of genitalic characters. In a few genera, such as *Macronemum* and *Leptocella*, genitalia have not given complete diagnosis, and color and proportions have been used.

There is a large amount of information in the literature regarding the immature stages of Trichoptera. Much of this is referred to in various places throughout the text of this report. Additional articles of considerable interest and value are the following: Denning (1937), Elkins (1936), Milne & Milne (1938, 1939), Margery Milne (1939) and Ulmer (1902, 1906*b*).

Terminology

The terms used commonly in the keys for wing venation and structural parts are illustrated in figs. 20 and 21 which include terms used for larvae, pupae and adults.

Material Studied

This report is based on extensive collecting over many years, during which a large amount of material has accumulated. We estimate that approximately 750,000 specimens were actually collected and checked over. Most of the specimens proved to be females or larvae which could be identified only to genus. About 150,000 specimens have been identified to species, and these constitute the basis for most of this report.

Disposition of Material

Unless otherwise noted, Illinois material recorded here is in the collection of the Illi-

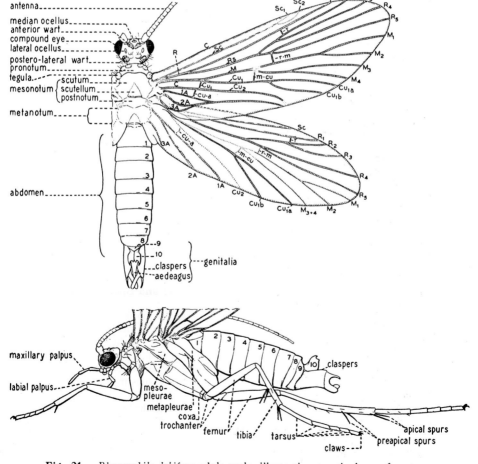

Fig. 21.—*Rhyacophila lobifera* adult male, illustrating terminology of parts.

nois Natural History Survey at Urbana. Some material is cited which belongs to other institutions, and this is usually indicated by letters following the record; these letters are as follows:

BC—Betten Collection, Ithaca, New York.

UM—University of Minnesota, St. Paul, Minnesota.

FM—Chicago Natural History Museum, Chicago, Illinois (formerly Field Museum).

MCZ—Museum of Comparative Zoology, Cambridge, Massachusetts.

Records Outside Illinois

Many records for states other than Illinois which are cited in this report are the first for these states. Those not taken from the literature are from Illinois Natural History Survey files, which are accessible for procuring additional locality and seasonal data.

KEY TO FAMILIES

Larvae

1. Pro-, meso- and metanotum each with a single, sclerotized shield embracing the entire notum, fig. 557 2
Either meso- or metanotum or both without sclerites or with sclerotized shield subdivided into separated plates, figs. 36, 37 3

2. Abdomen with many conspicuous branched gills, fig. 281; larva living in a nest, fig. 4 . . . .**Hydropsychidae**, p. 76
Abdomen without gills; larva living in a definite case, fig. 465 . . . .**Hydroptilidae**, p. 117

3. Anal legs projecting beyond, and free from, membranous lobes of tenth segment, fig. 22; note especially fig. 23 4
Anal legs appearing as lateral sclerites of membranous lobes of tenth segment, fig. 20 6

4. Sclerotized shield present on dorsum of ninth abdominal segment, fig. 22 . . . .**Rhyacophilidae**, p. 30
Dorsum of ninth abdominal segment entirely membranous 5

5. Labrum with anterior and lateral portions expanded into a wide, membranous area, fig. 24 . . . .**Philopotamidae**, p. 44
Labrum shorter, entirely sclerotized, fig. 25 . . . .**Psychomyiidae**, p. 51

6. Claws of hind legs very small, those of middle and front legs large, fig. 26 . . . .**Molannidae**, p. 205
Claws of hind legs as long as those of middle legs, fig. 27 7

7. Antennae long, at least eight times as long as wide, and arising at base of mandibles, fig. 28 . . . .**Leptoceridae**, p. 209
Antennae much shorter, fig. 709, not more than three or four times as long as wide, often very inconspicuous, and arising at various points, figs. 29, 30 8

8. Mesonotum submembranous except for a pair of parenthesis-like, sclerotized bars as in fig. 764 . . . .**Leptoceridae**, p. 209
Mesonotum without such bars 9

9. Meso- and metanotum entirely membranous or with only minute sclerites, figs. 561–566 . . . .**Phryganeidae**, p. 161
Mesonotum and usually metanotum with some conspicuous sclerotized plates 10

10. Labrum with a row of about 20 stout setae across middle, fig. 31 . . . .**Calamoceratidae**, p. 209
Labrum without such a row of setae, usually with 6–8 long setae, not in a row, and other scattered small setae, fig. 32 11

11. Anal hooks with a long comb of teeth, fig. 33; larva living in a case shaped exactly like a snail shell, fig. 906 . . . .**Helicopsychidae**, p. 266
Anal hooks with accessory teeth, but these not forming a comb, fig. 34; case not at all snail-like 12

12. Metanotum with a wide, straplike anterior sclerite, a pair of oblong lateral sclerites and a posterior thin sclerite, as in fig. 36, the posterior sclerite frequently difficult to distinguish . . . .**Odontoceridae**, p. 209
Metanotum not with this grouping of sclerites, usually with only 1 or 2 round, small and more or less indefinite sclerites, fig. 37 13

13. Anal hooks formed of 2 or 3 long teeth situated one over another, fig. 35 . . . .**Sericostomatidae**, p. 266
Anal hooks formed of a single large tooth with 1 or more small teeth on its dorsal edge, fig. 34 14

14. Pronotum with a deep furrow running almost the full width of the sclerite, figs. 892, 896, 897, the posterior margin of the furrow forming a sharp and slightly overhanging carina . . . .**Brachycentridae**, p. 260
Pronotum either without any trace of a

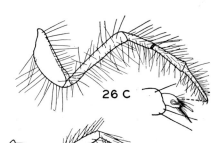

Fig. 22.—*Rhyacophila lobifera* larva, apex of abdomen.

Fig. 23.—*Agapetus illini* larva, apex of abdomen.

Fig. 24.—*Chimarra feria* larva, labrum.

Fig. 25.—*Polycentropus interruptus* larva, labrum.

Fig. 26.—*Molanna uniophila* larva, legs. *A*, front leg; *B*, middle leg; *C*, hind leg.

Fig. 27.—*Triaenodes tarda* larva, legs. *A*, front leg; *B*, middle leg; *C*, hind leg.

Fig. 28.—*Leptocerus americanus* larva, antenna (*a*).

Fig. 29.—*Lepidostoma liba* larva, antenna (*a*).

Fig. 30.—*Limnephilus submonilifer* larva, antenna (*a*).

Fig. 31.—*Ganonema americanum* larva, labrum.

Fig. 32.—*Limnephilus submonilifer* larva, labrum.

Fig. 33.—*Helicopsyche borealis* larva, anal hooks.

Fig. 34.—*Brachycentrus numerosus* larva, anal hooks.

Fig. 35.—*Sericostoma* sp. larva, anal hooks. (After Ulmer.)

Fig. 36.—*Psilotreta* sp. larva, thorax.

Fig. 37.—*Goera* sp. larva, thorax. (After Ulmer.)

Fig. 38.—*Beraea* sp. larva, hind leg. (After Ulmer.)

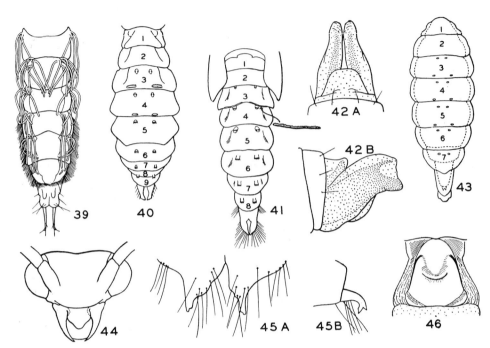

Fig. 39.—*Limnephilus submonilifer* pupa, venter of abdomen.

Fig. 40.—*Hydropsyche orris* pupa, abdomen.

Fig. 41.—*Macronemum zebratum* pupa, abdomen.

Fig. 42.—*Rhyacophila lobifera* pupa, abdomen, ♂, *A*, dorsal aspect; *B*, lateral aspect.

Fig. 43.—*Rhyacophila lobifera* pupa, abdomen, ♀.

Fig. 44.—*Ochrotrichia anisca* pupa, head.

Fig. 45.—*Beraea* sp. pupa, apical processes. (After Ulmer.) *A*, dorsal aspect; *B*, lateral aspect.

Fig. 46.—*Molanna uniophila* pupa, first abdominal tergite.

transverse furrow or with a gently concave depression across the sclerite............................ 15

Fig. 47.—*Molanna uniophila* pupa, hook plates.

Fig. 48.—*Oecetis inconspicua* pupa, hook plates.

15. Hind tarsal claws extremely long and narrow, as long as tibia, as in fig. 38................**Beraeidae**, p. 208
Hind tarsal claws much shorter, as in fig. 27......................... 16

16. Mesonotum divided into 2 pairs of plates, fig. 37.......**Goeridae**, p. 256
Mesonotum not divided into plates, but forming a single, rectangular sclerite with only a mesal fracture line, fig. 20...................... 17

17. Antennae situated very close to eye, fig. 29; first abdominal tergite without a hump......................
............**Lepidostomatidae**, p. 258
Antennae situated either midway between eye and margin of head or closer to margin of head than to eye, fig. 30; first abdominal tergite with a hump, fig. 20..................
.............**Limnephilidae**, p. 176

Pupae

1. Apex of abdomen membranous, without definite lobes except ventral

membranous ones which contain developing genitalic parts, figs. 42, 43   2
Apex of abdomen with definite, projecting, platelike processes, figs. 570, 571, or finger-like or triangular processes in addition to lobes containing developing parts of genitalia, figs. 20, 49–54   4

2. Mandibles without teeth or serrations, fig. 44 . . . . **Hydroptilidae**, p. 117
Mandibles with either serrations, fig. 97, or distinct teeth, fig. 158   3

3. Mandibles with teeth grouped near apex, figs. 158–161 . . . .
. . . . **Philopotamidae**, p. 44
Mandibles with teeth near middle, or mandibles only serrate, figs. 97–100
. . . . **Rhyacophilidae**, p. 30

4. Fifth tergite with only anterior pair of hook-bearing plates, third or fourth tergites with both anterior and posterior pairs, figs. 40, 41 . . . .
. . . . **Hydropsychidae**, p. 76
Fifth tergite with both anterior and posterior hook-bearing plates, third and fourth tergites at most with anterior pair, fig. 20   5

5. Seventh abdominal tergite without a pair of sclerotized plates   6
Seventh abdominal tergite with a pair of sclerotized hook-bearing plates, fig. 20   9

6. Apical processes of abdomen short, appearing triangular from dorsal view, sharply curved ventrad from lateral view, fig. 45 . . . **Beraeidae**, p. 208
Apical processes of abdomen either much longer, fig. 49, or not curved ventrad   7

7. First abdominal tergite with a short, arcuate ledge near middle of segment, fig. 46; sclerotized plates of

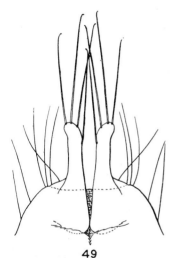

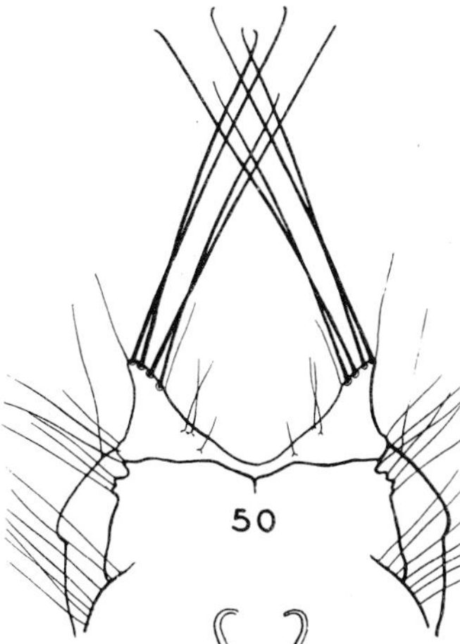

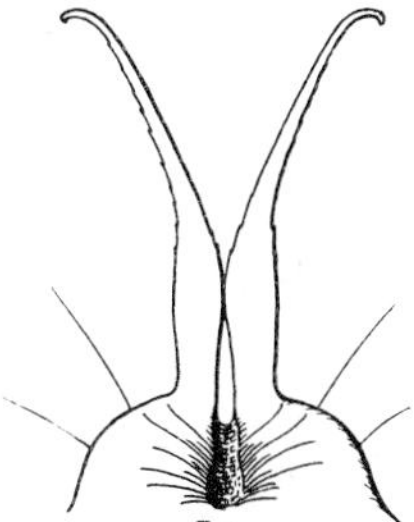

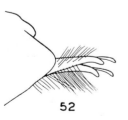

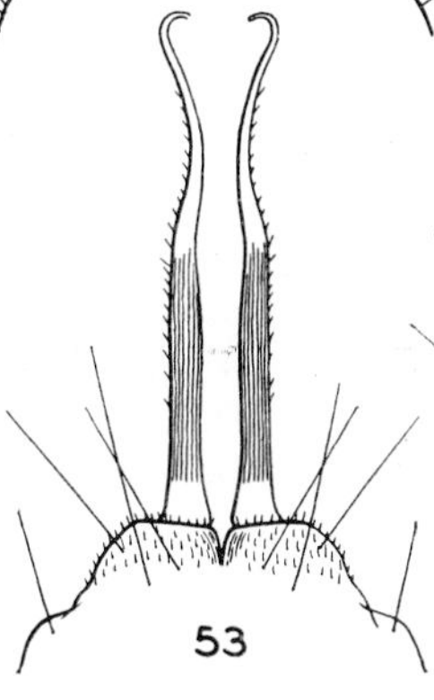

Fig. 49.—*Helicopsyche borealis* pupa, apical processes, dorsal aspect.

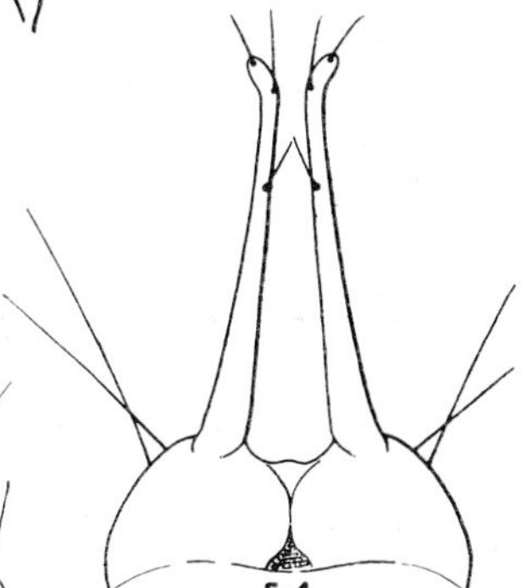

Fig. 50.—*Lepidostoma liba* pupa, apical processes, dorsal aspect.

Fig. 51.—*Psilotreta* sp. pupa, apical processes, dorsal aspect.

Fig. 52.—*Sericostoma* sp. pupa, apical processes, lateral aspect. (After Ulmer.)

Fig. 53.—*Goera* sp. pupa, apical processes, dorsal aspect. (After Ulmer.)

Fig. 54.—*Limnephilus submonilifer* pupa, apical processes, dorsal aspect.

fifth and sixth segments wide, with 4 to 8 hooks, fig. 47..............
................**Molannidae**, p. 205
First abdominal tergite without a ledge except at apex, fig. 20; sclerotized plates of fifth and sixth segments narrow, some or all with only 2 or 3 hooks, fig. 48.............. 8

8. Apical processes of abdomen narrow and finger-like, and with apical black hairs as long as the process, fig. 49.
.............**Helicopsychidae**, p. 266
Apical processes of abdomen either not finger-like, or without long, apical hairs, figs. 721–726..............
................**Leptoceridae**, p. 209

9. Abdomen without a fringe of hair; apical processes as in figs. 205–207
..............**Psychomyiidae**, p. 51
Abdomen with a lateral fringe of hair, fig. 39........................ 10

10. Abdomen with a pair of almost linear, transverse lines of hooks (plate 5*P*) between fifth and sixth tergites, figs. 888, 889.....**Brachycentridae**, p. 260
Abdomen with these areas of hooks not as thin, at least as broad as in fig. 618........................ 11

11. Apical processes of abdomen short and stubby, appearing platelike from dorsal view, figs. 570, 571........
..............**Phryganeidae**, p. 161
Apical processes of abdomen finger-like, at least as long as in fig. 50, often styliform, fig. 49........... 12

12. Apical processes of abdomen short, widely separated and bearing black spines many times as long as the processes, fig. 50.................
...........**Lepidostomatidae**, p. 258
Apical processes either close together or much longer, figs. 51–54........ 13

13. Mandibles produced at apex into a narrow, whiplike style, fig. 55.....
..............**Odontoceridae**, p. 209
Mandibles pointed but not produced into a style, figs. 56, 57.......... 14

14. Dorsum of abdomen with transverse patches of dense, fine hair, these patches forming bands on some segments, fig. 58....................
...........**Calamoceratidae**, p. 209
Dorsum of abdomen without patches of hair, with only isolated setae, fig. 20........................ 15

15. Apical processes with slender, terminal appendage, fig. 52..............
...........**Sericostomatidae**, p. 266
Apical processes without appendage.. 16

16. Antennae twice length of body, looped several times around apical processes
..............**Leptoceridae**, p. 209

Antennae much shorter, not looped around apical processes............ 17

17. Apical processes extremely slender at apex, threadlike and sinuate, fig. 53
..................**Goeridae**, p. 256
Apical processes not greatly narrowed at apex, with apical hairs and not sinuate, fig. 54..**Limnephilidae**, p. 176

Adults

1. Mesoscutellum with posterior portion forming a triangular, flat area with steep sides, figs. 438–446; mesoscutum without warts; front tibiae never with more than 1 spur. Small, hairy individuals not over 6 mm. long...........**Hydroptilidae**, p. 117
Either mesoscutellum evenly convex, without a triangular posterior portion set off by sharp sides, figs. 80, 83, or mesoscutum with warts, figs.

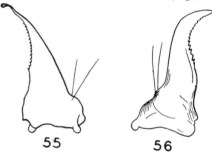

55   56

57

58

Fig. 55.—*Psilotreta* sp. pupa, mandible.
Fig. 56.—*Sericostoma* sp. pupa, mandible. (After Ulmer.)
Fig. 57.—*Goera* sp. pupa, mandible. (After Ulmer.)
Fig. 58.—*Calamoceratidae* sp. pupa, dorsum of abdomen.

81–90. Includes a size range of 5 to
  40 mm.................................... 2

2. Ocelli present, fig. 21.............. 3
  Ocelli absent....................... 8

3. Maxillary palpi 3-segmented, fig. 65..
    ....♂ **Limnephilidae**, p. 176
  Maxillary palpi 4- or 5-segmented.... 4

4. Maxillary palpi 4-segmented, fig. 64..
    ....♂ **Phryganeidae**, p. 161
  Maxillary palpi 5-segmented, fig. 63..   5

5. Maxillary palpi with fifth segment two
  or three times as long as fourth, fig.
  61.............**Philopotamidae**, p. 44
  Maxillary palpi with fifth segment not

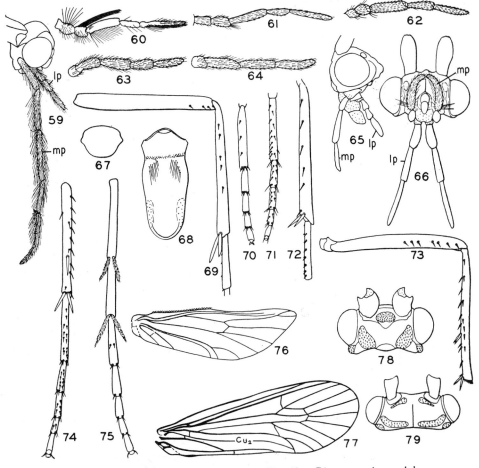

Fig. 59.—*Triaenodes tarda* ♂, head; *lp*, labial palpus; *mp*, maxillary palpus.

Fig. 60.—*Psilotreta* sp. ♂, maxillary palpus.

Fig. 61.—*Dolophilus shawnee* ♂, maxillary palpus.

Fig. 62.—*Rhyacophila lobifera* ♂, maxillary palpus.

Fig. 63.—*Banksiola selina* ♀, maxillary palpus.

Fig. 64.—*Banksiola selina* ♂, maxillary palpus.

Fig. 65.—*Limnephilus submonilifer* ♂, head; *lp*, labial palpus; *mp*, maxillary palpus.

Fig. 66.—*Lepidostoma liba* ♂, head; *lp*, labial palpus; *mp*, maxillary palpus.

Fig. 67.—*Rhyacophila lobifera*, labrum.

Fig. 68.—*Phryganea cinerea*, labrum.

Fig. 69.—*Beraea gorteba*, middle leg.

Fig. 70.—*Beraea gorteba*, middle tarsi.

Fig. 71.—*Sericostoma crassicornis*, middle tarsi.

Fig. 72.—*Sericostoma crassicornis*, middle tibia.

Fig. 73.—*Molanna uniophila*, middle leg.

Fig. 74.—*Brachycentrus numerosus*, middle tibia and tarsi.

Fig. 75.—*Theliopsyche corona*, middle tibia and tarsi.

Fig. 76.—*Helicopsyche borealis*, hind wing.

Fig. 77.—*Sericostoma crassicornis*, front wing.

Fig. 78.—*Sericostoma crassicornis*, head.

Fig. 79.—*Brachycentrus numerosus*, head.

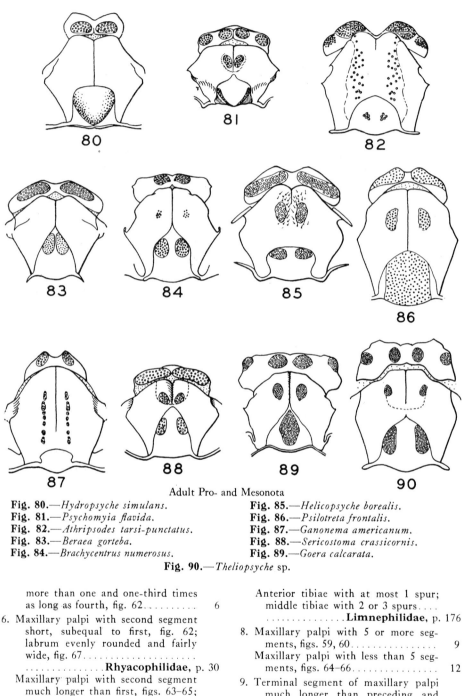

Adult Pro- and Mesonota

Fig. 80.—*Hydropsyche simulans.*
Fig. 81.—*Psychomyia flavida.*
Fig. 82.—*Athripsodes tarsi-punctatus.*
Fig. 83.—*Beraea gorteba.*
Fig. 84.—*Brachycentrus numerosus.*

Fig. 85.—*Helicopsyche borealis.*
Fig. 86.—*Psilotreta frontalis.*
Fig. 87.—*Ganonema americanum.*
Fig. 88.—*Sericostoma crassicornis.*
Fig. 89.—*Goera calcarata.*

Fig. 90.—*Theliopsyche* sp.

more than one and one-third times as long as fourth, fig. 62.......... 6

6. Maxillary palpi with second segment short, subequal to first, fig. 62; labrum evenly rounded and fairly wide, fig. 67.....................
...............**Rhyacophilidae,** p. 30
Maxillary palpi with second segment much longer than first, figs. 63–65; labrum with a wide basal portion set off by a crease from a long, tonguelike apex, fig. 68.......... 7

7. Anterior tibiae with 2 or more spurs; middle tibiae with 4 spurs........
...............**Phryganeidae,** p. 161

Anterior tibiae with at most 1 spur; middle tibiae with 2 or 3 spurs....
...............**Limnephilidae,** p. 176

8. Maxillary palpi with 5 or more segments, figs. 59, 60............... 9
Maxillary palpi with less than 5 segments, figs. 64–66............... 12

9. Terminal segment of maxillary palpi much longer than preceding and with close, suture-like, cross striae, which are not possessed by the other segments, figs. 214, 321.......... 10
Terminal segment of maxillary palpi without such striae and similar in general structure to fourth segment,

figs. 59, 63, usually of same length, or some segments with long hair brushes, fig. 60.   12

10. Anterior tibiae with a preapical spur as in fig. 21. . . . .
. . . . **Psychomyiidae**, p. 51
Anterior tibiae without a preapical spur.   11

11. Hind wings with R almost or entirely normal in its course, with 4 or all 5 branches distinct and the stem distinct from Sc, fig. 334; anal area at least as large as in fig. 333; mesoscutum without warts, fig. 80. . . . .
. . . . **Hydropsychidae**, p. 76
Hind wings with R much reduced, the stem either absent or fused with Sc and only 3 or 4 branches present, figs. 212, 213; anal area reduced to a small area as in fig. 212; mesoscutum with a pair of small warts, fig. 81. . .
. . . . **Psychomyiidae**, p. 51

12. Middle tibiae without preapical spurs and with a row of black spines, fig. 69.   13
Middle tibiae with preapical spurs, with or without a row of spines, figs. 73–75.   17

13. Pronotum consisting of a lateral pair of erect, platelike warts separated by a wide, mesal, excavated collar which is usually hidden by the produced, angulate margin of the mesonotum, fig. 82; mesonotum with short scutellum and with scutal warts represented by a long, irregular line of setate spots; antennae always very long and slender, fig. 863. . . . . **Leptoceridae**, p. 209
Pronotum with warts much closer together, not platelike, and usually prominent, fig. 83; mesonotum with scutal warts either small, fig. 85, or absent, fig. 83; antennae as stout as or not longer than those in fig. 702   14

14. Hind wings each with anterior margin cut away beyond middle, fig. 76, with a row of hamuli along straight basal portion of margin . . . .
. . . . **Helicopsychidae**, p. 266
Hind wings each with anterior margin straight or evenly rounded, fig. 874   15

15. Middle and hind tarsi with a crown of 4 black spines at apex of each segment and only a few preapical spines arranged in a single row on the basitarsus, fig. 70; apical spurs of middle tibiae nearly half length of basitarsus, fig. 69. . . . . **Beraeidae**, p. 208
Middle and hind tarsi with apical spines more separated and not forming a crown, and with numerous pre-

apical spines on all segments, arranged in a double row on the basitarsus, fig. 71; apical spurs of middle tibiae not more than one-third length of basitarsus, fig. 72.   16

16. Mesoscutum with a deep, antero-mesal fissure with scutal warts near meson, fig. 88; head with posterior warts diagonal and tear-shaped, fig. 78; front wings with a long crossvein between R_1 and R_2 and with Cu_2 joining apex of Cu_{1b} directly, fig. 77
. . . . **Sericostomatidae**, p. 266
Mesoscutum with only a shallow antero-mesal crease, with scutal warts some distance from meson, fig. 84; head with posterior warts linear and transverse, fig. 79; front wings without a crossvein between R_1 and R_2 and with Cu_2 connected to apex of Cu_{1b} with a crossvein, fig. 890. . . . .
. . . . **Brachycentridae**, p. 260

17. Middle femora each with a row of 6–10 black spines on antero-ventral face, fig. 73. . . . . **Molannidae**, p. 205
Middle femora each with none to 2 black spines on antero-ventral face   18

18. Mesonotum with small, rectangular scutellum, and with scutal warts represented by a linear area of small, setate spots extending the full length of the scutum, fig. 87. . . . .
. . . . **Calamoceratidae**, p. 209
Mesonotum with longer and pointed scutellum, and with scutal warts oval or lanceolate and short, fig. 84   19

19. Mesoscutellum with a single large oval or round wart which extends the full length of the scutellum, fig. 89, and may occupy almost the entire scutellum, fig. 86.   20
Mesoscutellum with 2 warts which are smaller and confined to the anterior half of the scutellum, figs. 84, 90. . .   21

20. Mesoscutellum round and distinctly domelike, the wart appearing to occupy most of the sclerite; scutum with mesal line only faintly indicated, fig. 86; tibial spurs not hairy; maxillary palpi of males 5-segmented
. . . . **Odontoceridae**, p. 209
Mesoscutellum triangular, only slightly convex, the wart elongate and occupying only the mesal portion of the sclerite; scutum with distinct mesal depression, fig. 89; tibial spurs hairy; maxillary palpi of males 3-segmented. . . . . **Goeridae**, p. 256

21. Middle tibiae with an irregular row, middle tarsi with a long double row of spines, preapical spurs of tibiae bare, shorter and situated about

two-thirds distance from base of
tibiae, fig. 74....................
............**Brachycentridae,** p. 260
Middle tibiae without spines, their
tarsi with only a scattered few in
addition to apical ones, preapical
spurs of tibiae hairy, longer and situated at middle of tibiae, fig. 75.....
..........**Lepidostomatidae,** p. 258

RHYACOPHILIDAE

The adults, both sexes, of the Rhyacophilidae have five-segmented maxillary palpi.
Two distinct groups are included in the
Illinois representatives of this family; the
subfamily Rhyacophilinae has free-living,
predaceous larvae and the subfamily Glossosomatinae has saddle-case making larvae.
This remarkable difference in habits of the
larvae has no apparent outstanding counter-
part in the adults. The southwestern genus
Atopsyche has been placed in the subfamily
Hydrobiosinae, but until the larvae of this
genus are discovered its true position is
enigmatic.

KEY TO GENERA

Larvae

1. Anal larvapods with long, large hooks,
   figs. 22, 91. Free living without
   cases.............**Rhyacophila,** p. 32
   Anal larvapods with very small, re-
   tractile hooks, fig. 23. Living in
   saddle-shaped cases constructed of
   small stones...................... 2
2. Pronotum notched only at extreme
   antero-lateral angle, at which point
   the legs are attached, fig. 92......
   ....**Glossosoma,** p. 39
   Pronotum narrow from anterior margin to middle, the legs attached at
   this central point, fig. 93......... 3
3. Dorsal plate of last segment with 4
   long, apical setae; pronotum with
   only a few scattered setae; anal hook
   divided into many teeth, fig. 96...
   ....**Protoptila,** p. 41
   Dorsal plate of last segment with 6
   long, apical setae, fig. 94; pronotum
   with a line of setae near posterior
   margin, and with a brush of setae
   along each anterior corner, fig. 93;
   anal hook with only 1 large and 1
   small tooth, fig. 95.....**Agapetus,** p. 39

Pupae

1. Mandibles with inner margin minutely
   serrate, and with apical inner tooth

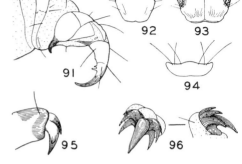

Fig. 91.—*Rhyacophila lobifera* larva, anal
hook.
Fig. 92.—*Agapetus illini* larva, pronotum.
Fig. 93.—*Glossosoma intermedium* larva,
pronotum.
Fig. 94.—*Agapetus illini* larva, plate of
tenth tergite.
Fig. 95.—*Agapetus illini* larva, anal hooks.
Fig. 96.—*Protoptila lega* larva, anal hooks.

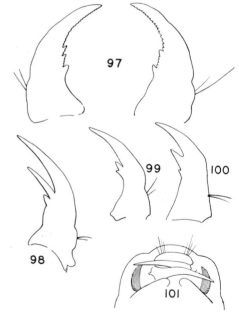

Fig. 97.—*Rhyacophila lobifera* pupa, mandibles.
Fig. 98.—*Protoptila lega* pupa, left mandible.
Fig. 99.—*Agapetus illini* pupa, left mandible.
Fig. 100.—*Glossosoma intermedium* pupa,
left mandible.
Fig. 101.—*Protoptila lega* pupa, head, ventral aspect.

no larger than basal one; each mandible with 2 or 3 inner teeth, fig. 97
.................**Rhyacophila**, p. 32
Mandibles with inner margin not serrate, and with apical inner tooth

larger than basal one; each mandible
with 2 inner teeth.............. 2

2. Apical inner tooth of mandibles half
as long as apical blade and sub-
parallel with it, fig. 98; mandibles in
repose over-reaching side of head,
fig. 101; size small, less than 4 mm.
...................**Protoptila**, p. 41
Apical inner tooth of mandibles much
shorter, fig. 100; mandibles in repose not reaching side of head; size
larger, over 5 mm................ 3

3. Apical inner tooth of mandibles only
slightly larger than basal one, fig. 99;
apical segments of abdomen only
slightly curled ventrad............
...................**Agapetus**, p. 39
Apical inner tooth of mandibles many
times larger than basal one, fig. 100;
apical segments of abdomen curled
ventrad and slightly forward......
.................**Glossosoma**, p. 39

Adults

1. Front tibiae with apical spurs absent
or hairlike, fig. 102....**Protoptila**, p. 41
Front tibiae with both apical spurs
prominent and sclerotized, fig. 103   2

2. Front tibiae with a preapical spur, fig.
104..............**Rhyacophila**, p. 32
Front tibiae never with preapical spur,
fig. 103...................... 3

3. Pronotum with mesal pair of warts
nearly touching; posterior warts on
head large, arcuate, tapered to a
curved, narrowed point, the two
nearly meeting on meson, fig. 105..
.................**Palaeagapetus**, p. 38
Pronotum with mesal pair of warts
well separated by a concave area;
posterior warts of head oval or round
and widely separated on meson,
fig. 108....................... 4

4. Head with 1 or both pairs of dorsal
warts connected by sutures running
across epicranial stem, fig. 107; hind
wings with radial sector apparently
2-branched, fig. 109....**Agapetus**, p. 39
Head with neither pair of dorsal warts
connected by sutures, fig. 108; hind
wings with radial sector 4-branched,
fig. 110...........**Glossosoma**, p. 39

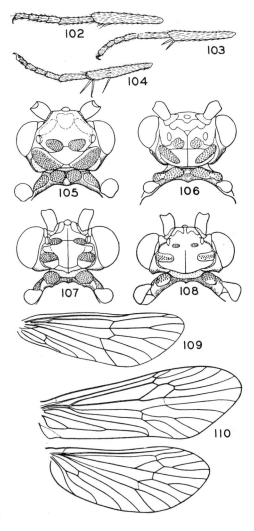

Fig. 102.—*Protoptila maculata*, front tibia.
Fig. 103.—*Agapetus illini*, front tibia.
Fig. 104.—*Rhyacophila vibox*, front tibia.
Fig. 105.—*Palaeagapetus celsus*, head and
pronotum.
Fig. 106.—*Rhyacophila vibox*, head and pro-
notum.
Fig. 107.—*Agapetus illini*, head and prono-
tum.
Fig. 108.—*Glossosoma intermedium*, head
and pronotum.
Fig. 109.—*Agapetus illini*, hind wing.
Fig. 110.—*Glossosoma intermedium*, wings.

RHYACOPHILINAE

The larva is free living, in all the Illinois
species without external gills; it constructs
a dome-shaped cocoon of pebbles for pupation. The pupa is formed within an ellipsoid,
translucent pupal chamber anchored at each
end within the cocoon. The adults have

short antennae, very simple and similar front and hind wings and five-segmented maxillary palpi in both sexes.

Rhyacophila Pictet

Rhyacophila Pictet (1834, p. 181). Genotype, here designated: *Rhyacophila vulgaris* Pictet.

In Illinois we have taken five species of this genus. Four of them occur in streams which are temporary but which are rapid and clear when running; the fifth occurs in a set of small, clear, spring-fed brooklets at Elgin. Over 70 species of *Rhyacophila* inhabit North America, most of them restricted to the rapid, clear streams of mountainous terrain or northern country.

Westwood (1840, p. 51) lists *vulgata* Pictet as the genotype. This is undoubtedly an emendation of *vulgaris* Pictet, since Pictet did not list a species by the name of *vulgata* in his description of *Rhyacophila*.

KEY TO SPECIES

Larvae

1. Second segment of anal larvapods with a long, bladelike, dorso-lateral spur, fig. 111................**fuscula**, p. 36
Second segment of larvapods without a distinct spur, fig. 112............. 2
2. Second segment of maxillary palpus much longer than first, fig. 115.... 3
Second segment of maxillary palpus not longer than first, fig. 114.......
...................**glaberrima**, p. 35
3. Front and middle legs almost the same size and shape, fig. 116; baso-ventral sclerotized rod of anal prolegs produced into a short, sharp, curved hook, fig. 91............**lobifera**, p. 35
Front femora much stouter than middle femora, giving the two legs different shapes, fig. 117; baso-ventral sclerotized rod of anal prolegs not hooked, fig. 112................. 4
4. Head wide and short, fig. 118; anal hooks without teeth on inner margin, fig. 113....................
..........**ledra**, p. 37; **fenestra**, p. 36
Head narrower and longer, fig. 119; anal hooks with at least one small inner tooth, fig. 112........**vibox**, p. 36

Adults

1. Apex of abdomen with long claspers (males)........................ 2

Apex of abdomen cylindrical (females) 8
2. Apical segment of clasper deeply incised to form a long dorsal point, fig. 120...............**lobifera**, p. 35
Apical segment of clasper either only

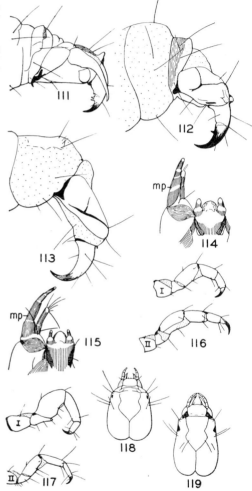

Fig. 111.—*Rhyacophila fuscula* larva, anal leg.
Fig. 112.—*Rhyacophila vibox* larva, anal leg.
Fig. 113.—*Rhyacophila fenestra* larva, anal leg.
Fig. 114.—*Rhyacophila glaberrima* larva, maxilla and labium; *mp*, maxillary palpus.
Fig. 115.—*Rhyacophila fenestra* larva, maxilla and labium; *mp*, maxillary palpus.
Fig. 116.—*Rhyacophila lobifera* larva, front and middle legs.
Fig. 117.—*Rhyacophila fenestra* larva, front and middle legs.
Fig. 118.—*Rhyacophila fenestra* larva, head.
Fig. 119.—*Rhyacophila vibox* larva, head.

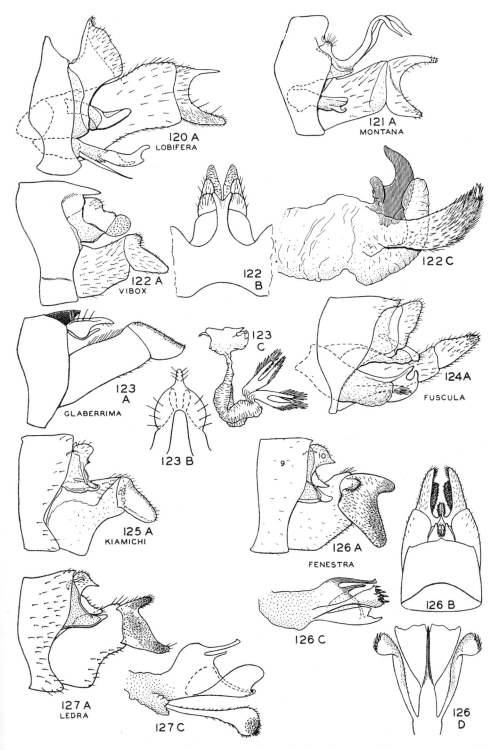

Figs. 120–127.—*Rhyacophila*, male genitalia. *A*, lateral aspect; *B*, dorsal aspect; *C*, aedeagus, lateral aspect; *D*, aedeagus, dorsal aspect.

moderately incised, fig. 126, or not incised at all, fig. 124.............   3

3. Ninth tergite produced into a long, narrow, forked process which extends over tenth tergite, fig. 122...
....................................**vibox,** p. 36
Ninth tergite not produced into a forked process, fig. 123...........   4

4. Tenth tergite heart shaped and pointed at apex, fig. 123, long and shallow; aedeagus with a U-shaped process at the end of the lateral arms of the aedeagus............**glaberrima,** p. 35
Tenth tergite short and deep, divided down meson, not forming a round, dorsal plate; aedeagus without U-

shaped processes at the end of the lateral arms, figs. 124, 126........   5

5. First segment of claspers with ventral margin almost straight from base to apex; aedeagus without a ventral plate, fig. 124...........**fuscula,** p. 36
First segment of claspers with ventral margin humped to form a definite shoulder near base; aedeagus with large, scoop-shaped ventral plate below central portion, fig. 126.....   6

6. Apical segment of clasper incised to form a definite dorsal heel, figs. 126, 127...........................   7
Apical segment of clasper not incised, only sinuate, fig. 125, so that the

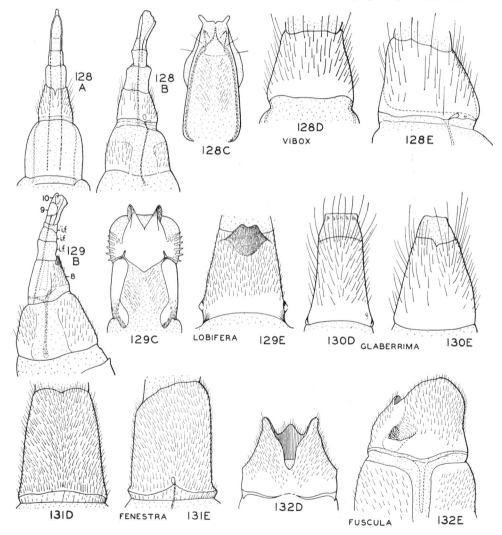

Figs. 128–132.—*Rhyacophila*, female genitalia. *A* and *B*, apex of abdomen, ventral and lateral aspect; *C*, tenth tergite; *D*, eighth sternite; *E*, eighth segment, lateral aspect.

dorsal portion is low and rounded instead of forming a distinct heel. .
. . . .**kiamichi**, p. 37

7. Apical segment of clasper with a mesal, setose flap; arms of aedeagus at apex with several stout spines, each surrounded by smaller setae, fig. 126. . . . .**fenestra**, p. 36
Apical segment of clasper without a mesal flap; arms of aedeagus with a brush of setae of almost equal size, fig. 127. . . . .**ledra**, p. 37

8. Eighth segment with apex of sternite deeply excavated and apex of tergite bi-emarginate, fig. 132. . .**fuscula**, p. 36
Eighth segment neither with sternite deeply incised nor with tergite bi-emarginate 9

9. Apex of eighth sternite with a produced mesal plate which is differentiated in texture from remainder of segment, fig. 129; tenth tergite sclerotized and spined, fig. 129. . . .
. . . .**lobifera**, p. 35
Eighth sternite without such a plate; tenth tergite chiefly membranous, without spines, fig. 128. 10

10. Eighth sternite short and stout, venter distinctly bulged near base, fig. 128
. . . .**vibox**, p. 36
Eighth sternite longer and more slender, without ventro-basal bulge, fig. 130. 11

11. Eighth tergite with an apical incision, fig. 131; entire segment with only moderately long hair; size larger, 10 mm. or more. . . . .
. . . .**fenestra**, p. 36; **ledra**, p. 37
Eighth tergite without a marked incision, fig. 130; entire segment clothed with long hair; size smaller, 8 mm. or less. . . . . . .**glaberrima**, p. 35

Rhyacophila lobifera Betten

Rhyacophila lobifera Betten (1934, p. 131); ♂, ♀, larva.

Larva.—Length 15 mm.; head and pronotal shield straw color, with scattered brown dots; body greenish.
Adults.—Length 11–13 mm.; color dark bluish gray, with some yellowish patches of hair on head, body and wings. Legs yellow to greenish. Male genitalia, fig. 120, with claspers very long, the apical segment incised to form a sharp dorsal point; tenth tergite large and somewhat triangular. Female genitalia as in fig. 129 (note the intersegmental folds, *i.f.*, between segments 8 and 9).

This species at times has been considered a synonym of *montana* Carpenter, described from the Great Smoky Mountains of North Carolina, but the two differ radically in the shape of the tenth tergite. That of *montana* has long, slender, sclerotized processes, fig. 121, and that of *lobifera* comprises a single, stout, triangular protuberance.

Originally described from Lake Bluff, Illinois, *lobifera* has since been taken in widely scattered localities in the state, principally in the eastern portion. It frequents small, rapid, clear streams that are of a temporary nature in drought years. The adults appear during April and May in southern Illinois and during May and June in northern Illinois.

Known also from Indiana, Ohio, Oklahoma.

Illinois Records.—Many males, females and pupae, taken April 3 to June 3, and many larvae and cases, taken March 5 to May 1, are from Alto Pass (Union Spring Creek), Brockton (Catfish Creek), Carbondale (Clay Lick Creek), Dixon Springs, Eddyville (Eddy Creek), Filson, Fox Ridge State Park, Grayville, Harrisburg (Blackman Creek), Herod (Gibbons Creek), Hill (tributary of Bishop Creek), Hurd (small stream), Marshall, Mazon (Mazon Creek), Muncie (Stony Creek), New Columbia (Clifty Creek), Oakwood (West Branch), Red Bud, Ritchie (small stream), Rosecrans, St. Elmo (South Fork Creek), Toledo, Tuscola, Urbana, Waltersburg, Watson, Willow Springs.

Rhyacophila glaberrima Ulmer

Rhyacophila glaberrima Ulmer (1907*b*, p. 85); ♂.
Rhyacophila fairchildi Banks (1930*a*, p. 130); ♂.
Rhyacophila andrea Betten (1934, p. 127); ♂.

Larva.—Length 12 mm. Body long and slender. Head, pronotum, legs and anal sclerites light yellow with suffused brown markings. Anal hooks stout, each with one large and one small inner tooth.
Adults.—Length 7–8 mm. Head and body dark brown; legs pale, slightly greenish; wings dark, without pattern. Male genitalia, fig. 123, with tenth tergite projecting; claspers very long, and with curious "forks" at apex of lateral appendages of aedeagus. Female genitalia, fig. 130, with

eighth segment simple in structure, with very long, fine hair.

Allotype, female.—Gatlinburg, Tennessee: Sept. 4, 1940, B. D. Burks.

Our only Illinois records are a single mature male pupa taken under a damp stone in the dry bed of Gibbons Creek at Herod, October 7, 1937, Ross & Burks, and 4 larvae taken in a small, spring-fed stream 2 miles away, May 30, 1940, B. D. Burks. These records are from the heart of the Illinois Ozarks region. The main range of *glaberrima* is in the Appalachian states; the species is known from Massachusetts, New York, North Carolina, Nova Scotia, Tennessee and Virginia. In view of this, our Illinois record is a significant extension of its range.

Rhyacophila vibox Milne

Rhyacophila vibox Milne (1936, p. 101); ♂, ♀.

LARVA.—Length 11 mm. Body stout. Head golden yellow with most of dorsal area brownish; pronotum golden yellow; legs and anal sclerites pale yellow. Abdomen whitish with purplish blotches.

ADULTS.—Length 8–10 mm. Color of body and appendages various shades of brown; head and wings without definite pattern. Male genitalia, fig. 122, with ninth tergite produced into a long dorsal process bifid at apex; tenth tergite forming a complex of small, paired plates; claspers short; aedeagus with a central hook and lateral, spinose lobes. Female genitalia, fig. 128, with eighth sternite stocky, short and simple.

In Illinois we have taken this species only in the small, spring-fed brooks in the Elgin Botanical Gardens. In view of the other known captures of the species, from Ontario and Quebec, it would appear that the species is chiefly northern and its occurrence in Illinois represents a localized capture at the extreme edge of the present range.

Illinois Records.—ELGIN: April 19, 1939, Burks & Riegel, 1 larva; May 9, 1939, Ross & Burks, 5 larvae; May 23, 1939, Burks & Riegel, 2 pupae; June 6, 1939, Burks & Riegel, 2 ♂ ; June 13, 1939, Frison & Ross, 3 ♂, many ♂ and ♀ pupae; Sept. 19, 1939, Ross & Mohr, 1 larva; preceding Elgin records from Botanical Gardens; Trout Spring, May 7, 1940, Burks & Mohr, 4 larvae.

Rhyacophila fuscula (Walker)

Neuronia fuscula Walker (1852, p. 10); ♂.

This species is the most common *Rhyacophila* found in a large number of the eastern states. It has not yet been taken in Illinois, but may eventually be found within the state. Known from Maine, Michigan, New Brunswick, New Hampshire, New York, North Carolina, Nova Scotia, Ontario, Pennsylvania, Quebec, Tennessee, Virginia, West Virginia.

Rhyacophila fenestra Ross

Rhyacophila fenestra Ross (1938a, p. 102); ♂, ♀.

LARVA.—Fig. 133. Length 14 mm. Body stocky. Head orange, spotted with brown at the side, most of dorsum brown enclosing an orange spot in the center of the frons; pronotum, front legs and anal hooks orange, pronotum with brown spots; middle and

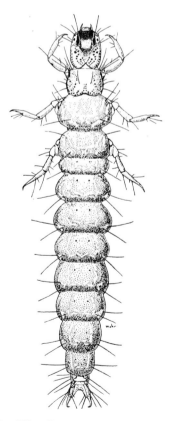

Fig. 133.—*Rhyacophila fenestra* larva.

hind legs pale yellow. Abdomen with an irregular purplish pattern.

Adults.—Fig. 134. Length 10–12 mm. Head, body and legs various shades of light and medium brown; fronto-dorsal area of head with a distinct, dark, quadrate spot;

Fig. 134.—*Rhyacophila fenestra* ♀.

wings fenestrate with light and dark brown. Male genitalia, fig. 126, with short, beaked tenth tergite; claspers short, the apical segment incised; aedeagus with a central scoop-like structure and lateral processes. Female genitalia as in fig. 131, eighth segment simple in shape.

This species, known only from Illinois, is with one exception restricted to the Ozarkian area, where it is abundant in all the clear, rapid streams, most of them flowing only in winter and spring.

The one exception is a single colony of *fenestra* located in a small, temporary stream at Oakwood.

Illinois Records.—Many males, females and pupae, taken April 21 to June 6, and many larvae and cases, taken March 23 to May 26, are from Aldridge, Alto Pass, Carbondale, Dixon Springs, East Peoria, Eddyville, Eichorn, Elizabethtown, Golconda, Herod (Gibbons Creek), Jonesboro, Karbers Ridge, New Columbia (Clifty Creek), Oakwood, Vienna, Wolf Lake.

Rhyacophila ledra Ross

Rhyacophila ledra Ross (1939a, p. 65); ♂.

Similar to *fenestra* in color and general structure, differing in characters of the male genitalia, fig. 127, particularly the apical segment of the claspers, the lateral arms of the aedeagus and the humped central ridge of the aedeagus. To date, characters have not been found to separate the larvae or females of these two species.

Our sole Illinois record for this species consists of two fully matured male pupae collected in Union Spring, a small, temporary stream near Alto Pass in the Ozark Hills of southern Illinois, May 26, 1940, Mohr & Burks. The species is known otherwise only from the type material collected in Tennessee.

Rhyacophila kiamichi new species

Male.—Length 9 mm. Color dark brown with very little mottling, the wings with only slight indications of an irrorate pattern. General structure typical for genus. Male genitalia, fig. 125: ninth segment cylindrical, considerably narrowed near ventral margin, tenth tergite composed of a pair of dorsal lobes which are round, project over the rest of the tergite, and bear a short, sclerotized tooth on the posterior margin; below this is a group of small sclerites very similar to those in other members of the *carolina* group; claspers with basal segment very wide at base, the ventral margin conspicuously angulate just beyond base and curving gradually to a narrowed apex; apical segment of clasper with dorsal corner rounded and short, posterior margin only slightly concave, the ventral portion of the segment wide and rounded at apex, the mesal face with an irregular peripheral brush of short, flat setae arranged as illustrated; aedeagus very similar to that of *fenestra*, with a sharp, dorsal, keel-like structure divided at apex into dorsal and ventral prongs, ventral portion large and scoop shaped, and lateral arms membran-

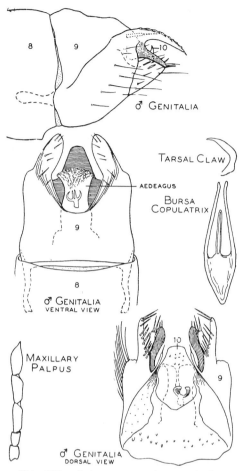

Fig. 135.—*Palaeagapetus celsus*, genitalia.

ous, tipped with a broad brush of curved spines.

Holotype, male.—Cloudy Creek near Cloudy, Oklahoma: May 4, 1940, Mrs. Roy Weddle.

Paratypes.—Same data as for holotype, 1 ♂.

The broad, scoop-shaped ventral portion of the aedeagus places this species immediately as a member of the *carolina* group. It is distinguished from all the previously described species of this group, however, by the absence of a well-developed dorsal heel on the apical segment of the clasper and by the shape of the tenth tergite.

The species has not been collected in Illinois. The types are from the Kiamichi Mountains of Oklahoma and may indicate an extensive range through the Ozarks, in which case it might eventually be found in Illinois.

Palaeagapetus Ulmer

Palaeagapetus Ulmer (1912, p. 35). Genotype, monobasic: *Palaeagapetus rotundatus* Ulmer (described from Baltic amber).

No representative of this genus has yet been taken in Illinois. The only species known from the eastern states, *celsus*, has been collected in North Carolina and Tennessee and is easily recognized in the male by the curious genitalia, fig. 135. Larva unknown. The genus may belong to the Rhyacophilinae.

GLOSSOSOMATINAE

This subfamily embraces several genera, three of which have been found in Illinois. The larvae make a saddle case formed of a dome-shaped upper portion with a flat strap across the underside, figs. 136, 137; the larva moves along with the anal portion protruding on one side of the strap and the front end protruding from the other. Before pupation the bottom strap is cut away and the dome-shaped upper portion is cemented to a rock or other support. The adults resemble *Rhyacophila* in shape and

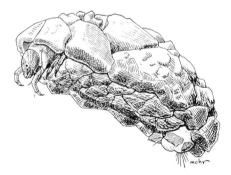

Fig. 136.—*Glossosoma intermedium* case.

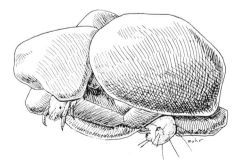

Fig. 137.—*Protoptila maculata* case.

general characteristics, and in general appearance differ from each other chiefly in size. The adults are secretive in habit and are very seldom captured except around their stream; the notable exception is *Protoptila*, which is taken frequently at lights in large numbers.

The larvae of this entire subfamily are very uniform in shape and appearance, differing chiefly in the characters mentioned in the key to genera. Reliable characters have not yet been discovered in the larvae for separating the species within the genus.

Glossosoma Curtis

Glossosoma Curtis (1834, p. 216). Genotype, monobasic: *Glossosoma boltoni* Curtis.

Mystrophora Klapálek (1892, p. 19). Genotype, monobasic: *Mystrophora intermedia* Klapálek. New synonymy.

The group of species with the short and platelike apical spur on the hind tibiae of the male has usually been considered as a separate genus, *Mystrophora*. Since there appears to be no corresponding diagnostic character in either the females or larvae, I am considering this division as of subgeneric importance at the most.

Only one species has been captured in Illinois; two others occur in the eastern states and many are known from the Rocky Mountain region.

Glossosoma intermedium (Klapálek)

Mystrophora intermedia Klapálek (1892, p. 19).

LARVA.—Fig. 136. Length 6–9 mm. Head, pronotum, legs and anal sclerites dark brown, body pinkish to very light brown.

ADULTS.—Length 7–10 mm. Body appendages dark brown, appearing almost black. Male with a flattened apical spur on hind tibiae, fig. 140. Male genitalia, fig. 138: tenth tergite divided to base into large lobes pointed at apex and provided at base with a long, sclerotized rod; claspers narrow at base, expanded at apex. Female genitalia, fig. 139, typical in general proportions for subfamily; eighth sternite deeply incised to form a deep, narrow V on meson.

This species, described and recorded from various points in Europe, has recently been found in Illinois, Minnesota and Missouri. In Illinois, it is apparently confined to the

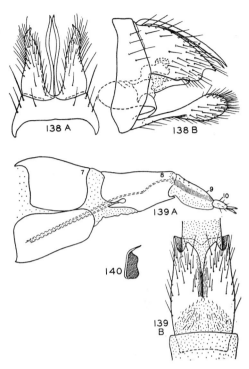

Fig. 138.—*Glossosoma intermedium*, male genitalia. *A*, dorsal aspect; *B*, lateral aspect.
Fig. 139.—*Glossosoma intermedium*, female genitalia. *A*, lateral aspect; *B*, ventral aspect.
Fig. 140.—*Glossosoma intermedium* ♂, spur of hind tibia.

small set of spring-fed brooks in the Elgin Botanical Gardens, where the species occurs in such numbers that the cases literally pave the bottoms of the streams.

Illinois Records.—ELGIN: April 19, 1939, Burks & Riegel, 1 pupa; May 9, 1939, Ross & Burks, ♂ ♂, ♀ ♀, many pupae and larvae; May 23, 1939, Burks & Riegel, 3 ♂, 1 ♀; June 6, 1939, Burks & Riegel, 2 ♂, 3 ♀; June 13, 1939, Frison & Ross, 6 ♂, 7 ♀; Sept. 19, 1939, Ross & Mohr, ♂ ♂, ♀ ♀, many larvae and pupae; March 20, 1940, B. D. Burks, 5 ♂, 2 ♀, 1 ♂ pupa, 1 mating pair; all of preceding Elgin records from Botanical Gardens; Rainbow Spring, May 19, 1939, Ross & Burks, 3 ♂, 2 ♀.

Agapetus Curtis

Agapetus Curtis (1834, p. 217). Genotype, by subsequent designation of Westwood (1840, p. 51): *Agapetus fuscipes* Curtis.

Only one species, *illini*, has been taken in Illinois. Three other species occur in the Ozarks and neighboring hills of nearby states. These resemble our Illinois form in size and color, but are readily separable on the basis of male genitalia as follows:

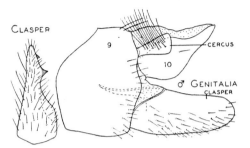

Fig. 141.—*Agapetus artesus.*

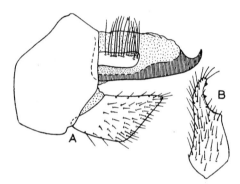

Fig. 142.—*Agapetus crasmus.*

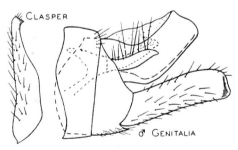

Fig. 143.—*Agapetus medicus.*

artesus, fig. 141, known from Missouri, has a somewhat pear-shaped, pointed tenth tergite and medium length, rounded claspers; *crasmus*, fig. 142, known from Tennessee, has a long tenth tergite with a hook at apex and very short, truncate claspers; and *medicus*, fig. 143, known from Arkansas, has a cleaver-shaped tenth tergite and long, rectangular claspers. Satisfactory characters have not yet been found to identify the females of species in this group.

Agapetus illini Ross

Agapetus illini Ross (1938a, p. 106); ♂, ♀.

LARVA.—Similar in size and color to that of *Glossosoma.*

ADULTS.—Length 7–8 mm. Body and appendages dark brown. Male genitalia, fig. 144, with apex of tenth tergite irregularly and sharply serrate, claspers tapering to apex. Female genitalia as in fig. 145.

Restricted in Illinois to clear streams in the Ozarkian region, where it becomes very abundant in early spring in these temporary streams. It has one generation per year.

Known also from Arkansas, Kentucky, Missouri and Oklahoma; apparently confined to the Ozarkian uplift and adjacent hilly regions.

Illinois Records.—East of ALDRIDGE: May 14, 1940, Mohr & Burks, 3 pupae, many larvae. ALTO PASS, Union Spring:

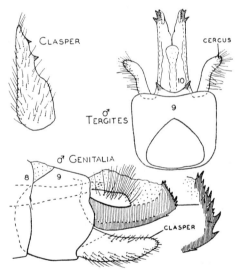

Fig. 144.—*Agapetus illini.*

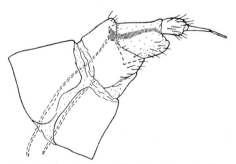

Fig. 145.—*Agapetus illini,* female genitalia.

May 26, 1940, Mohr & Burks, 1 ♂. EDDY-
VILLE, Lusk Creek: June 1, 1940, B. D.
Burks, 9 ♂. EICHORN: May 11, 1935, C.
O. Mohr, 4 ♂. HEROD: May 29, 1928,
T. H. Frison, 1 ♂; Gibbons Creek, May
29, 1928, T. H. Frison, ♂ ♂; May 10,
1935, C. O. Mohr, ♂ ♂, 1 ♀; May 29, 1935,
Ross & Mohr, ♂ ♂, 7 ♀; July 11, 1935,
Ross & DeLong, 1 ♂; May 1, 1936, Ross
& Mohr, ♂ ♂, 1 ♀; May 12, 1936, Mohr &
Burks, 7 ♂, 3 ♀; May 29, 1936, Ross &
Mohr, 1 ♀; May 13, 1937, Frison & Ross,
♂ ♂, 7 ♀.

Protoptila Banks

Clymene Chambers (1873, p. 114); preoccupied. Genotype, monobasic: *Clymene aegerfasciella* Chambers (described in Lepidoptera,
placed here by Banks).
   Protoptila Banks (1904*d*, p. 215). Genotype,
by original designation: *Beraea? maculata*
Hagen.

Of the 10 known Nearctic species, 3 have
been taken in Illinois and 2 others, known
from neighboring states, may ultimately turn
up here. No differences have been found to

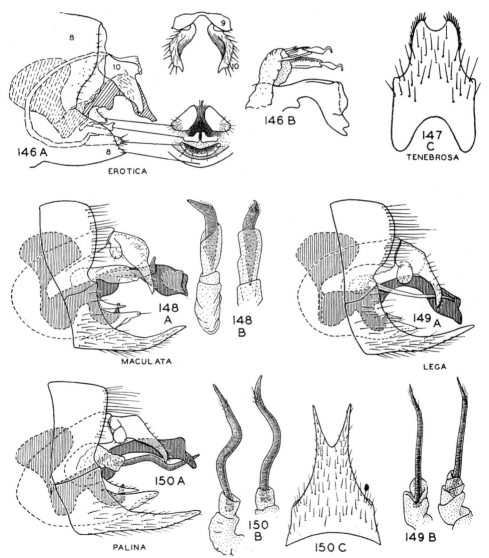

Figs. 146–150.—*Protoptila*, male genitalia.   *A*, lateral aspect; *B*, aedeagus or its spines;
C, eighth sternite.

divide the larvae to species. The adults of all species resemble each other very closely in appearance and general structure, differing chiefly in characters listed in the key.

KEY TO SPECIES

Adults

1. Apex of abdomen with assemblage of sclerotized rods and plates (males), fig. 146......................... 2
   Apex of abdomen cylindrical (females), fig. 151......................... 6
2. Eighth sternite scoop-shaped, not produced into a bifid process, fig. 146.. ....**erotica,** p. 44
   Eighth sternite produced into a bifid process, fig. 150................. 3
3. Eighth sternite with apico-lateral corner produced into a brushy lobe, and with apex massive and deeply and widely excavated, fig. 147..... ....**tenebrosa,** p. 43
   Eighth sternite with apico-lateral corner angulate, not produced, and

with apex more slender, fig. 150.... 4
4. Lateral spine of aedeagus stout and abruptly angled near apex, fig. 148. ....**maculata,** p. 43
   Lateral spine of aedeagus slender and only gradually curved, fig. 150.... 5
5. Lateral spine of aedeagus curved only near apex; apex of aedeagus abruptly narrowed at base, fig. 149...... ....**lega,** p. 43
   Lateral spine of aedeagus sinuate; apex of aedeagus only gradually narrowed at base, fig. 150........ ....**palina,** p. 43
6. Internal plate of ninth tergite with a dorsal, bandlike prolongation which is joined to the base of the tenth tergite, fig. 152*B*; apico-lateral lobes of eighth sternite long, trianguloid, fig. 152*A*...................... **maculata,** p. 43; **lega,** p. 43; **palina,** p. 43
   Internal plate of ninth tergite without dorsal prolongation, fig. 151*B*; apico-lateral lobes of eighth sternite narrow, fig. 151*A*.................. 7
7. Internal sternal "whip" attached to a

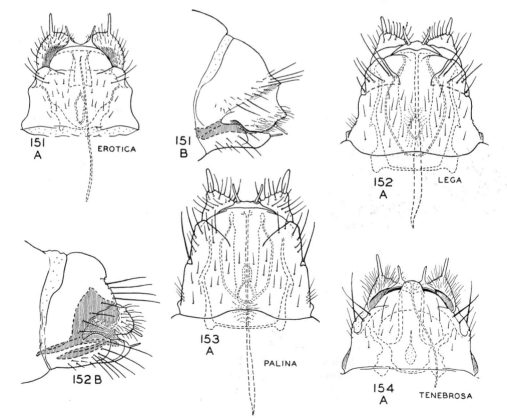

Figs. 151–154.—*Protoptila*, female genitalia. *A*, ventral aspect; *B*, lateral aspect.

small, projecting, mesal sclerite; lobes of tenth tergite conical, fig. 154..................**tenebrosa**, p. 43
Internal sternal "whip" attached to large, rounded plate which spans almost the entire width of the segment, fig. 151*A*.........**erotica**, p. 44

Protoptila maculata (Hagen)

Beraea? maculata Hagen (1861, p. 296); ♂.
Protoptila lloydi Mosely (1934*b*, p. 151); ♂.

LARVA.—Length 3–4 mm. Head, legs and body sclerites yellow.

CASE.—Fig. 137. Constructed of small, flat stones and forming a typical saddle case, complete with ventral strap. Due to its small size and somewhat irregular appearance it is overlooked easily when collecting.

ADULTS.—Length 3–4 mm. Head and body medium and light shades of brown, wings dark brown with a whitish band across the "cord" of the front wings. Both wings long and narrow, front ones with crossveins grouped to form an irregular cord near middle. Male genitalia, fig. 148: eighth sternite produced into a long, narrow, bifid process; tenth tergite produced into a divided, beaklike portion narrow at tip; aedeagus with a large, ovoid, internal lobe, a pair of lateral, style-bearing lobes and a sinuate central portion expanded at apex; styles short, stout and sharply curved at tip. Female genitalia similar to those in fig. 152, with essentially the same shaped internal whip and plates.

Allotype, female.—Momence, Illinois, along Kankakee River: May 29, 1939, Frison & Ross.

This species has been taken in Illinois from only two points on its eastern margin, in the Salt Fork River and the Kankakee River. Mature pupae have been collected in the Kankakee River. Adult records from May to August indicate two or more generations per year.

The range of the species is extensive through the northeastern states, with records from the District of Columbia, Illinois, Indiana, Kentucky, New York and Pennsylvania; these indicate that our Illinois records are near the western limit of its range.

Illinois Records.—MOMENCE: Kankakee River, May 29, 1939, Frison & Ross, ♂ ♂, 1 mating pair; Aug. 21, 1936, Ross & Burks, ♂ ♂, 2 ♂ (reared); Kankakee River, May 26, 1936, H. H. Ross, ♂ ♂.

OAKWOOD: June 14, 1935, C. O. Mohr, 1 ♂.

Protoptila lega Ross

Protoptila lega Ross (1941*b*, p. 48); ♂, ♀.

LARVA.—Not associated, but undoubtedly present in material collected in the Salt Fork River and not distinguished from *maculata.*

ADULTS.—Similar in size, color and general structure of genitalia to *maculata*; differing in the long, straight lateral styles of the aedeagus and the shape of the apex of the aedeagus, fig. 149. Female genitalia variable in minute details, a typical condition shown in fig. 152, but with variations occurring which are very similar to fig. 153.

To date this species has been taken in Illinois only from the upper Sangamon River, Salt Fork River, Middle Fork River and Embarrass River; confined to the stony riffles of these relatively clear streams. Mature pupae, linking the larvae with the adults, were collected in the Middle Fork River at Danville.

Known also from Missouri and Wisconsin.

Illinois Records.—CHARLESTON: Sept. 8, 1931, H. H. Ross, 1 ♂, 1 ♀. DANVILLE, Middle Fork River: Aug. 27, 1936, 1 ♂, 1 ♀. MAHOMET: Aug. 3, 1937, Ross & Burks, ♂ ♂, ♀ ♀. OAKWOOD: Aug. 14, 1935, C. O. Mohr, 5 ♂, 2 ♀; June 14, 1935, C. O. Mohr, 5 ♂, 3 ♀.

Protoptila palina Ross

Protoptila palina Ross (1941*b*, p. 46); ♂, ♀.

This species frequently occurs in company with *maculata* and *erotica.* Since both of these last species occur in Illinois, there is a good possibility that *palina* will eventually be taken in this state also. It is known from Kentucky, Pennsylvania and West Virginia.

Protoptila tenebrosa (Walker)

Hydroptila tenebrosa Walker (1852, p. 134); ♂, ♀.

This species has not yet been taken in Illinois but is known from Arkansas, Montana, Ontario, Wisconsin and Wyoming, and may eventually be found in one of the colder Illinois streams.

Protoptila erotica Ross

Protoptila erotica Ross (1938a, p. 113); ♂, ♀.

LARVA.—Not associated, but undoubtedly present in material collected from the Kankakee River and undifferentiated from *maculata*.

ADULTS.—Length 3.0–3.5 mm. Head and body brown, front wings with a narrow, light band across "cord." Male genitalia, fig. 146: eighth sternite short and scoop-like; tenth tergite divided into a pair of beaklike processes; aedeagus with a large, ovoid, internal lobe, a pair of lateral, style-bearing arms and a heavy, angled central portion. Female genitalia as in fig. 151.

This widely distributed northern species has been taken only at Momence, along the Kankakee River, in which the larvae undoubtedly live in company with *maculata*. Adult records from May to August indicate two or more generations per year.

Known from Illinois, Wisconsin and Wyoming.

Illinois Records.—MOMENCE: Aug. 21, 1936, Ross & Burks, 6 ♂ ; Kankakee River, May 26, 1936, H. H. Ross, ♂ ♂ ; May 24, 1937, H. H. Ross, 1 ♂ ; June 4, 1932, Frison & Mohr, 1 ♂, 1 ♀ ; Aug. 24, 1936, Ross & Burks, 2 ♂ .

PHILOPOTAMIDAE

Of the three North American genera belonging to this family, two have been taken in Illinois, and the third occurs in Indiana at a locality 17 miles from the Illinois state line.

The larvae frequent rapid streams or brooks. They are very active and make silken nets which form long, narrow pockets shaped like a long funnel. When the net is taken out of the water the whole structure collapses into a mass of silken folds.

For pupation each larva constructs an ovoid cocoon of small stones and debris which is lined with several folds of silk. This is attached on the underside of a stone or other object in the water.

The adults of *Trentonius* and *Dolophilus* are secretive; those of *Chimarra*, slightly less so. They can be collected by sweeping foliage hanging over water or in humid shady portions of the stream's course, especially during early evening.

KEY TO GENERA

Larvae

1. Apex of frons markedly asymmetrical, with a large or pointed left lobe and a smaller right one, figs. 155, 179–182. . . . .**Chimarra,** p. 48
   Apex of frons at most slightly asymmetrical, as in fig. 156.   2

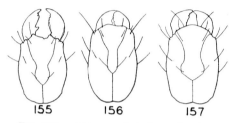

Fig. 155.—*Chimarra feria* larva, head.
Fig. 156.—*Trentonius distinctus* larva, head.
Fig. 157.—*Dolophilus shawnee* larva, head.

2. Frons almost perfectly symmetrical, with posterior portion widened, separated by a constriction from anterior portion, fig. 157. . . . .
   . . . .**Dolophilus,** p. 45
   Frons slightly asymmetrical, without constriction, posterior portion uniform in width, fig. 156. . . . .
   . . . .**Trentonius,** p. 47

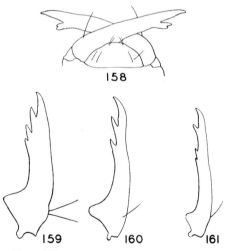

Fig. 158.—*Chimarra obscura* pupa, mandibles.
Fig. 159.—*Trentonius distinctus* pupa, mandibles.
Fig. 160.—*Dolophilus shawnee* pupa, mandibles.
Fig. 161.—*Dolophilus moestus* pupa, mandibles.

Pupae

1. Mandibles with a single, incised cusp below apical tooth, fig. 158......
    ....**Chimarra**, p. 48
    Mandibles with 2 or 3 sharp teeth below apical tooth, fig. 159........   2
2. Mandibles broad, subapical teeth close together, fig. 159..........
    ....**Trentonius**, p. 47
    Mandibles narrower, subapical teeth farther apart, figs. 160, 161......
    ....**Dolophilus**, p. 45

Adults

1. Wings reduced to stubs, fig. 171.....
    ....**Trentonius**, p. 47
    Wings normal, reaching beyond apex of abdomen, fig. 170..............   2
2. Front tibiae with 1 apical spur......
    ....**Chimarra**, p. 48
    Front tibiae with 2 apical spurs.....   3

Fig. 162.—*Trentonius distinctus*, front wing.
Fig. 163.—*Dolophilus shawnee*, front wing.

3. Front wings with vein R₂₊₃ branching beyond radial crossveins, near margin of wing, fig. 162..............
    ....**Trentonius**, p. 47
    Front wings with vein R₂₊₃ either branching at or near radial crossveins, or not branched, fig. 163....
    ....**Dolophilus**, p. 45

Dolophilus McLachlan

Dolophilus McLachlan (1868, p. 303). Genotype, monobasic: *Dolophilus copiosus* McLachlan.

Paragapetus Banks (1914, p. 202). Genotype, monobasic: *Paragapetus moestus* Banks.
Dolophiliella Banks (1930*b*, p. 230). Genotype, by original designation: *Dolophiliella gabriella* Banks.

Of the nine described North American species, only two have been taken in Illinois. The remainder have been collected only as far east as Oklahoma with the exception of one species, *major*, which occurs in the Great Smoky Mountains of North Carolina and Tennessee.

KEY TO SPECIES

Larvae

1. Apex of fore coxae with a stout, curved spur, fig. 164..........**shawnee**, p. 46

Fig. 164.—*Dolophilus shawnee* larva, front leg.
Fig. 165.—*Dolophilus moestus* larva, front leg.

Apex of fore coxae with a slender spur, fig. 165...............**moestus**, p. 47

Adults

1. Apex of abdomen with a pair of 2-segmented claspers (males).......   2
    Apex of abdomen simple and tubular (females)......................   3
2. Claspers with basal segment short and bulbous, apical segment much longer and spatulate; apico-mesal projection of seventh sternite short, fig. 166..................**shawnee**, p. 46
    Apical segment of claspers subequal in

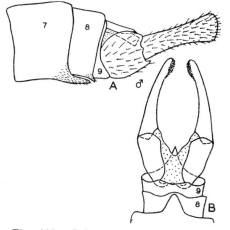

Fig. 166.—*Dolophilus shawnee*, male genitalia. *A*, lateral aspect; *B*, ventral aspect.

length to basal segment; apico-mesal process of seventh sternite very long, fig. 167......**moestus,** p. 47

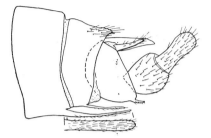

Fig. 167.—*Dolophilus moestus,* male genitalia.

Fig. 168.—*Dolophilus moestus* ♀, maxillary palpus.

Fig. 169.—*Dolophilus shawnee* ♀, maxillary palpus.

3. Maxillary palpi with second segment cylindrical, of the same diameter as first segment, fig. 168....**moestus,** p. 47
   Maxillary palpi with second segment swollen on the mesal side, so that at this point it is considerably wider than the first segment, fig. 169....
   ....**shawnee,** p. 46

Dolophilus shawnee Ross

Dolophilus shawnee Ross (1938a, p. 133); ♂, ♀.

LARVA.—Length 11–12 mm. Body slender. Head, pronotum, legs and anal hooks golden yellow. Head with a few long, scattered setae and with a pair of transverse brown bars near the posterior angle of the frons; mandibles relatively small with fine teeth near apex, fig. 173. Pronotum with a row of scattered setae along the anterior margin and another similar row across the segment at the point of the attachment of the legs. Body whitish when preserved, each segment with two pairs of slender setae. Anal hooks without inner teeth. Legs of similar shape and proportions, only the first pair with coxal spur.

ADULTS.—Fig. 170. Length 7–9 mm. Color of head, body and legs varying shades

of brown; antennae annulate with tawny and dark brown; wings uniformly gray. Head and thorax bearing tufts of thick tawny hair, and wings with fine, short, black setae which give them a purplish shade. Male genitalia, fig. 166, with claspers long, the apical segment twice the length of the basal segment.

This species is very abundant locally in clear, rapid, temporary streams in the Ozark Hills of southern Illinois. The adults are secretive and seldom captured even in localities where the larvae and pupae are abundant beneath almost every stone. The species is single brooded, the adults appearing in early spring.

In addition to Illinois, known only from Hopkinsville, Kentucky.

Illinois Records.—ALTO PASS, Union Spring: May 26, 1940, Mohr & Burks, 3 larvae, 5 pupae. EDDYVILLE, Lusk Creek: May 24, 1940, Mohr & Burks, 5 larvae, 6 pupae; June 1, 1940, B. D. Burks, 1

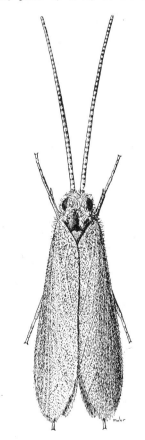

Fig. 170.—*Dolophilus shawnee.*

larva, 1 pupa. EICHORN: May 11, 1935, C. O. Mohr, 1 larva. ELIZABETHTOWN, Hog Thief Creek: May 10, 1935, C. O. Mohr, many larvae. GOLCONDA: May 11, 1935, C. O. Mohr, many larvae; April 30, 1940, Burks & Mohr, many larvae. HEROD, Gibbons Creek: March 10, 1935, C. O. Mohr, 1 pupa; May 10, 1935, C. O. Mohr, many larvae, 1 pupa; May 29, 1935, Ross & Mohr, 6 pupae; May 26, 1936, Mohr & Burks, 1 ♂ (reared); May 29, 1936, Ross & Mohr, 5 ♂, 8 ♀; May 15, 1941, Mohr & Burks, 1 larva. KARBERS RIDGE: May 11, 1935, C. O. Mohr, 1 pupa. WALTERSBURG: April 30, 1940, Mohr & Burks, 1 larva.

Dolophilus moestus (Banks)

Paragapetus moestus Banks (1914, p. 202); ♂.
Dolophilus breviatus Banks (1914, p. 254); ♂, ♀.

LARVA.—Length 10–11 mm. Similar in size and general structure to *shawnee*, differing in lacking the stout coxal spine on the front legs and in having the transverse bars of the frons only faintly indicated.

ADULTS.—Size 6–8 mm. Similar in general appearance and structure to those of *shawnee*. Male abdomen with long apical processes on seventh and eighth sternites; genitalia, fig. 167, with short, stocky claspers.

Our only Illinois records are from a group of small, spring-fed brooks in the Elgin Botanical Gardens, where we have taken larvae, mature pupae and adults. This species shares with *Chimarra feria* the distinction of being one of the earliest Illinois caddis flies to appear on the wing, adults having been taken as early as March 7.

The species is widespread throughout the eastern portion of the continent. In addition to Illinois, it is known from Georgia, Indiana, New York, North Carolina, Ohio, Ontario, Tennessee, Virginia, West Virginia and Wisconsin.

Illinois Records.—ELGIN: May 9, 1939, Ross & Burks, 2 ♂; May 23, 1939, Burks & Riegel, 1 ♂; June 13, 1939, Frison & Ross, 3 ♀; Sept. 19, 1939, Ross & Mohr, 1 larva, 1 pupa, 2 ♂, 1 ♀; preceding Elgin records from Botanical Gardens; Trout Spring, March 7, 1940, Burks & Mohr, 3 ♀.

Trentonius Betten & Mosely

Trentonius Betten & Mosely (1940, p. 11). Genotype, by original designation: *Philopotamus distinctus* Walker.

Apparently only the genotype occurs in the northeastern states. For many years this genus has been identified in North American literature as *Philopotamus*.

Trentonius distinctus (Walker)

Philopotamus distinctus Walker (1852, p. 104); ♂, ♀.
Philopotamus americanus Banks (1895, p. 316); ♂.

This species has not yet been captured in Illinois, but is known from Turkey Run State Park, Indiana, which is only 17 miles from the Illinois state line. It is distributed throughout the northeastern states, with records available for Indiana, Maine, Maryland, Michigan, Minnesota, New Brunswick, North Carolina, Nova Scotia, Ontario, Pennsylvania, Tennessee and Virginia.

This species is remarkable because of the production of adults during the entire year, including the winter months, and the wingless condition of most of the females, fig. 171. Extensive records in the Illinois Natural History Survey files indicate that fe-

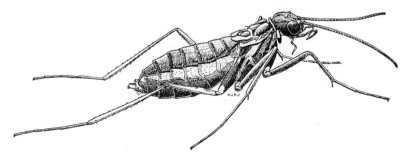

Fig. 171.—*Trentonius distinctus.*

males produced during the colder months are all wingless. Examination of pupae shows that in these brachypterous females the wings are abortive even in the pupal stage. Winged females have been taken only during the warmer months of the year. No

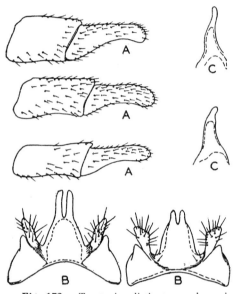

Fig. 172.—*Trentonius distinctus*, male genitalic parts, showing variation. *A*, claspers; *B*, tenth tergite, dorsal aspect; *C*, tenth tergite, lateral aspect.

intergradations between the normally winged specimens and practically wingless specimens have been observed. It would seem from this that these two conditions of the wings are probably caused by a temperature reaction influencing the late larvae, similar in behavior to certain characters observed in genetic studies of *Drosophila*. There is considerable variation in the relative proportions of the claspers in this species, apparently correlated to a large degree with size of individual: large individuals have the claspers very wide; smaller specimens have them much narrowed, fig. 172. As a general rule, the larger specimens of the males occur during the colder months of the year, so there is also an apparent correlation between width of clasper and seasonal appearance.

Chimarra Stephens

Chimarra Stephens (1829, p. 318). Genotype, monobasic: *Phryganea marginata* Linnaeus.

Chimarrha Burmeister (1839) and many other authors, an emendation.

Four species of this genus occur in Illinois and a fifth may be taken in future collecting. The larvae and adults of all our species are identical in external appearance, differing in the characters mentioned in the key.

LARVAE.—Length 11–12 mm. Head and pronotum golden brown, legs and anal hooks straw colored. Body whitish with two or three pairs of fine setae on each segment. Legs having short claws with a short tooth at base; anal hooks small and without inner teeth.

ADULTS.—Length 6–8 mm. Color dark brown, almost black, the sides of the abdomen and sometimes portions of the femora creamy white.

KEY TO SPECIES

Larvae

1. Apex of frons bearing a pair of large, rounded lobes, fig. 179 . . . .
. . . .**obscura,** p. 51
Apex of frons bearing smaller, pointed lobes, figs. 180–182   2

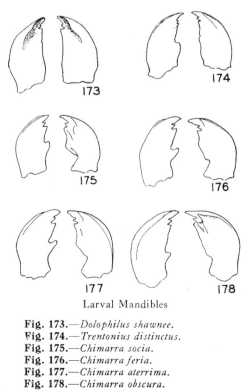

Larval Mandibles

Fig. 173.—*Dolophilus shawnee.*
Fig. 174.—*Trentonius distinctus.*
Fig. 175.—*Chimarra socia.*
Fig. 176.—*Chimarra feria.*
Fig. 177.—*Chimarra aterrima.*
Fig. 178.—*Chimarra obscura.*

2. Basal incision of right mandible very deep, fig. 175.............**socia**, p. 51
   Basal incision of right mandible shallow, fig. 177................... 3
3. Marginal lobes of frons slightly farther apart, fig. 181; basal incision of right mandible more conspicuous, fig. 176.................**feria**, p. 50
   Marginal lobes of frons slightly closer together, fig. 182; basal incision of right mandible less conspicuous, fig. 177.................**aterrima**, p. 50

Adults

1. Apex of abdomen with a pair of well differentiated claspers (males); all characters for couplets 2–5 are illustrated in fig. 183................. 2
   Apex of abdomen without claspers (females)......................... 6
2. Clasper with upper portion elongated into a narrow, rounded, finger-like lobe; ventro-mesal process of ninth sternite long and projecting, e.g., *obscura*......................... 3
   Clasper with upper portion short, either pointed or rounded and

blunt; ventro-mesal process of ninth sternite short and triangular, e.g., *angustipennis, feria*.............. 4
3. Aedeagus ending in a heavy, sclerotized hook; ventro-mesal process of ninth sternite long and narrow....
   ....**obscura**, p. 51
   Aedeagus ending in a pair of semimembranous lobes sclerotized at the

Apex of Larval Frons

Fig. 179.—*Chimarra obscura*.
Fig. 180.—*Chimarra socia*.
Fig. 181.—*Chimarra feria*.
Fig. 182.—*Chimarra aterrima*.

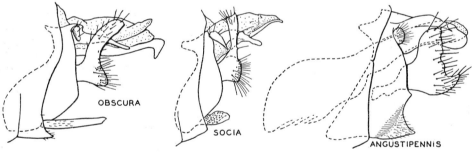

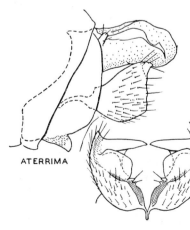

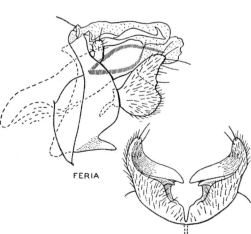

Fig. 183.—*Chimarra*, male genitalia.

sides; ventro-mesal process of ninth
tergite shorter and spatulate......
.........................**socia**, p. 51

4. Ventral margin of claspers produced
into a slightly upturned lobe......
................**angustipennis**, p. 51
Ventral margin of claspers not produced, forming a rounded lobe
e.g., *feria*....................... 5

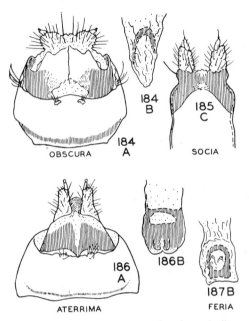

184
B

185
C

184
A
OBSCURA

SOCIA

186
A

186B

187B

ATERRIMA   FERIA

Figs. 184–187.—*Chimarra*, female genitalia.
A, ventral aspect; *B*, bursa copulatrix; *C*, dorsal
aspect.

5. Claspers with caudal face flat, transverse dorsal spur straight and dorsal
shoulder projection small or lacking
....................**aterrima**, p. 50
Claspers with caudal face excavated,
transverse dorsal spur curved basad
and dorsal shoulder projection high
and triangular...........**feria**, p. 50

6. Ninth tergite constricted sharply near
apex, fig. 185.............**socia**, p. 51
Ninth tergite with lateral margins
straight to apex................ 7

7. Ninth sternite produced into well-
defined, lateral, sclerotized "ears";
bursa copulatrix with only a single,
delicate, U-shaped sclerite, fig. 184
....................**obscura**, p. 51
Lateral margin of ninth sternite without lateral extensions; bursa copulatrix with at least a complete sclerotized ring, figs. 186, 187.......... 8

8. Sclerite of bursa copulatrix ringlike,
with a circular central clear area,

fig. 187..................**feria**, p. 50
Sclerite of bursa copulatrix purselike,
with a semicircular central clear
area, fig. 186.........**aterrima**, p. 50

Chimarra aterrima Hagen

Chimarrha aterrima Hagen (1861, p. 297); ♂,
♀.

Our only Illinois records for this species
are from small, spring-fed brooks in the
northern fourth of the state. Our records
are from April and May, indicating a single
generation per year in Illinois. In northern
states the species has been collected throughout the summer months.

This species is very abundant throughout
the eastern states, fig. 17, with records from
Florida, Illinois, Indiana, Kentucky, Maine,
Michigan, Minnesota, New Brunswick,
New York, North Carolina, Nova Scotia,
Ontario, Pennsylvania, Tennesse, Virginia,
West Virginia and Wisconsin. Illinois appears, therefore, to be on the western limit
of its main range. It has been collected
farther west only once, at Malvern, Arkansas.

Illinois Records.—COUNCIL HILL, tributary of Galena River: April 9, 1941, Ross
& Mohr, many larvae. DUNDEE: May 23,
1939, Burks & Riegel, ♂ ♂, ♀ ♀, many
larvae. UTICA, Split Rock Brook: May
24, 1941, 1 ♂.

Chimarra feria Ross

Chimarrha feria Ross (1941*b*, p. 51); ♂, ♀.

This species is very common in many of
the rapid clear streams in the Ozark region
of southern Illinois. Most of these streams
are dry during the summer and autumn
period. In these dry situations we have collected larvae of this species in a normal,
active, healthy condition under stones in portions of the river bed which were damp beneath the surface. The adults are among
the earliest caddis flies to appear on the
wing in this state, having been found at
Herod as early as March 28.

The range of the species embraces roughly the western edge of the oak-hickory forest
region, fig. 17. Records are available from
Arkansas, Illinois, Kansas, Minnesota, Missouri, Oklahoma, Texas and Wisconsin.
Illinois is on the extreme eastern edge of
its range.

Illinois Records.—DIXON SPRINGS: July
9, 1935, DeLong & Ross, 1 ♂. GOLCONDA:

May 11, 1935, C. O. Mohr, 1 larva. HEROD: Grand Pierre Creek, July 29, 1898, Hart, many larvae; Gibbons Creek, March 28, 1935, Ross & Mohr, ♂ ♂, ♀ ♀, many pupae, pupal skins and larval parts; June 21, 1935, DeLong & Ross, ♂ ♂; July 11, 1935, DeLong & Ross, ♂ ♂, 2♀; May 1, 1936, Ross & Mohr, ♂ ♂; May 12, 1936, Mohr & Burks, 2♂; June 24, 1936, DeLong & Ross, 5♂; Gibbons Creek, Sept. 11, 1937, H. H. Ross, 3 larvae; Oct. 7, 1937, Ross & Burks, 1♂; July 27, 1938, Burks & Boesel, 3♂, 1 mating pair; Oct. 1, 1941, B. D. Burks, many larvae. VIENNA: May 29, 1939, Burks & Riegel, ♂ ♂, ♀ ♀, 1 mating pair; May 1, 1940, Mohr & Burks, 2♂, 1♀. WALTERSBURG: March 24, 1939, Ross & Burks, 8 larvae. WEST VIENNA, Branch Cache River: May 13, 1939, Burks & Riegel, ♂ ♂, 6 larvae.

Chimarra angustipennis Banks

Chimarrha angustipennis Banks (1903*a*, p. 242); ♂.

This species, not yet taken in Illinois, occurs in Oklahoma and Arkansas. It is a close relative of the two preceding species. The larva is unknown.

Chimarra obscura (Walker)

Beraea? obscura Walker (1852, p. 121); ♂.
Wormaldia plutonis Banks (1911, p. 358); ♂.
Chimarrha lucia Betten (1934, p. 175); ♂, ♀.

Frequenting rapid and clear streams, this species has been taken at many points in northern, eastern and extreme southern Illinois. In each case our catches have been small, except in a few localities in the Ozark Hills of southern Illinois. Mature male pupae have been collected from many localities.

This species is the most widely distributed in the genus, fig. 18, being known from Arkansas, Illinois, Indiana, Kentucky, Maine, Maryland, Michigan, Minnesota, Missouri, New York, Ohio, Oklahoma, Ontario, Pennsylvania, Texas, Virginia and Wisconsin.

Illinois Records.—Many males and females and three pupae, taken May 11 to October 5, and many larvae, taken April 10 to August 27, are from Aurora, Danville (Middle Fork River), Golcondo, Herod (Grand Pierre Creek), Jonesboro

(Clear Creek), Kankakee (Kankakee River, Rock Creek), Momence, Oakwood (Salt Fork River), Oregon, Spring Grove, West Havana, West Vienna, Wilmington (Kankakee River), Wolf Lake (Hutchins Creek).

Chimarra socia Hagen

Chimarrha socia Hagen (1861, p. 297).
Wormaldia femoralis Banks (1911, p. 358).

Our only records for Illinois are along the Kankakee River. The species is apparently restricted to the northern and eastern states, and these collections for Illinois represent a local occurrence at the extreme western edge of its range. Association of larvae and adults is on the basis of a mature male pupa collected at Spooner, Wisconsin.

Known from Florida, Georgia, Indiana, Kentucky, Maine, Maryland, Michigan, New Brunswick, New York, Ohio, Ontario, Pennsylvania, Quebec, South Carolina and West Virginia in addition to Wisconsin.

Illinois Records.—KANKAKEE, Kankakee River: Aug. 1, 1933, Ross & Mohr, 6 larvae. MOMENCE, Kankakee River: May 26, 1936, H. H. Ross, 2♂.

PSYCHOMYIIDAE

The adults of this family range in size from fairly large species which might readily be confused with the Hydropsychidae to very small ones which, in general sorting, are frequently confused with Hydroptilidae. The larva, fig. 188, is active and spins a long silken net; when taken out of the water the net collapses and appears only as an irregular mass from which the larva wriggles free. Certain species are restricted to rapid streams, whereas others have an extremely wide ecological tolerance and are found in situations varying from lakes to rapid rivers.

The group formerly was divided into two families, the Psychomyiidae, containing *Psychomyia, Lype* and *Tinodes,* and the Polycentropidae, containing *Phylocentropus,*

Fig. 188.—*Polycentropus interruptus* larva.

Neureclipsis, Plectrocnemia, Polycentropus, Holocentropus, Nyctiophylax and *Cyrnellus.* An interesting link between the two groups, *Cernotina,* was recently described.

KEY TO GENERA

Larvae

1. Anal hooks with a row of 4 or 5 long teeth along inner ventral margin, fig. 189; tenth segment short, with scarcely any ventral margin, fig. 191; mentum forming a pair of distinct, sclerotized plates, fig. 194.......
.................**Psychomyia,** p. 75
Anal hooks with at most very short, inner teeth, fig. 190; tenth segment longer and tubular, figs. 192, 193; mentum not divided into two sclerotized plates, fig. 195............ 2
2. Mandibles short and triangular, each

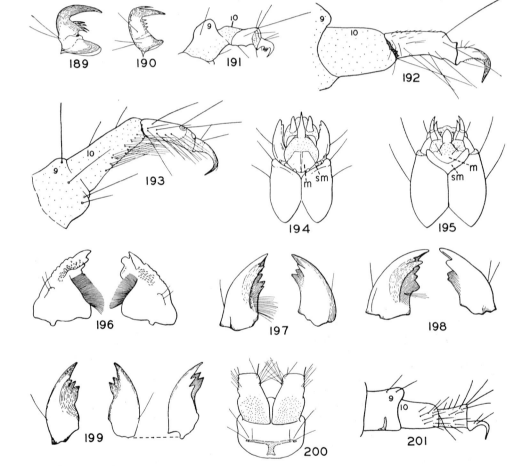

Fig. 189.—*Psychomyia flavida* larva, anal hook.

Fig. 190.—*Psychomyiid Genus A* larva, anal hook.

Fig. 191.—*Psychomyia flavida* larva, apex of abdomen.

Fig. 192.—*Neureclipsis crepuscularis* larva, apex of abdomen.

Fig. 193.—*Polycentropus interruptus* larva, apex of abdomen.

Fig. 194.—*Psychomyia flavida* larva, head, ventral aspect; *m,* mentum; *sm,* submentum.

Fig. 195.—*Polycentropus interruptus* larva,
head, ventral aspect; *m,* mentum; *sm,* submentum.

Fig. 196.—*Phylocentropus placidus* larva, mandibles. (After Vorhies.)

Fig. 197.—*Neureclipsis crepuscularis* larva, mandibles.

Fig. 198.—*Polycentropus interruptus* larva, mandibles.

Fig. 199.—*Psychomyiid Genus A,* mandibles.

Fig. 200.—*Psychomyiid Genus B,* venter of ninth and tenth segments.

Fig. 201.—*Psychomyiid Genus B,* apex of abdomen.

with a large, thick brush on the mesal side, fig. 196..............
..............**Phylocentropus**, p. 54
Mandibles longer, fig. 197, with only a thin brush on left mandible, none on right........................ 3

3. Right mandible with a single dorsal tooth which only partially hides the ventral row of teeth; on the left mandible the dorsal row of teeth does not hide the ventral row, figs. 197, 198....................... 4
Right mandible with two large dorsal teeth which completely overhang and hide the ventral row; on the left mandible the dorsal row of teeth overhangs and hides the ventral row, fig. 199.................... 5

4. Basal segment of anal appendages (tenth segment) without hair, fig. 192; left mandible with basal tooth small and with a linear brush on mesal face near base, fig. 197.....
.................**Neureclipsis**, p. 56
Basal segment of anal appendages (tenth segment) with long hair, fig. 193; left mandible with basal tooth large, subequal to one above and with brush small, fig. 198........
..............**Polycentropus**, p. 58

5. Ninth sternite with a wide, T-shaped, reticulate area; tenth segment short, with an extensive patch of minute spinules on venter, figs. 200, 201...
........**Psychomyiid Genus B**, p. 74
Ninth sternite without a reticulate area; tenth segment long, without spinules but with an extensive patch of long hair on venter, similar to fig. 193.....**Psychomyiid Genus A**, p. 73

Pupae

1. Apex of mandibles with a long, terminal "whip," fig. 202.............
.................**Psychomyia**, p. 75

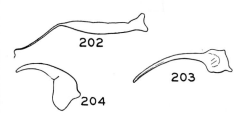

Fig. 202.—*Psychomyia flavida* pupa, mandible.
Fig. 203.—*Polycentropus cinereus* pupa, mandible.
Fig. 204.—*Phylocentropus placidus* pupa, mandible. (After Vorhies.)

Apex of mandibles without a terminal "whip," fig. 203.................. 2

2. Terminal segment of abdomen with 4 bushy processes, 2 apical and 2 baso-lateral.........**Phylocentropus**, p. 54
Terminal segment with only 2 apical bushy processes, fig. 205.......... 3

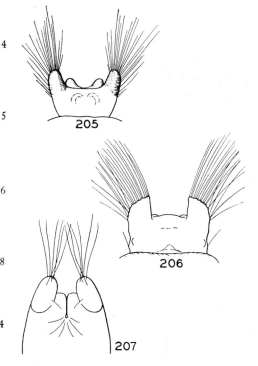

Fig. 205.—*Polycentropus cinereus* pupa, apical processes.
Fig. 206.—*Neureclipsis crepuscularis* pupa, apical processes.
Fig. 207.—*Psychomyia flavida* pupa, apical processes.

3. Apical lobes of abdomen evenly rounded at apex, fig. 205..........
.................**Polycentropus**, p. 58
Apical lobes of abdomen with mesal margin straight, mesal angle sharp and outer margin curved, fig. 206..
.................**Neureclipsis**, p. 56

Adults

1. Front tibiae with a preapical spur.... 2
Front tibiae without a preapical spur 6

2. Both pairs of wings with R_2 present and branching from R_3 at radial crossvein, fig. 208.
..............**Phylocentropus**, p. 54
Both pairs of wings with R_2 either

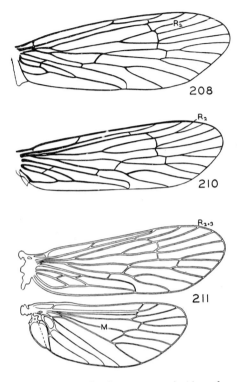

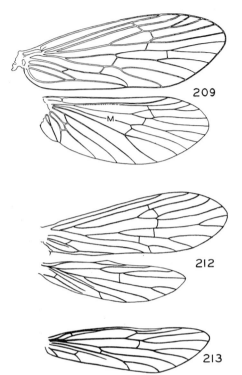

Fig. 208.—*Phylocentropus placidus*, front wing.

Fig. 209.—*Neureclipsis crepuscularis*, front and hind wings.

Fig. 210.—*Polycentropus cinereus*, wings.
Fig. 211.—*Nyctiophylax vestitus*, wings.
Fig. 212.—*Psychomyia nomada*, wings.
Fig. 213.—*Lype diversa*, hind wing.

     absent or branching from R_3 near margin of wing, fig. 210........... 3
3. Hind wings with M 3-branched, fig. 209..............**Neureclipsis**, p. 56
    Hind wings with M 2-branched, fig. 211.............................. 4
4. Front or hind wings, or both, with R_2 present, fig. 210...**Polycentropus**, p. 58
    Both wings with R_2 absent, fig. 211... 5

5. Maxillary palpi with second segment long, third only slightly longer than second, fifth short, fig. 214........ ....**Cyrnellus**, p. 71
    Maxillary palpi with second segment short, third three times as long as second, fifth long, fig. 215........ ....**Nyctiophylax**, p. 69
6. Maxillary palpi with second segment only one-half to one-third as long as third segment and with the apex enlarged into a small cushion, fig. 216 ....**Cernotina**, p. 72
    Maxillary palpi with second segment as long as third and uniformly cylindrical, fig. 217................. 7
7. Hind wings with apex evenly rounded, fig. 213...................**Lype**, p. 74
    Hind wings with apex tapering and somewhat pointed, fig. 212........ ....**Psychomyia**, p. 75

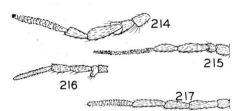

Fig. 214.—*Cyrnellus marginalis*, maxillary palpus.
Fig. 215.—*Nyctiophylax vestitus*, maxillary palpus.
Fig. 216.—*Cernotina oklahoma*, maxillary palpus.
Fig. 217.—*Lype diversa*, maxillary palpus.

Phylocentropus Banks

♦ *Phylocentropus* Banks (1907a, p. 130). Genotype, by original designation: *Holocentropus placidus* Banks.

Acrocentropus Betten (1934, p. 213). Genotype, monobasic: *Polycentropus lucidus* Hagen.

Only one species of this genus has been taken in the state. A second species, *lucidus*, occurs in the northeastern states and may eventually be found in Illinois. We have not reared this genus in Illinois, but descriptions of the larvae by Vorhies (1909) and others indicate characters for a clear-cut generic diagnosis.

KEY TO SPECIES

Adults

1. Apex of abdomen with dorsal and ventral appendages, figs. 218, 219 (males) 2
   Apex of abdomen conical with a pair of flaplike ventral appendages, figs. 220, 221 (females) 3
2. Tenth tergite sclerotized and produced into a heavy, upturned hook; apex of aedeagus sharp, fig. 218 . . . . **lucidus**, p. 56
   Tenth tergite broad and truncate, not sclerotized; aedeagus tubular with the apex obliquely truncate, fig. 219 . . . . **placidus**, p. 55

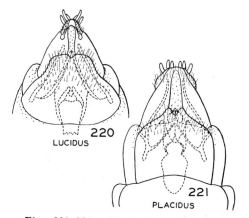

Figs. 220–221.—*Phylocentropus*, female genitalia.

3. Apex of eighth sternite broad, the mesal incision forming 2 wide lobes, fig. 220 . . . . **lucidus**, p. 56
   Apex of eighth sternite narrowed and divided into 2 small lobes, fig. 221 . . . . **placidus**, p. 55

Phylocentropus placidus (Banks)

Holocentropus placidus Banks (1905*b*, p. 15); ♂.

Phylocentropus maximus Vorhies (1909, p. 711); ♂, larva and pupa.

LARVA (after Vorhies).—Length 15–16 mm. Head, pronotum and legs straw yellow, pronotum with posterior half of lateral border and all posterior border black; body colorless. Labium elongate and styliform. Mandibles short and stocky, dorsal surface with more or less granular teeth and mesal portion provided with a dense large brush.

ADULTS.—Length 9–11 mm. Color various shades of brown; wings finely and almost evenly speckled with light brown. Front wings with R_s angled near base and touching stem of M. Male genitalia, fig. 219: cerci ovate, tenth tergite wide, unsclerotized and almost truncate at apex; claspers appearing ovate from side view, ventral aspect more or less quadrate with a dense brush of black setae along mesal margin; aedeagus tubular, the apex obliquely truncate. Female genitalia, fig. 221: eighth sternite tapered at apex and incised to form a pair of small lobes.

Our Illinois records of this species are from two southern localities in the Ozark Hills. The account of its biology is given by Vorhies, who found it making tubular

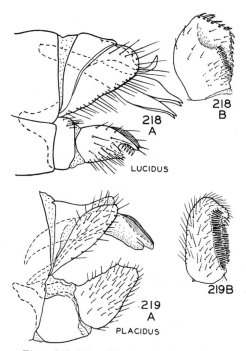

Figs. 218–219.—*Phylocentropus*, male genitalia. *A*, lateral aspect; *B*, claspers, caudoventral aspect.

cases embedded in the sand bottoms of southern Wisconsin streams. These cases he records as sometimes 65 mm. long, the greater portion buried, only 10–20 mm. of the case projecting from the stream bed. Within this case the pupa spins its cocoon.

This species is fairly widely distributed throughout the Northeast. Our records from Indiana and Illinois appear to be on the southern limit of the western portion of the range. It is known from Georgia, Illinois, Indiana, Maine, Michigan, Minnesota, New Brunswick, New York, Nova Scotia, Ohio, Ontario, Quebec and Wisconsin.

Illinois Records.—GOLCONDA: April 17, 1930, Frison & Ross, 2 ♂, 1 ♀. HEROD: May 10, 1935, C. O. Mohr, 1 ♀.

Phylocentropus lucidus (Hagen)

Polycentropus lucidus Hagen (1861, p. 294); ♂.

This species has not yet been taken in Illinois. It is known from New York, Nova Scotia, Pennsylvania and Tennessee. In the front wing R_s does not join M, and on this basis the species was referred to a new genus, *Acrocentropus*, by Betten. The structures of the male and female genitalia, however, indicate clearly that it belongs with *placidus*. The female is similar to the male in color and in general structure; the genitalia, fig. 220, have the eighth sternite heavily sclerotized, the apex broad, slightly indented on the meson, resulting in very wide lobes; bursa copulatrix long, semimembranous, and attached to sclerotized rods of the ninth segment.

Allotype, female.—Bear Brook near Blue Mountain Lake, New York: June 19, 1941, Frison & Ross.

Neureclipsis McLachlan

Neureclipsis McLachlan (1864, p. 30). Genotype, monobasic: *Phryganea bimaculata* Linnaeus.

Of the three species known from North America, two have been taken from Illinois, and the third occurs to the northeast. We have reared only *crepuscularis*; this larva agrees very well with Ulmer's description of *bimaculatus*, and it is possible that all three species have larvae similar in color and general structure.

KEY TO SPECIES

Adults

1. Genitalia with a distinct aedeagus, figs. 222–224 (males)   2
   Genitalia without an aedeagus, figs. 225–227 (females)   4
2. Base of left clasper with a large dorsal projection near base, fig. 222 . . . . . .
   . . . .**validus**, p. 58
   Base of left clasper without a dorsal projection, dorsal margin almost uniformly straight from base to apex, fig. 223   3
3. Cerci represented by long, heavily sclerotized filaments, fig. 223; tenth tergite very long . . . .**bimaculatus**, p. 57
   Cerci lobelike and not heavily sclerotized, fig. 224; tenth tergite short . . . .**crepuscularis**, p. 57
4. Eighth sternite with a long, high mesal ridge, the lateral lobes long and nar-

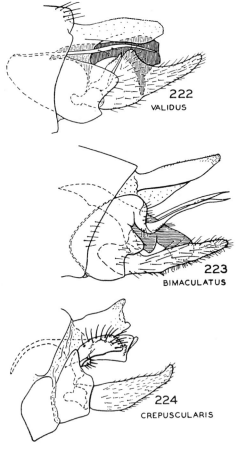

Figs. 222–224.—*Neureclipsis*, male genitalia.

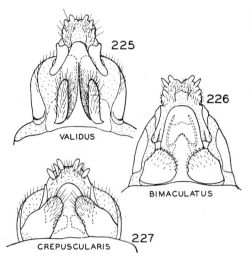

Figs. 225–227.—*Neureclipsis*, female genitalia.

row, fig. 225............**validus**, p. 58
Eighth sternite without a long mesal
ridge, the lateral lobes short and
wide, fig. 226................... 5
5. Apex of eighth sternite projecting beyond lateral lobes the length of the
lobes; ninth sternite with a heavily
sclerotized, vasiform structure, fig.
226..............**bimaculatus**, p. 57
Apex of eighth sternite projecting only
a short distance beyond lateral
lobes; ninth sternite with only indistinct structures, fig. 227........
................**crepuscularis**, p. 57

Neureclipsis crepuscularis (Walker)

Brachycentrus crepuscularis Walker (1852,
p. 87); ♀.
Neureclipsis parvula Banks (1907*b*, p. 163);
♂.

LARVA.—Length 12 mm. Head, prono-
notum and legs straw color with black setae,
the head and pronotum with dark brown
spots; those on the frons arranged as in
fig. 233; body pale with irregular purplish
areas on the dorsum and lateral portion
of each segment.
ADULTS.—Length 7.5 mm. Color reddish
brown, the legs and venter straw color.
Male genitalia, fig. 224: cerci ovate with a
round ventral lobe; claspers long, evenly
tapering from base to apex, tip curved
mesad; tenth tergite long, tapering and
semimembranous. Female genitalia, fig.
227: eighth sternite with distinct corners
and a rounded apex projecting a distance

beyond lateral lobes; lateral lobes fairly
broad, rounded at apex and with abundant
setae; internal sclerites of ninth segment
semimembranous and irregular.
A study of large series of males and
females leaves no doubt regarding the association of the two sexes, thus upholding
the synonymy of *parvula* with *crepuscularis*,
as proposed by Milne (1936).
In Illinois this species is widely distributed over the entire state. It is most abundant along the larger rivers. It is seldom
taken in large numbers, but we have at
times captured large series along the Mississippi River. The adults emerge over a
wide period; our records extend from May
3 to October 2. The association of larvae
and adults is made on the basis of mature
pupae collected in Wisconsin and Indiana.
The range of the species includes most
of the Northeast, with a southwestward
extension through the Ozarks. We have
records from Arkansas, Illinois, Indiana,
Kentucky, Michigan, Missouri, New Brunswick, New York, North Carolina, Nova
Scotia, Ohio, Pennsylvania, Tennessee, Virginia and Wisconsin.
Illinois Records.—Many males and females, taken May 3 to October 2, are from
Alton, Champaign, Danville, Deer Grove
(Green River), Elizabethtown, Florence,
Fort Massac State Park, Grafton (wing
dam), Grand Tower, Hardin (Illinois
River), Harrisburg, Havana (Spoon Riv-
er), Homer (Salt Fork River), Kamps-
ville, Kankakee, Keithsburg, La Rue (Mc-
Cann Spring), Milan (Rock River), Mo-
mence (Kankakee River), Monticello,
Mount Carmel, Morris, Oakwood, Pontiac,
Quincy (Burton Creek), Rock Island, Rosi-
clare, Savanna, Serena (Indian Creek),
Sterling, Venedy Station (Kaskaskia River).

Neureclipsis bimaculatus (Linnaeus)

Phryganea bimaculata Linnaeus (1758, p.
548).

LARVA.—Similar to that of *crepuscularis*,
according to Ulmer (1909, p. 229).
ADULTS.—Length 7.5–9.0 mm. Color
brown, the venter and legs straw color.
Male genitalia, fig. 223: cerci ribbon-like,
produced into long, fairly straight ribbons as
long as claspers; claspers slender, elongate
and straight; tenth tergite semimembranous,
long and slightly rounded at apex; aedeagus

with a straight base and with the apex divided by a ventral incision into two large lobes. Female genitalia, fig. 226: eighth sternite projecting far beyond lateral lobes, the apex rounded; lateral lobes short and somewhat ovate; ninth segment with a somewhat vasiform, sclerotized, internal structure in addition to other membranous parts.

The few Illinois records for this species are scattered from the extreme northern portion to the southern tip of the state. The species is Holarctic, its distribution on this continent extending southeastward to Quebec, Wisconsin and Illinois. It has been taken in a variety of habitats, and the records indicate an adult emergence which continues through the warmer months of the summer.

Illinois Records.—GOLCONDA: April 17, 1930, Frison & Ross, 1 ♀. HOMER: July 6, 1927, at light, Frison & Glasgow, 1 ♀. SAVANNA: June 2, 1942, at light, H. Hersey, ♂ ♂, 6 ♀. North of WADSWORTH, Des Plaines River: July 7, 1937, Frison & Ross, 1 ♂. WAUKEGAN: July 16, 1938, Ross & DeLong, 1 ♀.

Neureclipsis validus (Walker)

Polycentropus validus Walker (1852, p. 100); ♂.
Hydropsyche dubitans Walker (1852, p. 113); ♀.
Polycentropus signatus Banks (1897, p. 30); ♂.

This species has not yet been taken in Illinois but has been recorded from Ontario and western New York.

Polycentropus Curtis

Polycentropus Curtis (1835*a*, pl. DXLIV). Genotype, by subsequent designation of Westwood (1840, p. 49): *Polycentropus irroratus* Curtis.

Many of the species included under this genus were formerly placed in *Plectrocnemia* and *Holocentropus*. The characters of the larvae and pupae, as well as certain characters of the adults, indicate that these species together form a single unit as contrasted with other generic groups in the family. I am making no attempt at this time to judge the validity of either *Plectrocnemia* or *Holocentropus*; the study of larvae of the species from various conti-

nents, as well as a critical study of the genotypes, will be necessary before the names can be applied even to subgeneric categories of North American species.

About 25 species are known in North America, of which 9 have been taken in Illinois. Many of the species are rare but widely distributed, and it is probable that further collecting will yield new state records in this genus.

KEY TO SPECIES

Larvae

The following larval key is based on relative characters and few species. For these reasons it should not be used indiscriminately for specific identifications. It is of considerable use for separating to species larvae in a particular habitat of known taxonomic composition, and it should be used primarily for this purpose.

1. Basal segment of anal appendages with setae fairly short and distributed uniformly over ventral surface, fig. 228............................... 2
   Basal segment of anal appendages with setae longer and grouped in two lateral linear areas, fig. 228........ 3

2. Spots on upper part of frons definite and forming an angle, fig. 230..... ....**cinereus,** p. 67
   Spots on upper frons indefinite and forming a straight line or even arc, fig. 231...............**centralis,** p. 64

3. Head almost uniformly brown, spots present but of only a slightly differ-

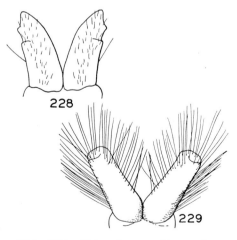

Fig. 228.—*Polycentropus cinereus* larva, lobes of tenth segment, ventral aspect.
Fig. 229.—*Polycentropus interruptus* larva, lobes of tenth segment, ventral aspect.

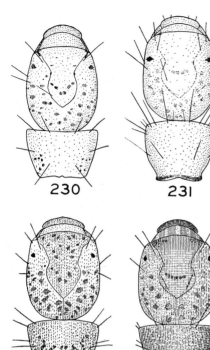

Polycentropus Larvae, Heads

Fig. 230.—*P. cinereus.*
Fig. 231.—*P. centralis.*
Fig. 232.—*P. remotus.*
Fig. 233.—*P. interruptus.*

ent shade than background.......
...........................**flavus,** p. 68
Head with spots conspicuous........　4
4. Upper part of frons long, subequal in
   length to lower portion, fig. 232;
   hair on basal segment of anal appendages in irregular lateral areas..
   ....**remotus,** p. 67
   Upper part of frons shorter than lower
   portion, fig. 233; hair on basal segment of anal appendages in regular
   rows, fig. 229....................　5
5. Dorsum of head usually clouded with
   reddish brown; major pair of setae
   of upper frons with a small pale area
   around base........**interruptus,** p. 69
   Dorsum of head usually not clouded
   with reddish brown; major pair of
   setae of upper frons with a brown
   ring around base......**glacialis,** p. 68

Adults

1. Genitalia complex, with an aedeagus,
   figs. 234–248 (males).............　2

Genitalia without an aedeagus, figs.
   249, 250 (females)...............　16
2. Eighth sternite produced into a long,
   apical projection, figs. 234, 235....　3
   Eighth sternite not produced into an
   apical projection, fig. 236.........　4
3. Apical projection of eighth sternite
   wide and incised on meson, fig. 234
   ....**aureolus,** p. 64
   Apical projection of eighth sternite
   narrow and pointed, fig. 235......
   ....**crassicornis,** p. 64
4. Cerci with dorsal angle produced into
   a long, down-curved, sclerotized
   needle, fig. 242..................　5
   Cerci without such a sclerotized process, fig. 236.....................　11
5. Ninth sternite narrow; cerci with a
   narrow, finger-like projection from
   latero-caudal margin, fig. 242.....
   ....**pentus,** p. 65
   Ninth sternite wide; cerci without a
   finger-like projection from latero-
   caudal margin, fig. 243...........　6
6. Aedeagus long and U-shaped, fig. 243
   ....**maculatus,** p. 65
   Aedeagus straight or only slightly
   curved, figs. 244, 246.............　7
7. Baso-dorsal appendage of clasper
   almost sessile, without a definite
   stalk, fig. 244, and projecting laterad of clasper.........**confusus,** p. 65
   Baso-dorsal appendage with a definite
   stalk so that the dark mesal point is
   some distance from the basal part of
   the clasper, figs. 246, 247, and not
   projecting laterad of it...........　8
8. Ventral aspect of claspers wide on
   basal portion, tapering suddenly to
   a narrow apex, figs. 245, 246......　9
   Ventral aspect of claspers tapering
   gradually or imperceptibly from base
   to apex, figs. 247, 248............　10
9. Claspers with base wide and subparal-
   lel two-thirds of its length, the apex
   short and digitate; filaments of cerci
   long and sinuate, their apex curved
   dorsad; baso-dorsal appendage of
   clasper with a subtriangular apex
   well differentiated from stalk, fig.
   245....................**elarus,** p. 65
   Claspers with base wide for only one-
   third its length, the apex long and
   curved; filaments of cerci curved
   ventrad and closer to basal portion;
   baso-dorsal appendage with apex
   smaller and merging gradually with
   stalk, fig. 246.......**carolinensis,** p. 66
10. Baso-dorsal lobe of claspers long and
    narrow, the mesal point round, the
    entire lobe arched; aedeagus widened
    at tip, fig. 247.............**pixi,** p. 66

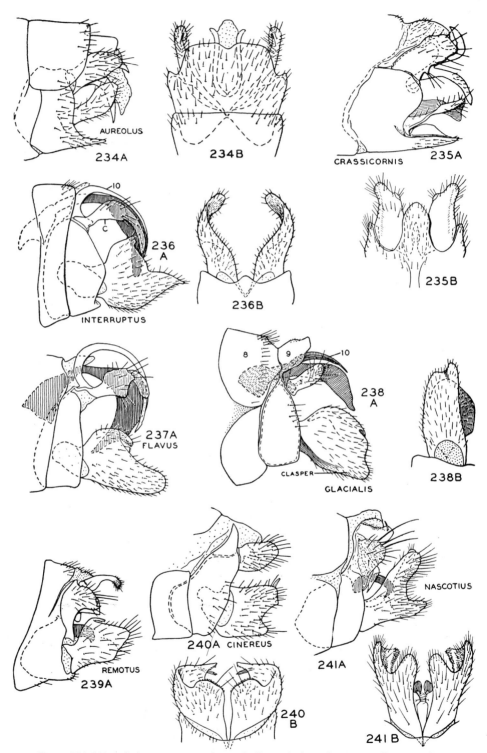

Figs. 234–241.—*Polycentropus*, male genitalia. *A*, lateral aspect; *B*, ventral aspect, usually showing only the claspers.

Baso-dorsal lobe of claspers shorter and wide, the mesal point sharp, the entire lobe erect; aedeagus narrowed at tip, fig. 248........... ....**centralis**, p. 64

11. Processes of tenth tergite long, sclerotized and arched, fig. 236....... 12
Processes of tenth tergite either semimembranous or short, fig. 239..... 14

12. Apex of cerci long and tapering to a sharp point, fig. 236............. ....**interruptus**, p. 69
Apex of cerci shorter, rounded at apex, fig. 237........................ 13

13. Aedeagus and filaments of tenth tergite long; claspers with only a short dorso-mesal flap, fig. 237.... ....**flavus**, p. 68
Aedeagus and filaments of tenth tergite short; claspers with a large, rhomboidal dorso-mesal flap, fig. 238.................**glacialis**, p. 68

14. Tenth tergite with a pair of curved,

hornlike, sclerotized processes, fig. 239..................**remotus**, p. 67
Tenth tergite without such processes, fig. 240........................ 15

15. Claspers with lateral aspect quadrate, posterior margin only narrowly incised, fig. 240..........**cinereus**, p. 67
Claspers with lateral aspect expanded at apex, posterior margin deeply and widely incised, fig. 241........ ....**nascotius**, p. 68

16. Genital segment long and tapering, lateral lobes of eighth sternite with footlike base and stylelike blade on meso-apical corner, fig. 249....... ....**crassicornis**, p. 64
Genital segment shorter and broader, lateral lobes of eighth sternite not so shaped, fig. 250................. 17

17. Base of eighth sternite with a pointed elevation, fig. 250........**flavus**, p. 68
Base of eighth sternite without a pointed elevation, fig. 251........ 18

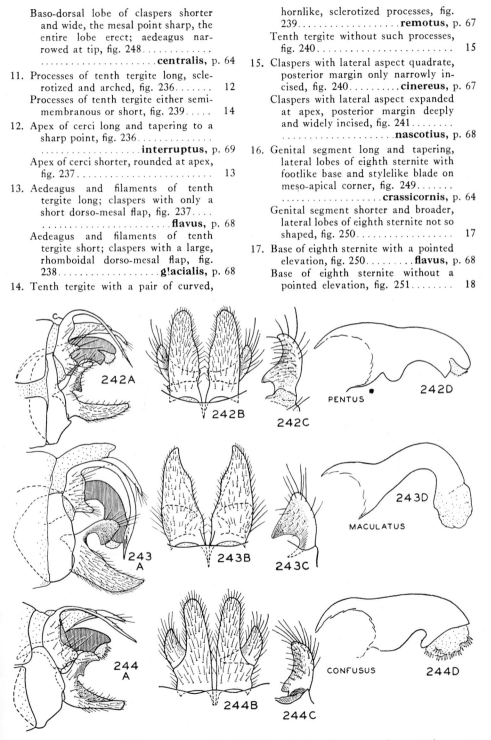

Figs. 242-244.—*Polycentropus*, male genitalia. *A*, lateral aspect; *B*, ventral aspect; *C*, baso-dorsal appendage of clasper; *D*, aedeagus.

18. Lateral lobes of eighth sternite long and narrow, figs. 251, 253........ 19

    Lateral lobes of eighth sternite shorter and wider, almost quadrate, figs. 260, 261...................... 27

19. Base of eighth sternite with a definite shelf or ledge with a sharp edge, situated between lateral lobes, figs. 251, 252...................... 20

    Base of eighth sternite without a ledge situated between lateral lobes, figs. 253–259........................ 21

20. Eighth sternite with basal ledge narrow; lateral lobes long, slightly expanded near apex and with an angulate foot, fig. 251...**interruptus**, p. 69

    Eighth sternite with basal ledge wide; lateral lobes therefore farther apart,

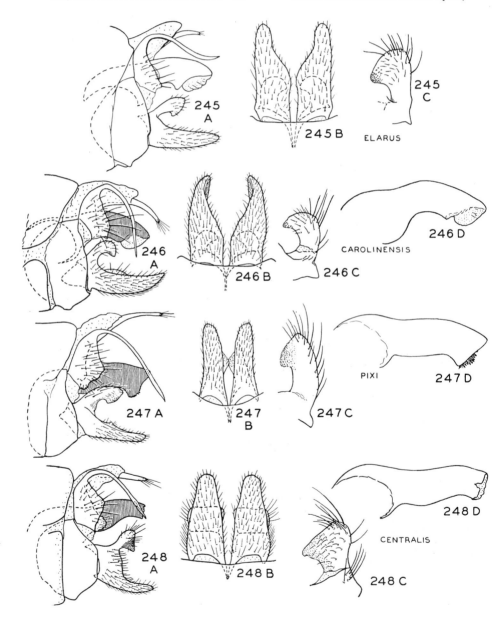

Figs. 245–248.—*Polycentropus*, male genitalia. *A*, lateral aspect; *B*, ventral aspect; *C*, baso-dorsal appendage of clasper; *D*, aedeagus.

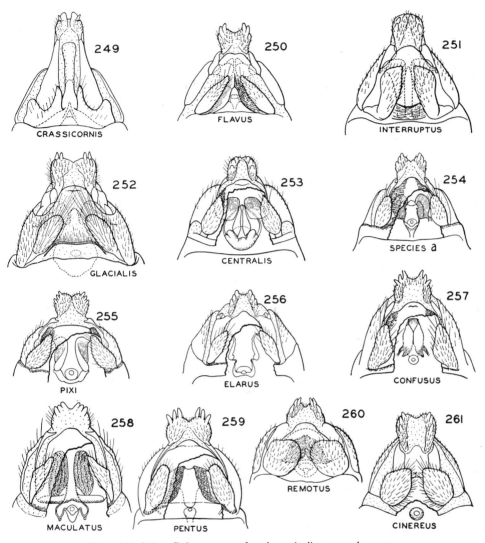

Figs. 249–261.—*Polycentropus*, female genitalia, ventral aspect.

shorter, without expanded apex and with foot not angulate, fig. 252....
................................**glacialis**, p. 68

21. Bursa copulatrix with a wide base and long, vasiform, sclerotized apical structures; internal structure of ninth segment as in fig. 253, with rounded, nearly approximate apical lobes which are sclerotized only at apex................**centralis**, p. 64

Bursa copulatrix shaped differently, figs. 254–259; internal structure with longer lobes which are farther apart.......................... 22

22. Ninth sternite with ovoid sclerotized lobes on each side of bursa; eighth sternite nearly triangular with the sides slightly sinuate, fig. 254......
......................**species a**, p. 66

Ninth sternite without ovoid lobes as in fig. 254; eighth sternite with apex more rounded, often nearly truncate, figs. 255–259.................. 23

23. Ninth sternite without sclerotized bands; bursa supports sometimes heavily sclerotized, figs. 255–257.. 24

Ninth sternite with sclerotized bands in addition to supports of bursa copulatrix, figs. 258, 259.......... 26

24. Upper portion of bursa supports thick, wide and twisted, fig. 255, and lower portion forming a thick bridge below bursa......................**pixi**, p. 66

Bursa supports much more slender,

fig. 256, or very little sclerotized, fig. 257................................. 25

25. Bursa supports distinct, sclerotized, slender and sinuate, fig. 256......
    ....**elarus**, p. 65
    Bursa supports chiefly membranous, with only a small basal portion and a curious sclerotized forklike piece near bursa, fig. 257.............
    ....**confusus**, p. 65

26. Sclerotized bands of ninth tergite more rectangular, parallel, and closer together at base, fig. 258....
    ....**maculatus**, p. 65
    Sclerotized bands of ninth tergite sinuate, pointed at apex, wide apart at base, and converging rapidly to apex, fig. 259............**pentus**, p. 65

27. Ninth sternite with a pair of somewhat quadrate sclerotized plates pointed at apex; bursa copulatrix not heavily sclerotized, fig. 260.......
    ....**remotus**, p. 67
    Ninth sternite without sclerotized plates; bursa copulatrix heavily sclerotized, fig. 261........**cinereus**, p. 67

Polycentropus crassicornis Walker

Polycentropus crassicornis Walker (1852, p. 101); ♂, ♀.
Plectrocnemia adironica Banks (1914, p. 256); ♂.
Pletrocnemia australis Banks (1907a, p. 131); ♀.

LARVA.—Unknown.
ADULTS.—Length 9–10 mm. Color brown, the front wings irrorate over their entire surface with brown and yellowish spots. Male genitalia, fig. 235: ninth segment produced into a long, pointed tongue which projects to the apex of claspers; cerci short and ovate; claspers very heavily sclerotized, lateral margin narrow, apical margin expanded, with a sharp mesal tooth at apex pointed ventrad; tenth tergite submembranous and small; connecting this and the cerci is a heavily sclerotized plate which is divided at its apex into a pair of heavily sclerotized prongs, one angled sharply dorsad, the other curved ventrad; aedeagus with a tubular base, the apex narrowed and consisting of membranous folds and internal sclerotized rods. Female genitalia, fig. 249, forming a long, tapering, heavily sclerotized structure, divided on the venter by a long, narrow tongue, at the base of which are lateral lobes produced into sharp, long points on their meso-apical corner.

We have only four Illinois records for this species, two from marsh areas in the extreme northeastern corner of the state (see p. 12), another from the east-central margin and the fourth from the extreme southern portion. Little is known regarding the biology of the species or its habitat preference. It is widespread throughout the eastern United States and Canada, with records from Florida, Illinois, Massachusetts, Michigan, New York, Ontario and South Dakota.
Illinois Records.—ALTO PASS, Union Spring: May 26, 1940, Mohr & Burks, 1 ♀. ROSECRANS, Des Plaines River: June 9, 1938, at light, Ross & Burks, 1 ♂, 1 ♀. URBANA: June 1, 1938, light trap, G. T. Riegel, 1 ♂. ZION, Dead River: June 3, 1938, Mohr & Burks, 1 ♂.

Polycentropus aureolus (Banks)

Plectrocnemia aureola Banks (1930a, p. 130); ♂, ♀.

Described from Nova Scotia, this species has been taken also in New Hampshire and Minnesota. It has not yet been taken in Illinois.

Polycentropus centralis Banks

Polycentropus centralis Banks (1914, p. 258); ♂.

LARVA.—Length 11 mm. Head, pronotum and legs yellow, the head with very indistinct spots arranged in the same pattern as in fig. 231; posterior margin of pronotum dark brown.
ADULTS.—Length 7–9 mm. General color brown with irregular light areas on the wings and definite pale spots around their border. Male genitalia, fig. 248: cerci stocky, apical filament fairly short; claspers short, the baso-dorsal appendage trapezoidal, its inner point sharp and serrulate; aedeagus slightly sinuate but its general outline straight. Female genitalia, fig. 253: eighth sternite broad, its apical margin fairly evenly rounded, lateral lobes moderately short and pointed at apex; ninth sternite with two short, broad, rounded lobes; bursa copulatrix porelike, its supports forming a broad base and a pair of fusiform supports which run close together to give the entire structure a more or less vasiform appearance.

Allotype, female.—Wolf Lake, Illinois, along Hutchins Creek: May 31, 1940, B. D. Burks.

In Illinois we have taken this species only in the extreme southern portion and in the extreme northwestern corner. In the former area we found the species very abundant in Hutchins Creek where larvae, pupae and adults were associated. All our records are along small, fairly clear and rapid streams.

The range of the species includes the Ozarks and adjacent ranges with a northeastward extension into New York. We have records from the following states: Arkansas, Illinois, Missouri, New York and Oklahoma.

Illinois Records.—GALENA, Sinsinawa River: June 5–6, 1940, Mohr & Burks, 1 ♂. HEROD: May 29, 1936, Ross & Mohr, 1 ♀. LA RUE, McCann Spring: May 26, 1939, Burks & Riegel, 4 ♂, ♀ ♀. WOLF LAKE, Hutchins Creek: Oct. 5, 1938, Frison & Burks, 4 ♀ ; May 25, 1940, Mohr & Burks, 1 ♀ ; May 31, 1940, B. D. Burks, ♂ ♂, ♀ ♀.

Polycentropus pentus Ross

Polycentropus pentus Ross (1941*b*, p. 71); ♂, ♀.

LARVA.—Unknown.

ADULTS.—Length 8–10 mm. General color mottled brown, the wings with a few light spots along periphery. Male genitalia, fig. 242: cerci narrow, with a finger-like projection near middle, apical filament relatively short; ninth segment narrow; claspers long, ventral aspect slightly irregular and tapering slightly toward apex, baso-dorsal appendage long, the apex pointed and the mesal point sharp; aedeagus slightly curved with a large hump on ventral margin near base. Female genitalia, fig. 259: eighth sternite wide, apex fairly evenly curved and slightly produced at tip, lateral lobes long and lanceolate; ninth sternite with a pair of sclerotized bars wide apart at base and converging markedly toward apex; bursa copulatrix conical, its supports poorly defined except for the apical rods, which are narrow and sinuate.

Our only record for this species in Illinois is a single male collected at Split Rock Brook, Utica, July 11, 1941, Ross & Ries (see p. 7).

The range of the species is not well defined, but it is apparently widely distributed through the Northeast, our Illinois record being the most western point from which it is known. Records are available from Illinois, New Hampshire and Ontario.

Polycentropus maculatus Banks

Polycentropus maculatus Banks (1908*a*, p. 65); ♂.

This species has not been taken in Illinois but is distributed through the eastern states. Records are available from Newfoundland, New Hampshire, New York and Tennessee. The male genitalia, fig. 243, are distinctive. The female is similar to the male in color and general structure and is readily distinguished by the widely separated, narrow and frequently angulate lateral lobes of the eighth sternite and the parallel, rugose, sclerotized bands of the ninth sternite, fig. 258.

Allotype, female.—Chimneys Camp Grounds, Great Smoky Mountains National Park, Tennessee: July 16, 1939, at light, A. C. Cole.

Polycentropus confusus Hagen

Polycentropus confusus Hagen (1861, p. 293); ♂, ♀.

While not as yet found in Illinois, this species is almost certain to be taken with additional collecting. Its range, apparently general throughout the Northeast, extends southwestward through the Ozarks, and includes Arkansas, Michigan, Missouri, New York, Ohio, Ontario, Quebec and Tennessee.

As explained in a previous article (Ross 1941*b*, p. 71), the type male lacks the abdomen, and the male characters are based on the plesiotype male set up in that paper. Since the specific characters for the female of this species have not been pointed out and illustrated before, I am designating a specimen to represent the female sex.

Plesio-allotype, female.—Costello Lake, Algonquin Park, Ontario: July 11, 1938, Cage No. 4, W. M. Sprules.

Polycentropus elarus new species

MALE.—Length 8.5 mm. Color various shades of brown, the hind tibiae not markedly annulate, the front wings with numerous inconspicuous light areas forming an indistinct, irrorate pattern. General structure typical for genus. Front and hind wings with R_2 present. Male genitalia, fig. 245, typical in general for the *maculatus* group; ninth sternite deep; cerci fairly stocky, the ventral corner fairly sharp, the dorsal angle produced into a long, slender, sclerotized, sinuate rod which curves dorsad at the tip; claspers with baso-dorsal lobe of moderate length, its neck long and slender, the apex large and produced into a large mesal point; ventral aspect of claspers with base large and rectangular, narrowing suddenly to a slender and somewhat digitate tip; aedeagus curved ventrad and slightly enlarged at apex.

Female.—Length 9.5 mm. In color and structure similar to male. Genitalia, fig. 256, with eighth sternite fairly narrow, its extreme apex produced into a slight lobe; lateral lobes wide apart at base, fusiform and narrow.

Holotype, male.—Costello Lake, Algonquin Park, Ontario: June 22, 1939, Cage No. 1, W. M. Sprules.

Allotype, female.—Same data as for holotype.

Paratypes.—New York.—Bear Brook near Blue Mountain Lake, Adirondack State Park: June 19, 1941, Frison & Ross, 1 ♂.

Ontario.—Same data as for allotype, 1 ♀ ; same data except June 11, 1 ♂ .

The elongate, sinuate and upturned filament of the cerci will distinguish this species from others in the *maculatus* group, to which it belongs. The ventral aspect of the claspers, fig. 245, is also unique for the group.

Not known from Illinois but may be taken in future collecting.

Polycentropus species a

Larva.—Unknown.

Adults.—Length 7–9 mm. Male unknown. Female genitalia, fig. 254, with eighth sternite almost evenly tapering from base to apex, more or less triangular, the lateral margins sclerotized; lobes slender and pointed. Ninth segment with ovate sclerotized processes which are short, rounded at apex, and connected to conical bursa copulatrix by a narrow ribbon which forms a narrow ventral bridge ventrad of bursa.

This form is known only from Herod,

Illinois, and Hopkinsville, Kentucky. It is either the female of *carolinensis* or represents a new species.

Illinois Records.—Herod: May 8, 1936, Ross & Mohr, 1 ♀ ; May 10, 1935, C. O. Mohr, 2 ♀.

Polycentropus carolinensis Banks

Polycentropus carolinensis Banks (1905a, p. 217); ♂.

This species, known only from the unique male type, has not been taken in Illinois. There is a possibility, however, that the unassociated female, *Polycentropus species a*, may be *carolinensis*. This has no statistical basis but is a possibility because, in the *maculatus* group of seven species, *carolinensis* is the only male with which a female has not been associated definitely, and *species a* is the only female not definitely associated with a male.

Polycentropus pixi new species

Male.—Length 7 mm. Color various shades of brown, the legs paler, the hind tibiae dark brown with a basal white annulus, the front wings with only a few indistinct light spots. General structure typical for genus. Wing venation with R_2 present in both wings, but only faintly indicated in the hind wings. Male genitalia, fig. 247, typical for the *maculatus* group in general structure as follows: ninth sternite deep; cerci fairly wide, the apical needle-like projection nearly straight and extending considerably posterad, not recurving toward ventral margin of cerci; tenth tergite long, the pair of sclerotized styliform processes very long; claspers with ventral aspect only slightly narrowed at apex, the dorsal margin with a sharp lateral edge and with the mesal margin produced into a sharp tooth near middle; baso-dorsal lobe of clasper long, arched, the mesal point not sharp but well differentiated at the end of the long, necklike portion; aedeagus only slightly curved at apex, which is slightly enlarged.

Female.—Length 8 mm. In color and general structure similar to male. Eighth sternite, fig. 255, very broad, the corners heavily sclerotized; lateral lobes of sternite long, narrow and widely separated at base.

Holotype, male.—North Woodstock, New Hampshire: June 21, 1941, at light, Frison & Ross.

Allotype, female.—Same data as for holotype.

Paratypes. — NEW HAMPSHIRE. — Same data as for holotype, 1 ♀.

NEW YORK.—EUBA MILLS, Adirondack State Park: June 20, 1941, Frison & Ross, 1 ♂. VARYSBURG: June 18, 1941, Frison & Ross, 1 ♀.

This species is most closely related to *centralis*, from which it differs in the long, arched, baso-dorsal lobe of the claspers, in having the mesal angle of this point round, in the widened tip of the aedeagus, and other characters of the genitalia.

Although not yet taken in Illinois, because this species is fairly widely distributed in the northeastern states, it may be taken here in future collecting.

Polycentropus cinereus Hagen

Polycentropus cinereus Hagen (1861, p. 293); ♂, ♀.
Polycentropus canadensis Banks (1897, p. 31); ♂.
Holocentropus flavicornis Banks (1907b, p. 162); ♂.
Plectrocnemia pallescens Banks (1930b, p. 231); ♂, ♀.
Plectrocnemia lutea Betten (1934, p. 219); ♂, ♀.

LARVA.—Fig. 230. Length 14 mm. Head, pronotum and legs straw color, head and sometimes pronotum with conspicuous brown spots, those of the upper portion of frons arranged in an angle; sometimes, also, the dorsal part of head is suffused with yellowish brown. Remainder of body pale, without markings.

ADULTS.—Length 7–9 mm. Color various shades of brown, the wings mottled with brown and light areas resulting in a checkerboard mottling. Front and hind wings with R_2 present. Male genitalia, fig. 240: tenth tergite short, stocky and semimembranous; cerci short and ovate; claspers appearing quadrate from lateral view, the posterior margin incised to form a dorso-mesal hook and a ventro-mesal lobe. Female genitalia, fig. 261: eighth sternite short, lateral lobes large and somewhat circular; ninth segment with its structures membranous; bursa copulatrix dark, cone-like and conspicuous.

This species has been taken commonly in all parts of Illinois. It is found in a wide variety of situations, ranging from lakes to large rivers, showing a marked preference for cool and clear water. Adult emergence occurs from May to September. Larvae are found chiefly under stones. Association of larval and adult forms was established by collections of all stages in Channel Lake.

The range of the species is very wide, occurring throughout the eastern states, north and westward through Canada and the northern states to the Pacific Coast and extending southwestward through the Ozarks to Oklahoma. We have records from British Columbia, the District of Columbia, Illinois, Indiana, Kentucky, Maine, Maryland, Michigan, Minnesota, Missouri, New Brunswick, New Hampshire, New York, North Carolina, Nova Scotia, Ohio, Oklahoma, Ontario, Pennsylvania, Saskatchewan, South Dakota, Tennessee, Washington and Wisconsin.

Illinois Records.—Many males and females and seven pupae, taken May 24 to September 20, and many larvae, taken May 5 to October 28, are from Algonquin, Antioch, Channel Lake, Danville (Middle Fork River), Eddyville (Lusk Creek), Eldorado, Elgin (Botanical Gardens), Fox Lake, Galena (Sinsinawa River), Homer, Johnsburg (Fox River), Kankakee (Kankakee River), McHenry, Momence (Kankakee River), Oakwood, Pontiac, Richmond, Round Lake, St. Joseph, Serena (Indian Creek), Spring Grove (Nippersink Creek), Wilmington (Kankakee River), Zion (Dead River).

Polycentropus remotus Banks

Polycentropus remotus Banks (1911, p. 359); ♂.

LARVA.—Length 14 mm. Head, pronotum and legs straw color, the head with well-marked spots. Upper portion of frons subequal in length to lower portion, fig. 232. Body pale, without markings.

ADULTS.—Length 7–9 mm. Color various shades of brown with a checkered pattern of small pale areas on the brown wings. Both pairs of wings with R_2 present. Male genitalia, fig. 239: tenth tergite composed chiefly of a pair of stocky, outcurved horns, slightly expanded and provided with a short spine at apex; cerci long and leaflike, the upper portion produced into a lobe, and the ventro-mesal corner bearing a stout, heavily sclerotized projection curved ventrad at apex; claspers appearing quadrate from lateral view, with a slender, digitate dorsomesal projection. Female genitalia, fig. 260: eighth sternite short, its lateral lobes large, almost quadrate, and close together along meson, covered with short setae; ninth sternite with a pair of distinctive, small, quadrate sclerotized plates which are narrowed and pointed at apex; other internal structures membranous or irregular.

Allotype, female.—Zion, Illinois, along Dead River: June 6, 1940, Mohr & Burks.

As with *flavus*, this species has been taken in Illinois chiefly along the Dead River, and our main collection is a series of larvae, pupae and adults taken along with the allotype. This species is widely distributed, occurring from the Atlantic to the Pacific. So few collections are known, however, that a very local distribution is indicated. Records are available from British Columbia, Illinois, Minnesota, New Hampshire and New York.

Illinois Records.—RICHMOND: June 4, 1938, Ross & Burks, 2♀. SPRING GROVE: Aug. 12, 1937, at light, Ross & Burks, 1♀. ZION, Dead River: June 3, 1938, Mohr & Burks, 1♂; June 6, 1940, Mohr & Burks, 2♂, 4♀, 3 larvae.

Polycentropus nascotius Ross

Polycentropus nascotius Ross (1941*b*, p. 73); ♂.

Not yet taken in Illinois, but to be looked for in future collecting. It is a rare species with a wide distribution, known from New Brunswick, Nova Scotia and Wisconsin.

Polycentropus flavus (Banks)

Holocentropus flavus Banks (1908*a*, p. 66); ♂.

LARVA.—Length 14 mm. Head somewhat uniformly reddish brown of a dusky shade, the typical spots present but inconspicuous, being almost the same color as the ground color. Pronotum and legs yellowish brown. Remainder of body pale without markings.

ADULTS.—Length 7–9 mm. Color brown with a checkered pattern on the wings similar to that of *nascotius*. Front wings with R_2 present, hind wings with R_2 absent. Male genitalia, fig. 237: tenth tergite with a pair of very long, curved sclerotized rods following the curve of the aedeagus; cerci

fairly long and narrow, the apex provided with a short, appendage-like prolongation; claspers with a high lobe at base, apex narrow and rounded; at the top of the lobe is a small, triangular flap projecting mesad, and below this there is frequently a tooth-like projection. Female genitalia, fig. 250: eighth sternite long, slightly incised at apex, and extending well beyond the lateral lobes, which are narrow and pointed; between them the eighth sternite is raised into a pyramid, sloping sharply at the sides.

Allotype, female.—Zion, Illinois, along Dead River: June 6, 1940, Mohr & Burks.

Our only recent Illinois records are from the extreme northeastern portion of the state. The two sexes and immature stages were associated by a series of males, females, pupae and larvae collected at Zion in and along the Dead River (see p. 12).

The species has been recorded over a wide but scattered range, probably indicating a very local distribution. Records are available from Illinois, Newfoundland, New York and Ontario.

Illinois Records.—URBANA: May 17, 1887, C. A. Hart, 1♂, 1♀; May 19, 1887, C. A. Hart, 1♂, 2♀; May 20, 1887, C. A. Hart, 1♀; June 20, 1888, Forbes, Marten & Hart, 1♀. ZION, Dead River: May 20, 1940, Mohr & Burks, 2 larvae; June 6, 1940, Mohr & Burks, 1♂, 3♀.

Polycentropus glacialis (Ross)

Holocentropus glacialis Ross (1938*a*, p. 135); ♂.

LARVA.—Length 13 mm. Head, pronotum and legs yellowish, the head frequently with slight brownish suffusions; spots on head distinct, the two major setae on upper part of frons surrounded by a small brown area. Remainder of body without markings.

ADULTS.—Length 8–9 mm. Color, general structure and venation similar to those of *flavus*. Male genitalia, fig. 238: tenth tergite composed of a pair of long, curved, sclerotized rods; cerci narrow and spatulate, without an appendage; claspers appearing somewhat quadrate from lateral view, the dorsal margin curved over into a trapezoidal flap projecting meso-ventrad. Female genitalia, fig. 252: eighth sternite with fairly short, ovate, lateral lobes which are wide apart at base; between them is a wide, transverse ledge without abrupt apical margin; internal structures forming a pair of wide, lateral lobes and a single mesal lobe.

Allotype, female.—Spring Grove, Illinois: May 22, 1938, Ross & Mohr.

In Illinois this species has been taken principally in the vicinity of the glacial lakes in the northeastern part of the state (see p. 10). It was recorded from Diamond Lake, Illinois, May 30, as *Holocentropus species 1* Betten (1934, p. 223). Apparently only one generation of adults appears each year as indicated by our collection records, which run from May 9 to August 12.

The range of the species is poorly known. In addition to our Illinois records we have only the following: Michigan (Nottawa) and Wisconsin (Mukwonagon).

Illinois Records.—ANTIOCH: July 1, 1931, Frison, Betten & Ross, ♂ ♂ ; July 6, 1931, Frison *et al.*, 5 ♂ ; July 6, 1932, Frison *et al.*, 9 ♂ ; July 7, 1932, at light, Frison & Metcalf, 1 ♂. CHANNEL LAKE: May 27, 1936, H. H. Ross, 1 ♂ pupa; June 11, 1936, Ross & Burks, 3 ♂. Fox LAKE: July 1, 1931, Frison, Betten & Ross, ♂ ♂ ; June 30, 1935, DeLong & Ross, 3 ♂ ; May 28, 1936, in weeds, H. H. Ross, ♂ ♂, 3 larvae; May 13, 1938, 1 ♀. HAVANA: May 9, 1896, Butler, 1 ♂. SPRING GROVE: Aug. 12, 1937, at light, Ross & Burks, 2 ♂ ; May 20, 1938, Ross & Burks, 1 ♂ ; May 22, 1938, Ross & Burks, 1 ♂, 1 ♀ ; May 23, 1938, Ross & Burks, 3 ♂ ; June 4, 1938, Mohr & Burks, 1 ♂ ; May 31, 1 ♂ ; June 10, 1 ♂ (reared). OTTAWA: June 3, 1938, Mohr & Burks, 1 ♂.

Polycentropus interruptus (Banks)

Holocentropus interruptus Banks (1914, p. 257); ♂.
Holocentropus orotus Banks (1914, p. 257); ♂, ♀.
Holocentropus longus Banks (1914, p. 258); ♂.

LARVA.—Fig. 233. Length 15 mm. Head yellowish with distinct dark spots and with most of the dorsum clouded with reddish brown, the major pair of setae of the upper frons with a small, pale area around base. Pronotum and legs yellowish brown. Remainder of body pale.

ADULTS.—Length 9–10 mm. Color various shades of brown, the wings marked with pale areas making a somewhat checkerboard pattern. Front wings with R_2 present, hind wings with R_2 absent. Male genitalia, fig.

236: tenth tergite with a pair of long, curved processes which are sclerotized, slender and curved to follow the outline of the aedeagus; cerci with the basal portion long and widened at apex, bearing a short, sausage-shaped apical projection; claspers broad at base, tapering to a sharp, upcurved point, and with only small flaps on the mesal base. Female genitalia, fig. 251: eighth sternite long and rounded at apex, lateral lobes long and spatulate, with a footlike angular base; between these lobes there is a deep depression in the tergite; ninth sternite with a pair of long, sclerotized rods.

In Illinois we have taken this species recently only in lakes and ponds in the extreme northeastern corner of the state. The larvae were taken in weed beds and beneath stones in these situations and locally were very abundant. Our adult records indicate only one generation per year, all falling between May 26 and July 15. Numerous mature pupae from Channel Lake, Fox Lake and Dead River (see p. 12) have established the association of the larvae and adults.

The range of the species is extensive, including Colorado, Illinois, Massachusetts, Michigan, New Hampshire and New York. These records, however, are based on a minimum of definite localities, so that the species appears to be very local in its occurrence.

Illinois Records.—Many males, females and pupae, taken May 26 to July 15, and many larvae, taken May 27–28, are from Algonquin, Antioch, Channel Lake, Fox Lake, Grass Lake, Pistakee Lake, Richmond, Spring Grove, Urbana, Volo, Zion.

Nyctiophylax Brauer

Nyctiophylax Brauer (1865, p. 419). Genotype, monobasic: *Nyctiophylax sinensis* Brauer.

Only two Nearctic species are known for this genus, one of them from Illinois, the other from the Northeast. The larva has not been associated with the adult, although one species is very common and widespread (see *Genus A* and *Genus B*, pp. 73 and 74).

KEY TO SPECIES

Adults

1. Apex of abdomen with cerci and claspers, figs. 262, 263 (males).... 2

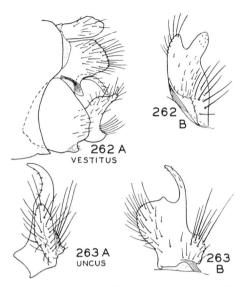

Figs. 262–263.—*Nyctiophylax*, male genitalia. *A*, lateral aspect; *B*, clasper, caudal aspect.

Apex of abdomen with platelike lateral
 lobes, fig. 264 (females) . . . .
 . . . . not keyed
2. Posterior aspect of claspers with mesal
 lobe produced into a long finger,
 fig. 263 . . . . **uncus,** p. 70
 Posterior aspect of claspers with mesal
 lobe no higher than lateral lobe,
 fig. 262 . . . . **vestitus,** p. 70

Nyctiophylax vestitus (Hagen)

Polycentropus vestitus Hagen (1861, p. 293);
 ♀.
Polycentropus affinis Banks (1897, p. 30); ♂.
Nyctiophylax moestus Banks (1911, p. 359);
 ♂.

LARVA.—Unknown.

ADULTS.—Length 5–7 mm. Color various
shades of brown, the wings with light spots
in an irregular pattern. Male genitalia, fig.
262: tenth tergite semimembranous, short,
narrowed at apex; cerci forming a somewhat ovate lobe with a sharp process on the
mesal face near venter; claspers appearing
narrow from lateral view, the extreme base
produced into a short shelf, the apical portion with a broad, concave, posterior face
which is divided at apex into a pair of short
lobes, the inner one small. Female genitalia, fig. 264: lateral lobes of eighth sternite short and wide; bursa copulatrix variable, but always with a shieldlike structure.

In Illinois this species occurs associated
with a wide variety of small to large streams
over most of the state. Adult emergence
begins in May and continues until at least
September.

The species is apparently widespread
through the Northeast and continues south-
westward through the Ozarks to Oklahoma.
We have records from Arkansas, Illinois,
Indiana, Kentucky, Maryland, Michigan,
Minnesota, New York, North Carolina,
Ohio, Oklahoma, Ontario, Quebec, Tennes-
see and Wisconsin.

Illinois Records.—Many males and females, taken May 19 to September 20, are
from Algonquin, Alto Pass (Union Spring),
Antioch, Apple River State Park, Bartonville (Kickapoo Creek), Charleston, Council Hill (Galena River), Danville (Middle

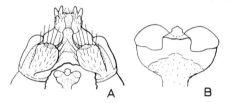

Fig. 264.—*Nyctiophylax vestitus*, female genitalia. *A*, ventral aspect; *B*, dorsal aspect of
bursa copulatrix.

Fork River), Downs (Kickapoo Creek),
Eddyville (Lusk Creek), Eichorn (Hicks
Branch), Elgin (Botanical Gardens), Fox
Lake, Galena (Sinsinawa River), Grass
Lake, Herod, Kankakee (Kankakee River),
McHenry, Momence (Kankakee River),
Mount Carroll, Muncie, Oakwood (Salt
Fork, Middle Fork, Vermilion River), Ore-
gon, Ottawa, Pontiac, Quincy (stream near
Cave Spring), Serena (Fox River, Indian
Creek), Springfield (Sangamon River),
Spring Grove (Nippersink Creek), Sugar
Grove, Venedy Station (Kaskaskia River),
Wadsworth (Des Plaines River), Wauke-
gan, White Pines Forest State Park, Wil-
mington.

Nyctiophylax uncus new species

MALE.—Length 6.5 mm. Color various
shades of brown, the wings only indistinctly
spotted, the antennae and legs straw colored
except for the hind tibiae which have the
apical five-sixths dark brown, forming a
conspicuous pale annulus at base. Wings
with R_2 absent. Male genitalia with gen-

eral features as in fig. 262: ninth sternite narrowed on ventral margin and produced on meson into a low, sharp hump; tenth tergite short, semimembranous, and divided at apex into just a pair of short approximate points; cerci broad, rounded at apex with a long, curved sclerotized hook arising from ventral mesal corner; claspers, fig. 263, appearing narrow from lateral view, the extreme base produced into a hump, the posterior face wide, slightly convex, with a wide, lateral, setate area, the apical mesal corner produced into a long, slender, sclerotized rod curved dorsad; aedeagus somewhat tubular with a pair of dorsal sclerotized rods and with a cushion of short, black spines at apex.

FEMALE.—Size 7.5 mm. In color and general structure similar to male. Eighth sternite with lateral lobes large and ovate; bursa copulatrix very similar to that in fig. 264.

Holotype, male.—Blue Mountain Lake, Adirondack State Park, New York: June 19, 1941, Frison & Ross.

Allotype, female.—Same data as for holotype.

Paratypes.—NEW YORK.—Same data as for holotype, 5♂, 1♀. LIMA: June 19, 1941, Frison & Ross, 2♂.

NEW HAMPSHIRE.—WOODSTOCK: June 21, 1941, at light, Frison & Ross, 1♀.

This species is closely related to *vestitus*, differing in the male in the large, expanded lateral lobe and the elongate mesal lobe of the apex; the female differs little in the shape of the bursa copulatrix.

Although not yet taken in Illinois, the species is so widely distributed to the north and northeast that it can be expected in the state in future collecting.

Cyrnellus Banks

Cyrnellus Banks (1913, p. 88). Genotype, by original designation: *Cyrnellus minimus* Banks.

Only one North American species, *marginalis*, is known for this genus. The immature stages have never been discovered. The significant generic characters for this complex (which includes *Nyctiophylax*) have not been worked out clearly, but I am following Mosely (1934a) in assigning *marginalis* to *Cyrnellus*. Future association of adults and larvae will help to clarify the status of these genera.

Cyrnellus marginalis (Banks)

Nyctiophylax marginalis Banks (1930b, p. 231); ♂.

Cyrnellus zernyi Mosely (1934a, p. 142); ♂.

LARVA.—Unknown.

ADULTS.—Length 4.5–5.5 mm. Color various shades of brown; antennae, legs and venter much paler. Male genitalia, fig. 265: tenth tergite semimembranous and subquadrate; cerci lanceolate, with a short, ventral, styliform process; claspers long and nearly straight, the apex with a sharp, large, black mesal triangle. Female genitalia, fig. 266, with parts weakly sclerotized; eighth sternite short, slightly carinate between lateral lobes, which are large, approximate on

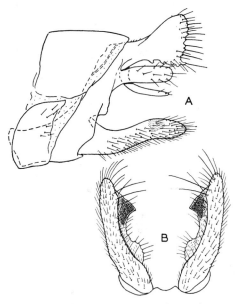

Fig. 265.—*Cyrnellus marginalis*, male genitalia. *A*, lateral aspect; *B*, ventral aspect of claspers.

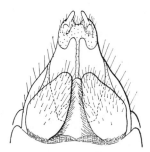

Fig. 266.—*Cyrnellus marginalis*, female genitalia.

meson and reach beyond sternite; ninth segment long and somewhat vasiform, without conspicuous internal processes.

Taken in all parts of the state, this species shows a marked preference for large rivers such as the Illinois, Kaskaskia and Mississippi; however, we have taken it in numbers along many small streams. Usually it is taken in only small numbers, but occasionally large swarms are encountered. The adult emergence occurs from May until October.

The species is widely distributed through the central states; records include Alabama, Arkansas, Illinois, Kentucky, Michigan, Minnesota, Missouri, Ohio, Oklahoma, Tennessee and Wisconsin. It is also known from near the mouth of the Amazon River in South America.

Illinois Records.—Many males and females, taken May 29 to October 10, are from Algonquin, Antioch, Bartonville (Kickapoo Creek), Danville, Deer Grove (Green River), Dixon, East Dubuque, Elgin (Botanical Gardens), Grafton, Hamilton, Hardin, Havana (Spoon River), Herod, Kankakee (Kankakee River), Milan (Rock River), Olive Branch (Horse Shoe Lake), Ottawa, Palos Park (Mud Lake), Pontiac, Ripley (La Moine River), Rockford, Rock Island, Springfield (Sangamon River), Spring Grove, Thebes, Venedy Station (Kaskaskia River).

Cernotina Ross

Cernotina Ross (1938*a*, p. 136). Genotype, by original designation: *Cernotina calcea* Ross.

No larva of this genus has been discovered. The adults of both sexes are 5–6 mm. long, with the head, body and appendages straw color, the wings and parts of the legs darkened with brown hair. The female genitalia are similar in all species known, the genital segments forming a conical structure with only simple parts, fig. 267.

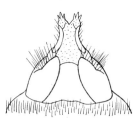

Fig. 267.—*Cernotina calcea*, female genitalia.

Of the six North American species, only one has been taken in Illinois, but three others are known from Michigan and Ohio and may eventually be found in the state.

KEY TO SPECIES

Males

1. Cerci with 3 or 4 long, black teeth on mesal side near base, fig. 268......
   ....**calcea**, p. 72
   Cerci without long, black mesal teeth   2
2. Apex of cerci long and ribbon-like, the inner margin just beyond apex set with a row of 5 to 7 small teeth, fig. 269.....................**pallida**, p. 73
   Apex of cerci shorter and whiplike, the inner margin without teeth, fig. 270   3
3. Base of clasper with a sclerotized, ovoid plate attached underneath it, fig. 270.................**spicata**, p. 73
   Base of clasper without this plate, fig. 271....................**ohio**, p. 73

Cernotina calcea Ross

Cernotina calcea Ross (1938*a*, p. 137); ♂, ♀.

ADULTS.—Length 5–6 mm. Head and body straw color, typical for genus. Male genitalia, fig. 268: tenth tergite merging with ninth, the resulting structure with a deep, V-shaped incision on meson; cerci with three to four large, black mesal teeth near middle, the apex lengthened into a long, slender sinuate rod; claspers stocky, the apex formed into a clawlike structure, and the dorsal margin with a slender arm at middle; aedeagus tubular and only slightly sclerotized. Female genitalia, fig. 267, conical, without heavily sclerotized internal parts or supports.

Our only Illinois records are from Kankakee and Oakwood. The species is always found along clear, cool streams. Adult emergence extends over a considerable period; our Illinois records indicate a span from June 29 to August 1.

The range of the species is incompletely known. It is apparently quite widely but locally distributed in cooler streams as indicated by records from Illinois, Florida, Missouri, Oklahoma and Texas.

Illinois Records.—KANKAKEE: Aug. 1, 1933, Ross & Mohr, 1 ♀ ; July 21, 1935, Ross & Mohr, 1 ♂ ; June 29, 1939, Burks & Ayars, 2 ♂. OAKWOOD: July 18, 1933, Ross & Mohr, 1 ♂.

Cernotina pallida (Banks)

Cyrnus pallidus Banks (1904*d*, p. 214); ♂.

This species, described from Maryland, has not yet been taken in Illinois but has been found as close as central Ohio. It is

Cernotina spicata Ross

Cernotina spicata Ross (1938*a*, p. 138); ♂.

This species has not yet been found in Illinois. Records from Maine, Michigan and Oklahoma indicate a widely scattered range

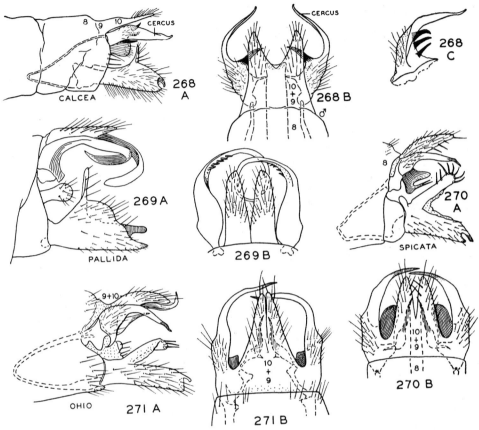

Figs. 268–271.—*Cernotina*, male genitalia. *A*, lateral aspect; *B*, dorsal aspect; *C*, cercus showing inner teeth.

similar in general appearance to *calcea*, differing in the long, whiplike cerci, which are armed with small teeth near the apex, instead of long black teeth near the base.

Cernotina ohio Ross

Cernotina ohio Ross (1939*b*, p. 628); ♂.

This species has not been taken in Illinois but occurs in Ohio. It is a close relative of *spicata* but may be readily distinguished by the male genitalia, fig. 271. The cerci lack a baso-mesal plate and the claspers have fewer setae on their dorsal arms.

and the possibility of its being found in Illinois in future collecting.

Psychomyiid Genus A

LARVA.—Fig. 272. Length 9 mm. Head cream with a dorsal, spotted, purplish brown pattern; pronotum cream around edges, central portion brown; legs white; body colorless. Mandibles with dorsal and ventral rows of teeth, fig. 199, in both mandibles the dorsal row concealing the ventral row. Legs spinose, tarsal claws long and sharp. Tubular processes of tenth segment long; anal legs and hooks large, very similar to

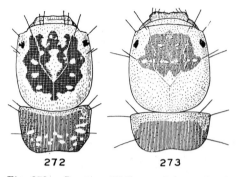

Fig. 272.—*Psychomyiid Genus A*, larva, head.
Fig. 273.—*Psychomyiid Genus B*, larva, head.

those in fig. 201; anal hooks with inner teeth minute, fig. 190.

ADULTS.—Unknown.

This curious larva has been taken in small to medium-sized, rapid streams, including the Salt Fork River and Rock Creek. Only scattered records are available, a few in the northern half of Illinois, and others from Florida, Michigan and Wisconsin. No accurate statement can be made as to the identity of this larva, but it is probably one of those now known only from the adult stage, such as *Nyctiophylax*, *Cyrnellus* or *Cernotina* (see the following).

Illinois Records.—BARTELSO: Aug. 16, 1898, on logs, C. A. Hart, 1 larva. ERIE, Rock Creek: June 5, 1940, Mohr & Burks, 1 larva. OAKWOOD: June 6, 1920, T. H. Frison, 2 larvae.

Psychomyiid Genus B

LARVA.—Fig. 273. Length 8 mm. Head creamy yellow with a large brown mark covering most of anterior portion of dorsum;

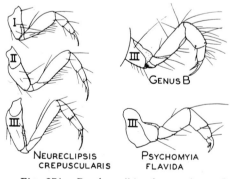

NEURECLIPSIS CREPUSCULARIS   PSYCHOMYIA FLAVIDA

Fig. 274.—Psychomyiidae larvae, legs. I, front leg; II, middle leg; III, hind leg.

pronotum brown with anterior margin yellow; legs cream to white. General structure of mandibles and legs similar to above, fig. 274; ninth sternite bearing a T-shaped, reticulate area and having tubular processes of tenth segment short, with an extensive patch of minute spinules, figs. 200, 201.

ADULTS.—Unknown.

We collected a single specimen of this larva in rapids of the Kankakee River at Momence, Illinois, May 26, 1936, H. H. Ross. The similar mandibles and anal hooks show a marked affinity with the larva described above as *Genus A*; they will doubtless prove to be *Nyctiophylax*, *Cyrnellus* or *Cernotina*.

Lype McLachlan

Lype McLachlan (1879, p. 422). Genotype, here designated: *Lype phaeopa* (Stephens).

To date only one species of the genus has been recorded for North America. We have one record of it from Illinois.

In recent years there has been considerable juggling of generic names in this complex. I believe that the genital structures indicate clearly that Betten's (1934) definition of this and the following genus is correct.

Larvae of this genus are not available for study. The genotype has been reared in Europe, but no North American species have had the adults and larvae associated.

Lype diversa (Banks)

Psychomyia diversa Banks (1914, p. 253); ♂.
Lype griselda Betten (1934, p. 229); ♂.
New synonymy.

ADULTS.—Length 5–7 mm. General color very dark, almost black, with only a few irregular light marks along the sutures. Male genitalia, fig. 275: tenth tergite large and hood shaped, with a dorsal horn; cerci long and lanceolate; claspers long and narrow; aedeagus arcuate. Female genitalia, fig. 276, produced into a long, tapering ovipositor, without conspicuous processes.

Allotype, female.—Elkmont, Tennessee, along Little River: June 12, 1938, T. H. Frison & T. H. Frison, Jr.

The dorsal horn of the male tenth tergite varies conspicuously from a very short, sharp projection to a long, sinuate structure enlarged at the tip. The type of *diversa*

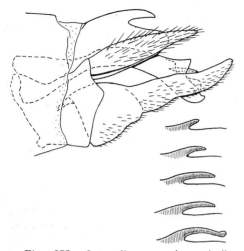

Fig. 275.—*Lype diversa*, male genitalia, showing variations of dorsal horn of tenth tergite.

represents the latter, the type of *griselda* a more or less intermediate condition. Examination of considerable material indicates that this entire range is merely variation within the species. Representative conditions found, showing the two extremes and intermediate steps, are illustrated in fig. 275.

Our only Illinois record of this species is a male collected along Quiver Creek at Havana, May 29, 1936, Mohr & Burks.

The range of the species is widespread through the eastern states, extending westward to Wisconsin and Illinois. We have records from Florida, Michigan, New Hampshire, New York, North Carolina, Ohio, Ontario, Tennessee, Vermont, Virginia and Wisconsin.

Psychomyia Pictet

Psychomyia Pictet (1834, p. 222). Genotype, here designated: *Psychomyia annulicornis* Pictet.
Quissa Milne (1936, p. 89). Genotype, monobasic: *Psychomyia flavida* Hagen.

Of the three described North American species, only *flavida* has been taken in Illinois. Of the other two species, *nomada* is known only from the eastern states, and *lumina* is known only from Oregon.

The genus was described without any included species. Pictet was the first to place species in the genus, and since no genotype has apparently been designated, I propose his first included species, *annulicornis*, in that capacity.

Psychomyia flavida Hagen

Psychomyia flavida Hagen (1861, p. 294); ♀.
Psychomyia pulchella Banks (1899, p. 217); ♀.
Psychomyia moesta Banks (1907a, p. 131); ♀.

Larva.—Fig. 277. Length 6 mm. Head and pronotum yellowish brown, other scle-

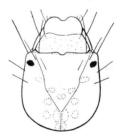

Fig. 277.—*Psychomyia flavida* larva, head.

rites straw color, body green. Frons with anterior margin sinuate. Legs short, claws short and angled, fig. 274.

Adults.—Length 4–6 mm. Head, body and appendages straw color with a slight purplish tinge on many areas. Male genitalia, fig. 278: tenth tergite divided into two large, flaplike lateral lobes to which are fused the cerci; claspers short, flat and truncate; aedeagus with a central arcuate

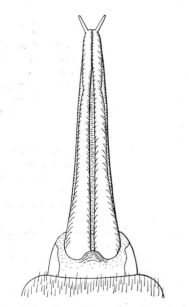

Fig. 276.—*Lype diversa*, female genitalia.

stem ending in a knob, with a pair of long needle-like styles following the stem, and another pair of styles arising from a ventral complex of internal sclerites. The short dorsal processes of the male genitalia are

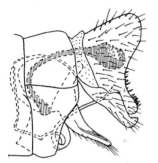

Fig. 278.—*Psychomyia flavida*, male genitalia.

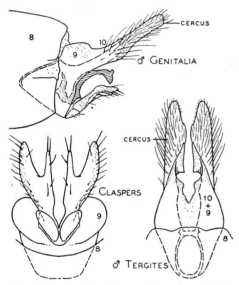

Fig. 279.—*Psychomyia nomada*, male genitalia.

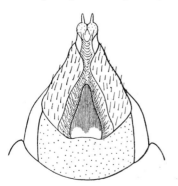

Fig. 280.—*Psychomyia flavida*, female genitalia.

in marked contrast to the long structures of the other eastern species, *nomada*, fig. 279. Female genitalia, fig. 280, conical with a single ventral sclerite.

This species is rare in Illinois. We have collected it in only two places, along the Kankakee River at Momence, and in Apple River Canyon State Park, in the northeast and northwest parts of the state, respectively. Immature stages were collected in Apple River Canyon State Park in one of the swift rapids of the Apple River.

The species has a very wide and extensive range which almost completely encircles the Great Plains. It is restricted to swift, cold streams in which it is frequently taken in enormous numbers. Records are available for the following: Arkansas, Colorado, Idaho, Illinois, Indiana, Kentucky, Michigan, Missouri, Montana, New Hampshire, New York, North Carolina, Ohio, Oklahoma, Ontario, Pennsylvania, Saskatchewan, Tennessee, West Virginia, Wisconsin and Wyoming.

Illinois Records.—APPLE RIVER CANYON STATE PARK: May 24, 1940, H. H. Ross, 1 pupa; June 6, 1940, Mohr & Burks, 1 ♀. MOMENCE: June 4, 1932, Frison & Mohr, 1 ♀.

HYDROPSYCHIDAE

Unquestionably this family is the most abundant caddis fly group in Illinois. Not only is our fauna rich in species, but various species of Hydropsychidae form the most abundant faunal element in most of the rivers and streams. This same condition holds true for almost the entire Corn Belt. By far the largest genus is *Hydropsyche*. Next comes *Cheumatopsyche*; then the remaining genera contain at the most a few species each.

The adults are diverse in size, shape and numerous structural characteristics. Both sexes have five-segmented maxillary palpi. All genera lack scutal warts, ocelli and preapical spurs on the front tibiae.

The larvae of all genera are remarkably uniform in habits and appearance. They are wormlike, active and pugnacious, and possess rows of bushy abdominal gills, fig. 281. They prefer the more rapid locations in streams, usually being concentrated around riffles, spillways and rapids, although they may also be found wherever there is an appreciable current. They make a retreat under and about trash, logs, stones and any other haven. In front of this retreat they build a net which is reputed to strain food from the flowing water, fig. 4. For

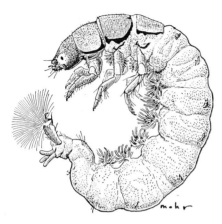

Fig. 281.—*Hydropsyche simulans,* larva.

pupation they spin an ovoid cocoon near the retreat, generally using sand, stones and bits of trash.

Characters of both mature and immature stages show no real benefit to be derived by dividing this family in subfamilies. Because it simplifies the keys to treat the entire family as a unit with no established groupings and combinations of genera to follow, subfamily treatment has been disregarded.

KEY TO GENERA

Larvae

1. Head with a broad, flat dorsal area set off by an extensive arcuate carina, fig. 415....**Macronemum,** p. 114
Head without a dorsal area set off by a carina, fig. 304................. 2
2. Left mandible with a high thumblike, dorso-lateral projection, fig. 282...
.....................**Genus A,** p. 83
Left mandible without a dorso-lateral projection, at most with a carina, fig. 283......................... 3
3. Stridulator of front leg forked, fig. 291 4
Stridulator of front leg not forked, fig. 292............................ 5
4. Prosternal plate with a pair of posterior sclerites, fig. 293. Basal tooth of mandibles single, fig. 284.......
................**Hydropsyche,** p. 86
Prosternal plate without a pair of sclerites posterior to it, fig. 294. Basal tooth of mandibles double,

fig. 285......**Cheumatopsyche,** p. 108
5. Gula rectangular and long, separating genae completely, fig. 296; each branched gill with all its branches arising at top of basal stalk, fig. 298.......................... 6
Gula triangular and short, genae therefore fused for most of their length,

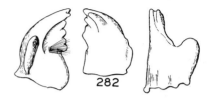

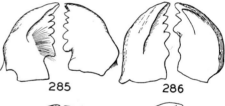

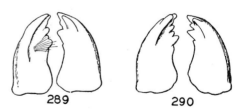

Hydropsychidae Larvae, Mandibles

Fig. 282.—*Hydropsychid Genus A.*
Fig. 283.—*Potamyia flava.*
Fig. 284.—*Hydropsyche cheilonis.*
Fig. 285.—*Cheumatopsyche campyla.*
Fig. 286.—*Diplectrona modesta.*
Fig. 287.—*Smicridea fasciatella.*
Fig. 288.—*Macronemum zebratum.*
Fig. 289.—*Parapsyche cardis.*
Fig. 290.—*Arctopsyche grandis.*

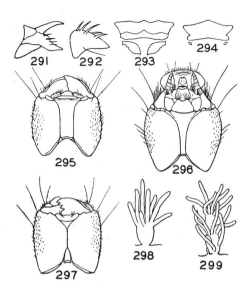

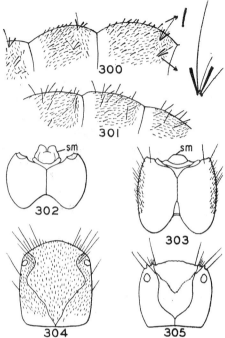

Fig. 291.—*Hydropsyche cheilonis* larva, stridulator of front leg.

Fig. 292.—*Smicridea fasciatella* larva, stridulator of front leg.

Fig. 293.—*Hydropsyche cheilonis* larva, prosternal plates.

Fig. 294.—*Cheumatopsyche campyla* larva, prosternal plates.

Fig. 295.—*Parapsyche cardis* larva, head, ventral aspect.

Fig. 296.—*Arctopsyche* sp. larva, head, ventral aspect.

Fig. 297.—*Diplectrona modesta* larva, head, ventral aspect.

Fig. 298.—*Parapsyche cardis* larva, gill with terminal branches.

Fig. 299.—*Diplectrona modesta* larva, gill with terminal branches.

Fig. 300.—*Parapsyche cardis* larva, portion of abdomen.

Fig. 301.—*Arctopsyche* sp. larva, portion of abdomen.

Fig. 302.—*Potamyia flava* larva, submentum (sm).

Fig. 303.—*Diplectrona modesta* larva, submentum (sm).

Fig. 304.—*Diplectrona modesta* larva, head, dorsal aspect.

Fig. 305.—*Smicridea fasciatella* larva, head, dorsal aspect.

fig. 297; each branched gill with branches arising from both sides and top of basal stalk, fig. 299 7

6. Gula rectangular and of even width, fig. 295; abdomen with stout, short, black, scalelike hairs arranged in tufts along dorsum near sides, frequently with broad scales scattered between them, fig. 300 . . . .
. . . .**Parapsyche**, p. 83
Gula narrowed posteriorly, fig. 296; abdomen without distinct setal tufts, with coarse hairs of varying lengths, some of them scalelike but narrow and long, fig. 301 . . . .
. . . .**Arctopsyche**, p. 83

7. Mandibles with winglike dorso-lateral flanges along basal half, fig. 283; submentum cleft, fig. 302 . . . .
. . . .**Potamyia**, p. 85
Mandibles without distinct dorso-lat-

eral flanges, fig. 286; submentum sub-conical, not cleft, fig. 303 8

8. Frons expanded laterad, its lateral extensions sharp, fig. 304 . . . .
. . . .**Diplectrona**, p. 84
Frons not expanded laterad, its lateral extensions scarcely produced, fig. 305 . . . .**Smicridea**, p. 85

Pupae

N. B.—*In connection with this key, characters of the mandibles should be used for checking identifications, fig. 316.*

1. Apical processes sharply recurved, fig. 306*B*, excavated along caudo-ventral aspect and tip without points, fig. 306 . . . .**Parapsyche**, p. 83
Apical processes not recurved, fig. 307, either not excavated along caudoventral aspect or with tip bifid 2

2. Apical processes rounded at apex, not bifurcate, figs. 308, 309.......... 3

Apical processes bifurcate at apex, figs. 310–313..................... 4

3. Apical processes flat, wide and appressed, hairy along lateral and dorsal margins, fig. 308; second hook-bearing plate of third segment narrow and linear................ ....Macronemum, p. 114

Apical processes finger-like and widely separated, hairy chiefly at apex, fig. 309; second hook-bearing plate of third segment ovoid........... ....Smicridea, p. 85

4. Tips of apical processes very long and sharp, fig. 310.....Diplectrona, p. 84

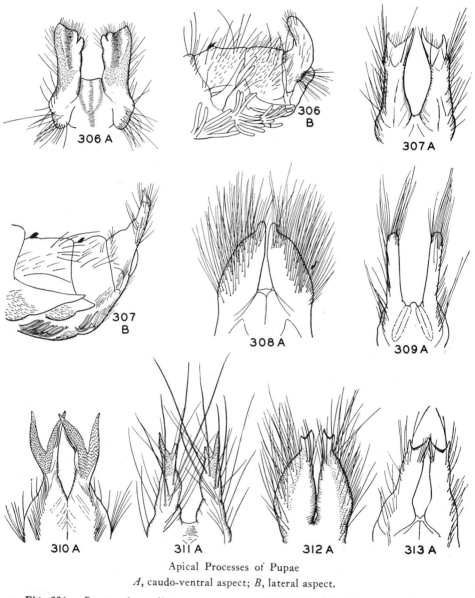

Apical Processes of Pupae

A, caudo-ventral aspect; *B*, lateral aspect.

Fig. 306.—*Parapsyche cardis.*
Fig. 307.—*Hydropsyche simulans.*
Fig. 308.—*Macronemum zebratum.*
Fig. 309.—*Smicridea fasciatella.*

Fig. 310.—*Diplectrona modesta.*
Fig. 311.—*Arctopsyche sp.*
Fig. 312.—*Potamyia flava.*
Fig. 313.—*Cheumatopsyche campyla.*

Tips of apical processes not so long or
sharp, figs. 311, 312   5

Fig. 314.—*Cheumatopsyche campyla* pupa, hook-bearing plate 3P.

Fig. 315.—*Hydropsyche orris* pupa, hook-bearing plate 3P.

5. Apical processes with a group of 3 or
   4 long, stout spines and with mesal
   point much shorter than lateral
   point, fig. 311 . . . . . . **Arctopsyche,** p. 83
   Apical processes without such a group
   of spines and with mesal point as
   long as or longer than lateral point,
   fig. 307   6
6. Apical processes with base large and
   inflated, apex short and narrow,
   fig. 312 . . . . **Potamyia,** p. 85
   Apical processes fairly uniform in

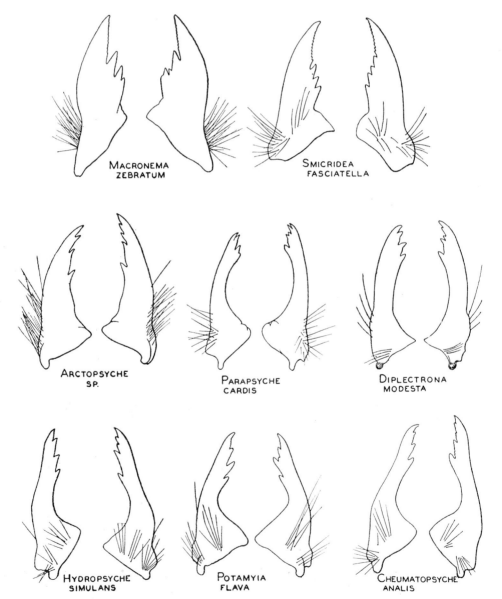

Fig. 316.—Hydropsychidae, pupal mandibles.

width, apex not narrowed, figs. 307,
313............................ 7

7. Third abdominal tergite with posterior
plates ovoid, fig. 314............
............**Cheumatopsyche**, p. 108
Third abdominal tergite with posterior
plates long and linear, fig. 315.....
.................**Hydropsyche**, p. 86

Adults

1. Head with anterior warts large and
swollen, posterior warts much
smaller, fig. 317; slender species
with very long antennae and with
pictured wings, fig. 420..........
.................**Macronemum**, p. 114
Head with anterior warts small or indistinct, posterior warts large, figs.
318–320...................... 2

2. Front wings with R_4 and R_5 running
very close together at base and forming a long, narrow $\vee$, fig. 330.....
.................**Smicridea**, p. 85
Front wings with R_4 and R_5 separating
rapidly at base and not running
close together, figs. 331–334...... 3

3. Hind wings with apex round and
with Sc and R_1 bowed deeply at
apex, fig. 331.......**Diplectrona**, p. 84
Hind wings either with Sc and R_1 not
markedly bowed, fig. 333, or both
wings with apical margin incised,
fig. 332...................... 4

4. Second segment of maxillary palpi
distinctly shorter than third segment, fig. 322.................. 5
Second segment of maxillary palpi as
long as or longer than third segment,
fig. 323...................... 8

5. Genitalia with aedeagus and claspers
(males)....................... 6
Genitalia without aedeagus or claspers
(females)...................... 7

6. Eighth segment with sternite forming
a short, wide projection extending
under genital capsule...........
...................**Parapsyche**, p. 83
Eighth segment with sternite not projecting under genital capsule......
.................**Arctopsyche**, p. 83

7. Middle tibiae with basal two-thirds
almost cylindrical, fig. 324.......
.................**Parapsyche**, p. 83
Middle tibiae greatly widened and
flattened, fig. 325...............
.................**Arctopsyche**, p. 83

8. Front tibiae without apical spurs, fig.
326..............**Potamyia** ♂, p. 85
Front tibiae with well-developed spurs,
fig. 327...................... 9

9. Eyes situated distinctly forward from
posterior margin of head, figs., 318,
319; front and hind wings similar in
shape, figs. 332, 333............. 10
Eyes situated at or near posterior
margin of head, fig. 320; front wings

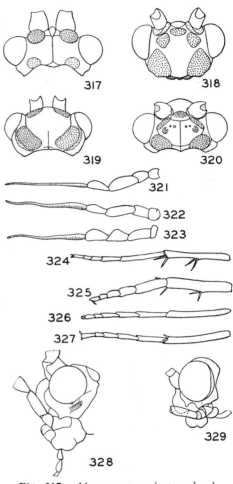

Fig. 317.—*Macronemum zebratum*, head.
Fig. 318.—*Oropsyche howellae*, head.
Fig. 319.—*Aphropsyche aprilis*, head.
Fig. 320.—*Potamyia flava*, head.
Fig. 321.—*Macronemum zebratum*, maxillary palpus.
Fig. 322.—*Arctopsyche lagodensis*, maxillary palpus.
Fig. 323.—*Hydropsyche betteni*, maxillary palpus.
Fig. 324.—*Parapsyche elsis* ♀, middle tibia.
Fig. 325.—*Arctopsyche lagodensis* ♀, middle tibia.
Fig. 326.—*Potamyia flava* ♂, front tibia.
Fig. 327.—*Potamyia flava* ♀, front tibia.
Fig. 328.—*Potamyia flava* ♀, head.
Fig. 329.—*Cheumatopsyche campyla*, head.

narrow with straight hind margin, much different in shape from hind wings, which have the hind margin arcuate, fig. 334................ 11

10. Both wings with apical margins incised; front wings with first fork of R_s as far basad as first fork of M, fig. 332.............**Oropsyche**, p. 83

Both wings with apical margins evenly rounded; front wings with first fork of R_s distad of first fork of M, fig. 333..............**Aphropsyche**, p. 83

11. Malar space wide, fig. 328; flagellum with first two segments partly or completely fused, fig. 328; body and wings straw color with tawny or

light brown on dorsum..........
.................**Potamyia** ♀, p. 85

Malar space narrow, fig. 329; flagellum with first two segments always separated by a distinct annular suture; body and wings darker, wings either dark or irrorate, figs. 392, 393..... 12

12. Males............................. 13
Females........................... 14

13. Base of aedeagus cylindrical, figs. 358–383..............**Hydropsyche**, p. 86
Base of aedeagus bulbous, figs. 394–403........**Cheumatopsyche**, p. 108

14. Sternal plates of eighth segment separated to base of segment, fig. 391 ....**Cheumatopsyche**, p. 10

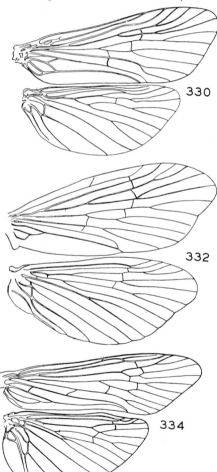

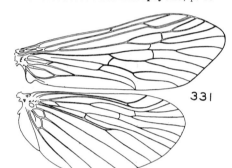

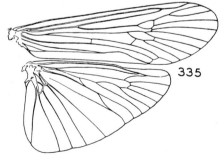

Hydropsychidae Wings

Fig. 330.—*Smicridea fasciatella.*
Fig. 331.—*Diplectrona modesta.*
Fig. 332.—*Oropsyche howellae.*

Fig. 333.—*Aphropsyche aprilis.*
Fig. 334.—*Hydropsyche simulans.*
Fig. 335.—*Macronemum zebratum.*

Sternal plates of eighth segment separated only two-thirds distance to base of segment, fig. 390.........
................**Hydropsyche**, p. 86

Parapsyche Betten

Parapsyche Betten (1934, p. 181). Genotype, monobasic: *Arctopsyche apicalis* Banks.

No species of this genus have been recorded from Illinois. Two species, *apicalis* and *cardis*, are recorded from the eastern states.

Arctopsyche McLachlan

Arctopsyche McLachlan (1868, p. 300). Genotype, monobasic: *Aphelocheira ladogensis* Kolenati.

As with the preceding, no species of this genus have been taken in Illinois. Two eastern species, *ladogensis* and *irrorata*, have been recorded from the eastern states and eastern Canada.

Oropsyche Ross

Oropsyche Ross (1941*b*, p. 79). Genotype, by original designation: *Oropsyche howellae* Ross.

This primitive genus has not yet been taken from Illinois and is known only from

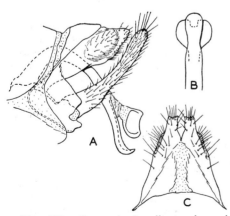

Fig. 336.—*Oropsyche howellae*, male genitalia. *A*, lateral aspect; *B*, aedeagus, ventral aspect; *C*, tenth tergite.

the genotype, described from North Carolina. The distinctive genitalia, fig. 336, will serve to verify identifications of this species.

Aphropsyche Ross

Aphropsyche Ross (1941*b*, p. 78). Genotype, by original designation: *Aphropsyche aprilis* Ross.

Only one species of this genus is known, the genotype, described from Tennessee. The male genitalia, fig. 337, are distinctive.

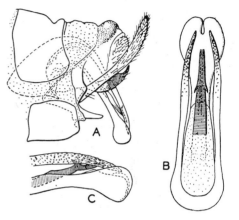

Fig. 337.—*Aphropsyche aprilis*, male genitalia. *A*, lateral aspect; *B* and *C*, aedeagus, dorsal and lateral aspects.

Although we have no definite adult record for this species in Illinois, there is considerable suspicion that the larva of the genotype might be *Genus A* described below. This larva was found in the stream at Parksville, Tennessee, along which the type series of the genotype was collected.

Hydropsychid Genus A

LARVA.—Fig. 338. Head bright brownish yellow with a few darker suffusions along the frontal area; thoracic shields and legs brownish yellow with irregular darker markings. Head with gula small and triangular, frontal area without prominent carinae; mandibles stout, fig. 282, the left

Fig. 338.—*Hydropsychid Genus A*, head.

one much larger than the right, with a large dorsal projection from the lateral margin, this projection somewhat thumb shaped and very high; a single brustia is present; and the row of teeth is even. The right mandible has only a slight flange on the dorsal lateral portion, a large tooth dorsad of the regular series, the regular series itself composed of three or four irregular teeth.

ADULTS.—Unknown.

Larvae of this distinctive form have been taken in small numbers at the mouth of Union Spring, a small underground river in the Ozark Hills near Alto Pass, Illinois, as well as at Parksville, Tennessee (see *Aphropsyche aprilis*). Efforts to rear this species have so far been unsuccessful, but such a large proportion of the genera of the Hydropsychidae are known that there seems good likelihood of this species proving to belong to one of the rare primitive genera such as *Aphropsyche*.

Diplectrona Westwood

Diplectrona Westwood (1840, p. 49). Genotype, by original designation: *Hydropsyche flavo-maculata* Stephens *nec* Pictet = *Diplectrona felix* McLachlan.

Only a single species of this genus occurs in Illinois. In addition to this one species, *californica* is known from the western states, and another species, *doringa*, has been described from New Hampshire. Dr. Milne informs me that the holotype of the latter may be lost; hence no diagnosis of the genitalia can be given.

Diplectrona modesta Banks

Diplectrona modesta Banks (1908*b*, p. 266); ♂, ♀.

LARVA.—Length 15 mm. Color of head, thoracic shields, and legs dark reddish brown to almost black; if reddish brown, the head has several indistinct darker markings. Head convex, frons sharply widened at middle, fig. 304. Mandibles sharp and stocky without lobes on the lateral margin, and with the teeth of both mandibles irregular in size, fig. 286. Abdomen with a mixture of short, appressed pubescence and erect, flattened hairs; each segment has in addition two pairs of tufts of a few long, slender hairs.

ADULTS.—Length 12–14 mm. Color of head, body and wings dark brown with a reddish tinge, the wings without mottling or pattern. Male genitalia composed of quite simple parts, fig. 339: tenth tergite

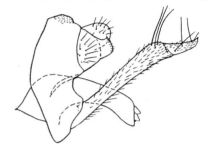

Fig. 339.—*Diplectrona modesta*, male genitalia.

divided into a mesal and a lateral pair of lobes; claspers with basal segment very long, apical segment short and narrow; aedeagus tubular and curved, with sharp sclerites set in the apex.

We have taken this species commonly in two spring-fed streams in Illinois, one of them at Elgin in the northern part of the state, the other at Alto Pass in extreme southern Illinois. Scanty Illinois collections have been made along other small spring-fed streams, also. The adult emergence is confined to late spring and early summer, May and June. In more northern states adults have been taken as late as July, and in southern states as early as the month of April.

The species ranges throughout the wooded portions of the eastern states and extends through the Ozarks into Oklahoma. Throughout its range it frequents rapid, clear brooks and streams. We have records for Arkansas, Florida, Georgia, Illinois, Indiana, New Hampshire, New York, North Carolina, Oklahoma, Ontario, Pennsylvania, South Carolina, Tennessee and West Virginia.

Illinois Records.—ALTO PASS, Union Spring: May 31, 1938, B. D. Burks, 2 larvae, 1 ♀ ; May 12, 1939, Burks & Riegel, 1 larva, 1 ♀ ; May 23, 1939, Ross & Burks, many larvae; May 29, 1939, Burks & Riegel, 1 ♀ ; May 14, 1940, Mohr & Burks, 3 larvae; May 26, 1940, Mohr & Burks, many larvae, 2 ♂, 2 ♀ ; May 31, 1940, B. D. Burks, many larvae; June 20, 1940, Mohr & Riegel, 1 ♂. ELGIN, Botanical Gardens: April 19, 1939, Burks & Riegel, 1 larva; May 9, 1939, Ross & Burks, 4 pupae, 3 larvae; May 23, 1939, Burks & Riegel, 2♂, 1♀, 3 larvae; June 6, 1939, Burks & Riegel, 4♂, 3♀; June 13, 1939, Frison & Ross, 3♂, many larvae; Sept. 19, 1939, Ross & Mohr, 3 larvae. FOUNTAIN BLUFF: May 14, 1932, Frison, Ross & Mohr, 1♀; May 15, 1932, Ross & Mohr, 1♀. OAKWOOD, small tributary Middle Fork River: July 14, 1939, Burks & Riegel, 1 larva. UTICA, Split Rock Brook: Feb. 1, 1941, Frison, Ries & Ross, 2 larvae; May 24, 1941, Ross & Burks, 1♀.

Smicridea McLachlan

Smicridea McLachlan (1871, p. 134). Genotype, here designated: *Smicridea fasciatella* McLachlan.

This genus has not yet been recorded from Illinois. The genotype has been taken commonly in Texas and Oklahoma and may ultimately be found in southern Illinois. The distinctive larval mandibles, fig. 287, pupal mandibles and apical processes, figs. 309, 316, adult venation, fig. 330, and male genitalia, fig. 340, will readily identify this

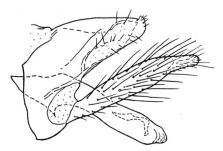

Fig. 340.—*Smicridea fasciatella*, male genitalia.

species. The larvae have been collected in small spring-fed streams in both Texas and Oklahoma. I have found the adults especially abundant in this latter state.

Potamyia Banks

Potamyia Banks (1900a, p. 259). Genotype, by original designation: *Macronema flavum* Hagen.

Only one species of this genus is known. In structure the female is very similar to that of *Hydropsyche*, but the male, larva and pupa are so distinctive that there is no question as to the separate generic status of *Potamyia*.

Potamyia flava (Hagen)

Macronema flavum Hagen (1861, p. 285); ♂.

Hydropsyche kansensis Banks (1905b, p. 15); ♀.

LARVA.—Length 13 mm. Head, thoracic sclerites and legs brownish yellow, the frontal area of head with a reddish cast, and the thoracic sclerites bordered by a narrow, black line. Frons subtriangular. Mandibles, fig. 283, with long, wide, lateral flanges along basal half. Hair on abdomen short and appressed.

ADULTS.—Length 10–11 mm. Color almost uniformly light brownish yellow, with a slight pinkish tinge. Male with very long, slender antennae and without spurs on the front tibiae; male genitalia, fig. 341, with simple parts. Female with shorter antennae and normal spurs on front tibiae, in both these respects resembling *Hydropsyche*.

This is one of the most common large-stream to large-river species, not only in Illinois but throughout the Middle West. We have abundant records of the species from all parts of Illinois and have taken it repeatedly in huge swarms along such rivers as the Illinois, Mississippi, Ohio and Rock. The adults begin emerging in May and continue through September.

An interesting feature of the species' habits has been observed in a few small streams where the larvae were accessible. Here it was found that, instead of hiding under the rocks, the larvae tended to frequent less rapid portions of the stream and construct their retreats on top of the rocks. In many of these situations their nets could be seen sticking up into the current like miniature fences.

The range of the species seems to be restricted to midwestern and southern states, with a preference for the larger and slower

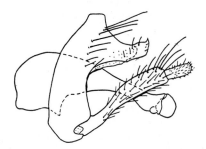

Fig. 341.—*Potamyia flava*, male genitalia.

streams. Records are available for Arkansas, Georgia, Illinois, Indiana, Iowa, Kansas, Kentucky, Michigan, Minnesota, Missouri, Ohio, Oklahoma, South Dakota, Tennessee, Texas and Wisconsin.

Illinois Records.—Many males, females and pupae, taken May 6 to October 10, and many larvae, taken April 24 to September 11, are from Alton, Apple River Canyon State Park, Arcola, Aurora, Bath, Cairo, Carbondale, Charleston, Clinton, Como (below mouth of Elkhorn Creek, Rock River), Crystal Lake near Gulfport, Danville (Middle Fork River), Dixon (Rock River), Downs, Dundee, East Dubuque, Effingham, Eichorn, Elgin (Botanical Gardens, Fox River), Elizabethtown, Florence, Fox Lake, Freeport, Fulton, Galena (Sinsinawa River), Gilman, Golconda, Grafton (Mississippi River), Grand Tower, Gulfport (Crystal Lake), Hamilton, Hanover, Hardin (Illinois River), Harrisburg, Harvard, Havana, Henry, Herod, Hillsdale, Homer, Horse Shoe Lake, Jerseyville, Kampsville, Kankakee (Kankakee River), Kappa (Mackinaw River), Keithsburg, Lawrenceville, Le Roy, Massac County, Meredosia, Metropolis, Milan (Rock River), Momence, Monticello, Morris, Mount Carmel, Muncie, New Boston, New Milford (Kishwaukee River), Oakwood (Salt Fork River), Oregon (Castle Rock, Rock River), Oswego, Ottawa, Pere Marquette State Park, Pontiac, Putnam (Lake Senachwine), Quincy (Burton Creek, Mississippi River), Richmond, Ripley (La Moine River), Rockford, Rock Island, Rockton, Rosiclare, Savanna (Mississippi River), Serena (Indian Creek, Fox River), Shawneetown, Shelbyville, South Beloit, Springfield (Sangamon River), Sterling (Rock River), Sugar Grove, Thebes, Urbana, Valley City (Illinois River), Venedy Station (Kaskaskia River), Wadsworth (Des Plains River), Waukegan, Wilmington, Yorkville, Zeigler, Zion.

Hydropsyche Pictet

Hydropsyche Pictet (1834, p. 199). Genotype, here designated: *Hydropsyche cinerea* Pictet.

In Illinois we have taken 18 species of this genus, the various species living in practically every kind of permanent stream in the state. Some are found abundantly in large rivers; others appear restricted to small spring-fed brooks.

The genus contains about 50 species, for a large proportion of which females and larvae have been identified. It is interesting to note that in the *scalaris* group the larvae can be identified with considerable ease, but in the *bifida* group few characters have yet been found by which to identify them. In the females the opposite is true; those of the *scalaris* group present many small complexes in which final specific identification is extremely critical and unreliable, whereas in the *bifida* group reliable specific characters are known for most of the species.

Fine pioneer work outlining diagnostic characters for the females of *Hydropsyche* and *Cheumatopsyche* has been done by Denning (1943). Denning has used the median plate as a source of supplementary characters. Due to the difficulty of seeing this plate in many species, its characters are not used in the present keys, and for information regarding them the student is referred to Denning's work.

Westwood (1840, p. 49) designated *instabilis* Curtis as the genotype of *Hydropsyche*, but since this name was not included in the original description of the genus, it cannot function as the type species. *H. cinerea* Pictet, an originally included species, is here designated the genotype. Pictet's species *cinerea* is considered a synonym of *instabilis*.

KEY TO SPECIES

Larvae

1. Frons with two short, upturned, stocky "horns" on anterior margin, fig. 346.................**orris,** p. 106
   Frons without teeth on anterior margin............................. 2

2. Frons with anterior margin produced into a low, wide, angular portion, fig. 347.............**phalerata,** p. 102
   Frons with anterior margin almost straight........................ 3

3. Head entirely black or blackish brown, including extreme posterior portion, excepting only a small area around eye which is yellowish, fig. 348....
   ....**betteni,** p. 99
   Head with at least red or yellowish areas leading from eye to posterior part of head or venter, fig. 352; usually with venter or back of head yellowish, figs. 351, 355......... 4

4. Dorsum of abdomen with wide, short, scalelike hairs mixed with plain hairs, fig. 342, these scales sometimes sparse but usually conspicuous on the sixth, seventh or eighth tergites...................... 5

Dorsum of abdomen with only narrow, long, scalelike hairs mixed with plain hairs, fig. 344.................. 10

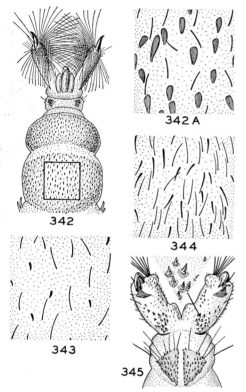

Fig. 342.—*Hydropsyche simulans* larva, apex of abdomen, dorsal aspect; *A*, enlarged portion of epidermis.

Fig. 343.—*H. arinale* larva.

Fig. 344.—*H. recurvata* larva.

Fig. 345.—*H. aerata* larva, apex of abdomen, ventral aspect.

5. Head chiefly yellow or straw color with a dorsal mark resembling a cross, fig. 349, the surface shining and without short, black hair; base of anal legs with a patch of brown, flat spines, fig. 345.....**aerata**, p. 101

Head either with more extensive dark markings, fig. 354, or with abundant, short, black hair, or base of anal legs without a patch of spines..... 6

6. Entire dorsum and lateral portion of head bright brownish red, uniform except for a fine pattern of yellow-

ish spots, fig. 350; preclypeus with sclerotized areas at sides, labrum with yellow or pale hair...**cuanis**, p. 100

Dorsum of head with either a definite pale and yellow pattern, fig. 353, or mostly dark brown; preclypeus without lateral sclerotized areas, labrum usually with pale hair....... 7

7. Scale-hairs sparse on dorsum of abdomen, on sixth segment no more abundant than in fig. 343........
...................**arinale**, p. 104

Scale-hairs at least as abundant as in fig. 342......................... 8

8. Head with dorsal pattern merging gradually and not contrasting much with ground color, fig. 352........
...................**simulans**, p. 104

Head with a well-delimited dorsal, dark brown mark contrasting with ground color, figs. 353, 354....... 9

9. Dorsal mark on head wider, extending full width of head, ending in line with eyes, cut off with a sharper and straighter margin, fig. 353; simple hairs on abdomen as dark and conspicuous as scale-hairs...**hageni**, p. 103

Dorsal mark of head not extending to margin of head, margin irregular, fig. 354; simple hairs on abdomen much lighter than scale-hairs.....
...................**frisoni**, p. 105

10. Head mostly black or blackish brown with one or two mesal yellow squares, fig. 355......**slossonae**, p. 99

Head with a definite checkered pattern, the checks either surrounded by black, fig. 356, or indicated by dark bars on a yellow ground, fig. 357......**bifida**, p. 97; **bronta**, p. 98; **cheilonis**, p. 98; **recurvata**, p. 99

Adults

1. Genitalia with a prominent aedeagus, fig. 358 (males)................ 2

Genitalia without an aedeagus, fig. 390 (females)................... 28

2. Aedeagus with a pair of ovoid, dorsal sclerites near apex, figs. 358–367.. 3

Aedeagus without a pair of ovoid, dorsal sclerites near apex, figs. 368–383........................... 13

3. Apex of aedeagus with a lateral pair of membranous arms directed basad, fig. 358....................... 4

Apex of aedeagus with lateral processes sessile or lacking, fig. 361.... 6

4. Aedeagus just basad of dorsal sclerites bearing a dorsal pair of large, stout hooks curved laterad, fig. 358....
...................**walkeri**, p. 96

Aedeagus with a dorsal pair of small
hooks, figs. 359, 360.............   5

5. Lateral arms of apex of aedeagus with
end containing a protrusible bundle
of pale but sclerotized spicules, fig.
359......................**vexa**, p. 97
Lateral arms of apex of aedeagus with
end surmounted by a ring of short
setae but without a bundle of
spicules, fig. 360.........**piatrix**, p. 97

6. Dorso-lateral arms of aedeagus with a
conspicuous lateral spine before
apex and a bundle of spicules at
apex, fig. 361............**sparna**, p. 97
Dorso-lateral arms of aedeagus with
spine either absent or apical, fig.
362, or arms absent.............   7

7. Main body of aedeagus sinuate, almost Z-shaped, fig. 362.........
....................**slossonae**, p. 99

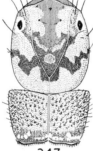

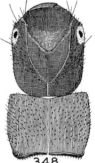
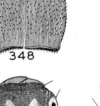

346   347   348   349

350   351   352   353

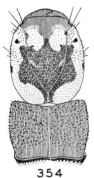

354   355   356   357

Hydropsyche Larvae, Head and Pronotum

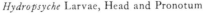

Fig. 346.—*H. orris.*
Fig. 347.—*H. phalerata.*
Fig. 348.—*H. betteni.*
Fig. 349.—*H. aerata.*
Fig. 350.—*H. cuanis.*
Fig. 351.—*H. arinale.*

Fig. 352.—*H. simulans.*
Fig. 353.—*H. hageni.*
Fig. 354.—*H. frisoni.*
Fig. 355.—*H. slossonae.*
Fig. 356.—*H. bifida.*
Fig. 357.—*H. recurvata.*

Figs. 358–367.—*Hydropsyche*, male genitalia.   *A*, lateral aspect; *B*, dorsal aspect; *C*, *D* and *E*, respectively, aedeagus, lateral, ventral and dorsal aspects; *F*, apex of clasper.

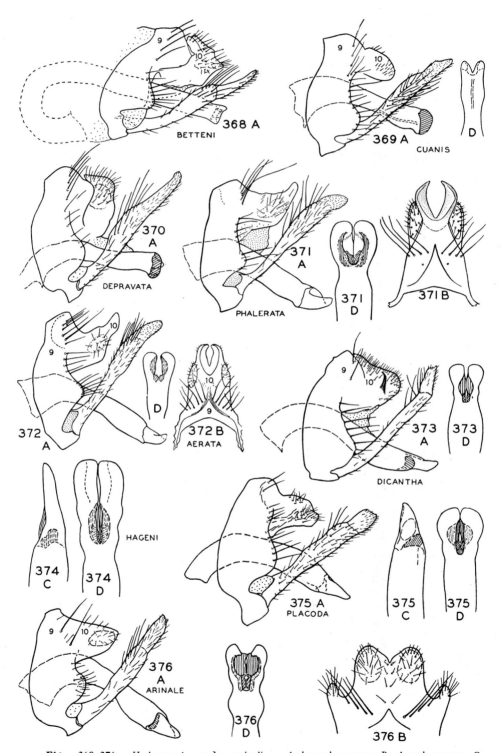

Figs. 368–376.—*Hydropsyche*, male genitalia. *A*, lateral aspect; *B*, dorsal aspect; *C*, aedeagus, lateral aspect; *D*, aedeagus, ventral aspect.

Main body of aedeagus with only the
angle at base pronounced, fig. 363.. 　8

8. Lateral arms tipped with an upturned
spur, fig. 363........**recurvata**, p. 99
Lateral arms tipped with no spur or
one that is not upturned.......... 　9

9. Spur of lateral arms long, robust and
hanging down with tip well below
ventral margin of aedeagus, figs.
364, 365...................... 　10
Spur of lateral arms shorter, flat, fig.
366, finger-like, fig. 367, or sometimes absent.................. 　11

10. Apex of aedeagus with lateral pockets
scarcely extruded and containing
only a few weak spicules, fig. 364..
......................**bronta**, p. 98
Apex of aedeagus with lateral pockets
extruded to form a sessile flap containing a cluster of strong, dark
spicules, fig. 365......**cheilonis**, p. 98

11. Spur of lateral arms large and flat, as
in fig. 366..............**morosa**, p. 98
Spur of lateral arms small and finger-
like, fig. 367, sometimes even smaller
or absent...................... 　12

12. Apical segment of clasper with apex
appearing attenuated, as in fig. 367,
seen from side...........**bifida**, p. 97
Apical segment of clasper conical, its
apex appearing pointed, as seen
from side, fig. 363....**recurvata**, p. 99

13. Apex of aedeagus round, fig. 369, or
truncate, fig. 368................ 　14
Apex of aedeagus produced into a
flattened area composed of two
lateral processes and a mesal body,
figs. 371–383.................... 　16

14. Aedeagus curved at base to form a
complete semicircle, fig. 368......
......................**betteni**, p. 99
Aedeagus curved not more than 90
degrees, fig. 370................. 　15

15. Vertical cleft at apex of aedeagus deep
and not containing extruded mesal
plates, fig. 369..........**cuanis**, p. 100
Vertical cleft at apex of aedeagus
shallower and containing a pair of
prominent mesal plates, fig. 370...
...................**depravata**, p. 100

16. Apex of tenth tergite turned up and
deeply cleft, fig. 371............ 　17
Apex of tenth tergite rounded and at
most cleft as deeply as shown in
fig. 376....................... 　18

17. Apex of aedeagus as wide as stem,
without an open area between lateral
processes, fig. 371....**phalerata**, p. 102
Apex of aedeagus narrower than stem,
with an open area between lateral
processes, fig. 372.......**aerata**, p. 101

18. Tenth tergite armed on each side with
a stout, long spine, fig. 373.......
....................**dicantha**, p. 102
Tenth tergite without such a conspicuous spine....................... 　19

19. Aedeagus with lateral lobes produced
far beyond mesal cavity, fig. 374...
.....................**hageni**, p. 103
Aedeagus with lateral lobes produced
only slightly beyond mesal cavity.. 　20

20. Apical segment of claspers appearing
obliquely truncate, from side view,
fig. 375...............**placoda**, p. 103
Apical segment of claspers appearing
sinuate, from side view, fig. 376... 　21

21. Apex of aedeagus moniliform, fig. 376
.....................**arinale**, p. 104
Apex of aedeagus with only one constriction and that at base......... 　22

22. Apex of aedeagus robust and surmounted by a shallow caplike continuation of the basal portion, fig. 377
...................**simulans**, p. 104
Apex of aedeagus either not surmounted by a "cap" or dorso-ven-
trally flattened, fig. 380........... 　23

23. Apex of aedeagus with lateral processes thin and long, as in fig. 378..
.....................**valanis**, p. 105
Apex of aedeagus with lateral processes
much more robust............... 　24

24. Apex of aedeagus with mesal dome
elevated above level of lateral flange
and also above level of stem and
forming a distinct angle with it,
fig. 379................**frisoni**, p. 105
Apex of aedeagus with mesal dome
either not elevated above level of
lateral flange or confluent with dorsal margin of stem, figs. 380–383... 　25

25. Apex of aedeagus with lateral flanges
wide, the apical portion of each
almost as large as the entire mesal
cavity; dorso-lateral edge of flange
confluent with dorsal line of stem,
fig. 380...............**scalaris**, p. 106
Apex of aedeagus with lateral flanges
narrow, the mesal cavity occupying
all of the apex except narrow lateral
and apical portions; dorso-lateral
edge of flange various............ 　26

26. Apex of aedeagus with a long, narrow
profile, and with two-thirds of mesal
cavity open ventrad, fig. 381......
...................**incommoda**, p. 106
Apex of aedeagus with a shorter, stock-
ier profile and with mesal cavity
only one-third open ventrad...... 　27

27. Apex of aedeagus with apico-lateral
corners of flange sharp, projecting
almost directly posterad and as wide
as in fig. 382..........**bidens**, p. 107

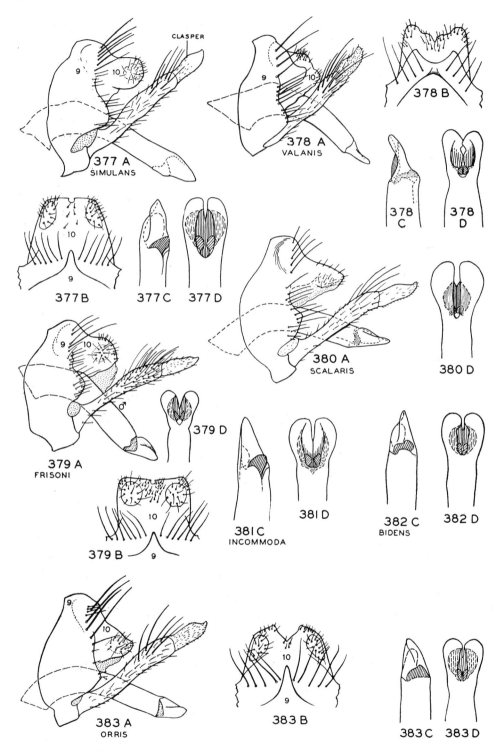

Figs. 377–383.—*Hydropsyche*, male genitalia. *A*, lateral aspect; *B*, dorsal aspect; *C*, aedeagus, lateral aspect; *D*, aedeagus, ventral aspect.

Apex of aedeagus with apico-lateral corners of flange blunt, in profile appearing to merge with apex of dome, and narrow, as in fig. 383...
..........................**orris**, p. 106

28. Eighth tergite with ventral margin concave, the apico-lateral lobe bearing a wide, compact brush of long setae, fig. 384*B*; clasper receptacle appearing deeply invaginated, large and round, especially as seen from dorsal aspect, fig. 385............
.....**betteni**, p. 99; **depravata**, p. 100
Either ventral margin of eighth tergite with no apico-lateral lobe or only a small brush, fig. 384*A*, or clasper receptacle much smaller or more slender, fig. 387..................... 29

29. Clasper groove not well-marked, clasper receptacle either not evident or appearing from lateral view as only a shallow crescent beneath dorsal cap, fig. 386*A–D*................ 30
Either clasper groove well marked, fig. 387*A*, or clasper receptacle represented by a definite pocket, fig. 387*B–I*, or by an invagination, fig.

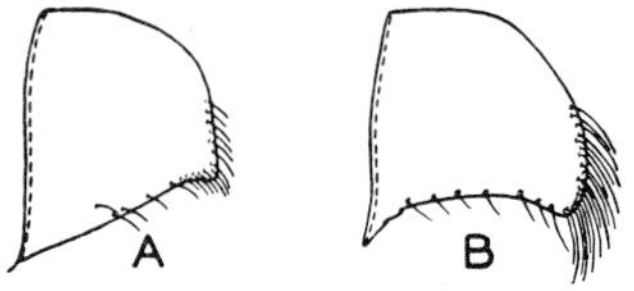

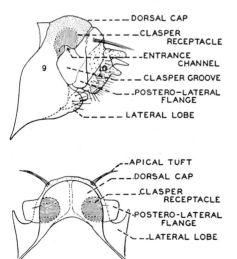

Fig. 384.—*Hydropsyche*, lateral aspect of female eighth tergite. *A, bifida*; *B, betteni*.

DORSAL CAP
CLASPER RECEPTACLE
ENTRANCE CHANNEL
CLASPER GROOVE
POSTERO-LATERAL FLANGE
LATERAL LOBE
9

APICAL TUFT
DORSAL CAP
CLASPER RECEPTACLE
POSTERO-LATERAL FLANGE
LATERAL LOBE

Fig. 385.—*Hydropsyche betteni*, female tergites. Upper figure, lateral view including tenth tergite; lower figure, dorsal view of ninth tergite alone.

386*H–N*, projecting beneath dorsal cap............................ 36

30. Ninth tergite with lateral lobe not developed; clasper groove small and very shallow, scarcely any indentation visible beneath dorsal cap from dorsal view, fig. 386*A*............
....................**dicantha**, p. 102
Ninth tergite with lateral lobe distinctly developed, either narrow, fig. 386*K*, or broad, fig. 386*C*; clasper groove well-marked, larger and forming a deep concavity visible beneath dorsal cap from dorsal view 31

31. Clasper groove with a small, distinct pit near dorsal margin, fig. 386*B*...
....................**placoda**, p. 103
Clasper groove without a pit........ 32

32. Lateral lobes of eighth sternite with mesal and lateral margins parallel, fig. 388*C*; head and thorax mostly dark purplish brown, basal segments of antennae pale, with only light V-marks, wings without irrorate pattern............**cuanis**, p. 100
Lateral lobes of eighth sternite with mesal margin sloping decidedly laterad toward apex, fig. 388*D*; either body much lighter, wings with irrorate wing pattern or basal segments of antennae with very dark V-marks 33

33. Lateral lobe of ninth tergite thickened at base, triangular in cross section, fig. 386*D*........**hageni**, p. 103
Lateral lobe of ninth tergite thin and leaflike.......................... **34**

34. Clasper groove, from dorsal view, appearing wider and slightly angulate at middle, fig. 386*E*...........
....................**arinale**, p. 104
Clasper groove shallower and evenly rounded, fig. 386*F, G*............ 35

35. Clasper groove, from dorsal view, appearing shallower, narrowing more rapidly anteriorly, fig. 386*F*.......
....................**phalerata**, p. 102
Clasper groove deeper, the anterior portion wide, fig. 386*G*...**aerata**, p. 101

36. Clasper groove forming a well-marked, curved trough, the upper end of which projects only slightly under dorsal cap, fig. 387*A*.....**walkeri**, p. 96
Clasper groove either indistinct, fig. 386*K*, or running into a pocket-like clasper receptacle, fig. 387*B*...... 37

37. Clasper receptacle forming a wide triangular, crescentic or irregular pocket which is not narrowed ventrad, fig. 386*H–N*................ 38
Clasper receptacle forming a pouch with a narrow ventral opening, fig. 387*B–I*....................... **44**

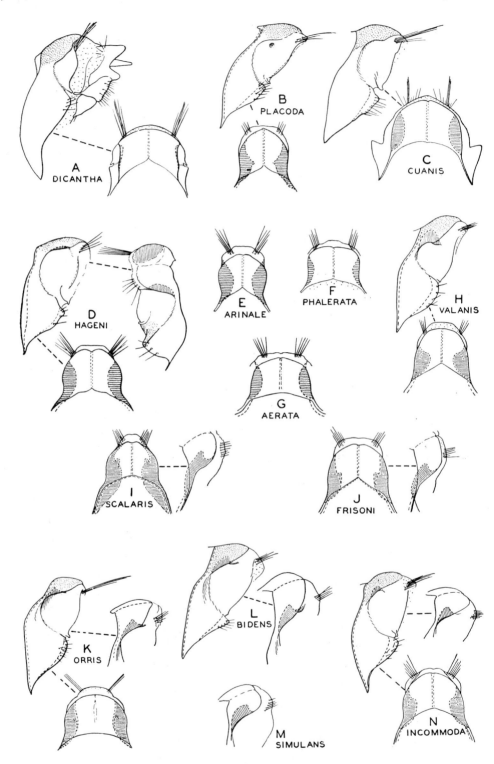

Fig. 386.—*Hydropsyche*, female ninth tergite.

38. Clasper receptacle large, nearly as high as long, fig. 386*H*...**valanis**, p. 105
    Clasper receptacle much shallower, but usually wide, fig. 386*K–N*..... 39
39. Lateral lobes of eighth sternite close together at base, mesal margins forming a wide V, figs. 389*A*, 390... 40
    Lateral lobes of eighth sternite farther apart, their mesal margins diverging less, fig. 389*B*.............. 41
40. Clasper receptacle appearing, from dorsal view, with a swollen portion basad of dorsal point, fig. 387*I*....
    ....**scalaris**, p. 106
    Clasper receptacle appearing, from dorsal view, with basal portion confluent in outline with dorsal point, fig. 387*J*...............**frisoni**, p. 105
41. Clasper receptacle appearing, from lateral view, with dorsal point acute and near middle, its posterior "tail" slender, long and slightly concave dorsad, fig. 386*K, L*...... 42

Clasper receptacle appearing, from lateral view, with dorsal point rounded or near posterior margin and with posterior "tail" consequently short, fig. 386*M, N*....... 43
42. Antero-lateral lobe of ninth tergite long and narrow, its apex rounded, its contour following its demarcation line, fig. 386*K*............**orris**, p. 106
    Antero-lateral lobe of ninth tergite narrower at base, wider at apex, which is produced as a somewhat angulate lobe, fig. 386*L*.......
    ....**bidens**, p. 107
43. Clasper receptacle with dorso-mesal portion narrow, fig. 386*N*........
    ....**incommoda**, p. 106
    Clasper receptacle with dorso-mesal portion wide and arcuate, with a pronounced posterior loop, fig. 386*M*
    ....**simulans**, p. 104
44. Clasper receptacle nearly globular and small, fig. 387*B*..........**bronta**, p. 98

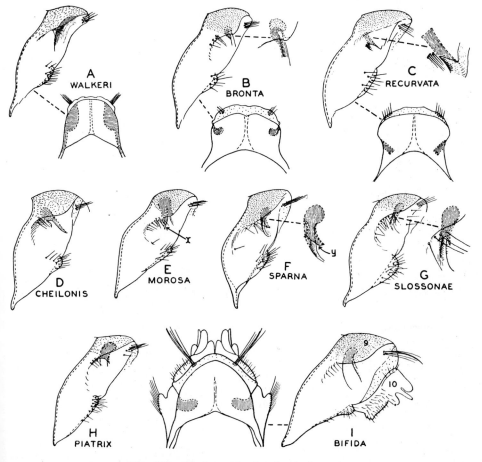

Fig. 387.—*Hydropsyche*, female ninth tergite.

Clasper receptacle tubular, fig. 387*C–I*   45
45. Clasper receptacle directed nearly anterad, diagonal to segment, fig. 387*C, D*   46

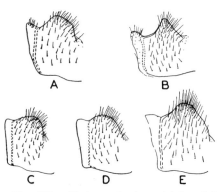

Fig. 388.—*Hydropsyche*, lateral lobe of female eighth sternite. *A, bifida; B, recurvata; C, cuanis; D, phalerata; E, betteni.* This set is drawn at right angles to the face of the lateral lobe.

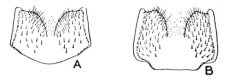

Fig. 389.—*Hydropsyche*, female eighth sternite. *A, scalaris; B, incommoda.*

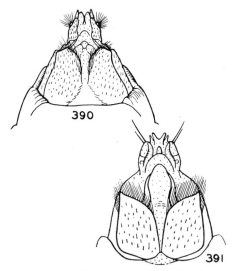

390

391

Fig. 390.—*Hydropsyche scalaris*, female genitalia, ventral aspect.
Fig. 391.—*Cheumatopsyche campyla*, female genitalia, ventral aspect.

Clasper receptacle directed or curved dorsad or posterad, fig. 387*E–I* . . .   47
46. Clasper receptacle narrow and truncate at tip, fig. 387*C* . . . .
. . . .**recurvata,** p. 99
Clasper receptacle wider and rounded at tip, fig. 387*D* . . . .**cheilonis,** p. 98
47. Clasper receptacle long, the anterior side of its entrance channel with a long, overhanging flange, *x*, fig. 387*E* . . . .**morosa,** p. 98
Either clasper receptacle much shorter, or the anterior side of entrance channel with only an inconspicuous flange, fig. 387*G*   48
48. Posterior side of entrance channel to clasper receptacle with a sinuate overhanging flange, *y*, fig. 387*F* . . .
. . . .**sparna,** p. 97
Posterior side of entrance channel with no flange extending down ventral portion   49
49. Entrance channel reduced to a narrow slit, fig. 387*G* . . . .**slossonae,** p. 99
Entrance channel much wider, fig. 387*H, I*   50
50. Clasper receptacle long, narrowed and with tip markedly curved, fig. 387*I* . . . .**bifida,** p. 97
Clasper receptacle shorter and more bulbous   51
51. Clasper receptacle situated near middle of tergite . . . .**vexa,** p. 97
Clasper receptacle situated along lower edge of posterior side of tergite, fig. 387*H* . . . .**piatrix,** p. 97

Bifida Group

Hydropsyche walkeri Betten & Mosely

Hydropsyche maculicornis Walker (1852, p. 113); ♂. Preoccupied.
Hydropsyche walkeri Betten & Mosely (1940, p. 23). New name.

To date this species has not been discovered in Illinois, although it may eventually be taken in the northern part of the state. It was originally described from Ontario; we have additional specimens from New York, Quebec and Wisconsin.

FEMALE.—Length 10 mm. In color and general structure similar to male, which in these characters is practically indistinguishable from *bifida*, described below. Female genitalia, fig. 387*A*, with clasper groove well marked, wide and curved at apex, the upper portion of the groove partly invaginated beneath dorsal cap of ninth tergite; lateral lobe long but narrow, with abundant setae; from dorsal view the clasper groove appears as a well-marked posterior swelling.

Allotype, female.—Niagara Falls, New York: June 23, 1941, J. A. Ross. The allotype is one of a mating pair.

Hydropsyche vexa Ross

Hydropsyche vexa Ross (1938a, p. 148); ♂.

This species is known only from the states of Minnesota and Wisconsin. As with *Hydropsyche walkeri*, it may ultimately be taken in Illinois. The female genitalia are illustrated by Denning (1943).

Hydropsyche piatrix Ross

Hydropsyche piatrix Ross (1938a, p. 148); ♂.

This species has been taken at the mouth of large springs in Missouri and Arkansas, but so far has not been taken in Illinois.

FEMALE.—Length 9 mm. Color and general structure typical for group as described for *bifida* below. Female genitalia, fig. 387H, with clasper groove more or less indistinct, leading to the distinct clasper receptacle invaginated under the dorsal cap of the ninth tergite. The receptacle is large, wide and fairly long, slightly swollen dorsad and curving slightly posterad; its ventral opening is wide. Lateral lobe of ninth tergite of moderate length but narrow, with scattered setae.

Allotype, female.—Greer Springs, Missouri: June 7, 1937, H. H. Ross. This is the type locality for the species.

Hydropsyche bifida Banks

Hydropsyche bifida Banks (1905b, p. 15); ♂, ♀.

LARVA. — Fig. 356. Length 14 mm. Ground color of head yellow with a dorsal checkerboard pattern; thoracic sclerites light brown, legs brownish yellow; abdomen gray with brown hair. Frons slightly concave, its interior margin straight. Hair of abdomen a combination of slender appressed hair with a few erect, flattened but narrow hairs.

ADULTS.—Length 8–10 mm. Head, thorax and abdomen various shades of brown; legs straw color; antennae alternate bands of straw color and brown; wings with a mottled irrorate pattern resulting in a salt-and-pepper mixture which is slightly checkered. Male genitalia, fig. 367: apical processes of tenth tergite finger-like and round; apical segment of clasper long and slender; aedeagus with dorso-lateral processes tipped with a small short spur; this spur may be absent in some specimens. Female genitalia, fig. 387, with the eighth tergite bearing an apical comb, fig. 384A, and with the lobes of the sternite produced, slightly flared ventrad and rather densely haired, fig. 388A; ninth tergite as in fig. 387I.

This is one of the very common species of *Hydropsyche* in several streams in northern Illinois, in particular the rapid portion of the Rock River, Apple River and Nippersink Creek. To date all o·r records of the species are confined to the northern fourth of the state. The adults begin emerging early in May and continue through September.

As is common with many other predominantly northeastern species with a wide seasonal emergence, *bifida* has a heavy flight early in the season and a lesser one for the remainder of the summer.

The species has a wide range, appears to be most abundant in the northcentral states, and has not yet been taken east of central New York. Records are available for the following: Colorado, Illinois, Minnesota, New York, Oklahoma, Ontario, Wisconsin and Wyoming.

Illinois Records.—Many males, females and pupae, taken May 10 to August 23, and many larvae, taken June 5 to June 12, are from Amboy (Green River), Apple River Canyon State Park, Dundee, Erie (Rock Creek), Galena, Oregon, Rockford, Rockton, Savanna, Spring Grove (Nippersink Creek), Sycamore (tributary South Kishwaukee River).

Hydropsyche sparna Ross

Hydropsyche sparna Ross (1938a, p. 150); ♂, ♀.

This distinctive species has not yet been taken in the state. It has been captured in extreme southwestern Michigan and can be looked for in future collecting in Illinois. It occurs abundantly to the north and east, including Georgia, Michigan, Minnesota, New York, North Carolina, Nova Scotia, Ontario, South Carolina, Virginia and West Virginia.

Hydropsyche morosa Hagen

Hydropsyche morosa Hagen (1861, p. 287); ♂.

Hydropsyche chlorotica Hagen (1861, p. 290); ♂.

Larva.—Unknown.

Adults.—Size, color and general structure identical with *bifida*. Male genitalia, fig. 366, differing from *bifida* chiefly in the aedeagus, which has the base larger, the stem slightly sinuate, and the membranous dorsal appendages tipped with a flat, sclerotized denticulate plate.

We have not taken this species in Illinois in our recent survey, but the locality, "Chicago" was mentioned by Hagen in his original description of *chlorotica*. These Chicago specimens, however, prove to be females of the genus *Cheumatopsyche* so that we still have no definite record for the state.

The species is known from Michigan, New York, Ontario, Virginia and West Virginia and may ultimately be found in Illinois.

Hydropsyche bronta Ross

Hydropsyche bronta Ross (1938a, p. 149); ♂, ♀.

Larva.—Length 14 mm. In coloration similar to *bifida*, especially with reference to the checkered type of pattern on the head. As with *bifida*, there is considerable variation in the details of this pattern.

Adults.—In size, color and general structure similar to *bifida*. Male genitalia, fig. 364, with apical processes of tenth tergite short and finger-like; apical segment of claspers conical; aedeagus with dorsal membranous processes tipped by a long, spinose spur which is directed ventrad and projects considerably beyond the ventral margin of the stem. Female genitalia similar in general with those of *bifida*, differing in characters of the clasper receptacle, fig. 387B.

In Illinois this species is restricted with few exceptions to small and medium-sized streams in northern Illinois. Most of these are spring fed; all are permanent. The adults emerge from April to the latter part of August.

The range of the species includes most of the Northeast, as follows: Illinois, Maryland, Michigan, New Brunswick, Ohio, Ontario, Pennsylvania and Virginia; in addition we have a large collection from Wyoming.

Illinois Records.—Many larvae, taken March 2 to May 30, and many females and two pupae, taken April 25 to August 23, are from Amboy (Green River), Apple River Canyon State Park, Cedarville, Council Hill (Galena River), Elgin (Botanical Gardens), Fox Lake, Galena (Sinsinawa River), Havana (Quiver Creek), Leland, Marengo, Momence, Mount Carroll, Oregon, Rock City, Sycamore (tributary South Kishwaukee River), Utica (Split Rock Brook), White Pines Forest State Park, Wilmington.

Hydropsyche cheilonis Ross

Hydropsyche cheilonis Ross (1938a, p. 149); ♂, ♀.

Larva.—Similar to *bifida* in size and color, especially in the checkered head pattern, as in fig. 356.

Adults.—In size, color and general structure identical with *bifida*. Male genitalia, fig. 365, differing from those of *bronta* chiefly in aedeagus, which has shorter membranous lobes tipped by a narrow spur constricted at the base; in addition, the apical bulb of the aedeagus has four pockets (two meso-dorsal and two lateral), each bearing a group of at least 6 relatively long and heavy sclerotized spicules, the lateral pockets exserted on a short stalk. Female typical for the *bifida* group, genitalia as in fig. 387D.

To date this species has been found in Illinois only in the Middle Fork and Salt Fork of the Vermilion River in the neighborhood of Oakwood. In these streams this species is fairly abundant, and the only member of the *bifida* group occurring in them. A scattering of adults has been taken from May 4 to September 20.

Practically nothing can be stated regarding the range of this species, since we have only two records from Michigan (Aurelius and East Lansing) in addition to the Illinois records. This indicates a spotted and local distribution pattern.

Illinois Records.—Muncie: Sept. 20, 1935, Frison & Mohr, 2 ♂ ; May 4, 1936, Ross & Burks, 1 ♂ ; July 6, 1936, Mohr & Burks, 1 larva. Oakwood: Salt Fork River, July 18, 1933, Ross & Mohr, 3 ♂ , 7 ♀ , many larvae; Middle Fork River, July 18, 1933, Ross & Mohr, 1♂; Sept. 20, 1935, DeLong & Ross, 7♂, 9♀; May 21, 1936, Mohr & Burks, 1 larva, 1 pupa; Salt Fork River, Aug. 25, 1936, H. H. Ross, many larvae; Middle Fork River, July 14, 1939, Burks & Riegel, 2 larvae.

Hydropsyche slossonae Banks

Hydropsyche slossonae Banks (1905*b*, p. 14); ♂, ♀.

LARVA.—Fig. 355. Length 16 mm. Head, thoracic sclerites and legs dark brown, frequently approaching black, with the following areas yellowish: retracted posterior portion of head, one or two small quadrate marks on the dorso-mesal line, and irregular portions of the legs; abdomen purplish gray.

ADULTS.—In size, color and general structure similar to *bifida*. Male genitalia, fig. 362, with the apical processes of the tenth tergite long, enlarged at middle, the mesal face concave, and the two forming a horseshoe-like structure; claspers with apical segment long, narrow and curved mesad; aedeagus with base large, markedly sinuate, the dorsal membranous lobes tipped by a short, sharp spur, and with the apical bulb provided with one mesal and two lateral pockets of spicules. Female typical for the *bifida* group, genitalia as in fig. 387*G*.

In Illinois we have records for this species from only three localities. One of these is the small stream at Elgin fed by Rainbow Springs, in which this species was taken in great abundance. Our Illinois collections, supplemented by those from other states, show that the adult emergence occurs from May to August. The larval head pattern is diagnostic.

The range of this species, fig. 16, includes most of the northeastern states. We have records from Illinois, Michigan, Minnesota, New Hampshire, New York, North Carolina, Pennsylvania, Saskatchewan and Wisconsin.

Illinois Records.—ELGIN, Rainbow Springs: April 19, 1939, Burks & Riegel, many larvae; May 9, 1939, Ross & Burks, many larvae, 4♂, 2♀, 1 pupa; June 6, 1939, Burks & Riegel, ♂♂, ♀♀; Aug. 9, 1939, Burks & Riegel, 3♂; April 25, 1941, Ross & Burks, many larvae; May 7, 1941, Mohr & Burks, 1 larva. GALENA: June 28, 1892, Hart & Shiga, 2♂ pupae. SPRING GROVE: May 29, 1938, Mohr & Burks, 1♂.

Hydropsyche recurvata Banks

Hydropsyche slossonae var. *recurvata* Banks (1914, p. 253); ♂.
Hydropsyche codona Betten (1934, p. 187); ♂, ♀.

LARVA.—Length 14 mm. Head varying from the dark checkered pattern in fig. 356 to almost entirely yellow with a few brown markings outlining a skeleton checkerboard, fig. 357; thoracic sclerites and legs usually entirely yellow with a few dark lines, varying to brownish yellow.

ADULTS.—In size, color and general structure similar to *bifida*. Male genitalia, fig. 363, with apical processes of tenth tergite short; claspers with apical segment short, conical and pointed; aedeagus with stem long and nearly straight, dorsal membranous lobes tipped by a stout recurved spur (rarely absent or reduced) and with the apical bulb forming a pair of membranous lobes, each with a pocket of spicules. Female genitalia typical for members of the *bifida* group, ninth tergite as in fig. 387*C*.

Of unusual interest is our only Illinois larval record of this species. At Evanston we found the larvae and pupae under rocks in Lake Michigan, in water which was 2 to 3 feet deep at that time. A few adults were taken around buildings along the beach. Collecting in situations away from Lake Michigan has persistently failed to disclose representatives of this species in the state.

The species is normally taken in swift, cold rivers to the north, fig. 16, including Michigan, Minnesota, New York, Ontario, Quebec, Saskatchewan and Wisconsin, with adult emergence occurring from May to September.

Illinois Records.—EVANSTON, Lake Michigan: May 22, 1938, Ross & Burks, 3♂, 1♀, many pupae and larvae. WAUKEGAN, Lake Michigan: June 9, 1938, at light, Ross & Burks, 2♂, 1♀.

Depravata Group

Hydropsyche betteni Ross

Hydropsyche betteni Ross (1938*a*, p. 146); ♂, ♀.

LARVA.—Fig. 348. Length 16 mm. Head and thoracic sclerites dark brown, frequently approaching black, with a light spot surrounding eye; legs yellow to yellowish brown. Frons small, flat, the anterior margin straight. Dorsum of abdomen with conspicuously flattened hairs scattered among the simple appressed ones.

ADULTS.—Length 12–13 mm. Various shades of brown, antennae with first seven segments of flagellum having a dorsal black V-mark; wings reticulate with various shades of brown, resembling closely the pattern of *bifida*. Male genitalia, fig. 368, with tenth tergite somewhat hood shaped; claspers with apical segment long and tapering; and aedeagus long, curled at base, with stem straight and apex almost truncate. Female similar to male in size, color and structure. Eighth tergite with a long brush on apicoventral corner and with lobes of eighth sternite somewhat produced at apex. Ninth tergite with large clasper receptacle, fig. 385.

This species was treated as *incommoda* by Betten (1934, p. 188). It frequents a variety of small streams throughout the northern two-thirds of Illinois. It has been taken in abundance many times, both in Illinois and elsewhere, in the shallow, swift film of water running over the spillways of small dams. Otherwise its favorite haunt seems to be the riffles of small to medium-sized streams. The adults emerge from April to September.

The species' range seems to include a sort of crescentic area through much of the Northeast and continuing south through the Appalachians. We have records from Georgia, Illinois, Indiana, Michigan, New York, Ohio, Ontario and Wisconsin.

Illinois Records.—Many males, females and pupae, taken April 11 to August 23, and many larvae, taken March 2 to August 13, are from Apple River Canyon State Park, Clinton (Weldon Springs), Elgin (Botanical Gardens, Rainbow Springs), Galena, Gibson City, Havana (Quiver Creek), Marengo (Coon Creek), Matanzas Lake, McHenry, Milan, Momence, Mount Carroll, Oregon, Richmond, Rock City, St. Anne, Utica, Watson, White Pines Forest State Park.

Hydropsyche depravata Hagen

Hydropsyche depravata Hagen (1861, p. 290); ♀.

This species is southern in distribution, roughly occupying the area south of the

range of *betteni*. It has not yet been taken in Illinois, but from both Kentucky and Indiana we have records which are very close to the Illinois state line, and it is almost certain that the species will eventually be found in Illinois. At present it is known from Georgia, Indiana, Kentucky and Tennessee.

Cuanis Group

Hydropsyche cuanis Ross

Hydropsyche cuanis Ross (1938a, p. 147); ♂, ♀.

LARVA.—Fig. 350. Length 15 mm. Head and thoracic sclerites bright brownish yellow, the head with an irregular, fine, reddish brown pattern, the pronotum with fine, reddish brown speckling; legs yellow. Frons almost flat, the apical margin straight. Dorsum of abdomen, especially on the seventh and eighth segments, with conspicuous flattened setae interspersed among the simple appressed ones.

ADULTS.—Length 10–11 mm. Head and body black with irregular areas of reddish brown; antennae with V-marks faint; wings with a purplish cast, mottled with various shades of brown and without a definite pattern. Male genitalia, fig. 369, with tenth tergite simple and hoodlike, divided into a pair of round lobes; claspers with apical segment oblique at apex; aedeagus curved, rounded at apex, incised on the meson. Female, fig. 386, with eighth tergite having only a very short and inconspicuous apical ventral fringe, eighth sternite with apicomesal corner only moderately produced, fig. 388C. Ninth tergite, fig. 386C, very similar to that in *scalaris* group.

Most of our Illinois records of this species are from various points along the Kankakee River; in addition we have taken it from two other points in the extreme northeastern corner of the state. The larvae are extremely abundant in swift rapids of the Kankakee River at Wilmington, and here we have taken large flights of the adults. In this locality the spring emergence, during May, is very heavy. Adults continue to emerge later in the year until August but never in the large numbers that we have taken in May.

The range of the species appears to be very restricted, the known records including only Illinois, Indiana and Michigan.

Illinois Records.—Des Plaines, Fox River: May 26, 1936, H. H. Ross, 2 larvae. Kankakee, Kankakee River: May 17, 1935, H. H. Ross, 2 pupae; Aug. 8, 1935, Ross & DeLong, 1 larva. Momence: May 17, 1931, Ross & Burks, 1 ♂ ; June 4, 1932, Frison & Mohr, 4 ♂ ; Aug. 1, 1935, Ross & Burks, 1 ♂ ; May 26, 1936, H. H. Ross, 1 ♂ ; July 14, 1936, B. D. Burks, 1 ♂, 2 larvae; Aug. 3, 1936, C. O. Mohr, 1 ♂ ; Aug. 4, 1936, Frison & Burks, ♂ ♂ ; May 17, 1937, Ross & Burks, ♂ ♂, 1 ♂ pupa; Sept. 7, 1937, Frison & Ross, 1 ♂ ; May 5, 1938, Ross & Burks, 3 ♂. St. Charles: June 18, 1931, T. H. Frison, 1 ♂. Spring Grove: May 14, 1936, Ross & Mohr, 3 ♂, 1 ♀, 2 pupae, 8 larvae; June 12, 1936, Ross & Burks, 5 ♂, 1 ♀, 1 ♂ pupa; Nippersink Creek, May 19, 1938, Ross & Burks, 2 ♂. Wilmington, Kankakee River: April 23, 1930, Ross & Mohr, 1 pupa; April 10, 1935, Ross & Mohr, many larvae; April 23, 1935, Ross & Mohr, 7 pupae, many larvae; May, 1935, reared in cage, Ross & Mohr, many pupae; May 12, 1935, Frison & Ross, ♂ ♂, ♀ ♀ ; May 17, 1935, H. H. Ross, ♂ ♂, ♀ ♀ ; May 27, 1935, Ross & Mohr, ♂ ♂, ♀ ♀, many pupae and larvae; June 6, 1935, Ross & Mohr, ♂ ♂, 7 ♀, many larvae; May 17, 1937, Ross & Burks, ♂ ♂, ♀ ♀. Wilmington: Aug. 3, 1937, at light, Ross & Burks, 1 ♂.

Scalaris Group

Hydropsyche aerata Ross

Hydropsyche aerata Ross (1938a, p. 144); ♂, ♀.

Larva.—Fig. 349. Length 13 mm. Head, thoracic sclerites and legs yellow, dorsum of the head with a somewhat cross-shaped dark brown mark, pronotum minutely speckled with brown. Frons almost flat, anterior margin straight. Head and pronotum with only a few scattered long hairs, in general appearing polished.

Adults.—The two sexes are very dissimilar in general appearance. Male, fig. 392: length 9 mm.; head and body dark brown, antennae and legs white; wings white with definite brown markings forming a distinctive pattern; eyes very large, twice as wide as the antero-dorsal distance between them; genitalia, fig. 372, with tenth tergite upturned and deeply incised; apex of aedeagus with an open area between lateral processes. Female: length 10 mm.; color dark brown, the wings mottled with various shades of brown and resembling other females of the genus, similar to fig. 393; genitalia as in fig. 386G.

Myriads of this uniquely marked species have been taken at Illinois localities along the Kankakee River, in the rapids of which the larvae and pupae have been found. Other than in this area, we have taken only one or two records from the eastern part of the state. The adults emerge from May through most of August.

The present known range of the species is very small, fig. 15, and includes Illinois, Indiana and southern Michigan. All the records indicate a preference for medium-sized to large, rapid rivers.

Illinois Records.—Aurora: July 17, 1927, at light, Frison & Glasgow, 1 ♂. Kankakee, Kankakee River: Aug. 1, 1933, Ross & Mohr, 1 ♂ ; May 26, 1935, Ross &

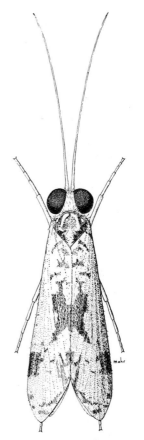

Fig. 392.—*Hydropsyche aerata*, ♂.

Mohr, 1♂ (reared); June 6, 1935, Ross & Mohr, ♂♂, ♀♀; July 21, 1935, Ross & Mohr, ♂♂; Aug. 8, 1935, Ross & De-Long, 1♂, 1♀, 4 larvae; May 17, 1937, Ross & Burks, ♂♂, ♀♀; May 6, 1938, Ross & Burks, 7♂; May 31, 1938, Mohr & Burks, 1♂; June 29, 1939, Burks & Ayars, 1♂. MOMENCE: Kankakee River, May 26, 1936, H. H. Ross, 1♂; Aug. 4, 1936, Frison & Burks, 4♂; Aug. 21, 1936, Ross & Burks, 1♂, 2 larvae; Kankakee River, March 24, 1937, H. H. Ross, 1♂; May 17, 1937, Ross & Burks, 3♂. MOUNT CARMEL: July 3, 1906, 1♂. SPRING GROVE: May 20, 1938, at light, Ross & Burks, 2♂. WILMINGTON: April 23, 1935, Ross & Mohr, 2 larvae; May 12, 1935, Frison & Ross, ♂♂, 7♀; Kankakee River, May 17, 1935, H. H. Ross, ♂♂, ♀♀; May 27, 1935, Ross & Mohr, 1 larva, 1 pupa; June 6, 1935, Ross & Mohr, 7♂, 7 larvae; July 1, 1935, DeLong & Ross, 1♂; Aug. 20, 1935, DeLong & Ross, 2♂; Kankakee River, May 17, 1937, Ross & Burks, 1♂; June 13, 1938, B. D. Burks, ♂♂.

Hydropsyche phalerata Hagen

Hydropsyche phalerata Hagen (1861, p. 287); ♀.

LARVA.—Fig. 347. Length 13 mm. Head, thoracic sclerites and legs with ground color yellow; superimposed on this is an irregular, dark, somewhat T-shaped area on the head bearing a scattering of small black setae, and scattered brown spots on the pronotum and mesonotum, each bearing numerous short, black setae. Frons almost flat and with the apical margin produced into a low triangular point.

ADULTS.—Length 9–10 mm. Head and body brown, wings tawny with brown areas small and forming only a light and indefinite pattern. Eyes of male medium sized, slightly larger than half the area between them. Male genitalia, fig. 371, with tenth tergite upturned and incised to form forceps-like lobes; aedeagus stout throughout, the apex large, the lateral processes close together, and the mesal cavity almost completely open. Female genitalia, fig. 386F, very similar to those of *aerata*.

Until the selection of a lectotype by Banks (1936b, p. 126), the status of this species had been confused. The species considered as *phalerata* by Betten (1934, p. 189) is *sparna*; and the species considered as *Hydro-*

psyche species 3 by Betten (1934, p. 192) is true *phalerata*. The color pattern of the adults is fairly distinctive but requires actual comparison with specimens to be of practical use.

In Illinois this species is apparently confined to the northern fourth of the state, where it has been taken abundantly in the Kankakee River and in small numbers along the Rock River and other creeks. Larvae and pupae have been taken in rapids of the Kankakee River. The adults emerge from May to October. As in the case of *bifida*, the heaviest flights of *phalerata* are taken during the early summer months.

The range of the species, fig. 15, extends from the southern portion of the eastern states to areas north of Illinois, and includes Georgia, Kentucky, Illinois, Indiana, Michigan, North Carolina, Ohio, Tennessee, Virginia and Wisconsin.

Illinois Records.—Many males, females and pupae, taken May 1 to September 7, and many larvae, taken April 23 to October 28, are from Como (Rock River), Dixon (Rock River), Frankfort (Clear Creek, Hickory Creek), Kankakee, Lyndon (Rock River), Momence (Kankakee River), New Milford (Kishwaukee River), Oregon, Rockford, Rock Island, Rockton, Sterling, Wilmington (Kankakee River).

Hydropsyche dicantha Ross

Hydropsyche dicantha Ross (1938a, p. 146); ♂.

This species, readily distinguished by the unique male genitalia, fig. 373, has been taken in extreme southwestern Michigan and may eventually be found in Illinois, although we have not as yet taken it here. Few records are available for the species, but they indicate a wide, scattered range, as follows: District of Columbia, Kentucky, Michigan, New York and Ontario.

FEMALE.—Length 9 mm. Color and general stucture as described for male. Ninth tergite, fig. 386A, with areas forming clasper groove small and only indistinctly concave, scarcely any indentation visible beneath dorsal cap from dorsal view; lateral lobe apparently absent, the margin of the segment in this region with a few setae.

Allotype, female.—Costello Lake, Algonquin Park, Ontario, from Station 4, Ontario Fisheries Research Laboratory: July 7, 1938, W. M. Sprules.

Hydropsyche hageni Banks

Hydropsyche hageni Banks (1905*b*, p. 14); ♂.

LARVA.—Fig. 353. Length 15 mm. Head and thoracic sclerites brown, legs yellowish brown; head with lateral and posterior portions yellowish, limiting the dark brown of the dorsum to a broad T of which the crosspiece is broad and rather sharply cut off laterally; the brown T area of head and all of the pronotum finely granulate with paler marks. Frons flat, its apical margin straight, the area surrounding the anterior portion of the fronto-genal suture set with abundant, short, black spines.

ADULTS.—Length 10–11 mm. Color dark brown, the wings mottled with various shades of brown and typical of the common pattern of the *scalaris* group, as in fig. 393. Eyes of male large, each equal to the area between them on the dorsum. Male genitalia, fig. 374, with tenth tergite short and pointed slightly ventrad; aedeagus with straight stem and with lateral processes greatly elongated, flattened and almost truncate at tip. Female readily distinguished from other species of the *scalaris* group by the thickened lateral lobe of the ninth tergite, fig. 386*D*.

Allotype, female.—Momence, Illinois: May 17, 1937, Ross & Burks.

Our Illinois records of this species are confined to the Kankakee River, with the exception of male specimens taken along the Rock River. Along the Kankakee we have taken it consistently but always in small numbers and have found the larvae and pupae in the rapids. The adults have been taken from May to late August.

The range of the species is poorly delineated. Our only records are from Illinois, Kentucky and Maryland. These indicate a marked preference for large, rapid rivers.

Illinois Records.—KANKAKEE: June 12, 1931, Frison & Mohr, 1 ♂ ; June 6, 1935, Ross & Mohr, 1 ♂ ; May 6, 1938, Ross & Burks, 9 ♂ ; May 31, 1938, Burks & Mohr, 1 ♂. MOMENCE: May 26, 1936, H. H. Ross, ♂ ♂, 6 larvae; Aug. 3, 1936, C. O. Mohr, 1 ♂ ; Aug. 4, 1936, Frison & Burks, 3 ♂ ; May 24, 1937, H. H. Ross, 1 ♂ ; May 5, 1938, Ross & Burks, 4 ♂, 3 larvae; Oct. 28, 1938, Ross & Burks, 2 larvae; preceding Momence records from Kankakee River; Aug. 21, 1936, Ross & Burks, 2 ♂, 1 pupa; May 17, 1937, Ross & Burks, 1 ♂ pupa, 5 ♂, 1 ♀, 4 larvae; May 5, 1938, Ross & Burks, 4 ♂, 3 larvae; Aug. 16, 1938, Ross & Burks, 1 ♂ ; June 24, 1939, Burks & Ayars, 1 ♂. ROCKFORD: June 12, 1931, Frison & Mohr, 1 ♂ ; May 30, 1936, H. H. Ross, 1 ♂. WILMINGTON, Kankakee River: June 6, 1935, Ross & Mohr, 1 ♂.

Hydropsyche placoda Ross

Hydropsyche placoda Ross (1941*b*, p. 87); ♂, ♀.

LARVA.—Unknown.

ADULTS.—Length 10–11 mm. General color typical for most members of the *scalaris* group, the male differing in having the eyes reddish and the wings slightly lighter. Eyes of male very large, each one equal to the dorsal area between them and almost completely hiding the head from side view. Male genitalia, fig. 375, with tenth tergite somewhat beaklike; apical segment of claspers short and markedly truncate; aedeagus of fairly uniform thickness, the lateral processes triangular from side view and dorsal margin almost confluent with the stem, and the mesal cavity more than half closed. Female with small eyes; genitalia, fig. 386*B*, distinguished by the pit at dorsal portion of clasper groove.

In Illinois this species has been taken in numbers only near the dam on the Illinois River at Starved Rock State Park. Other records are represented by few specimens. We have not yet obtained larvae, but it is probable that they occur in the race below the dam at Starved Rock State Park.

This species has been taken in many of the north central states and as far east as Niagara Falls. In addition to this New York locality, we have records from Illinois, Minnesota, Montana, South Dakota and Wisconsin.

Illinois Records. — ELGIN: Botanical Gardens, June 6, 1939, Burks & Riegel, 1 ♂ ; Rainbow Springs, June 6, 1939, Burks & Riegel, 1 ♂. KANKAKEE: June 12, 1931, Frison & Mohr, 1 ♂. OTTAWA: June 3, 1938, Mohr & Burks, 1 ♂. RICHMOND: June 7, 1938, at light, Ross & Burks, 1 ♂. ROCKFORD: June 29, 1938, at light, B. D. Burks, 2 ♂. ROCK ISLAND: June 23, 1928, at light, Frison & Hottes, 1 ♂ ; June 24, 1931, at light, C. O. Mohr, 1 ♂. SERENA: Fox River, June 3, 1938, Ross & Burks, 3 ♂. STARVED ROCK STATE PARK: June 28, 1937, G. T. Riegel, 9 ♂, 2 ♀ ; June 28, 1937,

Ross & Burks, 4♂, 5♀; June 15, 1938, D. T. Ries, 5♂; June 17, 1938, Frison & Mohr, 4♂; June 18, 1938, Ries & Werner, 6♂; June 22, 1938, D. T. Ries, 6♂; June 27, 1938, F. Werner, 1♂, 1♀; June 5, 1941, Floyd Werner, 1♂, 1♀; July 11, 1941, D. T. Ries, 1♂. SUGAR GROVE: June 13, 1939, Frison & Ross, 1♂.

Hydropsyche arinale Ross

Hydropsyche arinale Ross (1938a, p. 143); ♂.

LARVA.—Fig. 351. Length 15 mm. Head mostly brown with yellowish markings around and under the eyes, on the ventral surface and the postero-lateral angles. Thoracic sclerites and legs brownish yellow. Frons flat, its anterior margin straight. Setae on the dorsum of the abdomen relatively sparse.

ADULTS.—Length 9–10 mm. Color various shades of brown similar to the typical pattern for the *scalaris* group, as in fig. 393. Male with eyes of medium size, each equal to at least two-thirds of the dorsal area between them. Male genitalia, fig. 376, with tenth tergite somewhat hood shaped and declivous; claspers with apical segment sinuate and pointed; aedeagus with stem constricted near middle, appearing somewhat moniliform from ventral view, the lateral processes wide and the mesal cavity almost entirely open. Female similar in color and general structure to other members of the *scalaris* group. Ninth tergite as in fig. 386E.

Allotype, female.—Serena, Illinois, along Indian Creek: May 12, 1938, Ross & Burks.

We have taken this species at various points in the northern half of the state. It shows a preference for such streams as Indian Creek, which is relatively clear and provided with many riffles or rapids. Our only large collections of adults were taken early in May, but emergence continues through August.

The range of the species seems to follow rather closely the outer fringe of the oak-hickory forest. We have records from Arkansas, Kansas, Missouri, Oklahoma and Wisconsin; these all indicate the same type of stream preference as do our Illinois records and increase the seasonal emergence of adults from April to September.

Illinois Records.—Many males and females and two pupae, taken May 12 to September 5, and many larvae, taken May 12 to May 16, are from Algonquin, Aurora, Baker, Des Plaines (Fox River), Oregon, Pontiac, Quincy (stream near Cave Spring), Richmond, Serena (Indian Creek), Starved Rock.

Hydropsyche simulans Ross

Hydropsyche simulans Ross (1938a, p. 139); ♂, ♀.

LARVA.—Fig. 352. Length 18 mm. Head dark brown with irregular light areas on the sides, posterior portion and venter; pronotum brown, remainder of thoracic sclerites and legs straw color to brownish yellow. Frons flat, its apical margin straight. Dorsum of abdominal segments with flattened setae relatively abundant.

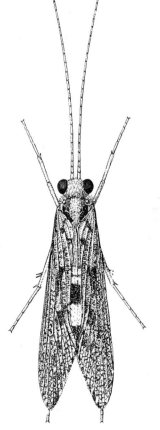

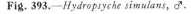

Fig. 393.—*Hydropsyche simulans*, ♂.

ADULTS.—Length 13–15 mm. Color pattern various shades of brown, fig. 393, the pattern typical of many species of the *scalaris* group. Male with eyes of medium size, each equal to about half the dorsal area between them. Male genitalia, fig. 377: tenth tergite somewhat hoodlike, the apex almost truncate; claspers with apical segment long, sinuate and pointed; aedeagus with stem straight and a dorsal continuation of it extending over the apical portion; lateral plates rounded at apex, the lateral flange sharp and sinuate, mesal plates long and curved ventrad, and the mesal cavity about half closed. Female with ninth tergite, fig. 386*M*, very similar to that of *incommoda*.

This species has been taken in abundance at various points along most of the large Illinois rivers; the records cover the entire state. It occurs also in smaller streams, as for example, in Quiver Creek near Havana, where the larvae and pupae were taken in large numbers from a small rapid. It is, however, by no means as widespread along the largest rivers as *orris*. The adlts emerge throughout the warmer monn s, from April to late September.

The range of the species, fig. 14, includes most of the Corn Belt states with extensions westward to Texas and eastern Colorado. States for which we have records are Colorado, Illinois, Indiana, Iowa, Kansas, Kentucky, Minnesota, Missouri, Ohio, Oklahoma, Tennessee and Wisconsin.

Illinois Records.—Many males and females, taken April 15 to September 20, and many larvae, taken May 5 to July 8, are from Alton (Mississippi River), Deer Grove (Green River), Freeport, Grafton, Hardin (Illinois River), Havana (Quiver Creek), Homer, Kankakee, Kappa (Mackinaw River), Lawrenceville, Momence (Kankakee River), Mount Carmel (Wabash River), Oakwood, Olney, Pontiac, Quincy, Rockford, Rock Island, Rockton, Savanna, Shawneetown, Spring Grove, Sterling, Topeka (Quiver Creek), Urbana, Wilmington.

Hydropsyche valanis Ross

Hydropsyche valanis Ross (1938*a*, p. 144); ♂.

LARVA.—Unknown.
ADULTS.—Length 9–10 mm. Color tawny with irregular flecking of light brown over the entire surface of the wings, forming a slightly lighter mottling than that found in *simulans*. Male with eyes large, each slightly larger than dorsal width between them. Male genitalia, fig. 378: tenth tergite short, stubby, and incised on meson; claspers with apical segment sinuate and rounded at apex; aedeagus with stem slightly curved; apex with lateral plates narrow from lateral view, and mesal margin notched, the two overlapping at apex; mesal cavity almost completely open. Female with small eyes, and color pattern slightly lighter than on most of the species. Ninth tergite, fig. 386*H*, with very large clasper receptacle.

Allotype, female.—Noblesville, Indiana: Aug. 10, 1938, Ross & Burks.

We have found this species at scattered localities in northern Illinois, never in great abundance. It has been taken along some of the larger streams only, such as Indian Creek and the Kankakee River. The dates of capture indicate adult emergence from May to late August. To date the larvae have not been identified.

Little is known about the range of the species. Aside from the Illinois records, it is known only from southern Minnesota and central Indiana where again it was found along fairly large rivers.

Illinois Records.—BAKER, Indian Creek: May 12, 1938, Ross & Burks, 1 ♂. KANKAKEE: July 21, 1935, Ross & Mohr, 1 ♂; Kankakee River, May 17, 1937, Ross & Burks, 3 ♂; May 6, 1938, Ross & Burks, ♂ ♂. PONTIAC: Aug. 22, 1938, H. H. Ross, ♂ ♂. ROCK ISLAND: June 23, 1928, Frison & Hottes, 1 ♂. ROCKTON: Rock River, July 2, 1931, Frison, Betten & Ross, ♂ ♂.

Hydropsyche frisoni Ross

Hydropsyche frisoni Ross (1938*a*, p. 142); ♂, ♀.

LARVA.—Fig. 354. Length 15 mm. Head straw color with a dorsal brown area covering the frons and a few irregular areas around it; thoracic sclerites and legs straw color to brownish yellow. Frons flat, its anterior margin straight.

ADULTS.—Length 12–13 mm. Body dark brown, similar in pattern to *simulans*, fig. 393. Male with eyes large, each equal to dorsal area between them. Male genitalia, fig. 379: tenth tergite short, almost truncate at apex; apical segment of clasper somewhat sinuate and pointed; aedeagus with stem straight, constricted at base of apical portion; apex of aedeagus angled dorsad, the lateral plates rounded at apex, the lateral flange considerably lower than mesal dome, mesal cavity half closed, and mesal plates short and somewhat triangular. Female with small eyes, color pattern typical for *scalaris* group. Ninth tergite as in fig. 386J.

This species has been taken commonly but not abundantly along the Middle Fork and Salt Fork rivers near Oakwood; aside from this area we have only a single record, from Indian Creek. The adult emergence continues from April to late August.

Little is known regarding the range of this species. Aside from Illinois, we have only three scattered records from lower Michigan. In this respect *frisoni* is remarkably similar to *cheilonis*, which has nearly the same known range and has never been found in Illinois outside the Oakwood area.

Illinois Records. — DANVILLE, Middle Fork River: Aug. 27, 1936, Ross & Burks, 1 pupa, 2 larvae. HOMER: July 11, 1927, at light, Frison & Glasgow, 1 ♂. MUNCIE: July 27, 1927, T. H. Frison, 2 ♂. OAKWOOD, Salt Fork River: April 24, 1925, T. H. Frison, 6 ♂, 1 ♀ ; June 6, 1925, T. H. Frison, 1 ♀ ; July 6, 1925, at light, Frison & Glasgow, 5 ♂ ; July 18, 1933, Ross & Mohr, 2 ♂ ; Aug. 25, 1936, H. H. Ross, 1 ♂. SERENA, Indian Creek: June 16, 1939, B. D. Burks, 1 ♂.

Hydropsyche scalaris Hagen

Hydropsyche scalaris Hagen (1861, p. 286); ♂, ♀.

This species has not yet been taken in Illinois but will almost certainly be found with future collecting, since it has been collected on practically all sides of the state, with records from Georgia, Indiana, Missouri, Oklahoma, Ontario and Wisconsin.

The name *scalaris* is the one under which many species have been confused. The selection of a lectotype by Banks (1936b, p. 127) has given us a definite concept of this species for the first time.

Hydropsyche incommoda Hagen

Hydropsyche incommoda Hagen (1861, p. 290); ♂.

LARVA.—Unassociated with adult.
ADULTS. — Length 13–14 mm. Color

brown with the typical mottled pattern similar to that in fig. 393. Male with eyes of moderate size, each subequal to one-half the dorsal area between them. Male genitalia, fig. 381, similar to *simulans* in shape of tenth tergite and male claspers; aedeagus with lateral plates long, lateral flange small, parallel with dorsal outline of stem, mesal cavity almost entirely open, and mesal plates large and projecting ventrad. Female with ninth tergite as in fig. 386N.

Allotype, female.—Tavares, Lake County, Florida: March 23, 1936, F. N. Young.

The species treated under the name *incommoda* by Betten (1934, p. 188) is not the true *incommoda*, but is *betteni* (see p. 99).

We have taken this species at several localities in the eastern, central and southern parts of Illinois, usually in small numbers, and never in a heavy flight. The collections are associated with medium-sized to large streams. The adults emerge over a long period, our records being scattered from April 24 to August 27.

In addition to Illinois, the species is known only from Florida, Georgia and North Carolina; presumably it occurs in suitable situations in the intervening area between these southeastern states and Illinois.

Illinois Records.—CARMI, Little Wabash River: April 24, 1935, T. H. Frison, 1 ♂. KAPPA, Mackinaw River: Sept. 14, 1937, Ross & Burks, 4 ♂. MAHOMET: Aug. 3, 1937, Ross & Burks, ♂ ♂, ♀ ♀. MOMENCE: Aug. 16, 1938, Ross & Burks, 1 ♂ ; Kankakee River, May 29, 1939, Frison & Ross, 1 ♂. MONTICELLO: May 7, 1936, Ross & Burks, 1 ♂. OAKWOOD: Sept. 20, 1935, DeLong & Ross, 1 ♂ ; Salt Fork River, July 31, 1939, Burks & Riegel, 1 ♂. PONTIAC: Aug. 22, 1938, H. H. Ross, 5 ♂. SHAWNEETOWN: May 27, 1928, at light, T. H. Frison, 1 ♂. VENEDY STATION, Kaskaskia River: Aug. 27, 1940, Mohr & Riegel, 9 ♂, 9 ♀.

Hydropsyche orris Ross

Hydropsyche cornuta Ross (1938a, p. 141); ♂, ♀. Preoccupied.
Hydropsyche orris Ross (1938d, p. 121). New name.

LARVA.—Fig. 346. Length 14 mm. Head brown with pale areas on lateral and posterior portions and frons; thoracic sclerites and legs straw colored to brownish yellow.

Frons slightly concave and always covered with a grayish hairy mass, the anterior margin straight across the middle, and provided with a pair of short, elevated teeth. Dorsal abdominal segments with abundant flattened setae.

ADULTS.—Length 12–13 mm. Color pattern brown, the mottling similar to that of *simulans,* fig. 393. Male with eyes small, each equal to less than half the dorsal area between them. Male genitalia, fig. 383: tenth tergite short, declivous and hooklike with a wide mesal incision; claspers with second segment long, sinuate and pointed at tip; aedeagus with stem straight, lateral plates upturned and meeting mesal dome on a line with the dorsal outline of stem, lateral flanges not sharp, and the tip of the plates rounded from side view, the mesal cavity two-thirds closed, and the mesal plates triangular and not projecting ventrad. Female with ninth tergite, fig. 386*K,* very similar to that of *bidens;* clasper receptacle with anterior and posterior dorsal margins usually of about equal slope.

This species is one of the most common along the larger rivers and has been taken quite generally in Illinois. Especially heavy flights have been seen along the Rock, Illinois and Mississippi rivers. Adult emergence continues from April to September.

The range of the species, fig. 14, covers the central Corn Belt states and widens toward the south to include most of the Gulf Coast states. We have records from Alabama, Arkansas, Georgia, Illinois, Indiana, Iowa, Kentucky, Michigan, Minnesota, Ohio, Tennessee, Texas and Wisconsin.

Illinois Records.—Many males and females and six pupae, taken April 24 to October 2, and many larvae, taken April 24 to July 23, are from Alton, Cairo, Chicago, Dixon, East Dubuque, Eddyville (Lusk Creek), Elgin (Botanical Gardens), Elizabethtown, Florence, Golconda, Grafton (Mississippi River), Grand Tower, Hamilton, Harrisburg, Havana (Spoon River), Herod, Homer (Salt Fork River), Horse Shoe Lake, Jerseyville, Kankakee, Keithsburg, Meredosia, Milan (Rock River), Momence (Kankakee River), Mount Carmel, New Boston, Oakwood (Salt Fork River), Oregon (Castle Rock), Ottawa, Putnam (Lake Senachwine), Quincy, Rockford, Rock Island, Rosiclare, St. Joseph, Savanna, Shawneetown, Sterling, Urbana, White Pines Forest State Park.

Hydropsyche bidens Ross

Hydropsyche bidens Ross (1938*a*, p. 142); ♂, ♀.

LARVA.—Not definitely reared; we have some statistical evidence that it might be similar to that of *orris.*

ADULTS. — Length 10–11 mm. Color brown, mottled as in *simulans.* Male with eyes small, each slightly smaller than half the dorsal area between them. Male genitalia similar to those of *orris* in structure of tenth tergite and claspers, differing chiefly in the shape of the aedeagus, fig. 382, which has the lateral plates parallel with the axis of the stem, the lateral flanges sharp and almost pointed at apex, and the mesal dome rounded and curving considerably ventrad to meet the apex of the lateral plates. Female ninth tergite, fig. 386*L,* very similar to that of *orris.* Extreme care must be exercised in identifying females of *bidens, orris, simulans* and *incommoda.* The differences between them are relative and subject to variation. For this reason, females of this group should not be used for isolated records.

This species is distributed over the entire state. It has been taken along a large variety of streams, ranging from small creeks to large rivers. Most of our collections have been of a few specimens, but occasionally large flights have been encountered. Adult emergence occurs from April to September. The species has been taken throughout most of the Corn Belt states, including Illinois, Indiana, Iowa, Michigan, Minnesota, Missouri, Ohio and Wisconsin.

Illinois Records.—Many males and females, taken April 24 to September 25, are from Alton, Apple River Canyon State Park, Carmi, Champaign, Charleston, Danville, Deer Grove (Green River), Dundee, East Dubuque, Elgin (Botanical Gardens, Rainbow Springs), Elizabethtown, Freeport, Fulton, Grafton (Mississippi River), Hardin, Havana, Homer, Kampsville, Kankakee (Kankakee River), Kankakee River at Illinois-Indiana state line, Marengo, Meredosia, Momence (Kankakee River), Mount Carmel, New Boston, New Memphis (Kaskaskia River), Oakwood, Pere Marquette State Park, Pike, Pontiac, Quincy (Burton Creek), Richmond, Rockford, Rock Island, St. Marie, Savanna, Spring Grove, Urbana, Venedy Station (Kaskaskia River).

Cheumatopsyche Wallengren

Cheumatopsyche Wallengren (1891, p. 142). Genotype, monobasic: *Hydropsyche lepida* Pictet.

Of the 18 species of this genus described from North America, we have taken 9 in Illinois. The remaining species are distributed in diverse parts of the continent. In Illinois, different members of the genus frequent almost every type of stream in the state. Not only do they occur in streams ranging from small brooks to the largest rivers but can frequently succeed to some extent in streams too polluted for almost any other caddis flies.

The female genitalia have definite concavities or invaginations in the sides of the ninth tergite. These seem to be correlated very closely in each species with the shape of the apical segment of the male claspers, and give definite indication of a "lock and key" relationship.

To date no structural characters have been found to identify the larvae to species. All five of the reared Illinois species have the larval frons notched in the middle, fig. 414, no conspicuous head or pronotal pattern, and a general habitus similar to that of *Hydropsyche*; *minuscula* differs in lacking the notch in the frons.

KEY TO SPECIES

Adults

1. Apex of abdomen with a pair of long claspers, fig. 397 (males)   2
   Apex of abdomen with no long appendages, fig. 391 (females) 11

2. Apical segment of claspers short, not produced into a tapered point, fig. 394   3
   Apical segment of claspers long, produced into a tapered point, figs. 396, 398   4

3. Apex of tenth tergite bearing a pair of pointed, dorsal lobes which are held close together, fig. 395 . . . .
   . . . . **minuscula**, p. 110
   Apex of tenth tergite bearing a pair of wide, lateral lobes which are not approximate on meson, fig. 394 . . . .
   . . . . **sordida**, p. 110

4. Apical segment of claspers half length of basal segment, fig. 396 . . . . **oxa**, p. 110
   Apical segment of claspers shorter, only one-fourth to one-fifth length of basal segment, fig. 397   5

5. Lobes of tenth tergite reflexed and upturned to form a sharp, pointed, apical ridge and just basad of it a digitate, setose lobe as in fig. 397 . . .
   . . . . **speciosa**, p. 114
   Lobes of tenth tergite not reflexed to form such distinct and apparently separated parts   6

6. Apical segment of claspers with a broad, triangular base and a short, tapered apex, fig. 398 . . . . **burksi**, p. 113
   Apical segment of claspers longer, with base not nearly so wide in relation to apex, fig. 400   7

7. Apical lobes of tenth tergite sharply angled, apex bent back and bearing an apical, thick cluster of stout, curved setae as in fig. 399 . . . **lasia**, p. 114
   Apical lobes of tenth tergite not sharply angled   8

8. Apical lobes of tenth tergite short, more or less circular and at right angles to linear body axis, fig. 400 . .
   . . . . **analis**, p.112
   Apical lobes at apex of tenth tergite either longer, fig. 402, or not at all circular, fig. 401   9

9. Apical lobes of tenth tergite appressed to tergite, appearing rounded at apex from both lateral and caudal view, and set diagonally to linear body axis, fig. 401 . . . . . **aphanta**, p. 111
   Apical lobes of tenth tergite not appearing rounded at apex from lateral and caudal view, and not set diagonally to linear axis, fig. 402 10

10. Apical lobes of tenth tergite perpendicular, rounded at apex and shorter, fig. 402 . . . . **campyla**, p. 113
    Apical lobes of tenth tergite angled caudad, pointed at apex and longer, fig. 403 . . . . **pasella**, p. 113

11. Ninth tergite without pouchlike lateral invaginations or pockets, figs. 404, 405 12
    Ninth tergite with pouchlike lateral invaginations or pockets, figs. 406– 413 13

12. Dorsal portion of ninth tergite wide; lateral portion with a small pit and a slightly raised line running ventrad from it, fig. 404 . . . . . **minuscula**, p. 110
    Dorsal portion of ninth tergite very narrow; lateral portion with a large concave area bounded toward anterior margin by a sinuate ridge and cutting beneath dorsal portion, fig. 405 . . . . **sordida**, p. 110

13. Lateral invagination short and small and situated far from postero-ventral point of segment, fig. 406 . . . . .
    . . . . **burksi**, p. 113

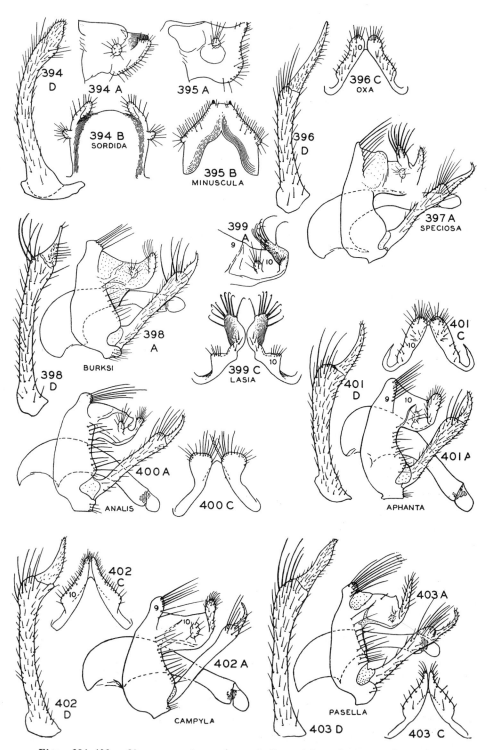

Figs. 394–403.—*Cheumatopsyche*, male genitalia. *A*, lateral aspect; *B*, dorsal aspect; *C*, caudal aspect of tenth tergite; *D*, claspers, caudal aspect.

Lateral invagination much longer and larger, usually approximate to postero-ventral point of segment, figs. 407–413 14

14. Lower margin of lateral invagination forming a wide, round lobe extending below postero-ventral corner, and with posterior corner upturned and level with anterior corner, fig. 408 .... **aphanta,** p. 111
Lower margin of lateral invagination either concave, fig. 411, or with anterior corner much higher than posterior corner, figs. 409, 410, never forming the rounded ventral lobe as above 15

15. Lateral margin of ninth tergite produced into a narrow, ventral angular point in which the lateral invagination ends and which projects slightly beyond the postero-ventral corner, fig. 409 .... **oxa,** p. 110
Lateral margin not forming a ventral angular projection, fig. 410 16

16. Lateral invagination with inner opening on mesal side, fig. 410 ....
.... **speciosa,** p. 114
Lateral invagination with inner opening on posterior side, figs. 411–413 17

17. Lateral invagination with lower posterior corner situated a short distance from postero-ventral corner of segment, fig. 407 .... **analis,** p. 112
Lateral invagination with lower posterior corner nearly touching postero-ventral corner of segment, fig. 411 18

18. Lateral invagination elongate and curved at apex, the two approximate on meson, fig. 413 .... **lasia,** p. 114
Lateral invagination shorter and not curved at apex, fig. 411 19

19. Lateral invagination smaller, the two divergent and very far apart, fig. 411 .... **campyla,** p. 113
Lateral invagination larger, the two parallel and closer together, fig. 412 .... **pasella,** p. 113

Cheumatopsyche sordida (Hagen)

Hydropsyche sordida Hagen (1861, p. 290); ♂, ♀.

ADULTS.—Length 6–8 mm. Head and body various shades of brown; antennae paler with a brown V-mark on the seven basal segments of the flagellum; wings uniformly dark brown without pattern. Male genitalia, fig. 394, with apical segment of claspers short and stubby; tenth tergite

wide, the mesal portion rounded with the apical lateral corners produced into short, flat, truncate lobes.

In Illinois we have taken this species only at Wilmington, along the Kankakee River. This is apparently along the western limits of the species' range; this range includes the denser portions of the beech-oak-hickory forest, with extensions southwestward through the Ozarks and neighboring ranges. Records are available from Arkansas, Illinois, Indiana, Kentucky, Michigan, Missouri, New York, Pennsylvania, Quebec and Wisconsin. Adults emerge from May to September.

Illinois Records.—WILMINGTON, Kankakee River: May 27, 1935, Ross & Mohr, ♂ ♂, ♀ ♀, 1 mating pair, 1 larva; June 6, 1935, Ross & Mohr, 11 ♂, 8 ♀ ; July 1, 1935, DeLong & Ross, 1 ♂, 1 ♀ .

Cheumatopsyche minuscula (Banks)

Hydropsyche minuscula Banks (1907a, p. 130); ♂, ♀.

This species has not yet been taken in Illinois but may eventually be found here. It is similar to *sordida* in its dark coloring and has a somewhat similar range, being known from Arkansas, Georgia, Kentucky, New York, Oklahoma, Ontario, Quebec, Tennessee and Wisconsin.

The tenth tergite and short apical segment of the claspers of the male distinguish the species from others in the genus.

Cheumatopsyche oxa Ross

Cheumatopsyche oxa Ross (1938a, p. 155); ♂, ♀.

ADULTS.—Length 8–9 mm. Color uniformly dark brown with only a few inconspicuous light areas near the anal angle of the wings. Male genitalia, fig. 396, with apical segment of the claspers very long, slender and pointed; apical lobes of tenth tergite, from caudal view, appearing fairly long, narrowed near middle and slightly widened at tip.

In Illinois, we have three scattered records of this species, each along a small, spring-fed stream. These and records from other states show the adult emergence to extend from March to middle or late October. Records from other states also indicate a preference for small, rapid streams, thus substantiating observations from our few Illinois records. The species usually occurs in small, local colonies.

The range of the species apparently covers most of the northeastern deciduous forest region with extensions westward through the Ozarks. We have records from Arkansas, Georgia, Illinois, Michigan, New York, North Carolina, Tennessee and West Virginia.

Illinois Records.—Herod: July 11, 1935, Ross & DeLong, 1 ♂. Springville: Roaring Spring Outlet, Oct. 17, 1938, Ross & Burks, 1 ♂, 1 ♀, many larvae. Utica: Split

Rock Brook, June 17, 1941, Burks & Riegel, 1 ♂.

Cheumatopsyche aphanta Ross

Cheumatopsyche aphanta Ross (1938a, p. 151); ♂, ♀.

Adults.—Length 7–9 mm. Color dark brown, the wings with a few indistinct, grayish, scattered spots and a large gray spot on the anal margin near apex. Male genitalia, fig. 401: clasper with apical segment long, curved, slender, and pointed at

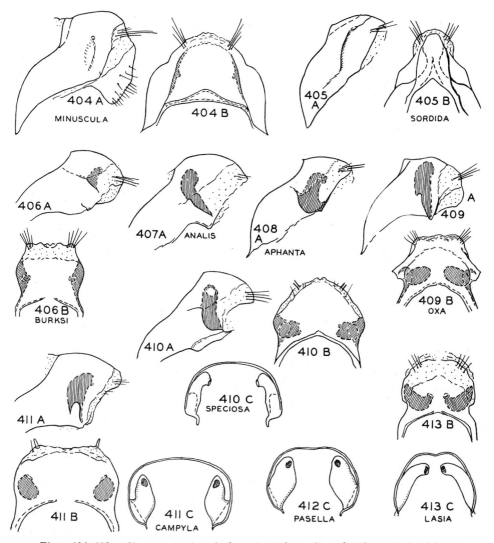

Figs. 404–413.—*Cheumatopsyche*, ninth and tenth tergites, females. *A*, lateral aspect; *B*, dorsal aspect; *C*, caudal aspect showing lateral invaginations.

apex; tenth tergite short, the apical lobes somewhat ovate, somewhat polished, and appressed on the diagonal to the apex of the tergite.

This species is common in small streams of the northern fourth of the state, in the vicinity of Oakwood and also in the center of the western margin of the state.

The species shows a decided preference for brooks and small creeks, especially those fed by springs and permanent in character. The only exception we have to this is a collection from Oregon, Illinois, which presumably came from the Rock River. The adult emergence extends from May to late September.

The range of the species is poorly delineated. In addition to Illinois records we have only one from Indiana and two from the heart of the Ozarks in western Arkansas.

Illinois Records.—Many males and females and 1 pupa, taken May 11 to September 20, are from Apple River Canyon State Park, Cedarville, Charleston, Chemung, (Piscasaw Creek), Danville (Middle Fork River), Deer Grove, Elgin, Galena (Sinsinawa River), Homer, Howardsville, Mahomet, Mount Carroll, Muncie, Oakwood, Oregon, Quincy (stream near Cave Spring), Rock City, Serena, Sycamore (tributary of South Kishwaukee River), Urbana, White Pines Forest State Park.

Cheumatopsyche analis (Banks)

Hydropsyche analis Banks (1903b, p. 243); ♂.

Hydropsyche pettiti Banks (1908b, p. 265); ♂.

ADULTS.—Length 9–12 mm. Color varying from almost entirely dark brown with few light spots on the wings to a lighter phase with many small, light spots and the two anal spots as described for *burksi*. Male genitalia, fig. 400: claspers with apical segment long, slightly sinuate and pointed; tenth tergite with apical lobes projecting slightly in front of mesal angle of tergite, low, and with the apex widened into a somewhat round plate which is nearly truncate at apex; these plates vary considerably in proximity to each other.

A re-examination of the type of *analis* convinces me that the curious structure of the tenth tergite of the type is due to mechanical injury, to wit, the breaking off of the apical lobes. The ridging of the tenth tergite, narrow aedeagus and shape of the

claspers leave no doubt in my mind that this is the same as *pettiti*, in which type the genitalia are intact. In the type of *analis*, the caudal aspect of the tenth tergite is asymmetrical and appears to end dorsad at fracture lines.

This species exhibits the interesting phenomenon of a dark color phase correlated with the earliest spring emergence and successively lighter color forms as the season advances into warmer weather. The same phenomenon is shown to a certain extent by other caddis flies, but I have observed none in which it is as marked as in this species.

In Illinois the species is very widespread. It shows a preference for small streams but occurs also in the larger rivers. With *campyla*, it is often found in streams carrying considerable pollution and in which few or no other caddis flies are found. It has a wide ecological tolerance.

The range of the species is extremely large, extending from the Atlantic to the Pacific through the northern states and from Georgia and Oklahoma in the south to Minnesota, Ontario and New Hampshire in the north.

Illinois Records.—Many males and females, taken April 16 to September 20, are from Amboy, Apple River Canyon State Park, Aurora, Baker (Indian Creek), Bourbonnais (Rock Creek), Cedarville, Charleston, Chemung (Piscasaw Creek), Chesterville, Clinton (Weldon Springs), Cora, Crescent City, Danville, Dixon Springs, Elgin (Botanical Gardens, Rainbow Springs), Erie, Freeport, Gibson City, Gilman, Greenup (Embarrass River), Halfday, Harrisburg, Havana (Quiver Creek), Herod, Homer, Horse Shoe Lake, Howardsville, Kankakee, Kappa (Mackinaw River), Leland, Mahomet (Sangamon River), Marengo, Mazon (Mazon Creek), McHenry, Momence (Kankakee River), Monticello, Morris, Mount Carroll, Muncie, Oak Hill, Oakwood, Oregon, Ottawa, Palos Park (Mud Lake), Pontiac, Quincy, Richmond, Rock City, Savanna, Serena (Indian Creek), Spring Grove (Nippersink Creek), Starved Rock State Park, Sycamore (tributary of South Kishwaukee River), Urbana (Salt Fork River), Utica (Split Rock Brook), Wadsworth (Des Plaines River), Waukegan, West Vienna, White Heath, White Pines Forest State Park, Wilmington (Kankakee River), Yorkville (Fox River).

Cheumatopsyche burksi Ross

Cheumatopsyche burksi Ross (1941*b*, p. 83); ♂, ♀.

ADULTS.—Length 9–10 mm. Color brown, the wings with abundant light flecks over the entire surface and with two fairly large white areas along the anal margin, one at the end of the anal veins, the other near the junction of the anal veins. Male genitalia, fig. 398: claspers with apical segment short, the caudal view with base wide and apex narrow and finger-like, the mesal margin straight, the segment in general somewhat triangular; tenth tergite long, the apical lobes short and lanceolate, armed with fairly long setae.

Our only record of this species in Illinois is the holotype male, taken at Havana, along the Spoon River, October 2, 1938, B. D. Burks. The only other record of the species is from Tavares, Florida; hence little can be said regarding the general range of the species.

Cheumatopsyche campyla Ross

Cheumatopsyche campyla Ross (1938*a*, p. 152); ♂, ♀.

ADULTS. — Length 10–12 mm. Color brown, wings irrorate with light brown and cream and with a large light spot on the anal margin near apex; the irrorate portion is irregularly marked. Male genitalia, fig. 402: claspers with apical segment long and pointed but much shorter than in *oxa* or *aphanta*; tenth tergite fairly long, the apical lobes appearing somewhat clavate at apex from side view, and shouldered and pointed from caudal view; in some specimens· this shoulder is more pronounced than in fig. 402.

This species is distributed very widely over Illinois. It seldom frequents small streams, preferring those at least as large as the Salt Fork at Oakwood. It is frequently taken in large numbers along the Illinois, Rock and Mississippi rivers. Adult emergence covers a wide span, from April to October. As mentioned under *analis*, this species is frequently found in streams which are quite unattractive to most caddis flies. The larval head is illustrated in fig. 414.

This species also has a very wide range. It is most abundant through the Corn Belt states but is found over almost all other parts of the continent, with records from Arkansas, Georgia, Idaho, Illinois, Indiana, Iowa, Kansas, Michigan, Minnesota, Missouri, Montana, New Mexico, New York,

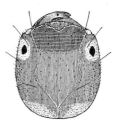

Fig. 414.—*Cheumatopsyche campyla* larva, head.

Ohio, Ontario, Oregon, Pennsylvania, Texas, Utah, Wisconsin and Wyoming.

Illinois Records.—Many males and females, taken April 11 to October 11, are from Algonquin, Alton, Beardstown, Byron, Carmi (on bridge across Little Wabash River), Charleston, Danville (Middle Fork River), Deer Grove (Green River), Des Plaines, Dixon, Dundee, East Dubuque, Elgin (Botanical Gardens), Fieldon, Florence, Grafton, Grand Detour, Grand Tower, Hamilton, Hardin (Illinois River), Harrisburg, Havana, Homer, Horse Shoe Lake, Jerseyville, Kampsville, Kankakee (Kankakee River), Kappa (Mackinaw River), Keithsburg, Mahomet, McHenry, Meredosia, Momence, Montezuma, Morris, Mount Carmel, New Boston, Oakwood, Oregon, Ottawa, Pearl, Pontiac, Quincy (stream near Cave Spring), Richmond, Rockford, Rock Island, Rockton, St. Charles, Savanna, Serena (Fox River), Springfield, Spring Grove (Nippersink Creek), Starved Rock State Park, Sterling, Urbana, Valley City, Waukegan, Wilmington, Yorkville.

Cheumatopsyche pasella Ross

Cheumatopsyche pasella Ross (1941*b*, p. 84); ♂, ♀.

ADULTS.—Length 7–9 mm. Color dark brown with very few light spots. Male genitalia, fig. 403: claspers with apical segment long and sinuate, pointed at apex. Lobes of tenth tergite very long, angled dorso-caudad, appearing narrow and pointed from lateral view, from caudal view pointed but with the base widened.

We have only two widely separated records of this species for the state, one along the Kaskaskia River, the other along the Kankakee.

Other records from Georgia, Indiana, Kentucky, North Carolina, Pennsylvania, Tennessee and Wisconsin indicate that the main range of the species centers in the eastern states with a preference for rapid streams, and that our isolated records from Indiana, Wisconsin and Illinois are on the extreme western edge of the range.

Illinois Records.—MOMENCE, Kankakee River: May 26, 1936, H. H. Ross, 3 ♂. VENEDY STATION, along Kaskaskia River: Aug. 27, 1940, Mohr & Riegel, 1 ♂.

Cheumatopsyche lasia Ross

Cheumatopsyche lasia Ross (1938a, p. 154); ♂, ♀.

ADULTS.—Length 7 mm. Color brown, the wings with very fine, uniform and irrorate markings over the entire wing. Male genitalia, fig. 399: claspers with apical segment long, similar to those of *campyla*; tenth tergite with apical lobes produced into a wide, projecting, basal shoulder, the apical portion curved back against the tenth tergite and provided with a heavy brush of setae at the apex.

This species has been taken fairly widely throughout the state, usually along small streams, although occasionally taken along rivers such as the Rock. Many of the streams in which it is found are fairly heavily silted; it is interesting to note in this connection that to the southwest the species has been taken in abundance along heavily silted rivers. Adult emergence extends from May to August with a decided high peak toward July and August.

The range, fig. 12, extending to the south and west of Illinois, includes Illinois, Kansas, Missouri, Oklahoma and Texas; in addition we have a record from eastern Montana which indicates that the species might be fairly widespread in the relatively uncollected Great Plains area.

Illinois Records.—Many males and females, taken May 15 to August 31, are from Amboy (Green River), Bartonville (Kickapoo Creek), Deer Grove, Dixon, Downs (Kickapoo Creek), Elgin (Botanical Gardens), Kappa (Mackinaw River), Mahomet, Milan, Oak Hill (Kickapoo Creek),

Pontiac, Quincy (Burton Creek), Ripley, Serena (Indian Creek), Springfield, Spring Grove, White Pines Forest State Park, Wolf Lake.

Cheumatopsyche speciosa (Banks)

Hydropsyche speciosa Banks (1904d, p. 214); ♂, ♀.

ADULTS.—Length 7–8 mm. Head brown, wings brown with irregular, fine, light mottling and three large light spots as follows: a pair on the anterior and posterior margins just before the stigma, and the third on the anterior margin just beyond the stigma, sometimes the three marks running together. Male genitalia, fig. 397: claspers with apical segment long, very narrow, pointed, and curved at apex; apical lobes of tenth tergite sharply angled near middle, the apical portion recurved down and back along the tergite and then curved dorsad again, the whole giving the appearance of a pair of sharp, apical projections and a pair of preapical, somewhat hairy lobes.

We have taken this species at several scattered localities in northern Illinois and at one locality along the Wabash River in southern Illinois; this last record probably represents drifts from a nearby large colony at Shoals, Indiana. Our only large Illinois collections have been made at Momence, along the Kankakee River; here the species emerges in swarms. It has a marked preference for large rivers. The adults emerge from April until early September.

The species has a wide range, occurring through the eastern states, extending to the southwest through the Ozarks and to the northwest through Minnesota to Montana. We have records from Arkansas, Indiana, Kentucky, Maryland, Minnesota, Missouri, Montana, New York, Ohio, Oklahoma, Tennessee and Wisconsin.

Illinois Records.—Many males and females, taken May 17 to September 7, are from Champaign, Dixon, Kankakee (Kankakee River), Metropolis, Momence (Kankakee River), Mount Carmel, Putnam, Savanna, Urbana, Wilmington.

Macronemum Burmeister

Macronema Pictet (1836, p. 399). Genotype, monobasic: *Macronema lineatum* Pictet. Preoccupied.
Macronemum Burmeister (1839, p. 915). Emendation.

The larvae and pupae are readily distinguished from other members of the family by characters used in the key. The adults may be distinguished also by the large, slender outline, extremely long antennae, and the polished, brightly colored and patterned wings.

The species frequent large, rapid rivers. The larvae, which may attain a length of nearly an inch, frequently net together large areas of small and medium sized stones if a large number of larvae spin their retreats close together. Only three species have been described for Nearctic America. Two of them have been taken in Illinois, and the other occurs in Indiana not many miles away. At some time we may expect to find adults of this third species which have drifted into Illinois.

KEY TO SPECIES

Larvae

1. Head yellow, the posterior portion of the dorsal flange raised into a pair of tubercles, fig. 417.............
.................**transversum**, p. 117
Head reddish brown, the posterior portion of the dorsal flange even, not tuberculate, fig. 416.......... 2
2. Tubercles near eye larger, fig. 416....
.....................**carolina**, p. 116

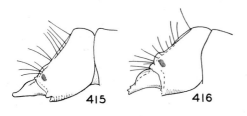
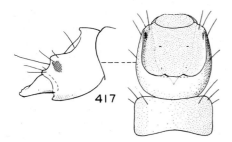

Fig. 415.—*Macronemum zebratum* larva, head.
Fig. 416.—*Macronemum carolina* larva, head.
Fig. 417.—*Macronemum transversum* larva, head.

Tubercles near eye smaller, fig. 415..
.....................**zebratum**, p. 115

Adults

1. Wings pale yellow with narrow, transverse brown stripes.............
....................**transversum**, p. 117
Wings brown with large yellow spots and stripes, fig. 420............. 2

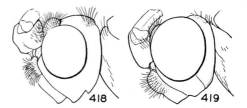

Fig. 418.—*Macronemum zebratum*, head.
Fig. 419.—*Macronemum carolina*, head.

2. Eyes small, malar space large, fig. 418
....................**zebratum**, p. 115
Eyes large, malar space narrow, fig. 419.................**carolina**, p. 116

Macronemum zebratum (Hagen)

Macronema zebratum Hagen (1861, p. 285); ♂, ♀.

LARVA.—Fig. 415. Length 22 mm. Head, thoracic sclerites and legs reddish brown. Head with a sharp, U-shaped ridge surrounding a flat area embracing almost all the dorsal portion of the head, this ridge elevated into a distinct tubercle above each eye. Mandibles with base very large and apex narrow, fig. 288. Front legs with a heavy brush on the tibiae.

ADULTS.—Fig. 420. Length 15–18 mm. Color of head and thorax metallic bluish brown; antennae dark brown at base, gradually becoming lighter toward apex; mouthparts and legs yellow. Front wings brown with yellow markings forming a pattern as in fig. 420. Eyes small, fig. 418, malar space large. Male genitalia with parts simple, fig. 421.

In Illinois we have taken this species at many localities in the northern half of the state, particularly along the Fox, Kankakee, Rock and Mississippi rivers. We have taken the larvae and pupae very abundantly in the rapids of the Kankakee River. Adult emergence begins during the latter part of May and continues into September. During the middle of the summer it is not unusual to encounter large flights of these beautifully colored insects.

The range includes most of eastern North America, with records available from Connecticut, Georgia, Illinois, Indiana, Kentucky, Maine, Michigan, Minnesota, New York, Ohio, Ontario, Pennsylvania, Virginia, West Virginia, Wisconsin; in addition we have an isolated record from Utah.

Illinois Records.—Many males and females, collected May 22 to September 7, and many larvae, collected April 27 to October 28, are from Algonquin, Antioch,

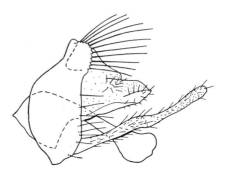

Fig. 421.—*Macronemum zebratum* ♂, genitalia.

Aurora, Como (Rock River), Dixon (Rock River), Hamilton, Kankakee (Kankakee River), Momence (Kankakee River), Normal, Oregon, Quincy (Mississippi River), Rockford, Rock Island, Sterling (Rock River), Wilmington (Kankakee River).

Macronemum carolina (Banks)

Macronema carolina Banks (1909, p. 342); ♂.

The genitalia appear identical with *zebratum*, but *carolina* is always smaller, 12–13 mm., has a slightly darker pattern, and has much larger eyes, resulting in a narrower malar space. The larvae, reared at Shoals, Indiana, are remarkably similar to those of *zebratum*, but the differences between them are very critical. It is advisable to use comparison material to aid identification.

Allotype, female.—Swainsboro, Georgia, along Ohoopee River: May 31, 1931, P. W. Fattig.

We have taken only a single specimen in Illinois, a female collected at light in Fox Ridge State Park, near the Embarrass River, July 9, 1944, Sommerman & Ross.

The species is fairly widely distributed through the southern states, and records are available from Florida, Georgia, Indiana, Louisiana, New York, Oklahoma, Pennsylvania and South Carolina.

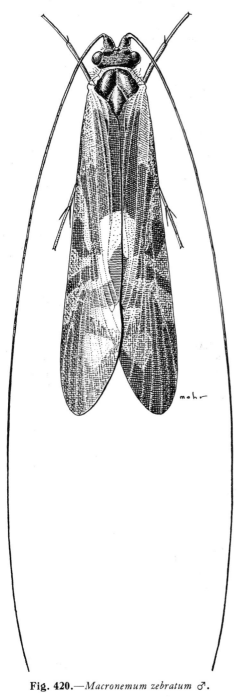

Fig. 420.—*Macronemum zebratum* ♂.

Macronemum transversum (Walker)

Hydropsyche transversa Walker (1852, p. 114); ♀.
Macronema polygrammatum McLachlan (1871, p. 129); ♂.
Macronema polygrammaticum Betten (1934, p. 204). *Misspelling.*

As in the case of *carolina*, we have not yet taken this species in Illinois but have found it in small numbers in the White River at Shoals and Petersburg, Indiana. We have not actually reared the yellow-headed larva of this genus which we are considering as this species. By a process of elimination, however, there seems no question as to the association. This larva, fig. 417, differs from the others not only in color but in having the posterior portion of the head ridge produced into a pair of tubercles.

Little is known regarding the distribution of the species. Available records are from Georgia and Indiana.

HYDROPTILIDAE

This family comprises most of the "micro" caddis flies. Various members of the family frequent diverse situations, and in Illinois one or more species may be found in almost any unpolluted lake or stream. Every known Nearctic genus has a representative in the central or eastern states.

The adults are hairy and usually have a mottled pattern; the maxillary palpi are five-segmented in both sexes and the wings have either reduced or compressed venation. The pupae, fig. 44, are very uniform in structure and no characters have been found to key them to genus.

The larvae are unique in possessing a modified type of hypermetamorphosis. In at least some genera (see *Ochrotrichia*, p. 125, and *Mayatrichia*, p. 160) the early instars have a slender body fitted for free, active life and have no case. These forms,

Fig. 422.—*Mayatrichia ayama*, apex of abdomen of early instar larva.
Fig. 423.—*Ochrotrichia* sp., apex of abdomen of early instar larva.

fig. 557, have a slender abdomen with the dorsum of each segment sclerotized. The *Mayatrichia* larva studied has structures similar to the mature form, fig. 422, but the *Ochrotrichia* larva differs in having long tarsal claws and long anal legs and claws, fig. 423. Later instars make a case and are modified for life in a case; the abdomen enlarges, at least some tarsal claws are stout, and the anal legs and hooks are reduced to small, stout hooks. Early instars are known for very few genera. Perhaps because they are exceedingly minute (about 1–2 mm. long), they are seldom collected.

The larvae and cases possess many generic characters and few specific characters, so that in the treatment of this family the generic characters are described in some detail under the first species in each genus.

Many of the genera of the Nearctic Hydroptilidae occur throughout the Americas, frequently with as many species in the Neotropical region as in the Nearctic, or more. Much pioneer work has been done in the study of the Neotropical fauna by Mosely, and the North American students of the group will find much valuable material in his two papers on the Mexican and Brazilian Hydroptilidae (Mosely 1937, 1939).

KEY TO GENERA

Larvae

1. Abdomen enlarged, at least some part of it much thicker than thorax, figs. 541; 557*B*, living in case (later instars).......................... 2
   Abdomen slender, not appreciably thicker than thorax, fig. 557*A*; free living, not with case (early instars) ....not keyed

2. Each segment of abdomen with a dark, sclerotized dorsal area, figs. 449, 464*A*.......................... 3
   Abdomen with at least segments 2–7 without dark, sclerotized dorsal area, at most with a small, delicate ring, fig. 464*B*.................... 4

3. Abdomen with dorsal sclerites solid; segments 1 and 2 small, 3–6 greatly expanded, fig. 449. Case translucent, ovoid and water-penny shaped, fig. 450..........**Leucotrichia**, p. 120
   Abdomen with dorsal sclerites membranous across middle, fig. 464*A*; segments 1–6 evenly expanded, as in fig. 541........**Ochrotrichia**, p. 125

4. Abdominal segments with lateral projections, fig. 456..................
.................**Ithytrichia**, p. 123
Abdominal segments without lateral
projections, fig. 541.............. 5

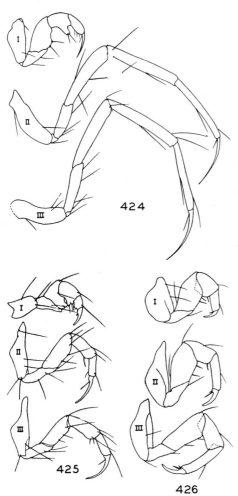

Middle and hind legs with tarsal claws
shorter or stouter, figs. 427, 429;
cases of various types........... 7

7. Anal legs distinctly projecting from
body mass, fig. 422; eighth abdominal tergite with a brush of setae,
fig. 433........................ 8
Anal legs apparently combined with
body mass and only the claws projecting, fig. 541; eighth abdominal
tergite with only one or two pairs of
weak setae, fig. 541.............. 9

8. Thoracic tergites clothed with long,
slender, erect, inconspicuous setae,
fig. 431; case of sand grains, evenly
tapered and without posterior slit
...................**Neotrichia**, p. 154
Thoracic tergites clothed with shorter,
stout, black setae which are conspicuous and appressed to the sur-

Fig. 424.—*Oxyethira dualis* larva, legs.
Fig. 425.—*Agraylea multipunctata* larva,
legs.
Fig. 426.—*Mayatrichia ayama* larva, legs.

5. Middle and hind legs almost three
times as long as front legs, fig. 424
...................**Oxyethira**, p. 133
Middle and hind legs not more than
one and one-half times as long as
front legs, fig. 425............... 6

6. Middle and hind legs with very long,
slender tarsal claws which are much
longer than tarsi, fig. 425; case
purselike, fig. 465.....**Agraylea**, p. 122

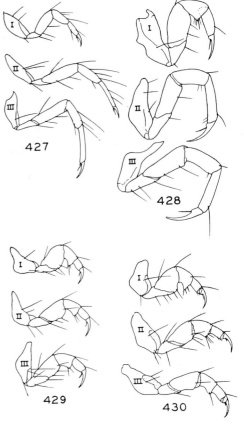

Fig. 427.—*Neotrichia* sp. larva, legs.
Fig. 428.—*Orthotrichia* sp. larva, legs.
Fig. 429.—*Hydroptila ajax* larva, legs.
Fig. 430.—*Ochrotrichia unio* larva, legs.

face of the body, fig. 432; case translucent, evenly tapered and with dorsal side either ringed or fluted with raised ridges, fig. 558.......
................**Mayatrichia**, p. 160

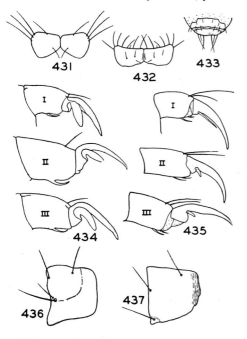

Fig. 431.—*Neotrichia* sp. larva, metanotum.
Fig. 432.—*Mayatrichia ayama* larva, metanotum.
Fig. 433.—*Mayatrichia ayama* larva, eighth tergite.
Fig. 434.—*Tascobia palmata* larva, tarsal claws.
Fig. 435.—*Ochrotrichia unio* larva, tarsal claws.
Fig. 436.—*Ochrotrichia tarsalis* larva, metanotum.
Fig. 437.—*Hydroptila waubesiana* larva, metanotum.

9. Tarsal claws with long, stout inner tooth, fig. 434; case purselike, robust..................**Tascobia**, p. 124
Tarsal claws without prominent inner tooth, fig. 435; case either purselike or cylindrical.................... 10

10. Middle and hind legs with tibiae cylindrical and long, fig. 428; case long, smooth and round in cross section, tapered at each end and with an indented slit at both ends......
................**Orthotrichia**, p. 139
Middle and hind legs with tibiae stout and widened at apex, fig. 429; case of purse type.................... 11

11. Metanotum with a distinct, widened ventro-lateral area, fig. 436.......
................**Ochrotrichia**, p. 125
Metanotum without a widened, lateral area, fig. 437......**Hydroptila**, p. 141

Adults

1. Ocelli absent.....................   2
Ocelli present.....................   4
2. Front tibiae with an apical spur.....
....................**Dibusa**, p. 121
Front tibiae without an apical spur..   3
3. Metascutellum almost rectangular, fig. 445..............**Orthotrichia**, p. 139
Metascutellum pentagonal to triangular, fig. 446........**Hydroptila**, p. 141
4. Metascutellum as wide as scutum, short and rectangular, fig. 438....
....................**Tascobia**, p. 124

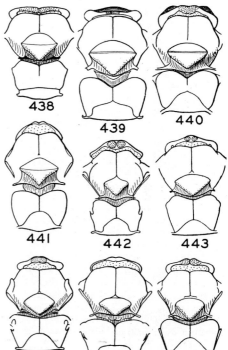

Hydroptilidae, Thorax
Fig. 438.—*Tascobia brustia.*
Fig. 439.—*Leucotrichia pictipes.*
Fig. 440.—*Metrichia nigritta.*
Fig. 441.—*Ochrotrichia tarsalis.*
Fig. 442.—*Agraylea multipunctata.*
Fig. 443.—*Oxyethira pallida.*
Fig. 444.—*Ithytrichia clavata.*
Fig. 445.—*Orthotrichia americana.*
Fig. 446.—*Hydroptila hamata.*

Fig. 447.—*Leucotrichia pictipes*, front coxae.
Fig. 448.—*Metrichia nigritta*, front coxae.

Metascutellum either triangular, fig.
    440, or markedly narrower than
    scutum, fig. 439. 5
5. Front tibiae with an apical spur. 6
    Front tibiae without an apical spur. . 7
6. Front coxae wide, fig. 447. . . . .
    . . . .**Leucotrichia**, p. 120
    Front coxae narrow, fig. 448. . . . . . .
    . . . .**Metrichia**, p. 121
7. Hind tibiae with only 1 preapical spur
    . . . .**Neotrichia**, p. 154
    Hind tibiae with 2 preapical spurs. . . 8
8. Middle tibiae without a preapical
    spur. . . . .**Mayatrichia**, p. 160
    Middle tibiae with a preapical spur. . 9
9. Mesoscutellum with a slightly arcuate,
    linelike fracture running from one
    lateral angle to the other, fig. 441,
    and dividing the area of the sclerite
    almost equally. . . .**Ochrotrichia**, p. 125
    Mesoscutellum without a transverse,
    linelike groove. 10
10. Mesoscutellum narrow and diamond-
    shaped, with a wide area posterior
    to postero-dorsal edge; metascutel-
    lum with sides parallel to median
    line and anterior margins forming
    a corner with sides, fig. 442. . . . . . .
    . . . .**Agraylea**, p. 122
    Mesoscutellum wider, anterior margin
    evenly curved, with postero-dorsal
    edge close to or touching posterior
    margin; metascutellum triangular,
    arcuate or nearly so, figs. 443, 444 11
11. Postero-dorsal edge of mesoscutellum
    touching posterior margin on meson;
    metascutellum with posterior mar-
    gin extending to lateral margin of
    segment, fig. 443. . . . .**Oxyethira**, p. 133
    Postero-dorsal edge of mesoscutellum
    separated from posterior margin by
    a narrow strip; metascutellum with
    posterior margin not extending to
    lateral margin but joined to it by a
    short, straplike piece, fig. 444. . . . .
    . . . .**Ithytrichia**, p. 123

Leucotrichia Mosely

Leucotrichia Mosely (1934*b*, p. 157). Genotype by original designation: *Leucotrichia melleopicta* Mosely.

Only one of the four Nearctic species
has been taken in Illinois. The remainder
are western or southwestern in distribution.
A key to Nearctic males is on page 271.

Leucotrichia pictipes (Banks)

Orthotrichia pictipes Banks (1911, p. 359);
♂, ♀.

LARVA (mature type).—Fig. 449. Length
4.5 mm. Sclerites dark brown. Segments of
thorax somewhat flattened, legs short and
stout. Abdomen with first two segments
very small, third to sixth greatly expanded;
each segment of abdomen with a conspicuous, rectangular, dark sclerite on the dorsum, each sclerite bearing several setae,
segments separated by a conspicuous constriction. Anal hooks sessile and fairly long.

CASE.—Fig. 450. Round and convex, similar in appearance to a leech egg, attached
like a water-penny, made of translucent material which appears gelatinous but is actually quite tough.
Underside of case
formed of a weak,
irregular sheet.

ADULTS.—Length
4.0–4.5 mm. Body
and appendages dark
brown to black, the
antennae and tarsi
banded with white,
the wings with a
few scattered, small
light areas.

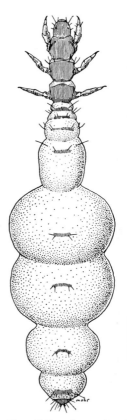

Fig. 449.—*Leucotri-
chia pictipes* larva.

Fig. 450.—*Leucotri-
chia pictipes* case.

Male genitalia, fig. 916, (see p. 272) : eighth sternite bilobed, forming a pair of widely spaced triangles; ninth tergite with a brush of long setae; claspers fused to form a short, broad spatula; aedeagus as in fig. 916. Female genitalia with segments simple; bursa copulatrix as in fig. 921 (see p. 273).

The larva was described by Lloyd (1915a) under the name *Ithytrichia confusa* (misidentification).

Our only Illinois records of this species are from the Apple River in Apple River Canyon State Park, situated in the Jo Daviess hills of extreme northwestern Illinois. In one or two of the swiftest rapids of the river we have taken larvae and pupae on large stones in the center of the current.

In the northern states, the species' range is practically transcontinental, with definite records from Colorado, Idaho, Michigan, Minnesota, New York, Oregon, Wisconsin and Wyoming.

Illinois Records.—APPLE RIVER CANYON STATE PARK: Aug. 23, 1939, Ross & Riegel, 7 ♂, 2 ♀ ; Apple River, May 24, 1940, H. H. Ross, 1 ♂, 2 larvae, many pupae; June 6, 1940, Mohr & Burks, 2 ♂ ; April 9, 1941, Ross & Mohr, many larvae.

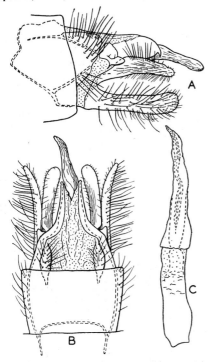

Metrichia Ross

Metrichia Ross (1938c, p. 9). Genotype, by original designation: *Orthotrichia nigritta* Banks.

The genotype is the sole species in the genus and is known from Texas and Okla-

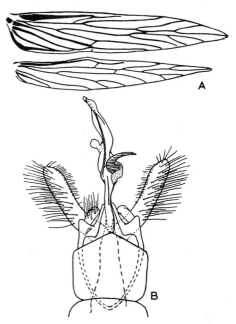

Fig. 451.—*Metrichia nigritta. A*, wings; *B*, male genitalia.

homa. The larva is unknown. The male genitalia and wings are illustrated in fig. 451.

Dibusa Ross

Dibusa Ross (1939a, p. 66). Genotype by original designation: *Dibusa angata* Ross.

In this genus, as in *Metrichia*, the genotype is the sole species. Originally described

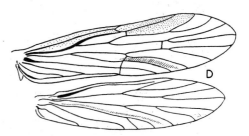

Fig. 452.—*Dibusa angata. A* and *B*, male genitalia, lateral and dorsal aspects; *C*, aedeagus; *D*, wings.

from North Carolina, it has since been collected in southeastern Oklahoma. The male genitalia and wings are illustrated in fig. 452; the female and larva are unknown.

Agraylea Curtis

Agraylea Curtis (1834, p. 217). Genotype, monobasic: *Agraylea multipunctata* Curtis.
Hydrorchestria Kolenati (1848, p. 103). Emended name.

Only one species of the genus, *multipunctata*, has been collected in Illinois. The

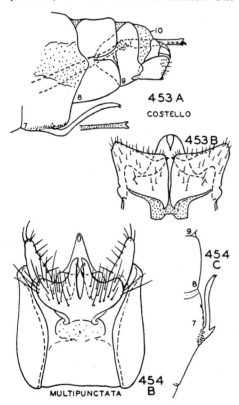

Figs. 453–454.—*Agraylea*, male genitalia. *A*, lateral aspect; *B*, ventral aspect; *C*, lateral process of seventh sternite.

only other eastern species, *costello*, differs markedly in the shape of the claspers, fig. 453.

Agraylea multipunctata Curtis

Agraylea multipunctata Curtis (1834, p. 217).
Allotrichia signata Banks (1904*d*, p. 215); ♂.
Agraylea fraterna Banks (1907*b*, p. 164); ♂.

Allotrichia flavida Banks (1907*b*, p. 164); ♀. New synonymy.

LARVA (mature type).—Length 5 mm. Head round and robust, front legs short and stocky, middle and hind legs longer, with exceptionally long tarsal claws. Abdominal segments enlarged gradually to beyond middle and decreasing to apex, segments separated by a constriction and without dorsal armature.

CASE.—Purselike, formed of two symmetrical ovate valves and with anterior and posterior slits. The case is carried erect. Construction of fibers often mottled.

ADULTS.—Length 4–5 mm. Color salt-and-pepper mottling to almost uniformly

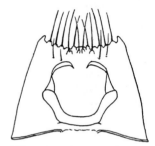

Fig. 455.—*Agraylea multipunctata*, female genitalia.

black. Venation relatively complete, much as in fig. 452. Male genitalia as in fig. 454. Female genitalia as in fig. 455.

Holarctic in distribution, this species is taken commonly throughout the northern states and Canada. In Illinois our records are most abundant in the northeastern corner. The larvae have been taken in both lakes and rivers. In addition to Illinois, we have records from British Columbia, Colorado, Maine, Manitoba, Michigan, Minnesota, New Brunswick, New York, Nova Scotia, Ontario, South Dakota, Virginia, Wisconsin.

Illinois Records.—ANTIOCH: July 1, 1931, Frison, Betten & Ross, 2♀; July 7, 1932, at light, Frison & Metcalf, ♂♂, ♀♀. FOX LAKE: July 1, 1931, Frison, Betten & Ross, 2♂, 6♀; Sept. 22, 1931, Frison & Ross, ♂♂, 6♀; Oct. 4, 1931, Ross & Mohr, ♂♂, 3♀; June 30, 1935, DeLong & Ross, ♂♂, ♀♀; May 28, 1936, in weeds, H. H. Ross, 3 larvae; June 10, 1936, Ross & Burks, 1♂. MCHENRY: June 30, 1931, Frison, Betten & Ross, 1♀. PALOS PARK: Mud Lake: Aug. 3, 1938, Ross & Burks,

1 ♂, 6 ♀. RICHMOND: June 20, 1938, Burks & Boesel, 5 ♀. SAVANNA: July 10, 1927, Frison & Glasgow, at light, 1 ♀. SPRING GROVE: Fish Hatchery, May 10, 1935, Frison & Ross, 1 ♂, 1 ♀; June 9, 1938, Burks & Mohr, 5 ♂, 5 ♀; June 17, 1938, at light, Burks & Boesel, 1 ♀; Nippersink Creek, June 17, 1938, B. D. Burks, 2 ♀; Fish Hatchery, July 11, 1938, Burks & Riegel, 4 larvae.

Ithytrichia Eaton

Ithytrichia Eaton (1873, p. 139). Genotype, monobasic: *Ithytrichia lamellaris* Eaton.

The curious hydroptilid larva described by Needham (1902) is probably of this genus. At the time Needham considered the larva (prepupa) with lateral appendages, fig. 456, to be a different phase of

Fig. 456.—*Ithytrichia?* larva. (After Needham.)

another larva without such appendages but collected with it. I have observed no such phenomenon in prepupae of other Hydroptilidae. Furthermore the larva under discussion fits descriptions of a European species of this genus (Morton 1888). I believe that two genera were involved in Needham's collecting. His larva without the lateral appendages (1902, fig. 1) may have been a species of *Oxyethira*; the one with lateral appendages (1902, figs. 2–5) was probably *Ithytrichia clavata*. Both were in cases apparently resembling fig. 465.

Both Nearctic species have been taken in Illinois. The female of one of these is unknown. The adults have the salt-and-pepper markings typical of many Hydroptilidae.

KEY TO SPECIES

Males

1. Claspers with ventral aspect narrowed to a slender apex; side plates of ninth segment with apex narrow, lateral aspect downcurved, ventral aspect flared, fig. 457............
   ....**clavata**, p. 124

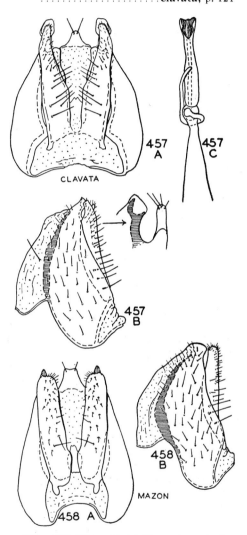

Figs. 457–458.—*Ithytrichia*, male genitalia. *A*, ventral aspect; *B*, lateral aspect; *C*, aedeagus.

Claspers with ventral aspect parallel sided, apex wide and truncate; side plates of ninth segment with apex wide, without flared end, fig. 458...
   ....**mazon**, p. 124

Ithytrichia clavata Morton

Ithytrichia clavata Morton (1905, p. 67); ♂.

LARVA.—What is possibly the larva of this species was illustrated by Needham (1902, p. 377, figs. 2–5). His drawing is reproduced here in fig. 456. No additional material of this form has been found.

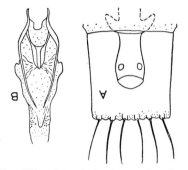

Fig. 459.—*Ithytrichia clavata*, female genitalia. *A*, ventral aspect; *B*, bursa copulatrix.

ADULTS.—Length 3 mm. Color dark brown with light mottling over body and wings. Male genitalia, fig. 457: ninth and tenth tergites entirely membranous dorsally, the lateral portion extending to apex of clasper and forming an apical portion with downcurved, truncate lateral aspect and a flared ventral aspect; below this is a thumb-like protuberance from which arises a finger-like process; claspers long and slender, tapering to a narrow apex; aedeagus long, with tubular base, distinct neck with a stout spiral process and long apex flattened and flanged at end. Female genitalia, fig. 459: eighth sternite membranous with six setae at apex, each on a separate basal tubercle; near middle of segment is a curious, head-like structure having internal lobes connected with its base; bursa copulatrix with base open, fig. 459B.

Allotype, female.—Cultus Lake, Sardis, British Columbia: July 23, 1936, H. H. Ross.

Our only Illinois collection of this species was made at light, along the Galena River, Council Hill, June 26, 1940, Mohr & Riegel, 7 ♂. We have female specimens from Muncie which may be this species. Since the female of *mazon* is not known and may be similar to that of *clavata*, it seems best to leave these Muncie specimens unidentified.

The species has a very wide range, at least transcontinental and perhaps Holarctic, with records from British Columbia, California, Illinois, New York, Oklahoma, Pennsylvania. Tjeder (1930) records the species from Sweden, but there is a doubt as to the correctness of his identification.

Ithytrichia mazon new species

MALE.—Length 3 mm. Color brown with light mottling over body and wings. General structure typical for genus. Male genitalia, fig. 458: ninth and tenth tergites not separated, both membranous; lateral area of ninth segment sinuate at base, with an arcuate, sclerotized dorsal thickening, the apex wide and without flared areas or processes; claspers nearly straight, ventral aspect parallel sided and truncate at apex; aedeagus with long, tubular base, round neck, and with spiral and apex similar to, but slightly narrower than, those in fig. 457C.

Holotype, male.—Mazon, Illinois, along Mazon Creek, June 16, 1938, B. D. Burks.

Known only from the holotype. This species resembles *lamellaris* Eaton most closely but differs in having no sclerotized dorsal rods beneath the base of the ninth tergite and in the truncate apex of the claspers. The type was collected at light along the banks of Mazon Creek, which is a small stream laden with pollution.

Tascobia new genus

LARVA (mature type).—Head rounded, all legs short and stocky. Abdomen gradually enlarged toward middle, tapering to posterior end, with moderate constrictions between segments. Anal hooks short and not projecting on "legs."

CASE.—Purselike, of fibrous construction.

ADULTS.—Length 3 mm. Color salt-and-pepper mottling. Ocelli present, lateral pair close to eye. Wings only moderately narrowed at apex. Legs with spur count of 1-3-4. Notum, fig. 438, with mesoscutellum divided by transverse line; metascutellum wide, short and rectangular.

Genotype.—*Stactobia palmata.*

This genus includes *palmata*, *brustia* and *delira*, all placed previously in the genus *Stactobia*. *Stactobia* is apparently restricted to Europe and is quite distinct from this new genus as evidenced by differences in larvae and genitalia. Characters to separate *Tascobia* from other Nearctic Hydroptilidae are given in the key to genera.

Tascobia palmata (Ross)

Stactobia palmata Ross (1938a, p. 116); ♂, ♀.

LARVA.—Length 3.5 mm. Sclerites cream to dusky, with dark lines and spots along sutures.

ADULT.—Size, color and structure as described for genus. Male genitalia, fig. 460: ninth segment forming a long internal shelf open ventrally; tenth tergite membranous; claspers short, ovate at apex; above them arise a pair of stalked processes divided at apex into three fingers; aedeagus simple and tubular. Female genitalia with a ring of spines at apex of eighth segment; bursa copulatrix as in fig. 463.

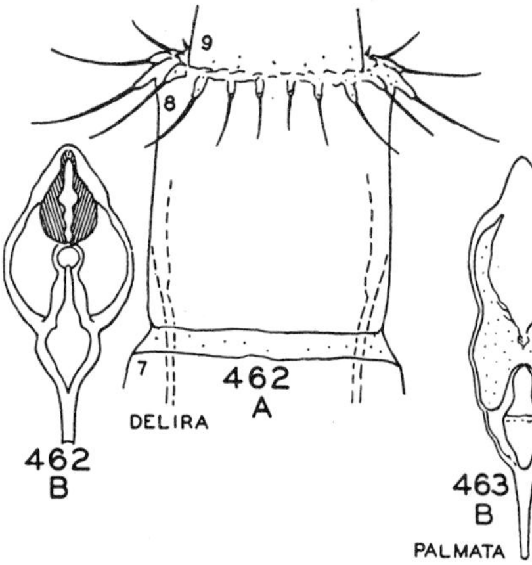

Figs. 462–463.—*Tascobia*, female genitalia. *A*, ventral aspect; *B*, bursa copulatrix.

Of the three species known in the genus, only this one has been taken in Illinois. Another, *delira*, occurs north and east of the state and may be taken in future collecting. The two species differ radically in genitalia, figs. 460, 461.

Adults have seldom been taken, but the larvae are found in numbers in several small and fairly swift streams, notably the Sangamon and Sinsinawa rivers. The cases are found on stones in riffles, and the larvae mature in early spring. Mature pupae have been collected from several localities.

Originally described from Illinois, Kentucky, Tennessee and Wisconsin, the species has since been taken in Oklahoma.

Illinois Records.—APPLE RIVER CANYON STATE PARK: May 24, 1940, H. H. Ross, many larvae; June 6, 1940, Mohr & Burks, ♂ ♂, ♀ ♀. COUNCIL HILL, Galena River: June 5, 1940, Mohr & Burks, 2 larvae. EDDYVILLE, Lusk Creek: May 24, 1940, Mohr & Burks, 1 ♂ (reared), 2 ♂, 1 ♀, 6 pupae, 6 larvae; June 1, 1940, B. D. Burks, 4 larvae, many pupae. GALENA: May 23, 1940, H. H. Ross, many larvae. KANKAKEE, Kankakee River: June 6, 1935, Ross & Mohr, 2 ♂; May 31, 1938, Mohr & Burks, 1 ♂, 3 ♀. MAHOMET, Sangamon River: June 6, 1940, Ross & Riegel, many pupae and larvae. SUGAR GROVE: June 13, 1939, Frison & Ross, 1 ♀.

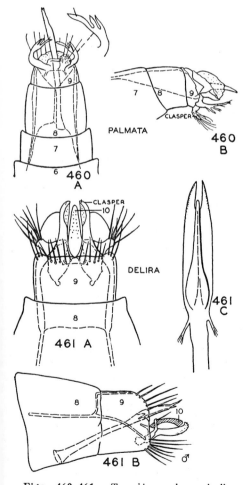

Figs. 460–461.—*Tascobia*, male genitalia. *A*, ventral aspect; *B*, lateral aspect; *C*, aedeagus.

Ochrotrichia Mosely

Polytrichia Sibley (1926b, p. 102). Genotype, monobasic: *Ithytrichia confusa* Morton. Preoccupied.

Ochrotrichia Mosely (1934*b*, p. 162). Genotype, by original designation: *Ochrotrichia insularis* Mosely.

The genus *Polytrichia*, erected in 1926 for the species *Ithytrichia confusa*, is preoccupied by a genus of snails and therefore cannot be used in the caddis flies. It is necessary to resurrect the genus *Ochrotrichia*, described in 1934, with *insularis* as its type. In 1937 Mosely sank his genus *Ochrotrichia* as a synonym of *Polytrichia*, but now Mosely's name must be applied to the large assemblage of species in North, Central and South America which have previously been placed under *Polytrichia*.

Ten of the 20 described Nearctic species have been taken in Illinois and one or two more may show up with additional collecting. All the species frequent clear and rapid streams, including some which dry in summer. Many of the species appear to be local in distribution, and the few known localities for any one of these species may be widely separated.

KEY TO SPECIES

Larvae

1. Abdominal tergites, fig. 464*A*, with an ovoid sclerite having a transverse, membranous center and with lateral, sclerotized, setate spots some distance from mesal sclerite; case tortoise-like, flat on the bottom . . . . . .
. . . . **riesi**, p. 132
Abdominal tergites, fig. 464*B*, ornamented only with inconspicuous sclerotized rings; case purselike, fig. 465 2
2. Head and thoracic sclerites almost entirely yellow or light brownish yellow, sometimes with a faint reddish tone 3

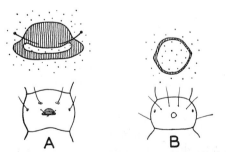

Fig. 464.—*Ochrotrichia* larvae, abdominal rings. *A*, *O. riesi*; *B*, *O. anisca*.

Head and thoracic sclerites mostly dark brown, sometimes shading to black 4

Fig. 465.—*Ochrotrichia unio*, larva and case.

3. Thoracic sclerites with distinct markings of fairly dark brown . . . .
. . . . **tarsalis**, p. 130
Thoracic sclerites with only indistinct suffusions of darker color; head and thorax frequently with a reddish tone . . . . **anisca**, p. 131
4. Head with a small, mesal pale spot or stripe . . . . **xena**, p. 130
Head without a mesal pale area . . . . . .
. . . . **unio,**
p. 129; **eliaga**, p. 132; **spinosa**, p. 132

Adults

1. Apex of abdomen with long claspers, fig. 466 (males) 2
Apex of abdomen tubular, fig. 478 (females) 12
2. Tenth tergite triangular or vasiform, figs. 466, 467, small, without long or hooked, sclerotized processes; both ninth segment and claspers long and narrow 3
Tenth tergite longer, with a set of definite, heavily sclerotized hooked or straight processes, fig. 471; ninth segment and claspers shorter 4
3. Claspers with two mesal brushes of black pegs at apex, fig. 466; tenth tergite triangular . . . . **xena**, p. 130
Claspers with only one mesal brush of black pegs at apex, fig. 467; tenth tergite vasiform . . . . **unio**, p. 129
4. Claspers shoelike, upcurved at apex, dorsal margin concave, fig. 468 5
Claspers sinuate, fig. 475 8
5. Left side of tenth tergite with a large, conspicuous spine near middle, curved mesad, fig. 471 . . . **tarsalis**, p. 130
Left side of tenth tergite without such a spine curved mesad 6
6. Tenth tergite with spine *C* filamentous and not angled from its base, fig. 468 . . . . **shawnee**, p. 131
Tenth tergite with spine *C* stout, curved away from and back to its parent sclerite, fig. 469 7
7. Tenth tergite with sclerite *A* very broad, *D* almost touching spiral of

B, and E short, tapering evenly to pointed apex, fig. 469 . . . .
. . . .**contorta**, p. 131

Sclerite A much narrower, D removed at least its own length from spiral of B, E long, obliquely truncate at apex and much closer to apex of F, fig. 470 . . . . **anisca**, p. 131

8. Claspers with a row of 4 or 5 long, stout, evenly spaced, black spines at middle shoulder, fig. 473   9
   Claspers with black spines irregular or clustered at middle shoulder, figs. 475–477 10

9. Hook of tenth tergite large and reaching beyond sclerite B; sclerites C and

D both slender, fig. 473 . . . .**riesi**, p. 132

Hook of tenth tergite small, sclerite B extending considerably beyond it; sclerite C very slender, sclerite D shorter and stout, fig. 474 . . . .
. . . .**confusa**, p. 133

10. Right clasper with middle of ventral portion angulate; the angle bears a spine well separated from the others, fig. 475 . . . .**spinosa**, p. 132
    Right clasper with middle of ventral portion evenly sinuate, fig. 476 11

11. Apex of claspers with a row of 4 to 6 black, peglike spines on the mesal face of the caudo-ventral arc, fig. 476 . . . .**eliaga**, p. 132

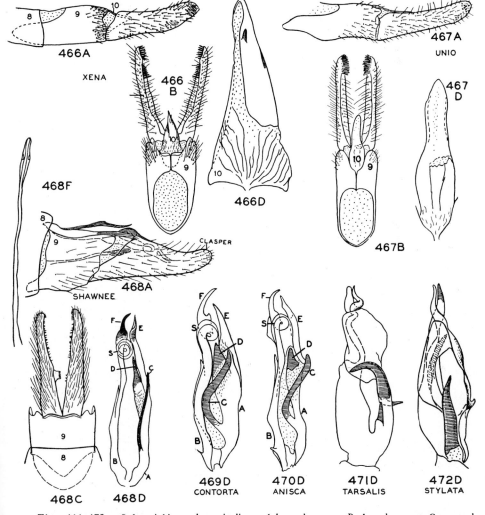

Figs. 466–472.—*Ochrotrichia*, male genitalia.   *A*, lateral aspect; *B*, dorsal aspect; *C*, ventral aspect; *D*, tenth tergite, dorsal aspect; *F*, aedeagus.

Apex of claspers with only 1 or 2 apico-mesal black spines, fig. 477..
............................**arva**, p. 132

12. Tenth tergite heart shaped, the apex pointed, the styles arising near meson; internal structure of eighth sternite not conspicuous, fig. 478..
..............**xena**, p. 130; **unio**, p. 129
Tenth tergite triangular, apex rounded, the styles arising from lateral

margin; internal structure of eighth sternite frequently sclerotized and conspicuous, figs. 479–484........   13

13. Eighth sternite with apical margin produced into a low, distinct lobe; mesal area of internal structure with spicules, fig. 479...**tarsalis**, p. 130
Eighth sternite with apical margin nearly straight or merged with ninth and the boundary between them in-

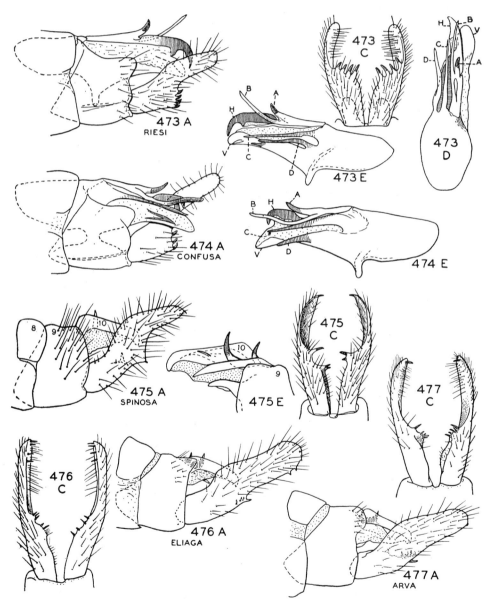

Figs. 473–477.—*Ochrotrichia*, male genitalia. *A*, lateral aspect; *C*, ventral aspect; *D*, tenth tergite, dorsal aspect; *E*, tenth tergite, right side.

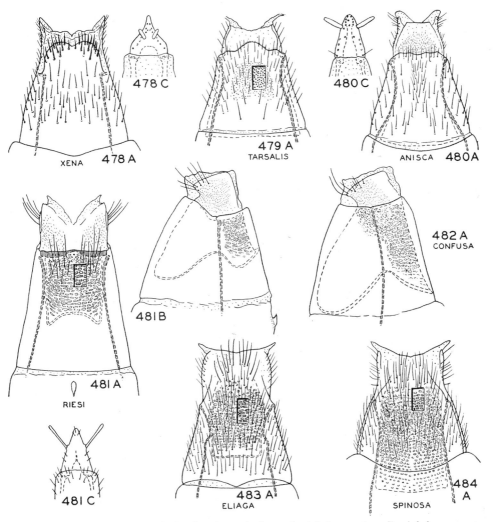

Figs. 478–484.—*Ochrotrichia*, female genitalia. *A*, eighth sternite; *B*, eighth segment, lateral aspect; *C*, tenth segment, dorsal aspect.

distinct, figs. 480, 484 14

14. Internal structure of eighth sternite with surface membranous and indistinct, fig. 480 . . . .
. . . . . . **shawnee**, p. 131; **anisca**, p. 131
Internal structure of eighth sternite with surface sclerotized and reticulate, figs. 481–484 15

15. Eighth sternite with apical margin distinct, separating it from ninth, fig. 481 16
Eighth sternite with apical margin merging with ninth sternite so that the division between the two is obliterated, fig. 483 17

16. Internal structure of eighth sternite short, reaching about middle of seg-

ment, fig. 481 . . . . **riesi**, p. 132
Internal structure of eighth sternite long, reaching almost to base of segment, fig. 482 . . . . **confusa**, p. 133

17. Internal structure of eighth sternite short, reaching only two-thirds distance to base, fig. 483 . . . . **eliaga**, p. 132
Internal structure of eighth sternite long, reaching well beyond base of segment, fig. 484 . . . . **spinosa**, p. 132

Ochrotrichia unio (Ross)

Polytrichia unio Ross (1941*b*, p. 56); ♂, ♀.

LARVA.—Fig. 465. Length 4 mm. Head and thoracic sclerites dark brown, shading to black, with pale ring around eyes and along some sutures. Abdominal tergites with an inconspicuous sclerotized mesal ring.

ADULTS.—Length 3–4 mm. Body and appendages dark brown to black with spots of white on body and legs and a narrow white band on front wings just before middle. Male genitalia, fig. 467: ninth segment long, slender and flattened; claspers long, symmetrical and nearly straight, each with a large brush of black, peglike setae on inner face at apex; tenth tergite small, vasiform and without processes. Female genitalia as in fig. 478: eighth sternite with apex produced into a broad, emarginate lobe set with fairly stout setae; internal rods straight; endoskeleton apparently absent; tenth segment heart shaped, cerci arising near meson.

To date we have records of this species only from southern Illinois. Here it occurs in several temporary streams in the Ozarkian region. The larvae usually occur in large colonies, although adults are seldom taken. We have many collections of mature male and female pupae. There are no records for other states.

Illinois Records.—East of ALDRIDGE: May 14, 1940, Mohr & Burks, 2 larvae. ALTO PASS, Union Spring: May 25, 1940, Mohr & Burks, ♂ ♂, 3 ♀, many pupae. CARBONDALE: Clay Lick Creek, April 17, 1935, H. H. Ross, many larvae; May 11, 1935, C. O. Mohr, many larvae, 7 pupae. ELIZABETHTOWN: Hog Thief Creek, May 10, 1935, C. O. Mohr, many larvae, 8 pupae. ETHERTON, Jackson County: May 15, 1940, Mohr & Burks, many larvae. GOLCONDA: May 11, 1935, C. O. Mohr, many larvae, 2 pupae; April 30, 1940, Burks & Mohr, many larvae. HEROD: May 10, 1935, C. O. Mohr, many pupae; May 29, 1935, Ross & Mohr, many pupae; Gibbons Creek, April 19, 1937, Ross & Mohr, many larvae; April 30, 1940, Mohr & Burks, many larvae and pupae. KARBERS RIDGE: May 11, 1935, C. O. Mohr, many larvae, 3 pupae. WALTERSBURG: April 30, 1940, Mohr & Burks, many larvae. WOLF LAKE, Hutchins Creek: May 12, 1939, Burks & Riegel, 7 larvae; May 31, 1940, B. D. Burks, 1 ♂.

Ochrotrichia xena (Ross)

Polytrichia xena Ross (1938a, p. 122); ♂.

LARVA.—Length 3.5 mm. Head and thoracic sclerites dark brown, except for a pale

ring around eyes and a small mesal pale spot or stripe down the front of the head. Otherwise similar to *unio*.

ADULTS.—Size and color as for *unio*. Male genitalia, fig. 466: ninth segment long, slender and flattened; claspers long, symmetrical, curved slightly dorsad, each clasper with two brushes of black, peglike setae on inner face, one brush at extreme apex, the other brush just beyond middle near ventral margin; tenth tergite triangular, the base membranous and wrinkled, the apex bearing a large sclerotized shield which bears two small peglike teeth. Female genitalia indistinguishable from *unio*, fig. 478.

Allotype, female.—Oakwood, Illinois: May 21, 1936, Mohr & Burks.

Known only from a few scattered localities in Illinois, this species is recorded chiefly from larval and pupal material. Better diagnosis of the larvae shows that most of the larvae I regarded as of this species in 1938 are in reality *unio*.

Illinois Records. — HEROD, Gibbons Creek: May 13, 1937, Frison & Ross, 4 ♂. MUNCIE, Stony Creek: May 1, 1935, H. H. Ross, many larvae; May 6, 1936, Ross & Mohr, many larvae. OAKWOOD: May 1, 1935, H. H. Ross, many larvae; May 21, 1936, Mohr & Burks, 3 ♂, 2 ♀.

Ochrotrichia tarsalis (Hagen)

Hydroptila tarsalis Hagen (1861, p. 275); ♂.
Polytrichia confusa Betten (1934, p. 154); *nec* Morton. Misidentification.

LARVA.—Length 4 mm. Head and thoracic sclerites almost entirely yellow or straw color, sometimes with a light brownish tint; thoracic sclerites with distinct dark brown markings along sutures; legs pale with dark brown markings along sutures. Case purselike.

ADULTS.—Size and color as for *unio*. Male genitalia: ninth segment short, claspers shoe shaped as in fig. 468, both claspers very similar, long and tapering as seen from ventral view; tenth tergite, fig. 471, with right portion produced into a long spiral process overlaid by a large plate; left process stout, with two small sclerotized points and a large sclerotized hook pointing mesad. Female genitalia, fig. 479: eighth sternite with apical margin sinuate, the mesal portion produced into a rounded lobe; internal rods sinuate; endoskeleton large, extending the full length of the segment and with the center area covered with small, sharp spicules; tenth tergite similar to that in fig. 480, long, somewhat triangular, rounded at apex, the cerci arising from the lateral margin.

Allotype, female.—Hollister, Missouri: July 14, 1938, Mrs. Vitae Kite.

The male genitalia extremely distinctive, resembling only those of *stylata*, fig. 472, which may be distinguished by the large, dark basal process of the tenth tergite. This latter species is apparently western in range (Montana to Oklahoma).

Showing a preference for clear, medium-sized streams, *tarsalis* occurs in several such streams in Illinois. We have established the identity of the larvae by collections of pupae from the Salt Fork River at Oakwood.

The range of *tarsalis* is widespread and includes Illinois, Indiana, Missouri, New York, Oklahoma, Ontario, Texas and Wisconsin.

Illinois Records.—DANVILLE, Middle Fork River: Aug. 27, 1936, Ross & Burks, 1 ♂, 1 ♀, many larvae. KANKAKEE: Aug. 1, 1933, Ross & Mohr, 1 ♂; July 21, 1935, Ross & Mohr, 2 ♂. MAHOMET, Sangamon River: June 6, 1940, Ross & Riegel, many larvae. MOMENCE: Aug. 21, 1936, Ross & Burks, 8 ♂; Kankakee River, May 26, 1936, H. H. Ross, 2 larvae; May 17, 1937, Ross & Burks, many larvae; June 22, 1938, Ross & Burks, 2 ♂; June 6, 1940, Ross & Riegel, many larvae. MORRIS: Aug. 22, 1938, H. H. Ross, 1 ♀. OAKWOOD, Salt Fork River: July 18, 1933, Ross & Mohr, 1 ♂. OTTAWA: July 3, 1937, at light, Werner, 1 ♀. WHITE PINES FOREST STATE PARK: Aug. 13, 1937, Ross & Burks, 1 ♀. WILMINGTON: July 1, 1935, DeLong & Ross, 1 ♂.

Ochrotrichia anisca (Ross)

Polytrichia anisca Ross (1941*b*, p. 58); ♂, ♀.

LARVA.—Length 4 mm. Head, thoracic sclerites, and legs light brownish yellow, frequently with a faint reddish tone; sometimes indistinct suffusions of a darker color are present but never forming distinct markings as in *tarsalis*. Abdominal tergites with only inconspicuous sclerotized rings. Case purselike.

ADULTS.—Size and color as for *unio*. Male genitalia with ninth segment and claspers similar to *shawnee*, fig. 468; tenth

tergite, fig. 470, with process, *C*, stout, curved mesad and then abruptly laterad; *D*, short and stout, situated more than its own length from spiral, *S*; the hook, *F*, longer and close to the spiral. Female genitalia, fig. 480: eighth sternite with apical margin slightly reticulate but not produced; internal rods markedly sinuate, following the shape of the membranous, indistinct endoskeleton. Tenth tergite somewhat triangular, the apex rounded, and the cerci arising from the lateral margin.

In Illinois this species frequents several small temporary streams in the Ozarkian region. These streams are rapid and clear in early spring when the larvae of the species mature. Collections of pupae at Wolf Lake have associated the larval and adult stages. A very large colony of larvae at this locality was unique in that each case had a comparatively large "anchor" stone attached to one side.

The range of the species extends through the Ozarks and neighboring mountains, with records for Arkansas, Illinois and Oklahoma.

Illinois Records.—LARUE, McCann School: May 26, 1939, Burks & Riegel, ♂ ♂, ♀ ♀. WOLF LAKE: Hutchins Creek, May 25, 1940, Mohr & Burks, many larvae; May 31, 1940, B. D. Burks, ♂ ♂, ♀ ♀.

Ochrotrichia contorta (Ross)

Polytrichia contorta Ross (1941*b*, p. 60); ♂.

This species is known from various localities in south central Missouri in the Ozarks and might be collected in Illinois.

Ochrotrichia shawnee (Ross)

Polytrichia shawnee Ross (1938*a*, p. 120); ♂, ♀.

LARVA.—Unknown.

ADULTS.—Size and color as for *unio*. Male genitalia, fig. 468: ninth segment short, claspers shoe shaped, both appearing long, slender and similar in shape from ventral view; tenth tergite divided into many parts; the right sclerite, *B*, formed near apex into a coiled spring, *S*, and beyond that forming a bent point, *F*; left process, *A*, with a long, slender style, *C*, arising near base, beyond this a mesal process, *D*, which has a sclerotized, narrow, pointed tip and at the extreme apex a pointed process, E. Female genitalia similar to *anisca*.

The original type material from Herod, Illinois, May 29, 1935, Ross & Mohr, is the only known collection of this species.

Ochrotrichia eliaga (Ross)

Polytrichia eliaga Ross (1941*b*, p. 57); ♂, ♀.

LARVA.—Length 4 mm. Head and thoracic sclerites dark brown to black with pale ring around each eye and along some sutures. Abdominal tergites with only inconspicuous sclerotized rings. Case purselike.

ADULTS.—Size and color as in *unio*. Male genitalia as in fig. 476: ninth segment short and high; claspers suddenly sinuate near base, the apex slightly enlarged and spatulate; from ventral view the base appears broad, suddenly tapering to a platelike apical portion, the shoulder thus formed bearing an uneven row of four to five sclerotized teeth, the extreme apex of the clasper bearing a row of four sclerotized teeth along the apico-ventral margin; tenth tergite with long keel-like structure, and teeth in processes on right side similar to *arva*. Female genitalia, fig. 483: eighth sternite merging imperceptibly with structures of the ninth segment; internal rods sinuate, touching the endoskeleton and then curving laterad; endoskeleton distinct, reaching about two-thirds the distance to the base of the segment and with the entire ventral surface fenestrate with rectangular reticulations; tenth segment as in *anisca*, fig. 480.

This species is known from only two states, Tennessee and Illinois. The Illinois record consists of a single male collected in company with a large flight of *anisca*, along Hutchins Creek, Wolf Lake, May 31, 1940, B. D. Burks.

Ochrotrichia spinosa (Ross)

Polytrichia spinosa Ross (1938*a*, p. 121); ♂.

LARVA.—Length 4 mm. Head and thoracic sclerites dark brown to black, similar to *eliaga*, as are also the inconspicuous sclerotized rings on the abdominal tergites and the purselike case.

ADULTS.—Size and color as in *unio*. Male genitalia, fig. 475: ninth segment short and high; claspers evenly sinuate, the apex narrowed and slightly pointed, with a sclerotized tooth at the tip, and with a triangular projection near the middle of the ventral side; from ventral view the base of each clasper appears broad, narrowing suddenly beyond middle to a bladelike apex; at the shoulder thus formed there is a small group of two or three sharp, black spines on the left clasper, and on the right clasper a small group of similar spines just below the middle, and a stout spur upon this and well separated from it. Female genitalia, fig. 484: eighth sternite merging imperceptibly with structures of the ninth segment; internal rods curving to meet and follow the endoskeleton; endoskeleton distinct and long, extending well beyond the base of the segment and fenestrate over most of its surface with rectangular reticulations.

Allotype, female.—North Lake, Wisconsin: June 5, 1938, Ross & Burks.

Our Illinois records are all from a single colony at Split Rock Brook (see p. 8), a small, spring-fed brook, where we have collected larvae and mature pupae. Association of males and females is based on a large collection of adults from a creek at North Lake, Wisconsin.

Few collections of this species have been made, but these indicate a wide range: Illinois, Kentucky (Harrodsburg), Oklahoma (Turner Falls State Park) and Wisconsin (North Lake).

Illinois Records.—UTICA, Split Rock Brook: Feb. 1, 1941, Frison, Ries & Ross, many larvae; June 17, 1941, Burks & Riegel, 4 ♂, 7 pupae, many larvae.

Ochrotrichia arva (Ross)

Polytrichia arva Ross (1941*b*, p. 58); ♂.

Originally described from Martin Springs, Tennessee, the species has not yet been taken in Illinois.

Ochrotrichia riesi new species

LARVA (mature type).—Length 4 mm. Color of sclerites black or dark brown. Head and thorax small but rounded; legs short and stocky. Abdominal segments gradually enlarged to beyond middle and tapering to apex, segments separated by constrictions; each segment having an ovoid, dorsal sclerite with a curious, transverse, membranous center and lateral sclerotized spots bearing setae situated at some distance from the mesal sclerite.

CASE.—Tortoise-shell-like with top piece ovoid, high and convex, the bottom piece forming a plate which covers all but the front and back of bottom opening. Made from fibrous material, opaque, sometimes with other matter attached.

MALE.—Length 2.8 mm. Color and general structure as given for *unio*. Genitalia, fig. 473: ninth segment short and stocky, its dorsal portion cutting away nearly to base to receive the tenth tergite; tenth tergite with a rounded internal base shaped like an inverted scoop; apical portion of tergite divided into many parts, conspicuous among them being stylelike sclerites *B*, *C* and *D*, spurlike *A*, the stout, apical hook *H*, and the ventral lobe *V* which has a small preapical tooth; the entire structure is produced on each side into a sclerotized attachment stub which is anchored to the internal lateral portion of the ninth sternite; claspers sinuate, the base fairly wide, suddenly constricted near middle to form a broad shoulder bearing four dark spurs and an apical flaplike portion; aedeagus simple and filiform, typical for the genus.

FEMALE.—Similar to male in size, color and general structure. Genitalia, fig. 481: eighth sternite set off distinctly from structures of the ninth, its apical margin fairly heavily sclerotized and almost straight; the segment has an internal bell-shaped structure whose ventral surface is fenestrate with oblong and linear reticules; bursa copulatrix typical for the genus.

Holotype, male.—Utica, Illinois, Split Rock Brook: July 11, 1941, Ross & Ries.

Allotype, female.—Same data as for holotype.

Paratypes.—ILLINOIS: PORT BYRON: May 14, 1942, Ross & Burks, 2♂, 3♀.

This species is related to *confusa*, differing from it in the shorter apical process of the clasper, the much larger hook of the tenth tergite, shorter style *B*, and other details.

A colony of larvae of this peculiar species has been found, existing in a short stretch of the spring-fed brook at Split Rock, Utica, Illinois. Unique for the genus is the tortoise-shell-like case and the conspicuous, sclerotized plates on the tergites of the larvae. In genitalia the adults suggest nothing peculiar, very plainly being a derivative of the *spinosa* group. In this group the larvae

and cases are very similar to those of the primitive *unio* group.

Ochrotrichia confusa (Morton)

Ithytrichia confusa Morton (1905, p. 69); ♂.

Although known only from New York and Tennessee, this species may be found in Illinois with future collecting. The larva has not been discovered. The larva accredited to this species by Lloyd (1915a) was misidentified; it was *Leucotrichia pictipes*.

Oxyethira Eaton

Oxyethira Eaton (1873, p. 143). Genotype, here designated: *Hydroptila costalis* Curtis.
Loxotrichia Mosely (1937, p. 165). Genotype, by original designation: *Loxotrichia azteca* Mosely. New synonymy.
Dampfitrichia Mosely (1937, p. 169). Genotype, by original designation: *Dampfitrichia ulmeri* Mosely.

The species of this genus frequent a wide variety of situations, and many of them are very widely distributed geographically. We have taken only four species in Illinois, but it is likely that others will be found in future collecting. No characters have been found to separate the larvae to species.

KEY TO SPECIES

Adults

1. Apex of abdomen with various sclerotized rods and plates (males), fig. 485. 2
   Apex of abdomen cylindrical (females), fig. 494. 10
2. Eighth tergite with apico-lateral margins produced into long, serrate processes, fig. 485. . . . . . . **serrata**, p. 136
   Eighth tergite without apico-lateral processes, fig. 489. 3
3. Aedeagus divided at neck into two twisted, sclerotized filaments which cross each other near apex, fig. 486 . . . . **pallida**, p. 137
   Aedeagus not divided into twisted filaments. 4
4. Aedeagus with prominent spiral process at neck, figs. 487–489. 5
   Aedeagus with spiral process inconspicuous or absent, figs. 492, 493. . 7
5. Apex of eighth segment toothed and serrate; claspers projecting, upturned and bootlike, fig. 487. . . . . **coercens**, p. 137

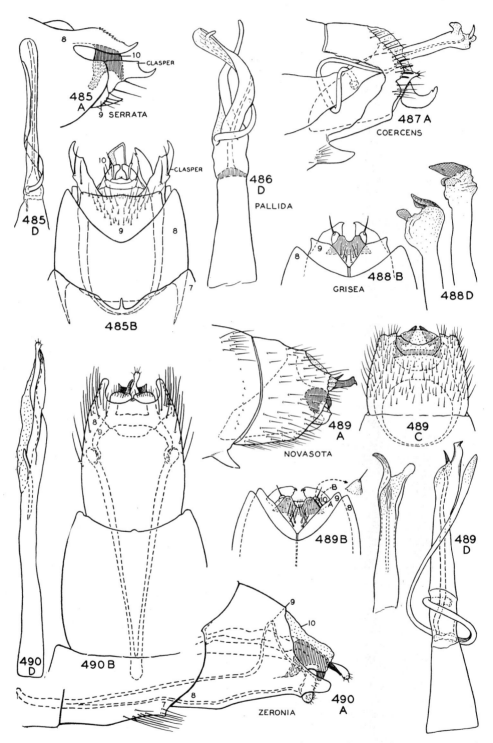

Figs. 485–490.—*Oxyethira*, male genitalia. *A*, lateral aspect; *B*, ventral aspect; *C*, dorsal aspect; *D*, aedeagus.

Apex of eighth segment only minutely serrate; claspers not projecting and upturned, fig. 489 6

6. Apex of aedeagus bulbous, with both apical processes smooth, the larger one short and stout; plate formed by claspers narrow, fig. 488 . . . .**grisea**, p. 138

Apex of aedeagus only slightly enlarged, with a long, smooth process and a round, platelike, serrate one; plate formed by claspers much wider, fig. 489 . . . .**novasota**, p. 138

7. Ninth sternite produced to form a long, narrow, ventral internal plate which is four or five times as long as

the posterior part of the segment, fig. 490 . . . .**zeronia**, p. 139

Ninth sternite not produced into such a long plate, the internal narrowed part never more than twice the length of posterior portion of segment, fig. 491 8

8. Aedeagus with a long, stout tooth just beyond neck, fig. 491 . . . .**verna**, p. 139

Aedeagus without a tooth; at most with a short, slender thread, fig. 492   9

9. Aedeagus with a neck, a weak, slender thread and a slender apex tipped with a small plate, fig. 492 . . . .**forcipata**, p. 139

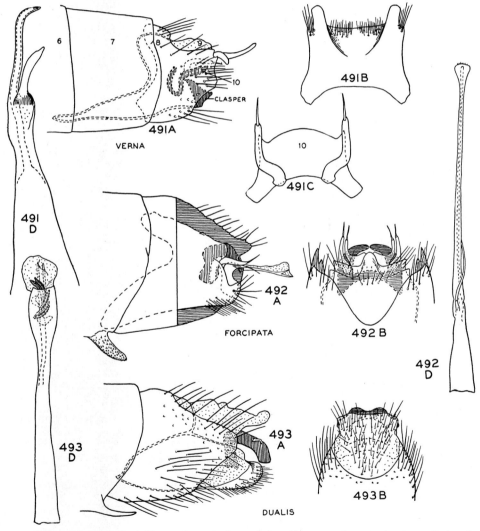

Figs. 491–493.—*Oxyethira*, male genitalia. *A*, lateral aspect; *B*, ventral aspect; *C*, dorsal aspect; *D*, aedeagus.

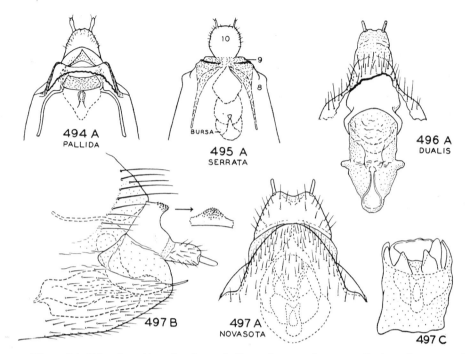

Figs. 494–497.—*Oxyethira*, female genitalia. *A*, ventral aspect; *B*, lateral aspect; *C*, bursa copulatrix.

Aedeagus with neither neck nor thread, with the tip enlarged and vasiform and containing an eversible group of 5–6 sclerotized spines, fig. 493... ....**dualis**, p. 139

10. Eighth sternite truncate, fig. 495, or emarginate, fig. 494.............. 11
    Eighth sternite produced into a rounded apex, fig. 497............ 12

11. Bursa copulatrix short, with a ventral, sclerotized bridge, fig. 494....... ....**pallida**, p. 137
    Bursa copulatrix elongate, without a sclerotized ventral bridge, fig. 495.. ....**serrata**, p. 136

12. Bursa copulatrix with a semisclerotized, large, vasiform base, fig. 496 ....**dualis**, p. 139
    Bursa copulatrix with base membranous and not vasiform, fig. 497.... ....**novasota**, p. 138

Oxyethira serrata Ross

Oxyethira serrata Ross (1938a, p. 117); ♂, ♀.

LARVA (mature type).—Length 3 mm. Head rounded. Middle and hind legs much more slender than front legs. Abdomen without dorsal sclerites and only slightly widened at middle, the segments not set off by constrictions.

CASE.—Fig. 498. Constructed of transparent, sheetlike material, without sand grains, narrow at end and tapering evenly to front, end slightly flattened.

ADULTS.—Length 2.5–3.0 mm. Color light and mottled. Wings tapered to a slender apex; hind wings slender. Tibial spur count 0-3-4. Ocelli present. Male genitalia, fig. 485: claspers elongate; tenth segment beaklike; aedeagus with a short base and elongate, cylindrical apex, with a ribbon-like spiral which apparently fuses with the apical portion; eighth segment with a pair of long, lateral processes which are serrate along the dorsal margin. Female genitalia, fig. 495: eighth sternite wide and slightly emarginate, ninth segment narrow and sclerotized, with a pair of long, internal rods; tenth segment nearly ovate; bursa copulatrix composed of three saclike lobes.

This species is apparently confined in Illinois to the glacial lakes in the northeastern corner of the state. The cases have been found in large numbers under stones in 2 or 3 feet of water along open beaches. Adult emergence seems confined to the earlier part

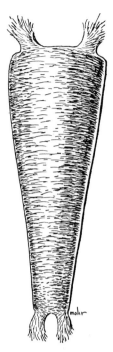

Fig. 498.—*Oxyethira serrata*, case.

of the year, from May to the middle of July; the number of generations per year has not been determined. In local areas around these lakes the species sometimes occurs in tremendous numbers, swarming around lights.

Little is known concerning the range of the species, with records available only from Illinois, New York and Wisconsin. All records, however, indicate a restriction to lakes and connecting channels.

Illinois Records.—ANTIOCH: July 7, 1932, Frison & Metcalf, 4♂, ♀♀. CHANNEL LAKE: May 27, 1936, H. H. Ross, ♂♂, 5♀. FOX LAKE: July 15, 1935, at light in town, DeLong & Ross, ♂♂, ♀♀; May 15, 1936, Ross & Mohr, ♂♂, ♀♀, many pupae, 2 larvae; May 28, 1936, H. H. Ross, ♂♂, 1♀; June 10, 1936, Ross & Burks, 1♀. JOHNSBURG, Fox River: May 28, 1936, H. H. Ross, ♂♂, ♀♀.

Oxyethira pallida (Banks)

Orthotrichia pallida Banks (1904*d*, p. 215); ♂.

Oxyethira viminalis Morton (1905, p. 71); ♂.

ADULTS.—Length 3 mm. Color a salt-and-pepper combination of cream and light brown, the general tone light. Male genitalia, fig. 486, with aedeagus split and curiously twisted. Female genitalia, fig. 494: eighth sternite produced into a wide, emarginate lobe which is sclerotized along the sides; tenth segment fairly long; ninth segment with very long and curved internal rods which extend below and to the side of the bursa copulatrix; bursa copulatrix short, with a ventral sclerotized bridge.

Allotype, female.—Wilmington, Illinois: Aug. 20, 1934, DeLong & Ross.

This species was first recorded from Illinois in the original description of *viminalis*, in which Morton recorded material from Lake Forest, collected October 15, 1902, by Professor Needham. We have since taken it in scattered localities in the northern half of the state. Adult emergence occurs throughout the warmer months of the year, from June to October. Our records indicate that the species frequents streams, lakes and artificial ponds. This is very likely the species which has been taken in large numbers as larvae by various fish in certain experimental lakes investigated by the Natural History Survey.

The distribution of the species apparently occupies most of the eastern and central part of the continent, with records available for the District of Columbia, Illinois, Nebraska, New York, Oklahoma, Texas, Virginia and Wisconsin.

Illinois Records.—COUNCIL HILL, Galena River: June 26, 1940, Mohr & Riegel, ♂♂, ♀♀. DOWNS, Kickapoo Creek: July 31, 1940, Ross & Riegel, 2♂. FOX LAKE: Sept. 22, 1931, Frison & Ross, 2♂; Oct. 4, 1931, Ross & Mohr, 1♂. KANKAKEE: July 21, 1935, Ross & Mohr, 1♂. LIVERPOOL: Oct. 7, 1931, T. H. Frison, 3♂, ♀♀. McHENRY: Oct. 4, 1931, Ross & Mohr, 1♂. MOMENCE: June 22, 1938, Ross & Burks, 1♂. PALOS PARK, Mud Lake: Aug. 3, 1938, Ross & Burks, 9♀. QUINCY, Burton Creek: June 25, 1940, Mohr & Riegel, 1♀. SPRING GROVE: Aug. 12, 1937, at light, Ross & Burks, 9♀. WHITE PINES FOREST STATE PARK: Aug. 13, 1937, Ross & Burks, ♂♂, ♀♀. WILMINGTON: Aug. 20, 1934, DeLong & Ross, 2♂, 8♀.

Oxyethira coercens Morton

Oxyethira coercens Morton (1905, p. 70); ♂.

ADULTS.—Length 3 mm. Color a salt-and-pepper mottling of cream and brown.

Male genitalia, fig. 487: eighth segment spiny at sides; claspers projecting and upturned at apex; aedeagus with a long, ribbon-like spiral and with apex knobbed and bearing a pair of sharp, short processes.

Our only records of this species in Illinois have been taken along the Kankakee River at Momence during May. Nothing is known regarding its biology.

Records of this species are very scattered but indicate an extensive range stretching from New York to Oklahoma, with records available for Indiana, New York and Oklahoma as well as Illinois.

Illinois Records.—MOMENCE, Kankakee River: May 17, 1937, Ross & Burks, 1 ♂ ; May 24, 1937, H. H. Ross, 1 ♂ .

Oxyethira novasota new species

MALE.—Length 3 mm. In color and general structure similar to the preceding, the diagnostic characters apparently confined to the male genitalia.

Genitalia as in fig. 489. Eighth segment very simple, without sclerotized processes, both dorsal and ventral margins of the apex circularly incised, the dorsal incision bearing membranous folds; there is a distinct angle where the dorsal margin and the lateral margin join. Ninth segment short; the venter with a wide, triangular emargination, the dorsum reduced to a narrow bridge. Tenth tergite somewhat inverted U-shaped, the base large and the apex pointed; the basal portion is bridgelike and the apex is divided into a pair of lobes appearing somewhat triangular, as viewed from above, and pointed mesad, not quite touching at apex, and armed at tip with a minute spine. Below the tenth tergite is a pair of semimembranous horns, each surmounted by a long seta. Below this are two plates, a short wide one with a slightly concave posterior margin and below that a longer one divided into a pair of rounded lobes separated by a rounded mesal incision, the ventral margin armed with a cluster of long setae. Aedeagus with a wide, tapered, tubelike basal portion; a sinuate, wide "neck" from which arises a long, stout spiral encircling the structure one and one-half times, proceeding as far toward the posterior as the remaining genitalia and ending in a clavate tip; and an apical tube which tapers from the base to the middle, then expands slightly, and is divided at the extreme apex into a sclerotized point and a semisclerotized lobe

which appears beaked from lateral view and ovate from dorsal view.

FEMALE.—Length 3.2 mm. Color and general structure as for male. Genitalia as in fig. 497. Eighth segment with tergite simple, bearing at apex an irregular row of long setae. Eighth sternite with its apical margin produced into a long, rounded projection which merges with the ninth sternite. Ninth tergite fairly heavily sclerotized, its baso-ventral angle produced into a long, internal rod, its baso-dorsal region produced into a rounded projection bearing a cushion of short, thick, black spines and its apex tapering to meet the tenth tergite. Tenth tergite appearing narrow from lateral view and wide and emarginate from ventral view with a pair of styles arising from each lateral hump. From the inner margin of the apex of the eighth arises a series of semimembranous folds which encircle the bursa copulatrix. This structure is irregular in shape, somewhat like a truncate cylinder, the posterior margin with a wide opening around the ventral margin from which arises a group of semisclerotized, irregular, toothlike lobes.

Holotype, male. — Marquez, Texas, along Novasota River: April 16, 1939, J. A. & H. H. Ross.

Allotype, female.—Same data as for holotype.

Paratypes.—TEXAS.—Same data as for holotype, 1 ♂ .

On the basis of genitalia, this species is most closely related to *grisea* from which it differs in the two-lobed apex of the aedeagus and other characters of the genitalia.

This species has not yet been taken in Illinois. The river along which it was collected in Texas is a sluggish, silty river much like some of the rivers of southern Illinois, and there is a good possibility that it may be found in Illinois with additional collecting.

Oxyethira grisea Betten

Oxyethira grisea Betten (1934, p. 162); ♂.

ADULTS.—Length 3 mm. Color a salt-and-pepper mottling of cream and brown. Male genitalia, fig. 488, similar in general features to those of the preceding species, differing chiefly in the apex of the aedeagus and smaller cleft of the fused claspers.

The holotype of this species may be lost. There seems little doubt, however, that our material is the species described by Betten. The coiled spiral of the aedeagus and the lobes of the aedeagus head indicate this; in Betten's illustration of the side view of the genitalia (1934, pl. 14, fig. 5), the apparent hook of the eighth segment is undoubtedly a silhouette of the hooklike tenth tergite.

We have only a single male from Illinois, collected along a small creek near Momence, June 22, 1938, Ross & Burks. The only other available records for the species are from Indiana and New York. It is probable that this species, like many others in the genus, has a wide but scattered range.

Oxyethira verna Ross

Oxyethira verna Ross (1938a, p. 118); ♂.

ADULTS.—Length 2.7 mm. Color a salt-and-pepper mixture of cream and brown, predominantly light. Male genitalia, fig. 491, with ninth segment produced internally into a long, ventral lobe; claspers fused on meson, tenth tergite somewhat platelike, with a pair of styliform appendages, and aedeagus simple, with a large tooth near base of apical portion.

To date we have only two Illinois records for this species, both of them in the extreme northeastern corner of the state. Nothing is known regarding the biology or habitat preference of the species. The only record outside of Illinois is from New Brunswick, indicating a wide but probably local range.

Illinois Records.—SPRING GROVE: June 12, 1936, Ross & Burks, 1 ♂. WILLOW SPRINGS: 2 ♂.

Oxyethira forcipata Mosely

Oxyethira forcipata Mosely (1934b, p. 153); ♂.

Not yet taken in Illinois. It occurs to the north and east, with records available for New York, Ontario, Virginia and Wisconsin.

Oxyethira zeronia Ross

Oxyethira zeronia Ross (1941a, p. 15); ♂.

ADULTS.—Length 2.5 mm. Color a salt-and-pepper combination of yellow and brown. Male genitalia, fig. 490: eighth segment produced into a pair of earlike apico-ventral lobes; ninth segment appearing tri-

angular from side view with a very long internal ventral projection which is narrow and pointed; claspers minute and biscuit-like; tenth tergite hooklike; aedeagus with a slender base, no distinct neck, the apical portion divided into two slender rods, one pointed, the other sinuate with a round apical knob.

Originally described from upper Michigan, this species has been identified since from only two localities in extreme northeastern Illinois. Nothing is known of its immature stages or general distribution.

Illinois Records.—RICHMOND: Aug. 15, 1936, Ross & Burks, 1 ♂. SPRING GROVE: Aug. 12, 1937, at light, Ross & Burks, 1 ♂.

Oxyethira dualis Morton

Oxyethira dualis Morton (1905, p. 71); ♂.

Not yet taken in Illinois. It is very widely distributed, occurring across the entire continent, but has not been taken many times. We have a record from Meramec Springs at St. James, Missouri, which is only a short distance from Illinois. Records are available for California, Missouri, New Mexico, New York, Texas and Virginia.

The female, which has not been described before, has the following diagnostic characters, fig. 496: eighth sternite tapering and produced at apex into a rounded lobe; tenth segment short and relatively wide; bursa copulatrix with a sclerotized, vasiform basal portion to which is attached an apical, membranous portion culminating in a somewhat lock-shaped ventral process.

Allotype, female.—Pecos River, Carlsbad, New Mexico: April 29, 1939, J. A. & H. H. Ross.

Orthotrichia Eaton

Orthotrichia Eaton (1873, p. 141). Genotype, here designated: *Hydroptila angustella* McLachlan.

Only two Nearctic species in this genus are known; both occur in Illinois. To date I have found no characters to separate these two in the larval stages.

KEY TO SPECIES

Adults

1. Apex of abdomen with platelike, conspicuous appendages, fig. 499 (males)   **2**

Apex of abdomen simple and tubular, without platelike or produced appendages, fig. 501 (females)...... 3

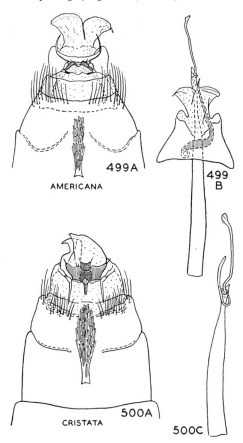

499A
AMERICANA
499 B

500A
CRISTATA
500C

Figs. 499–500.—*Orthotrichia*, male genitalia. *A*, ventral aspect; *B*, dorsal aspect; *C*, aedeagus.

2. Claspers wide, with a sharp, projecting, apico-lateral corner; plate back of claspers small and truncate, fig. 500 ....**cristata**, p. 141

Claspers narrow, converging, together forming a trapezoidal, dark block; plate back of claspers with a pair of long hornlike arms, each tipped with a long seta, fig. 499 ....**americana**, p. 140

3. Eighth sternite with median process not flared out at a wide angle toward base; this mesal portion of sclerite distinctly but not heavily sclerotized, fig. 502.........**cristata**, p. 141

Eighth sternite with median process flared out at a wide angle toward base; this mesal portion membranous, fig. 501.......**americana**, p. 140

Orthotrichia americana Banks

Orthotrichia americana Banks (1904*b*, p. 116); ♂, ♀.
Oxyethira dorsalis Banks (1904*d*, p. 216); ♀. New synonymy.
Orthotrichia brachiata Morton (1905, p. 70); ♂.

LARVA (mature type).—Length 4 mm. Head and thorax brown and robust. Front legs stocky, middle and hind legs very long, with tarsi elongate. Abdomen elliptical, widest near middle but not distended and with the segments not separated by constrictions.

CASE.—Modification of the purse type; composed of two equilateral halves, the case almost round in cross section, long and with the slits at each end visible from the ventral view only.

ADULTS.—Length 2.5–3.5 mm. Color mottled with a salt-and-pepper combination over the entire body, and with a pale stripe down meson when wings are folded. Seventh sternite of male with a mesal process covered with a brush of long scales. Male genitalia, fig. 499: ninth segment mostly membranous; tenth tergite forming a pair of long, wide membranous lobes; claspers small, fused to form a bifid plate; above these arise a pair of long horns, each bearing a long seta at tip; aedeagus very long, with a sclerotized, eversible penis; lying near and above aedeagus is a curved, sclerotized blade. Female genitalia, fig. 501: eighth sternite with a wide, membranous ventral area; bursa copulatrix nearly circular.

This species was recorded by Morton (types of *brachiata*) from Lake Forest, Illi-

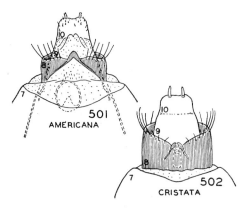

501
AMERICANA

10
9
7
502
CRISTATA

Figs. 501–502.—*Orthotrichia*, female genitalia.

nois. In our recent collecting we have taken the species at various points in the north-eastern part of the state and found the larvae frequenting ponds and lakes. Adult records extend from June 9 to August 15, probably indicating more than one generation per year.

Although collections are not common, the range of the species is wide, as shown by records from the District of Columbia, Illinois, Kentucky, Maryland, Minnesota, New York, Texas, Virginia.

Illinois Records.—ANTIOCH: Aug. 1, 1931, Frison, Betten & Ross, 1 ♂ ; July 7, 1932, at light in town, Frison & Metcalf, 2 ♂, 1 ♀. Fox LAKE: June 30, 1935, De-Long & Ross, 1 ♂, 1 ♀. PALOS PARK, Mud Lake: Aug. 3, 1938, Ross & Burks, ♂ ♂, ♀ ♀. RICHMOND: Aug. 15, 1938, Ross & Burks, 5 ♀. ROSECRANS, Des Plaines River: June 19, 1938, Ross & Burks, 2 ♂. SPRING GROVE: Aug. 12, 1937, at light, Ross & Burks, 3 ♂, 3 ♀ ; June 9, 1938, Mohr & Burks, 6 ♂, 6 ♀.

Orthotrichia cristata Morton

Orthotrichia cristata Morton (1905, p. 73); ♂.

LARVA.—Not differentiated from *americana*.

ADULTS.—Size and color as for *americana*. Seventh sternite with a mesal process bearing a large brush of long scales. Male genitalia, fig. 500: similar in general organization to *americana*; claspers larger, black and produced into lateral processes; process above, small, quadrate, with two small apical spines; no large, curved blade present. Female genitalia, fig. 502, with only a small, membranous mesal area.

Allotype, female. — Belton, Montana: July 10, 1940, at light, H. H. & J. A. Ross.

In Illinois we have taken this species in fewer numbers but in more widespread localities than *americana*, including localities along small streams, lakes and ponds. Adult emergence continues from June to August.

The range of the species is widespread, with records from British Columbia, Illinois, Michigan, Montana, Oklahoma, Tennessee, Texas.

Illinois Records.—ANTIOCH: at light in town, July 7, 1932, Frison & Metcalf, 1 ♀. Fox LAKE: June 30, 1935, DeLong & Ross, 1 ♂, 2 ♀. OAKWOOD, Salt Fork River: July 18, 1933, Ross & Mohr, 1 ♀. PALOS PARK, Mud Lake: Aug. 3, 1938, Ross & Burks,

1 ♂, 2 ♀. SPRING GROVE: at light, Aug. 12, 1937, Ross & Burks, 5 ♂, 5 ♀ ; June 9, 1938, Mohr & Burks, 6 ♂, 6 ♀. WHITE PINES FOREST STATE PARK: Aug. 13, 1937, Ross & Burks, 1 ♂.

Hydroptila Dalman

Hydroptila Dalman (1819, p. 125). Genotype, monobasic: *Hydroptila tineoides* Dalman.
Phrixocoma Eaton (1873, p. 132). Genotype, here designated: *Hydroptila sparsa* Curtis.

This genus embraces about 35 Nearctic species, comprising one-third of the Hydroptilidae. The habits of the various species are diverse. Several species have a known range covering most of the continent. Fourteen species have been taken in Illinois, nine of which we have reared. No structural differences have been found to separate the larvae to species, so that color has been the only guide to separation. This varies so much in some species, and is so similar in other species, that it seems impossible at present to make a key which would be accurate. Instead, a short diagnosis is presented drawing attention to the few characters so far discovered.

DIAGNOSIS OF LARVAE

1. Head yellowish or brown, without definite markings—paler specimens are usually **ajax**, darker specimens usually **angusta**, and nearly black specimens **consimilis**, fig. 503.

2. Head and pronotum pale yellow with scattered, small, dark spots as in fig. 504: **spatulata.**

3. Head and thoracic sclerites with a contrasting pattern as in fig. 505, the head always with a light, postero-mesal streak, the nota always with a pair of lateral, light areas: **albicornis.**

4. Head yellow, marked only with a pair of posterior dark bars, and each thoracic notum with a transverse dark bar in addition to that posterior margin, fig. 506: **armata.**

5. Head entirely yellow except for a wide, black V across top of frons, fig. 507; pronotum variable in color: **hamata.** In darker specimens the posterior portion of the head is darker and the black V-mark enlarges anteriorly to a pentagon.

6. Head yellowish, with both a wide posterior dark band and a V-shaped dark mark above frons, fig. 508; each thoracic notum with anterior portion and two vague lateral areas pale, intervening areas brownish: **grandiosa.** In darker specimens the V-mark enlarges to form a hollow diamond.

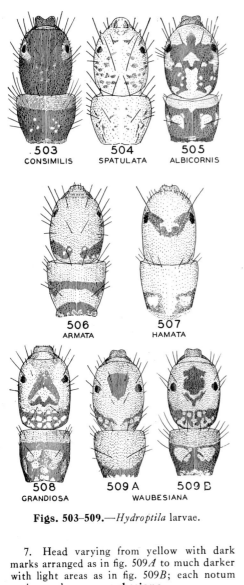

Figs. 503–509.—*Hydroptila* larvae.

7. Head varying from yellow with dark marks arranged as in fig. 509*A* to much darker with light areas as in fig. 509*B*; each notum varies as shown: **waubesiana.**

8. Head and pronotum almost entirely black, head with at most an indistinct light area between posterior and anterior dark dorsal areas: probably dark specimens of **hamata.**

KEY TO SPECIES

Adults

1. Apex of abdomen with complicated set of appendages, figs. 510–526 (males).......................... 2
   Apex of abdomen tubular and with simple parts, figs. 527–539 (females) 17

2. Seventh sternite with a long median process either expanded at apex, straight or sinuate, fig. 515....... 3
   Seventh sternite with a short, spur-like, median process, fig. 520...... 9

3. Tenth tergite with apex divided into a pair of long, stout, heavily sclerotized arms curved sharply mesad at apex, fig. 510............**xella,** p. 148
   Tenth tergite divided only into semi-membranous lobes................ 4

4. Eighth sternite with an apico-mesal, heavily sclerotized projection; median process of seventh sternite sinuate and suddenly narrowed at apex, fig. 511................**virgata,** p. 148
   Eighth sternite without a mesal projection; median process of seventh sternite expanded and flanged at apex, or of even thickness, figs. 512, 515............................ 5

5. Claspers short and beaklike, tenth tergite projecting beyond them, fig. 513............................ 6
   Claspers long and slender, as long as tenth tergite, figs. 514–516....... 7

6. Aedeagus with apex divided into a pair of very slender rods, one straight and the other sharply right-angled close to end, fig. 512......
   ....**hamata,** p. 149
   Aedeagus without one apical rod so sharply angled, at most as in fig. 513.................**amoena,** p. 150

7. Apex of aedeagus with a definite knob beyond lateral spur near tip, fig. 514
   ....**spatulata,** p. 148
   Apex of aedeagus with lateral spur at tip, figs. 515, 516................ 8

8. Tenth tergite with apex blunt and un-expanded, fig. 515.........**vala,** p. 148
   Tenth tergite with apex divided into a pair of laterally directed, sharp points, fig. 516.........**armata,** p. 147

9. Tenth tergite with apex divided into a pair of hornlike spikes directed laterad, fig. 517....**waubesiana,** p. 150
   Tenth tergite without such apical structures, fig. 518.............. 10

10. Tenth tergite with apex divided into a pair of lateral, slender, sinuate filaments curved under the apico-dorsal projections of the claspers, fig. 518
    ....**delineata,** p. 151
    Tenth tergite without such apical structures, figs. 519–525.......... 11

11. Eighth sternite with a row of 4 to 6 stout black spines at each apico-dorsal corner, fig. 519............
    ....**grandiosa,** p. 151
    Eighth sternite without stout black spines....................... 12

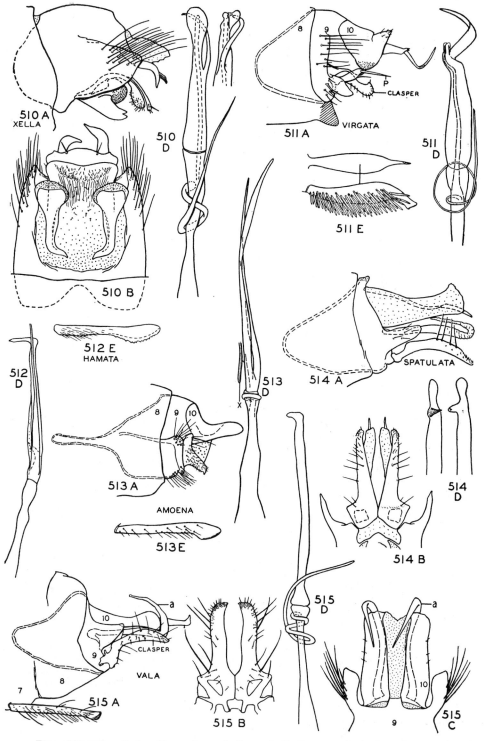

Figs. 510–515.—*Hydroptila*, male genitalia. *A, B, C,* respectively lateral, ventral and dorsal aspects; *D,* aedeagus; *E,* process of seventh sternite.

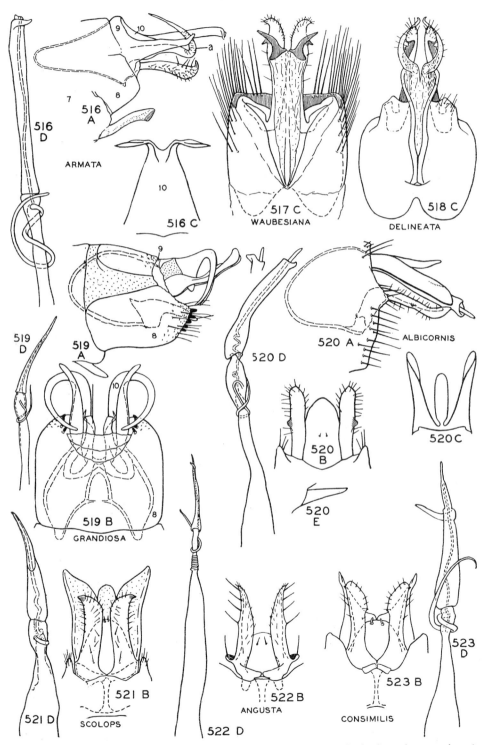

Figs. 516–523.—*Hydroptila*, male genitalia. *A, B, C,* respectively lateral, ventral and dorsal aspects; *D,* aedeagus; *E,* process of seventh sternite.

12. Claspers with dark sclerotized elevation near lateral margin midway between base and apex, fig. 520......
.................**albicornis**, p. 151
Claspers with dark sclerotized points only along mesal or apical margins, figs. 521–525................... 13

13. Spiral process of aedeagus short and slender, fig. 521.......**scolops**, p. 152
Spiral process of aedeagus long and stout, fig. 522.................. 14

14. Claspers saber shaped, pointed at apex, with a dark, sclerotized point beyond middle of mesal margin, figs. 522, 523.................. 15
Claspers with mesal margin concave and without sclerotized point, apex slightly curled latero-ventrad and bearing a sclerotized point at each corner, figs. 524, 525............. 16

15. Apical portion of aedeagus short and slender, its extreme apex with only a short curved process, fig. 522....
....................**angusta**, p. 152
Apical portion of aedeagus longer and stouter, its extreme apex with a long, stout process, fig. 523.......
..................**consimilis**, p. 153

16. Extreme apex of aedeagus bent at a right angle to form a narrow, sharp process, fig. 524; tenth tergite with a

sclerotized, clavate, mesal strip with the lateral areas membranous
.....................**perdita**, p. 153
Extreme apex of aedeagus straight, fig. 525; tenth tergite divided by membranous strips into a mesal and 2 lateral sclerotized fingers...**ajax**, p. 153

17. Apex of eighth sternite formed as in fig. 527, with a pair of sharp corners between which arises a truncate tongue bearing about 6 long, stout setae...................**xella**, p. 148
Apex of eighth tergite not formed as in fig. 527.......................... 18

18. Apex of eighth sternite with a pair of flat, ovate lobes, each bearing 3 long setae, fig. 528......**amoena**, p. 150
Apex of eighth sternite without a pair of flat, ovate lobes bearing 3 long setae.......................... 19

19. Eighth sternite bearing a pair of transverse, sclerotized bars below apex, fig. 529..........**hamata**, p. 149
Eighth sternite not bearing such a pair of bars..................... 20

20. Eighth sternite with a group of 6 long radiating hairs at apex, figs. 530, 532............................ 21
Eighth sternite without a group of 6 long radiating hairs at apex, figs. 533–539; hairs absent or short.... 24

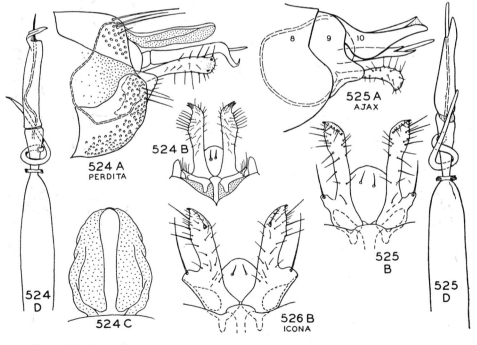

Figs. 524–526.—*Hydroptila*, male genitalia. *A, B, C,* respectively lateral, ventral and dorsal aspects; *D,* aedeagus.

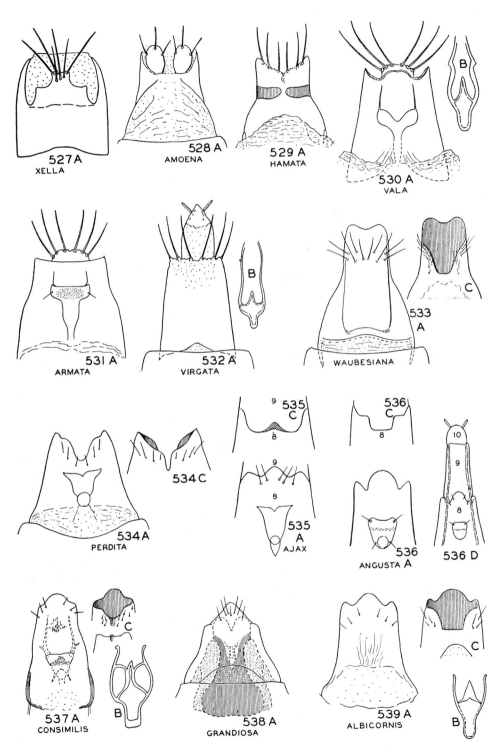

Figs. 527–539.—*Hydroptila*, female genitalia.   *A*, eighth sternite;   *B*, bursa copulatrix;   *C*, eighth tergite;   *D*, apex of abdomen.

21. Eighth sternite with a long, T- or Y-
    shaped area marked on middle,
    fig. 530   22
    Eighth sternite without central orna-
    mentation, fig. 532   23
22. Mesal sclerite of eighth sternite Y-
    shaped, without imbrications, fig.
    530 . . . .**vala**, p. 148
    Mesal sclerite of eighth sternite with
    posterior margin truncate and the
    wide portion imbricate, fig. 531 . . . .
    . . . .**armata**, p. 147
23. Eighth sternite with apical 6 setae
    situated on individual stalks along
    margin; tenth segment triangular,
    fig. 532 . . . .**virgata**, p. 148
    Eighth sternite with apical 6 setae
    clustered on a mesal lobe as in fig.
    531; tenth segment semicircular . . .
    . . . . .ʼ. . . . .**spatulata**, p. 148
24. Apex of eighth sternite produced into
    a long shield extending half the
    length of the segment beyond meson
    of tergite, fig. 533 . .**waubesiana**, p. 150
    Apex of eighth sternite not produced
    into a long shield   25
25. Surface of eighth sternite bearing a
    single mesal plate near middle, fig.
    534   26
    Surface of eighth sternite not bearing
    a mesal plate, fig. 539   29
26. Apex of eighth sternite incised on
    meson, fig. 534 . . . .**perdita**, p. 153
    Apex of eighth sternite produced on
    meson, fig. 535   27
27. Mesal plate of eighth sternite bell
    shaped, long and narrow, fig. 535 . .
    . . . .**ajax**, p. 153
    Mesal plate of eighth sternite trapezoi-
    dal, short and wide, figs. 536, 537 . .   28
28. Apex of eighth tergite with a narrow,
    straight-sided, straight-bottomed in-
    cision without a mesal thickening,
    fig. 536 . . . .**angusta**, p. 152
    Apex of eighth tergite with incision
    shallower, wider and with a mesal
    thickening, fig. 537 . .**consimilis**, p. 153
29. Eighth segment with a large, spatulate,
    internal plate, best seen from ven-
    tral aspect, fig. 538 . . .**grandiosa**, p. 151
    Eighth segment without a large in-
    ternal plate, fig. 539 . . . .
    . . . .**albicornis**, p. 151

Hydroptila armata Ross

Hydroptila armata Ross (1938a, p. 123); ♂,
♀.

Larva (mature type).—Fig. 506. Length
about 5 mm. Head yellow with an interrupted posterior band; each thoracic notum
yellow with a central and a posterior dark
band. Body, fig. 541, similar in shape and
general appearance to that of *Ochrotrichia*
except for key characters. Each segment of
abdomen with a very small, inconspicuous
rectangular sclerite, difficult to detect.

Case.—Shape as in fig. 465. Length about
5 mm. Purselike type, generally narrower
in cross section than *Ochrotrichia*, sometimes constructed of sand grains.

Adults.—Length 2–4 mm. (generally
quite variable within this genus). Color
a mottled, salt-and-pepper combination of
white, gray, brown and dark brown. Seventh sternite of male with a long, sinuate
process. Male genitalia, fig. 516: tenth tergite wide at base, tapering toward apex, and
divided at extreme apex into a pair of sharp
lobes directed laterad; beneath the tenth
arise a pair of long processes which pro-
ceed beyond the apex of the tenth tergite
and then curve back above it; claspers long,
extreme tip sclerotized and upturned; aedeagus with small neck, long spiral process, and
long, slender apex which is armed at tip
with a short arm at right angles to stem.
Female genitalia, fig. 531: eighth segment
short, semimembranous, with a T-shaped,
ventral, imbricated area, and with an apical
lobe bearing six long setae.

Association of males, females and larvae
was established by a collection of larvae and
mature pupae in Nippersink Creek at Spring
Grove, Illinois. In Illinois, as in other
states, the species has been taken only in
riffles of clear and moderately swift streams
of various sizes. The adults appear contin-
uously from May through September. They
are usually rare, but occasionally a fairly
large colony is found.

The range of the species, including Illinois, Indiana, Michigan, Oklahoma and
Wisconsin, seems to follow the western portion of the oak-hickory forest.

Illinois Records.—Fox Lake: July 15,
1935, DeLong & Ross, 2♂. Momence:
Aug. 21, 1936, Ross & Burks, 1♂ ; May
17, 1937, Ross & Burks, 1♂, 6♀ (reared);
May 24, 1937, H. H. Ross, 7♂ ; June 22,
1938, Ross & Burks, ♂ ♂. Oakwood, Salt
Fork River: Sept. 20, 1935, DeLong & Ross,
1♂. Spring Grove: Nippersink Creek,
May 14, 1936, Ross & Mohr, 1♂, 3♀
(reared), many larvae and pupae; June 12,
1936, Ross & Burks, 1♂. Wilmington:
July 1, 1935, DeLong & Ross, 2♂.

Hydroptila vala Ross

Hydroptila vala Ross (1938a, p. 123); ♂, ♀.

LARVA.—Unknown.

ADULTS.—In size and color similar to *armata*. Seventh sternite of male with a long, straight process. Male genitalia, fig. 515: tenth tergite divided into a pair of thick, rectangular lobes; beneath these arise a pair of long arms which curve back over the tergite; claspers with apical portion long and flattened, curved slightly mesad at tip; aedeagus with apical portion long, simple and sharply turned at tip, and with a long spiral. Female genitalia, fig. 530: eighth segment semimembranous; sternite with a central Y- or T-shaped structure without imbrications, and with an apical, detached plate bearing six long setae.

Originally described from Herod, Illinois, the species has since been collected at another locality near Herod and in the Kiamichi Mountains of Oklahoma.

Illinois Records.—EDDYVILLE, Lusk Creek: June 19–20, 1940, Mohr & Riegel, ♂ ♂. HEROD: May 29, 1935, Ross & Mohr, ♂ ♂, ♀ ♀.

Hydroptila xella Ross

Hydroptila xella Ross (1941b, p. 65); ♂, ♀.

Not yet taken in the state but perhaps to be expected in future collecting. The species is known only from south central Tennessee, where it occurred along a creek similar to several found in southern Illinois. Both sexes are readily identified by means of the genitalia; the larvae are unknown.

Hydroptila spatulata Morton

Hydroptila spatulata Morton (1905, p. 66); ♂.

LARVA.—Fig. 504. Head and body sclerites tawny yellow, head and pronotum with a scattering of small, dark spots.

ADULTS.—Size and color as for *armata*. Seventh sternite of male with a long, straight process, oblique at apex. Male genitalia, fig. 514: tenth tergite membranous, with a pair of sinuate, sclerotized rods running through it; beneath tenth tergite arise a pair of recurved, membranous processes, frequently difficult to see due to poor refraction; claspers spatulate; aedeagus very long

and slender, spiral small, tip provided with a lateral spur and beyond this spur a knob. Female genitalia without ventral ornament on eighth sternite, the apical setae of this sternite grouped on a semicircular lobe as in fig. 531.

Allotype, female.—Kankakee, Illinois: June 6, 1935, Ross & Mohr.

Our only abundant records in Illinois are along the Kankakee River. Here the larvae occur in the rapids, where we have collected mature pupae. Other records are from the Oakwood region. Adult records extend from June to late in August, indicating successive summer generations.

The range of the species extends throughout the Northeast; definite records are available for Illinois, Indiana, Michigan, New York, Quebec, Wisconsin.

Illinois Records. — DANVILLE, Middle Fork River: Aug. 27, 1936, Ross & Burks, 3 larvae. KANKAKEE: Kankakee River, Aug. 1, 1933, Ross & Mohr, 4 ♂, 1 ♀, many larvae, 2 pupae; June 6, 1935, Ross & Mohr, ♂ ♂, 6 ♀. MOMENCE: July 14, 1936, B. D. Burks, 1 larva; strip mines, Aug. 21, 1936, Ross & Burks, ♂ ♂, many larvae and pupae; Kankakee River, Aug. 24, 1936, Ross & Burks, 4 ♂ ; May 17, 1937, Ross & Burks, many larvae; Kankakee River, May 24, 1937, H. H. Ross, ♂ ♂ ; at light, June 24, 1939, Burks & Ayars, 1 ♂. MORRIS: Aug. 22, 1938, H. H. Ross, ♂ ♂, ♀ ♀. OAKWOOD: Salt Fork River, July 18, 1933, Ross & Mohr, 2 ♂, 3 ♀ ; Middle Fork, Vermilion River, July 18, 1933, Ross & Mohr, 1 ♂ ; May 21, 1936, Mohr & Burks, 1 ♂. PUTNAM, Lake Senachwine: July 11, 1933, C. O. Mohr, 4 ♂. WILMINGTON: July 1, 1934, DeLong & Ross, 4 ♂ ; Aug. 20, 1934, DeLong & Ross, 4 ♂, 16 ♀ ; Kankakee River, May 27, 1935, Ross & Mohr, 1 ♂, many larvae and pupae; Kankakee River, June 6, 1935, Ross & Mohr, ♂ ♂ ; July 1, 1935, DeLong & Ross, ♂ ♂.

Hydroptila virgata Ross

Hydroptila virgata Ross (1938a, p. 125); ♂, ♀.

LARVA.—Unknown.

ADULTS.—Size and color as for *armata*. Seventh sternite of male with mesal process sinuate and abruptly narrowed at tip. Eighth sternite of male with apico-mesal portion forming a heavily sclerotized, rudder-like projection. Male genitalia, fig. 511:

tenth tergite pointed and conical; claspers short and sinuate; near base of each clasper arises a short style tipped with a long seta, *P*; aedeagus with long, slender spiral and a sickle-like hook at tip. Female genitalia, fig. 532: eighth segment cylindrical, almost membranous, without ventral ornament; its apical margin straight, the ventral margin bearing six evenly spaced setae, each situated on an individual stalk; bursa copulatrix with end short and robust. Tenth segment triangular, unique in the genus.

In Illinois this species is restricted to the Ozark Hills where it has been collected along the streams peculiar to that region (see p. 6). The seasonal appearance of the adults is distinctly vernal, as indicated by records not only for Illinois but for all other states from which the species is known. Although the adults have been taken in large numbers, no larvae have yet been discovered.

The known distribution records are scanty, including only Arkansas, Illinois and Oklahoma, but indicate a restriction to the Ozarks and nearby mountains.

Illinois Records.—Eddyville, Lusk Creek: June 1, 1940, B. D. Burks, 6 ♂, 6 ♀. Eichorn, Hicks Branch: May 29, 1935, Ross & Mohr, 1 ♂. Herod: May 10, 1935, C. O. Mohr, 1 ♂; May 29, 1935, Ross & Mohr, ♂ ♂, ♀ ♀; May 13, 1937, Frison & Ross, ♂ ♂.

Hydroptila hamata Morton

Hydroptila hamata Morton (1905, p. 67); ♂, ♀.

Larva.—Fig. 507. Color variable. Light extreme has head yellow, with black V across top of frons, and pronotum mostly yellow; darker individuals have head with a dusky posterior band and a black pentagonal central area, and pronotum dark with pale anterior margin.

Adults.—Fig. 540. Size and color as for *armata*, except for the femora, which are dark brown or black (they are tawny in other members of the genus). Seventh sternite of male with a long mesal process expanded at apex and flared laterad, the flared edges serrate. Male genitalia, fig. 512: ninth segment with long, finger-like internal arms; tenth tergite simple; claspers short, with a beaked ventral portion and a finger-like, style-bearing, dorso-lateral portion; aedeagus very long, the apical portion divided

into a long, slender filament and a long rod bent sharply at apex. Female genitalia, fig. 529: eighth sternite with six apical setae along incised apical margin, and with a pair of transverse sclerotized bands near middle.

Although we have collections of this species from many widely scattered localities in the state, it must be classed as a rarity

Fig. 540.—*Hydroptila hamata* ♂.

for Illinois. It occurs in some of our northeastern glacial lakes and in clear rivers and streams in various other localities, but is almost always collected in very small numbers. We have associated larvae and adults on the basis of mature pupae from Channel Lake and Lusk Creek. The adults appear from spring to late summer.

The species ranges throughout most of the mountainous and predominantly hilly country from southern Mexico to at least Washington in the west and to New York and Ontario in the east. It is frequently abundant in such areas as the Ozarks and hilly parts of Oklahoma. Records are available from Arizona, Arkansas, Illinois, Indiana, Kentucky, Michigan, Missouri, New Mexico, New York, North Carolina, Oklahoma, Ontario, Oregon, Pennsylvania, Texas, Virginia, Washington, Wyoming, Mexico.

Illinois Records.—Channel Lake: May

16, 1936, Ross & Mohr, 4♂, 1♀. DAN-
VILLE, Middle Fork River: Aug. 27, 1936,
Ross & Burks, 2 larvae. EDDYVILLE, Lusk
Creek: June 19–20, 1940, Mohr & Riegel,
5♂, 5♀, 1 pupa. ELIZABETHTOWN: June
25, 1932, Ross, Dozier & Park, 1♂. Fox
LAKE: June 30, 1935, DeLong & Ross,
1♀. HARRISBURG: June 15, 1934, DeLong
& Ross, at light, 1♂. HEROD: June 20,
1940, Mohr & Riegel, 1♂. HOMER: Aug.
5, 1931, H. H. Ross, 1♂. MOMENCE: Aug.
21, 1936, Ross & Burks, 1♂. OTTAWA:
July 3, 1937, at light, Werner, 1♂.

Hydroptila amoena Ross

Hydroptila amoena Ross (1938a, p. 124); ♂.

LARVA.—Unknown.
ADULTS.—Size and color as for *armata*.
Seventh sternite of male with a long mesal
process which is curved ventrad and slightly
indented at apex, the apical margin slightly
rounded and neither flanged nor serrate.
Invaginated lateral portion of ninth segment long and narrow. Male genitalia, fig.
513: tenth tergite narrow and projecting;
claspers short, with a wide base and narrow
apex, slightly beaked at tip; aedeagus with
very short spiral wound tightly around the
short neck, the apical portion long and
divided almost to base to form long processes. Female genitalia, fig. 528: eighth
sternite tapering and semimembranous, with
a pair of ovate lobes at apex, each bearing
three long setae.
Allotype, female.—Broken Bow, Oklahoma, along small creek near town: June
8, 1940, Mrs. Roy Weddle.
Our only records for this species are collections of males from Herod, Illinois, and
Turner Falls State Park, Oklahoma (the
type series) and a subsequent collection of
both sexes from Broken Bow, Oklahoma.
Presumably this species is a spring form
inhabiting small streams in the Ozarks and
neighboring ranges.
Illinois Records.—HEROD: May 29, 1935
Ross & Mohr, 1♂; Gibbons Creek, April
19, 1937, Ross & Mohr, 1♂.

Hydroptila waubesiana Betten

Hydroptila waubesiana Betten (1934, p. 160);
♂, ♀.

LARVA.—Figs. 509, 541. Color extremely
variable. Light extreme has head and tho-

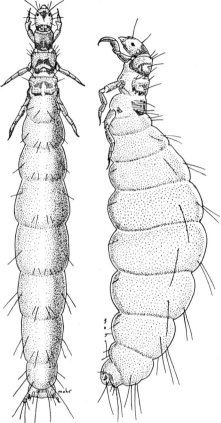

Fig. 541.—*Hydroptila waubesiana* larva.
Dorsal aspect, left; lateral aspect, right.

racic terga yellow with small black marks
as in fig. 509*A*; dark extreme has head mostly black with thoracic terga having large
dark areas.
ADULTS.—Size and color as for *armata*.
Male genitalia, fig. 517: ninth segment almost entirely retracted within eighth; tenth
tergite divided into a pair of long processes,
closely appressed and with apexes pointed
laterad, truncate and sclerotized; claspers
long, slender and hooked at apex, reaching
beyond apex of tenth tergite; aedeagus
simple, rodlike. Female genitalia, fig. 533:
eighth segment sclerotized, the ventral portion produced into a long, tonguelike flap
which is emarginate at tip, tergite deeply
incised on meson.
Interesting among the habits of this species is its ability to thrive in both lakes and
streams. In Illinois it occurs over the entire

state; in the northeastern portion it inhabits the glacial lakes and over the remainder it inhabits a variety of clear streams and large rivers. We have collections of larvae and mature pupae from Fox Lake and from Quiver Creek near Havana. Adult emergence occurs from April through October.

In addition to Illinois, the species is known from Indiana, Michigan, Ohio, Ontario, Saskatchewan and Wisconsin.

Illinois Records.—Many males, females and pupae, taken April 29 to October 5, and many larvae, taken April 25 to May 29, are from Amboy, Antioch, Council Hill, Fox Lake, Galena, Grand Tower, Havana, Kankakee, La Rue, Mahomet, McHenry, Momence, Palos Park, Pere Marquette State Park, Quincy, Richmond, Spring Grove, White Pines Forest State Park, Wolf Lake.

Hydroptila delineata Morton

Hydroptila delineatus Morton (1905, p. 66); ♂.

Not yet taken in Illinois; it is known from Indiana, New York and Nova Scotia. Only the male is known, readily distinguished by the genitalia, fig. 518.

Hydroptila grandiosa Ross

Hydroptila grandiosa Ross (1938a, p. 126); ♂.

Larva.—Fig. 508. Head tawny yellow with dark posterior band and a dark V across top of frons, this V sometimes closed in front to form a dark, hollow diamond; each thoracic tergum with an anterior light margin and a pair of lateral light areas outlined by a darker background.

Adults.—Size and color as for *armata*. Male genitalia, fig. 519: eighth sternite large and scoop shaped, bearing four to six black, peglike setae on each lateral margin; ninth segment small and retracted within eighth; tenth tergite divided into a pair of large, sclerotized hooks broad at base and sharp at tip; below these arise a pair of long, sinuate rods around which the hooks curl; claspers small, short and truncate; aedeagus short, with a slender spiral and tapered apex. Female genitalia, fig. 538: eighth segment short, wide at base and narrowing rapidly toward apex; sternite without external plates but with apex produced

into a triangle set with short setae; internal skeleton large and conspicuous, dark and expanding anteriorly.

Allotype, female. — Oakwood, Illinois, along Salt Fork River: July 18, 1933, Ross & Mohr.

To date this species has been taken only in the northern half of Illinois, in clear rivers and small, permanent streams. In only one or two cases have more than a few specimens been taken at one time. The adults emerge over the entire summer, our records including May through September. Larvae and both sexes of the adults were associated by collections of larvae and pupae from the Sinsinawa River near Galena, and from the Apple River.

Known from Illinois, Indiana, Missouri, Oklahoma and Wisconsin, the species has a range that seems to follow the better streams of the western oak-hickory forest, much as with *armata*.

Illinois Records.—Amboy, Green River: July 7, 1939, Mohr & Riegel, 2♀. Apple River Canyon State Park: Aug. 23, 1939, Ross & Riegel, 1♂ ; Apple River, May 24, 1940, H. H. Ross, many larvae and pupae. Danville, Middle Fork River: Aug. 27, 1936, Ross & Burks, 1♂, 1 pupa, 4 larvae. Galena: May 23, 1940, H. H. Ross, 2♂, 3♀, many pupae and larvae. Momence: May 17, 1937, Ross & Burks, 7♂ ; Kankakee River, May 24, 1937, H. H. Ross, 2♂. Muncie: June 27, 1932, H. H. Ross, 1♀. Oakwood: Salt Fork River, July 18, 1933, Ross & Mohr, 2♀ ; Salt Fork River, July 18, 1933, Ross & Mohr, 2♂, 2♀ ; Salt Fork River, Sept. 20, 1935, DeLong & Ross, 1♂ ; May 21, 1936, Mohr & Burks, 1 pupa. Richmond: Aug. 15, 1938, Ross & Burks, 1♀. Rock City: June 6, 1940, Mohr & Burks, 1♂. Sugar Grove: June 13, 1939, Frison & Ross, 1♂, 2♀.

Hydroptila albicornis Hagen

Hydroptila albicornis Hagen (1861, p. 275); ♂.

Larva.—Fig. 505. Head patterned with pale yellow and dark brown, always with a postero-mesal pale streak; each thoracic notum dark brown with anterior margin and a pair of lateral areas pale.

Adults.—Male, fig. 520: tenth tergite divided into a mesal and a pair of lateral semimembranous lobes, each narrow. Claspers as long as tenth tergite, slender, situated some distance apart; the mesal margin is nearly straight, the apex is rounded and curved slightly dorsad, and near the lateral margin is a sclerotized point midway between base and apex. Above the claspers is a round plate bearing a pair of small setae near the middle. Aedeagus with spiral slender, neck large, and tip of apical portion with a short lateral projection. Female, fig. 539: eighth segment semisclerotized, tubular, without internal plates or external ornamentation; tergite with a flat-bottomed mesal depression; sternite with meson produced into a rounded lobe.

Allotype, female.—Kankakee, Illinois: July 22, 1935, at light, DeLong & Ross.

As pointed out in the lectotype designation (Ross 1938c, p. 9), the type is in reality a male, although the original description notes it as a female.

Our only Illinois records for this species are from various points along the Kankakee River (see p. 6). Here it is abundant; we have taken larvae and pupae from the river at Momence and Kankakee. Records for the species are widespread but not numerous, including Illinois, Indiana, Missouri, Ontario and Wisconsin. All specimens were taken along large, swift, clear rivers, including the St. Lawrence, Kankakee, White (in Indiana), Gasconade and White (in Missouri), and Namekagon (in Wisconsin). The adults emerge throughout the warmer months (May through September).

Records given under the name *albicornis* by Betten (1934) probably refer to some other species; the illustrations indicate *hamata*.

Illinois Records.—KANKAKEE: Kankakee River, Aug. 1, 1933, Ross & Mohr, many larvae; July 22, 1935, DeLong & Ross, 1 ♂, 1 ♀. MOMENCE: July 14, 1936, B. D. Burks, many pupae and larvae; Aug. 21, 1936, Ross & Burks, ♂ ♂, many pupae and larvae; Kankakee River, Aug. 24, 1936, Ross & Burks, 1 ♂ ; May 17, 1937, Ross & Burks, 5 ♂, many pupae and larvae; Kankakee River, May 24, 1937, H. H. Ross, ♂ ♂. WILMINGTON: Aug. 20, 1934, DeLong & Ross, 3 ♀ ; Kankakee River, May 17, 1937, Ross & Burks, 2 ♂.

Hydroptila scolops Ross

Hydroptila scolops Ross (1938a, p. 128); ♂.

LARVA.—Unknown.

ADULTS.—Size and color as for *armata*.

Male genitalia, fig. 521: tenth tergite membranous, divided into two large lateral lobes and a small mesal lobe; claspers fairly long and straight, with an apico-lateral sclerotized point and only small setae; aedeagus short, basal portion flared, neck distinct, spiral small and apical portion large at base, tapering gradually to a pointed tip. Female unknown.

This species is known only from the holotype, collected along the Ohio River at Shawneetown, Illinois, May 11, 1935, at light, C. O. Mohr.

Hydroptila angusta Ross

Hydroptila angusta Ross (1938a, p. 130); ♂, ♀.

LARVA.—Head and thoracic sclerites varying from tawny yellow to fairly dark brown, the color fairly uniform over the entire area and not forming a pattern.

ADULTS.—Male, fig. 522: tenth tergite wide, divided down meson by a deep, angular cleft, with only lateral margins sclerotized. Claspers with a wide "foot," the upper portion bladelike; blade with a small, sclerotized point on mesal margin beyond middle, with a row of irregular setae on lateral margin and with tip pointed. The rounded plate above the claspers bears a pair of short setae near apex. Aedeagus very long, with an imbricated portion below neck, a narrow neck, a long, stout spiral and a long, slender apical portion which has a sinuate, small finger at tip. Female, fig. 536: eighth segment semimembranous, tapering; apex of tergite with a truncate incision; sternite with somewhat stocky, mesal plate near middle and with a mesal, tongue-like projection at apex.

Association of larvae and adults was established by collections of larvae and pupae from the Middle Fork River near Danville, and from other localities.

In Illinois the species has been collected from widespread localities. It prefers moderate-sized to large streams and rivers, and is frequently encountered in large numbers. The adults emerge over a wide span; we have records from May 1 to October 16.

The range of the species extends from the arid plains of western Texas and eastern New Mexico to Ohio, with records from Illinois, Indiana, Missouri, New Mexico, Ohio, Oklahoma and Texas.

Illinois Records.—Many males, females

and two pupae, taken May 1 to October 16, and many larvae, taken August 1 to August 27, are from Amboy, Charleston, Danville, Galena, Homer, Kankakee, Mahomet, Milan, Momence, Morris, Mount Carroll, Muncie, Oakwood, Ottawa, Putnam, Richmond, Rock City, Rock Island, Serena, Spring Grove, Sugar Grove, Wilmington.

Hydroptila consimilis Morton

Hydroptila consimilis Morton (1905, p. 65); ♂.

LARVA.—Fig. 503. Head and thoracic nota mostly black; head sometimes with a narrow pale area between posterior and anterior dark areas; thoracic nota with anterior margin pale.

ADULTS.—Male, fig. 523: similar in most structures to the preceding species, but differing as follows: claspers wider, rounder at apex; the apex of the aedeagus robust and shorter, with a long, finger-like, lateral process at tip. Female, fig. 537: eighth segment semimembranous, tapering; tergite with a wide, shallow incision at apex, the bottom of the incision with a sclerotized, mesal thickening; sternite with a somewhat trapezoidal mesal ornament and a rounded, mesal projection.

Allotype, female.—Utica, Illinois, Split Rock Brook: July 11, 1941, Ross & Ries.

Although taken several times, this species must be classed as a rarity in Illinois. We have taken it in numbers only in two peculiar and restricted situations, at Elgin and Split Rock (Utica). Other records are from clear, permanent streams, most of them in the northern quarter of the state. All our records are in June and July, but records for other states indicate that the adults emerge from April to September.

The range of the species is extensive and seems to cover all the mountainous and much of the heavily wooded areas from Texas to British Columbia in one direction and New York in the other. Records are available from Arizona, British Columbia, Illinois, New York, Oklahoma, Oregon, Tennessee, Texas, Utah, Virginia and Wyoming.

Illinois Records.—Many males, females and eight pupae taken June 5 to August 15, and five larvae taken May 23 to June 6, are from Apple River Canyon State Park, Council Hill (Galena River), Dixon, Elgin (Rainbow Springs), Galena, Mount Carroll, Muncie, Oakwood (Middle Fork Vermilion River), Utica (Split Rock Brook), White Pines Forest State Park.

Hydroptila perdita Morton

Hydroptila perdita Morton (1905, p. 67); ♂.

LARVA.—Unknown.

ADULTS.—Male, fig. 524: tenth tergite large, somewhat hood shaped, almost entirely membranous except for a mesal, clavate sclerotized strip. Claspers with a distinct foot, the blade long, slightly out-curved at apex, and with a dark, sclerotized point at each apical angle. Aedeagus with a stout spiral and with the tip of the apical portion bent to form a sharp, right-angled process. Female, fig. 534: eighth segment wide at base and semimembranous; tergite with sloping apex and a narrow mesal incision; sternite with sinuate apical margin and a wide, rounded incision; near the center of the sternite is a bell-shaped plate.

Allotype, female.—Washington County, Arkansas: June 19, 1940, M. W. Sanderson.

To date we have only two records of this species for Illinois, from the Kankakee and Salt Fork rivers, both on the extreme eastern edge of the state. These, together with other localities, indicate a preference for large, clear, rapid streams, with adult emergence from May to October.

Available records are from Arkansas, Illinois, Michigan, New York, Ontario and Pennsylvania.

Illinois Records.—MOMENCE, Kankakee River: May 24, 1937, H. H. Ross, 1 ♂. OAKWOOD, Salt Fork River: July 18, 1933, Ross & Mohr, 1 ♀. SPRING GROVE: Aug. 12, 1937, at light, Ross & Burks, 3 ♂.

Hydroptila ajax Ross

Hydroptila ajax Ross (1938a, p. 127); ♂, ♀.

LARVA.—Head and thoracic sclerites tawny yellow, varying somewhat in exact shade but not forming a pattern.

ADULTS.—Size and color as for *armata*. Male genitalia, fig. 525: tenth tergite hoodlike, divided by membranous darts into a mesal and pair of lateral lobes; claspers having a distinct foot and a fairly long, narrow blade with the apex outcurved and a sclerotized point on each apical corner;

aedeagus large, with a large spiral and the apical portion straight at tip. Female genitalia, fig. 535: eighth tergite with apex widely and deeply emarginate and with a sclerotized nodule at base of depression; sternite with a long, bell-shaped central plate and with the apical margin undulate to form a pair of low, lateral humps and a higher mesal projection.

The species *icona*, described from Mexico and since taken in Texas and Oklahoma, might be confused with this species, but *icona* differs radically in having short claspers, fig. 526.

This is one of the more common Illinois species of the genus, having been taken in large numbers in a considerable variety of creeks and small rivers in the northern half of the state. Larvae and pupae have been collected in several localities. The adults appear throughout the warmer months, from May through September.

The range of the species extends from Oklahoma to New York, with Illinois as the apparent density center. We have records for Illinois, Indiana, New York and Oklahoma.

Illinois Records.—Many males and females and four pupae, taken May 24 to September 20, and many larvae, taken May 21 to June 6, are from Amboy (Green River), Apple River Canyon State Park, Downs (Kickapoo Creek), Howardsville, Kappa (Mackinaw River), Mount Carroll, Muncie, Oakwood (Middle Fork, Vermilion River, Salt Fork River), Quincy (stream near Cave Spring, Burton Creek), Rock City, Serena, Spring Grove, White Pines Forest State Park.

Neotrichia Morton

Cyllene Chambers (1873, p. 124); preoccupied. Genotype, monobasic: *Cyllene minutisimella* Chambers.

Neotrichia Morton (1905, p. 72). Genotype, monobasic: *Neotrichia collata* Morton.

Exitrichia Mosely (1937, p. 170). Genotype, by original designation: *Exitrichia anahua* Mosely.

Dolotrichia Mosely (1937, p. 177). Genotype, by original designation: *Dolotrichia canixa* Mosely.

Guerrotrichia Mosely (1937, p. 179). Genotype, by original designation: *Guerrotrichia caxima* Mosely.

Lorotrichia Mosely (1937, p. 181). Genotype, by original designation: *Lorotrichia hiaspa* Mosely.

This genus contains the smallest caddis flies in North America. Of the 11 species known from the United States, 6 have been captured in Illinois. All the species frequent clear-water streams, and some of them are extremely local in their distribution. The genus has developed a large fauna in the Neotropical region, which seems to be the center of distribution for many "micros" that range from southern Mexico to Oklahoma, Illinois and New York.

Characters of the genitalia separate the species in both males and females, but, to date, reliable characters have not been found for separating the larvae. We have associated larvae and adults of *minutisimella, okopa, collata* and *riegeli.*

KEY TO SPECIES

Adults

1. Apex of abdomen with several sets of plates or processes (males)........   2
   Apex of abdomen simple and tubular (females)......................   9

2. Ninth segment with outer lateral process *B* divided to form long dorsal and ventral fingers; plate *E* behind claspers twice as long as claspers, fig. 542.................**kitae**, p. 158
   Ninth segment with outer lateral process simple; plate behind claspers short or inconspicuous, figs. 543–549............................   3

3. Aedeagus with a pair of stout, sclerotized hooks, figs. 543–545..........   4
   Aedeagus without stout, sclerotized hooks, figs. 546–549..............   6

4. Claspers slender, almost three times longer than wide, fig. 543........ ....**collata**, p. 159
   Claspers almost quadrate, no longer than wide, fig. 544..............   5

5. Aedeagus with both sclerotized hooks subequal and alike; apex of claspers with a steplike break, fig. 544..... ....**falca**, p. 159
   Aedeagus with sclerotized hooks very dissimilar in length and shape; apex of claspers truncate, fig. 545.. ....**riegeli**, p. 159

6. Aedeagus ending in a uniform, sclerotized cylinder; claspers heavily sclerotized and black, fig. 546..... ....**okopa**, p. 158
   Aedeagus not cylindrical or sclerotized at apex; claspers not as above, fig. 547........................   7

7. Claspers fused to form a long ventral

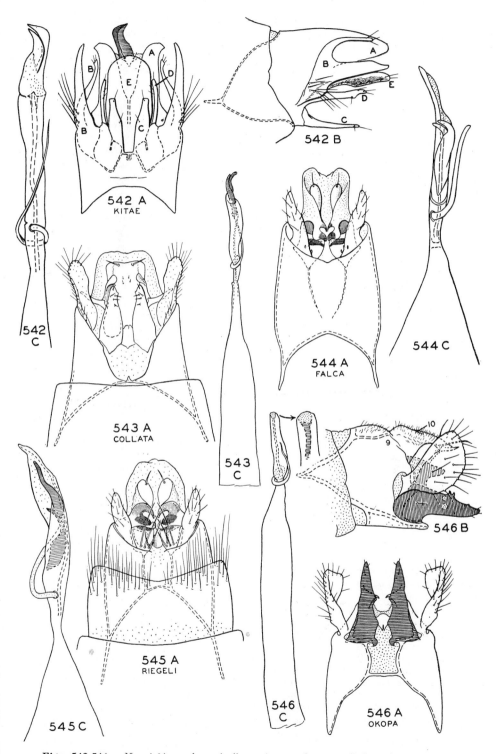

Figs. 542-546.—*Neotrichia*, male genitalia.   *A*, ventral aspect; *B*, lateral aspect; *C*, aedeagus, the basal portion omitted in 542.

plate covered with long setae and narrowed and upturned at apex, fig. 547............**minutisimella,** p. 157
Claspers not forming a plate, figs. 548, 549.............................. 8

10. Sclerotized plate of eighth sternite narrow and angular, fig. 550 ....
.....................**edalis,** p. 158
Sclerotized plate of eighth sternite wide and arcuate, figs. 551, 552... 11

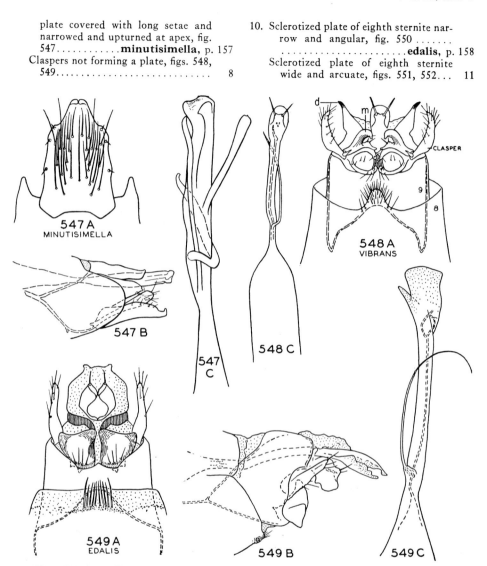

Figs. 547-549.—*Neotrichia*, male genitalia. *A*, ventral aspect; *B*, lateral aspect; *C*, aedeagus, the basal portion omitted in 547 and 548.

8. Apex of aedeagus flattened and elliptic, with a pair of long, apical setae; apex of tenth tergite divided into a pair of divergent, pointed, sclerotized lobes, fig. 548.....**vibrans,** p. 159
Apex of aedeagus flattened, but with a membranous "thumb" instead of setae; tenth tergite entirely membranous, fig. 549........**edalis,** p. 158

9. Eighth sternite with a heavily sclerotized, arcuate or angular plate, figs. 550, 551....................... 10
Eighth sternite without a sclerotized plate, fig. 553.................... 12

11. Sclerotized plate of eighth sternite evenly arcuate along apical margin, fig. 551.................**riegeli,** p. 159
Sclerotized plate of eighth sternite with a mesal emargination, fig. 552
.......................**falca,** p. 159

12. Eighth sternite with a large mesal body, angulate at apex, occupying a full third of the width of the segment, fig. 553...........**kitae,** p. 158
Eighth sternite with mesal body either much smaller, fig. 556, or of a different shape, fig. 554; note also differences in bursa copulatrix..... 13

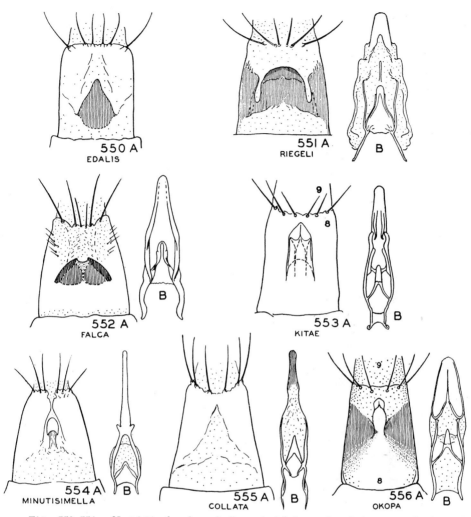

Figs. 550–556.—*Neotrichia*, female genitalia.   *A*, eighth sternite; *B*, bursa copulatrix.

13. Apex of bursa copulatrix forming a
    long, narrow, tapered rod, figs. 554,
    555................................. 14
    Apex of bursa copulatrix forming a
    wide, bilobed structure, fig. 556... 15
14. Median portion of bursa copulatrix
    with a pair of sclerotized projections
    at base of apical rod, fig. 554......
    .... **minutisimella,** p. 157
    Median portion of bursa copulatrix en-
    tirely membranous, without pro-
    jections, fig. 555 .... **collata,** p. 159
15. Eighth sternite sclerotized and dark-
    ened to form a distinct V, fig. 556..
    .... **okopa,** p. 158
    Eighth sternite slightly sclerotized but
    not darkened; without an evident
    V-shaped pattern....... **vibrans,** p. 159

Neotrichia minutisimella (Chambers)

Cyllene minutisimella Chambers (1873, p. 125); ♂.

LARVA (mature type).—In general shape similar to fig. 557. Length 2 mm. Head somewhat cone shaped, narrowed toward front. Legs short but slender. Abdomen abruptly enlarged at juncture of thorax, the second segment slightly the widest and the abdomen tapering almost evenly from that point to the end; lateral margins with a delicate, small fringe of hair. Anal hooks situated on short, stubby but distinct "legs."

CASE.—Short and elliptic, tapered at the base without a bottom opening; composed of sand grains woven into an even, fairly smooth surface. Top opening closed for pupation by an irregular silky layer.

ADULTS. — Length 1.5–2.0 mm. Color strawlike, wings with only indistinct markings. Male genitalia, fig. 547: tenth tergite large, bilobed and submembranous; ventral plate (probably consisting of the fused claspers) large, clothed with long setae and narrowed and upturned at apex; aedeagus with a large spiral process at neck, the apical portion submembranous with one or two accessory finger-like lobes. Female genitalia, fig. 554: eighth sternite practically colorless, divided down meson by membranous incision which flares out at the base; within this area at the base arises an ovate structure with rounded apex and membranous base; bursa copulatrix with long, slender, apical style and a pair of horns at its base.

Allotype, female.—Kankakee, Illinois: July 22, 1935, at light, DeLong & Ross.

No record of this species, the smallest known caddis fly in North America, has been published since its original description from Covington, Kentucky. It is the commonest species of the genus in Illinois, especially abundant in the upper Sangamon River, where we have reared it, and has been taken also from the Kankakee River and a few small streams.

The species is known to range through Missouri, Oklahoma, Illinois, Indiana and Kentucky.

Illinois Records.—KAMPSVILLE: July 2, 1931, Frison, Betten & Ross, 1 ♂. KANKAKEE: Kankakee River, Aug. 1, 1933, Ross & Mohr, 1 ♂; July 22, 1935, at light, DeLong & Ross, 2 ♂, 1 ♀. MAHOMET, Sangamon River: June 6, 1940, Ross & Riegel, 2 pupae. OAKWOOD, Middle Fork River: Sept. 7, 1936, DeLong & Ross, 1 ♀. QUINCY, Burton Creek: June 25, 1940, Mohr & Riegel, 1 ♀. URBANA: Aug. 3, 1931, light trap, W. P. Flint, 7 ♂. WHITE HEATH: Aug. 2, 1940, Ross & Riegel, 1 ♀.

Neotrichia okopa Ross

Neotrichia okopa Ross (1939b, p. 629); ♂, ♀.

ADULTS.—Length 2 mm. Body and appendages dark brown, the wings mottled. Male genitalia, fig. 546: tenth tergite membranous with a mesal lobe, a pair of long setae and a pair of lateral extensions; beneath it are a pair of sclerotized processes;

lateral appendages spatulate; aedeagus with a very long, cylindrical, basal portion, narrow neck with a prominent spiral process and the apical portion more or less cylindrical and heavily sclerotized. Female genitalia, fig. 556: eighth sternite with sclerotized portions forming a dark V; above the base of the V is a small, rounded structure the base of which is divided into two lobes; bursa copulatrix as in fig. 556B.

This species, not previously recorded from Illinois, has been taken at only widely separated localities in the state. It was especially abundant in Lusk Creek in the Ozark Hills, where it was reared in company with *collata* and *riegeli*. Its known range includes scattered localities in Illinois, Ohio, Oklahoma and Pennsylvania. Our collecting in Illinois indicates its preference for small, clear streams.

Illinois Records.—APPLE RIVER CANYON STATE PARK: Aug. 23, 1939, Ross & Riegel, 1 ♂. COUNCIL HILL, Galena River: June 26, 1940, Mohr & Riegel, 1 ♂, many pupae. EDDYVILLE, Lusk Creek: June 19–20, 1940, Mohr & Riegel, ♂ ♂, ♀ ♀. MOMENCE: June 22, 1938, Ross & Burks, 8 ♂. UTICA, Split Rock Brook: June 17, 1941, Burks & Riegel, ♂ ♂, ♀ ♀. WHITE PINES FOREST STATE PARK: Aug. 13, 1937, Ross & Burks, 1 ♂, ♀ ♀. WILMINGTON: July 1, 1935, DeLong & Ross, 1 ♀.

Neotrichia kitae Ross

Neotrichia kitae Ross (1941b, p. 60); ♂, ♀.

To date this species has not been taken in Illinois. It is known only from Hollister, Missouri. This species resembles the others of the genus in general size and shape, but is readily distinguished on the basis of genitalia, figs. 542, 553.

Neotrichia edalis Ross

Neotrichia edalis Ross (1941b, p. 62); ♂, ♀.

Although not yet taken in Illinois, this species frequents streams in eastern Oklahoma which are very similar to some in southern and western Illinois and may possibly be taken in the state in the future. The genitalia of both sexes, figs. 549, 550, are diagnostic for the species; the triangular subgenital plate of the female eighth sternite is unusual in the genus and distinctive.

Neotrichia vibrans Ross

Neotrichia vibrans Ross (1938a, p. 119); ♂.

ADULTS.—Length 2 mm. Body and appendages mottled with black, brown and whitish. Male genitalia, fig. 548: eighth sternite with an apico-mesal lobe; genitalia with claspers small, curved and hooklike, arising from a platelike, basal sclerite; tenth tergite produced into a pair of widely divergent pointed lobes; lateral appendages long and fusiform; aedeagus with a broad base, very narrow neck bearing a long, slightly curved, spiral process, and a long, narrow apical portion which has its tip enlarged and ovate, and bears a pair of prominent setae. Female genitalia similar to those of *okopa* in structure of eighth segment and bursa copulatrix; differing in lacking dark coloration so that the sternite has no distinct pattern.

Allotype, female.—Hollister, Missouri: July 14, 1938, Mrs. Vitae Kite.

Originally described from a single male from Oakwood, Illinois, this species has since been collected in large numbers at Hollister, Missouri. The Illinois records indicate a preference for small, clear streams. Little can be said regarding the range of the species.

Illinois Records.—MUNCIE: June 27, 1932, H. H. Ross, 1♀. OAKWOOD, Middle Fork River: Sept. 7, 1936, DeLong & Ross, 1♂.

Neotrichia falca Ross

Neotrichia falca Ross (1938a, p. 119); ♂.

ADULTS.—Length 2.5 mm. Color a salt-and-pepper mixture of cream and brown. Male genitalia, fig. 544: tenth tergite membranous; cerci long, slightly sinuate and with sparse setae; claspers short, the apical margin steplike and with two black, sclerotized cushions; above them membranous folds end in a pair of blunt black lobes and a pair of small black hooks; above these are a pair of ovate membranous lobes tipped by a seta; aedeagus with flared base, a long finger-like lobe rising from neck and a slender, curved apical portion with two teeth which are almost superimposed one over the other. Female genitalia, fig. 552: eighth sternite with a central sclerite with arcuate apical margin and a minute incision at tip; bursa copulatrix as in fig. 552B.

Allotype, female.—Quincy, Illinois, stream near Cave Spring: July 6, 1939, Mohr & Riegel.

We have taken this species in scattered localities in the northern two-thirds of the state, in every case along a small and fairly clear stream. Adult emergence is continuous throughout the warmer months, with records from June through most of September. No collections are known outside Illinois.

Illinois Records.—COUNCIL HILL, Galena River: June 26, 1940, Mohr & Riegel, 1♂. MOMENCE: June 22, 1938, Ross & Burks, ♂ ♂, ♀ ♀. MUNCIE, Stony Creek: Sept. 20, 1935, Frison & Mohr, 1♂. QUINCY: stream near Cave Spring, July 6, 1939, Mohr & Riegel, ♂ ♂, ♀ ♀; Burton Creek, June 25, 1940, Mohr & Riegel, 1♀. SUGAR GROVE: June 13, 1939, Frison & Ross, 1♂. WHITE PINES FOREST STATE PARK: Aug. 13, 1937, Ross & Burks, 4♀.

Neotrichia riegeli Ross

Neotrichia riegeli Ross (1941b, p. 61); ♂, ♀.

ADULTS.—Length 2.0–2.5 mm. Straw colored, with irregular light brown marks on body and wings. Male genitalia, fig. 545: similar in general structure to *falca*; claspers short, nearly quadrate, with a dense black area at apex; above, the black hooks are large with a black cushion at base; aedeagus with sclerotized hooks set one beyond the other. Female genitalia, fig. 551: eighth sternite with a large, sclerotized mesal lobe with the arcuate apical margin thickened; bursa copulatrix as in fig. 551B.

This species is known only from the type series, containing a large collection of males and females, from Lusk Creek near Eddyville, Illinois, June 19–20, Mohr & Riegel. Mature pupae also were collected here, linking larval and adult forms. This set was taken in company with *collata* and *okopa*.

Neotrichia collata Morton

Neotrichia collata Morton (1905, p. 72); ♂, ♀.

ADULTS.—Size 2.0–2.5 mm. Color mottled brown and tawny. Male genitalia, fig. 543: tenth tergite membranous; cerci fairly long; claspers long and tapering, with a small mesal tooth at apex; above it is a rectangular plate with a pair of apical setae; aedeagus very long, neck long and narrow, spiral long, apex with a pair of appressed sclerotized hooks. Female genitalia, fig. 555: eighth sternite without central ornamentation; bursa copulatrix with an elongate, tenpin-like process.

Our only Illinois record of this species is a large collection of males, females and pupae from Lusk Creek near Eddyville, June 19–20, 1940, Mohr & Riegel. These were taken in company with *okopa* and *riegeli*. Lusk Creek is a clear, rapid stream in the Ozark Hills of southern Illinois.

The only available records are from Illinois, Kentucky and New York.

Mayatrichia Mosely

Mayatrichia Mosely (1937, p. 182). Genotype, by original designation: *Mayatrichia ayama* Mosely.

This genus contains three North American species, of which only one, *ayama*, has been taken in Illinois. The other two are known from Oklahoma and Texas. The three species are readily distinguished on the basis of male genitalia, but differences between the females have not yet been worked out. A key to the males, followed by descriptions of the out-of-state species, is given on p. 278.

Mayatrichia ayama Mosely

Mayatrichia ayama Mosely (1937, p. 182); ♂.

LARVA (mature type).—Fig. 557. Length 2 mm. Head and body sclerites cream colored with only a few slightly darker lines around the edges of some sclerites; body white. Similar in general to *Neotrichia*, with cone-shaped head and slender legs. Abdomen wedge shaped, with lateral contours very even and possessing lateral fringe, similar in this respect to the Leptoceridae.

LARVA (free-living young form).—Fig. 557. Similar to mature type but with abdomen small and tapering, all segments partially sclerotized and provided with stout setae. Anal legs close together at base, fig. 552, claws as in mature form.

CASE.—Fig. 558. Somewhat wedge shaped, fibrous, ventral surface flat, dorsal surface convex, raised into either longitudinal ridges, transverse ridges, or sometimes a combination of both. Posterior end closed; anterior

end sealed for pupation by a circular, brown, membranous cap.

ADULTS.—Length 2–3 mm. Color brown without conspicuous markings. Sixth segment with a long, slender spine, fig. 559. Male genitalia, fig. 929, p. 279; ninth seg-

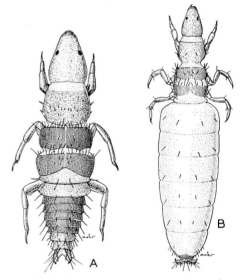

Fig. 557.—*Mayatrichia ayama. A*, free living, early instar; *B*, case making, later instar.

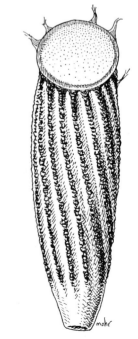

Fig. 558.—*Mayatrichia ayama*, case.

ment with a large, clasper-like lobe on the postero-lateral margin, this lobe with the apical margin rounded dorsally and tapering to a somewhat pointed ventral corner; tenth tergite membranous and somewhat hood shaped; claspers with a broad base, a small, finger-like dorso-lateral projection and a wide ventro-mesal lobe the apical margin of which is rounded and which bears four to six setae; above the claspers is a

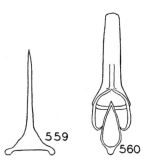

Fig. 559.—*Mayatrichia ayama* ♂, spine of sixth sternite.
Fig. 560.—*Mayatrichia ayama* ♀, bursa copulatrix.

stout, wide lobe with a long, sharp ventral beaked apex; aedeagus long, slender and simple, the extreme apex divided into a three-pronged sclerotized plate. Female genitalia simple and tubular, with bursa copulatrix large and shaped as in fig. 560.

This species is the one described by Betten (1934, p. 164) as an undetermined genus and species.

In Illinois, we have taken the species commonly in the northern fourth of the state and have, in addition, a record from southern Illinois. We have taken the larvae and pupae abundantly in the riffles of the Galena River at Council Hill, Illinois, thus associating the larvae, males and females; we have made similar collections in the Kankakee River at Momence. This species has a distinct preference for the more rapid and clear Illinois rivers and streams. Adult emergence extends from June to early September, indicating a continuous cycle of generations.

The range of the species extends from extreme southern Mexico to New York and Montana; most of the records follow fairly closely the confines of the deciduous forests, ranging through Texas into Florida and more northern eastern states; in the northwestern states our only record is from Mon-

tana. Although the records are scattered over a wide area, the species is quite rare and not commonly taken. We have records from Florida, Georgia, Illinois, Iowa, Kentucky, Missouri, Montana, New York, Oklahoma, Pennsylvania, Tennessee and Texas.

Illinois Records.—Many males, females and pupae, taken June 21 to September 10, and many larvae, taken June 6 to August 21, are from Amboy (Green River), Apple River Canyon State Park, Council Hill (Galena River), Dixon, Elizabethtown, Kankakee, Momence, Oregon, Ottawa, Rock Island, Serena.

PHRYGANEIDAE

In this family the maxillary palpi are four segmented in the male, five in the female. The larvae construct cases which in most genera are long and built in a spiral. Characteristic of the larvae are their membranous meso- and metanotum, each with a lateral tuft of long setae; in addition, the lateral gills are covered with hair, and the lateral line of the abdomen is represented by a fairly wide area of short hair.

The generic limitations in this family have previously been established on the basis of wing venation and vestiture. Both of these characters, however, vary so much in some genera that it is impractical to use these as a basis for generic differentiation in this family. The best characters for this purpose seem to be the female genitalia, which present some striking evidences of both differentiation and affinities, and the generic groupings outlined here are based on these characters.

The genus *Neuronia* Leach, used commonly in the past as a caddis fly genus of this family, apparently belongs to the Plecoptera, with *Phryganea fusca* Linnaeus as the type.

In general, the family favors marshes and lakes for its abode, but some species are taken in rivers and streams.

KEY TO GENERA

Larvae

1. Frons with a median black line, fig. 561.................................... 2
   Frons without a median black line, fig. 564.......................... 3
2. Pronotum with anterior margin black,

fig. 561, and without a diagonal black line..........**Phryganea**, p. 174

Pronotum with a diagonal black line, fig. 562, anterior margin mostly yellow.........**Banksiola selina**, p. 169; **Agrypnia straminea**, p. 165

3. Mesonotum with a pair of small sclerites near anterior margin, fig. 563   4

Mesonotum without a pair of sclerites, sometimes with a very small sclerotized area around the base of 1 seta, fig. 564..................   5

4. Mature larvae attaining length of 30 mm...............**Eubasilissa**, p. 168

Mature larvae attaining length of only 20 mm.......**Oligostomis**, p. 167

5. Pronotum with anterior margin black, fig. 564, and without a diagonal black line.....**Agrypnia vestita**, p. 166

Pronotum with a diagonal black line, fig. 565, anterior margin mostly yellow.........................   6

6. Diagonal marks on pronotum meeting at posterior margin to form a V-mark, fig. 566...................
.........**Phryganeid Genus A**, p. 167

Diagonal marks on pronotum not reaching posterior margin but join-

561

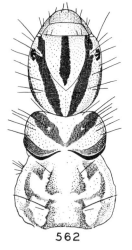

562

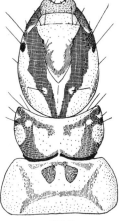

563

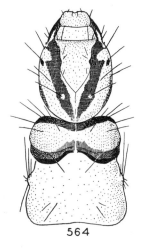

564

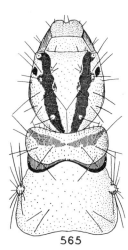

565

566

Larvae of Phryganeidae

Fig. 561.—*Phryganea* sp.
Fig. 562.—*Banksiola selina.*
Fig. 563.—*Oligostomis ocelligera.* (After Lloyd.)

Fig. 564.—*Agrypnia vestita.*
Fig. 565.—*Ptilostomis ocellifera.*
Fig. 566.—*Phryganeid Genus A.*

ing each other on meson to form an arcuate mark, fig. 565............
................**Ptilostomis**, p. 171

Pupae

1. Mandibles short and fleshy, sometimes with a small mesal point but without an apical blade, much shorter than labrum, fig. 567...... 2
   Mandibles long, with a sclerotized apical blade, figs. 568, 569........ 5

2. Apical processes of abdomen long and not widely separated, fig. 570.....
   ....**Banksiola**, p. 169
   Apical processes of abdomen short and their apical points very widely separated, fig. 571................. 3

3. Posterior plate of fifth tergite with 6 teeth forming one row, fig. 574; apical projection of first tergite elongate, membranous and truncate.....**Phryganeid Genus A**, p. 167
   Posterior plate of fifth tergite with

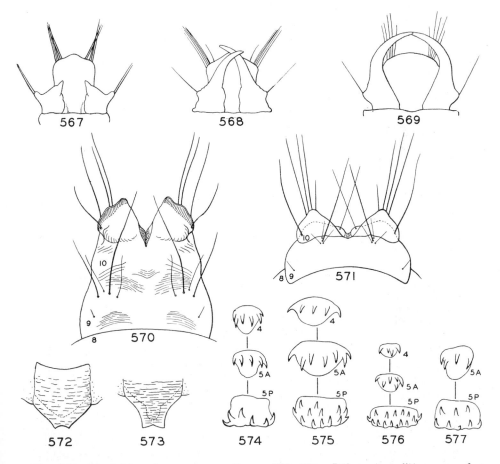

Fig. 567.—*Banksiola selina* pupa, mandibles and labrum.

Fig. 568.—*Agrypnia vestita* pupa, mandibles and labrum.

Fig. 569.—*Phryganea sayi* pupa, mandibles and labrum.

Fig. 570.—*Banksiola selina* pupa, apex of abdomen.

Fig. 571.—*Phryganeid Genus A* pupa, apex of abdomen.

Fig. 572.—*Ptilostomis ocellifera* pupa, first tergite.

Fig. 573.—*Eubasilissa pardalis* pupa, first tergite. (After Lloyd.)

Fig. 574.—*Phryganeid Genus A* pupa, hook bearing abdominal plates.

Fig. 575.—*Ptilostomis ocellifera* pupa, hook bearing abdominal plates.

Fig. 576.—*Phryganea sayi* pupa, hook bearing abdominal plates.

Fig. 577.—*Agrypnia vestita* pupa, hook bearing abdominal plates.

10–12 teeth forming two rows, fig. 575; apical projection of first tergite bifid, figs. 572, 573..............   4

4. Apical projection of first tergite only moderately produced, the apex wide, fig. 572......**Ptilostomis**, p. 171
Apical projection of first tergite forming a long structure with a narrow apex, fig. 573......**Eubasilissa**, p. 168

5. Mandibles greatly curved and sickle shaped, fig. 569; fourth tergite with a normal sized, hook-bearing, sclerotized plate, fig. 576, which nearly equals size of anterior plate on fifth tergite.............**Phryganea**, p. 174
Mandibles only slightly curved, fig. 568; fourth tergite with hook-bearing plate absent or not more than half size of anterior plate on fifth tergite, fig. 577......**Agrypnia**, p. 165

Adults

1. Maxillary palpi 4-segmented, fig. 64; genitalia with an aedeagus, figs. 580, 594 (males)......................   2
Maxillary palpi 5-segmented; genitalia without an aedeagus, figs. 582, 598 (females)......................   8

2. Ninth sternite produced as a toothed shelf beyond the bases of the claspers, fig. 594........**Ptilostomis**, p. 171
Ninth sternite not shelflike, figs. 580, 585............................   3

3. Claspers produced posterad into a short, slightly upturned point, but rounded and low dorsad, appearing spoon shaped from the side and biscuit shaped from below, figs. 603, 604..............**Phryganea**, p. 174
Claspers produced dorsad into either a long process or into appendage-like blades, figs. 580, 585.........   4

4. Tenth tergite forming two long, black, sclerotized rods, fig. 590; ninth sternite with a pair of sharp points, fig. 590. Hind wings banded with black and dark yellow, fig. 588........
.................**Eubasilissa**, p. 168
Tenth tergite not rodlike; ninth sternite sometimes with 1 mesal point but not 2. Hind wings not so banded......................   5

5. Hind wings almost entirely black, fig. 587.............**Oligostomis**, p. 167
Hind wings with only black spots or markings on a gray or clear ground color..........................   6

6. Ninth tergite forming a transverse, somewhat hood-shaped area arising above base of tenth tergite and bearing a brush or pair of brushes of

long setae, figs. 580, 581.........
....................**Agrypnia**, p. 165
Ninth tergite continuous with outline of tenth tergite and usually not bearing a brush of long setae......   7

7. Middle tibiae thorny, the black spines sticking out prominently and about as long as the tibia is thick; wings shiny with a conspicuous pattern of black markings, fig. 591..........
.................**Banksiola**, p. 169

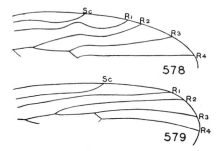

Fig. 578.—*Banksiola selina*, front wing.
Fig. 579.—*Ptilostomis semifasciata*, front wing.

Middle tibiae not appearing thorny, the black spines not sticking out prominently, shorter than the tibia is thick; wings dull, tawny brown and with only a faint, fine, irrorate pattern...............**Fabria**, p. 166

8. Ninth sternite divided at apex into three long processes, which are stout and close together, figs. 589, 605............................   9
Ninth sternite either not divided into three points or these very short, figs. 586, 601....................   10

9. Both wings checkered with black and orange, the hind wings black at base with two bands at apex, fig. 588; ninth sternite with apical processes shorter and converging, fig. 589...
.................**Eubasilissa**, p. 168
Neither pair of wings with orange, the hind wings pale at least at base; ninth sternite with apical processes longer and divergent, fig. 605.....
.................**Phryganea**, p. 174

10. Ninth sternite forming an extremely wide, flat, emarginate plate, fig. 584*C*.................**Fabria**, p. 166
Ninth sternite not forming such a plate, figs. 582, 593..............   11

11. Ninth sternite with a semimembranous apical lobe set off by a constricted neck, fig. 582..**Agrypnia**, p. 165
Ninth sternite not produced into such a lobe, figs. 586, 593..............   12

12. Ninth sternite almost triangular, tapering evenly to a narrow apex, fig. 586..............**Oligostomis**, p. 167
Ninth sternite wide at apex, figs. 593, 601............................ 13
13. R₁ markedly sinuate in both front and hind wings, fig. 578..............
...................**Banksiola**, p. 169
R₁ nearly straight in both front and hind wings, fig. 579............
...................**Ptilostomis**, p. 171

Agrypnia Curtis

Agrypnia Curtis (1835a, p. 540). Genotype, monobasic: *Agrypnia pagetana* Curtis.
Agrypnetes McLachlan (1876, p. ii). Genotype, monobasic: *Agrypnetes crassicornis* McLachlan.
Dasystegia Wallengren (1880, p. 73). Genotype, by subsequent designation of Milne (1934, p. 7): *Phryganea obsoleta* Hagen.
Phryganomyia Banks (1907a, p. 122). Genotype, by original designation: *Asynarchus alascensis* Banks.
Prophryganea Martynov (1924, p. 210). Genotype, by original designation: *Prophryganea principalis* Martynov.
Jyrvia Milne (1934, p. 3). Genotype, by original designation: *Neuronia vestita* Walker.

The size, color, wing venation and vestiture all vary through a wide range in this genus, but the curious ninth sternite of the female, fig. 582, and the structure of the male genitalia leave no doubt but that this forms a compact generic unit well differentiated from the rest of the family.

Only two species of the genus have been taken in Illinois. A third occurs in Wisconsin, and the remaining seven or eight occur to the north. Several of these occur through the subarctic regions of Alaska and Canada.

KEY TO SPECIES

1. Wings almost uniformly tawny, at most with a few brownish streaks in the forewing........**straminea**, p. 165
Front wings with a definite pattern of brown and gray; hind wings clear with an apical band of dark brown
....................**vestita**, p. 166

Agrypnia straminea Hagen

Agrypnia straminea Hagen (1873, p. 425); ♂.
Agrypnetes curvata Banks (1900a, p. 252); ♂.
Phryganomyia obscura Banks (1907a, p. 122); ♂.

LARVA.—Not reared in Illinois. A specimen determined as this species by Elkins, loaned through the courtesy of Professor C. E. Mickel, University of Minnesota, appears identical with our specimens of *Banksiola selina* (see p. 169).

ADULTS.—Length 14 mm. Head, body and appendages almost uniformly yellowish brown, the front wings with a few slightly darker streaks and with a very fine and faint pattern of irrorations. Legs with only a scattering of short, tawny spines. Male genitalia, fig. 580: ninth segment with a pair of slightly projecting lateral areas, each bearing a brush of long setae; tenth tergite almost hemicylindrical; claspers with a large

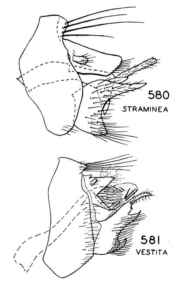

Figs. 580–581.—*Agrypnia*, male genitalia.

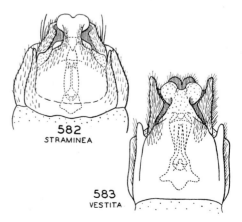
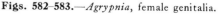

Figs. 582–583.—*Agrypnia*, female genitalia.

base, tapering dorsally to a narrow apex divided into two sharp points and bearing a bladelike apical segment which extends between and beyond these two points. Female genitalia, fig. 582, with ninth sternite constricted at apex and then expanded into a wide, semimembranous orbicular lobe.

Dr. Betten (1934) has recorded this species in an insect drift along Lake Michigan at Lake Forest, Illinois. This catch was made by Professor Needham on August 12, and constitutes the only known record for the state. The species was reared by Elkins (1936) from Minnesota.

The range of the species is widespread through the northern states and Canada from Alaska to Quebec, with records available for Alaska, Colorado, Illinois, Manitoba, Michigan, Minnesota, Quebec, Saskatchewan and Wisconsin.

Agrypnia vestita (Walker)

Neuronia vestita Walker (1852, p. 10); ♂, ♀.
Neuronia commixta Walker (1852, p. 10); ♂.

LARVA.—Fig. 564. Length 25 mm. Head, pronotum and legs yellow; head with a pair of black lines following the boundaries of the frons and with another short, black line on the lateral margin; pronotum with anterior and posterior margins black, without diagonal marks.

CASE.—About 45 mm. long, slender and of spiral construction.

ADULTS.—Length 18–22 mm. Color brown with dense, matted hair on most of the body; front wings variegated brown, the posterior and apical margins with grayish cream-colored areas which form a sinuate pattern when the wings are folded; hind wings clear with an apical dark brown margin. Tibiae with long, pale spines which stand out conspicuously and give the legs a tawny appearance. Male genitalia, fig. 581, similar in general structure to *straminea*, differing chiefly in the long, sharp, mesal projection of the base of the clasper. Female genitalia, fig. 583, with the orbicular lobe of the ninth sternite larger and stouter than in *straminea*.

This species has frequently been placed in *Phryganea* or *Dasystegia*.

In our recent collections we have found this species confined in Illinois to the lakes and marshes of the northeastern corner of the state. We have, however, a single early record (1894) from Havana, near the center of the state. The species was recorded from Lake Forest and Diamond Lake, Illinois, by Betten (1934). We have reared the larvae from the Dead River at Zion, Illinois, where the cases were found in abundance in mats of aquatic smartweed and other plants. Adult records extend from May to mid August and indicate the possibility of more than one generation per year; our own records are confined chiefly to May and June, so that undoubtedly the greatest wave of adult emergence occurs at this time.

The range of the species includes most of the Northeast and East; records are known for the District of Columbia, Georgia, Illinois, Indiana, Massachusetts, New York and Ohio.

Illinois Records.—ALGONQUIN: June 9, 1909, 1 ♂ ; June 11, 1910, at light, 1 ♀ ; June 20, 1910, at light, 1 ♀. CHICAGO: June 17, W. J. Gerhard, 1 ♂, FM. HAVANA: 1894, 1 ♀. NORTHERN ILLINOIS: 1 ♀ ; Aug. 13, 1898, 1 ♀. PALOS PARK: July 4, 1905, W. J. Gerhard, 1 ♀, FM. PISTAKEE LAKE: May 28, 1936, H. H. Ross, 1 ♀. SAND LAKE: June 15, 1892, Hart & Shiga, 1 ♀. WILLOW SPRINGS: June 26, 1910, W. J. Gerhard, 1 ♀, FM. ZION, Dead River: May 28, 1938, Mohr & Burks, 1 ♂, 1 reared pupa and larval parts; May 20, 1940, Mohr & Burks, 9 larvae; June 6, 1940, Mohr & Burks, 2 ♀, 4 pupae, 2 larvae; June 16, 1940, Mohr & Burks, 1 ♂, 1 ♀, 7 larvae (reared).

Fabria Milne

Fabria Milne (1934, p. 9). Genotype, by original designation: *Neuronia inornata* Banks.

This genus is readily distinguished in the female by the extremely broad ninth sternite. The male is distinguished by the combination of drab color and genitalia, as outlined in the key.

One of the two North American species has been taken in Illinois.

Fabria inornata (Banks)

Neuronia inornata Banks (1907a, p. 117); ♂.

LARVA.—See following genus.

ADULTS.—Length 20–24 mm. Color light brown, the wings with a very fine reticulation of slightly darker brown marks. Front wings with R_1 very sinuate at apex, hind wings with R_1 also sinuate. Male genitalia, fig. 584: tenth tergite stocky and somewhat hood shaped; claspers with a large, broad basal segment bearing a short, sharp tooth at apex which is nearly as long as the short, sinuate second segment. Female genitalia very wide, the ninth sternite as in fig. 584C.

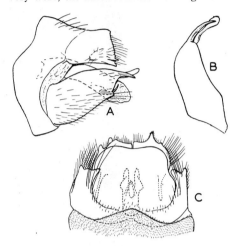

Fig. 584.—*Fabria inornata*, genitalia. *A*, male, lateral aspect; *B*, clasper, caudal aspect; *C*, female, ventral aspect.

In Illinois we have taken this species only at Zion, where adults have been collected at lights beside the Dead River. In this locality we reared all the species of larvae that we found except one, described below as *Genus A*. Similarly, all the Phryganeidae adults which we collected there were reared except one, *Fabria*. There is a very good possibility, therefore, that *Genus A* is the larva of this species. Little is known regarding the range of the species. It was described from Minnesota, and this is only the second state record for it.

Illinois Records.—ZION, Dead River: July 7, 1937, Frison & Ross, 2 ♀; May 28, 1938, Mohr & Burks, 1 ♂; June 3, 1938, Mohr & Burks, 2 ♂; June 4, 1938, Ross & Burks, 2 ♂, 1 ♀; June 6, 1940, Mohr & Burks, 5 ♂.

Phryganeid Genus A

LARVA.—Fig. 566. Length 22 mm. Head, pronotum and legs yellow; head with no mesal line but with two pairs of dark lines, one outside the frons, the other on the lateral margin; pronotum with posterior margin black, and each half with a diagonal black line, the two not meeting posterad on

the meson. Meso- and metanotum without any sclerites near the meson and with a dark purple line on each side of the meson.

Of the many phryganeid larvae collected in the Dead River at Zion, Illinois, this species alone was not reared. As explained in the discussion of the preceding species, circumstantial evidence indicates that this might be the larva of *Fabria inornata*. This larva has been taken only in the Dead River, where it was quite common in the smartweed beds (see p. 11). We found that it differed from others inhabiting the same location in being unable to withstand our rearing conditions, which were accompanied, unfortunately, by rather high, unseasonable temperatures.

Illinois Records.—ZION, Dead River: May 18, 1940, Mohr & Burks, 1 larva; May 20, 1940, Mohr & Burks, 2 pupae, many larvae; June 6, 1940, Mohr & Burks, 4 larvae; June 16, 1940, Mohr & Burks, 3 larvae; June 28, 1940, Mohr & Riegel, 2 larvae.

Oligostomis Kolenati

Oligostomis Kolenati (1848, p. 80). Genotype, by subsequent designation of Milne (1934, p. 8): *Phryganea reticulata* Linnaeus.

We have only one species of this genus in North America, *ocelligera*, which has not been taken in Illinois. This species is very striking in coloration, fig. 587, having reticulate black front wings and black hind wings

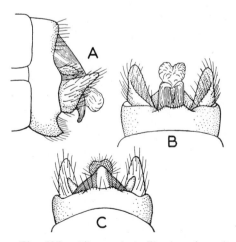

Fig. 585.—*Oligostomis ocelligera*, male genitalia. *A*, lateral aspect; *B*, ventral aspect; *C*, dorsal aspect. (After Betten & Mosely.)

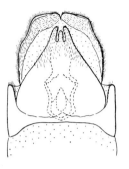

Fig. 586.—*Oligostomis ocelligera*, female genitalia.

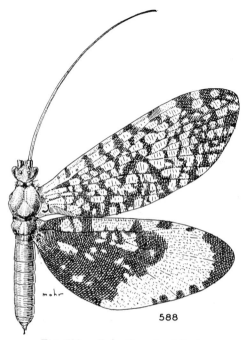

Fig. 588.—*Eubasilissa pardalis* ♀.

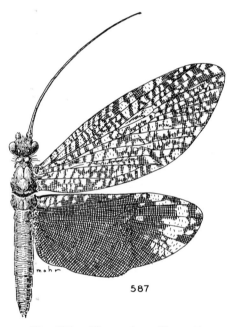

587

Fig. 587.—*Oligostomis ocelligera* ♂.

which has not been taken in Illinois. This species, fig. 588, is so brightly colored with orange and black that it could be confused with many of the brighter Lepidoptera. The genitalia are distinctive for both sexes, figs. 589, 590. The species is known only from the Northeast, including New Hampshire, New York, Nova Scotia and Quebec. Lloyd (1921, p. 21) has described the immature stages and case under the name *Neuronia pardalis*. This is the most colorful North American caddis fly. In Europe, however,

with a bandlike group of yellow reticulations near apex. It has been reared by Lloyd (1921, p. 26), who described the larva under the name *Neuronia stygipes*, which is a synonym of *ocelligera*. The genitalia of both sexes are distinctive, figs. 585, 586.

Eubasilissa Martynov

Regina Martynov (1924, p. 215); preoccupied. Genotype, by original designation: *Neuronia regina* McLachlan.
Eubasilissa Martynov (1930, p. 88). New name for *Regina*.

This genus is represented in North America by only the brightly colored *pardalis*,

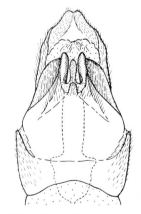

Fig. 589.—*Eubasilissa pardalis*, female genitalia.

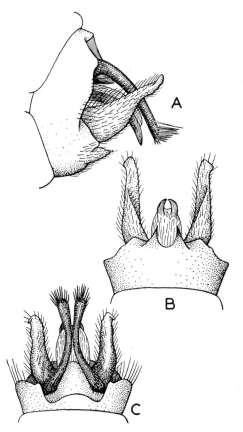

Fig. 590.—*Eubasilissa pardalis*, male genitalia. *A*, lateral aspect; *B*, ventral aspect; *C*, dorsal aspect. (After Betten & Mosely.)

there are several closely related species which are larger and more strikingly colored.

Banksiola Martynov

Banksiola Martynov (1924, p. 216). Genotype, by original designation: *Neuronia concatenata* Walker.

This genus is distinguished by the sinuate apex of R_1 in both wings, the spiny tibiae, the reticulate and spotted wings, and in particular the quadrate brown spots on the otherwise clear hind wings. At the present time five species are recognized in the Nearctic region. One of these, *canadensis*, was placed in *Oligostomis* by Milne (1934); it seems better placed in *Banksiola* on the basis of the venation and spiny legs. The genitalia, however, are extremely aberrant. Unquestionably a review of the world fauna

will necessitate changes in some of these generic groupings.

Only one species has been taken in Illinois.

Banksiola selina Betten, new species

Larva.—Fig. 562. Length 20 mm. Head, pronotum and legs yellow; head with a mesal and two lateral lines, the latter converging toward the back of the head but not actually meeting; pronotum with posterior margin black, and with the disk having a pair of black lines which usually touch on the meson. Mesonotum and metanotum entirely membranous, with irregular purplish blotches.

Adults.—Fig. 591. Length of male 12–15 mm.; of female 16–20 mm. Head mostly yellow; ocelli yellow, sometimes greenish yellow, with their bases dark brown, the area between lateral ocelli with some round, dark brown spots each with a stout bristle; posterior warts brown, covered with yellowish bristles; in some specimens the brown color of the head predominant; antennae with alternate dark brown and yellowish bands, the basal part of each segment dark; palpi brownish yellow and covered with darker bristles. Thorax various shades of brown, the bristles yellowish. Legs brownish yellow, the spurs brown, the spines black. Forewings with pale, cream-colored background, covered with a close reticulation of dark brown; larger dark brown spots at base and tip of subcosta, at tips of anals, and often between anal veins; the dark spot at tips of anals and one beyond on Cu_{1a} are generally noticeable in the mid-dorsal line when wings are roofed over abdomen. Hind wings clear at base, a dark brown area on the line of anastomosis and brown reticulations from there out to the wing tip; M_3 and M_4 fused in the males, separate for some distance in the females. Abdomen yellowish brown, darker above; a transverse sclerotized line on sternites 4–7 in the male, 3–6 in the female; a blunt sclerotized tooth projects from meson on the sixth sternite of the female, a smaller tooth appears on the seventh and, rarely, one on the fifth; these are usually absent on the male abdomen.

Male Genitalia.—Fig. 592. Ninth segment sclerotized and ringlike, the anterior margin curved and telescoped into the eighth segment, the posterior margin nearly straight and bearing dorsally many long

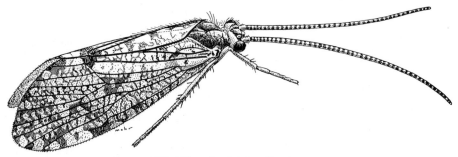

Fig. 591.—*Banksiola selina* ♀.

bristles. Tenth tergite forming a dorsal roof which narrows from its base and is notched at the posterior margin; on each side near the base is a lateral projection. Aedeagus with a blunt membranous stalk beneath which extends a dark brown, heavily sclerotized flat strap; arising from the base of the aedeagus is a membranous appendage which has on the upper margin of its tip a large number of stout, reddish bristles; this appendage curves down along the side of the aedeagus, generally on the left side. Claspers very heavy, each terminating in a strong dorsal hook and with strong teeth along the posterior margin; seen from below the bases of the claspers meet in a straight line.

Female Genitalia.—Fig. 593. Terminal dorsal segment of abdomen rooflike, not unlike that of the male; near its base is a transverse line of bristles and two bunches of these are located toward the tip. Embedded in the ventral wall of the eighth ventral segment is a dark brown, corneous structure, thin in the middle and with inflated lobes at the sides; at the posterior end of this structure there are two spinose arms and between these a shorter, generally broad and rounded projection also covered with spines. These parts vary greatly.

Holotype, male.—Zion, Illinois, along Dead River: June 3, 1938, Mohr & Burks.

Allotype, female.—Zion, Illinois: larva from Dead River, emerged June 12, 1940, Mohr & Burks.

Paratypes.—Illinois.—Zion: Same data as for holotype, 4 ♀; July 7, 1937, Frison & Ross, 1 ♂, 1 ♀; same data as for allotype, 2 ♀. Four paratypes are deposited in the collection of Dr. Betten.

Additional specimens have been examined from Illinois, Massachusetts, Michigan, Minnesota, New York and Ontario.

This species has heretofore always been identified as *concatenata*. The type of the latter (described by Betten & Mosely 1940) is a female in which M_3 and M_4 are separate nearly to the line of anastomosis, much farther than is ordinarily the case in *selina*; the genitalia of *concatenata* resemble those of *dossuaria* more than those of *selina*.

The above description was kindly sent to us by Dr. Betten for inclusion in this report.

In Illinois, with the exception of a single male taken at lights in Champaign, all our records are from the extreme northeastern corner. We have found the species breeding abundantly in the Dead River near Zion, and apparently its main range in the state is in the region containing similar marsh

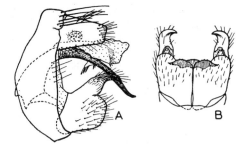

Fig. 592.—*Banksiola selina*, male genitalia. *A*, lateral aspect; *B*, claspers, ventral aspect.

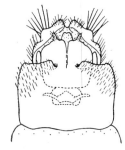

Fig. 593.—*Banksiola selina*, female genitalia, ventral aspect.

areas. There is only a single generation per year, the adults being present in June and early July.

Illinois Records. — ALGONQUIN: June 30, 1906, 1 ♀ ; May 25, 1908, 1 ♀ ; July 9, 1909, 1 ♀ ; July 12, 1910, 1 ♀, all by W. A. Nason. CEDAR LAKE: June 19, 1892, H. S. Shiga, 1 ♀. CHAMPAIGN: at electric light, June 17, 1886, Hart, 1 ♂. ZION: many larvae, pupae and adults (including the type series) taken in or near Dead River from May 15 to July 7.

Ptilostomis Kolenati

Ptilostomis Kolenati (1859*b*, p. 198). Genotype, monobasic: *Ptilostomis kovalevskii* Kolenati.

All the species of this genus are brown, frequently with an angulate dark brown mark in the hind wings. The shelflike projection of the male ninth sternite and the broad ninth sternite of the female, with its two lateral finger-like processes and mesal triangular process, are diagnostic. The larvae have no mesal dark line down the frons and have the diagonal marks on the pronotum forming an arcuate mark, fig. 565. To date no characters have been found to separate the larvae to species. They make

a long cylindrical case of spiral formation similar to that of other members of the family.

Four species of the genus are recognized, three of which occur in Illinois. The genotype, *kovalevskii*, described from Alaska, has never been identified definitely, and we do not know whether it constitutes a fifth Nearctic species of the genus or whether it is the same as one of the four treated below.

KEY TO SPECIES

Adults

1. Maxillary palpi 4-segmented (males)   2
   Maxillary palpi 5-segmented (females)   5
2. Apex of tenth tergite with a pair of long, curved, filiform blades, fig. 594 . . . . **semifasciata**, p. 173
   Apex of tenth tergite at most with long setae, fig. 595 3
3. Base of tenth tergite with two pairs of processes which arise from it, then angle suddenly and run parallel with the segment; the dorsal pair is very long, the lateral pair short, fig. 595 . . . . **postica**, p. 173
   Base of tenth tergite at most with a lateral pair of processes, figs. 596, 597 4
4. Tenth tergite flat and rectangular, with

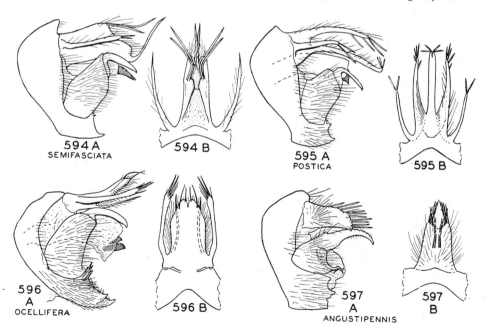

594 A
SEMIFASCIATA
594 B

595 A
POSTICA
595 B

596 A
OCELLIFERA
596 B

597 A
ANGUSTIPENNIS
597 B

Figs. 594–597.—*Ptilostomis*, male genitalia. *A*, lateral aspect; *B*, tenth tergite, dorsal aspect.

a tuft of long setae at apex and long, lateral processes, fig. 596. . . . .
. . . . **ocellifera**, p. 172
Tenth tergite convex, with a pair of dorsal rows of setae and without lateral processes, fig. 597. . . . .
. . . . **angustipennis**, p. 174

5. Bursa copulatrix with a high, triangular ventral keel, fig. 598. . . . .
. . . . **semifasciata**, p. 173
Bursa copulatrix with a short ventral process which forms a transverse fork or short plate, figs. 599–601. . .   6

6: Ventral process of bursa forming a short fork which is narrow and small, fig. 599. . . . .**postica**, p. 173
Ventral process of bursa transverse and platelike, its tip emarginate and sometimes forming a very broad V, figs. 600, 601.   7

7. Ventral process of bursa with the anterior face forming a short mesal keel, fig. 600. . . .**angustipennis**, p. 174
Ventral process of bursa with the anterior face slightly carinate at each lateral margin where it joins with base, fig. 601, but without a mesal keel. . . . .**ocellifera**, p. 172

Ptilostomis ocellifera (Walker)

Neuronia ocellifera Walker (1852, p. 8); ♂.
Neuronia simulans Betten & Mosely (1940, p. 107); ♀. New synonymy.

LARVA.—Length 27 mm. Head, pronotum and legs yellow; head with two pairs of black lines, one on each side of the frons and one on the lateral margin; pronotum with posterior margin black and with an arcuate dark brown line starting at each anterolateral corner and running to about the middle of the mesal margin.

CASE.—Very long, usually about 50 mm.

ADULTS.—Length 21–24 mm. Color yellowish brown, the front wings minutely speckled with darker brown, hind wings sometimes with a V-shaped dark brown mark which is small or even completely absent in some specimens. Male genitalia, fig. 596: tenth tergite long and somewhat rectangular with a pair of long, stout lateral arms arising from base, and a pair of spiny processes arising from ventral margin near middle; the apex of the tergite bears a pair of long, curved setae; ninth sternite produced beneath and beyond base of claspers, the apex of the ventral margin forming two stout teeth, the dorsal margin with a row of irregular teeth. Female genitalia, fig. 601: bursa copulatrix with a relatively short body bearing a ventral transverse projection which extends platelike at right angles to the surface and is usually emarginate at apex; this projection is anchored at its base with a short carinate brace at each lateral

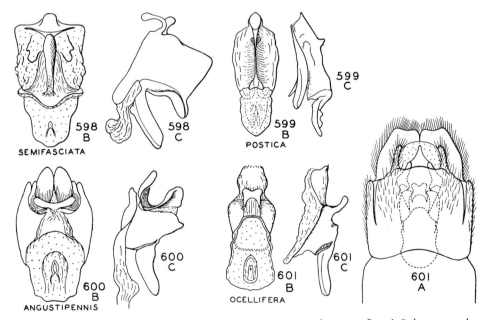

598
B
SEMIFASCIATA

598
C

599
C

599
B
POSTICA

600
B
ANGUSTIPENNIS

600
C

601
B
OCELLIFERA

601
C

601
A

Figs. 598–601.—*Ptilostomis*, female genitalia.   *A*, ventral aspect; *B* and *C*, bursa copulatrix, ventral and lateral aspects.

margin; posterior to this projection is a fairly wide and long, heavily sclerotized piece.

This species has been collected at scattered points in the central and northern portions of Illinois. At Oakwood we reared it from larvae collected in the back waters of a small stream. At other localities we have taken unreared larvae of this genus in similar situations. Our adult records extend from April to late June, indicating that we may have only a single early summer emergence of adults in Illinois. In more northern states, the species emerges later.

This species is widespread through the Northeast; records are known from Illinois, Indiana, Michigan, New Jersey, New York, Nova Scotia, Ohio, Ontario, Pennsylvania, Quebec and Wisconsin.

Illinois Records. — Algonquin: June 17, 1907, W. A. Nason, 1♀ ; June 16, 1908, 1♀ ; June 29, 1909, at light, Nason, 2♂ ; June 20, 1910, at light, Nason, 3♂. Chicago: June 28, 1908, 1♀ ; June 4, W. J. Gerhard, 1♂, 1♀, fm. Harvard: Chas. Faust, 1♂. Havana: Chas. Faust, 1♂. Northern Illinois: 1♂ ; May, Peabody Collection, 1♂. Oakwood: April 10, 1936, Ross & Mohr, 1♀, 2 larvae, 1 larva (reared); May 27, 1936, Ross & Mohr, 2♂, 5♀ ; June 1, 1936, Ross & Mohr, 1♀ ; June 13, 1936, Ross & Mohr, 1♀. Palos Park: June 20, 1908, W. J. Gerhard, 1♂, fm. Urbana: June 12, 1886, Hart, 1♂.

Ptilostomis semifasciata (Say)

Phryganea semifasciata Say (1828, pl. 44).
Neuronia fusca Walker (1852, p. 9); ♂.
Neuronia dubitans Betten & Mosely (1940, p. 105); ♀. New synonymy.

ADULTS.—In size and color similar to the preceding species. Male genitalia, fig. 594: tenth tergite, very complex, having a pair of long, widely separated dorso-lateral appendages arising from extreme base, a pair of setal tufts arising from central portion, and with the lateral margins modified at apex into a pair of sclerotized plates which end in a long, narrow upturned blade; ninth segment with apex of shelflike portion bearing four teeth on the emarginate ventral margin and an irregular group of teeth on the dorsal margin. Female genitalia, fig. 598, with bursa copulatrix bearing a large, long keel on the venter, this keel being the most prominent part of the entire structure.

Neotype, male. — Momence, Illinois: June 4, 1932, Frison & Mohr.

The traditional identification of this species has been quite uniform for many years, and in order to avoid any ambiguity I have selected the above neotype since Say's type is lost.

This species, like the preceding, has been taken at scattered localities in the northern half of Illinois. Our adult records are entirely from June and July, indicating a single adult brood. Specimens have been taken in the proximity of both lakes and streams, with a preponderance of records from localities near streams.

The range of the species is apparently widespread through the Northeast; records are available from Illinois, Kentucky, Ohio, Quebec, South Dakota and Wisconsin.

Illinois Records. — Algonquin: June 10, 1905, W. A. Nason, 1♂ ; June 13, 1905, W. A. Nason, 1♂ ; July 10, 1905, W. A. Nason, 1♂ ; July 13, 1905, W. A. Nason, 1♂ ; June 13, 1910, W. A. Nason, 1♀ ; June 20, 1910, at light, W. A. Nason, 1♂. Channel Lake: June 15, 1928, T. H. Frison, 1♀. Charleston: June 11, 1931, at light, H. H. Ross, 1♀. Elgin, Botanical Gardens: June 6, 1939, Burks & Riegel, 1♀. Fithian: June 18, 1919, at light, 1♀. Homer: June 30, 1927, at light, Frison & Glasgow, 1♀. Momence: June 4, 1932, Frison & Mohr, 1♂, 1♀ ; 3 miles east, June 22, 1938, Ross & Burks, 1♀. Oregon: June, 1930, Sauer, 1♀. Palos Park: July 2, 1910, W. J. Gerhard, 1♀, fm. Richmond: June 4, 1938, Ross & Burks, 1♂. St. Joseph: July 30, 1929, T. H. Frison, 1♂. Urbana: July 18, 1885, 1♀. Wadsworth, Des Plaines River: July 7, 1937, Frison & Ross, 1♀.

Ptilostomis postica (Walker)

Neuronia postica Walker (1852, p. 9); ♀.

ADULTS.—Length 19–20 mm. Color as in *ocellifera*. Male genitalia, fig. 595: tenth tergite with central portion long and styliform, with two pairs of processes which arise from it, then angle suddenly and run parallel with the segment; the dorsal pair is very long, the lateral pair short; apical shelflike projection of ninth sternite with a pair of ventral, low teeth and an arcuate row of smaller, irregular teeth. Female genitalia, fig. 599, with bursa copulatrix having a long, ventral blade which bears near its middle a short fork which is narrow and small.

The male of this species was described by Betten & Mosely (1940, p. 108) as the male of their new species *simulans* (the female type of *simulans* is *ocellifera*).

In Illinois we have only three scattered collections for this species, all of them along fairly large rivers, including the Kankakee, Rock and Kaskaskia. Our few records extend from May until late September.

The range of the species is poorly known but apparently is extensive through much of the Northeast; records include Georgia, Illinois, Michigan, New Jersey and New York.

Illinois Records.—MOMENCE: June 4, 1932, Frison & Mohr, 1 ♂. NEW MEMPHIS, Kaskaskia River: Sept. 25, 1939, Frison & Ross, 2 ♀. OLIVE BRANCH: Oct. 4, 1909, W. J. Gerhard, 1 ♀, FM. OREGON: May, 1929, Sauer, 1 ♀.

Ptilostomis angustipennis (Hagen)

Neuronia angustipennis Hagen (1873, p. 400); ♂, ♀.

This species has not yet been taken in the state but may be found with subsequent collecting. We have records from Massachusetts, Michigan and New Jersey.

Phryganea Linnaeus

Phryganea Linnaeus (1758, p. 547). Genotype, by subsequent designation of Westwood (1840, p. 49): *Phryganea grandis* Linnaeus.

The adults of this genus are all large, with a conspicuous pattern of brown and gray, most noticeable in repose, fig. 602. The female ninth sternite, fig. 605, and the short, biscuit-shaped claspers of the male, fig. 603, are diagnostic for the genus.

Only three species are recognized in North America, and two of these have been taken in Illinois. Larvae of these two species have been reared, but no characters have yet been found to distinguish them.

KEY TO SPECIES

1. Hind wings with basal two-thirds smoky, apical third dark brown or blackish gray............**sayi**, p. 176
   Hind wings uniformly gray or brownish, marked at apex only with a few slightly darker darts along the veins,

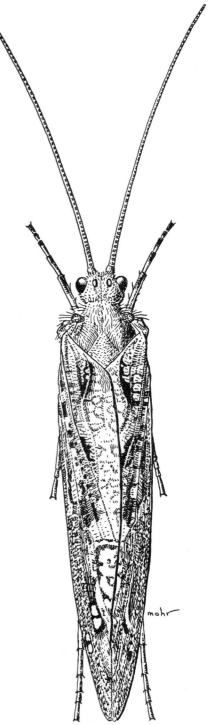

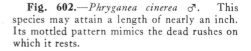

Fig. 602.—*Phryganea cinerea* ♂. This species may attain a length of nearly an inch. Its mottled pattern mimics the dead rushes on which it rests.

but with no suggestion of an apical
band..................**cinerea**, p. 175

Phryganea cinerea Walker

Phryganea cinerea Walker (1852, p. 4); ♂,
♀.

LARVA.—Fig. 561. Length 35 mm. Head,
pronotum and legs yellow; head with a
mesal dark line down the frons, a pair of
oblique dark lines, one on each side of the
frons; and a second pair of dark lines, one
along each lateral margin of the head. Pronotum with anterior and posterior margins
black, the two lines frequently meeting on
meson.

CASE.—Very long, usually 65–70 mm.,
and of the usual spiral type of construction.

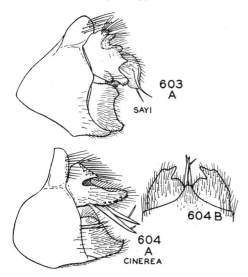

Figs. 603–604.—*Phryganea*, male genitalia.
A, lateral aspect; *B*, claspers, ventral aspect.

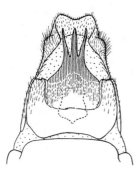

Fig. 605.—*Phryganea cinerea*, female genitalia.

ADULTS.—Length 21–25 mm. Color predominantly gray or brown, the front wings
with an irregular pattern of various shades
of brown with light gray patches along the
posterior margin, these forming triangular
marks when the wings are folded; hind
wings uniformly gray, with a few slightly
darker darts along the extreme tips of the
veins. Male genitalia, fig. 604: tenth tergite divided into a pair of cercus-like organs
with a short but broad dorsal spur and a
group of stout, black spines at apex; claspers short, somewhat spoon shaped as seen
from lateral view, rounded and biscuit
shaped as seen from ventral view. Female
genitalia, fig. 605, characterized by the tri-
dentate apex.

In Illinois we have taken this species only
in the northeastern part of the state where
it is apparently confined to glacial lakes and
marshes. We reared the species from the
Dead River at Zion, where the larvae were
taken in aquatic smartweed beds in company
with *sayi* (see p. 11). Our adult records
are chiefly from June and July, indicating
a heavy early summer emergence with strag-
glers beyond that time.

The adults are crepuscular, flying chiefly
in the first hours after dark. During the
day they rest on rushes and sedges around
lakes or marshes. When at rest, with wings
folded, they blend into their surroundings.

The species is widely distributed through
the northern states and Canada, extending
as far west as the Rocky Mountains; our
Illinois records represent apparently the
most southern points at which the species
has been taken. Records are available for
Alberta, Colorado, Illinois, Maine, Manitoba, Massachusetts, Michigan, Minnesota,
Montana, New York, Ontario, Saskatchewan, South Dakota, Wisconsin and Wyoming.

Illinois Records.—ANTIOCH: July 1,
1931, Frison, Betten & Ross, 1 ♂, 1 ♀.
CHANNEL LAKE: Aug. 13, 1906, 1 ♂. CHI-
CAGO: Wescott, 1 ♂. Fox LAKE: July 1,
1931, Frison, Betten & Ross, 1 ♂; June 30,
1935, DeLong & Ross, 3 ♂. GRASS LAKE:
July 1, 1926, Frison & Hayes, 1 ♂, 1 ♀.
NORTHERN ILLINOIS: July 28, 1898, 1 ♀.
ZION, Dead River: July 7, 1937, Frison &
Ross, 4 ♂, 1 ♀; June 12, 1940, Mohr &
Burks, 1 ♀ (reared); June 28, 1940, Mohr
& Riegel, 3 ♂, 2 ♀; June 16, 1940, Mohr
& Burks, 4 ♂, 3 ♀, 1 ♂ (reared); July 1,
1940, Mohr & Burks, 1 ♀.

Phryganea sayi Milne

Phryganea interrupta Say (1828, pl. 44); preoccupied.

Phryganea sayi Milne (1931, p. 228). New name.

LARVA AND CASE.—Indistinguishable from those of *cinerea*.

ADULTS.—Length 20–25 mm. In color similar to *cinerea*, differing chiefly in the hind wings, which are grayish yellow with the apical third dark brown and forming a distinct band. Male genitalia, fig. 603, with the tenth tergite much broader and shorter than in *cinerea*. Female genitalia very similar to those of *cinerea* in regard to both external and internal parts.

We have scattered records of this species from the northern half of Illinois. Larvae were collected and reared from the Dead River at Zion, in company with those of *cinerea*. Our adult records extend from June 6 to August 27. Indications are that this species has a longer adult life than many caddis fly species. The larva illustrated for this species by Lloyd (1921) is apparently a misidentification; his larva, described under the old name *interrupta*, has diagonal marks on the pronotum, whereas Vorhies (1909) found (and we did, also) that the marks followed the margin as in *cinerea*. I do not know what species Lloyd actually had.

The range of the species is apparently confined principally to the Northeast. Records are available from the District of Columbia, Illinois, Massachusetts, Michigan, Missouri, New Jersey, New York, Pennsylvania and Wisconsin.

Illinois Records.—ALGONQUIN: Aug. 27, 1908, 1♀. HAVANA: June 12, 1894, C. A. Hart, 1♂; June 14, 1894, C. A. Hart, 1♀; June 23, 1894, C. A. Hart, 1♂. OAKWOOD, Salt Fork River: July 18, 1933, Ross & Mohr, 1♀. SPRINGFIELD: July 2, 1885, at light, C. A. Hart, 1♀. URBANA: Aug. 2, 1886, at light, C. A. Hart, 1♀; Aug. 18, 1886, at light, C. A. Hart, 1♀; Aug. 23, 1886, at light, C. A. Hart, 1♂; Aug. 22, 1938, G. T. Riegel, light trap, 1♀. ZION, Dead River: June 6, 1940, Mohr & Burks, 1♂, 1♀; June 12, 1940, Mohr & Burks, 1♂ (reared); June 16, 1940, Mohr & Burks, 1♂ (reared), 1♀ (reared), 2♂, 2♀; June 28, 1940, Mohr & Burks, 1♂; July 1, 1940, Mohr & Burks, 1♀; July 15, 1940, Mohr & Burks, 1♂.

LIMNEPHILIDAE

This is one of the largest families of caddis flies in North America, represented by over 20 genera and nearly 200 species. It is characterized by having the maxillary palpi of the male three segmented, by distinct ocelli in both sexes, and other structural characters as outlined in the key. The larvae are quite variable in many characters, but in all of them the antennae are situated midway between the eye and the base of the mandible. All species are case makers, many of which are illustrated by Lloyd (1921).

Discovery of its larva shows that the genus *Neothremma*, previously placed in the Sericostomatidae, belongs definitely in the Limnephilidae. The genus *Farula* also was placed in the Sericostomatidae, but since it possesses distinct ocelli, I am removing it tentatively to the Limnephilidae.

Most of the genera and species of the Limnephilidae are western or northern in distribution, and Illinois occurs on the southern fringe of the main range of the family. Only a small proportion of the species have been taken in Illinois, and many of these are rare or locally distributed.

In many cases the genera are only imperfectly defined, and we are awaiting information on females or larvae, which are as yet unknown for many genera and species.

KEY TO GENERA

Larvae

1. Anterior margin of mesonotum with a mesal, rectangular emargination, fig. 606; at this point it is connected to pronotum by a short, sclerotized strap; head with malar space nearly twice height of head above eye, fig. 609 . . . .**Neophylax**, p. 202
   Anterior margin of mesonotum evenly rounded and not emarginate, fig. 607; head with malar space no longer than height of head above eye, fig. 610 2

2. Front femora slender, the apical margin short, fig. 611; pronotum slightly incised along anterior margin; always with sclerotized portions of head and body black or nearly so. . . . .**Dicosmoecus**, p. 181
   Front femora somewhat chelicerate, widened, with the apical margin very oblique and nearly as long as the lower margin, fig. 612 3

3. Gills arising singly, fig. 613 4
   Gills arising in groups of two or more 5
4. Seventh abdominal tergite with an antero-mesal gill; postero-lateral corner of mesonotum with a linear black mark...... **Astenophylax,** p. 183
   Seventh abdominal tergite with no antero-mesal gill; postero-lateral corner of mesonotum with either a spot or no black mark, as in fig. 20..... .... **Pycnopsyche,** p. 193
5. Pronotum with dense, short black spines, especially anterior margin, fig. 608; legs banded with red and black, fig. 612... **Glyphopsyche,** p. 200
   Pronotum without dense black spines, clothed primarily with long setae, fig. 607; legs not so banded........ 6
6. Anal legs with a group of about 10 setae on the bulbous ventral portion .... **Frenesia,** p. 199
   Anal legs with no setae on bulbous ventral portion.................. 7
7. Dorsal gills of first few abdominal segments with 6–12 branches forming a fanshaped spread, figs. 615, 616.... 8

606

607

608

609

610

611A
611B

612A
612B

613

614

615

616

617

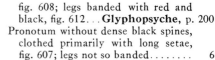

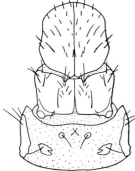

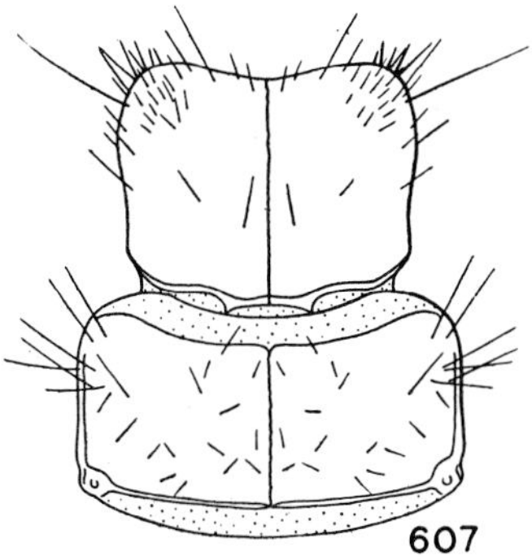

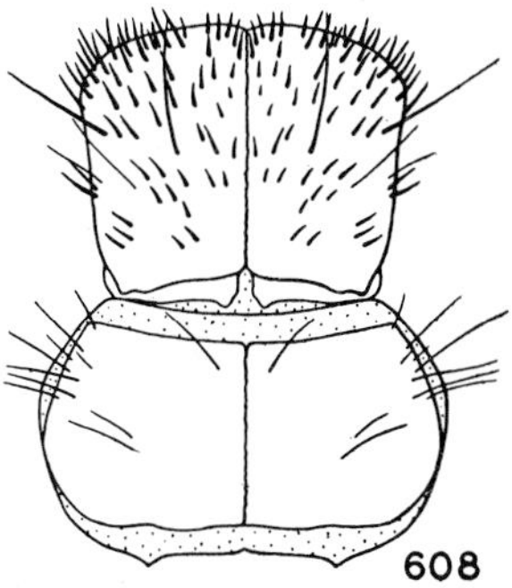

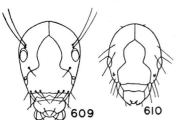

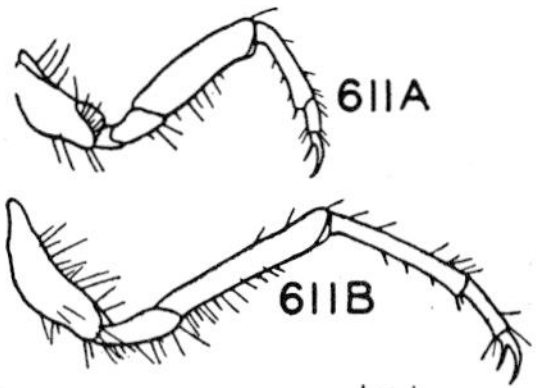

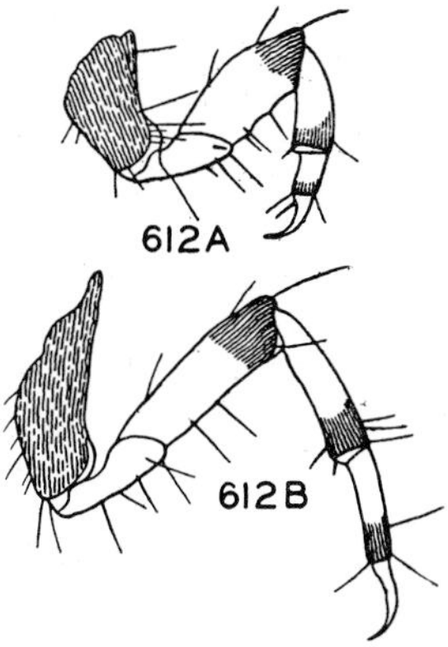

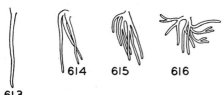

Fig. 606.—*Neophylax autumnus* larva, thorax.

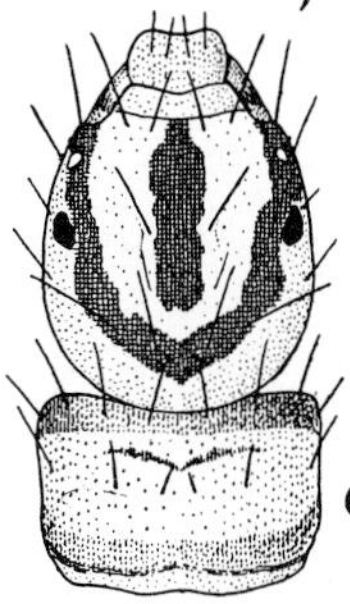

Fig. 607.—*Frenesia missa* larva, thorax.

Fig. 608.—*Glyphopsyche missouri* larva, thorax.

Fig. 609.—*Neophylax autumnus* larva, head.

Fig. 610.—*Frenesia missa* larva, head.

Fig. 611.—*Dicosmoecus* sp. larva, legs. *A*, front leg; *B*, hind leg.

Fig. 612.—*Glyphopsyche missouri* larva, legs. *A*, front leg; *B*, hind leg.

Fig. 613.—*Pycnopsyche subfasciata* larva, abdominal gill.

Fig. 614.—*Limnephilus submonilifer* larva, abdominal gill.

Fig. 615.—*Hesperophylax designatus* larva, abdominal gill.

Fig. 616.—*Caborius* sp. larva, abdominal gill.

Fig. 617.—*Glyphotaelius* sp. larva, head and pronotum.

Dorsal gills of first few abdominal segments with 2 or 3 branches at the most, not spreading fanlike, fig. 614   9

8. Dorsal gills at base of abdomen with about 12 branches each, fig. 616...
.....................**Caborius**, p. 196
Dorsal gills at base of abdomen with about 6 branches each, fig. 615....
..............**Hesperophylax**, p. 183

9. Head with a narrow, dark line along meson of frons and with a dark, U-shaped line running through eyes and above frons, fig. 617.........
..............**Glyphotaelius**, p. 183
Head either with wider dark areas, fig. 648, or without indication of dark lines, fig. 646...................   10

10. Prosternal horn short, not projecting beyond apexes of front coxae......
................**Limnephilus**, p. 185
Prosternal horn projecting distinctly beyond apexes of front coxae......
..............**Platycentropus**, p. 181

Pupae

1. Dorsal plates *5P* transverse, narrow and with two rows of about 24 teeth each, fig. 618.......**Neophylax**, p. 202
Dorsal plates *5P* much more ovate or nearer square, fig. 620, with rows of not more than 12 teeth each, fig. 619   2

2. Dorsal abdominal gills arising in groups of 5 or 6 or threadlike, usually crushed into a small, shapeless bundle..........**Hesperophylax**, p. 183; probably **Caborius** also, p. 196
Dorsal abdominal gills finger-like and distinct, figs. 622, 623, never with more than 3 or 4 gills in a group...   3

3. Dorsal abdominal gills stout, very long, and arising singly...............   4
Dorsal abdominal gills more slender, arising in bunches of two or more..   5

4. Dorsal plates *5P*, 6 and 7 with about 17, 5 and 4 teeth, respectively, fig. 619.............**Astenophylax**, p. 183
Dorsal plates *5P*, 6 and 7 with about 7 and 2 teeth and 1 tooth, respectively, fig. 621....**Pycnopsyche**, p. 193

5. Second antennal segment with a tuft of long, black hair, fig. 624........
................**Dicosmoecus**, p. 181
Second antennal segment with at most a tuft of very short setae, fig. 625..   6

6. Postero-dorsal gills of second abdominal segment and antero-dorsal gills of third segment with some filaments reaching fifth segment and a few others nearly as long, fig. 622......
..............**Platycentropus**, p. 181
Postero-dorsal gills of second abdominal segment and antero-dorsal gills of third never reaching more than a short distance on fourth segment, fig. 623......**Limnephilus**, p. 185; **Glyphopsyche**, p. 200; **Frenesia**, p. 199

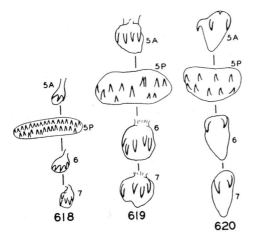

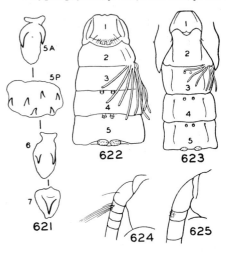

Fig. 618.—*Neophylax autumnus* pupa, hook-bearing plates.

Fig. 619.—*Astenophylax argus* pupa, hook-bearing plates.

Fig. 620.—*Limnephilus submonilifer* pupa, hook-bearing plates.

Fig. 621.—*Pycnopsyche subfasciata* pupa, hook-bearing plates.

Fig. 622.—*Platycentropus radiatus* pupa, portion of abdomen.

Fig. 623.—*Glyphopsyche missouri* pupa, portion of abdomen.

Fig. 624.—*Dicosmoecus* sp. pupa, base of antenna.

Fig. 625.—*Platycentropus radiatus* pupa, base of antenna.

Adults

1. Front wings with apical abscissa of
   vein 2*A* atrophied, fig. 626........
   ....**Platycentropus**, p. 181
   Front wings with vein 2*A* complete,
   fig. 628........................ 2
2. Front wings with Sc ending in a short,
   straight, oblique crossvein, fig. 627
   ....**Radema**, p. 181
   Front wings with Sc not ending in an
   oblique crossvein, figs. 628, 629... 3
3. Hind wings with M_{1+2} undivided, fig.
   637; head with a small pair of warts
   between lateral ocelli and posterior
   warts..............**Neophylax**, p. 202
   Hind wings with M_{1+2} divided into M_1
   and M_2, fig. 638; head without warts
   between lateral ocelli and posterior
   warts............................ 4
4. Apex of front wings scalloped and
   posterior corner sharp, fig. 628....
   ....**Glyphotaelius**, p. 183

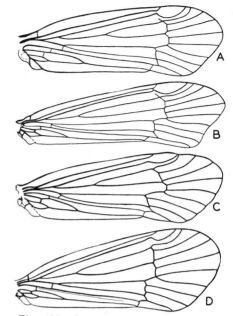

Fig. 631.—Limnephilidae front wings. *A,
Glyphopsyche missouri; B, Glyphopsyche irrorata; C, Grensia praeteritum; D, Frenesia missa.*

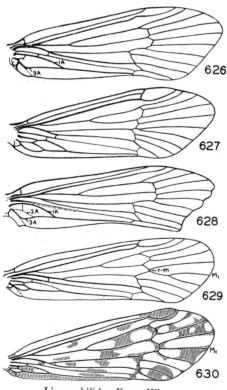

Limnephilidae Front Wings

Fig. 626.—*Platycentropus radiatus.*
Fig. 627.—*Radema stigmatella.*
Fig. 628.—*Glyphotaelius hostilis.*
Fig. 629.—*Phanocelia canadensis.*
Fig. 630.—*Chilostigma areolatum.*

   Apex of front wings either evenly
   rounded or incised without scalloped
   condition, figs. 629, 631*B*......... 5
5. Dorsum of head and pronotum greatly
   lengthened, with a deep, narrow
   groove running their entire length,
   fig. 644..........**Leptophylax**, p. 184
   Dorsum of either head or pronotum,
   or both, much shorter, and head
   without mesal groove............ 6
6. Front wings with fork of M_{1+2} considerably beyond crossvein *r-m*, fig.
   629...............**Phanocelia**, p. 201
   Front wings with fork of M_{1+2} at or
   near crossvein *r-m*, fig. 630........ 7
7. Dorsum of head bright yellow, highly
   polished and with only a few short,
   black setae......**Astenophylax**, p. 183
   Dorsum of head either dark, dull or
   with long or abundant setae...... 8
8. Vertex and anal portion of front wings
   covered with close, appressed, silky
   hair..........**Hesperophylax**, p. 183
   Vertex without close, appressed hair 9
9. Front wings with a short, rounded
   stigma (bordered below by R_1) and
   with R_2 also curved parallel with it
   or even more curved, figs. 630, 631;
   never with a longitudinal silvery
   line............................ 10
   Front wings either with a longitudinal
   silvery line, fig. 633, or with stigma

longer if well marked, and with R_2 less sharply curved or straight, figs. 633, 636 14

10. Wings transparent, colorless and glassy with definite solid brown markings, fig. 630; veins and membrane with very short, sparse hair; cord following a zigzag course . . . . **Chilostigma**, p. 199

    Wings either mostly brown, or with abundant hair on veins or membrane; cord more regular, as in fig. 631 11

11. Apical margin of front wings deeply incised and with cell Cu_{1b} very narrow, long and parallel-sided, fig. 631*B* . . . . **Glyphopsyche**, p. 200

    Apical margin not incised; cell Cu_{1b} narrowing gradually for most of its length, fig. 631*A*, *C* 12

12. Front wings with cord aligned with base of stigmatic area, fig. 631*D* . . . . **Frenesia**, p. 199

    Front wings with cord not forming a line with base of stigma, fig. 631*A*, *C* 13

13. Front wings with apex of R_2 almost

fusing with apex of stigma, fig. 631*C* . . . . **Grensia**, p. 201

    Front wings with R_2 paralleling stigma and definitely not approaching it, fig. 631*A* . . . . **Glyphopsyche**, p. 200

14. Front wings with fork of R_{2+3} much basad of fork of R_{4+5}, at least as much as in fig. 632, and last tarsal segment of all legs without black spines 15

    Either front wings with fork of R_{2+3} more nearly on a level with fork of R_{4+5}, fig. 636, or last tarsal segment of at least 1 or 2 legs with 1 or more short black ventral spines 16

15. Hind tibiae with 2 spurs; small, slender species about 10 mm. long . . . . **Ironoquia**, p. 184

    Hind tibiae with 4 spurs; large, robust species about 15 mm. long . . . . **Caborius**, p. 196

16. Front wings as in fig. 633, with R_1 sinuate and upcurved at apex to delimit a stigmatic area, and R_2 close to and parallel with R_1 from base of stigma; wing very long and narrow; last tarsal segments never with black spines . . . . . **Psychoglypha**, p. 201

    Front wings either very wide or with R_2 following R_1 no closer than in fig. 636; note that R_2 does not follow R_1 at base of stigma; last tarsal segments sometimes with 1 or 2 black spines 17

17. Hind wings with R_5 bordered with a

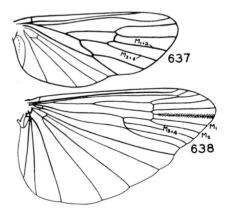

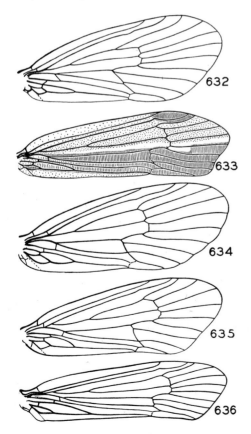

Limnephilidae Front Wings

Fig. 632.—*Caborius kaskaskia.*
Fig. 633.—*Psychoglypha avigo.*
Fig. 634.—*Drusinus uniformis.*
Fig. 635.—*Pycnopsyche subfasciata.*
Fig. 636.—*Limnephilus submonilifer.*
Fig. 637.—*Neophylax autumnus,* hind wing.
Fig. 638.—*Grammotaulius* sp., hind wing.

black streak, fig. 638.............
.............**Grammotaulius,** p. 185
Hind wings with R₅ not bordered with
a dark streak................... 18

18. Front wings with first cell 1*A* much
more than half as long as second
cell 1*A*, fig. 634................ 19
Front wings with first cell 1*A* at most
only half as long as second cell 1*A*,
fig. 636....................... 20

19. Front wings with post-apical margin
rounded, fig. 634, and last tarsal segment of all legs without black
spines...............**Drusinus,** p. 202
Front wings with post-apical margin
oblique, fig. 635, and last tarsal segment of 1 or more legs with 1 or
more short, black ventral spines...
................**Pycnopsyche,** p. 193

20. Mesonotum with mesoscutal warts
represented by a poorly defined,
linear area of setae, some of them
stout; head either with 1
or 2 pairs of long, stout macrochaetae in postocellar area or with only
a few, stout setae on posterior
warts, fig. 639....**Limnephilus,** p. 185
Mesonotum with mesoscutal warts
ovate, well delimited and with long,
silky hair, fig. 640; head with scattered hair over postocellar area and
with long, silky hair on posterior
warts, fig. 640................... 21

21. Last tarsal segments without black
ventral spines; male claspers distinctly 2-segmented; female genitalia
of eastern species with tenth segment vasiform....**Dicosmoecus,** p. 181
Last tarsal segment of at least 1 or 2
legs with 1 or more short, black ventral spines; male claspers with only
1 segment, figs. 673–678; female
genitalia with apical portion not
vasiform, fig. 680...............
................**Pycnopsyche,** p. 193

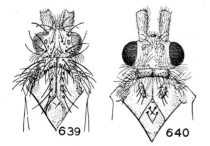

Fig. 639.—*Limnephilus submonilifer,* head
and thorax.
Fig. 640.—*Pycnopsyche subfasciata,* head
and thorax.

Radema Hagen

Radema Hagen (1864, p. 799). Genotype,
monobasic: *Radema infernale* Hagen.
Apatidea McLachlan (1874, p. 33). Genotype, here designated: *Apatidea copiosa* Mc-
Lachlan.
Apatelia Wallengren (1886, p. 78). Genotype, here designated: *Apatania (Apatelia)
inornata* Wallengren.
Apatania of authors, not Kolenati.

No Illinois species of this genus have yet
been reported, but several are known in the
northeastern states. In general, the group
is Arctic and Subarctic, occurring as far
south as New York and Connecticut.

This group was formerly called *Apatania*.
The genus *Apatania,* however, has as its
only included species one which belongs to
the genus *Molanna; Apatania,* therefore,
must be considered a synonym of *Molanna*.

Dicosmoecus McLachlan

Dicosmoecus McLachlan (1875, p. 122). Genotype, here designated: *Stenophylax palatus*
McLachlan.

No species of this genus is known to occur
in Illinois, but *quadrinotatus* occurs in the
Northeast.

Platycentropus Ulmer

Platycentropus Ulmer (1905*a*, p. 13). Genotype, by original designation: *Halesus maculipennis* Kolenati.
Hylepsyche Banks (1916, p. 121). Genotype,
by original designation: *Halesus indistinctus*
(Walker).

Of the three species described in the genus
only one is known from Illinois.

Platycentropus radiatus (Say)

Phryganea radiata Say (1824, p. 308).
Limnephilus indicans Walker (1852, p. 23);
♀. New synonymy.
Halesus maculipennis Kolenati (1859*b*, p.
176); ♂. New synonymy.
Hallesus hostis Hagen (1861, p. 266); ♂.
New synonymy.

Larva.—Length 24 mm. Head and pronotum with ground color yellowish brown,
nearly orange, irregularly speckled with
small black dots which are arranged to form
a small design on the frons. Mesonotum

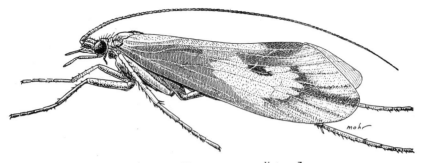

Fig. 641.—*Platycentropus radiatus* ♂.

and legs brownish yellow with irregular darker markings. Pronotum with a transverse depression. Abdominal gills long and single beyond base, arising in groups of one to three. Lateral line conspicuous.

CASE.—Length 23 mm., constructed of fiber and wood fragments to form a round and very thick case of log-cabin construction and usually very fuzzy in appearance.

ADULTS.—Fig. 641. Length 20–23 mm. General color a medium shade of brown, the wings with a very distinct pattern of various shades of brown ranging from almost cream color to chocolate, as in fig. 641. Fifth, sixth and seventh sternites in both sexes with a row of projecting sclerotized teeth. Male genitalia, fig. 642: cerci small and cushion shaped, bearing a black mesal area; tenth tergite forming a pair of long, pointed processes which are black and striate on the dorsal surface; claspers small and inconspicuous. Aedeagus as in fig. 642. Female

genitalia, fig. 642, simple, without long or complicated processes.

Neotype, male.—Northern Illinois, Peabody Collection.

The neotype fits Say's description well, and records indicate that the species occurs throughout the bounds of the old "Northwest Territory," which included Illinois, Michigan, Minnesota and Wisconsin.

The occurrence of specimens of this species in old collections, such as Peabody's, may indicate that *radiatus* was more abundant in earlier years. This circumstance is undoubtedly true of some of Say's other species.

In Illinois this species has been taken at Palos Park (near Chicago) and along the Kankakee River at Momence (see p. 5). At this locality one female was taken at lights; in addition to this we took moderate numbers of the larvae on drift along the river bank after a very heavy flood. We have taken larvae of this species in abundance in some of the small streams in northwestern Indiana which are the headwaters of the Kankakee River, but we have taken the larvae at Momence only after a flood stage of water. We think it highly probable that this species does not normally live in the river at Momence but is periodically washed down from small streams. Larvae from Momence were reared.

The range of the species extends through the East and Northeast; records are known from Georgia, Illinois, Indiana, Manitoba, Massachusetts, Michigan, Minnesota, Newfoundland, New York, Ontario and Wisconsin.

Illinois Records.—MOMENCE, Kankakee River: June 4, 1932, Frison & Mohr, 1♀; May 19, 1937, Ross & Burks, many larvae, 1♂ pupa (reared). PALOS PARK: June 19, 1909, W. J. Gerhard, 1♂, FM; June 24, 1922, W. J. Gerhard, 1♀, FM.

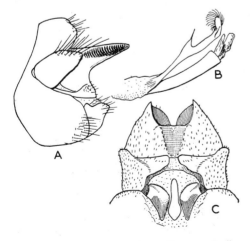

Fig. 642.—*Platycentropus radiatus*, genitalia. *A*, male; *B*, aedeagus; *C*, female.

Glyphotaelius Stephens

Glyphotaelius Stephens (1837, p. 211). Genotype, monobasic: *Limnephilus pellucidus* De Geer (spelled *pellucidulus* by Stephens).
Glyphidotaulius Kolenati (1848, p. 36). Emended name.

Only one species has been recorded from North America, *hostilis*. This species has not been taken in Illinois but is distributed throughout the Northeast.

Astenophylax Ulmer

Astenophylax Ulmer (1907b, p. 51). Genotype, monobasic: *Phryganea arga* Harris.

The genus contains only one species, *argus*, which has not yet been taken in Illinois.

This large and very showy caddis fly has been taken throughout the northeastern states from Maine to Wisconsin. The wings are medium brown with large areoles which are almost transparent, and the apical third of the wing is almost entirely transparent except for the brown veins.

Hesperophylax Banks

Hesperophylax Banks (1916, p. 118). Genotype, by original designation: *Platyphylax occidentalis* Banks.

The adults of this genus usually have a longitudinal silvery mark on the front wings; this is very prominent in the larger western species. The genitalia of both sexes, fig. 935, are uniform in general structure throughout the entire genus.
Of the described North American species only one occurs in Illinois.

Hesperophylax designatus (Walker)

Limnephilus designatus Walker (1852, p. 24); ♂, ♀.

LARVA.—Length 15 mm. Head, thoracic sclerites and legs yellowish brown; head and pronotum speckled with irregular small brown spots; legs with an orange tinge. Pronotum with a transverse crease. Abdominal gills mostly branched, the dorsal gills and meso-ventral gills of the first few segments with five or six branches and forming a fan, fig. 615. First abdominal sternite with many black, conspicuous setae.

CASE.—Length 18 mm., constructed chiefly of small stones and sand grains; in very young forms the case is strongly tapered and almost horn shaped; in mature specimens it is nearly cylindrical but slightly curved.

ADULTS.—Fig. 643. Length 20 mm. Color brown, the wings with a definite pattern of light and dark brown, and in addition a silver stripe through cell first R_5. Male genitalia, fig. 935: claspers appearing somewhat triangular from lateral view; tenth tergite produced into a dorso-mesal knob; claspers elongate, tapering from base to a narrow apex; aedeagus with a pair of bunches of sclerotized, serrate and appressed spurs. Female genitalia, fig. 938, without conspicuous or complicated processes.

Structurally this species is closely related to others in the genus. In the past there has been considerable confusion as to whether or not certain forms were varieties or species, but differences in the cerci and tenth tergite appear to separate these clearly. A key to the Nearctic species is given on page 281.

Our Illinois records are all from the spring-fed brooks in the Botanical Gardens at Elgin. The species is very abundant in this set of streams (see p. 7), and larvae, pupae and adults have been collected there. Our adult emergence was apparently confined to May.

The species is widely distributed through the Northeast; records are known from Illinois, Michigan, New Hampshire, New York, Nova Scotia, Ontario and Wisconsin.

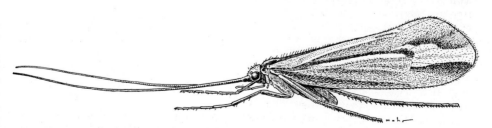

Fig. 643.—*Hesperophylax designatus* ♂.

Illinois Records.—ELGIN: April 19, 1939, Burks & Riegel, 3 pupae; May 9, 1939, Ross & Burks, 2 ♂, 2 larvae; May 14, 1939, Ross & Burks, 1 ♂, 3 ♀; May 20, 1939, 33 cases, 1 ♂ pupa, 3 ♀ pupae; June 13, 1939, Frison & Ross, many larvae; May 7, 1941, Mohr & Burks, 1 ♂, 1 ♀; preceding Elgin records from Botanical Gardens; Rainbow Springs, April 19, 1939, Burks & Riegel, 7 pupae; Trout Spring, March 7, 1940, Burks & Mohr, 8 larvae.

Ironoquia Banks

Ironoquia Banks (1916, p. 121). Genotype, by original designation: *Chaetopterygopsis parvula* Banks.

This genus contains only one species, the genotype, described from New Brunswick, New Jersey. It has not been taken in Illinois.

Leptophylax Banks

Leptophylax Banks (1900a, p. 252). Genotype, monobasic: *Leptophylax gracilis* Banks.

Only one species is known for the genus, and this has been taken in Illinois.

Leptophylax gracilis Banks

Leptophylax gracilis Banks (1900a, p. 252); ♀.

LARVA.—Unknown.
ADULTS.—Fig. 644. Length 14–16 mm. Color tawny, the antennae and anal portion of the wings darker brown. Form elongate, the head and pronotum long, fig. 644. Male genitalia, fig. 645: cerci large, the apical margin sclerotized and the apico-dorsal corner forming a sclerotized point; tenth tergite forming two long, narrow blades; claspers narrow, long and pointed, the apex tipped with black. Female genitalia with apical segments large, and the lateral lobes of the tenth tergite long and pointed.

We have no recent record of this species from Illinois, but it has been collected in earlier years from Chicago and Algonquin. Nothing is known of the biology of the species. It is widespread through the Northeast; records are known from Illinois, Michigan, Minnesota, New York and South Dakota.

Illinois Records.—ALGONQUIN: July 3,

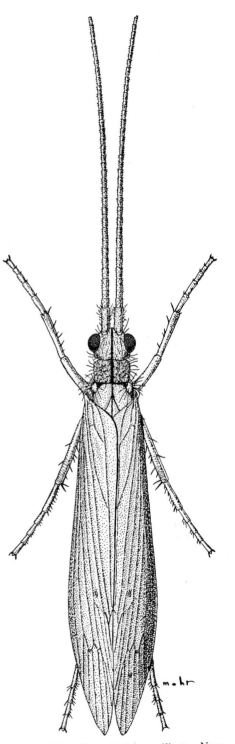

Fig. 644.—*Leptophylax gracilis* ♀. Now a rarity, but apparently abundant in Illinois at one time.

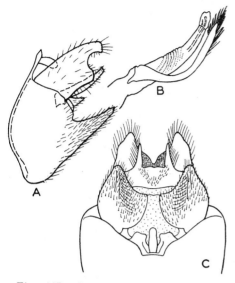

Fig. 645.—*Leptophylax gracilis*, genitalia. *A*, male; *B*, aedeagus; *C*, female.

1909, 1 ♀ ; July 10, 1909, 3 ♀ ; July 3, 1910, 4 ♂, 1 ♀ ; July 7, 1910, 1 ♀ ; July 28, 1910, 1 ♀ ; all W. A. Nason. Chicago: June 23, 1907, Lincoln Park, 1 ♂ ; June 11, W. J. Gerhard, 1 ♀, fm ; June 17, W. J. Gerhard, 1 ♂ .

Grammotaulius Kolenati

Grammotaulius Kolenati (1848, p. 38). Genotype, by subsequent designation of Milne (1935, p. 50): *Phryganea interrogationis* Zetterstedt.

No representatives of this genus have been taken in Illinois. The species are all large and Arctic or Subarctic in distribution. The genotype is known as far south as Minnesota. The genus was revised by Denning (1941*b*).

Limnephilus Leach

Limnephilus Leach (1815, p. 136). Genotype, monobasic: *Phryganea rhombica* Linnaeus.
Anabolina Banks (1903*a*, p. 244). Genotype, by original designation: *Anabolina diversa* Banks.
Apolopsyche Banks (1916, p. 121). Genotype, by original designation: *Stenophylax minusculus* Banks.
Algonquina Banks (1916, p. 121). Genotype, by original designation: *Stenophylax? parvula* Banks.

Rheophylax Sibley (1926*b*, p. 107). Genotype, by original designation: *Limnephilus submonilifer* Walker.

The species treated under this genus include those placed by previous writers not only in *Limnephilus* but in *Anabolia*, *Anabolina*, *Arctoecia* and *Colpotaulius*. I have been unable to find characters which will key out either the males or the females to these groups; available characters intergrade to such an extent that they cannot be used for accurate separation. I have not listed certain of these genera as synonyms because the genotypes involve European species which cannot be placed quite definitely in relation to the North American forms.

The characteristics of the genus are varied, and the only diagnostic characters which I have found are included in the key. This is probably one of the largest genera in North America, containing 60 or 70 species. Of these we have taken only 9 in Illinois, one of which is very common and widespread, the others locally distributed and rare.

KEY TO SPECIES

Larvae

1. Head yellow, with scattered brown dots, without dark areas or lines, fig. 646. . . . .**consocius,** p. 190
   Head with dark areas at least as extensive as in fig. 647.   2
2. First abdominal tergite with only a few setae beside dorsal hump and above lateral swellings, fig. 650. . . .
   . . . . **submonilifer,** p. 192
   First abdominal tergite with many setae in each of these areas, fig. 651   3
3. Mesal and lateral dark areas of head separated by a wide pale area, fig. 648. . . . .**rhombicus,** p. 190
   Mesal and lateral dark areas of head separated by a narrow pale area, fig. 649. . . . .**indivisus,** p. 191

Adults

1. Antennae 3-segmented (males).   2
   Antennae 5-segmented (females). 11
2. Front basitarsus only half length of second tarsal segment and with a black, curved apical spur. . . . .
   . . . .**submonilifer,** p. 192
   Front basitarsus longer than second tarsal segment and with a straight, yellow apical spur.   3

3. Cerci with a deep lateral incision dividing them into long dorsal and ventral lobes, fig. 653...**ornatus**, p. 189
   Cerci with posterior margin slightly or not at all incised............ 4

4. Cerci very large, long and wide, dwarfing the other parts of the genitalia, especially the minute tenth tergite, fig. 654............**rhombicus**, p. 190
   Cerci either small, fig. 655, or less than twice length of tenth tergite, fig. 659............................ 5

5. Cerci short, either widened at apex

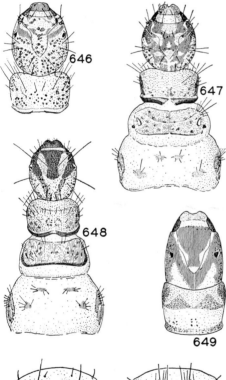

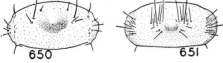

Fig. 646.—*Limnephilus consocius* larva, head and thorax.
Fig. 647.—*Limnephilus submonilifer* larva, head and thorax.
Fig. 648.—*Limnephilus rhombicus* larva, head and thorax.
Fig. 649.—*Limnephilus indivisus* larva, head and thorax.
Fig. 650.—*Limnephilus submonilifer* larva, first abdominal tergite.
Fig. 651.—*Limnephilus rhombicus* larva, first abdominal tergite.

and spatulate, or with apical margin incised, figs. 655–658............ 6
   Cerci long and rounded or pointed at apex, figs. 659–661............... 9

6. Claspers reduced to a small, sharp triangle; processes of tenth tergite narrow and sharp, projecting below level of cerci, fig. 655...**sericeus**, p. 192
   Claspers large, fig. 656, or projecting as finger-like processes, fig. 657; processes of tenth tergite projecting between cerci and at least partially hidden by them in lateral view.... 7

7. Cerci with apical margin uniformly black and heavily sclerotized, emarginate, forming a produced dorsal lobe, fig. 656; mesal face of cerci without row of teeth near base....
   ....**consocius**, p. 190
   Cerci with apical margin not black but with mesal, sclerotized teeth black; apical margin nearly straight, with the dorsal corner rounded, figs. 657, 658; mesal face of cerci with a row of black, sclerotized teeth near base, fig. 658................... 8

8. Claspers broad, nearly as broad as cerci; lateral arms of aedeagus ending in a membranous, diamond-shaped lobe with a dense brush of spines, fig. 657........**hyalinus**, p. 191
   Claspers finger-like, much narrower than cerci; lateral arms of aedeagus bladelike and with a dorsal angulation, bearing a definite dorsal row of setae, fig. 658........**indivisus**, p. 191

9. Claspers small and platelike, without any projecting parts, fig. 659......
   ....**moestus**, p. 191
   Claspers with a long, pointed apical portion, fig. 660................. 10

10. Cerci longer, more slender at tip and curved slightly ventrad, fig. 660...
    ....**sordidus**, p. 189
    Cerci shorter and stouter, straight and tapered at tip to a point, fig. 661...
    ....**bimaculatus**, p. 189

11. Cerci represented only as slight swellings at base of tenth tergite, which forms a simple tube, fig. 662......
    ....**submonilifer**, p. 192
    Cerci present as distinct processes above or beside tenth tergite, figs. 663–671........................ 12

12. Tenth segment very short and broad, cerci long; ninth tergite broad and bandlike, fig. 663......**ornatus**, p. 189
    Tenth segment more than half length of cerci, fig. 665, usually as long as or longer than cerci, fig. 666...... 13

13. Dorsal portion of tenth segment produced into a long, thin spatula

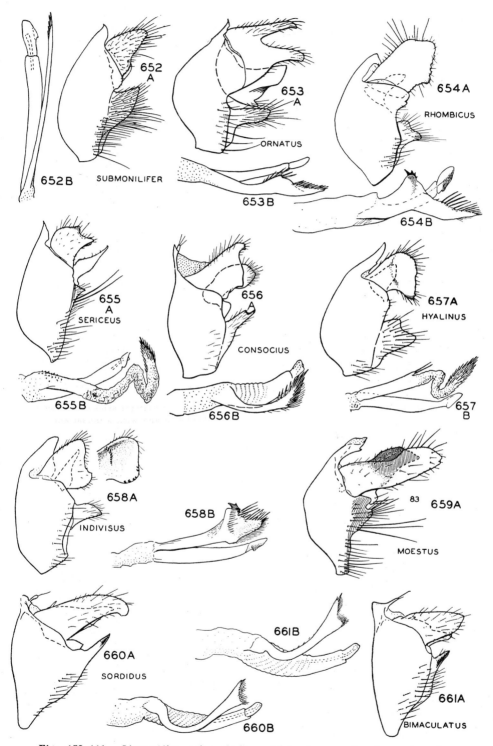

Figs. 652–661.—*Limnephilus*, male genitalia. *A*, lateral aspect; *B*, aedeagus, lateral aspect, showing one of the lateral arms.

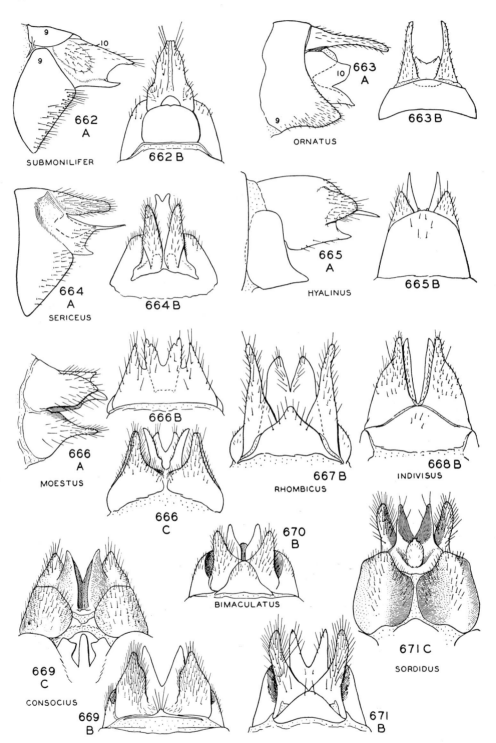

Figs. 662–671.—*Limnephilus*, female genitalia. *A*, lateral aspect; *B*, dorsal aspect; *C*, ventral aspect.

slightly emarginate at apex, fig. 664
...................................**sericeus**, p. 192
Dorsal portion of tenth tergite either
divided at least half way to base,
fig. 665, or not much produced beyond ventral margin.............   14

14. Dorsal portion of tenth segment modified into a pair of narrow, needle-
like blades, fig. 665....**hyalinus**, p. 191
Dorsal portion of tenth segment with
wide blades, fig. 666.............   15

15. Ninth sternite prolonged into long,
finger-like processes, the apices of
which are separated by half the
width of the segment, as in fig. 666
...................................**moestus**, p. 191
Ninth sternite forming a pair of short,
stocky processes, figs. 667–671....   16

16. Cerci long, slender, spindly, and widely separated to base, tenth tergite
very much stouter, its halves appressed, fig. 667.....**rhombicus**, p. 190
Cerci stout, shorter and wider, fig.
668, tenth tergite not stouter than
cerci...............................   17

17. Cerci close together at base and apex,
forming with the tenth segment a
definitely conical structure, fig. 668
...................................**indivisus**, p. 191
Cerci either diverging, fig. 671, or wide
apart at base, fig. 669............   18

18. Ninth tergite with only a small sclerotized button, cerci wide apart at
base; ninth sternite with lobes
rounded ventrad, tenth tergite with
lateral halves solid and pyramidal,
fig. 669............**consocius**, p. 190
Ninth tergite with a fairly large, triangular sclerite, cerci fairly close
together at base; ninth sternite with
lobes angular ventrad, tenth tergite
with lateral halves thin and curved,
fig. 671...........................   19

19. Cerci with a large, nearly bulbous
basal portion which narrows to a
small, short apex, fig. 670........
...................**bimaculatus**, p. 189
Cerci with a small basal portion and
a long, thin apex, fig. 671........
...................................**sordidus**, p. 189

Limnephilus sordidus (Hagen)

Anabolia sordida Hagen (1861, p. 264); ♂.
Anabolia longicercus Denning (1941a, p.
195); ♂, ♀.

LARVA.—Unknown.
ADULTS.—Length 16–18 mm. Color dark
reddish brown, the dorsum and antennae almost black, the front wings very dark brown

with irregular light dots scattered over the
entire surface of the wing, giving it a salt-
and-pepper appearance. Head and thorax
with black dorsal macrochaetae, those on
head sparse. Front basitarsus of male much
longer than succeeding segment. Male genitalia, fig. 660, with long cerci which are
narrowed at apex and have a few small
sclerotized teeth along the apico-mesal margin; lobes of tenth tergite also long and
reaching nearly to apex of cerci; claspers
smooth, long and sharp; lateral arms of
aedeagus sclerotized, curved, widened and
obliquely truncate at apex. Female genitalia, fig. 671, with ninth tergite triangular,
cerci long and diverging, lateral halves of
tenth segment thin and long, ninth sternite
produced into large angulate protuberances.

Our only Illinois record of this species
is a female collected at Galena, Illinois,
bearing the number 1062; this specimen was
recorded by Hagen and is probably part of
the Kennicott Collection.

The range of this species is poorly understood. It was originally described from the
Red River valley (North Dakota–Minnesota), but undoubtedly specimens of this
species had been recorded under the name
bimaculatus, and few definite locality records can be given until this material is re-
studied.

Limnephilus bimaculatus Walker

Limnephilus bimaculatus Walker (1852, p.
30); ♂.

This species occurs throughout the northern states from Colorado to the Atlantic
Coast. Betten mentions a record from
northern Illinois in Hagen's specimens, but
these specimens are the preceding species,
sordidus. We have no definite Illinois records of this species, although it might be
taken in future collections.

Limnephilus ornatus Banks

Limnephilus ornatus Banks (1897, p. 27); ♀.
Limnephilus elegans Mosely (1929, p. 504);
♂.

LARVA.—Unknown.
ADULTS.—Length 17–18 mm. Color yellowish brown, the front wings with longitudinal silvery stripes which contrast with
the chocolate brown ground color. Dorsum
of head and thorax with a mixture of tawny

and silvery setae. Front basitarsus of male longer than second segment. Male genitalia, fig. 653, with cerci deeply incised to form long dorsal and ventral lobes; tenth tergite large and stocky; claspers with wide base and fairly long apical portion; lateral arms of aedeagus with a wide foliaceous apex bearing rows of spines. Female genitalia, fig. 663, with cerci long and slender, tenth segment short and forming a wide tube.

Dr. Betten (1934) reports this species from Lake Forest, Illinois, in June. In addition to this record, we have a single female bearing the data "Northern Illinois," a male collected at Zion, Illinois, June 26, 1936, Frison & DeLong, and a female collected at Chicago, Illinois, May 17, W. J. Gerhard, FM.

The species has been recorded from scattered localities over a very wide range from Greenland, across America, to Japan; on the North American continent records are available for Alaska, Illinois, Maine, Massachusetts, Newfoundland, New Hampshire, New York and Ontario.

Limnephilus rhombicus (Linnaeus)

Phryganea rhombica Linnaeus (1758, p. 548).
Limnephilus combinatus Walker (1852, p. 28); ♂.

LARVA.—Length 20 mm. Head, thoracic sclerites and legs yellowish brown with scattered brown dots; head with a distinct brown area down the center of the frons, a pair of brown lines on each side of the frons, and an irregular brown area occupying much of the lateral and ventral portions of the head; pronotum sometimes with anterior half dark.

CASE.—Fig. 672. Length 20 mm., stout and round, constructed of short wood fragments woven together in an irregular pattern.

ADULTS. — Length 19–20 mm. Color brownish yellow, the wings with a distinct pattern of cream color and chocolate brown arranged in somewhat oblique stripes. Head and thorax armed with silvery or tawny macrochaetae. Front basitarsus of male longer than succeeding segment. Male genitalia, fig. 654, with very long, wide cerci which have a row of ventro-mesal sclerotized teeth; tenth tergite very small, claspers small. Female genitalia, fig. 667, with minute ninth tergite, long and spindly cerci and stout tenth segment.

We have taken this species in Illinois only in the spring-fed brooks in the Botanical Gardens at Elgin (see p. 7). To date we have actually captured only three larvae and one female of this species there, so that it is a rarity with us.

This species is widely distributed throughout the Northeast. All stages were described

Fig. 672.—*Limnephilus rhombicus*, case.

by Vorhies (1909) and Lloyd (1921), and records are available from Greenland, Illinois, Maine, Newfoundland, New York, Saskatchewan and Wisconsin, in addition to records from Eurasia.

Illinois Records. — ELGIN: Botanical Gardens, June 19, 1939, H. H. Ross, 1 ♀ ; Trout Spring, March 7, 1940, Burks & Mohr, 3 larvae.

Limnephilus consocius Walker

Limnephilus consocius Walker (1852, p. 33); ♂.
Colpotaulius medialis Banks (1905*b*, p. 8); ♂.

LARVA.—Length 20 mm. Head and pronotum yellow, with small brown spots scattered over the entire surface, fig. 646. Other sclerites yellow with variable brown spots.

CASE.—Length 20 mm. Constructed chiefly of wood and leaf fragments, irregular in outline, but fairly stoutly constructed.

ADULTS.—Length 14–16 mm. Color almost entirely a rich reddish brown, the front wings finely marbled with a darker shade of brown but without a definite pattern. Setae of head and thorax reddish brown. Front basitarsus longer than the succeeding segment. Male genitalia, fig. 656, with cerci short and broad at apex, the posterior margin heavily sclerotized along the mesal edge; claspers narrow, with a pair of sclerotized points at apex; tenth tergite projecting beyond cerci; aedeagus with stout, curved, spinose, lateral arms. Female genitalia, fig. 669, with cerci stout and tenth tergite with the lateral halves thick and pyramidal; ninth sternite developed into large rounded protuberances.

This species has been taken at various points in the northeastern quarter of the state. Dr. Betten found it abundant in the ravines at Lake Forest, Illinois, but in our recent collections we have taken adults only in small numbers at various localities. Lloyd (1921) has described the immature stages. Our adult records for Illinois are scattered from early June to late August.

The range of the species occupies most of the Northeast; records are available from Illinois, Maine, Michigan, New Hampshire, New York, Ontario and Wisconsin.

Illinois Records.—CHICAGO: Aug. 3–12, W. J. Gerhard, 1 ♂, 2 ♀, FM. KANKAKEE: June 17, 1939, B. D. Burks, 1 ♂. PALOS PARK: June 19, 1933, Ross & Mohr, 2 ♀; Sept. 11, 1910, W. J. Gerhard, 1 ♀, FM. SEYMOUR: June 13, 1929, Frison & Hottes, 1 ♂, 1 ♀. URBANA: Aug. 24, 1896, at light, C. A. Hart, 1 ♂. WAUKEGAN: July 6, 1932, Frison *et al.*, 2 ♂.

Limnephilus indivisus Walker

Limnephilus indivisus Walker (1852, p. 34).
Limnephilus subguttatus Walker (1852, p. 34).

LARVA.—Length 20 mm. Head and pronotum with a pattern of light and dark markings as in fig. 649. Legs and other sclerites yellow with indefinite brown marks.

CASE.—Length 20 mm. Constructed in log-cabin style, as in fig. 833, of small twigs, grass stems and other short and narrow pieces.

ADULTS.—Length 15–16 mm. Color in general tawny to straw color, the front wings with scattered irregular brown marks which give a slightly banded impression. Setae of head and thorax tawny. Front basitarsus longer than the succeeding segment. Male genitalia, fig. 658: cerci short and triangular, narrow at base, the posterior margin bearing sclerotized teeth, the mesal face with a row of sclerotized teeth near base; tenth tergite with lobes long and narrow; claspers short, lateral arms of aedeagus sclerotized, with a sharp dorsal fin. Female genitalia, fig. 668, with the parts compactly arranged to give the general impression of a tube.

Our only Illinois record of this species is a single male collected at Antioch, August 1, 1930, Frison, Knight & Ross. The species is widely distributed through the Northeast with about the same range as that for the preceding. Lloyd (1921) has described the immature stages.

Limnephilus hyalinus Hagen

Limnephilus hyalinus Hagen (1861, p. 258); ♂.

LARVA.—Unknown.

ADULTS.—Length 13–14 mm. Entire insect straw colored except for the black spines on the middle and hind legs; front wings usually without any pattern, hyaline; with very sparse, short hair; sometimes with faint brownish markings along the posterior margin. Front basitarsus longer than succeeding segment. Male genitalia, fig. 657, with cerci short, narrow at base, and with a mesal ridge of sclerotized teeth near base, this ridge, continuing faintly near ventral margin to postero-ventral corner; lobes of tenth tergite fairly wide but short, claspers wide and short, the apex emarginate; aedeagus with lateral arms terminating in an extensile membranous organ tipped with a diamond-shaped brush of spines. Female genitalia, fig. 665, with ninth tergite and cerci short and broad, tenth segment developed into a pair of long and needle-like processes.

The only Illinois record for this species is a single female in the Field Museum Collection taken at Chicago, August 29, W. J. Gerhard. The species has a very widespread range extending across the entire northern portion of the continent, with records from British Columbia, Colorado, Illinois, New York, the Northwest Territory (Canada) and Ontario.

Limnephilus moestus Banks

Limnephilus moestus Banks (1908a, p. 62); ♂, ♀.
Limnephilus hingstoni Mosely (1929, p. 504); ♂.

LARVA.—Unknown.

ADULTS.—Length 12–13 mm. Color dark brown; front wings with cubital and anal areas tawny, remainder of wing chocolate brown with cream-colored spots, some of these spots forming a fairly large, light area around the cord. Front basitarsus of male longer than succeeding segment. Male genitalia, fig. 659, with very long and slightly sinuate cerci, long and pointed tenth tergite, and claspers reduced to a small plate bearing numerous short setae and a few long ones. Female genitalia similar to those in fig. 666, with cerci and tenth segment long, and ninth sternite developed into a pair of long, finger-like processes.

We have only one record of this species in Illinois, a male collected at Dixon, at lights along the Rock River, June 27, 1935, DeLong & Ross. The species is widespread through the northern part of the continent from Greenland to Colorado, with records from Colorado, Greenland, Illinois, Newfoundland, Nova Scotia, Ontario, Quebec and Wisconsin.

Limnephilus sericeus (Say)

Phryganea sericeus Say (1824, p. 309).
Limnephilus despectus Walker (1852, p. 31); ♂, ♀. New synonymy.
Limnephilus multifarius Walker (1852, p. 32); ♀. New synonymy.
Limnephilus perforatus Walker (1852, p. 33); ♀. New synonymy.
Limnephilus eminens Betten (1934, p. 323); ♂. New synonymy.

This species has not been taken in Illinois but occurs to the north from Alaska to New York. Records are available for Alaska, Minnesota, New York, Northwest Territory (Canada), Ontario, Pennsylvania and Quebec.

I am designating as a neotype a female from Duluth, Minnesota, well differentiated on the basis of its genitalia, fig. 664, and characters given in the preceding key. The species was originally described from the old Northwest Territory, which included Minnesota. Of the various species known from that general region, this particular one fits Say's description quite well, especially in the unusual black mark on the forewing.

Neotype, female.—Duluth, Minnesota.

Limnephilus submonilifer Walker

Limnephilus submonilifer Walker (1852, p. 33); ♀.
Limnephilus pudicus Hagen (1861, p. 262); ♂.

Larva.—Length 16–17 mm. Head, thoracic sclerites and legs fairly dark brown; head with frons almost entirely brown and with small light patches at apex and sides, dorso-lateral portions variegated with yellowish brown; legs lighter yellowish brown than the head. See fig. 20, page 20.

Case.—Length 16-20 mm., made of leaf and grass stem fragments neatly arranged in linear order to form a fairly loosely constructed straight and almost cylindrical case.

Adults.—Length 13–16 mm., slender. Color brown, the dorsum darker and the wings variegated with irregular lighter and darker spots; leg spines black. Head and thorax armed dorsad with long, stout macrochaetae. Front legs with a linear brush of stout, black spines on underside of femur and tibia; basitarsus only one-half length of next segment. Male genitalia, fig. 652, with cerci and claspers triangular, tenth tergite short and hooked dorsad, aedeagus with lateral arms sclerotized, filiform, very long and tipped with a small row of short spurs. Female genitalia, fig. 662, with ninth and tenth segments and cerci fused to form a single tubular structure.

This is our common temporary pond and marsh species in Illinois. We have taken it at scattered localities throughout the state, especially in the temporary ponds along railroad rights-of-way and in shallow spring marsh ponds in the northeastern corner of the state. In these situations the larvae are difficult to see since they build their cases from the dead grass stems and leaves in the bottom of the ponds, and, although they frequently practically cover the bottom, it is scarcely possible to detect them until they move.

This species has two very definite generations, at least in the general region of Illinois. The first matures early in spring, in the vicinity of Urbana the adults emerging about the first of May. Soon after this date the ponds invariably dry up, filling up again with the late summer rains. When this occurs, a second generation is developed which matures into the adults in late August and September. This same phenomenon has been noticed by previous writers. Vorhies gave evidence of this two-brooded habit from Wisconsin material, and Betten observed the same phenomenon in his studies with the species in the vicinity of Lake Forest, Illinois.

The range of the species is extensive to the north and east of Illinois; records include the District of Columbia, Illinois, Indiana, Maine, Maryland, Massachusetts, Michigan, Newfoundland, New Hampshire, New York, Ohio, Ontario, Quebec, Rhode Island, South Dakota and Wisconsin.

Illinois Records.—Many males, females

and pupae, taken April 30 to October 17, and many larvae and cases, taken March 3 to May 7, are from Arcola, Cary, Champaign, Chicago, Grayslake, Leslie, Neoga, Oakwood, Rantoul, Rosecrans (Des Plaines River), Savoy, Seymour, Spring Grove, Urbana, Volo, Watson, Waukegan, West Pullman, Zion.

Pycnopsyche Banks

Pycnopsyche Banks (1905*b*, p. 9). Genotype, by original designation: *Limnephilus scabripennis* Rambur.

Allegophylax Banks (1916, p. 118). Genotype, by original designation: *Phryganea subfasciata* Say. New synonymy.

Eustenace Banks (1916, p. 118). Genotype, by original designation: *Stenophylax limbatus* McLachlan. New synonymy.

The general shape and color of the wings, the heart-shaped subgenital plate of the female and the structure of the male genitalia, especially the aedeagus, indicate that the species grouped under this genus form a very compact and homogenous unit. There is considerable variation in particular points of the venation and to an even greater degree in the spur count, but these differences are not substantiated by any indications of phylogenetic importance.

Many species occur in the eastern states, but to date only three have been taken in

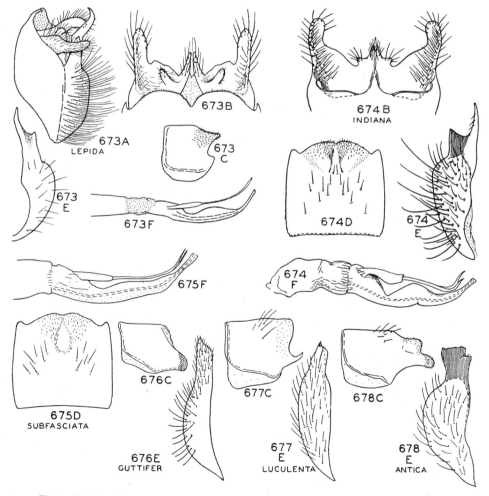

Figs. 673–678.—*Pycnopsyche*, male genitalia. *A* and *B*, lateral and dorsal aspect respectively; *C* and *D*, eighth tergite, lateral and dorsal aspect respectively; *E*, clasper, caudal aspect; *F*, aedeagus.

Illinois. Three others, however, have been taken within a few miles of Illinois and are to be expected here in future collecting.

The larvae of several species of this genus have been reared, but to date no characters have been found to separate them to species.

KEY TO SPECIES

Adults

1. Front wings irregularly speckled over entire surface with small, dark brown spots............**antica,** p. 196

Aedeagus long, narrow, dorsal spines thrice length of their base; mesal area of eighth tergite with a depression, fig. 675...**subfasciata,** p. 194

6. Lateral lobes of eighth tergite widely separated, enlarged and covered with dense, black spines, fig. 676..
.....................**guttifer,** p. 196
Lateral lobes of eighth tergite small and bare, fig. 677.....**luculenta,** p. 196

7. Tenth segment with dorsal portion tapering gradually to apex, without lateral expansions, fig. 680........ 8
Tenth segment with lateral, flangelike

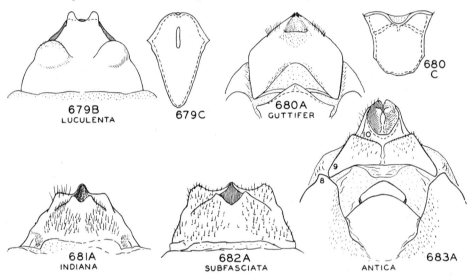

Figs. 679–683.—*Pycnopsyche,* female genitalia. *A,* ventral aspect; *B,* dorsal aspect; *C,* bursa copulatrix.

Front wings at most with dark brown marks near center and along apical margin........................ 2

2. Maxillary palpi 3-segmented (males) 3
Maxillary palpi 5-segmented (females) 7

3. Apico-mesal angle of clasper projecting dorsad as a long, sharp point, fig. 673........................ 4
Apico-mesal angle of claspers not produced into a long point, fig. 676.... 6

4. Eighth tergite with an abrupt, quadrate mesal notch and with an apical brush of short, black spines, fig. 673
.....................**lepida,** p. 195
Eighth tergite not abruptly notched and with triangular patches of spines instead of an apical brush... 5

5. Aedeagus short, stocky, dorsal spines only twice as long as their base; mesal area of eighth tergite not excavated, fig. 674........**indiana,** p. 196

expansions on dorsal portion, fig. 681............................. 9

8. Bursa copulatrix long and triangular; ventral margin of tenth segment bilobed and extending beyond dorsum, fig. 679.............**luculenta,** p. 196
Bursa copulatrix shorter and ovate; ventral margin of tenth segment slightly emarginate but not extending beyond dorsum, fig. 680.......
.....................**guttifer,** p. 196

9. Ventral portion of tenth segment narrowed to a very small, apical opening, fig. 681...........**indiana,** p. 196
Ventral portion of tenth segment narrowed, but with the apical opening wide, fig. 682.......**subfasciata,** p. 194

Pycnopsyche subfasciata (Say)

Phryganea subfasciata Say (1828, pl. 44).

LARVA.—Length 18–20 mm. Head, thoracic sclerites and legs shades of reddish brown; head and pronotum with abundant small dark brown dots; legs with tibiae and tarsi darker and redder than preceding segments. Gills very long and single. First abdominal segment with a pair of very small sclerites near meson of venter and with only a few scattered setae on the rest of the venter and on the dorsum. Pronotum with distinct and fairly deep transverse furrow.

CASE.—Length 20 mm. Constructed of stones, sand and wood fragments; robust and straight, frequently with a long twig or a group of small twigs cemented to the sides so that they trail behind the case; the variety of materials used varies from place to place, sometimes the stone material predominating, sometimes the wood fragment material, so that there is great variation in the general appearance of the case.

ADULTS. — Length 19–20 mm. Color brown, front wings usually with two dark brown marks, a transverse one which ends just in front of *m-cu*, and a more or less angulate mark along the cord; in addition the apex of the wing and a narrow border along the tips of the veins are darkened. Male with eighth tergite rounded at apex and bearing a pair of triangular areas covered with short, brown spines, fig. 675. Male genitalia, fig. 675, with claspers produced into a long dorsal process which usually has a low lateral shoulder at its base; tenth tergite with mesal processes fairly long; aedeagus elongate with a pair of long, needle-like dorsal styles, each of which has a long, tubular base. Female genitalia, fig. 682: tenth segment with lateral flangelike expansions on dorsal portion, ventral portion wide and emarginate on meson, the apical opening wide; subgenital plate and bursa copulatrix as in fig. 682.

Neotype, male. — McHenry, Illinois: Oct. 4, 1931, Ross & Mohr.

This species is very abundant in scattered localities in the state, especially in the northern and eastern parts. It occurs in such rivers as the Salt Fork and Kankakee and also in the glacial lakes in the northeastern corner. There is only a single generation per year. In this state the larvae become full grown not later than June, then aestivate until September, when the adults emerge. In localities to the north, adult emergence may take place in August, as in *Neophylax*.

This species is widespread through the Northeast; records are available for Illinois, Michigan, Minnesota, New York, Pennsylvania, South Dakota and Wisconsin.

Illinois Records. — CHANNEL LAKE: May 16, 1936, Ross & Mohr, many larvae; May 27, 1936, H. H. Ross, 2 larvae. Fox LAKE: Sept. 22, 1931, Frison & Ross, ♂ ♂. GOLCONDA: April 17, 1930, Frison & Ross, 1 larva. HAVANA: June 16, 1894, C. A. Hart, 4 larvae; Sept. 21, 1894, C. A. Hart, 2 pupae; April 9, 1895, 2 larvae; Quiver Creek, April 29, 1937, Ross & Mohr, 1 ♂, 1 ♀, 2 larvae. HOMER: Sept. 24, 1927, T. H. Frison, 1 ♀. KANKAKEE: June 6, 1935, Ross & Mohr, 1 larva. KANKAKEE COUNTY, Kankakee River: June 1, 1901, Laske & Wright, 4 larvae. McHENRY: Oct. 4, 1931, Ross & Mohr, ♂ ♂. MOMENCE: Sept. 19, 1937, Ross & Burks, many larvae and pupae, ♂ ♂, ♀ ♀ (all reared), 1 ♂; Kankakee River, May 26, 1936, H. H. Ross, 3 larvae; July 14, 1936, B. D. Burks, 1 larva; Aug. 21, 1936, Ross & Burks, 2 larvae; Sept. 17, 1937, B. D. Burks, 7 larvae, many pupae, 1 ♀; Sept. 20, 1937, Ross & Burks, 3 larvae; Kankakee River, Oct. 4, 1937, Ross & Burks, 2 ♀. WILMINGTON, Kankakee River: May 17, 1935, H. H. Ross, 1 larva.

Pycnopsyche lepida (Hagen)

Enoicyla lepida Hagen (1861, p. 269); ♂.

LARVA AND CASE.—Similar to those of *subfasciata*.

ADULTS.—In size and color similar to *subfasciata*. Eighth tergite of male with posterior margin sharply incised and with a brush of black setae along entire margin. Male genitalia, fig. 673, differing from those of *subfasciata* chiefly in always having a large, sharp, concave shoulder at the base of the apical process of the claspers. Female unknown; the specimen so labeled by Betten & Mosely (1940, p. 156) is only a provisional assignment as stated by the authors, and we have no well-associated females for the species.

We have only a single record of this species from Illinois, a male collected along the Kankakee River at Momence, September 7, 1937, Frison & Ross. Apparently its life cycle is the same as for *subfasciata*.

The range of the species is very similar to that of *subfasciata*: through the North-

196 ILLINOIS NATURAL HISTORY SURVEY BULLETIN *Vol. 23, Art. 1*

east; records are available from Illinois, Michigan, New York, Pennsylvania, Virginia, West Virginia and Wisconsin.

Pycnopsyche guttifer (Walker)

Halesus guttifer Walker (1852, p. 16); ♂, ♀.
Pycnopsyche similis Banks (1907a, p. 122); ♂.

LARVA AND CASE.—Similar to those of *subfasciata*.

ADULTS.—In size and color similar to *subfasciata*; the dark marks of the front wing quite variable in size, shape and degree of darkness. Eighth tergite of male with postero-lateral corners produced into long lobes which bear a dense cushion of black spines along the apex. Male genitalia, fig. 676, with tenth tergite produced into narrow sclerotized hooks, claspers with apex long, flattened and oblique at tip, aedeagus very similar to that of *subfasciata*. Female genitalia with tenth segment narrowed toward apex, the dorsum forming a pair of narrow flanges, the ventral margin incised.

Dr. Betten has collected this species from Lake Forest, Illinois, but we have not taken it in our recent survey. The streams around Lake Forest have changed greatly since Dr. Betten collected there in about 1905-06, and it is entirely possible that the colony of *guttifer* which he located has become extinct in that area.

The species is widely distributed through the Northeast; records are available for Georgia, Illinois, Michigan, New Hampshire, New York, Nova Scotia, Ontario, Saskatchewan, South Dakota and Tennessee.

Pycnopsyche antica (Walker)

Neuronia antica Walker (1852, p. 9); ♀.

This species has not yet been taken in Illinois, but J. S. Ayars has taken it in the extreme southwestern corner of Michigan at Almena, not far from Illinois.

As pointed out by Betten & Mosely (1940, p. 144), there is some question regarding the identity of Rambur's species *scabripennis*, under which name the present species has usually been listed in North American literature. Collections from North Carolina indicate that the male here illustrated is the one associated with the type of *antica*. Its range extends through some of the eastern

states; records are available from Georgia, Michigan, North Carolina and West Virginia.

Pycnopsyche indiana (Ross)

Stenophylax indiana Ross (1938d, p. 121); ♂, ♀.

This species has not yet been taken in Illinois, although it occurs nearby in southern Indiana. It is possible that some of the unidentified *Pycnopsyche* larvae which we have obtained from southern Illinois streams may belong to this species, but we have not yet been able to differentiate the larvae of *indiana* from other related species in the genus.

Records for the species, which are very limited, include only Rogers, Indiana, and Athens, Ohio; this may indicate that the range of the species is south and west of the main range of *subfasciata*, to which it is most closely allied.

Pycnopsyche luculenta (Betten)

Stenophylax luculentus Betten (1934, p. 345); ♂, ♀.

Although we have not yet taken this species in Illinois, we have reared it in southern Indiana close to Illinois, so that it may be found in this state with future collecting. The larvae are apparently indistinguishable from others in the genus. It is widespread in distribution, although apparently local, and seldom collected. Records are available for Indiana, New York and North Carolina.

Caborius Navás

Allophylax Banks (1907a, p. 119); preoccupied. Genotype, by original designation: *Halesus punctatissimus* Walker.
Caborius Navás (1918, p. 362). New name for *Allophylax* Banks.
Carborius used by Betten (1934), Milne (1935) and Ross (1938a); misspelling.

Both previously described species of this genus have been taken in Illinois, and a third form, until now undescribed, has also been captured. All of them are short and stocky and have broad wings.

No North American species have yet been reared. We have located many colonies of larvae in Illinois, but all efforts to rear them have failed. The larvae are about 15 mm. long, the head and pronotum are yellowish brown with brown spots, and the gills at the base of the abdomen are short and very bushy, each forming a compact fan with 10 to 12 filaments, fig. 616. These agree perfectly with the description of the European species of this genus, the peculiar gills being diagnostic. The case is usually slightly curved and made of wood fragments.

We have taken these larvae in temporary ponds and in small streams, most of which became dry in summer. In each collection we made, the larvae were full grown late in April or early in May. They appear to aestivate under roots and other objects close to or under the bank of the stream or pond. We never were able to locate the larvae after the stream or pond dried up, and the cultures which we had in cages in various streams were all killed by a fungus growth. Our adult records are all late in the season, ranging from September into October, although in other states adult records are earlier. It is very likely that this genus has essentially the same habits as *Neophylax* (see p. 202).

As it is impossible to be sure of the association of any of the larvae with definite species, the records of the larvae for the entire genus are grouped together as follows.

Illinois Records of *Caborius* Larvae: Des Plaines, Fox River: May 26, 1936, H. H. Ross, 1 larva. Fox Ridge State Park: April 12, 1941, B. D. Burks, 1 larva. Hurd, small stream: April 15, 1936, Ross & Mohr, many larvae. Oakwood: April 10, 1936, Ross & Mohr, 1 larva; May 6, 1936, Ross & Mohr, 2 larvae; May 7, 1936, Ross & Mohr, 1 larva. Rantoul, temporary pond: April 10, 1936, Ross & Mohr, 1 larva. Red Bud: March 23, 1939, Ross & Burks, 2 larvae. Seymour: March 20, 1929, H. H. Ross, 1 larva. Watson: April 15, 1936, Ross & Mohr, 2 larvae; April 16, 1936, Ross & Mohr, 1 larva.

KEY TO SPECIES

Adults

1. Maxillary palpi 3-segmented (males) 2
   Maxillary palpi 5-segmented (females) 3
2. Apex of aedeagus cleft and lyre shaped at apex, claspers rounded at apex, fig. 684 . . . . **lyratus**, p. 198

Apex of aedeagus divided into a pair of bulging, sharp plates with a membranous dorsal pocket, claspers bluntly pointed at apex, fig. 685 . . . . **punctatissimus**, p. 197
3. Ninth and tenth tergites separated by a distinct, suture-like groove; ninth sternite without an internal plate ventrad of bursa copulatrix, fig. 686 . . . . **kaskaskia**, p. 198
   Ninth and tenth tergites fused and scarcely separable, fig. 687; ninth sternite with a round or rectangular internal plate ventrad of bursa, figs. 687, 688 4
4. Ninth sternite with an internal rectangular plate ventrad of bursa copulatrix, fig. 688 . . . . **punctatissimus**, p. 197
   Ninth sternite with internal plate much smaller and semicircular, fig. 687 . . . . **lyratus**, p. 198

Caborius punctatissimus (Walker)

Halesus punctatissimus Walker (1852, p. 17); ♂.

Adults.—Length 16–18 mm. Color almost uniformly yellowish brown, the front

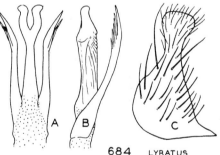

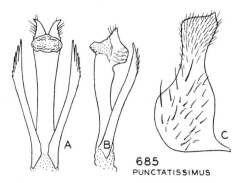

Figs. 684–685.—*Caborius*, male genitalia. *A*, aedeagus, ventral aspect; *B*, aedeagus, lateral aspect; *C*, clasper.

wings a darker bown with small, light dots scattered over the entire surface to give it a peppered look. Face with genae produced into sharp points. Male genitalia, fig. 685, with the claspers pointed at apex, the aedeagus with its extreme tip forming a pair of somewhat triangular lobes having a dorsal membranous fold. Female genitalia, fig. 688, with ninth and tenth tergites fused and with the ninth sternite bearing an internal, rectangular, sclerotized plate ventrad of the bursa copulatrix.

Allotype, female. — Columbia Crossroads, Pennsylvania: July 7, 1931, R. M. Leonard.

Our only Illinois record of this species is a female collected at Champaign, October 6, 1938, C. O. Mohr. Dr. Mohr captured this specimen in the grass and weeds at the edge of a small stream which forms the headwaters of the Embarrass River.

The species is widespread through the

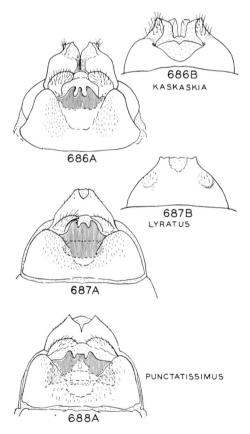

Figs. 686–688.—*Caborius*, female genitalia. *A*, ventral aspect; *B*, dorsal aspect.

Northeast; definite records are available from Illinois, Indiana, Maryland, Michigan, New York, Nova Scotia and Ohio.

Caborius lyratus Ross

Carborius lyratus Ross (1938a, p. 163); ♂.

Adults.—Length 16–18 mm. In color similar to *punctatissimus*, yellowish brown, the front wings darker brown with small light dots scattered over the entire surface. Face with genae not unusually produced. Male genitalia, fig. 684, with the claspers rounded at apex, the aedeagus with its extreme tip forming a divided, lyre-shaped fork without any dorsal membranous fold. Female genitalia, fig. 687, with ninth and tenth tergites fused and with the ninth sternite bearing an internal, semicircular, semisclerotized plate ventrad of the bursa copulatrix.

Allotype, female. — Oakwood, Illinois: Sept. 20, 1935, DeLong & Ross (this is the same data as for the holotype).

In Illinois this species has been taken only at Oakwood, the collection comprising the holotype and allotype, both bearing the data given above. *Caborius* larvae were collected in a small tributary of the Salt Fork near the point at which the adults were taken at lights. These larvae were not relocated in the fall after they had gone into aestivation and the stream had dried up. The range of the species is very poorly known, the only available records being from Illinois, Pennsylvania and Wisconsin.

Caborius kaskaskia new species

Female.—Length 16 mm. Color light brown, the front wing slightly darker brown with small light dots scattered over the entire surface of the wing. General structure typical for the genus. Genitalia, fig. 686: subgenital plate with three processes, the lateral ones wide at base and tapering to a rounded apex; ninth and tenth segments separated on the dorsum by a sharp declivity; ninth segment with the apical portion divided from the base by a furrow; bursa copulatrix without a plate ventrad of it.

Holotype, female.—New Memphis, Illinois, along Kaskaskia River: Sept. 25, 1939, Frison & Ross.

Paratype.—Same data as for holotype, 1 ♀.

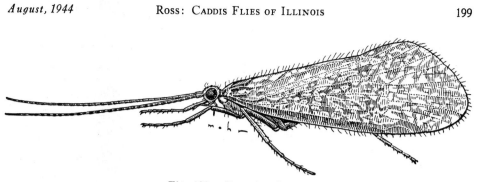

Fig. 689.—*Frenesia missa* ♀.

This species is distinguished from the others in the genus by characters given in the preceding key. It is represented only by the single collection of the type series. Considering the frequency with which the larvae are found, and the few records of the adults, there is every indication that we may have in this genus a more extensive fauna than has hitherto been considered. All our records for Illinois and Indiana were taken in September and October, a time when little general collecting is done for this order.

Chilostigma McLachlan

Chilostigma McLachlan (1876, p. 187). Genotype, monobasic: *Chilostigma sieboldi* McLachlan.

There is only one North American species in the genus, *areolatum*, described from "Arctic America," with records from Ontario and Labrador. It has never been taken in Illinois.

Frenesia Betten & Mosely

Frenesia Betten & Mosely (1940, p. 165). Genotype, by original designation: *Limnephilus difficilis* Walker.

Of the two North American species, only *missa* has been found in Illinois. The other species, *difficilis,* is eastern in distribution.

Frenesia missa (Milne)

Chilostigma missum Milne (1935, p. 35); ♂, ♀.

LARVA.—Length 11 mm. Head, thoracic sclerites and legs reddish brown, the head with only very indistinct lighter spots, the legs slightly lighter than the head. Pro-

notum with only a very indistinct transverse groove.

CASE.—Length 12 mm., constructed of small stones; slender, cylindrical and fairly rigid.

ADULTS.—Fig. 689. Length 13–14 mm. Head and body varying from almost black to various shades of brown; legs beyond coxae yellowish brown; wings with a ground color of brown with small, translucent dots scattered uniformly and abundantly over the entire surface, giving it a salt-and-pepper

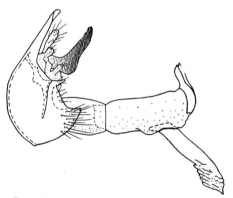

Fig. 690.—*Frenesia missa*, male genitalia.

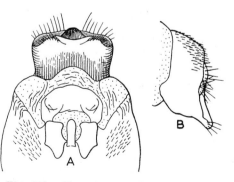

Fig. 691.—*Frenesia missa*, female genitalia. *A*, ventral aspect; *B*, lateral aspect.

appearance. Male genitalia, fig. 690, with tenth tergite forming a pair of appressed, heavily sclerotized, narrow plates angled sharply dorsad; cerci short and clavate; claspers small and padlike. Female genitalia, fig. 691, with the ninth segment appearing as a thick collar almost completely surrounding the tubular tenth, the cerci reduced to indistinct small cushions on the posterior margin of the "collar."

The eastern species, *difficilis*, is illustrated by Betten & Mosely (1940).

For years we were puzzled by two females of this species in the Illinois Natural History Survey collection labeled "Havana, Ill., November 8, 1912." Diligent search in the vicinity of Havana did not produce any caddis flies still on the wing at this date. Finally, however, a large series of the species was taken along a small, clear, spring-fed brook just south of Havana at Matanzas. At this time only a few cases were found in the stream. Continuing the search the next year, it was discovered that the larvae were congregated in a little seepage area near the bank and were thriving in water scarcely deep enough to cover their cases. Many of the individuals were feeding on leaves and twigs so that most of the insect and its case was actually out of water. Later we found that odd specimens would live in the stream itself; and, since the seepage areas frequently dried up, it is possible that this reservoir in the stream is chiefly responsible for the preservation of the species in this area.

The habits of this species certainly represent an intermediate stage between the typical caddis fly and one or two humus inhabiting species reported from Europe.

We have taken the species nowhere else in Illinois. The center of its range is apparently in the Northeast; records are available from the District of Columbia, Maryland, Massachusetts, Michigan, Minnesota, New Hampshire, New York, Pennsylvania and Virginia.

Illinois Records.—HAVANA, Matanzas Lake: Nov. 15, 1939, Ross & Burks, 5 ♂, 4 ♀, 5 mating pairs, many larvae; June 2, 1940, H. H. Ross *et al.*, many larvae; Sept. 30, 1940, Mohr & Burks, many larvae.

Glyphopsyche Banks

Glyphopsyche Banks (1904c, p. 141). Genotype, by original designation: *Glyphopsyche bryanti* Banks.

Contains only two species: *irrorata*, known from Arctic America, British Columbia and Ontario; and *missouri*.

Glyphopsyche missouri new species

LARVA.—Length 14 mm. Head, thoracic plates and coxae mostly black, with a few reddish blotches; trochanters dark red;

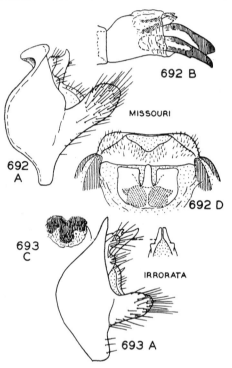

Figs. 692–693.—*Glyphopsyche*, genitalia. *A*, male, lateral aspect; *B*, aedeagus; *C*, spiny area of male eighth tergite; *D*, female, ventral aspect.

femora, tibiae and tarsi red with apical black band. Pronotum with short, stout black spines.

CASE.—Irregular and cylindrical, constructed of a mixture of stones and pieces of twigs.

MALE.—Length 11 mm. Color mottled shades of brown, without distinct pattern. General structure typical for the genus. Eighth tergite with a black cushion of short setae, the cushion divided into a mesal and two lateral lobes. Male genitalia, fig. 692, remarkably similar to *irrorata*, fig. 693. Tenth tergite short and sharp. Cerci bilobed and small. Claspers long and stout, with the apex slightly concave on mesal side.

Aedeagus short, with a ventral, bifid, sclerotized scoop and a pair of short, dorsal sclerotized spurs.

FEMALE.—Similar to male in color and general structure. Genitalia, fig. 692, with small subgenital plate, the lateral lobes relatively narrow, the mesal tongue long; ninth and tenth segments fused to form a wide, very short, compressed tube with dorso-lateral expansions.

Holotype, male.—Meramec Springs, St. James, Missouri: Oct. 8, 1938, Ross & Burks.

Allotype, male.—Same data as for holotype.

Paratypes.—Same data as for holotype, 257 ♂, 44 ♀.

Known only from a single large colony at Meramec Springs, which are more in the nature of an underground river. This colony was located on September 29, 1938, by Frison & Yeager, who collected larvae and pupae and reported them literally paving spring and stream. Ross & Burks visited the spot a few days later and collected large numbers of all stages. The adults were found in floating beds of water cress; when the water cress was pushed under water the caddis fly adults came to the surface and were collected in large numbers.

The short wings of this species, fig. 631*A*, are very dissimilar to those of the genotype, fig. 631*B*, and suggest immediately that a new genus should be erected for this new species. The male genitalia, however, are so similar in the two forms that there is no doubt that *irrorata* and *missouri* are practically sister species.

Grensia new genus

ADULTS.—General structure typical for family. Head and mesonotum without unusually large macrochaetae. Mesoscutum with elongate oval warts. Tibial spur count 1-2-2. Front wings, fig. 631*C*, with stigma very wide and short, R_2 curving with stigma, gradually becoming closer to it, the two nearly or distinctly touching at apex; cord irregular, distinctly not in line with base of stigma; R_3 curving markedly. Hind wings typical for group.

Genotype.—*Limnephilus praeteritus.*

The only known representative is the genotype, recorded from Arctic portions of North America. It has not been taken in Illinois.

Phanocelia Banks

Phanocelia Banks (1943, p. 354). Genotype, by original designation: *Apatania canadensis* Banks.

The genotype, described from Manitoba, is the only known North American species in this genus, and has never been taken in Illi-

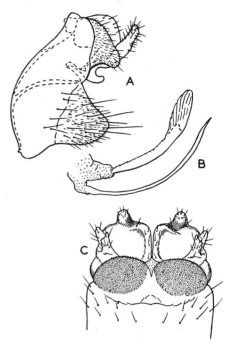

Fig. 694.—*Phanocelia canadensis*, male genitalia. *A*, lateral aspect; *B*, aedeagus; *C*, dorsal aspect.

nois. The female is not known, but the male is readily distinguished by the genitalia, fig. 694.

Psychoglypha new genus

ADULTS.—General structure typical for family. Male palpi long and slender. Last tarsal segment of all legs without black spines. Dorsal macrochaetae of head not conspicuously longer or stouter than surrounding setae; area between and behind lateral ocelli bare except for a group of five or six silvery setae near each ocellus. Mesonotum with a pair of well-defined and ovate scutal warts; meso-scutellum with a pair of rows of five or six well-separated setae. Front wings as in fig. 633, with a distinct stigma which is usually colored red, the red extending past R_1 almost to R_2; the lower portion of the stigma is defined by R_1, which is abruptly sinuate at base of stigma and then curves evenly to the front margin of the wing; R_2 curves sharply toward R_1 and follows parallel to it to the front margin of the wing; the wing is very long and narrow and characterized by a silvery streak which runs through the first and second R_5 cells, usually with a short spur into cell M_1.

Genotype.—*Glyphopscyche avigo.*

This genus contains most of the species which have previously been placed in *Glyphopsyche*, the genotype of which does not belong here.

Most of the species are western or Subarctic in distribution. None have been taken in Illinois. One, *subborealis*, occurs in the eastern states and has been taken as far south as central Michigan.

Drusinus Betten

Drusinus Betten (1934, p. 359). Genotype, by original designation: *Drusinus uniformis* Betten.

In this genus the front wings are broad and anal cells large. The genotype is the only species so far collected in Illinois. The larva of the genus is unknown.

Drusinus uniformis Betten

Drusinus uniformis Betten (1934, p. 360); ♂, ♀.

Adults. — Length 14–16 mm. Color brown, dorsum darker, front wings with a distinctly purplish cast over the brown. Tibiae and tarsi with numerous black spines. Eighth tergite of male with a bilobed cushion of black, peglike setae. Male genitalia, fig. 695, with elongate cerci and stocky tenth tergite which is divided and upturned to form a pair of black, narrow, sclerotized processes. Female genitalia simple, with no long processes.

The male genitalia are very similar in general structure to those of *virginicus*; in this latter species, however, the cerci are larger, and the lateral apical processes of the tenth tergite are developed into a distinct shoulder at base, fig. 696.

Our only Illinois collection of this species was made at Elgin, along one of the small spring-fed brooks in the Botanical Gardens, June 6, 1939, Burks & Riegel, 1 ♂, 1 ♀. To

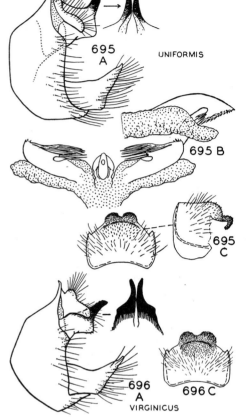

Figs. 695–696.—*Drusinus*, male genitalia. *A*, lateral aspect; *B*, aedeagus; *C*, eighth tergite.

date we have not found the larva of this species.

Little is known regarding the range of the species. It is apparently widespread but local, as evidenced by the scattered available records from Illinois, New York and Tennessee.

Neophylax McLachlan

Neophylax McLachlan (1871, p. 111). Genotype, monobasic: *Neophylax concinnus* McLachlan.

Acronopsyche Banks (1930b, p. 227). Genotype, by original designation: *Acronopsyche pilosa* Banks.

In addition to characters mentioned in the key, the short, triangular front wings are characteristic of the adults. The larva has a unique long head and usually lacks the prosternal horn.

The genus is represented in the eastern states by many species, but we have taken only one in Illinois. Two others occur in nearby states and have been included in the key.

The biology of the genus in this latitude is unique in having a long aestivation period, the larvae usually maturing early in the spring, and the adults emerging late in autumn. All three species treated here have been reared, but no satisfactory key characters have been found to separate the larvae.

KEY TO SPECIES

Adults

1. Maxillary palpi 3-segmented (males)   2
   Maxillary palpi 5-segmented (females)   4
2. Claspers with a long, curved, heavily sclerotized mesal arm, fig. 697.....
   ....**autumnus**, p. 203
   Claspers without a heavily sclerotized arm, at most with a mesal flange as in fig. 698.......................   3
3. Claspers long, wide apart at base, with a mesal flange, fig. 698; ninth sternite slightly incised on meson.....
   ....**ayanus**, p. 205
   Claspers short, close together, without a mesal flange, fig. 699; ninth sternite with a short, truncate mesal projection..............**fuscus**, p. 205
4. Subgenital plate with 2 pairs of prominent lobes, fig. 700...**autumnus**, p. 203
   Subgenital plate with a mesal, spatulate style and a pair of low, lateral lobes, fig. 701...................
   ....**fuscus**, p. 205; **ayanus**, p. 205

Neophylax autumnus Vorhies

Neophylax autumnus Vorhies (1909, p. 669); ♂, ♀, larva.

LARVA.—Length 8–9 mm. Head varying from reddish brown to blackish brown, sometimes with a paler mesal stripe and always with round pale spots on dorsal portion. Thoracic sclerites and legs brownish yellow with narrow black areas along some sutures. Head long, malar space twice as long as distance from eye to top of head; upper portion of frons produced into a low but definite hump; antennae situated on a slight protuberance. All legs the same shape, the front ones only slightly modified for grasping. Pronotum velvety and produced into a rounded anterior portion under which the head may be retracted. Gills single and

short. Sternites 3, 4 and 5 with an oval sclerotized ring.

CASE.—Length 8–10 mm. Constructed of stones, slightly curved, nearly cylindrical, with larger stones situated along each side to give it a broadened appearance. Before aestivation, the anterior portion of the case is capped with a single flat stone, around the edge of which are small vents.

ADULTS.—Fig. 702. Length 9-12 mm. Head and body brownish yellow; front wings fairly dark brown with irregular, small, lighter areas scattered over most of

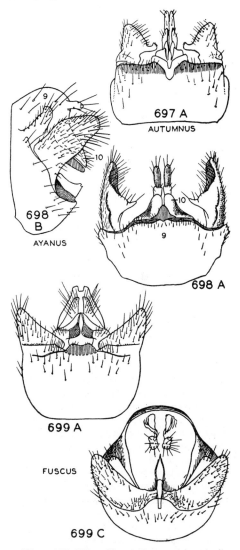

Figs. 697–699.—*Neophylax*, male genitalia. *A*, *B* and *C*, respectively ventral, lateral and caudal aspects.

the surface and with a pair of large, yellow marks along the posterior margin; in repose these two yellow marks form a double, diamond-shaped, mesal pattern. Male genitalia, fig. 697, with ninth and tenth tergites both narrow and beaked, ninth sternite nearly truncate, and claspers short with a long, sclerotized, constricted mesal arm

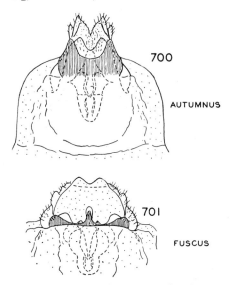

Figs. 700–701.—*Neophylax*, female genitalia.

which is enlarged at tip; aedeagus simple and tubular. Female genitalia, fig. 700, with ninth and tenth segments narrow and small, subgenital plate wide and with two pairs of fairly long projections.

This species has been found in the northern portion of Illinois and also in the Ozark Hills streams of southern Illinois. In both areas it is confined to small, clear and rapid streams with predominantly rock bottoms. In all areas but one, adults and pupae have been taken only late in the year, from September into October. The one exception was a large colony in Split Rock Brook at Utica, where the adults emerged in large numbers in April. The reason for this deviation from the usual seasonal cycle we do not know, but it is the only record of adults in the spring for the entire genus anywhere on the continent.

Of unique interest is the adaptation of this species to streams which become dry in summer, such as those in the Ozark Hills. In these situations the larvae mature at least by April, fasten their cases under stones and aestivate until autumn; in September the larvae change to the pupae, and shortly thereafter the adults emerge. When the stream becomes dry, a very high proportion of the aestivating larvae die from desiccation, but those which are situated under a rock which remains even slightly damp are able to survive and mature. We have observed successful emergence of the adults at Herod when the stream was still dry, the pupae leaving the moist cases with no mishaps. After a stream has been dry for a spring and summer, it is startling to find that the next spring, when it is again a rapid stream, the rocks are almost covered with the larvae of this species.

The species has not been taken very frequently, but the records are scattered through most of the Northeast; records include Illinois, Michigan, New York, Ontario and Wisconsin.

It has been suggested by Betten and others that this species might be the same as the genotype, which was described from New York. It certainly is closely related to the genotype, *concinnus*, but until information is available regarding the type, it seems advisable to treat the two as distinct.

Illinois Records.—ALTO PASS, Union Spring: Oct. 18, 1938, Ross & Burks, many pupae and larvae; March 23, 1939, Ross & Burks, many larvae; May 26, 1940, Mohr & Burks, many larvae; May 31, 1940, B. D. Burks, many larvae; May 12, 1939, Burks & Riegel, many larvae. BELVIDERE, Kishwaukee Creek: June 18, 1938, B. D. Burks, 1 larva. DUNDEE: May 23, 1939, Burks & Riegel, many larvae. ELGIN: April 19, 1939, Burks & Riegel, 1 larva; May 9, 1939, Ross & Burks, 6 larvae; Sept. 19, 1939, Ross & Mohr, 1 ♂, 1 ♀; preceding Elgin records are from Botanical Gardens; Trout Spring, March 7, 1940, Burks & Mohr, 5 larvae. HEROD, Gibbons Creek: March 28, 1935, Ross & Mohr, 2 larvae; May 29, 1935, Ross & Mohr, many larvae; Aug., 1936, Ross & Burks, many larvae; April 19, 1937, 4 larvae; Sept. 11, 1937, H. H. Ross, 4 larvae; Oct. 3, 1937, Ross & Burks, many larvae, pupae and pupal skins; and the following specimens which were reared, emerging on the dates shown: Oct. 8, 1937, Ross & Burks, 5 pupae; Oct. 18, 1937, 1 ♂, 1 ♀; Oct. 21, 1937, 3 ♂; Oct. 25, 1937, 1 ♀; Oct. 29, 1937, 6 ♀; Nov. 1, 1937, 1 ♂; Nov. 2, 1937, 2 ♂; Nov. 3, 1937, 1 ♀; Nov. 5, 1937, 2 ♂. LARUE, McCann Spring:

Oct. 17, 1938, Ross & Burks, 8 larvae; March 23, 1939, Ross & Burks, many larvae and pupae. Spring Grove: May 14, 1936, Ross & Mohr, many larvae; June 12, 1936, Ross & Burks, many larvae. Starved Rock State Park: April 25, 1933, Frison & Mohr, 1 larva. Utica, Split Rock Brook: Feb. 1, 1941, Frison, Ries & Ross,

Molanna Curtis

Molanna Curtis (1834, p. 214). Genotype, monobasic: *Molanna angustata* Curtis.
Apatania Kolenati (1848, p. 75). Genotype, monobasic: *Phryganea vestita* Zetterstedt.

The larva of this genus, fig. 709, is characterized by the long frons, antennae of

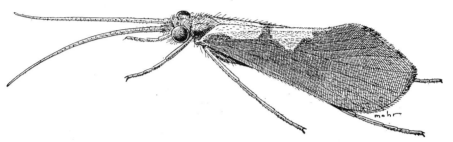

Fig. 702.—*Neophylax autumnus* ♂.

many larvae, 1 pupa; April 25, 1941, T. H. Frison, 1 ♂, many larvae and pupae.

Neophylax fuscus Banks

Neophylax fuscus Banks (1903b, p. 242); ♂, ♀.

Not yet taken in Illinois, but found in the Meramec River near Steelville, Missouri, which is west of St. Louis and not far from Illinois. In addition to Missouri, the species is known from Michigan, New Hampshire and Virginia. The species recorded as *fuscus* by Betten (1934) is not *fuscus* but a species identical with or closely related to *stolus*.

Neophylax ayanus Ross

Neophylax ayanus Ross (1938a, p. 168); ♂, ♀.

Not yet taken in Illinois. The only records for this species are from Louisville, Kentucky, and Cataract, Indiana; the latter is only about 40 miles from the Illinois line, near Terre Haute.

MOLANNIDAE

This family is represented in the Illinois fauna by only one genus, *Molanna*. The genus *Beraea* has frequently been placed in the family Molannidae but is treated as a separate family in this paper.

medium length situated above base of mandibles, and the curious, reduced hind tibia and claw. The curious, flanged case, fig. 710, is also characteristic of the genus, although a similar case is made by some species of *Athripsodes* (see p. 228). The adults have the maxillary palpi five segmented in both sexes. When at rest the adults sit with the wings curled around the body and with the body held at an angle to the surface upon which the insect rests, its mottled gray color giving the insect in this position a remarkable resemblance to a rusty nail head or a very small twig.

Five North American species are known, of which three have been taken in Illinois, and it is quite possible that stray specimens of the other two may eventually turn up from this state.

No characters have yet been discovered to give certain identification of the females and larvae. For this reason it is necessary to disregard for the present the species *cinerea*, represented by the female type of which only fragments remain.

KEY TO SPECIES

Males

1. Femora and tibiae yellow, except for indefinite areas on femora, contrasting sharply with coxae; tenth tergite forming a simple hook, fig. 703 ....**flavicornis**, p. 208
Coxae and femora the same color, dark

brown or gray; tenth tergite with dorsal or beaklike expansions, figs. 704–707........................ 2

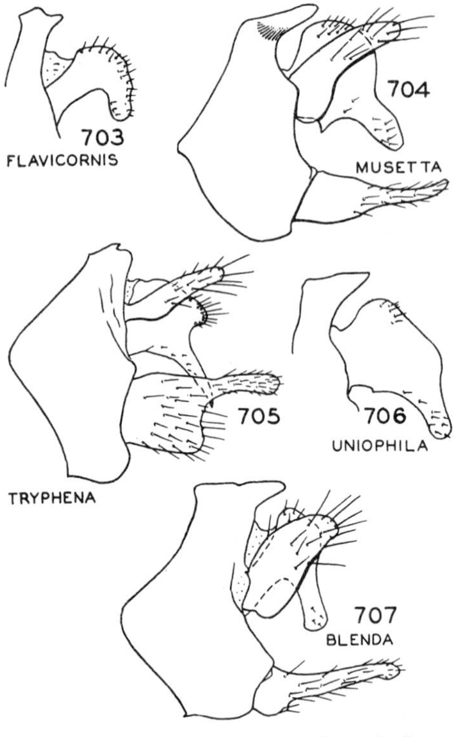

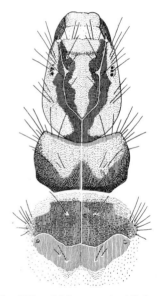

Figs. 703–707.—*Molanna*, male genitalia.

Fig. 708.—*Molanna musetta*, hind wing.

2. A long furrow of black scales in hind wings, fig. 708........**musetta**, p. 207
    No furrow of scales in hind wings.... 3
3. Lateral aspect of tenth tergite with a long, pointed, ventral process, fig. 705, and with a small dorsal lobe.. ....**tryphena**, p. 207
    Lateral aspect of tenth tergite rounded at apex and with a larger or less definite dorsal lobe, figs. 706, 707.. 4
4. Tenth tergite with large dorsal lobe and small ventral lobe, fig. 706.... ......•............**uniophila**, p. 206
    Tenth tergite with small dorsal lobe and very long, truncate ventral lobe, fig. 707, shaped like a duck's bill... ....**blenda**, p. 208

Molanna uniophila Vorhies

Molanna uniophila Vorhies (1909, p. 705); larva, pupa, ♂, ♀.

LARVA.—Fig. 709. Length 18 mm. Head, pronotum and legs yellow, head with a Y-shaped black mark, posterior portion of pronotum black; mesonotum brown, subdivided by an irregular line into an anterior and posterior portion. Head long, frons also long, the anterior portion not expanded. Mandibles short and stocky with three teeth along apical margin. Gula almost rectangular, longer than wide. Mesonotum with a semicircular, small antero-mesal plate, the remaining membranes with a lateral tuft of long setae. Gills long and filiform, most of them triple, those on the second and third abdominal tergites with five branches. Lateral line forming a fringe on segments 3–7, eighth segment with a sinuate lateral line

Fig. 709.—*Molanna uniophila* larva.

divided into an anterior portion of branched, short, appressed hairs and a posterior portion of about eight very long double hairs. Anal hooks large with one or two dorsal teeth.

CASE.—Fig. 710. Length 25 mm. Width 11–13 mm., the lateral margins built out into wide flanges so that the entire dorsal surface is uniformly convex and formed of sand and gravel; the ventral aspect has the middle tube made of fine grains.

ADULTS.—Length 16 mm. Body and appendages various shades of brown and gray, the wings with light areas in the middle forming a more or less checkered pattern. Male genitalia, fig. 706: tenth tergite somewhat hood shaped, produced into a short, rounded beak at apex; claspers with a small basal portion which merges gradually into a long, apical blade; at the extreme base of

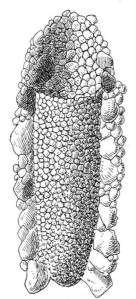

Fig. 710.—*Molanna uniophila*, case.

the clasper there arises a short, mesal, flat process bearing short setae at its apex; aedeagus tubular and slightly curved, containing an eversible group of long spines. Female genitalia very simple, bursa copulatrix small and without complicated structures.

In Illinois this species has been collected only in the glacial lakes and connecting streams in the northeastern part of the state. In these localities the larvae are found on gravel bars where they may occur in large local colonies. Our adult records are all for May and June, indicating a single generation per year.

The curious case of this insect has been the cause of frequent remarks by students of aquatic insects. Vorhies reared this species from Wisconsin, and we have reared it from Channel Lake, Illinois.

The range of the species is extensive through the Northeast. Records are available for Michigan, Minnesota, New Brunswick, New York, Ohio, Pennsylvania, Quebec and Wisconsin.

Illinois Records.—ANTIOCH: July 1, 1931, Frison, Betten & Ross, 1 ♂ ; July 6, 1932, Frison *et al.*, 6 ♂ ; June 11, 1936, Ross & Burks, ♂ ♂, ♀ ♀ ; June 12, 1936, Ross & Burks, 2 ♂, 1 ♀. CHANNEL LAKE: May 16, 1936, Ross & Mohr, many pupae which were reared, adults emerging June 1–3, 1936, Urbana; May 27, 1936, H. H. Ross, ♂ ♂, ♀ ♀, many pupae, larvae and cases; May 31, 1938, Mohr & Burks, 1 larva. FOURTH LAKE, Lake County: Aug. 2, 1887, C. A. Hart, 1 ♂. FOX LAKE: June 30, 1935, DeLong & Ross, ♂ ♂, ♀ ♀ ; May 28, 1936, H. H. Ross, 3 ♂ ; June 10, 1936, Ross & Burks, 1 ♂, 1 ♀. GRASS LAKE: July 14, 1926, Frison & Hayes, 1 ♂. JOHNSBURG, Fox River: May 28, 1936, H. H. Ross, ♂ ♂, 3 ♀. ROUND LAKE: June 26, 1936, at light, Frison & DeLong, ♂ ♂, ♀ ♀. SAND LAKE: June 17, 1893, Hart & Shiga, 1 ♂. SOUTH CHICAGO: June 9, 1880, 1 ♂. ZION, Dead River: May 20, 1940, Mohr & Burks, 2 larvae.

Molanna musetta Betten

Molanna musetta Betten (1934, p. 248); ♂.

LARVA.—Unknown.

ADULTS.—In size, color and general structure similar to *uniophila*. Hind wing with a long, arcuate, conspicuous furrow of scales running from the apical corner down below the middle and to the base of the wing, fig. 708. Male genitalia almost identical with *uniophila*, the tenth tergite with the dorsal portion larger, fig. 704.

We have only one record of this species for Illinois, a male collected along the Kankakee River at Wilmington, August 20, 1934, DeLong and Ross. This species apparently has a scattered range through the Northeast with a southwestward extension through the Ozarks into Oklahoma. We have records from Illinois, New York, Oklahoma and Ontario.

Molanna tryphena Betten

Molanna tryphena Betten (1934, p. 248); ♂, ♀.

Not yet taken in Illinois. This species occurs in Michigan, New York and Wisconsin. Dr. Betten (1902) has reared it in New York, recording it as *cinerea*.

Molanna blenda Sibley

Molanna blenda Sibley (1926*b*, p. 105); larva.

Molanna blenda Betten (1934, p. 245); ♂, ♀.

LARVA.—Very similar to that of *uniophila*. Sibley's illustrations indicate that the pronotum is darker, but since there is some variation of this character in *uniophila*, it is doubtful whether this is a safe criterion for identification.

ADULTS.—Length 10–11 mm. Similar in general appearance to those of *uniophila*. Front wings of male with a wide furrow running through the length of the wing, the furrow filled with scales. Male genitalia, fig. 707, similar in general structure to those of *uniophila* but with the tenth tergite shaped more like a duck's head and bill, the apico-ventral projection long and almost truncate.

We have only one Illinois record for this species, a male collected along one of the spring-fed brooks in the Botanical Gardens at Elgin, June 13, 1939, Frison & Ross. Aside from Illinois, records are available only for New York and Wisconsin.

Molanna flavicornis Banks

Molanna flavicornis Banks (1914, p. 261); ♂, ♀.

This species has not yet been taken in Illinois but has been recorded only a few miles away at Madison, Wisconsin. This species is common through the northern part of the continent with a distinct preference for lakes. Records are available for Colorado, Manitoba, Michigan, Minnesota, New York, Quebec, Saskatchewan, South Dakota and Wisconsin.

BERAEIDAE

Contains only the genus *Beraea*. No larvae of this family have been recognized from North America, the key characters used here being taken from Ulmer (1909).

Beraea Stephens

Thya Curtis (1834, p. 216); preoccupied.
Beraea Stephens (1836, p. 158). Genotype, by present designation: *Beraea marshamella* Stephens = *pullata* (Curtis).

Only two species of the genus have been found in North America, and neither of these in Illinois. Banks described the first, *nigritta*, from Long Island, New York.

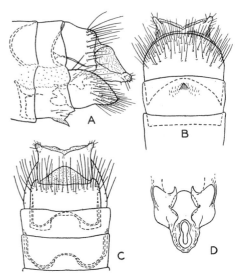

Fig. 711.—*Beraea nigritta*, female genitalia. *A, B* and *C*, respectively lateral, ventral and dorsal aspects; *D*, bursa copulatrix.

The original collection consisted of females, and no other specimens have been found from that vicinity. The female genitalia, fig. 711, resemble those of the Molannidae and Odontoceridae in general structure. Recently a male of this genus was received from Georgia, and, since it cannot be associated definitely with *nigritta*, it is described as new.

Beraea gorteba new species

MALE.—Length 5 mm. Head and thorax brown; appendages yellowish or paler, covered with brown hair, the legs with black spines; wings hyaline with brown hair. General structure typical for family; maxillary palpi cylindrical and very hairy, five segmented, the first half as long as the second, the remainder subequal; tibial spur formula

Fig. 712.—*Beraea gorteba*, front wing.

2-2-4, leg spines as in fig. 69; wing venation reduced, front wing, fig. 712, with
radial sector only two branched, hind wing
narrow with a wide, curved band of black
scales extending above cubitus along the
basal two-thirds of the wing; seventh sternite of abdomen with a mesal, sclerotized
process, eighth sternite with a band of hair
along apex.

Male genitalia, fig. 713: tenth tergite
divided down meson to form a pair of long,

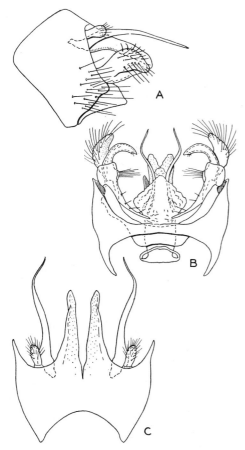

Fig. 713.—*Beraea gorteba*, male genitalia.
A, lateral aspect; *B*, ventral aspect; *C*, dorsal
aspect.

pointed, semimembranous lobes; arising near
its base are a pair of long, sclerotized, sinuate rods and a pair of short, ovate cerci;
claspers complex, their base fused on meson,
apex comprised of (1) a quadrate ventral
plate which is produced into a long, curved
basal filament, (2) a stout hook which
bears a small cushion of setae on the mesal

margin near base and (3) a curved, membranous dorsal lobe which bears long setae;
aedeagus short, its extreme base vasiform,
the apical portion forming a wide, convoluted ventral area with a pair of slender sclerotized styles, a pair of short membranous
lobes and a pair of sclerotized dorsal lobes.

Holotype, male.—Five miles southeast
of Roberta, Georgia: May 8, 1939, P. W.
Fattig.

This species is similar in general structure
to *nigritta*, differing in having smaller anterior warts on the head, only a very short
epicranial stem on the head, and the antero-
dorsal angle of the head much less produced
than in *nigritta*. Additional material may
show these characters to be only antigenetic.

ODONTOCERIDAE

The genus *Psilotreta* is the only representative of this family in the eastern states.
It contains a number of species which are
treated on page 285 and following.

CALAMOCERATIDAE

The family is represented in the eastern
states by two species: *Ganonema americanum*, a brown to black species with five-
segmented maxillary palpi, known from the
eastern and northeastern states; and *Anisocentropus pyraloides*, an orange-brown species with six-segmented maxillary palpi,
known only from Georgia. The larvae of
Ganonema make a case by hollowing out a
solid piece of twig (Lloyd 1915*b*).

LEPTOCERIDAE

All the larvae in this family make cases,
using a variety of materials and constructing
cases of various shapes. The adults are
slender, frequently exceedingly so, and have
long, slender antennae. The maxillary palpi
are similar and five segmented in both sexes.

This family is well represented in Illinois, and various genera and species occur
in a wide variety of streams, ponds and
lakes. At times large swarms of *Oecetis*
and *Athripsodes* occur along large rivers,
such as the Ohio and Illinois. Their most
conspicuous numbers, however, occur in the
glacial lakes of the northeastern part of
the state (see p. 10). Here they form the
dominant part of the caddis fly fauna.

Representatives of all seven Nearctic genera occur in Illinois. A large number of the species are widespread, some of them Holarctic. It is certain that a study of the Holarctic fauna of this family will show a good many more of the names based on North American material to be synonyms of European or Asiatic names.

In the entire family the pupal chamber has a slit and not a mesh in the closing cap at both ends. Through these slits the pupa pushes out all the larval sclerites, so that it is impossible to get associations of adult structures and larval sclerites in the same case. For this reason it is necessary to rear larvae in cages in order to associate immature and adult stages.

KEY TO GENERA

Larvae

1. Middle legs with claw stout and hook shaped, tarsus bent, fig. 714; case transparent........**Leptocerus**, p. 212
   Middle legs with claw slender, slightly curved, tarsus straight, fig. 715; case seldom transparent.......... 2
2. Maxillary palpi nearly as long as stipes, fig. 717; mandibles long, sharp at apex, the teeth considerably below apex..................**Oecetis**, p. 236
   Maxillary palpi short, about half length of stipes, fig. 718; mandibles shorter, blunt at apex, the teeth near or at apex.................. 3
3. Head with a suture-like line paralleling the epicranial arms, fig. 764....
   ....**Athripsodes**, p. 221
   Head without a suture-like line in addition to the epicranial arms, fig. 811   4
4. Mesonotum membranous with a pair of sclerotized, narrow, curved or angled bars, figs. 764, 769........
   ....**Athripsodes**, p. 221
   Mesonotum without such a pair of sclerotized bars, fig. 836.......... 5
5. Anal segment developed into a pair of sclerotized, concave plates, with spinose dorso-lateral and mesal carinae, and an overhanging ventral flap, fig. 719..........**?Setodes**, p. 256
   Anal segment convex and without carinae between anal hooks, fig. 720.. 6
6. Hind tibiae entirely sclerotized, without a fracture in middle, fig. 716; abdomen without gills............
   ....**Leptocella**, p. 213
   Hind tibiae with a fracture near middle which appears to divide tibiae into two segments, fig. 715; abdomen with at least a few gills.......... 7

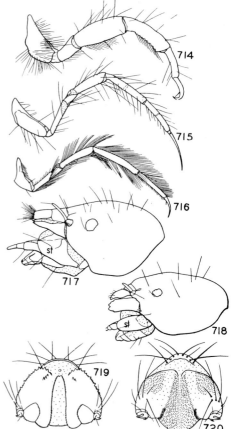

Fig. 714.—*Leptocerus americanus* larva, middle leg.
Fig. 715.—*Mystacides sepulchralis* larva, hind leg.
Fig. 716.—*Leptocella candida* larva, hind leg.
Fig. 717.—*Oecetis cinerascens* larva, head; *st*, stipes.
Fig. 718.—*Leptocella candida* larva, head; *st*, stipes.
Fig. 719.—*Setodes* sp. larva, anal segment.
Fig. 720.—*Mystacides sepulchralis* larva, anal segment.

7. Hind tibiae with a regular fringe of long hair, as in fig. 716...........
   ....**Triaenodes**, p. 244
   Hind tibiae with only irregularly placed hairs, fig. 715............
   ....**Mystacides**, p. 253

Pupae

1. Anal appendages wide at base with a sharp mesal corner, the apex tapering gradually to a sharp point, fig. 721.................**Leptocerus**, p. 212

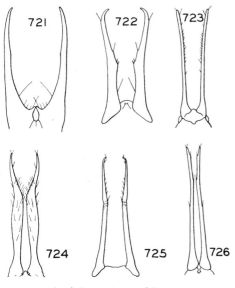

Anal Appendages of Pupae

Fig. 721.—*Leptocerus americanus.*
Fig. 722.—*Athripsodes tarsi-punctatus.*
Fig. 723.—*Oecetis inconspicua.*
Fig. 724.—*Triaenodes tarda.*
Fig. 725.—*Mystacides sepulchralis.*
Fig. 726.—*Leptocella* sp.

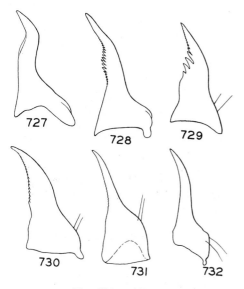

Mandibles of Pupae

Fig. 727.—*Leptocerus americanus.*
Fig. 728.—*Triaenodes tarda.*
Fig. 729.—*Oecetis inconspicua.*
Fig. 730.—*Athripsodes tarsi-punctatus.*
Fig. 731.—*Mystacides sepulchralis.*
Fig. 732.—*Leptocella* sp.

Anal appendages with the base narrow; shoulder, if present, situated at the middle, fig. 722........... 2

2. Mandibles with a definite area of teeth below the apical point, fig. 730; frequently stocky and triangular..... 3
Mandibles without teeth, sometimes with the apex minutely serrate, fig. 731; always with blade very narrow 5

3. Anal appendages slender, straight and of uniform thickness throughout, fig. 723...............**Oecetis,** p. 236
Anal appendages with a distinct shoulder at or near middle, beyond which the apex tapers evenly to a sharp point, fig. 722.............. 4

4. Mandibles with apex long and slightly twisted, teeth small and situated on a slight convex bulge, fig. 728.....
.................**Triaenodes,** p. 244
Mandibles with apex shorter and straight, either the teeth situated within an angulation or curve, fig. 730, or mandible short and triangular...............**Athripsodes,** p. 221

5. Mandibles with a large, bulbous base, the apical blade minutely serrate and little longer than base, fig. 731....
.................**Mystacides,** p. 253
Mandibles with base small, blade long and slender, not serrate, fig. 732...
.................**Leptocella,** p. 213

Adults

1. Front wings with stem of M atrophied, leaving only two main veins between convex R_1 and convex Cu_1, fig. 733
.................**Triaenodes,** p. 244
Front wings with stem of M present, so that three main veins are present

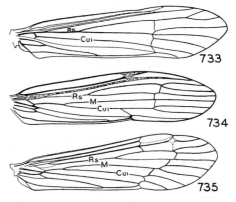

Fig. 733.—*Triaenodes injusta,* front wing.
Fig. 734.—*Oecetis inconspicua,* front wing.
Fig. 735.—*Mystacides sepulchralis,* front wing.

between convex R₁ and convex Cu₁, fig. 734.......................... 2

2. M apparently not branched, fig. 734 ....**Oecetis**, p. 236
   M obviously branched, fig. 735...... 3

3. Epicranial stem distinct, lateral sutures absent or indistinct, fig. 736; katepisternum constricted at apex, fig. 739....................... 4
   Epicranial stem absent or indistinct, lateral sutures well marked, fig. 738;

katepisternum truncate at apex, fig. 740.......................... 5

4. Dorsal triangle of head small, epicranial stem long, fig. 737; color whitish, straw yellow or light brown...... ....**Setodes**, p. 256
   Dorsal triangle of head large, epicranial stem short, fig. 736; color very dark brown or bluish black, including wings..........**Mystacides**, p. 253

5. Meso-epimeron membranous nearly to ventral margin, fig. 740; hind wings with most of R_s and its branches atrophied; ground color white..... ....**Leptocella**, p. 213
   Meso-epimeron with a wide sclerotized bridge between membranous area and ventral margin, fig. 741; hind wings with R_s and its branches present; ground color not white... 6

6. Front tibiae with 2 apical spurs..... ....**Athripsodes**, p. 221
   Front tibiae without apical spurs.... ....**Leptocerus**, p. 212

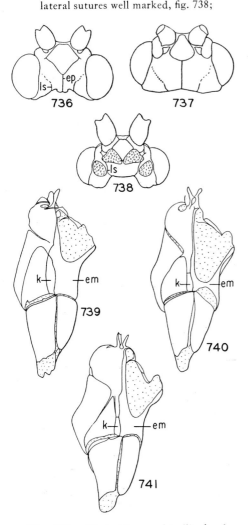

Fig. 736.—*Mystacides sepulchralis*, head.
Fig. 737.—*Setodes vernalis*, head.
Fig. 738.—*Athripsodes tarsi-punctatus*, head.
Fig. 739.—*Mystacides sepulchralis*, mesopleuron.
Fig. 740.—*Leptocella albida*.
Fig. 741.—*Athripsodes transversus*.
em, mesoepimeron; *ep*, epicranial stem; *k*, katepisternum; *ls*, lateral suture.

Leptocerus Leach

Leptocerus Leach (1815, p. 136). Genotype, monobasic: *Phryganea interrupta* Fabricius. *Ymymia* Milne (1934, p. 16). Genotype, monobasic: *Setodes americana* Banks.

The curious translucent case, the hooked middle leg and anal tufts of the larvae, and the genitalia of the adults readily distinguish the only North American species of this genus.

The type of case, structure of larva and adult venation leave no doubt but that *americanus* is congeneric with the genotype, which is European. This necessitates reducing *Ymymia* to synonymy and resurrecting *Setodes* for the group of species for which Milne used the name *Leptocerus*. It is interesting to note that within both these groups the male genitalia vary greatly in shape.

Leptocerus americanus (Banks)

Setodes americana Banks (1899, p. 215); ♂, ♀.
Setodes grandis Banks (1907a, p. 128); ♂.

LARVA.—Fig. 742. Length 6–7 mm. Head, pronotum and legs straw color, the head and pronotum with many black spots. Gula somewhat heart shaped. Mandibles short, truncate at end. Middle leg with claw hooked, tibiae with rounded mesal teeth.

Abdominal gills absent. Anal segment incised on meson, with brushes of black setae along the sides of the incision.

Case.—Length 7–8 mm.; slender, slightly curved and made entirely of secretion; pale green to straw color.

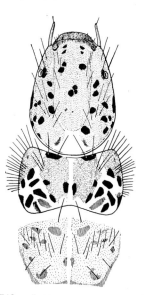

Fig. 742.—*Leptocerus americanus* larva.

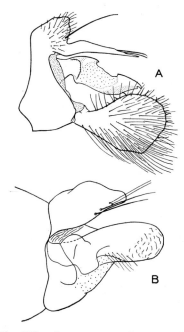

Fig. 743.—*Leptocerus americanus*, genitalia. *A*, male; *B*, female.

Adults.—Length 8 mm. Body very slender, dark brown in color. Both wings narrow and pointed. Male genitalia, fig. 743, with tenth tergite long and bladelike, aedeagus irregular; claspers short, narrow at base and expanding rapidly into a large, spatulate structure. Female genitalia, fig. 743, with tenth tergite large and semimembranous, lobes of the ninth tergite large and clasper-like, and bursa copulatrix small and somewhat circular.

This species is distributed over all parts of Illinois but has been taken in large numbers around only the glacial lakes and in the slow streams connecting them. In these places the larvae are almost invariably found in water horsetail.

Illinois Records.—Many males, females and pupae, taken May 6 to August 2, and many larvae, taken May 15 to June 12, are from Antioch, Carbondale, Channel Lake, Effingham, Eichorn (Hicks Branch), Fox Lake (Pistakee Bay), Fulton, Grand Tower, Grass Lake, Havana (Devil's Hole), Herod, McHenry, Momence, Olive Branch (Horse Shoe Lake), Ottawa, Pistakee Lake, Putnam (Lake Senachwine), Richmond, Savanna, Springfield, Wadsworth (Des Plaines River), West Havana, Zion (Dead River).

Leptocella Banks

Leptocella Banks (1899, p. 214). Genotype, by original designation: *Mystacides uwarowii* Kolenati.

In this genus the case and larva are always very long and narrow. The larva has a long, triangular gula, short mandibles with a broad apex divided into three or four teeth, and undivided tibiae. Hind legs with or without swimming brush.

The adults are very long and slender, chiefly white or gray, frequently with conspicuous patterns. They include some of our most beautiful caddis flies. This is the only genus in which it is essential to have material pinned instead of preserved in liquid. For satisfactory results the specimens must be handled extremely carefully. To obtain good study material, it is necessary to kill them a few at a time in a strong cyanide bottle, remove them to a temporary container where they will not rub, and then pin them up very carefully at the first opportunity, taking pains at all times to avoid rubbing off the hairs on the wings. These hairs form the color pattern, which is frequently essential for adult diagnosis.

No caddis fly genus has been subject to more conjecture regarding the differentiation and limits of its species than has *Leptocella*. In the past, some 14 species have been described from America north of Mexico. Most of these have been synonymized by Milne (1934, p. 13), who reduced the genus to two species with one species subdivided into 10 forms.

Early in our work on the Illinois caddis flies, we discovered that several species belonging to *Leptocella* occurred in Illinois

with conspicuous and constant differences in the larval forms. We have not as yet succeeded in rearing all of them but have reared three in controversial groups. This rearing led to a more detailed study of the adults in our search for specific characters and resulted in the discovery that size of eyes and certain differences in male genitalia could be used to supplement color pattern in the definite diagnosis of at least some species. Most of these adult characters are presented in the descriptions which follow.

I wish to emphasize that there are many

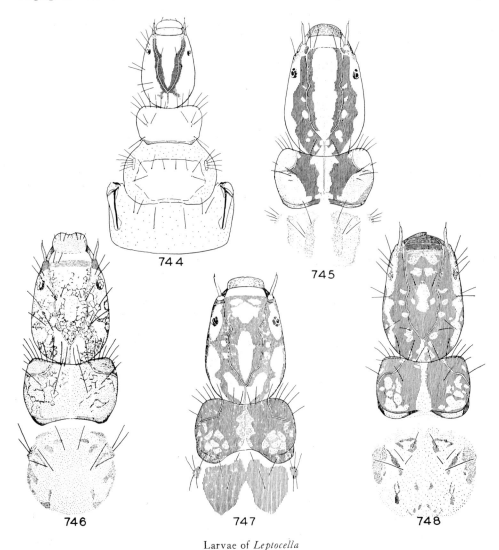

Larvae of *Leptocella*

Fig. 744.—*L. albida.*

Fig. 745.—*L. diarina.*

Fig. 746.—*L. exquisita.*   Fig. 747.—*L. pavida.*   Fig. 748.—*L. candida.*

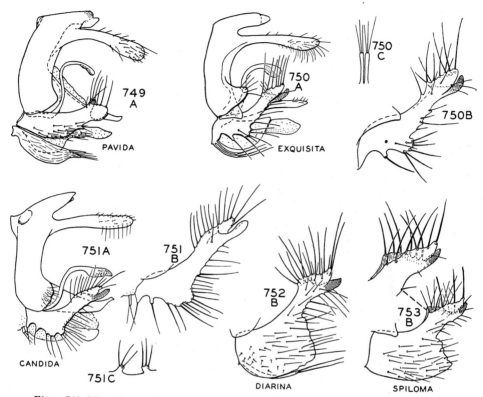

Figs. 749–753.—*Leptocella*, male genitalia. *A*, lateral aspect; *B*, claspers; *C*, styles at base of claspers.

species which have not yet been investigated sufficiently to determine their status. Such forms as *coloradensis, intervena* and *minuta* have not been satisfactorily diagnosed. I have been unable to find any appreciable difference in the male genitalia of these. Experience with the Illinois fauna leads me to believe that until cultures of these other species are reared, or until additional adult characters are found, it will be unwise to attempt definite placement of these names. There is a very good possibility that many of them represent distinct species. Not until we know how many species exist and what are their limits can we satisfactorily diagnose them.

KEY TO SPECIES

Larvae

1. Hind legs with only scattered hair. Head yellow with a definite ∨ mark, as in fig. 744..........**albida,** p. 220
   Hind legs with a definite swimming brush of long hair, fig. 716. Head with either large, irregular brown

areas or with parallel dark lines, figs. 745–748......................... 2
2. Head with parallel dark lines which are carried back on the pronotum, fig. 745...............**diarina,** p. 218
   Head with irregular dark areas or a dark network, fig. 746........... 3
3. Middle and hind legs almost entirely black beyond coxae; dorsum of head with fine reticulations, fig. 746....
   ....**?exquisita,** p. 217
   Middle and hind legs mostly yellow, at most with small dark areas; dorsum of head with solid lines or areas of brown or black, figs. 747, 748... 4
4. Legs pale, banded with dark brown or black.....................**sp. a,** p. 221
   Legs almost uniformly light colored.. 5
5. Head with an open network of dark brown or black lines, fig. 747......
   ....**pavida,** p. 218
   Head with more extensive dark areas as in fig. 748...........**candida,** p. 217

Adults

1. Genitalia with claspers and aedeagus, fig. 749 (males)................. 2

Genitalia without such structures (females)......................... 7

2. Apex of ninth sternite produced into a spoon-shaped lobe situated beneath aedeagus, fig. 749...... **pavida**, p. 218
   Apex of ninth sternite with a pair of long, or short, narrow processes... 3

3. Claspers with basal portion not produced into a wide flap, figs. 750, 751   4

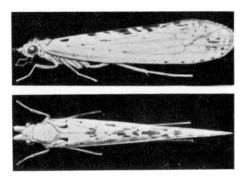

Fig. 754.—*Leptocella spiloma*, wing pattern.

Fig. 755.—*Leptocella exquisita*, wing pattern.

Fig. 756.—*Leptocella pavida*, wing pattern.

Claspers with basal portion produced into a wide flap, fig. 752......... 5

4. Wings with transverse yellowish bars in the membrane, fig. 755........
   ....**exquisita**, p. 217
   Wings without transverse yellowish bars in the membrane, fig. 757....
   ....**candida**, p. 217

5. Ventral aspect of head with eye width equal to distance between eyes, fig. 761..............**spiloma**, p. 219
   Ventral aspect of head with eye width less than distance between eyes, figs. 759, 760........................ 6

6. Wings in repose forming a distinct dorsal pattern of V-marks, as in fig. 754...............**diarina**, p. 218

No dorsal pattern formed by marks on wings, which have either indistinct apical rows of spots or the spots absent and the veins quite prominent, fig. 758...........**albida**, p. 220

7. Wings with transverse yellowish bars in the membrane, and with four black areas in membrane near apex of posterior margin, fig. 755......
   ....**exquisita**, p. 217
   Wings without transverse yellowish bars, sometimes with four black areas of hairs but never black areas in the membrane............... 8

8. Wings with four patches of black hair near apex of posterior margin, fig. 757.................**candida**, p. 217

Fig. 757.—*Leptocella candida*, wing pattern.

Fig. 758.—*Leptocella albida*, wing pattern.

Wings without patches of black hair in this region................... 9

9. Wings yellowish with small, well-delineated, scattered black spots, fig. 756...................**pavida**, p. 218

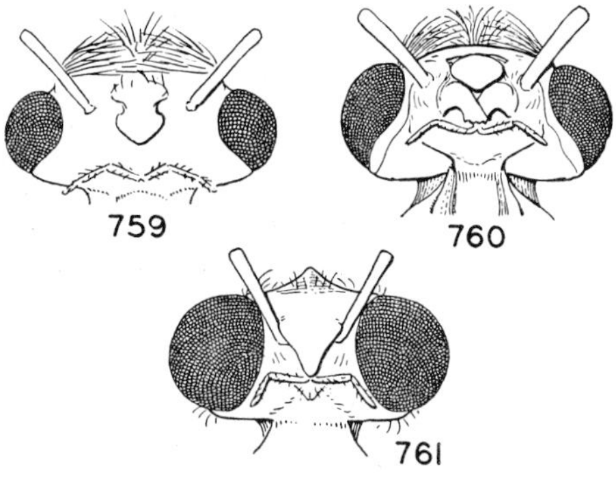

759   760

761

Heads, Ventral Aspect

Fig. 759.—*Leptocella albida*.
Fig. 760.—*Leptocella diarina*.
Fig. 761.—*Leptocella spiloma*.

Wings either with spots larger or less contrasting, figs. 754, 758........ 10

10. Wings with a dorsal pattern of V-marks, fig. 754, formed by dark areas along the posterior margin of the wings......................... 11

Wings without conspicuous dark marks on posterior margin, therefore without dorsal V-marks when the wings are folded in repose, fig. 758......
........................**albida**, p. 220

11. Wings chalky white, with conspicuous shoulder marks, spots contrasting and eyes occupying most of lateral aspect of head........**spiloma**, p. 219

Ground color of wings slightly tawny, shoulder mark usually absent and spots not as dark; eyes smaller, not occupying most of lateral aspect of head.................**diarina**, p. 218

Leptocella candida (Hagen)

Setodes candida Hagen (1861, p. 280); ♂.

LARVA.—Length 12 mm. Head and thoracic sclerites mottled with yellow and brown, as in fig. 748, the frons always with the upper portion almost entirely brown; legs entirely yellow, sometimes with very narrow dark lines at the joints. Hind legs with a long swimming brush of fine hair.

CASE.—About 20 mm. long, constructed of wood and leaf fragments molded into a fairly smooth exterior, frequently with one to several long twigs cemented to side; before pupation the case is reduced in length.

ADULTS.—Length 15 mm. Head and sclerites tawny, covered with white hair. Wing membrane transparent, with a definite pattern from a covering of hair; front wings white with rows of gray and black marks, and having four conspicuous tufts of black hair along the hind margin at apex, as in fig. 757. Male genitalia, fig. 751: ninth segment more or less cylindrical, produced into a meso-dorsal hood, below which arise a pair of long fingers; tenth tergite almost ventral in position, broad at base and tapering to a slightly upturned and narrow apex; at the base of the tenth tergite arise a pair of filaments curved like a swan's neck and expanded at apex into a reticulate plate; claspers narrow at base, with a slight projection of the ventral margin, this entire margin bearing rows of long setae; at apex the clasper is divided into a subapical, spoonlike, sclerotized mesal lobe and a lateral apical lobe with a very oblique margin

clothed with very long setae; between the bases of the claspers arise a pair of very short lobes bearing two or three setae at apex; aedeagus membranous with a spoonshaped ventral sclerite. Female genitalia very simple, consisting of one or two inconspicuous pairs of lobes.

Allotype, female.—Momence, Illinois: Aug. 16, 1938, Ross & Burks.

This species is widely distributed over the state. It frequents a wide variety of streams and rivers, ranging from Quiver Creek to the Mississippi River and has been found also in marshes adjoining these streams. Adult emergence continues from early June to late August, indicating more than one generation per year. Both adults and larvae are frequently taken in large numbers. Reared collections of larvae from Quiver Creek have established the association of larval and adult forms.

This species ranges through the central and southern states, with records from Florida, Illinois, Indiana, Iowa, Kentucky and Ohio.

Illinois Records.—Many males and females and three pupae, taken May 28 to September 20, and many larvae and four cases, taken May 14 to August 21, are from Council Hill (Galena River), Deer Grove (Green River), Dixon, East Dubuque, Elizabethtown, Erie (Rock Creek), Freeport, Hamilton, Havana (Quiver Creek), Henry, Hillsdale, Homer, Jackson Island (in Mississippi River opposite Hannibal, Missouri), Kampsville, Kankakee, Keithsburg, Milan, Momence (Kankakee River), Mount Carmel, Oakwood, Pontiac, Quincy, Rockford, Rock Island, Rosiclare, St. Joseph, Savanna, Shawneetown, Shelbyville, Vandalia, and Wilmington.

Leptocella exquisita (Walker)

Leptocerus exquisita Walker (1852, p. 72); ♀.

LARVA (not reared, see below).—Length 12 mm. Head and thoracic sclerites mottled with yellow and light brown to form pattern as in fig. 746; front legs and all coxae yellow, middle and hind legs mostly black beyond coxae.

CASE.—Length 20 mm., made of wood fragments and similar in general to that of *candida*.

ADULTS.—Length 17 mm., the female usually not over 11 mm. Head and thorax tawny, covered with white hair. Front wings with a very conspicuous pattern, composed of cross bands of brownish yellow and a series of four quadrate black spots on posterior margin near apex, as in fig. 755; the bands are actually pigmented areas in the wing membrane with hair which follows this pattern closely. Male genitalia, fig. 750, with structures typical for genus, the claspers with only a small basal projection and with a pair of long styles tipped with long setae arising between bases of claspers.

Our Illinois records are confined to the eastern and northern portions of the state, and the species has been taken in large numbers only around the glacial lakes in the northeast corner. The larva which is described above as belonging to this species was found abundantly in Channel Lake, from which our largest collections of adults were taken; it is the only *Leptocella* larva in this entire lake region which was not reared; so we feel fairly confident in identifying it as *exquisita*. Collection data indicate a single generation per year, the Illinois emergence ranging from late June to mid July.

This species is widely distributed through the East, with an extension westward through the Ozarks to Oklahoma. We have records from Arkansas, Florida, Georgia, Illinois, Indiana, Kentucky, Maine, Michigan, Minnesota, Missouri, New York, North Carolina, Ohio, Oklahoma, Ontario, Pennsylvania, Quebec, South Carolina, Tennessee, Vermont and Wisconsin.

Illinois Records.—ALGONQUIN: July 16, 1910, Nason, 1 ♂. ANTIOCH: July 7, 1932, Frison & Metcalf, ♂ ♂. RICHMOND: June 28, 1938, Ross & Burks, 3 ♂ ; June 29, 1938, Ross & Burks, 4 ♂. WILMINGTON: July 1, 1935, DeLong & Ross, 1 ♂, 4 ♀. YORKVILLE, Fox River: June 25, 1936, at light, Frison & DeLong, 5 ♂, 8 ♀.

Leptocella pavida (Hagen)

Setodes pavida Hagen (1861, p. 282); ♀.

LARVA.—Length 7 mm. Head with a definite pattern of brownish yellow and dark brown, pronotum mostly brown with yellowish marks, as in fig. 747; legs yellowish with a few dark marks near the joints.

CASE.—Length 9 mm. Constructed of leaf fragments and forming a slightly flattened capsule.

ADULTS.—Length 10 mm. Color very pale yellow, including both the front wing membrane and the hairs on the wing; front wing, in addition, with a scattering of small and very black dots over most of the surface, many of the dots arranged in rows but all of them well separated, fig. 756. Male genitalia, fig. 749: general structure typical for genus as regards most of the structures; diagnostic are the claspers, which have a basal flap, and the large scoop-shaped sclerite beneath the base of the claspers and extending to the end of the basal lobe of the claspers.

In Illinois this species is a rarity. We have taken only four specimens, three of them in the center of the state, and one in the southern tip. We have not found any larvae. A collection of larvae and pupae made at Poe Springs, Alachua County, Florida, April 15, 1935, J. S. Rogers, has given us the association of larvae and adults.

The range of the species includes the eastern states with extensions westward through the Ozarks into Oklahoma. Records are available from Arkansas, District of Columbia, Florida, Georgia, Illinois, Kentucky, Maryland, Massachusetts, Michigan, Missouri, New York, Oklahoma, Tennessee and Wisconsin.

Illinois Records. — HEROD: Aug. 16, 1937, at light, Ross & Ritcher, 1 ♀. MAHOMET: Aug. 3, 1937, Ross & Burks, 2 ♀. MONTICELLO: June, 1932, T. H. Frison, 1 ♂.

Leptocella diarina new species

LARVA.—Length 11 mm. Head and thoracic sclerites yellow with a pair of black lines running the full length of head and pronotum and frequently indicated on the mesonotum, fig. 745. Legs various shades of brown, hind legs with a swimming brush of long hair.

CASE.—Length 20 mm. Made from wood fragments or sand grains, usually with a long stick attached to the side and with wood fragments predominating in the construction.

MALE.—Length 14 mm. Head and body straw colored, the legs whitish, all covered with white hair. Antennae banded with black and white hair. Wings with membrane transparent, color pattern formed entirely of hair; color nearly white with light brown spots arranged in rows across the apical third of the wing and scattered indefinitely over the anterior two-thirds; along the dorsum the wings usually form three large V-marks with small ones between. Sometimes these V-marks are reduced in size, in which case the intermediate small ones disappear, leaving only widely spaced dots. The general appearance is much as in fig. 754; the chief difference is that the central part of the wing has a few more spots, and the apical portion does not have such black bars; frequently, also, the shoulder spot is present near the base of the wing (well shown in fig. 754), but usually it is absent. General structure typical for genus. Eyes moderately large, separated on venter by twice their width as seen from this view, fig. 760. Genitalia typical for the *albida* group; ninth segment with dorsal process finger-like, the tenth tergite in the "swan's neck" processes typical for the genus; claspers, fig. 752, with a large basal flap, short narrow neck, the apex divided into a mesal spoon-shaped mesal lobe and a lateral, truncate, apical lobe bearing long setae; on the mesal face of the clasper there is a seta-bearing ridge which runs from the base of the mesal, subapical lobe to the anterior corner of the apex, with considerable variation as to the exact detail of this region.

FEMALE.—Slightly shorter and a little stouter than the male but similar to it in color and general structure; the color pattern is almost always reduced in contrast as compared to that of males. Abdomen bright green.

Holotype, male.—Havana, Illinois: June 29, 1936, Mohr & Burks.

Allotype, female. — Havana, Illinois: June 27, 1936, Mohr & Burks (reared from same lot as holotype).

Paratypes.—ILLINOIS.—Same data as for holotype, including June 24 to June 29, 3 ♂, ♀ ♀. ALGONQUIN: Sept. 16, 1904, W. A. Nason, 1 ♂; July 2, 1905, W. A. Nason, 1; same but June 28, 1 ♂; same but July 26, 1 ♂; same but Aug. 14, 1 ♀. AURORA: July 17, 1927, at light, Frison & Glasgow, 1 ♀. RICHMOND: June 24, 1938, Ross & Burks, 1 ♂, 6 ♀; same but June 28, 1 ♀; same but June 29, 2 ♂, 1 ♀.

INDIANA.—CRAWFORDSVILLE, Honey Creek: Aug. 10, 1938, Ross & Burks, 1 ♀. NOBLESVILLE: Aug. 10, 1938, Ross & Burks, 2 ♂.

MICHIGAN.—NILES: July 13, 1914, at light, 1 ♂.

SOUTH DAKOTA.—BROOKINGS: July 11, 1919, H. C. Severin, 1 ♂, 1 ♀.

In characters of the genitalia this species belongs to the *albida* group and is most closely related to the *intervena-texana* complex. It differs from this latter, however, in lacking close, definite rows of brown marks near the base of the wings, and in having the V-marks on the dorsum (when the wings are folded) or in having three large V-marks separated by small dots. Subsequent rearing of Texas material may show that this species is just a variant of *texana*, but in the material at hand there seems to be a clear-cut line between the two.

In Illinois we have taken this species at only scattered places. The larvae have always been found in fairly swift, cool streams such as Quiver Creek and Nippersink Creek. Larvae from both of these localities were reared. Little data are available on adult emergence, but the few records are sufficiently scattered from June to September to indicate the possibility of two generations per year.

The larvae of this species have been taken in company with *candida* but quite evidently are much rarer than *candida*.

Available records are from Illinois, Indiana, Michigan and South Dakota. So little material has been seen, however, that these records may give little indication of the true range of *diarina*.

Illinois Larval Records.—EAST PEORIA, Farm Creek: Aug. 29, 1940, 5 larvae. HAVANA, Quiver Creek: Aug. 7, 1895, C. A. Hart, many larvae; June 11, 1896, E. B. Forbes, 1 larva; May 28, 1936, Mohr & Burks, many larvae; May 29, 1936, Mohr & Burks, 6 larvae; June 5, 1936, Mohr & Burks, many larvae; June 20, 1936, Mohr & Burks, 2 larvae, 1 ♂, 2 ♀. SPRING GROVE, Nippersink Creek: June 12, 1936, Ross & Burks, 1 larva; June 8, 1938, Mohr & Burks, 5 larvae (reared); June 20, 1938, B. D. Burks, 2 larvae, 5 cases, 1 pupa (reared).

Leptocella spiloma new species

LARVAE.—Unknown.

MALE.—Length 12 mm. Head and body straw colored, the legs whitish, all covered with white hair; antennae banded white and black; wings transparent, covered with hair to form a white and brown pattern, fig. 754. In this species the black shoulder mark is always present, and the spotting on the anterior three-fourths of the wing is always sparse, with heavy dorsal V-marks. General structure typical for genus. Eyes very large, occupying most of the lateral aspect of the head and, as seen from ventral view, as wide as the distance between them. Male genitalia almost identical with the preceding species; claspers, fig. 753, with a very wide basal flap and with the mesal ridge, which continues from the base of the short apical lobe, extending above the dorsal margin of the lateral lobe. There is considerable variation in the details of these parts.

FEMALE.—Length 11 mm. Slightly more robust than male and with the spots usually a little smaller but just as contrasting as in the male; abdomen bright green. The eyes are much smaller than in the male but considerably larger than the eyes of females of *diarina*. Genitalia typical for genus.

Holotype, male.—Junction City, Kansas: July 29, 1938, J. A. & H. H. Ross.

Allotype, female.—Douglas County, Kansas: July, at light.

Paratypes.—KANSAS.—Same data as for allotype, 10 ♂, 22 ♀.

TEXAS.—BROWNSVILLE: Feb. 3, George Dorner, 2 ♂; Feb. 4, George Dorner, 1 ♀.

This species is most closely related to the preceding, differing from it slightly in the pattern but chiefly in the large eyes which, as seen from ventral view, are as wide as the distance between them, fig. 761. The only other described species with large eyes is *stigmatica*, which is much darker than this species.

In all the specimens we have seen, the females of this species appear to have a ground color of almost snowy white, with the green of the abdomen showing through, whereas the females of *diarina* have a ground color which is closer to a straw color or a very pale tawny shade, with the green of the abdomen showing through.

We have taken only one specimen of this species in Illinois, a female collected at Quincy, July 6, 1937, Mohr & Riegel. Little is known regarding the habits of the species, but it appears to have a range centering around Texas and Kansas, extending northeastward with records in Missouri and Illinois. As with the preceding species, records are too few to give an adequate picture of the range.

Leptocella albida (Walker)

Leptocerus albidus Walker (1852, p. 71); ♂.
Setodes nivea Hagen (1861, p. 281); ♂.
?*Mystacides uwarowii* Kolenati (1859b, p. 249).

LARVA.—Fig. 744. Length 11 mm. Head, thoracic sclerites and front legs brownish yellow; the head with a V-shaped dark brown mark along frons, and with ventral portion dark brown; middle and hind legs dark brown to black with lighter areas at the joints, legs without swimming brushes.

CASE.—Length 20 mm., slender and tapering, constructed of sand grains and minute fragments of clam shells, smooth in outline and sometimes with a slender twig fastened to one side. Before pupation the lower portion is cut off, leaving a case about 15 mm. long which is cylindrical and truncate at both ends. The case for this species is illustrated in fig. 762.

ADULTS.—Length 16 mm. Head and thorax almost black, covered with white hair. Front wings nearly white with rows of small gray marks beyond the cord; after the adult has been flying for some time some of the wing hairs come off, after which the veins stand out fairly boldly as in fig. 758. Male genitalia similar to those of *diarina*, having the same type of clasper with a wide basal flap.

Until the fauna of Alaska is better known, it is impossible to place Kolenati's *uwarowii* with certainty, but his illustration of the insect seems to fit this species fairly well.

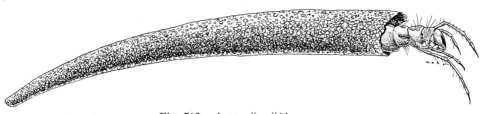

Fig. 762.—*Leptocella albida*, case.

Vorhies (1909) described all stages of this insect under the name *uwarowii*.

In Illinois the species centers around the glacial lakes in the northeastern part of the state. In these it is very abundant, being found under stones and among weeds near the shore. Our adult emergence records, including those from other states, extend from June to September, indicating more than one generation per year.

The species ranges widely through the North and Northeast; records are available from Illinois, Michigan, New Brunswick, New York, Ontario, Pennsylvania, Saskatchewan and Wisconsin. The range may be more extensive southward, but I have restricted identifications of this species to specimens about which there seems no doubt.

Illinois Records.—Many males, females and pupae, taken May 18 to August 14, and many larvae and cases, taken May 15 to June 11, are from Algonquin, Antioch, Aurora, Channel Lake, Chicago, Fox Lake, Grass Lake, Havana, Ottawa, Pistakee Lake, Richmond, Round Lake, Sand Lake, Spring Grove (Nippersink Creek), Volo, Zion (Dead River).

Leptocella species a

LARVA.—Length 12 mm. Head and pronotum with a mottling of brown and yellow very similar to that in *diarina*. Mesonotum yellow with brownish marks as in the same species. Legs yellow, the middle and hind pair with narrow black bands at apex. Hind legs with swimming brush of long hairs.

This larva has not been reared, nor have we any evidence which would link it with species known only from the adults. We have one larva from Illinois, from the Spoon River near Havana, October 2, 1938, B. D. Burks; in addition, material has been taken in Wisconsin and Michigan.

Athripsodes Billberg

Athripsodes Billberg (1820, p. 94). Genotype, by subsequent designation of Milne (1934, p. 18): *Phryganea albifrons* Linnaeus.

The larva is short and builds either a tapering, horn-shaped case, fig. 810, or one with lateral flanges, figs. 808, 809; gills are usually abundant and tufted, although difficult to distinguish and reduced in number in some forms; the mouthparts are short, the

mandibles with a blunt, toothed apex. The adults are brown or black, with wide hind wings.

A large number of species have been described from North America, of which 14 have been collected in Illinois. Eight species are known from the larval stage, and three additional unassociated forms have been recognized; characters have been found for separating these to species and also for separating the females for all the Illinois species in which this sex is known.

KEY TO SPECIES

Larvae

1. Mesonotum with many hairs, fig. 763; parafrontal areas originating at apex of frons............**mentieus**, p. 232
   Mesonotum with only two or three pairs of scattered hairs, fig. 765; parafrontal areas, if present, originating below apex of frons, fig. 764 2
2. Parafrontal areas absent, head pale without distinct markings........ ....**sp. a**, p. 235
   Parafrontal areas outlined distinctly at least somewhere along their boundary, fig. 764...............3
3. Head dark brown except for distinct pale lines on "false frons" and side, fig. 766; case with extended lateral margin, fig. 808................4
   Head either yellowish, or brown with many pale spots, fig. 764; case usually without extended lateral margin, fig. 810.....................5
4. Case twice as long as wide, fig. 808; frons nearly black......**ancylus**, p. 227
   Case broader, only one and one-half times as long as wide, fig. 809; reddish brown.........**?flavus**, p. 228
5. Sclerotized bars of mesonotum wide, with a mesal spur and a thickened area down the center, fig. 769; pronotum chocolate brown......... ....**sp. c**, p. 236
   Sclerotized bars of mesonotum linear, without a mesal spur or thickened central area, fig. 764; pronotum yellowish brown to colorless.......6
6. Ninth segment with only weak, short setae, variable in number, fig. 771.. 7
   Ninth segment with two dorsal pairs of long, black setae, fig. 770....... 8
7. Head with parafrontal areas nearly as wide as frons, fig. 772.....**sp. b**, p. 235
   Head with parafrontal areas much narrower than frons, fig. 773 ....**dilutus**, p. 231

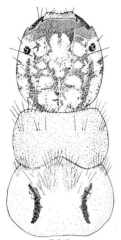

763

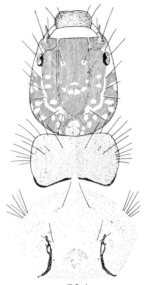

764

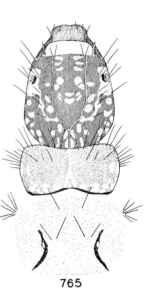

765

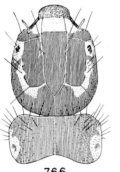

766

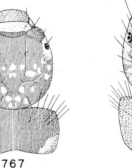

767

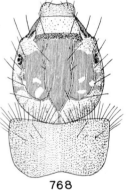

768

Larvae of *Athripsodes*

Fig. 763.—*A. mentieus.*
Fig. 764.—*A. alagmus.*
Fig. 765.—*A. tarsi-punctatus.*
Fig. 766.—*A. ancylus.*
Fig. 767.—*A. transversus.*
Fig. 768.—*A. cancellatus.*

8. Parafrontal area nearly as wide as frons, fig. 768; dorso-lateral sclerotized area over anal leg long and slender, rodlike.................. 9
   Parafrontal area only slightly wider than half width of frons, fig. 765; dorso-lateral sclerotized area over anal leg short and platelike....... 10
9. Anterior margin of pronotum with setae on central portion irregular in length and close together, fig. 768..
   ....**cancellatus,** p. 233

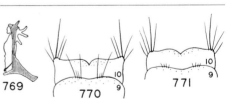

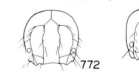

769   770   771   772 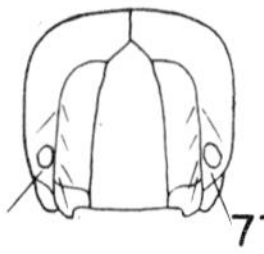   773

Fig. 769.—*Athripsodes species c,* larva, mesonotal bar.
Fig. 770.—*Athripsodes cancellatus* larva, ninth tergite.
Fig. 771.—*Athripsodes dilutus* larva, ninth tergite.
Fig. 772.—*Athripsodes species b* larva, head.
Fig. 773.—*Athripsodes dilutus* larva, head.

Anterior margin of pronotum with well-separated hairs of nearly equal length, fig. 767.....**transversus**, p. 233

10. Color pattern and spots more contrasting, fig. 765................ ....**tarsi-punctatus**, p. 229

Color pattern and spots less contrasting, fig. 764...........**alagmus**, p. 229

Adults

1. Genitalia with movable claspers, figs. 774–791 (males)................ 2

Genitalia without claspers, figs. 792-807 (females)................... 19

2. Claspers with a basal projection nearly as long as height of clasper, fig. 774 3

Claspers with either a short basal projection or none, figs. 780, 791..... 4

3. Basal projection of claspers evenly rounded, fig. 774.......**ancylus**, p. 227

Basal projection of claspers angled, fig. 775.................**flavus**, p. 228

4. Tenth tergite U-shaped, the base forming the bottom of the U, the ventral arm of the U divided into lateral halves, each tipped with a cluster of spines, fig. 776.........**saccus**, p. 234

Tenth tergite not U-shaped, sometimes long and necklike, fig. 778... 5

5. Claspers with a serrate, mesal lobe; tenth tergite divided by a narrow fissure into dorsal and ventral parts, the ventral lobe with a strong, long, lateral blade, fig. 777..**erraticus**, p. 235

Claspers without a serrate mesal lobe; tenth tergite not divided into dorsal and ventral parts................ 6

6. Basal segment of clasper with a long spur almost as stout and long as mesal process, fig. 778............ ....**erullus**, p. 235

Basal segment of clasper without such a spur, at most with a large seta on the mesal lobe, fig. 784.......... 7

7. Tenth tergite long, somewhat hooded, and with a pair of long, sclerotized arms arising at its base and reaching almost midway to apex, fig. 779 8

Tenth tergite either no longer than cerci, fig. 791, or without such a pair of arms, fig. 785............. 9

8. Lateral arms of tenth tergite only half length of tergite; spine of aedeagus upturned at tip, fig. 779.......... ....**nephus**, p. 230

Lateral arms of tenth tergite more than half length of tergite; spine of aedeagus curved ventrad, figs. 780, 781.......................... 9

9. Tenth tergite very long, with a sharp,

hooded apex, fig. 780; aedeagus slender.......**tarsi-punctatus**, p. 229

Tenth tergite shorter, as in fig. 781, with a blunt and slightly enlarged apex; aedeagus robust........... ....**alagmus**, p. 229

10. Claspers with body long and slender, with mesal process small, scarcely longer than width of apical lobe, and the body of the clasper with a mesal lobe just under mesal process, figs. 782, 783......................... 11

Claspers either with short body, fig. 790, longer mesal process, fig. 785, or without a mesal lobe below mesal process....................... 12

11. Base of clasper not produced into a spur, fig. 782, aedeagus small, with the base narrow and with two internal spines..........**dilutus**, p. 231

Base of clasper produced into a spur, fig. 783, aedeagus large, with a single internal spine and with the base greatly enlarged............ ....**annulicornis**, p. 232

12. Claspers with apical segment bent at right angles to basal segment, fig. 784.......................... 13

Claspers with apical segment at most slightly angled from basal segment, fig. 786....................... 14

13. Mesal lobe of clasper with a fusiform, pointed spine, fig. 784........... ....**angustus**, p. 231

Mesal lobe of clasper without a spine, fig. 785.............**resurgens**, p. 230

14. Tenth tergite with a long neck and a long, somewhat hood-shaped head, fig. 786...........**ophioderus**, p. 232

Tenth tergite without a definite, long neck and head, fig. 787.......... 15

15. Tenth tergite sickle shaped, the ventral margin evenly concave, fig. 787 ....**mentieus**, p. 232

Tenth tergite not at all sickle shaped, fig. 788....................... 16

16. Sclerotized mesal process of clasper stout, fig. 788; front wings dark brown, almost black, with a scattering of white scales............... 17

Sclerotized mesal process of clasper slender, fig. 790; front wing medium to light shades of brown without scales........................ 18

17. Tenth tergite with narrowed apical portion nearly as long as base, cylindrical and rounded at apex, fig. 788 ....**punctatus**, p. 234

Tenth tergite with narrowed apical portion short, tapering and truncate, fig. 789...........**submacula**, p. 235

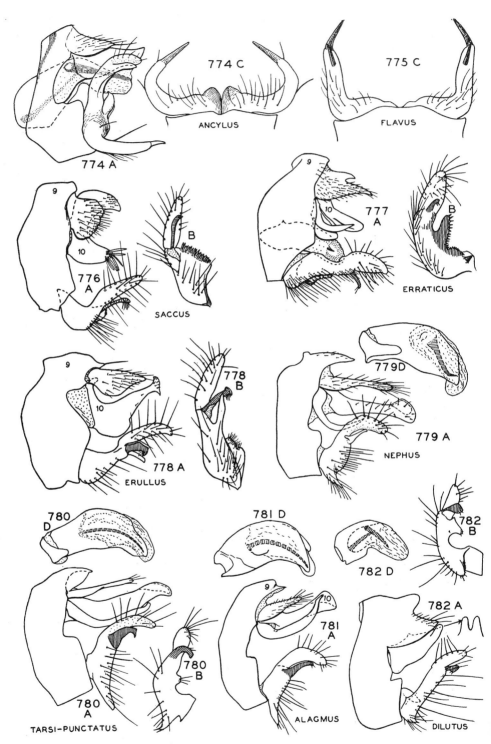

Figs 774–782.—*Athripsodes,* male genitalia. *A,* lateral aspect; *B* and *C,* claspers, respectively caudal and ventral aspects; *D,* aedeagus.

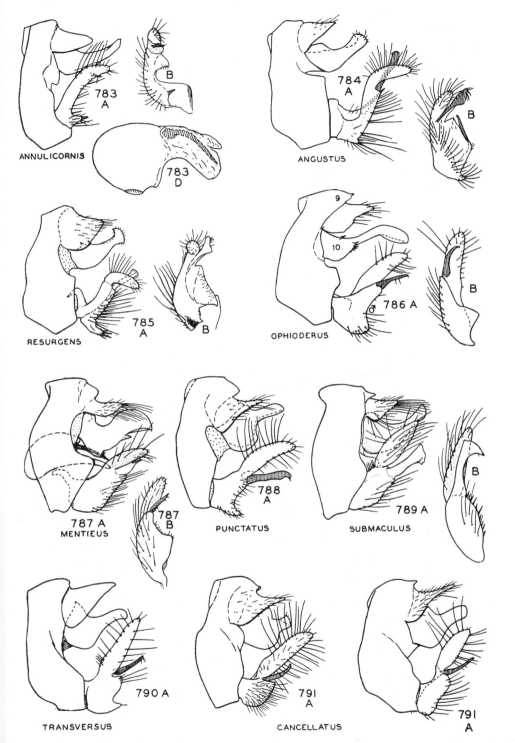

Figs. 783–791.—*Athripsodes*, male genitalia.　*A*, lateral aspect; *B* and *C*, claspers, respectively caudal and ventral aspects; *D*, aedeagus.

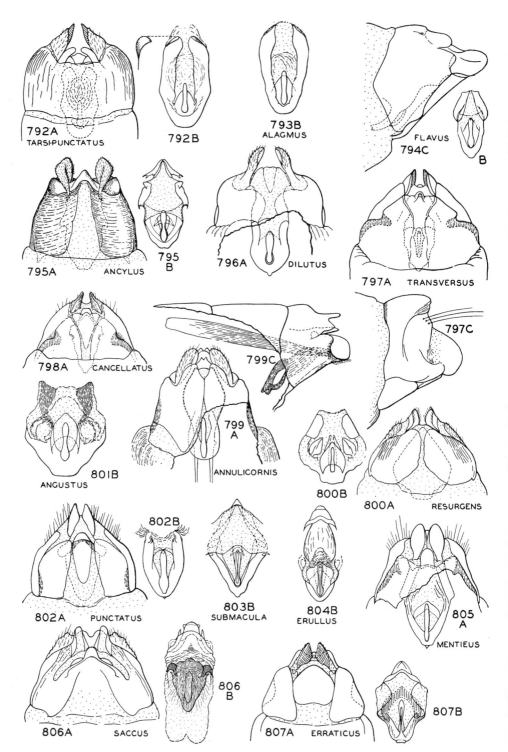

Figs. 792–807.—*Athripsodes*, female genitalia.   *A*, ventral aspect;   *B*, bursa copulatrix; *C*, lateral aspect.

18. Base of claspers with ventral margin produced into a lobe, fig. 790......
    ....**transversus**, p. 233
    Base of claspers with ventral margin rounded, fig. 791...**cancellatus**, p. 233

19. Ninth sternite with a pair of finger-like, apico-mesal lobes, fig. 792.... 20
    Ninth sternite without digitate lobes, at most with short points, fig. 794 21

20. Bursa copulatrix with lateral bands curved ventrad and convoluted near attachment; only a small, triangular sclerite between bursa and dorsal apodeme of tenth tergite, fig. 792
    ....**tarsi-punctatus**, p. 229
    Bursa copulatrix with lateral bands flat to attachment; a large sclerite almost filling space between bursa and dorsal apodeme of tenth tergite, fig. 793.............**alagmus**, p. 229

21. Ninth sternite with plates deeply concave, apico-mesal corners pointed, lateral margin upturned and angulate near base, fig. 794............ 22
    Ninth sternite not concave, not with lateral margin upturned or angulate, figs. 796–807................. 23

22. Sclerotized halves of ninth sternite sharply tapered to base, lateral margin sharply angulate; bursa copulatrix with sides appressed to body, fig. 794..........**flavus**, p. 228
    Sclerotized halves of ninth sternite almost truncate at base, lateral margin only rounded at projection; bursa copulatrix with sides flaring laterad, fig. 795........**ancylus**, p. 227

23. Tenth segment with lateral plates as long as ninth sternite, fig. 796.....
    ....**dilutus**, p. 231
    Tenth segment with lateral plates much shorter than ninth sternite, fig. 797........................ 24

24. Ninth sternite with lateral margins angling more mesad than caudad from base, the angled portion marked by an internal shelf, fig. 797 25
    Ninth sternite with lateral margins not angling so sharply, either the internal shelf absent or not angling mesad more than in fig. 805.... 26

25. Apical portion of ninth sternite wide, fig. 797............**transversus**, p. 233
    Apical portion of ninth sternite narrower, fig. 798.....**cancellatus**, p. 233

26. Bursa copulatrix situated on sclerotized ribbons which extend far past the bursa to the seventh segment, fig. 799.........**annulicornis**, p. 232
    Attachment ribbons of bursa copulatrix not extending anterior of bursa 27

27. Bursa copulatrix with wide lateral expansions, fig. 800................ 28
    Bursa copulatrix with lateral expansions absent or small, fig. 806...... 29

28. Attachment of bursa copulatrix chiefly membranous with a single pair of flat sclerites just above bursa, fig. 800................**resurgens**, p. 230
    Attachment of bursa copulatrix consisting chiefly of a sclerotized ribbon, fig. 801.............**angustus**, p. 231

29. Ninth sternite with large lateral plates and a narrow, mesal tongue, all heavily sclerotized, as in fig. 802...
    ....**punctatus**, p. 234
    Ninth sternite with mesal area indistinct or much wider, fig. 807...... 30

30. Bursa copulatrix triangular, fig. 803
    ....**submacula**, p. 235
    Bursa copulatrix U-shaped, figs. 804–807............................ 31

31. Bursa copulatrix attached at the end of a long, vasiform, sclerotized structure, fig. 804..........**erullus**, p. 235
    Bursa copulatrix attached to short membranous folds or to paired sclerotized ribbons................... 32

32. Bursa copulatrix oval, without latero-ventral points, fig. 805...........
    ....**mentieus**, p. 232
    Bursa copulatrix U-shaped or somewhat vasiform, with sharp latero-ventral points, figs. 806, 807...... 33

33. Points near top of bursa copulatrix; ninth sternite composed chiefly of a single, large sclerotized plate arcuate across apex, fig. 806.....**saccus**, p. 234
    Points near middle of bursa; ninth sternite composed of a pair of large, lateral sclerotized plates and a smaller, nearly square mesal plate, fig. 807.............**erraticus**, p. 235

Athripsodes ancylus (Vorhies)

Leptocerus ancylus Vorhies (1909, p. 691); ♂, ♀.

LARVA.—Fig. 766. Length 8 mm. Head very dark brown with pale area around eyes and subfrons, forming a pale U with a few dark dots in upper portion; pronotum dark brown with a lateral white spot; legs light brown. The frontal areas more than half width of frons. Pronotum with only long scattered hairs on anterior margin. Mesonotum with a lateral tuft of about 10 hairs, central area with only three or four scattered pairs of hairs, sclerotized bars thin and not at all sharply angled.

Case.—Fig. 808. Length 9 mm., 4.5–5.0 mm. wide, built solidly of sand grains, the dorso-lateral margins produced into a wide flange so that from above the case appears shaped like a water-penny.

Adults.—Length 11 mm. Color medium to dark shades of brown without conspicuous markings on scales. Male genitalia, fig. 774: cerci short and tenth tergite long;

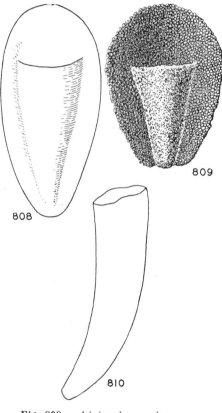

Fig. 808.—*Athripsodes ancylus*, case.
Fig. 809.—*Athripsodes ?flavus*, case.
Fig. 810.—*Athripsodes mentieus*, case.

claspers with a long prolongation of the base, as seen from ventral view forming a stout, curved, pencil-like pair of appendages, the remainder of the clasper upright, long and slender with a short mesal process and apical segment only slightly longer than the process. Female genitalia, fig. 795, with the ninth sternite divided into a pair of heavily sclerotized, markedly concave plates which are produced into a sharp apico-mesal point; bursa copulatrix as in fig. 795B.

We have only scattered records of this species from Illinois, from some of our best

aquatic habitats in the northern, central and southern parts of the state. All the material we have, both in Illinois and in other states, has a case conforming quite exactly to the above description. Lloyd (1921, p. 96) records a case markedly different in shape, but we have seen nothing that agrees with his description. Our larvae were collected in wide extremes of environment, including weed beds in the northeastern glacial lakes, and under stones in the rapid streams of the Ozark Hills. Adult emergence apparently is confined to May, June and July; this indicates a single generation per year.

The species is distributed widely through the northern and eastern states and also occurs in the Kiamichi Mountains in Oklahoma. Available records include Georgia, Illinois, New York, North Carolina, Ohio, Oklahoma and Wisconsin.

Illinois Records. — Chicago: July 8, 1939, G. T. Riegel, 1 ♂. Eddyville, Lusk Creek: May 24, 1940, Mohr & Burks, 1 pupa. Fox Lake: May 15, 1936, from weeds, Ross & Mohr, 2 larvae. Golconda: May 30, 1928, at light, T. H. Frison, 1 ♂. Johnsburg, Fox River: May 10, 1938, Ross & Burks, 2 cases. Momence: June 4, 1932, Frison & Mohr, 1 ♂. Wilmington: July 1, 1935, DeLong & Ross, 1 ♂.

Athripsodes flavus (Banks)

Leptocerus flavus Banks (1904d, p. 212); ♂, ♀.

Larva.—We have no definite rearing of this species but have taken several collections of a larva which is closely related to *ancylus*, differing in the wider lateral extensions of the case and the uniformly paler color of the larval sclerites. Since this species displays the proper taxonomic characters for such a placement and in addition is slightly smaller than *ancylus*, I am regarding this larva tentatively as *flavus*. The case is 8 mm. long and 5.5–6.0 mm. wide, fig. 809.

Adults.—Length 9 mm. Color various shades of light brown without conspicuous markings or white scales. Male genitalia, fig. 775, distinguished by the long basal projection of the clasper, which in this species is sharply angled at the base. Female genitalia, fig. 794, with the sclerotized halves of the ninth sternite sharply tapered to base, the lateral margin sharply angulate; bursa copulatrix with sides appressed to body so that, from ventral view, they do not flare.

This species has been taken in many scattered localities in Illinois, almost all of them along fairly large rivers such as the Ohio, Illinois and Kankakee. Our adult emergence records run from June 23 to July 14, indicating a single generation per year. The larvae which we are considering as of this species have been taken mainly in large rivers.

The species is known from adult collections from a limited number of eastern and northcentral states, including Illinois, Kentucky, Pennsylvania and Wisconsin; in addition, larvae considered as this species have been taken from Indiana and Minnesota.

Illinois Records.—Many males and females, taken June 23 to July 21, and many larvae, taken May 4 to October 30, are from Dixon, Elizabethtown (Ohio River), Fox Lake, Hardin, Hoopeston, Kampsville, Kankakee, Momence, Rockford, Rock Island, Saline Mines (Saline River), Springfield, Sterling, Wilmington.

Athripsodes tarsi-punctatus (Vorhies)

Leptocerus tarsi-punctatus Vorhies (1909, p. 694); ♂.

LARVA.—Length 6 mm. Head brown with indefinite pale spots, fig. 765. Pronotum and legs straw color to yellowish brown. Parafrons scarcely wider than half width of frons. Pronotum with long, well-separated hairs on anterior margin. Mesonotum with a lateral tuft of 6–8 hairs, mesal portion of tergite with only a few scattered hairs, sclerotized bars thin and gently curved.

CASE.—Length 7 mm., horn shaped, made of vegetable fragments and sand grains, the sand grains predominating in most situations.

ADULTS.—Length 11 mm. Color chocolate brown, the base of the tarsi ringed with white. Male genitalia, fig. 780: cerci long, the apex slender; tenth tergite very long, the extreme apex slightly downcurved, a stout sclerotized spur arising from the base and extending three-fourths distance to apex; clasper with a very long basal projection, its apical segment curved, the mesal projection stout and curved. Female genitalia, fig. 792: ninth sternite with a pair of fingerlike apico-mesal fingers which converge toward apex; bursa copulatrix with lateral bands curved ventrad and convoluted near

attachment and with only a small triangular sclerite between bursa and dorsal apodeme of tenth tergite, this sclerite sometimes almost entirely membranous.

Allotype, female.—Council Hill, Illinois, along Galena River: June 26, 1940, Mohr & Riegel.

This species occurs throughout the entire state, with a preponderance of records from the northern fourth. The larvae live in lakes and streams. They are abundant in many of the glacial lakes in northeastern Illinois; the streams they frequent are generally fairly clear, rapid and cool. There is usually only one generation a year, the large wave of adults occurring during May and June.

The species is apparently widespread through the eastern half of the continent, with records available for Arkansas, Georgia, Illinois, Indiana, Kentucky, Maine, Michigan, Minnesota, Missouri, New Brunswick, New York, Ontario, Pennsylvania, Saskatchewan, South Dakota and Wisconsin.

Illinois Records.—Many males and females, taken May 4 to August 19, and many larvae, taken May 4 to June 27, are from Amboy (Green River), Antioch, Carbondale, Channel Lake, Charleston, Chicago, Council Hill (Galena River), Dixon, East Fox Lake, Elgin (Rainbow Springs), Fox Lake, Grand Tower, Harrisburg, Havana (Quiver Creek), Johnsburg (Fox River), Kankakee, McHenry, Mineola (East Fox Lake), Momence, Ottawa, Pistakee Lake, Rock Island, Rosecrans (Des Plaines River), Savanna, Serena (Indian Creek), Shawneetown, Springfield, Spring Grove (Nippersink Creek), Sterling, Urbana, Wadsworth (Des Plaines River), West Fox Lake, Wilmington, Zion (Dead River).

Athripsodes alagmus Ross

Athripsodes alagmus Ross (1938a, p. 155); ♂.

LARVA.—Fig. 764. Length 7 mm. Head brown with definite pale spots which do not contrast greatly with the background. Pronotum and legs straw color to yellowish brown. Frons and other structural characters similar to those of *tarsi-punctatus*.

CASE.—Length 8 mm., horn shaped, made chiefly of vegetable fragments, very rarely with some sand grains mixed with these.

ADULTS.—Length 12 mm. Color chocolate brown, the base of the tarsi ringed with white. Male genitalia, fig. 781: cerci short; tenth tergite fairly long, slightly curved, fairly thick at apex, and with a pair of stout, sclerotized lateral arms which arise at the extreme base of the tergite and nearly reach the tip; claspers with long, pointed basal projection, curved apical segment and a stout, curved mesal projection. Female genitalia, fig. 793: ninth sternite with a pair of finger-like, apico-mesal lobes; bursa copulatrix with lateral bands flat to point of attachment; a large sclerite almost fills the space between the bursa and the dorsal apodeme of the tenth tergite.

Allotype, female.—Spring Grove, Illinois, reared from hatchery ponds: June 14, 1938, B. D. Burks.

This species has been taken at only a few localities in the northern part of the state. It is apparently single brooded, our emergence records being from June 14 to July 20. We have taken the larvae only in fish hatchery ponds at Spring Grove where they were very abundant. It is interesting to note that only a few miles away the somewhat similar larvae of closely related *tarsi-punctatus* were abundant in Fox Lake, but we experienced no difficulty in separating the two on comparative coloration and case construction, nor did the two appear to mix in either habitat.

Records for this species are scattered but restricted to the northeastern states, as follows: Illinois, Michigan, Minnesota, New York and Wisconsin.

Illinois Records.—Many males and females, taken June 14 to August 15, and many larvae, taken June 9 to 14, are from Antioch, Fox Lake, Fulton, Homer, McHenry, Momence, Richmond, Spring Grove, Waukegan, Wadsworth (Des Plaines River).

Athripsodes nephus new species

LARVA.—Unknown.

MALE.—Length 10 mm. Color various shades of brown, the wings an almost uniform shade and without white scales, the tarsi banded with light and dark. General structure typical for genus. Male genitalia, fig. 779: ninth segment fairly narrow and cylindrical, the dorsal portion projecting over the base of the tenth. Tenth tergite long and narrow, the central portion narrowed, the apex expanded into a definite

head; at the base of the tenth tergite arise a pair of sclerotized rods which are sharply curved at the middle and reach to the middle of the tenth tergite. Claspers stocky; basal segment short with a ventral pointed projection; apical segment stout and curved at middle, membranous and bearing long scattered setae; mesal process fairly slender and about half the length of the apical segment. Aedeagus ovate, the lateral sclerites deep, the internal sclerotized pair of rods short, wide at base, and sharply angled dorsad at apex.

Holotype, male. — Rosecrans, Illinois, along Des Plaines River: June 9, 1938, at light, Ross & Burks.

Paratypes.—ILLINOIS.—Same data as for holotype, 1 ♂.

OKLAHOMA.—Cloudy Creek near CLOUDY: May 4, 1940, Mrs. Roy Weddle, 1 ♂.

The species differs from all the previously described members of the *tarsi-punctatus* group in the short, sclerotized rod which arises from the base of the tenth tergite, the angled internal rod of the aedeagus, and also in the shape of the tenth tergite, notably the constricted central portion and expanded apex.

This is a very rare species in Illinois known only from the male and with nothing known regarding its biology. Probably locally distributed over a wide range.

Athripsodes resurgens (Walker)

Leptocerus resurgens Walker (1852, p. 70); ♂.
Leptocerus variegatus Hagen (1861, p. 278); ♂.
Leptocerus aspinosus Betten (1934, p. 255); ♂.

LARVA.—Unknown.

ADULTS.—Length 16 mm. Color grayish brown, the wings and body with a scattering of fairly large areas of white hair giving it a variegated and somewhat hairy appearance. Male genitalia, fig. 785: cerci short and rounded; tenth tergite elongate and upturned; claspers with a short, dark basal projection, very long basal segment, short and curved apical segment, and a mesal process which is straight and stout and usually extends slightly above the level of the apical segment. Female genitalia, fig. 800: ninth sternite only slightly sclerotized; bursa copulatrix with wide lateral extensions, the attachments fairly long, membranous except for a pair of plates which do not touch the bursa.

Allotype, female.—Brevort, Michigan: Aug. 8, 1936, C. Sabrosky.

Illinois records are confined entirely to the shore of Lake Michigan. The type of Hagen's *variegatus* was collected at Chicago, the types of *aspinosus* are from Lake Forest, and we have taken additional specimens at Waukegan. The larva, which is unknown, probably lives in Lake Michigan.

The range of the species extends throughout the Northeast, with a single isolated record from the Kiamichi Mountains in Oklahoma. Records include Illinois, Michigan, Minnesota, New York, Ohio, Oklahoma, Ontario, Quebec, Saskatchewan and Wisconsin.

Illinois Records.—CHICAGO: June 11–Aug. 27, W. J. Gerhard, 7 ♂, 3 ♀, FM. WAUKEGAN: July 7, 1937, at light, Frison & Ross, 3 ♀.

Athripsodes angustus (Banks)

Leptocerus angustus Banks (1914, p. 263); ♂.

LARVA.—Unknown.

ADULTS.—Length 13 mm. Color brown with scarcely any markings. Male genitalia, fig. 784, very similar to *resurgens*, differing in the longer apical segment of the clasper, more uniform tenth tergite, and the long, fusiform spine on the inner lobe of the clasper. Female genitalia, fig. 801, similar in general structure to *resurgens* but with supports of the bursa sclerotized for almost their entire length.

Allotype, female.—Lake Erie, Put-in-Bay, Ohio: Aug. 16, 1937, C. O. Mohr.

We have only a few scattered records of this species from the northern half of Illinois. Little is known about its habitat preference, and the larva is unknown.

The range of the species occupies a large portion of the Northeast, with a southwestward extension into the Kiamichi Mountains of Oklahoma. Records are available from Illinois, Maine, Michigan, Minnesota, New York, Ohio, Oklahoma, Ontario, Pennsylvania, Quebec and Wisconsin.

Illinois Records. — DANVILLE, Middle Fork River: Aug. 27, 1936, Ross & Burks, 3 ♂. Three miles east of MOMENCE: June 22, 1938, Ross & Burks, 1 ♂. OREGON:

July 18, 1927, at light, T. H. Frison & R. D. Glasgow, 2 ♂. RICHMOND: June 20, 1938, Burks & Boesel, 1 ♂.

Athripsodes dilutus (Hagen)

Leptocerus dilutus Hagen (1861, p. 277); ♂.

LARVA.—Length 6 mm. Head, pronotum and legs cream color to yellowish, the head with scattered, indistinct, brownish spots on upper portion. Parafrontal areas only about half width of frons. Mesonotum with only a few pairs of scattered hairs, the sclerotized bars narrow and not sharply angled. Ninth segment with only one or two very short and slender dorsal hairs.

CASE.—Length 7 mm., horn shaped, nearly round in cross section, constructed of sand grains cemented together to form a fairly smooth exterior.

ADULTS.—Length 6–7 mm. Color dark brown, the wings with a few patches of light hair. Male genitalia, fig. 782: cerci short, almost completely fused at base with genital capsule; tenth tergite fairly long, divided at apex into a pair of short, rounded lobes; claspers with basal segment very long, produced into a short ventral projection, apical segment short and somewhat elliptic; mesal process short, narrow at base and widened into a spatulate apex; aedeagus with two long, black internal spines situated one beyond the other. Female genitalia, fig. 796, with ninth sternite short and only slightly sclerotized, and tenth segment with lateral plates long and slender.

This species, originally described by Hagen from Chicago specimens, is apparently confined in Illinois to the vicinity of Lake Michigan and glacial lakes in the northeastern corner of the state. Our records are too incomplete to be sure of the number of generations, but large flights have been taken from May to mid August. It is possible that there is only a single generation and that the late emergence records are from cold water situations. Vorhies (1909, p. 688) reared this species in the lakes around Madison, Wisconsin, and described the larvae and adults. We have taken pupae commonly on stones in Channel Lake near Antioch, Illinois.

The range of the species apparently includes most of the Northeast, extending westward to Minnesota and south to Georgia. We have records from Georgia,

Illinois, Indiana, Minnesota, New York, Ohio, Ontario, Quebec and Wisconsin.

Illinois Records.—ANTIOCH: May 18, 1938, Ross & Burks, 3♂, 1♀ (reared in cage at Spring Grove). CHANNEL LAKE: May 27, 1936, H. H. Ross, 3♂, 4♀. CHICAGO: July 13, 1931, roof of Stevens Hotel, T. H. Frison, 8♂, 9♀; July 8, 1939, G. T. Riegel, 5♂, 7♀. FOX LAKE: May 15, 1936, Ross & Mohr, from stones, 7 pupae; May 28, 1936, H. H. Ross, 2♀. GRAYSLAKE: May 26, 1936, H. H. Ross, 1♂. North of WADSWORTH, Des Plaines River: July 7, 1937, Frison & Ross, 1♀. WAUKEGAN: Aug. 25, 1932, Ross & Mohr, 1♂; July 16, 1935, Ross & DeLong, ♂♂, ♀♀; May 25, 1936, H. H. Ross, 1♀; July 7, 1937, at light, Frison & Ross, ♂♂, ♀♀; Aug. 15, 1938, Ross & Burks, 6♀. ZION: Dead River, July 7, 1937, Frison & Ross, 4♂, ♀♀; June 4, 1938, Ross & Burks, 1♀; Aug. 15, 1936, Ross & Burks, 1♀.

Athripsodes annulicornis (Stephens)

Leptocerus annulicornis Stephens (1836, p. 199); ♂, ♀.
Leptocerus lugens Hagen (1861, p. 276); ♂, ♀.
Leptocerus recurvatus Banks (1908b, p. 265); ♂.
Leptocerus futilis Banks (1914, p. 264); ♂.
Athripsodes perplexus nordus Milne (1934, p. 15); ♂.

Not yet collected in Illinois, but a possible addition with future collecting. The range of the species covers the Holarctic region with North American records from Alaska, Colorado, New York, Ontario, Oregon, Quebec and Wisconsin.

Athripsodes mentieus (Walker)

Leptocerus mentieus Walker (1852, p. 71); ♂.
Leptocerus vanus Betten (1934, p. 262); ♂, ♀.
Leptocerus mentiens auct., misspelling.

LARVA.—Fig. 763. Length 6.5–7.0 mm. Head, pronotum and legs brownish yellow, the head with an irregular brown pattern. Parafrontal areas as long as frons, the three meeting at base of epicranial stem. Mesonotum relatively hairy with at least 20 pairs of hairs in addition to lateral tufts, and with sclerotized bars fairly wide. Ninth segment with two pairs of long black setae.

CASE.—Fig. 810. Length 10 mm., horn shaped and markedly curved; constructed of flattened sand grains cemented together to form an even and fenestrated exterior.

ADULTS.—Length 10 mm. Color dark brown, the tarsi ringed with white. Male genitalia, fig. 787: cerci short and ovate; tenth tergite stout, the apical portion long and expanded into a broad hood; claspers with basal segment large, produced into a mesal triangular lobe, the apical segment short and curved, the mesal process wide at base, fairly long and tapering to a sharp point. Female genitalia, fig. 805: ninth sternite only indistinctly sclerotized; bursa copulatrix oval and attached by a pair of sclerotized ribbons.

Our collections of adults have resulted in only a few scattered Illinois records of this species distributed from the extreme north to the extreme south end of the state. Bottom fauna collections made by R. E. Richardson show that in 1924-27 the larva of this species was an abundant midstream feature for almost the entire length of the Rock River. These Rock River collections have established the association of the larva and adults. Collections of adults and pupae indicate that emergence occurs from late June through August.

The few records available from Illinois, New York, Ontario and Wisconsin indicate the species to be distributed through the Northeast.

Illinois Records.—Many males, four females and many pupae, taken June 15 to August 7, and many larvae and cases, taken May 11 to August 29, are from Byron (Rock River), Como (Rock River), Dixon (Rock River), Erie (Rock River), Grand Detour, Grand Tower, Hamilton, Harrisburg, Keithsburg, Love's Park (Rock River), Lyndon (Rock River), Nelson (Rock River), Oregon (Rock River), Prophetstown (Rock River), Rockton, Sterling (Rock River).

Athripsodes ophioderus Ross

Athripsodes ophioderus Ross (1938a, p. 157); ♂.

LARVA.—Unknown.
ADULTS.—Length 10 mm. Color reddish brown, the wings with a few indistinct whitish spots. Male genitalia, fig. 786: cerci short but pointed at apex; tenth tergite

elongate, with a small, round, basal portion bearing a short cone of stout setae near apex, the tergite beyond this prolonged into a slender neck bearing a small hoodlike portion at tip; claspers with basal segment large, with an angular ventro-mesal elongation, the apical segment fairly long, the mesal process slender and curved. Female unknown.

This species was originally described from two specimens collected at Elizabethtown, Illinois, and since then only one other male has been found, from Hoopeston in the east-central part of the state. No generalizations can be made about either its distribution or habitat preference.

Illinois Records.—ELIZABETHTOWN: June 22, 1927, at light, Frison & Glasgow, 2 ♂. HOOPESTON: July 14, 1940, at light, J. S. Ayars, 1 ♂.

Athripsodes transversus (Hagen)

Leptocerus transversus Hagen (1861, p. 279); ♂, ♀.
Leptocerus maculatus Banks (1899, p. 214); ♀.

LARVA.—Fig. 767. Length 6 mm. Head yellowish brown with indistinct lighter spots. Mesonotum and legs straw colored. Parafrontal areas nearly as wide as frons. Pronotum with evenly spaced hairs along anterior margin. Mesonotum with only two or three pairs of hairs, the lateral tufts composed of three to four hairs, the sclerotized bars narrow but fairly sharply angled. Ninth tergite with two pairs of long black setae. Anal legs with a fairly long, sclerotized dorsal bar.

CASE.—Length 8 mm., horn shaped and constructed of sand grains, these generally irregular in size and shape, giving a more or less rough external appearance to the case itself.

ADULTS.—Length 10 mm. Color varying from bright reddish brown to lighter or darker shades of brown. Male genitalia, fig. 790: cerci fairly long, pointed at apex; tenth tergite with somewhat bulbous base and finger-like apex; claspers with basal segment short, provided with a short, stout ventral projection, apical segment long and straight, mesal process slender and much shorter than apical segment. Female genitalia, fig. 797: ninth sternite sloping abruptly mesad from base, the mesal portion forming a tonguelike rounded lobe, the sloping

portion marked by a distinct invagination; bursa copulatrix somewhat elliptic.

This species has been taken throughout the state, chiefly along the larger rivers and streams. The larvae were reared from Indian Creek and Nippersink Creek. The span of adult emergence is wide, from May to early September. The larvae are generally found under stones.

The range of the species is wide, extending from the eastern states southwestward to Texas and northwestward to Minnesota, with records from the following: Arkansas, District of Columbia, Georgia, Illinois, Indiana, Iowa, Kentucky, Minnesota, Missouri, New Brunswick, Ohio, Oklahoma, Pennsylvania, Tennessee, Texas and Wisconsin.

Illinois Records.—Many males, females and pupae, taken May 17 to September 11, and many larvae and seven cases, taken May 17 to August 12, are from Alton, Bartonville (Kickapoo Creek), Cairo, Charleston, Council Hill (Galena River), Dixon, Elgin (Botanical Gardens), Erie (Rock Creek), Hamilton, Hardin, Havana, Kampsville, Kankakee (Kankakee River), Lyndon, Mahomet (Sangamon River), Milan (Rock River), Momence (Kankakee River), Morris, Mount Carmel, Ottawa, Pontiac, Quincy, Rock Island, Savanna, Serena (Indian Creek), Spring Grove (Nippersink Creek), Venedy Station (Kaskaskia River), Wadsworth (Des Plaines River), Yorkville (Fox River).

Athripsodes cancellatus (Betten)

Leptocerus cancellatus Betten (1934, p. 256); ♂, ♀.

LARVA.—Length 6 mm. Head, pronotum and legs creamy white, the head with an indefinite light brownish pattern. Parafrontal areas nearly as wide as frons. Pronotum with a thick line of setae along anterior margin, the setae including long and short ones. Mesonotum with only three or four pairs of setae in addition to lateral tuft which consists of only two or three hairs.

CASE.—Length 8 mm., horn shaped, the main structure composed of fairly regular sand grains arranged in a somewhat fenestrate pattern, a few larger grains arranged along the side, giving very slightly the appearance of a lateral extension.

ADULTS.—Length 10–12 mm. Color dark brown with very few markings. Male genitalia similar to those of *transversus*, differing chiefly in the basal segment of the claspers, which lack the ventral projection, fig. 791. Considerable variation occurs in both tenth tergite and claspers, as shown in the two drawings. Female genitalia, fig. 798, also very similar to those of *transversus*, usually with the mesal lobe of the ninth sternite narrower and the sloping portion of the tergite longer.

This species has been collected commonly in northern Illinois, and we have also one or two scattered records from the central and southern parts of the state. It frequents medium to large streams and has an adult emergence ranging from June through August. We have reared the larvae from Nippersink Creek.

The species is widely distributed through the eastern states and westward through the Ozarks to Oklahoma. We have records from Arkansas, Georgia, Illinois, Indiana, Kentucky, Minnesota, Missouri, New York, Ohio, Oklahoma, Pennsylvania, Quebec, Tennessee and Wisconsin.

Illinois Records.—Many males and females, taken May 17 to August 2, and many larvae, taken May 17 to June 9, are from Dixon, Elgin (Botanical Gardens), Fox Lake, Freeport, Homer, Kankakee (Kankakee River), Keithsburg, Mahomet (Sangamon River), Milan (Rock River), Momence (Kankakee River), Ottawa, Richmond (Nippersink Creek), Rockford, Rock Island, Savanna, Serena (Indian Creek), Shawneetown, Spring Grove (Nippersink Creek), Wilmington, Yorkville (Fox River).

Athripsodes punctatus (Banks)

Mystacides punctatus Banks (1894, p. 180); ♀.

LARVA.—Unknown.

ADULTS.—Length 10 mm. Color black, the wings with a scattering of flat white scales. Male genitalia, fig. 788: cerci pointed; tenth tergite robust, with a digitate apical prolongation; claspers with basal segment short, apical segment long and lanceolate, the mesal process long and stout. Female genitalia, fig. 802: ninth sternite divided into a pair of wide lateral plates and a mesal tonguelike strip, these three areas

heavily sclerotized, and together making an arcuate apical margin; bursa copulatrix small and vasiform, the connectives chiefly membranous.

The male illustrated for this species by Betten (1934, p. 259) belongs to *uvalo*, which is distinguished by the pointed tenth tergite. The male which I am considering true *punctatus* has been taken in company with the female which agrees in structure of genitalia with a series of females belonging to the type lot, from Douglas County, Kansas.

Allotype, male. — Harrisburg, Illinois: June 15, 1934, at light, DeLong & Ross.

In Illinois we have taken this species at only two points, both of these in the southern part of the state. The nature of the terrain at these two points is such that these specimens could have flown to the lights from either the Ohio River or smaller sluggish and muddy streams such as the Saline, in the immediate vicinity.

The only definite records of this species which we have are from Arkansas, Illinois, Kansas and Maine.

Illinois Records.—ELDORADO: Sept. 8, 1933, Ross & Mohr, 1 ♀. HARRISBURG: June 15, 1934, DeLong & Ross, at light, 3 ♂, 1 ♀.

Athripsodes saccus Ross

Athripsodes saccus Ross (1938b, p. 89); ♂.

LARVA.—Unknown.

ADULTS.—Length 13 mm. Color almost entirely black, tarsi whitish, and front wings with one or two white marks and with a scattering of broad white scales over the entire wing. Male genitalia, fig. 776: cerci short and oval; tenth tergite large, U-shaped, the ventral arm of the U divided into large, lateral prolongations tipped with a cluster of long, peglike setae; claspers with basal segment broad, its apico-mesal margin bearing a dense cone of peglike setae, the apical segment long and lanceolate, the mesal process long and slender. Female genitalia, fig. 806: ninth segment with cerci well delineated; ninth tergite composed chiefly of a single large, sclerotized plate arcuate across the apex; bursa copulatrix U-shaped, with a pair of sharp points near the top, these points curving ventrad; bursa attached to short but heavy membranous folds, and with a rather thick ventral membranous "curtain" hanging down on the ventral side of the bursa.

Allotype, female.—Lake Erie, Put-in-Bay, Ohio: 1937.

Our only definite records for this species are two females collected at Chicago, Illinois, one on July 8, 1937, along the lake front, Frison & Ross, the other on June 24, 1925, A. C. Weed, FM. There is a third female bearing the data "Northern Illinois," but without other information.

The species was originally described from Lake Erie, where it is very abundant; otherwise it is known only from Quebec and Illinois.

Athripsodes erraticus Milne

Athripsodes erraticus Milne (1936, p. 58); ♂, ♀.

LARVA.—Unknown.

ADULTS.—Length 12 mm. Color black or nearly so, the anterior wings with a scattering of white scales. Male genitalia, fig. 777: tenth tergite divided into dorsal and ventral portions, the ventral portion with a lateral long curved blade; claspers with a large mesal lobe which is serrate with evenly spaced teeth on the mesal margin. Female genitalia, fig. 807: ninth sternite only slightly sclerotized; bursa copulatrix U-shaped with a pair of lateral points at middle and above these forming a slightly narrower, vasiform part.

Our only Illinois record of this species is a female bearing the data "Northern Illinois." The species is present in Lake Erie and has been taken in Quebec.

Athripsodes erullus Ross

Athripsodes erullus Ross (1938b, p. 90); ♂.

This species has not yet been taken in Illinois, but since it is common in company with both *saccus* and *erraticus* in Lake Erie, we might expect it in the northern part of the state. The male genitalia, fig. 778, are readily distinguished on the basis of characters in the key. The females resemble the males in black color and the white scales on the wings. They are readily distinguished from those of other species by the curious structure of the bursa copulatrix and the division of the ninth sternite into three fairly large areas, fig. 804.

Allotype, female.—Lake Erie, Put-in-Bay, Ohio: 1937.

Athripsodes submacula (Walker)

Leptocerus submacula Walker (1852, p. 70): ♂.

This species, like *errulus*, has not yet been taken in Illinois, although in Lake Erie it occurs in company with *erraticus* and *saccus*. As outlined by Betten & Mosely (1940, p. 70), only the male of the type series can be definitely assigned. Study of much material from Lake Erie shows that the female has the black head and white-scaled wings typical of the group, and small eyes, although slightly larger than eyes of related females; the ninth sternite is divided into extensive lateral lobes which are only moderately sclerotized, and the bursa copulatrix is ·heavily sclerotized and triangular, fig. 803.

Allotype, female.—Lake Erie, Put-in-Bay, Ohio: 1937.

Athripsodes species a, b and c

In addition to the larvae associated definitely with adults, there are three species of larvae segregated in our collection which have not been reared. Most likely these belong to species here treated in the adult stage only, which include *angustus*, *ophioderus*, *resurgens* and the entire complex of species with white-scaled wings such as *punctatus* and *erraticus*. These unreared larvae have been included in the key as an aid to the better recognition of the reared species and a stimulus for additional rearing work.

Species a.—Length 6 mm. Almost entirely straw colored, the sclerites scarcely darker than the body. Parafrontal areas indistinguishable. Mesonotum with only a few hairs in addition to lateral tufts of two or three hairs. This species makes a short horn case using fragments of fresh-water sponges in its construction so that it appears irregular, soft and fuzzy. We have taken this species in Nippersink Creek at Spring Grove, Illinois, in the Namekagon River at Spooner, Wisconsin, and in Meramec Springs at St. James, Missouri. This last collection had cases made of irregular pieces of stones and very little sponge material.

Species b.—Length 5 mm. Head, ·pronotum and legs very pale yellowish brown, not much darker than the straw-colored body; upper portion of head with scattered brown spots; parafrontal areas nearly as wide as frons. Mesonotum with only a few hairs in addition to lateral tuft of two or three hairs. Ninth segment with only one or two pairs of very weak, short setae. Case with lateral margins somewhat produced, although not as much so as in *ancylus*; constructed of sand grains and fairly smooth. We have a single collection from Apple River in Apple River Canyon State Park, Illinois, June 27, 1940, Mohr & Riegel.

Species c.—Length 8.5 mm. Head, pronotum and legs chocolate brown, the head with many light dots and dashes. Parafrontal areas only about half width of frons. Mesonotum with only a few scattered hairs in addition to lateral tufts composed of one or two hairs; sclerotized bars wide, sharply angled and almost L-shaped. Ninth segment with two pairs of long black hairs. Anal legs with long, dorsal sclerotized bars. Case made of flat stones, stout and almost cylindrical. These larvae have been collected in Lake Erie at Put-in-Bay, Ohio, and may be either *resurgens* or one of the *punctatus* group. They are conspicuous in that the abdomen is large and cylindrical, scarcely tapering toward apex. They were collected in deep water.

Oecetis McLachlan

Oecetis McLachlan (1877, p. 329). Genotype, here designated: *Leptocerus ochraceus* Curtis.

Setodina Banks (1907a, p. 130). Genotype, by original designation: *Setodina parva* Banks.

Oecetina Banks (1899, p. 215). Genotype, by original designation: *Oecetis incerta* of American authors, nec Walker = *inconspicua* (Walker).

Oecetodes Ulmer (1909, p. 144). Genotype, by subsequent designation of Milne (1934, p. 19): *Setodes avara* Banks.

Friga Milne (1934, p. 16). Genotype, by original designation: *Setodes immobilis* Hagen.

Quaria Milne (1934, p. 17). Genotype, monobasic: *Oecetis scala* Milne.

Yrula Milne (1934, p. 17). Genotype, by original designation: *Oecetina fumosa* Banks.

This genus is of unusual interest because of the predaceous habit of the larvae and the elongate, grasping type of mouthparts which have been developed in company with this habit. The adults may readily be distinguished by venation, the pupae by the mandibles and anal appendages.

In this genus we have possibly the most widely distributed caddis flies in North America and species which become abundant in very diverse situations. Only 15 species have been described from North America; of these we have taken 7 in Illinois. The females and larvae have both exhibited good key differences, but due to difficulties in rearing only five larvae have been associated with the adults.

KEY TO SPECIES

Larvae

1. Head brown with light spots and bars, fig. 811; case of log cabin type, fig. 833...............**cinerascens**, p. 241
   Head straw color, sometimes with brown spots or bars, fig. 812; case of stone construction............. 2

2. Dorsal hump of first abdominal seg-

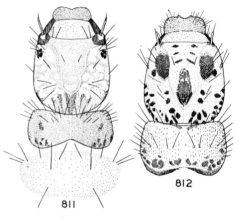

Fig. 811.—*Oecetis cinerascens*, larva.
Fig. 812.—*Oecetis species a* larva.

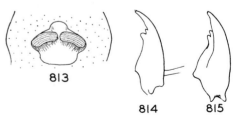

Fig. 813.—*Oecetis avara* larva, dorsal hump.
Fig. 814.—*Oecetis eddlestoni* larva, left mandible, ventral aspect.
Fig. 815.—*Oecetis species b* larva, left mandible, ventral aspect.

ment with 4–6 rows of micro-hooks, fig. 813..................**avara**, p. 240
Dorsal hump of first abdominal segment without micro-hooks........　3

3. First abdominal sternite with a row of hairs extending across the segment　4
First abdominal sternite with only one or two pairs of setae.............　6

4. Meso- and metanotum each with a lateral tuft of 10–20 hairs; first abdominal sternite with a row of about 50 hairs; ninth tergite with about 25 hairs; head spots very dark..... ....**ochracea**, p. 244
Meso- and metanotum without distinct lateral tufts; first abdominal sternite with a row of only 25 hairs; ninth tergite with only 8–10 hairs; head spots various..............　5

5. Head with three dark areas on and near frons, fig. 812.....**species a**, p. 244
Head without such dark areas, fig. 834 ....**inconspicua**, p. 242

6. Left mandible with ventral aspect slightly convex but without creases, fig. 814............**eddlestoni**, p. 240
Ventral aspect of left mandible with a deep crease running from apical tooth, fig. 815.........**species b**, p. 244

Adults

1. Apex of abdomen with movable claspers, figs. 816–824 (males)........　2
Apex of abdomen without claspers, figs. 825–832 (females)............　10

2. Tenth tergite consisting of a pair of long, slender, cylindrical, sclerotized rods, each bearing two stout, peglike setae, fig. 816.............　3
Tenth tergite either very short, composed of a single process, fig. 824, or with rods bladelike and without pegs, fig. 819....................　4

3. Claspers produced into a long, apical finger, fig. 816...........**scala**, p. 241
Claspers in general truncate at apex, fig. 817............**eddlestoni**, p. 240

4. Claspers somewhat kidney shaped, much higher than long, fig. 818.... ....**avara**, p. 240
Claspers elongate, longer than high...　5

5. Tenth tergite formed of a pair of bladelike structures wide at base and tapering to a downcurved, narrow apex; claspers with basal portion wide and apex with a very short projection, fig. 819.......**osteni**, p. 241
Tenth tergite formed of either a single mesal projection, fig. 821, or very short, fig. 820....................　6

6. Claspers with mesal margin incised to form a short mesal tooth, fig. 820.. ....**ochracea**, p. 244
Claspers with mesal margin straight or sinuate, not incised, figs. 821–824.........................　7

7. Abdomen with sixth and seventh or seventh and eighth tergites finely and distinctly reticulate; apical finger of claspers long and converging at apex, fig. 822..............　8
Abdomen with none of tergites recticulate; apical finger of claspers diverging, fig. 824.....................　9

8. Tenth tergite twice as long as cerci, fig. 821; seventh and eighth tergites reticulate...........**persimilis**, p. 243
Tenth tergite about as long as cerci, fig. 822; sixth and seventh tergites reticulate.........**cinerascens**, p. 241

9. Upper margin of claspers evenly sinuate, aedeagus elongate and with the apical beak projecting straight, fig. 823.................**immobilis**, p. 241
Upper margin of claspers deeply emarginate to form a prominent baso-dorsal lobe, aedeagus almost circular, the beak directed ventrad, fig. 824..........**inconspicua**, p. 242

10. Bursa copulatrix attached to a large, many-lobed, heavily sclerotized internal structure with a pair of long, anteriorly directed, sclerotized rods, fig. 825.............**persimilis**, p. 243
Bursa copulatrix not attached to a sclerotized, lobed internal structure, fig. 826........................　11

11. Eighth sternite with a purse-shaped, sclerotized area, fig. 826...**osteni**, p. 241
Eighth sternite without such an area, at most with sclerotized lines, fig. 827................................　12

12. Ninth sternite produced into a pair of short "ears" on each side of lobes of tenth segment, fig. 827; subgenital plate outlined by a more or less circular black line.................　13
Ninth sternite not produced into "ears"; subgenital plate outlined as a diamond-shaped or vasiform area, figs. 830–832..................　15

13. Subgenital plate angled outward across middle, the base membranous, the apical declivity with a pair of sclerotized plates together forming a shallow, concave basin, fig. 827.... ....**cinerascens**, p. 241
Subgenital plate with sclerotized plates weaker and occupying basal instead of apical portion, fig. 828.........　14

14. Bursa copulatrix as in fig. 828, with apex nearly truncate and basal por-

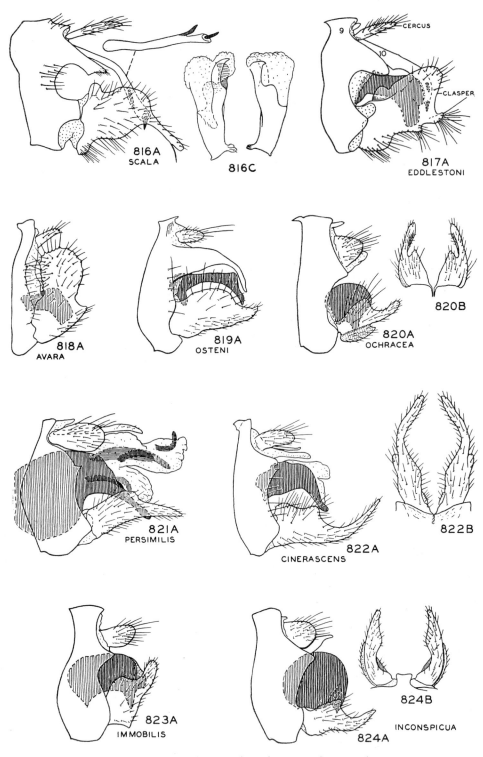

Figs. 816-824.—*Oecetis*, male genitalia. *A*, lateral aspect; *B*, ventral aspect; *C*, aedeagus.

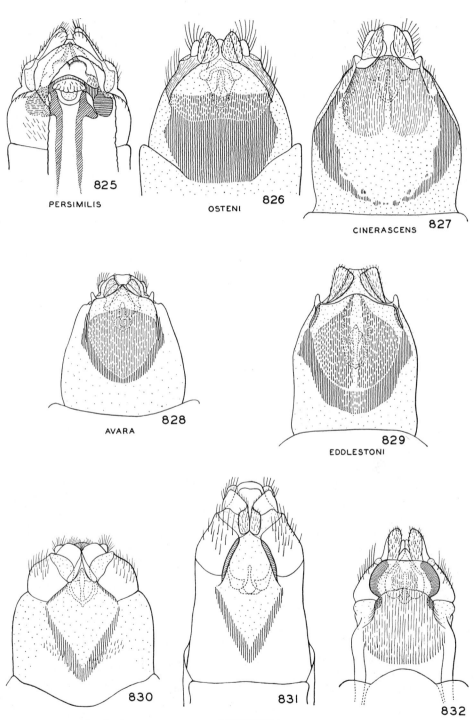

Figs. 825–832.—*Oecetis*, female genitalia. All figures showing ventral aspect; in fig. 825 the sternites partially cut away to show bursa copulatrix.

tion with sharp lateral extensions..
...................**avara**, p. 240
Bursa copulatrix as in fig. 829, with apex rounded and without sharp, lateral extensions....**eddlestoni**, p. 240

15. Subgenital plate diamond-shaped, the posterior sides of the diamond raised and fencelike, fig. 830......
...............**immobilis**, p. 241
Subgenital plate more vasiform, the posterior sides of the vase folded laterad and shelflike, fig. 831.....   16

16. Postero-lateral, shelflike margin of subgenital plate nearly straight, the anterior portion angulate and almost membranous, fig. 831.......
.............**inconspicua**, p. 242
Postero-lateral, shelflike margin of subgenital plate arcuate, the anterior portion of the sternite more ovate and distinctly sclerotized, fig. 832................**ochracea**, p. 244

Oecetis avara (Banks)

Setodes avara Banks (1895, p. 316); ♂.

LARVA.—Length 6.5 mm. Head, pronotum and legs straw color, top of head with short brown bars.

CASE.—Length 7 mm., horn shaped, constructed of large sand grains cemented together to form a fairly smooth exterior.

ADULTS.—Length 10–11 mm. Color straw yellow to light brown, the forewings with numerous dark brown spots in the membrane. Male genitalia, fig. 818: tenth tergite short, slender and curved, consisting of only a single mesal piece; cerci short and ovate; claspers somewhat kidney shaped; aedeagus short and tubular, the apex slightly expanded ventrad. Female genitalia, fig. 828, with ninth sternite wide, delineated by arcuate dark lines, bursa copulatrix with apex nearly truncate and basal portion with sharp lateral extensions.

Allotype, female.—Momence, Illinois: Aug. 21, 1936, Ross & Burks.

This species has been taken commonly in the northern and central portions of the state where it frequents fairly rapid streams of various sizes. Larvae have been collected and associated with the adults in the Galena River at Council Hill, Illinois. The adults emerge throughout the summer months from May until early September.

The range of the species covers most of the United States, southern Canada and Mexico. The spotting on the wings varies

to a considerable extent, and it is possible that the species *disjuncta* known from California may be simply a color variant of this species. We have records of *avara* from Alabama, British Columbia, Georgia, Idaho, Illinois, Indiana, Kentucky, Maine, Maryland, Michigan, Minnesota, Missouri, Montana, New Mexico, New York, Nova Scotia, Ohio, Oklahoma, Ontario, Oregon, Pennsylvania, Tennessee, Texas, West Virginia, Wisconsin and Wyoming.

Illinois Records.—Many males and females and four pupae, taken June 5 to September 7, and many larvae, taken May 5 to June 27, are from Apple River Canyon State Park, Charleston, Council Hill (Galena River), Danville (Middle Fork River), Homer, Kankakee (Kankakee River), Momence (Kankakee River), Oakwood (Middle Fork River), Oregon, Rock Island, St. Charles, Serena (Indian Creek), Wilmington, Yorkville (Fox River).

Oecetis eddlestoni Ross

Oecetis eddlestoni Ross (1938*a*, p. 160); ♂.

LARVA.—Length 5 mm. Head, pronotum and legs straw color, the head with brown bars and dots over most of its surface.

CASE.—Length 6 mm., constructed of sand grains, with a fairly smooth exterior.

ADULTS.—Length 10 mm. Color various shades of light brown, without conspicuous markings. Male genitalia, fig. 817: tenth tergite consisting of a pair of stout, cylindrical rods curved ventrad at apex, each bearing two stout spines and reaching almost to the apex of the claspers; cerci slender and lanceolate; claspers short and somewhat rhomboidal, the lower margin sinuate; aedeagus with a slender basal stalk and a footlike apex. Female genitalia, fig. 829, with the ninth sternite round, delineated by curved lines, bursa copulatrix rounded at apex and without lateral expansions at base.

Allotype, female.—Serena, Illinois: June 16, 1939, along Indian Creek, B. D. Burks.

We have collected this species in Illinois only along Indian Creek at Serena, from which locality the larvae were reared. It was originally described from Pennsylvania; we have additional records of this species only from Illinois, Ohio and Oklahoma, so that little can be said regarding its general habits and distribution.

Illinois Records.—SERENA, Indian

Creek: May 12, 1938, Ross & Burks, 7 larvae; May 17, 1938, Ross & Burks, 2 ♂, 2 ♀, 1 larva (all reared in cage at Spring Grove, Illinois); May 27, 1938, Ross & Burks, 1 larva; June 16, 1939, B. D. Burks, 1 ♀.

Oecetis scala Milne

Oecetis scala Milne (1934, p. 17); ♂.

Not yet taken in Illinois, but apparently with a widespread though scattered range, so that the species may be looked for in the state with future collecting. To date it has always been collected in small numbers, with records available from Maryland, New Jersey, North Carolina and Pennsylvania.

Oecetis osteni Milne

Oecetis osteni Milne (1934, p. 17); ♂, ♀.

Larva.—Unknown.
Adults.—Length 9 mm. Color various shades of brown without conspicuous markings. Male genitalia, fig. 819: tenth tergite composed of a pair of fairly long, sclerotized arms, wide at base, tapering to a curved apical beak; aedeagus narrow and arcuate, in repose fitting into the V of the beak of the tenth tergite; claspers with the basal portion somewhat rectangular, tapering to a short, apical point. Female genitalia, fig. 826, readily identified by the dark area on the eighth sternite and the simple bursa copulatrix.

In Illinois this species is restricted to the extreme northern portion of the state and has been taken most commonly around the glacial lakes in the northeastern corner. The adults have been taken from late June to the latter part of August. In other states the records are most frequently associated with lakes, but the species undoubtedly occurs also in rivers.

The range of the species includes a band through the Northeast from Minnesota eastward to New Brunswick. Records are available from Illinois, Massachusetts, Michigan, Minnesota, New Brunswick, New Hampshire, New Jersey, New York, Ontario, Quebec, Virginia and Wisconsin.

Illinois Records.—Antioch: July 7, 1932, at light, Frison & Metcalf, 4 ♂, 1 ♀. Fox Lake: June 30, 1935, DeLong & Ross,

♂ ♂, ♀ ♀; June 10, 1936, Ross & Burks, 1 ♀. Fulton: July 20, 1927, Frison & Glasgow, 1 ♀. Grass Lake: July 14, 1926, Frison & Hayes, 1 ♀. Grayslake: Aug. 20, 1939, Mohr & Riegel, 1 ♂. Richmond: June 25, 1938, Burks & Boesel, 1 ♀. Spring Grove: Aug. 12, 1937, at light, Ross & Burks, 1 ♂.

Oecetis immobilis (Hagen)

Setodes immobilis Hagen (1861, p. 283); ♂.

Larva.—Unknown.
Adults.—Length 9 mm. Color various shades of brown without conspicuous markings. Male genitalia, fig. 823: tenth tergite composed of a single semimembranous, fairly short process; cerci ovate; claspers fairly short, the dorsal margin sinuate, the apical process fairly short and the basal portion appressed for a considerable distance on meson; aedeagus stout at base, the apex forming a definite beak. Female genitalia, fig. 830, with ninth sternite diamond shaped, the posterior sides of the diamond raised and fencelike, bursa copulatrix almost circular.

In Illinois we have taken this species only in the extreme northern portion and, as with *osteni*, it has been taken abundantly only around the glacial lakes of the northeast corner of the state. All our records for Illinois are in late May, June and early July; records for other states, however, indicate an emergence which continues into August and September.

The range of the species includes most of the Northeast; records are from Illinois, Indiana, Michigan, New Brunswick, New York, Nova Scotia, Ohio, Ontario, Saskatchewan and Wisconsin.

Illinois Records.—Fox Lake: July 1, 1931, Frison, Betten & Ross, ♂ ♂, ♀ ♀; June 30, 1935, DeLong & Ross, ♂ ♂, ♀ ♀; May 28, 1936, H. H. Ross, ♂ ♂, 1 ♂ pupa; June 10, 1936, Ross & Burks, 9 ♂. Johnsburg, Fox River: May 28, 1936, H. H. Ross, 2 ♂, 2 ♀. Pistakee Lake: June 12, 1936, H. H. Ross, 1 ♂. Rock City: May 24, 1938, Ross & Burks, 1 ♂. Spring Grove: June 9, 1938, Mohr & Burks, 1 ♂.

Oecetis cinerascens (Hagen)

Setodes cinerascens Hagen (1861, p. 282); ♂.
Oecetina fumosa Banks (1899, p. 216); ♀.

LARVA.—Fig. 811. Length 7 mm. Head brown with spots of a lighter shade scattered over the entire surface. Pronotum and legs straw color, the pronotum finely speckled with light brown. Labrum with

Fig. 833.—*Oecetis cinerascens*, case.

hairs forming an irregular band across apical third, first abdominal segment with dorsal holding process large and without setae.

CASE.—Fig. 833. Length 8–10 mm., constructed of bits of stems and other debris into a somewhat irregular log-cabin case.

ADULTS.—Length 11–13 mm. Color medium shades of brown; in life somewhat hoary due to the pale hair; the wing membrane with several dark spots situated at the vein forks. Male genitalia, fig. 822: tenth tergite consisting of a single stylelike projection; cerci fairly long and parallel sided, apex rounded; claspers with a wide basal portion which tapers suddenly to a long apical curved filament; aedeagus fairly long, the apex produced into a projecting beak. Female genitalia, fig. 827, with ninth sternite large and almost circular, delineated by very distinct arcuate lines, the apical portion of the sternite composed of a pair of concave sclerites; bursa copulatrix simple.

The common log-cabin case of this species is one of the most abundant features of many lakes and streams scattered throughout the state. The species is frequently

taken in great numbers and occurs on the wing from May to late September, with a constant cycle of generations.

This species is widely distributed through the Northeast, and occurs south to Georgia, southwest through the Ozarks to Texas, and northwest to Saskatchewan. We have records from Arkansas, Georgia, Illinois, Maine, Massachusetts, Michigan, Minnesota, Missouri, New Brunswick, New York, Nova Scotia, Ohio, Oklahoma, Ontario, Pennsylvania, Quebec, Saskatchewan, South Dakota, Tennessee, Texas, Virginia and Wisconsin.

Illinois Records.—Many males and females and 1 pupa, taken May 7 to September 25, and many larvae and nine cases, taken April 15 to October 17, are from Algonquin, Antioch, Beardstown (Muscooten Bay), East Fox Lake, Elgin (Botanical Gardens), Fox Lake, Grass Lake, Havana (Quiver Lake, Thompson's Lake, Illinois River), Henry, Herod, Homer, Johnsburg (Fox River), Liverpool, McHenry, Meredosia, Milan, Momence, Mount Zion (Fork Lake), New Memphis (Kaskaskia River), Olive Branch (Horse Shoe Lake), Peoria, Pistakee Lake, Putnam (Lake Senachwine), Quincy (Willow Slough), Richmond, Rosecrans (Des Plaines River), Round Prairie, Savanna (Mississippi River), Springfield (Sangamon River), Spring Grove, Stewart Lake, Urbana (Crystal Lake), Wilmington, Wood River, Zion (Dead River).

Oecetis inconspicua (Walker)

Leptocerus inconspicuus Walker (1852, p. 71); ♂.
  Setodes sagitta Hagen (1861, p. 284); ♂.
  Setodes micans Hagen (1861, p. 283); ♂, ♀.
  Setodes flaveolata Hagen (1861, p. 282); ♀.
  Oecetina parvula Banks (1899, p. 215); ♀.
  Oecetina flavida Banks (1899, p. 216); ♂, ♀.
  Oecetina floridana Banks (1899, p. 216); ♂.
  Oecetina apicalis Banks (1907a, p. 129); ♂.
  Oecetina inornata Banks (1907a, p. 128); ♀.

LARVA.—Fig. 834. Length 8 mm. Sclerotized parts straw color to pale yellowish brown, the head varying from an almost immaculate condition to a distinct dark brown pattern as in fig. 834. First segment of abdomen with dorsal hump large and without setae.

CASE.—Length 9 mm. Constructed of stones and sand grains, frequently irregular and not very rigid in construction; a few larger stones are frequently attached at the sides.

ADULTS.—Length 10–12 mm. Color brown with a reddish cast, without distinct markings; specimens in liquid showing a con-

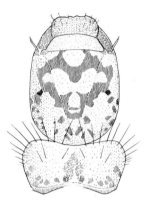

Fig. 834.—*Oecetis inconspicua* larva.

spicuous dark bar across the cord. Position of crossveins forming the cord extremely variable, ranging from a condition in which the three crossveins form an almost straight line to one in which they are far removed and steplike. Male genitalia, fig. 824: tenth tergite forming a single, straight, fairly long rod; cerci short and ovate; claspers with dorsal margin incised to form a conspicuous ventral lobe, their ventral margin somewhat angulate at base; aedeagus almost circular, with short beak. Female genitalia, fig. 831, with ninth sternite membranous and not bounded by dark lines, the apical shelf straight and bursa copulatrix simple.

This species is one of the most common caddis flies in Illinois and has been taken throughout the state. It is one of the few caddis flies abundant in artificial ponds. The larvae live in both lakes and streams. They are seldom encountered in field collections but are frequently present, together with those of *cinerascens*, in fish stomachs. The adults emerge throughout the warmer months, from May until early October, and frequently occur in immense numbers.

The species is very widely distributed throughout the North American continent and appears to be fairly rare only in the Northwest. We have records from Alabama, Arkansas, British Columbia, California, Cuba, Florida, Georgia, Illinois, Indiana, Iowa, Kansas, Kentucky, Maine, Massachusetts, Mexico, Michigan, Minnesota, Missouri, Nebraska, New Brunswick, New Hampshire, New York, Nova Scotia, Ohio, Oklahoma, Ontario, Oregon, Pennsylvania, Quebec, Saskatchewan, South Carolina, South Dakota, Texas, Utah, Virginia and Wisconsin. (See fig. 13.)

Illinois Records.—Many males, females and pupae, taken May 6 to October 10, and many larvae, taken May 20 to August 7, are from Algonquin, Alton, Amboy (Green River), Antioch, Apple River Canyon State Park, Bartonville (Kickapoo Creek), Brussels, Cairo, Carbondale, Champaign, Channel Lake, Charleston, Chicago (roof of Stevens Hotel), Clinton, Council Hill, Danville, Des Plaines, Downs, East Dubuque, East Fox Lake, Eldorado, Elgin, Elizabethtown, Fieldon, Fox Lake, Frankfort (Hickory Creek), Freeport, Galena (Sinsinawa River), Galesburg, Golconda, Grafton, Grand Tower, Grass Lake, Grayslake, Hamilton, Hardin (Illinois River), Harrisburg, Havana (Chautauqua Lake), Henry, Herod, Homer, Jackson Island (Mississippi River opposite Hannibal, Missouri), Jerseyville, Kampsville, Kappa (Mackinaw River), La Rue (McCann Spring), Le Roy, Libertyville, Liverpool, Mahomet, Meredosia, McHenry, Milan (Rock River), Momence (Kankakee River), Montezuma, Mount Zion (Fork Lake), Muncie, New Memphis (Kaskaskia River), Oakwood (Salt Fork River, Middle Fork Vermilion River), Olive Branch (Horse Shoe Lake), Ottawa, Palos Park (Mud Lake), Peoria, Pontiac, Putnam (Lake Senachwine), Quincy (stream near Cave Spring, Burton Creek), Richmond, Ripley (Lamoine River), Rockford, Rochelle, Rosiclare, Rome, Round Lake, ʼSavanna, Serena (Indian Creek), Springfield (Sangamon River), Spring Grove (Nippersink Creek), Starved Rock State Park, Sterling, Urbana, Utica, Venedy Station (Kaskaskia River), Wadsworth (Des Plaines River), Waukegan, White Pines Forest State Park, Wilmington, Yorkville, Ziegler, Zion (Dead River).

Oecetis persimilis (Banks)

Oecetina persimilis Banks (1907a, p. 129); ♂, ♀.

LARVA.—Unknown.

ADULTS.—Length 7–8 mm. Color light brown, venter and legs straw color; wings uniformly smoky, with long brown hair and dark shading along the cord. Abdomen of male with seventh and eighth tergites heavily sclerotized, and covered with minute and lacelike fenestrations. Male genitalia, fig. 821: tenth tergite consisting of a long stylelike projection twice as long as cerci; cerci ovate, wide and rounded at tip; claspers with a wide, long basal portion suddenly narrowed to an apical elongation; the apices of the two claspers curve mesad very much as in figure 822*B*, except that they curve more sharply and usually touch or overlap at the extreme tip; aedeagus large, with a greatly expanded bulbous base which narrows to a ventral beaklike spatula above which extrude several membranous folds which enclose three short hooks, a curved sclerotized rod twice as long as these hooks and another curved sclerotized rod stouter and longer than the preceding. Female genitalia, fig. 825, with ninth sternite mostly membranous but with the bursa copulatrix developed into several pairs of ovate sclerotized folds and with a basal pair of long sclerotized rods which project into the abdomen.

We have only a single record of this species from Illinois, a male collected at Principia College, Elsah, June 28, 1943, at light, C. L. Remington. The range of the species embraces many of the eastern states, including Georgia, Illinois, Kentucky, Maryland, Ohio, Tennessee, Virginia and Wisconsin. In spite of its wide distribution, collections of this species are infrequent, probably indicating a scattered type of distribution pattern.

Oecetis ochracea (Curtis)

Leptocerus ochraceus Curtis (1825, pl. 57).
Oecetis ochracea carri Milne (1934, p. 16); ♂, ♀. New synonymy.

Not yet taken in the state, but of very wide distribution to the north. This is a Holarctic species with records in North America from Alaska, Alberta, Manitoba, Minnesota, Saskatchewan, South Dakota and Wyoming.

Oecetis species a and *b*

We have segregated two distinctive larvae which have not yet been reared.
Species a.—Fig. 812. Length 6 mm. Head and body sclerites cream colored,

the head and pronotum with small dark spots or bars, the head with three additional dark areas on and near the frons. Case tubular, slightly horn shaped, constructed of sand grains and usually even in finish. The great similarity between the structural characters of this larva to *inconspicua* suggests strongly that this is the larva of *immobilis*; *immobilis* is most closely related on adult structures to *inconspicua* and occurs in some numbers around Fox and Channel lakes, in which this larva *a* has been found.

Illinois Records. — CHANNEL LAKE: May 31, 2 larvae. FOX LAKE: May 15, 1936, from stones, Ross & Mohr, 8 larvae. MINEOLA, East Fox Lake: June 9, 1938, Mohr & Burks, 4 larvae.

Species b.—Length 5.5 mm. Head, pronotum and legs cream colored with dark spots on head and pronotum; mesonotum with a pair of irregular dark areas on each side of the meson. Case horn shaped, constructed of sand grains and with a very smooth exterior. We have taken only one specimen of this larva, in Channel Lake near Antioch, Illinois, May 18, 1938, Ross & Burks. Aside from *immobilis*, the only species of adult taken in this region which has not been reared is *osteni*, and it is possible that this *species b* is the larva of *osteni*.

Triaenodes McLachlan

Triaenodes McLachlan (1865, p. 110). Genotype, by present designation: *Leptocerus bicolor* Curtis.
Triaenodella Mosely (1932, p. 308). Genotype, by original designation: *Triaenodella chelifera* Mosely.
Ylodes Milne (1934, p. 11). Genotype, by original designation: *Triaenodes grisea* Banks.

Diagnostic characters for the genus include the long body and case of the larva, its divided hind tibiae and lack of swimming brush on hind legs; the curious mandibles of the pupa, with their large base and slender blades; and, in the adult, the venation of the front wing, fig. 733, absence of epicranial stem on the head, and katepisternum truncate at apex. Most of the larvae make cases of short, slender twigs built into a spiral pattern, fig. 862.

The genus has been divided into *Ylodes* and *Triaenodella*; it seems best at the present time to consider these as subgenera.

The genus contains many North American species; a few are widespread, but many

are known from only a limited number of
localities. Eight species have been taken in
Illinois, of which one is represented by an
unidentified female. The specific characters
of the female sex have been worked out
sufficiently to show that this unidentified
eighth species is different from the other
seven taken in the state.

KEY TO SPECIES

Larvae

1. Head with pale antennae and with a
pattern of spots, only a few anterior
ones somewhat coalesced to form
weak lines, fig. 835.......**tarda,** p. 250
Head with definite lines reaching posterior portion of head, fig. 836, or
antennae black................... 2
2. Head lines broken into spots at posterior portion, fig. 836; pronotum
without extensive dark areas.....
....................**injusta,** p. 252
Head lines solid to posterior margin of
head, fig. 837; pronotum usually
with dark patches in addition to dark
spots on posterior portion......... 3
3. Lateral spots of head distinct and
separate, fig. 837...........**aba,** p. 249
Lateral spots of head connected by a

fuscous area to form lines, fig. 838..   4
4. Lateral portion of head mostly pale;
pronotum with only small dark
areas..............**marginata,** p. 251
Lateral portion of head mostly dark
with pale lines between the dark
areas; pronotum almost entirely
dark, fig. 838........**species b,** p. 253

Adults

1. Genitalia with claspers and aedeagus,
figs. 839–850 (males)............ 2
Genitalia without these structures,
figs. 851–861 (females)............ 13
2. Claspers consisting chiefly of a thin,
vertical plate, incised on apical margin, fig. 839..................... 3
Claspers consisting of a solid base the
mass of which is distributed hori-
zontally, and often bearing various
lateral or mesal lobes, figs. 841–850 4
3. Inner spur of clasper long, curved and
whiplike, fig. 839......**frontalis,** p. 249
Inner spur of clasper short, somewhat
angular and stocky, fig. 840......
......................**grisea,** p. 249
4. Tenth tergite forming a long fork, with
a basal stalk, figs. 841, 842........ 5
Tenth tergite single or vestigial, fig.
843.............................. 6

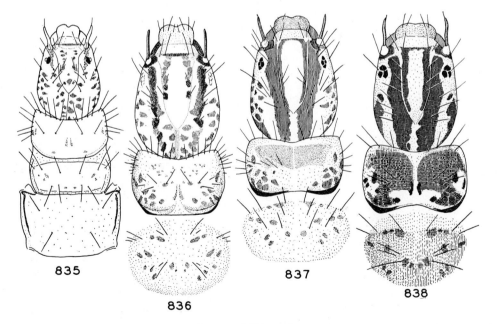

835

836

837

838

Larvae of *Triaenodes*

Fig. 835.—*T. tarda.*
Fig. 836.—*T. injusta.*

Fig. 837.—*T. aba.*
Fig. 838.—*T. species b.*

5. Arms of tenth tergite wide, short and divergent, fig. 841......**injusta**, p. 252
   Arms of tenth tergite narrow, long, parallel and curved to left at tip, fig. 842.................**ignita**, p. 252
6. Dorsal apex of tenth tergite vestigial, fig. 843...................**aba**, p. 249
   Dorsal apex of tenth tergite long, fig. 844............................ 7
7. Clasper with no postero-lateral or mesal projection, fig. 844.. **perna**, p. 250
   Clasper with postero-lateral and mesal projections, fig. 845.............. 8
8. Aedeagus scarcely exserted, with an ovate body and short beak, fig. 845 ....**phalacris**, p. 250

Aedeagus exserted to beyond base of claspers, forming a long, curved structure, fig. 846................ 9
9. Tenth tergite gradually tapering from near base to apex, fig. 846........ ....**flavescens**, p. 251
   Tenth tergite clavate, fig. 847...... 10
10. Lateral lobe of clasper only slightly longer than mesal lobe, fig. 847.... 11
    Lateral lobe of clasper at least nearly twice as long as mesal lobe, figs. 849, 850............................ 12
11. Cerci as long as tenth tergite, fig. 847. ....**baris**, p. 252
    Cerci about half as long as tenth tergite, fig. 848...........**dipsia**, p. 252

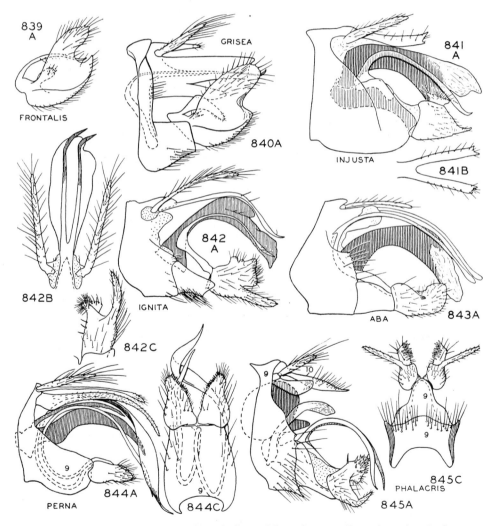

Figs. 839–845.—*Triaenodes*, male genitalia. *A*, lateral aspect; *B*, tenth tergite; *C*, claspers, ventral aspect.

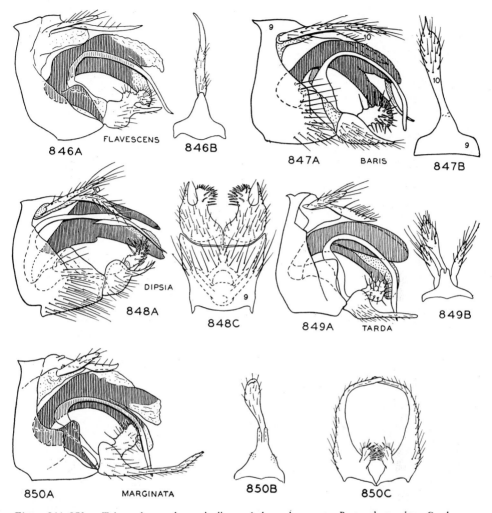

Figs. 846–850.—*Triaenodes*, male genitalia. *A*, lateral aspect; *B*, tenth tergite; *C*, claspers.

12. Apex of claspers straight, tenth tergite sharply pointed, fig. 849 . . . . . .
 . . . .**tarda,** p. 250
 Apex of claspers bent mesad at a considerable angle, tenth tergite spatulate, fig. 850 . . . .**marginata,** p. 251

13. Cerci present as earlike lobes; ventral margin of lateral plates of tenth segment angled to form a flat shelf, fig. 852 14
 Cerci absent, fig. 861; ventral margin of lateral plates of tenth tergite not angled 15

14. Bursa copulatrix situated at the end of a long, flat stalk, fig. 851 . . . .
 . . . .**grisea,** p. 249
 Bursa copulatrix sessile, attachments short, fig. 852 . . . .**frontalis,** p. 249

15. Plates of ninth sternite with ventral aspect forming a ∨ with swollen arms, lateral aspect pointed at both ends, fig. 853 . . . .**aba,** p. 249
 Plates of ninth sternite not shaped like the above, figs. 854–861 16

16. Apodeme of tenth segment long and sinuate, reaching far past bursa copulatrix almost to sixth segment, fig. 854 . . . .**perna,** p. 250
 Apodeme of tenth segment not reaching beyond apex of bursa copulatrix, fig. 855 17

17. Apodeme above bursa copulatrix long, ending in a swollen, emarginate, sclerotized plate, fig. 855 . . .**injusta,** p. 252
 Apodeme not extending above bursa copulatrix, fig. 856 18

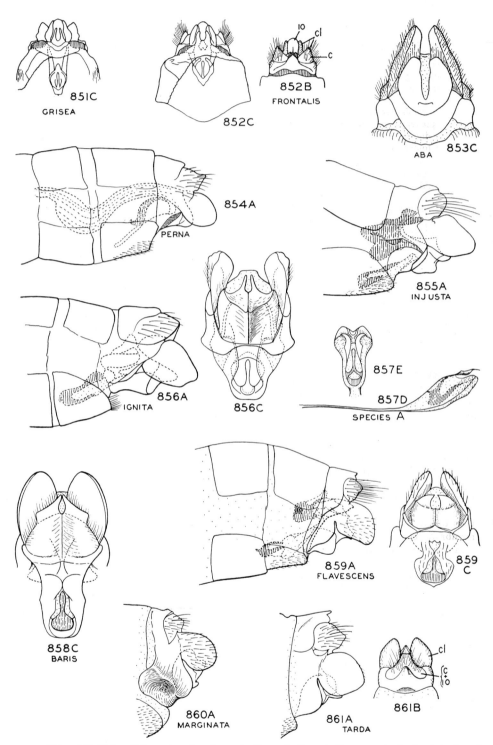

Figs. 851–861.—*Triaenodes*, female genitalia. *A*, *B* and *C*, respectively lateral, dorsal and ventral aspects; *D* and *E*, bursa copulatrix, respectively lateral and ventral aspects; *c*, cerci; *cl*, clasper.

18. Apex of ninth sternite produced into a pair of long, slender, pointed fingers, fig. 856..................**ignita**, p. 252
    Apex of ninth sternite not produced into long fingers, fig. 858......... 19
19. Bursa copulatrix with ventral folds forming long, shelflike, sclerotized bands, fig. 857, and base of apical hook heavily sclerotized around edge................**species a**, p. 253
    Bursa copulatrix with ventral folds either straplike and not shelflike or membranous, fig. 858, and base of apical hook uniformly sclerotized 20
20. Apical lobes of ninth sternite projecting more sharply posterad, fig. 858; a sclerotized bar, platelike at each end, is situated above base of bursa supports................**baris**, p. 252
    Apical lobes of ninth sternite not projecting so sharply, fig. 859; only an arcuate lobe above base of bursa supports...................... 21
21. One internal fold beyond base of clasper sclerotized, fig. 859.......
    ....**flavescens**, p. 251
    All internal folds beyond base of clasper membranous, fig. 860...... 22
22. Ventro-lateral margins of ninth segment sclerotized, flared and convoluted, fig. 860.....**marginata**, p. 251
    Ventro-lateral margins of ninth segment not flared and almost entirely membranous, fig. 861.....**tarda**, p. 250

Triaenodes frontalis Banks

Triaenodes frontalis Banks (1907a, p. 127); ♀.

Not yet taken in Illinois, but is known from Colorado and Saskatchewan, where it frequents ponds.

Triaenodes grisea Banks

Triaenodes grisea Banks (1899, p. 214); ♀.

Not yet taken in Illinois. It is known from Colorado, Manitoba and Saskatchewan; it frequents ponds. This and *frontalis* might be looked for in some of the marsh situations of northeastern Illinois.

Triaenodes aba Milne

Triaenodes sp. Milne (1934, p. 12); ♂.
Triaenodes aba Milne (1935, p. 20); ♂.

LARVA.—Fig. 837. Length 10 mm. Head, pronotum and legs cream color, the head

with a pair of dark stripes on the ventral aspect, with another pair on the dorsum and irregular small spots on the head and pronotum; the spots on the frons forming an interrupted pair of lines just inside the large stripes.

ADULTS.—Length 8–9 mm. Color reddish brown with a narrow dorsal stripe of pinkish brown when the wings are folded in repose. Male genitalia, fig. 843: tenth tergite with only a vestigial mesal process; cerci long and slender, not quite as long as aedeagus; claspers with large platelike mesal lobe, short lateral spur; aedeagus U-shaped. Female genitalia, fig. 853: ninth sternite forming a V with wide arms and a narrow cleft, from side view appearing shallow and pointed at both ends; abdomen thin, short and flat.

Allotype, female.—Zion, Illinois, along Dead River at Dunes Park: June 28, 1940, Mohr & Riegel.

This species is abundant in two marsh areas in northeastern Illinois, one the Des Plaines River at Rosecrans, the other the Dead River at Zion. It was reared from both localities. The larvae were found in weed beds, and their cases were very difficult to see in the mass of broken twigs which had accumulated in these areas. Betten (1934, p. 287) recorded the species from Lake Forest, Illinois. Our adult records are for June, July and August, indicating a single generation per year.

The range of this species is poorly defined but apparently includes most of the Northeast. Records are available from Illinois, Massachusetts, Michigan, New Hampshire, Ontario and Wisconsin.

Illinois Records.—CHICAGO: June 16, W. J. Gerhard, 2 ♂, FM. FOX LAKE: June 23, 1892, Hart & Shiga, 1 ♀ ; June 26, 1936, Frison & DeLong, 1 ♂. NORTHERN ILLINOIS: 1 ♂. ROSECRANS: June 14, 1938, Ross & Burks, 2 ♂ ; Des Plaines River, May 23, 1938, Ross & Burks, many larvae, ♂ ♂, ♀ ♀ (all reared); May 29, 1938, Mohr & Burks, 1 larva (reared); June 8, 1938, Ross & Burks, many larvae, 1 ♂ ; June 9, 1938, at light, Ross & Burks, ♂ ♂ ; June 13, 1938, Ross & Burks, 4 ♂ ; June 14, 1938, Ross & Burks, many larvae; June 15, 1938, Ross & Burks, 6 ♂ ; June 21, 1938, Ross & Burks, 1 ♀. SPRING GROVE: Aug. 12, 1937, at light, Ross & Burks, 1 ♂. URBANA: Aug. 25, 1892, McElfresh, 1 ♀. WADSWORTH, Des Plaines River: July 7,

1937, Frison & Ross, ♂ ♂. ZION, Dead River: July 7, 1937, Frison & Ross, ♂ ♂; May 23, 1938, Ross & Burks, 2 larvae and cases; June 3, 1938, Mohr & Burks, ♂ ♂; June 4, 1938, Ross & Burks, ♂ ♂, 5 ♀; Aug. 15, 1938, Ross & Burks, 1 ♀; Aug. 19, 1939, Mohr & Riegel, 1 ♀; May 20, 1940, Mohr & Burks, 2 larvae; June 28, 1940, Mohr & Riegel, 1 larva, 1 pupa, 1 ♀; June 5, 1941, Mohr & Burks, 4 ♂, 3 ♀.

Triaenodes perna Ross

Triaenodes perna Ross (1938*a*, p. 159); ♂, ♀.

LARVA.—Unknown.

ADULTS.—Length 9 mm. Color tawny, front wing with a definite pattern of cream color and brown; in repose the insect has a dorsal light stripe, a large light area along middle of front margin of wings, a dark brown area across wing at stigma, and a golden brown area beyond this along the apical margin. Male genitalia, fig. 844: tenth tergite long and hairlike with a slight thickening at apex; beneath this there is a long, membranous, curved process extending beyond the tenth tergite, claspers flat, the ventral aspect somewhat triangular, and the apico-mesal side with a row of black spines; basal whiplike processes of claspers very long, the right one convoluted and bladelike, the left one filamentous. Female genitalia, fig. 854: apex of ninth sternite forming a somewhat anvil-shaped projecting body with flat apical plates; these plates, from ventral aspect, appearing to form a sort of "hat" at the end of the anvil; most conspicuous is the very long internal apodeme of the tenth segment; this apodeme extends almost to the sixth segment, reaching far past the bursa, and has a definite enlarged central portion where it makes a sharp bend; bursa copulatrix short and inconspicuous, its apex terminating in indefinite membranous folds.

Our Illinois specimens of this species are confined to the type series of a male and two females collected at Eichorn, June 13, 1934, along Hicks Branch, DeLong & Ross. The only records which have come to our attention since that time are a male from Franklin County, Ohio, and a female from Broken Bow, Oklahoma.

Triaenodes phalacris Ross

Triaenodes phalacris Ross (1938*b*, p. 88); ♂.

Not yet taken in Illinois. It is known from Athens, Ohio, and may ultimately be taken in southern Illinois.

Triaenodes tarda Milne

Triaenodes marginata tarda Milne (1934, p. 12); ♂.
Triaenodes vorhiesi Betten (1934, p. 286); ♂, ♀. New synonymy.
Triaenodes mephita Milne (1936, p. 59); ♂, ♀. New synonymy.

LARVA.—Fig. 835. Length 10 mm. Sclerites straw color, the head with a definite pattern of small spots; the spots along the frons may be sharply coalesced to form an interrupted line. Case as in fig. 862.

ADULTS.—Length 12–13 mm. Color tawny with the same conspicuous cream and brown pattern as in fig. 863; in most specimens the dorsal stripe is divided into an elongate anterior area and a posterior diamond-shaped area. Male genitalia, fig. 849: tenth tergite long and fusiform; cerci fairly short and lanceolate; claspers with base bulbous, lateral angle produced into a long, sharp point, mesal portion produced into a knobbed lobe set with short, stout setae; aedeagus U-shaped and cleft at apex. Female genitalia, fig. 861, with apodemes entirely membranous, ninth sternite somewhat anvil shaped, its apical flanges not greatly produced on the meson.

This species is widely distributed in Illinois, occurring in both lakes and streams. We have taken it in abundance, however,

Fig. 862.—*Triaenodes tarda*, case.

only in the glacial lakes in the northeast part of the state. In these the larvae were taken in large numbers from weed beds and were reared from these collections. Our adult collections extend from May to late September, indicating that more than one generation may be produced in a year.

Female genitalia, fig. 860, similar in general structure to *tarda* but differing in the sclerotized, flared and convoluted ventro-lateral expansions of the ninth segment.

This species is a rarity in our Illinois collections; our records to date consist of only two males, from Chicago and Mo-

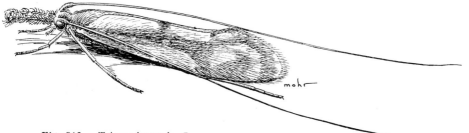

Fig. 863.—*Triaenodes tarda* ♂.

This species is widely distributed through the northeastern states and extends southwestward through the Ozarks into Oklahoma, with records from Arkansas, District of Columbia, Illinois, Minnesota, New Brunswick, New York, Ohio, Oklahoma, Ontario, Pennsylvania and Wisconsin. In addition, Milne lists the species from Arizona and British Columbia (paratypes of *tarda*).

Illinois Records.—Many males and females, taken May 31 to September 25, and many larvae, taken May 15 to August 13, are from Algonquin, Antioch, Champaign, Chicago, Elgin (Botanical Gardens), Fox Lake, Havana (Quiver Lake), New Memphis (Kaskaskia River), Richmond, Sand Lake, Spring Grove (Nippersink Creek), Urbana, Zion (Dunes Park).

Triaenodes marginata Sibley

Triaenodes marginata Sibley (1926a, p. 80); ♂, ♀.

LARVA (after Sibley, 1926b, p. 105).—Head and pronotum yellow; head with two pairs of dark lines and scattered spots; pronotum with only small dark markings on a pale background.

ADULTS.—Length 12–13 mm. Color tawny with a black and cream pattern as shown in fig. 863. Male genitalia, fig. 850, similar in general structure to *tarda*, differing chiefly in the spatulate tenth tergite and long lateral projections of the claspers, these processes curved sharply mesad at apex.

mence, both in the northeastern portion of the state.

The species has a wide range, including Arkansas, Illinois, Michigan, New Jersey, New York, Nova Scotia and South Dakota.

Illinois Records.—CHICAGO: Roof of Stevens Hotel, July 13, 1931, T. H. Frison, 1 ♂. MOMENCE: June 4, 1932, Frison & Mohr, 1 ♂.

Triaenodes flavescens Banks

Triaenodes flavescens Banks (1900a, p. 257); ♂.

LARVA.—Unknown.

ADULTS.—Length 12 mm. Color tawny with the cream and brown wing pattern shown in fig. 863. Male genitalia, fig. 846, similar in general structure to *tarda*, differing in the long, bladelike tenth tergite and the claspers with the shorter, pointed lateral projection and the larger mesal lobe. Female genitalia, fig. 859, similar in general structure to *tarda*, differing chiefly in having one internal fold beyond the base of the claspers sclerotized.

Allotype, female.—Wilmington, Illinois: Aug. 20, 1934, DeLong & Ross.

In Illinois we have taken only one collection of this species; it bears the same data as given for the allotype and contains two males and four females. Little is known regarding the habits of the species.

Its range includes the northeastern states, with records from Illinois, New Jersey, New York, Ohio and Pennsylvania.

Triaenodes baris Ross

Triaenodes baris Ross (1938b, p. 88); ♂.

LARVA.—Unknown.

ADULTS.—Length 11–12 mm. Color tawny with the cream and brown pattern shown in fig. 863. Male genitalia, fig. 847: tenth tergite fairly long, simple and fusiform; cerci very long; claspers with lateral projection short, mesal lobe very large, the basal, recurved rod fairly short, not reaching base of aedeagus; aedeagus somewhat U-shaped, apex deeply cleft. Female genitalia, fig. 858: similar in general appearance to *tarda* but with the apical lobes of ninth sternite projecting more sharply posterad and with a sclerotized bar situated above base of bursa supports, the bar enlarged and platelike at each end.

This species was originally described from Zion, Illinois, and has since been taken only at that locality. We obtained a pupa in the Dead River at Zion, living in a case typical for the genus and indistinguishable from cases of *tarda* and *aba* taken in company with it.

Our collection of this species is so small that there is some doubt as to the association of male and female. Our assignment of the above female must be considered tentative; hence no allotype is designated.

Illinois Records.—ZION: June 10, 1933, Mohr & Townsend, 1 ♂, 1 ♀; along Dead River, June 6, 1940, Mohr & Burks, 1 ♂.

Triaenodes ignita (Walker)

Leptocerus ignitus Walker (1852, p. 72); ♂.
Triaenodes dentata Banks (1914, p. 261); ♂. New synonymy.

LARVA.—Unknown.

ADULTS.—Length 11–12 mm. Color tawny with the cream and brown pattern of the wing shown in fig. 863. Male genitalia, fig. 842: tenth tergite divided near base into a pair of very long, slender filaments which curve sharply to the left near apex; cerci very long and slender; claspers with the lateral projection slightly curved and sharp, the mesal projection large and quadrate from lateral view, with small swellings on its dorsal margin, the basal filament ribbon-like at base, filamentous on the apical portion; aedeagus U-shaped, slender in the middle, and with a long, ventral portion. Female genitalia, fig. 856, with no sclero-

tized apodemes, ninth sternite produced at apex into a pair of long, slender fingers.

Our only Illinois record of this species is a single male taken at Vandalia, June 22, 1940, along the Kaskaskia River, Mohr & Riegel. The species has a scattered distribution over most of the eastern states, occurring west to Illinois and Oklahoma. Records are available for Alabama, Georgia, Illinois, New York, Nova Scotia, Oklahoma and Tennessee.

Triaenodes dipsia Ross

Triaenodes dipsia Ross (1938b, p. 89); ♂.

This species has not been taken in Illinois but is known from Athens, Ohio, and may possibly be taken in southern Illinois.

Triaenodes injusta (Hagen)

Setodes injusta Hagen (1861, p. 283); ♂.

LARVA.—Fig. 836. Length 10 mm. Head, pronotum and legs straw color, the head with two pairs of dorsal lines, the long pair from base of antennae to vertex, and a shorter, interrupted pair along inner margin of frons; pronotum with some irregular spots on posterior portion.

ADULTS.—Length 12 mm. Color tawny with the cream and brown pattern shown in fig. 863. Male genitalia, fig. 841: tenth tergite divided near base into a pair of wide, fairly short, heavily sclerotized divergent arms; cerci long and slender; claspers with lateral projection very short, dorsal projection large. Female genitalia, fig. 855, similar to *tarda* in general outline but distinct from all other species of the genus by the fairly long apodeme of the tenth segment, this apodeme produced at apex into a series of knoblike folds.

Allotype, female. — Antioch, Illinois: June 27, 1938, Ross & Burks.

We have taken this species very abundantly in the glacial lakes of northeastern Illinois; we have taken only scattered records from other parts of the state. In the lakes the larvae are found in weed beds. We have reared them from Channel Lake, near Antioch. Most of the adult emergence occurs during June and July. A few specimens have been collected in May and August. Data are insufficient to tell how many generations are produced per year.

Illinois Records.—Many males and fe-

males, taken May 18 to August 20, and
many larvae, taken May 16 to June 12,
are from Antioch, Channel Lake, Fox Lake,
Grass Lake, Grayslake, Pistakee Lake,
Richmond, Round Lake, Urbana, Wilmington, Zion.

Triaenodes species a

FEMALE.—Length 9 mm. Color tawny
with the brown and cream pattern typical
of the *tarda* group. Female genitalia, fig.
857: apex of ninth sternite not greatly
produced, typical in general form of the
tarda group; tenth tergite without conspicuous apodemes; bursa copulatrix with its
ventral bands folded, long and shelflike and
heavily sclerotized; the hook set in the apex
of the bursa is very heavily sclerotized,
especially the margins of the base, giving
it a hollow appearance from ventral view.

We have taken only one female of this
species, from Herod, Illinois, May 29, 1935,
Ross & Mohr. We have taken no male
which could be positively associated with it,
but it is definitely none of the other species
of which we have record from the state.
There is a possibility that it may be the
female of *phalacris* or *dipsia*, both taken
from southern Ohio, or it may be an entirely
different species.

Triaenodes species b

LARVA. — Fig. 838. Length 10 mm.
Ground pattern of sclerites straw color;
head with spots coalesced to form a pair
of long, broad lines down the central portion and a pair of short, broad lines on the
lateral margin, the ventral aspect almost
all dark so that only narrow pale areas
appear between the ventral and lateral dark
markings; pronotum mostly brown with a
pale mesal line, a pale postero-mesal area
and a pair of pale lateral spots. Case typical for genus.

This is an unreared larva of which we
have taken only one specimen, from Herod,
Illinois, May 15, 1941, Mohr & Burks.
It probably belongs to one of the species
recorded from southern Illinois on the basis
of adults, including *perna* and *species a*.

Mystacides Berthold

Mystacides Berthold (1827, p. 437). Genotype, by present designation: *Phryganea longi-*

cornis Linnaeus, one of species first included in
the genus by Burmeister (1839, p. 918).

Species of this genus construct a long,
slender, parallel-sided case adorned with
irregular pieces of leaf, wood or shell fragments; the case is not very rigid. The larvae have a distinct, rectangular gula, mandibles which are blunt at apex and armed
with several teeth, and single abdominal
gills varying in number, usually inconspicuous.

Three species are known from North
America, of which we have two in Illinois,
both restricted to the northeastern corner
of the state.

KEY TO SPECIES

Larvae

Head with a Y-shaped black mark
following epicranial stem and arms,
fig. 864...........**longicornis**, p. 255
Head with spots or parallel black lines,
not forming a Y, fig. 865..........
................**sepulchralis**, p. 254

Adults

1. Genitalia with a large ventral furca,
figs. 866, 867 (males)............ 2
   Genitalia without a ventral furca, fig.
   868 (females).................... 3
2. Apical process of ninth sternite forked,
   the arms long and slender, fig. 866
   ....**sepulchralis**, p. 254

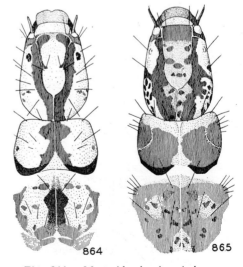

Fig. 864.—*Mystacides longicornis* larva.
Fig. 865.—*Mystacides sepulchralis* larva.

Apical process of ninth sternite single and wide, fig. 867...**longicornis**, p. 255

3. Color shining blue-black. Lateral lobes of ninth sternite not narrowed at ex-

treme base, fig. 868................

...............**sepulchralis**, p. 254

Color dull gray-black or brownish-black. Lateral lobes of ninth sternite markedly narrow at extreme base, fig. 869...........**longicornis**, p. 255

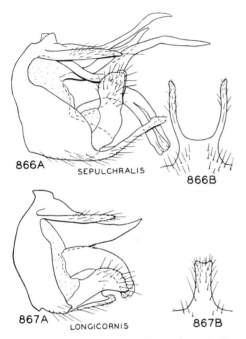

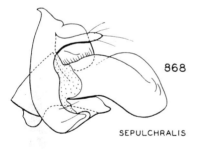

Figs. 866-867.—*Mystacides*, male genitalia. *A*, lateral aspect; *B*, tongue of ninth sternite.

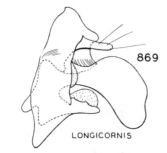

Figs. 868-869.—*Mystacides*, female genitalia.

Mystacides sepulchralis (Walker)

Leptocerus sepulchralis Walker (1852, p. 70); ♂, ♀.

LARVA. — Fig. 865. Length 10 mm. Ground color of head straw color with a pair of dark brown longitudinal lines (sometimes broken into spots) fading at the posterior margin, and with numerous small brown dots over most of the head area; pronotum ranging from entirely dark brown with a narrow mesal light area to brownish yellow with lateral irregular brown spots; legs straw color wtih narrow dark bands.

ADULTS.—Fig. 870. Length 9 mm. Color blue-black, the wings and thorax with an iridescent metallic sheen. Male genitalia, fig. 866, with apical process of ninth sternite divided at base into a pair of slender long processes; claspers short and stocky; tenth tergite subdivided into a group of intricate sinuate blades. Female genitalia as in fig. 868.

In our collecting we have found this species in Illinois only in the glacial lakes of the northeastern part. Betten (1934, p. 281) recorded the species both from this locality and from Charleston, Illinois. In other states, we have found, the species occurs in both lakes and streams; so it may do this in Illinois also.

We have found the larvae under and around stones in Channel Lake, near Antioch, and reared them from this locality. Adult emergence occurs from May into September; our records from Illinois are few, but abundant records from other states indicate this long seasonal range.

This species occurs through the Northeast, south to Georgia, and southwest through the Ozarks. Records are available from Arkansas, Georgia, Indiana, Illinois, Maine, Michigan, Minnesota, New Brunswick, New Hampshire, New York, Nova Scotia, Ohio, Ontario, Pennsylvania, Quebec, Saskatchewan and Wisconsin.

Illinois Records.—ANTIOCH: July 8, 1932, H. H. Ross, 3 ♂, 1 ♀. CHANNEL LAKE: May 27, 1936, H. H. Ross, 9 ♂, 9 ♀; May 18, 1938, Ross & Burks, 1 ♂, 1

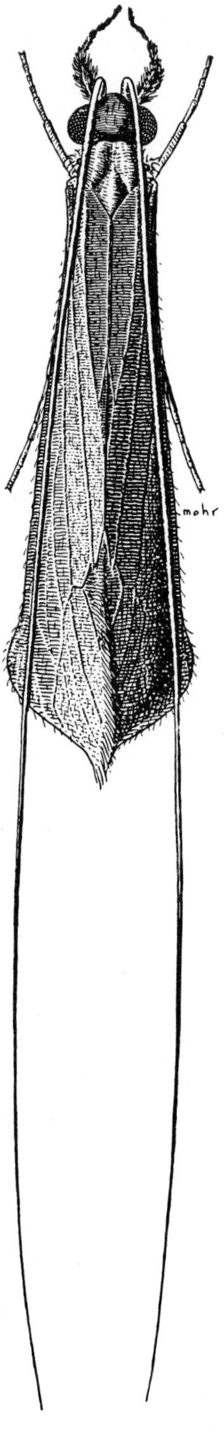

Fig. 870.—*Mystacides sepulchralis* ♂, metallic blue-black in color. This species is common in eastern states.

larva. Chicago: July 30, 1904, 1 ♂, fm; Aug. 4, 4 ♂, 1 ♀, fm. Fox Lake: May 28, 1936, H. H. Ross, 1 ♂, 2 ♀. Lake Villa: July 21, 1916, 1 ♀.

Mystacides longicornis (Linnaeus)

Phryganea longicornis Linnaeus (1758, p. 548).
Phryganea quadrifasciata Fabricius (1775, p. 308).
Oecetina interjecta Banks (1914, p. 262); ♀.
Mystacides canadensis Banks (1924, p. 448); ♂.

Larva.—Fig. 864. Length 10 mm. Head yellowish with a few spots and a large black Y following the epicranial stem and arms; pronotum varying from yellowish with a paired mesal black mark to almost entirely black with a light area in the middle of each lateral half; legs pale with narrow dark bands.

Adults.—Length 9 mm. Color rusty brown, the front wings frequently clothed with golden hair arranged to form alternate golden and brown bands; in rubbed specimens this banding never shows. Male genitalia, fig. 867, with apical process of ninth sternite long, narrow and only slightly incised at apex. Female genitalia as in fig. 869.

In Illinois we have taken this species only in company with the preceding species in glacial lakes of the northeastern part of the state (see p. 11). Betten's record (1934, p. 279) from Diamond Lake, Illinois, May 30, is in the same region. Larvae were collected and reared from Channel Lake. We found larvae of both species side by side making identical cases. Available records indicate an adult emergence throughout the warmer months of the year.

The range of the species is apparently much wider from east to west through the northern states than that of *sepulchralis*, but it does not extend as far south. We have records from Colorado, Illinois, Michigan, New York, Ontario, Pennsylvania, Quebec, Saskatchewan and Wisconsin; it is recorded from many localities in Eurasia.

Illinois Records.—Antioch: July 7, 1932, at light in town, Frison & Metcalf, 2 ♂ ; May 18, 1938, Ross & Burks, 1 larva, 1 ♂ (reared). Channel Lake: May 27, 1936, H. H. Ross, 2 ♂ pupae; June 11, 1936, Burks & Ross, 3 ♂. Fourth Lake: Aug. 9, 1887, C. A. Hart, 1 ♂. Fox Lake:

July 1, 1931, Frison, Betten & Ross, 1♀;
June 30, 1935, DeLong & Ross, 1♀; May
15, 1936, Ross & Mohr, 1 larva; May 28,
1936, H. H. Ross, 1♂, 2♀.

Setodes Rambur

Setodes Rambur (1842, p. 515). Genotype,
by subsequent designation of Milne (1934, p.
18): *Setodes punctella* Rambur.

This genus contains six or seven species,
all of them rare, of which we have taken
only one in Illinois. An additional species,
incerta, will likely be found in the state
with subsequent collecting.

No Nearctic larvae of this genus have
been reared, but Miss Thelma Howell
collected a leptocerid larva in Swain County,
North Carolina, which may belong to this
genus. It is characterized by a rectangular
gula, mandibles with a broad dentate apex,
filamentous abdominal gills which are single
or double, and the curious anal plate shown
in fig. 719.

Setodes oligia (Ross)

Leptocerus oligius Ross (1938a, p. 160); ♂,
♀.

Larva.—Unknown.
Adults.—Length 8 mm. Color almost

Fig. 872.—*Setodes incerta*, male genitalia.

cream, some sutures and veins light brown
but without definite pattern. Male genitalia, fig. 871: tenth tergite forming a long,
rectangular projection divided at apex into
a pair of long slender filaments; claspers
divided into a finger-like dorsal lobe and
truncate ventral lobe; aedeagus cylindrical
and curved; at its base originate a pair of
long, slender sclerotized filaments. Female
genitalia, fig. 871: tenth tergite hood shaped,
ninth with a pair of handlike lobes and with
extensive internal structures.

The genitalia of the male are radically
different from those of *incerta*, fig. 872, the
only other species of the genus which has
been taken near Illinois.

Our Illinois collection of this species consists of a single record of one male and three
females taken along the Kankakee River at
Wilmington, August 20, 1934, DeLong &
Ross. The species was described from this
series of specimens. In addition, we have
records from Michigan and Ontario.

GOERIDAE

This family is represented in North
America by the genera *Goera*, *Pseudogoera*
and *Goerita*, all occurring in the eastern
states. None of these have been reared in
North America, and our knowledge of the
immature stages is based chiefly on the descriptions of the immature stages of *Goera*
by European writers. The case resembles
that of *Neophylax autumnus* (p. 203). The
adults have the maxillary palpi three segmented in the male, five in the female.

KEY TO GENERA

Adults

1. Front wings with venation reduced,
R₄₊₅ partially fused with M; 2A and
3A absent, fig. 873..............
................**Pseudogoera**, p. 258

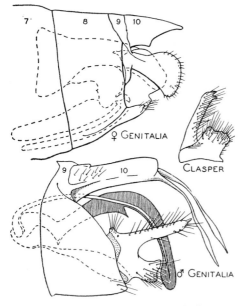

Fig. 871.—*Setodes oligia*, genitalia.

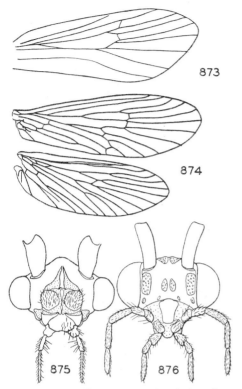

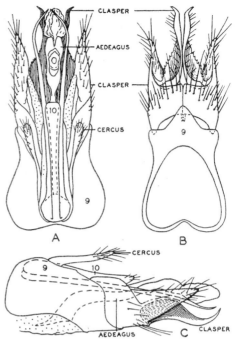

Fig. 877.—*Goera stylata*, male genitalia. *A*, dorsal aspect; *B*, ventral aspect; *C*, lateral aspect.

Fig. 873.—*Pseudogoera singularis*, front wing. (After Carpenter.)

Fig. 874.—*Goerita semata*, wings.

Fig. 875.—*Goerita semata* ♂, head.

Fig. 876.—*Goera calcarata* ♀, head.

Front wings without marked reduction in venation, R$_s$ not fused with M; 2A and 3A present, fig. 874.... 2

2. Eyes small, the head forming a high crown between them, fig. 875.....
..................**Goerita**, p. 258
Eyes much larger, with a smaller crown, fig. 876.........**Goera**, p. 257

Goera Curtis

Goera Curtis (1834, p. 215). Genotype, monobasic: *Phryganea pilosa* Fabricius.

Not known from Illinois. The males of this genus have complicated genitalia, as illustrated by *stylata*, known from Michigan, fig. 877.

A few pupae, presumably belonging to this genus, have been received from scattered localities in eastern states. All these pupae were collected from clear, cold, rapid streams. The stone cases were solid and tightly built.

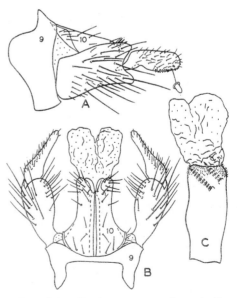

Fig. 878.—*Goerita semata*, male genitalia. *A*, lateral aspect; *B*, dorsal aspect; *C*, aedeagus.

Note ventral row of peglike teeth on apical segment of clasper in *A*; one of these teeth is illustrated separately below the clasper.

Goerita Ross

Goerita Ross (1938a, p. 171). Genotype, by original designation: *Goerita semata* Ross.

Not known from Illinois. The only known eastern species, *semata*, has not been recorded east of the Allegheny ranges. The male genitalia are distinctive, fig. 878.

Pseudogoera Carpenter

Pseudogoera Carpenter (1933, p. 37). Genotype, by original description: *Pseudogoera singularis* Carpenter.

This genus is known only from the type series of the genotype, described from North

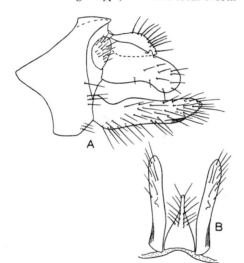

Fig. 879.—*Pseudogoera singularis*, male genitalia. *A*, lateral aspect; *B*, dorsal aspect.

Carolina. The distinctive male genitalia are illustrated in fig. 879.

LEPIDOSTOMATIDAE

In this family the maxillary palpi of the females are five segmented, and those of the males vary from three to a curiously modified structure which may appear only one segmented. As here defined it includes only two Nearctic genera, *Lepidostoma* and *Theliopsyche*. The larvae are known for many species of *Lepidostoma*; these bear a striking superficial resemblance to many genera of Limnephilidae but may be readily separated by the antennae, which are close to the eye, and by lacking a dorsal spacing

hump on the first abdominal segment. The larvae and pupae of *Theliopsyche* are unknown.

KEY TO GENERA

Adults

1. Head with posterior warts fairly wide, triangular or curved, fig. 880......
.................**Lepidostoma**, p. 258

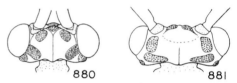

Fig. 880.—*Lepidostoma liba*, head.
Fig. 881.—*Theliopsyche* sp., head.

Head with posterior warts long, narrow and straight, fig. 881.........
...............**Theliopsyche**, p. 260

Lepidostoma Rambur

Mormonia Curtis (1834, p. 215); preoccupied. Genotype, monobasic: *Phryganea hirta* Fabricius.

Lepidostoma Rambur (1842, p. 43). Genotype, by present designation: *Lepidostoma squamulosum* Rambur = *hirtum* (Fabricius).

Nosopus McLachlan (1871, p. 114). Genotype, monobasic: *Nosopus podager* McLachlan.

Olemira Banks (1897, p. 29). Genotype, monobasic: *Olemira americana* Banks.

Pristosilo Banks (1899, p. 212). Genotype, monobasic: *Pristosilo canadensis* Banks = *togatum* (Hagen). New synonymy.

Atomyia Banks (1905b, p. 11). Genotype, by original designation: *Atomyia modesta* Banks. New synonymy.

Notiopsyche Banks (1905b, p. 11). Genotype, by original designation: *Notiopsyche latipennis* Banks. New synonymy.

Mormomyia Banks (1907a, p. 127). Genotype, by original designation: *Mormonia vernalis* Banks. New synonymy.

Alepomyia Banks (1908a, p. 64). Genotype, by original designation: *Alepomyia bryanti* Banks. New synonymy.

Phanopsyche Banks (1911, p. 357). Genotype, by original description: *Phanopsyche grisea* Banks. New synonymy.

Alepomyioides Sibley (1926b, p. 106). Genotype, by original designation: *Lepidostoma wisconsinensis* Vorhies = *bryanti* (Banks). New synonymy.

Arcadopsyche Banks (1930*a*, p. 129). Genotype, monobasic: *Arcadopsyche prominens* Banks. New synonymy.

Oligopsyche Carpenter (1933, p. 36). Genotype, by original designation: *Notiopsyche carolina* Banks. New synonymy.

Neuropsyche Carpenter (1933, p. 38). Genotype, by original designation: *Neuropsyche tibialis* Carpenter. New synonymy.

Jenortha Milne (1936, p. 119). Genotype, monobasic: *Jenortha cascadensis* Milne. New synonymy.

This genus is characterized in the adults by the arrangement of warts as outlined in the key. The females exhibit few characters upon which to base their classification, and to date I have been able to find no differences upon which to key most of them to species. Comparative lengths of the antennal segments, slight differences of venation, and some fairly striking differences in the female genitalia can be used to segregate the species into groups containing two or more. It is usually necessary, therefore, to rely upon association with males for specific identification of females.

An astonishing number of bizarre characters have been developed by the males. Some have leaflike legs, others extremely wide wings or folded-back portions which form large pockets filled with black scales; still others have the maxillary palpi variously developed into spoon-shaped structures with long extensile membranous organs. Organizing and correlating the differences found in both male and female genitalia give us ample evidence that this entire complex is a compact phylogenetic group. The secondary sexual characters so strikingly developed in the males appear to have no relation to the phylogeny of the true species groups in the genus. It seems necessary, therefore, to consider this entire complex one genus.

There are about 25 well-recognized species in the Nearctic region. Only one has been found in Illinois, but at least a dozen others have been taken in the eastern and northeastern states. Their distribution, however, is so local, especially west of the Alleghenies, that it is impossible to predict which ones might possibly be taken in Illinois with additional collecting.

An interesting feature of the genus is the local nature of many colonies. Only rarely are many species found occurring together in the same locality. Most species prefer streams or springs to lakes.

Lepidostoma liba Ross

Lepidostoma liba Ross (1941*b*, p. 120); ♂, ♀.

LARVA.—Fig. 882. Length 7.5 mm. Head, pronotum and metanotum dark chocolate brown; legs yellowish brown; the head has a pattern of small, lighter brown markings. Frontal area of head nearly flat, frons of only medium width; upper portion of head without long setae. Pronotum with an apical row of long setae and a few scattered ones in the middle. Mesonotum with an irregular group of setae around periphery. Metanotum with two pairs of small central dark spots, each bearing a long seta, and a longer lateral sclerite bearing several setae. Middle and hind legs slender and of medium length, front legs stout and short.

CASE.—Length 8 mm. Two distinct types are built, a square log-cabin type of wood fragments and a round type of stones. Both have a rough exterior, and frequently a case will be part one and part the other.

ADULTS.—Length 8.5–9.0 mm. Color various shades of brown, the dorsum darker, antennae, legs and venter much lighter, often tawny; the wings have patches of light hair which give the species an indistinctly checkered appearance. Male genitalia, fig. 883: ninth tergite with two large brushes of long setae, tenth tergite with a pair of lateral sclerotized irregular and short arms, and a pair of mesal, membranous triangular lobes; claspers with a long curved dorsobasal hook; from ventral view they appear slightly constricted just before apex, the apex itself irregular and oblique. Female

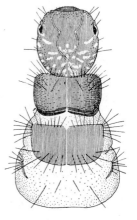

Fig. 882.—*Lepidostoma liba*, larva.

genitalia as in fig. 884, with no prominent processes; bursa copulatrix as in fig. 884B.

This species has been taken in considerable numbers in three spring-fed brooks in the state, one at Elgin (see p. 7), another

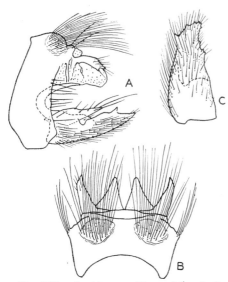

Fig. 883.—*Lepidostoma liba*, male genitalia *A*, lateral aspect; *B*, dorsal aspect; *C*, clasper

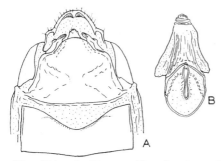

Fig. 884.—*Lepidostoma liba*, female genitalia. *A*, ventral aspect; *B*, bursa copulatrix.

at Cave Spring, Quincy, and the other at a spring near McCann School at La Rue. These are very widely scattered. In all three places we have taken the larvae in fairly good numbers, and at Quincy we collected mature pupae, linking the larval and adult forms. Our adults were taken in May, June and September, indicating a possible two-brooded cycle. Our observations at Quincy, however, where a large flight of adults was taken on September 15, indicates that the spring brood may have been skipped,

so that locally this species may have a highly irregular emergence period, as was found true in certain localities for *Neophylax* (see p. 202).

This species has not been collected outside of Illinois, so that nothing can be stated regarding its general range.

Illinois Records.—ELGIN, stream in Botanical Gardens: June 6, 1939, Burks & Riegel, 1 ♂, 2 ♀; June 13, 1939, Frison & Ross, 1 ♀. LA RUE, McCann Spring: May 12, 1939, Burks & Riegel, 1 ♀. QUINCY, Cave Spring: Sept. 15, 1939, Ross & Riegel, 3 ♂, ♀ ♀.

Theliopsyche Banks

Theliopsyche Banks (1911, p. 356). Genotype, monobasic: *Theliopsyche parva* Banks.
Subg. *Aopsyche* Ross (1938a, p. 174). Genotype, by original designation: *Theliopsyche corona* Ross.

No species of this genus has as yet been found in Illinois. It is represented by four species, all restricted to the eastern states.

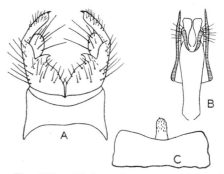

Fig. 885.—*Theliopsyche parva*, male genitalia. *A*, ventral aspect; *B*, aedeagus; *C*, eighth sternite.

The males are readily distinguished by the wide, flaplike process on the eighth sternite, fig. 885C. No larvae of this genus have been reared.

BRACHYCENTRIDAE

The maxillary palpi are three segmented in the male, five segmented in the female. The tibial spur count varies a great deal. The larvae are readily distinguished by having a sharp crease across the pronotum, a divided mesonotum and only two pairs of sclerites on the mesonotum; in addition, the antennae are small, closer to the mandibles than to the eyes, and situated under a carina.

The family contains two genera, represented over most of the continent.

KEY TO GENERA

Larvae

1. Middle and hind tibiae with an inner, apical, seta-bearing spur, fig. 886; hind coxae with a ventral, semicircular lobe bearing a row of long setae; mesonotum with sclerites long and narrow, plates of metanotum heavily sclerotized, fig. 896....
.............**Brachycentrus**, p. 263

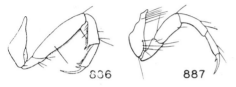

Fig. 886.—*Brachycentrus numerosus* larva, hind leg.
Fig. 887.—*Micrasema rusticum* larva, hind leg.

   Middle and hind tibiae without an apical spur, fig. 887; hind coxae without a ventral lobe; mesonotum with sclerites short and very wide, plates of metanotum only lightly sclerotized but recognized chiefly by their cluster of setae, fig. 892......
.................**Micrasema**, p. 261

Pupae

1. Hook plates of fifth and sixth segments with fewer, larger hooks, fig. 888...
.............**Brachycentrus**, p. 263

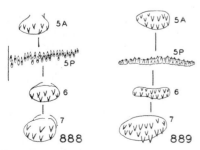

Fig. 888.—*Brachycentrus numerosus* pupa, hook plates.
Fig. 889.—*Micrasema rusticum* pupa, hook plates.

   Hook plates of fifth and sixth segments with more and smaller hooks, fig. 889..............**Micrasema**, p. 261

Adults

1. Front wings with R_1 suddenly arched and markedly sinuate at base of stigmal region, fig. 890..........
..............**Brachycentrus**, p. 263

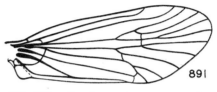

Fig. 890.—*Brachycentrus numerosus*, front wing.
Fig. 891.—*Micrasema rusticum*, front wing.

   Front wings with R_1 only faintly sinuate at base of stigmal region, fig. 891
.................**Micrasema**, p. 261

Micrasema McLachlan

Micrasema McLachlan (1876, p. 259). Genotype, here designated: *Oligoplectrum morosum* McLachlan.

This genus is very distinct from *Brachycentrus* on the basis of the larvae, but in the adults and pupae it is more difficult to make a separation. All the species of which we have larvae make round cases. Six species are known from North America; of these four are known from the eastern states, but only one has been found in Illinois.

Micrasema rusticum (Hagen)

Dasystoma rusticum Hagen (1868, p. 272); ♂, ♀.
Micrasema falcatum Banks (1914, p. 265); ♂.

Larva.—Fig. 892. Length 6 mm. Head yellow with brown spots, the lower part of the frons entirely brown; thoracic sclerites and legs yellowish. Frons with anterior portion wide.

Case.—Length 6 mm., constructed of

sand grains, circular in cross section and tapering fairly evenly. At pupation part of the narrow end is cut off, and the case then appears nearly cylindrical.

ADULTS.—Length 6–7 mm. Color uniform dark brown, appearing almost black in life. Male genitalia, fig. 893: cerci somewhat triangular, well separated to base;

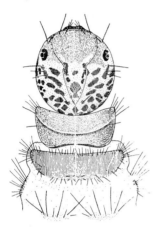

Fig. 892.—*Micrasema rusticum* larva.

tenth tergite forming a pair of lateral sclerotized processes enlarged at apex and bearing a group of short setae; at base of these processes is a pair of low tubercles bearing a seta; claspers long and straight, the posterior margin of the apex forming a slight tooth. Female genitalia simple, similar in general structure to those for *Brachycentrus*.

This species is very similar to *charonis* and *wataga*, both of which occur in the eastern states; the diagnostic differences in the genitalia are illustrated in figs. 894, 895; *charonis* is characterized by the bent apex of the clasper, *wataga* by the long style and heavily sclerotized lateral plates of the tenth tergite, *rusticum* by the short style, weaker tenth tergite and almost straight clasper.

In Illinois we have taken this species only in and along the Kankakee River at Momence and Kankakee. At Momence the cases were found under stones in the river, and mature pupae were obtained, thus linking the larval and adult stages. In this locality we have taken this species only in spring, indicating a single-brooded condition here. The species seems to follow the two *Brachycentrus* species in seasonal succession and has been taken in abundant swarms during the middle of May.

The species is widely distributed through the eastern states, extending southwestward into Oklahoma. It appears to be fairly scattered in distribution, since we do not have a large number of locality records, but is frequently taken in swarms. Records are available for Georgia, Illinois, Indiana, Michigan, New York, Oklahoma, Saskatchewan, Virginia and Wisconsin.

Illinois Records.—KANKAKEE: May 31, 1938, Mohr & Burks, 1 ♂ ; Kankakee River, May 21, 1940, Mohr & Burks, 8 ♂, 6 ♀. MOMENCE: Kankakee River, May 26, 1936, H. H. Ross, 1 ♀ ; May 17, 1937, Ross &

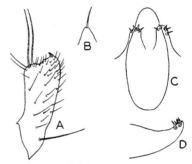

893   RUSTICUM

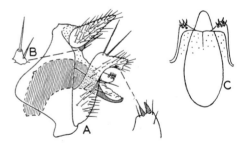

894   CHARONIS

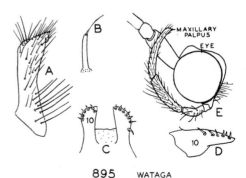

895   WATAGA

Figs. 893–895.—*Micrasema*, male genitalia. *A*, clasper; *B*, spine of tenth tergite; *C* and *D* tenth tergite, respectively dorsal and lateral aspects. *E*, male head.

Burks, ♂ ♂, ♀ ♀, 7 pupae, many larvae; Kankakee River, May 24, 1937, H. H. Ross, ♂ ♂, ♀ ♀; May 5, 1938, Ross & Burks, ♂ ♂, ♀ ♀, many pupae; Aug. 19, 1939, Ross & Burks, 1 larva; May 1, 1941, T. H. Frison, 5♂, 1♀.

Brachycentrus Curtis

Brachycentrus Curtis (1834, p. 216). Genotype, monobasic: *Brachycentrus subnubilus* Curtis.

Sphinctogaster Provancher (1877, p. 262). Genotype, monobasic: *Sphinctogaster lutescens* Provancher.

Oligoplectrum McLachlan (1868, p. 297). Genotype, by subsequent limitation of McLachlan (1876, p. 258): *Phryganea maculata* Fourcroy.

Subg. *Amiocentrus* Ross (1938a, p. 177). Genotype, by original designation: *Brachycentrus aspilus* Ross.

The larvae of this genus frequently construct the well-known chimney case, fig. 904, although the case may be cylindrical. Most of the diagnostic characters for the genus are given in the key.

Nine species are known from North America, two of which have been taken in the state, and another has been taken nearby in Wisconsin. To date characters have not been found for the separation of all females. Many of the larvae present characters useful in their diagnosis.

Of especial interest in this genus are two Say species, *lateralis* and *numerosus*. Both of these were described from along the Ohio River at Shippingsport, Kentucky (near Louisville), and recorded as occurring in vast numbers early in May, the wave of one species appearing after the wave of the other. We believe that in the Kankakee River at Momence, Illinois, we have found a duplication of this condition; in fact, so closely do our observations correspond on what are apparently these same two species (belonging to the genus *Brachycentrus*) that I am selecting neotypes from this Momence material.

KEY TO SPECIES

Larvae

1. Head entirely black..............
   ....**americanus,** p. 266
   Head with light marks, figs. 896, 897   2
2. Head with pattern predominantly

light or bright yellow and having narrow dark lines, fig. 897........
................**lateralis,** p. 265

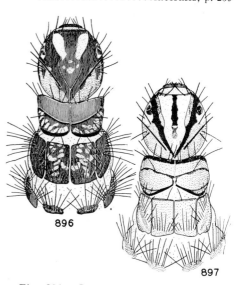

Fig. 896.—*Brachycentrus numerosus* larva.
Fig. 897.—*Brachycentrus lateralis* larva.

Head with lower portion dark brown and having a pair of cream marks, fig. 896............**numerosus,** p. 264

Adults

1. Genitalia with claspers, figs. 898–900
   (males).........................   2
   Genitalia without claspers, fig. 901
   (females).........................   4
2. Cerci fused on meson for at least basal half; apex of clasper with a lower, rounded platelike lobe, fig. 898...
   ....**americanus,** p. 266
   Cerci not fused on meson; apex of clasper without a platelike lobe, figs. 899, 900...................   3
3. Tenth tergite divided at apex, each lobe with a long macrochaeta at tip, fig. 899............**numerosus,** p. 264
   Tenth tergite without a pair of macrochaetae, in outline shaped as in fig. 900..............**lateralis,** p. 265
4. Lateral aspect of apical tergite robust and long, a crease setting off the apical third as a distinct area round at tip, fig. 903........**lateralis,** p. 265
   Lateral aspect of apical tergite short and truncate or with apical portion as long as base, figs. 901, 902......   5
5. Lateral aspect of apical tergite short, apical portion truncate and deeper

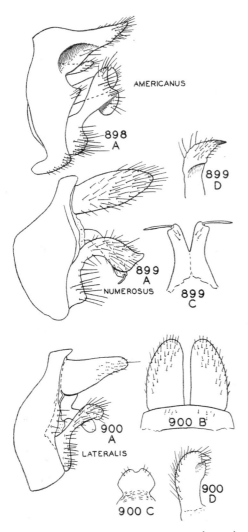

Figs. 898–900.—*Brachycentrus*, male genitalia. *A*, lateral aspect; *B*, dorsal aspect; *C*, tenth tergite, dorsal aspect; *D*, apex of clasper, ventro-caudal aspect.

than long; eighth sternite with apical lobes wide and large, fig. 902......
.......................**numerosus**, p. 264
Lateral aspect of apical tergite long, apical portion oblique and much longer than deep; eighth sternite with apical lobes narrower and smaller, fig. 901....**americanus**, p. 266

Brachycentrus numerosus (Say)

Phryganea numerosa Say (1823, p. 160).

LARVA.—Fig. 896. Length 12 mm. Head with ventral portion dark brown, dorsal

portion lighter brown, frons with a pair of cream-colored marks along lateral margin; thoracic sclerites dark brown. Legs with coxae brown, remainder of segments shading to a chestnut brown, the upper and lower edges of the femora black. Lateral fringe present on segments 3–7.

CASE.—Fig. 904. Length 12 mm., almost square in cross section and smooth in outline, constructed of wood fragments.

ADULTS.—Length 9–11 mm. Head, body, antennae and most of legs dark brown to black, tarsi whitish and abdomen with a wide lateral line; wings tawny, frequently almost white, with a series of pale spots giving a somewhat checkered appearance. Male genitalia, fig. 899: cerci ovate and widely separated to base; claspers curved, the base narrow, the curve narrow and necklike, the apical portion swollen, narrowed to a sharp tip; tenth tergite divided down meson into a pair of long apical processes, each bearing one or two long macrochaetae directed laterad. Female genitalia, fig. 902, consisting of simple plates and a small bursa copulatrix.

Neotype, male. — Momence, Illinois: May 4, 1937, Ross & Mohr.

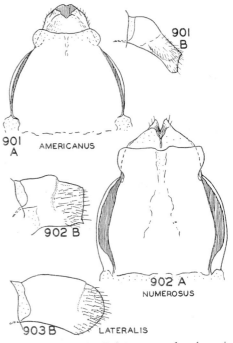

Figs. 901–903.—*Brachycentrus*, female genitalia. *A*, ventral aspect; *B*, lateral aspect of ninth and tenth tergites.

Neoallotype, female.—Same data as for neotype.

In Illinois we have taken this species at several widely scattered points. The larvae are restricted to the rapid riffles of some of our better streams such as the Kankakee

Fig. 904.—*Brachycentrus numerosus*, case.

River and Quiver Creek. There is only one generation a year, adult emergence taking place in late April and early May. The season timing of the species seems to be remarkably acute.

At Momence we have taken the adults in great swarms, although not in the clouds recorded by Say. Larval and adult associations have been made from pupae collected from both Quiver Creek near Havana, Illinois, and the Kankakee River at Momence.

This is the species recorded by Betten (1934) as *Brachycentrus nigrosoma*. The type of Banks' species is a female, and it seems advisable at the present to consider it of doubtful identity.

The range of the species is poorly known, but it is widespread through many of the northern and central states. We have records from Illinois, Indiana, Maryland, Massachusetts, New York, North Carolina, Quebec and Wisconsin.

Illinois Records. — DUNCANS MILLS, Spoon River: Sept. 2, 1910, 1 larva. GARDEN PRAIRIE: Aug. 13, 1926, 1 larva. HAVANA, Quiver Creek: Aug. 7, 1895, C. A. Hart, 9 larvae; June 11, 1896, E. B. Forbes, 1 larva; July 3, 1896, C. A. Hart, many larvae; April 24, 1898, C. A. Hart, 1 ♂, 2 ♀ ; Aug. 25, 1910, 1 larva; May 28, 1936, Mohr & Burks, 1 larva; May 29, 1936, Mohr & Burks, many larvae; June 5, 1936, Mohr & Burks, 1 ♂ (reared), 3 larvae, 2 pupae; June 20, 1936, Mohr & Burks, 6 larvae. HAVANA: White Oak Run, Oct. 5, 1910, rapid current, 2 larvae; June 20,

1936, Mohr & Burks, 6 larvae. MAHOMET, Sangamon River: June 6, 1940, Ross & Riegel, 4 larvae. MOMENCE: May 26, 1936, H. H. Ross, 2 larvae; Aug. 15, 1937, Ross & Burks, 6 larvae; Oct. 27, 1938, Ross & Burks, many larvae; Nov. 3, 1938, Mohr & Burks, many larvae; Dec. 21, 1938, Mohr & Burks, 6 larvae; May 7, 1940, B. D. Burks, ♂ ♂, ♀ ♀ ; May 8, 1940, Mohr & Burks, 7 pupae, 5 ♀ ; preceding Momence records are from Kankakee River; July 14, 1936, B. D. Burks, many larvae; Aug. 21, 1936, Ross & Burks, 3 larvae; May 4, 1937, Ross & Mohr, ♂ ♂, ♀ ♀, 3 mating pairs.

Brachycentrus lateralis (Say)

Phryganea lateralis Say (1823, p. 161).

LARVA.—Fig. 897. Length 12 mm. Head, thoracic sclerites and legs yellowish, head with three black lines on dorsum, femora with upper and lower edges black. Structures similar to those of *numerosus*.

CASE.—Length 12 mm. Of typical log-cabin construction as for *numerosus*.

ADULTS.—Length 9–11 mm. Color chiefly black with tawny wings as with *numerosus*. Male genitalia, fig. 900: cerci not fused on meson but close enough to appear hoodlike; claspers with narrow base, fairly long neck, the apex widened, the posterior face concave and with a short, sharp tooth; tenth tergite short, emarginate at apex and humped dorsally; aedeagus tubular. Female genitalia simple, similar to those of *numerosus* in general proportions.

Neotype, male. — Momence, Illinois: May 4, 1937, Ross & Mohr.

Neoallotype, female.—Momence, Illinois: May 17, 1937, Ross & Burks.

In recent years this species has been found in Illinois at Momence only, where it is abundant in the Kankakee River. It has a very definite place in the seasonal succession about 2 weeks after the peak of *numerosus*.

We have not reared the larva of *lateralis*, but there seems to be no doubt that the larva described above belongs to this species. It occurs abundantly in the Kankakee River along with larvae of *numerosus*, differing only in a tendency to prefer deeper and less rapid points in this stream. We have made many collections at Momence, where these two species occur, and have taken only the two species of *Brachycentrus* adults. At the time of spring emergence, the river is always in flood, so that we have been able to obtain pupae of only *numerosus*, which frequents shallower water than does *lateralis*.

Little is known regarding the range of the species. Records are available for Illinois, Kentucky and Michigan.

Illinois Records.—CHICAGO: 1 ♂, FM. MOMENCE: May 4, 1937, Ross & Mohr, 2 ♂; May 17, 1937, Ross & Burks, 3 ♂, ♀ ♀ ; June 12, 1938, Ross & Burks, 1 larva; Kankakee River, May 7, 1940, B. D. Burks, 5 ♂, 2 ♀ ; May 1, 1941, T. H. Frison, 2 ♂.

Brachycentrus americanus (Banks)

Oligoplectrum americanum Banks (1899, p. 210); ♂.
Brachycentrus similis Banks (1907a, p. 124); ♂, ♀.

Not as yet taken in Illinois. The species is extremely widespread through the northern part of the continent from coast to coast, with records from Alberta, California, Colorado, Michigan, Utah, Vermont, Wisconsin and Wyoming. Collections from Wisconsin are of peculiar interest because of the case-building habits of the larvae. Here we have found cases which were perfectly round in cross section rather than square, these round cases mingled with square ones, and frequently with cases which were round at the bottom and square at the top. Apparently the larva is quite as well able to make a circular case from its own secretion as to build the square case considered typical for the genus.

SERICOSTOMATIDAE

In North America this family contains only the genus *Sericostoma*. The Nearctic species have generally been placed in *Notidobia* by previous American authors. There are no Illinois representatives of this family, the species being restricted to the mountainous regions of the East and West. No Nearctic species have been reared.

As with the genus *Lepidostoma*, the genus *Sericostoma* has been divided into several genera, such as *Notidobia* and *Schizopelex*, almost entirely on the basis of the secondary sexual characters of the male. The uniformity of general characteristics in the females indicates that these differences are not of generic value; therefore I am considering the two names just mentioned as synonyms of *Sericostoma*.

HELICOPSYCHIDAE

The familiar snail case represents the only genus in this family, *Helicopsyche*. Various authors have commented upon the distinct features of this group, and Betten in particular (1934, p. 414) has given a very clear summary of the oddity of its characters. On the basis of the curious structures of both larvae and adults, it seems best to consider this as a distinct family.

Helicopsyche Hagen

Helicopsyche Hagen (1866, p. 252). Genotype, monobasic: *Notidobia borealis* Hagen.

Distinctive of the larva are the following characters: anal legs with a comb; head with frons wide, running close to eyes, with a ridge running from dorsal margin of eye to above mandible, antennae short, situated under this ridge and midway between eye and mandible; legs of medium length; pronotum long, mesonotum forming a large erect shield and divided into parts by pale areas as in fig. 905. Pupae have the anal appendages as in fig. 49. The adults are readily distinguished by the short mesoscutellum, with its narrow transverse wart, and the hamuli on the hind wings.

Four species are known from the United States, only one of which has been taken in Illinois. A key which will separate it from its allies is given on p. 288.

Helicopsyche borealis Hagen

Notidobia borealis Hagen (1861, p. 271); ♂.
Helicopsyche californica Banks (1899, p. 210); ♂. New synonymy.
Helicopsyche annulicornis Banks (1904d, p. 212); ♂.

LARVA.—Fig. 905. Length 8 mm. Head and thoracic sclerites brown, legs straw colored. Head, thoracic sclerites and legs with abundant long hair.

CASE.—Fig. 906. Built in the form of a spiral coil, its diameter about 5 mm., shaped like a snail shell, made of sand grains and small stones.

ADULTS.—Length 5–7 mm. Head, body and appendages straw colored, the body and wings suffused with varying shades of brown. Male genitalia, fig. 961, p. 288, with hand-shaped claspers, narrow and beaklike tenth tergite and cylindrical, curved aedeagus. An added diagnostic character is the

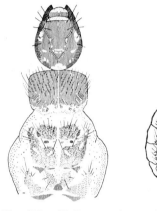

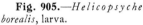

Fig. 905.—*Helicopsyche borealis*, larva.

slightly clavate, sclerotized spur of the sixth sternite. Female abdomen with very distinctive pattern of sclerites, those of the basal segments reticulate, as in fig. 907; bursa copulatrix small and stalked. The male abdomen has similar reticulation.

This species is widely distributed in Illinois but is confined to relatively clear and swift streams, such as the Kankakee and Salt Fork Rivers and Split Rock Brook, and is found also in the glacial lakes of the northeastern corner of the state. The larvae are found chiefly under stones. There is apparently a continuous succession of generations, our adult emergence ranging from May 28 to September 7.

This insect is one of the best known caddis flies and has received much attention. Vorhies (1909) has reared and described all stages very completely.

Betten (1934) also has illustrated characters of this species in considerable detail.

The curious snail-like case has attracted the attention of many entomologists and collectors of natural history objects. It is remarkably constant in structure, varying little in shape over the species range.

The continental range of the species is very wide, stretching from Mexico northeastward to Nova Scotia and westward to Montana and Oregon; the range embraces most of the forested areas of the continent, forming a complete circle around the Great Plains. Records are available for Arkansas, California, Colorado, Florida, Georgia, Illinois, Indiana, Kentucky, Michigan, Minnesota, Missouri, Montana, New Brunswick, New Hampshire, New York, Nova Scotia,

Fig. 906.—*Helicopsyche borealis*, case.

Ohio, Oklahoma, Ontario, Oregon, Pennsylvania, Saskatchewan, South Dakota, Texas, Virginia, West Virginia, Wisconsin and Wyoming.

Illinois Records.—Many males, females and pupae, taken May 14 to September 7, and many larvae, taken February 1 to October 30, are from Antioch, Apple River Canyon State Park, Baker (Indian Creek), Cedar Lake, Channel Lake, Chemung (Piscasaw Creek), Fox Lake, Herod (east fork of Grand Pierre Creek), Homer, Kankakee (Kankakee River), Leland, Martha Iron Furnace (Hog Thief Creek), McHenry, Momence (Kankakee River), Muncie (Stony Creek), Oakwood (Salt Fork River), Richmond, Rock Island, Serena (Indian Creek), Spring Grove, Sterling, Urbana (Salt Fork River), Utica (Split Rock Brook), Wilmington (Kankakee River).

Fig. 907.—*Helicopsyche borealis*, female abdomen, ventral aspect.

EXTRALIMITAL TRICHOPTERA

During the course of the foregoing study of the Illinois caddis flies it has been necessary to examine a large amount of material from other states. Detailed studies of some of the species involved have been necessary in order to establish the species limits of some components of the Illinois fauna. Descriptions of some of the more pertinent new forms are presented here, partly to supplement identification of Illinois species and partly to supplement the check list.

Rhyacophila banksi new species

This species is unique among North American forms in the narrow, angled and bifid dorso-mesal projection of the ninth tergite. Superficially it appears closely related to *invaria* but differs from this species not only in the projection of the ninth tergite but in many characters of the claspers and tenth tergite.

MALE.—Length 10 mm. Color brown, the wings without definite pattern except irregular spots of golden hair which occur over most of the surface. General structure typical for genus. Genitalia as in fig. 908. Ninth segment annular, narrowed ventrad, and with a prominent dorso-mesal projection which angles sharply dorsad, is narrow

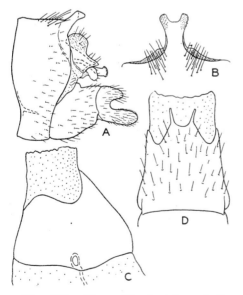

Fig. 908.—*Rhyacophila banksi*, genitalia. Male: *A*, lateral aspect; *B*, dorsal aspect. Female: *C*, lateral aspect; *D*, ventral aspect.

at base, and expanded and distinctly emarginate at apex. Tenth tergite with a prominent pair of dorsal lobes which are produced into a posterior point; below these is a central style with a rounded apex and narrow sinuate internal rodlike base. Claspers with basal segment short and stocky, as wide as long; apical segment almost as long as basal one, apical margin very deeply incised to form a large, rounded, dorsal lobe and a long, rounded, ventral lobe, the latter with a brush of short black setae on the mesal face. Aedeagus very similar to that of *invaria*, having a short, stocky membranous base with a mesal sclerotized body having a wide, "eared" dorsal portion and a ventral portion produced into an upturned sharp point, flanked by an extensile membranous lobe which bears a sclerotized, pointed blade.

FEMALE.—In size, color and general structure similar to male. Eighth segment, fig. 908, with ventral margin produced into a tongue, divided at tip into a pair of narrow fingers; lateral margin sinuate and dorsal margin deeply incised.

Holotype, male.—Warren, New Hampshire: June 21, 1941, Frison & Ross.

Allotype, female.—Same data as for holotype.

Paratypes.—NEW HAMPSHIRE. — Pemigewasset River, near WOODSTOCK: June 22, 1941, Frison & Ross, 1 ♂, 1 ♀. MOUNT WASHINGTON: June 22, in Tuckerman's Ravine, P. Darlington, 2 ♂, MCZ.

Rhyacophila harmstoni new species

The general structure of the genitalia indicates a close affinity between this species and *vofixa*; *harmstoni*, however, may be distinguished by the convex rather than concave tenth tergite and the short aedeagus with its two curved clusters of spines, fig. 909.

MALE.—Length 11 mm. Color various shades of brown, the wings irrorate over almost their entire surface. General structure typical for genus. Male genitalia as in fig. 909. Ninth segment annular, slightly narrowed ventrad. Tenth tergite short, the apex divided into a pair of snoutlike reticulate lobes, the central and upper portion convex, the dorsal angle produced into a slight hump. Claspers with basal segment stocky, longer than wide, its apical margin almost truncate and having a scattering of medium length setae; apical segment short and boot shaped, the dorsal heel small and pointed, the ventral toe large and somewhat triangular, with a brush of short setae on

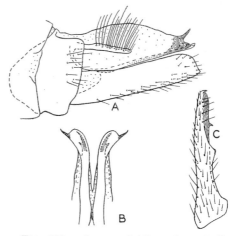

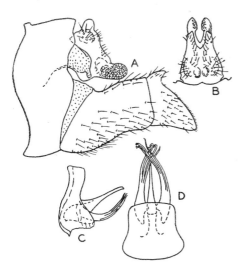

Fig. 909.—*Rhyacophila harmstoni*, male genitalia. *A*, lateral aspect; *B*, tenth tergite; *C* and *D* aedeagus, respectively lateral and ventral aspects.

Fig. 910.—*Agapetus iridis*, male genitalia. *A*, lateral aspect; *B*, tenth tergite; *C*, clasper.

the inner margin at apex. Aedeagus with dorsal portion very narrow, ventral portion expanded and wider; armature consisting of a mesal style which is widest at base and tapers rather rapidly to a slender straight apex, flanked on each side by a curved cluster of three or four spines fused on basal portion and sinuate at apex.

Holotype, male. — Strawberry Valley, Utah: July 15, 1938, Knowlton & Harmston.

Agapetus iridis new species

This species is most closely related to *pinatus*, differing from it in the truncate lateral aspect of the claspers and the conformation of the tenth tergite.

MALE.—Length 5 mm. Color dark brown, the legs beyond coxae whitish yellow with black spurs. General structure typical for genus. Genitalia as in fig. 910. Ninth segment cylindrical, its posterior margin truncate laterad and incised almost to the base on the dorsum. Cerci long and slender with a dorsal brush of long setae. Tenth tergite very long, the basal part robust, tapering

to apex; almost completely membranous except for a pair of stout sharp dorsal spines at apex and a pair of ventral sclerotized ribbons which are expanded and flat at apex and bearing on the lateral corner a fairly long, sharp spine. Claspers long, lateral aspect forming an elongate rectangle, the apico-ventral corner slightly pointed; mesal face with an apical and dorsal sclerotized tooth and with the ventro-mesal margin produced near middle into a wide, triangular lobe sclerotized at apex and evenly curved to meet the slightly wider base. Aedeagus semimembranous and tubular, typical for the genus.

FEMALE.—In size, color and general structure similar to male. Eighth segment bilaterally compressed, its apical margin slightly incised on meson and with the dorsal margin slightly shorter than the ventral one.

Holotype, male.—Small creek near Tahawus, New York, Adirondack State Park: June 20, 1941, Frison & Ross.

Allotype, female.—Same data as for holotype.

Paratypes.—NEW YORK.—Same data as for holotype, 1 ♂. Cedar River near INDIAN LAKE, June 20, 1941, Frison & Ross, 1 ♂.

Chimarra elia new species

This species is most closely related to *utahensis*, differing from it in the large, keel-like apical process of the ninth sternite, in addition to other differences in the genitalia.

From other species with the ventral keel, such as *aterrima*, this new species may be distinguished readily by the situation of the ventral keel immediately under the face of the clasper and also by the heavily sclerotized, serrate, lateral process of the tenth tergite.

MALE.—Length 6 mm. Color very dark brown, the legs whitish yellow except for the tarsi and spurs, which are brown; wings

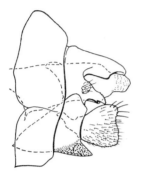

Fig. 911.—*Chimarra elia*, male genitalia.

without perceptible pattern; in life the insect looks almost black. General structure typical for genus. Male genitalia as in fig. 911. Ninth and tenth tergites fused, the anterior margin of the ninth with a short, stout, somewhat hook-shaped apodeme, the tenth tergite forming an irregular, almost membranous hood over the apex of aedeagus; ventrad of this hood are situated the small, round cerci and, beyond these, the lateral margin of the segment is produced into a sharp, minutely serrate point. Ninth sternite triangular, the apico-mesal line bearing a long, projecting, sharp keel which is slightly serrulate, is situated directly below the base of the claspers and occupies most of the exposed ventral margin of the sternite. Claspers somewhat triangular, the dorsal corner rounded and bearing several fairly long setae, the remainder of the clasper with shorter setae, the dorsal surface of the apico-mesal corner with a slender but strong black spine. Aedeagus typical in general proportions for the *aterrima* group, having the somewhat expanded internal base, beyond which it is cylindrical, the exserted apex membranous and narrow, not sclerotized.

Holotype, male.—Spring-fed stream west of Brackettville, Texas: April 17, 1939, H. H. & J. A. Ross.

Chimarra florida new species

This species is a close relative of *obscura*, differing from it, however, in the short mesal process of the ninth sternite, the longer claspers, which are wider at base and more slender at apex, and the longer and stouter lateral processes of the tenth tergite. From species of the *aterrima* group which also have the short mesal process of the ninth sternite, this new species may be distinguished by the hooked aedeagus.

MALE.—Length 7 mm. Color black, the wings without pattern, the femora sometimes brownish. General structure typical for genus. Male genitalia as in fig. 912. Tenth tergite with central part membranous, lateral area developed into strongly sclerotized curved processes rounded at apex; at the base of these is a ridgelike area representing the cerci. Ninth sternite produced dorsad to base of tenth tergite, narrow and sinuate, with a short, meso-ventral keel situated near base of segment. Claspers with ventral portion flared and somewhat saucer-like, its lateral margin appearing definitely crenulate due to the presence of fairly evenly spaced small humps, each bearing a large seta; dorsal portion of clasper elongate and evenly curved. Aedeagus with basal portion long and irregular, developed at apex into a single stout sclerotized hook.

FEMALE.—Size, color and general structure as for male. Genitalia very similar to those of *obscura*; reliable characters to separate the two have not been found.

Holotype, male.—Five miles southeast of Roberta, Georgia: May 4, 1939, P. W. Fattig.

Allotype, female.—Same data as for holotype.

Paratypes.—FLORIDA. — FREEPORT, Walton County: April 3, 1938, L. Berner, 1 ♂.

GEORGIA.—Same data as for holotype, 4 ♂, 1 ♀.

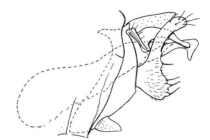

Fig. 912.—*Chimarra florida*, male genitalia.

Hydropsyche solex new species

This is most closely related to *californica*, differing from it in the extremely constricted aedeagus. In this regard it approaches *delrio*, but *delrio* is readily distinguished by the short, apical segment of the clasper and the mesal cavity of the aedeagus, which is almost entirely closed.

MALE.—Length 11 mm. Head and body black; antennae very slender and yellowish, with dorsal black V-marks on the first eight

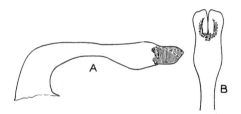

Fig. 913.—*Hydropsyche solex*, aedeagus. *A*, lateral aspect; *B*, ventral aspect.

segments of the flagellum; eyes red, legs yellowish brown, the femora darker; front wings tawny brown, irrorate, with abundant fenestrate cream-colored marks. General structure typical for genus. Male genitalia in general typical for the *scalaris* group. Ninth segment only slightly humped dorsad. Tenth tergite somewhat hood shaped, with a fairly wide mesal incision and with each lateral lobe produced into a very small point. Claspers slightly sinuate; apical segment nearly one-half as long as basal segment, the apex obliquely truncate. Aedeagus, fig. 913, with the base round, the stem constricted to a narrow central portion and greatly expanded at apex; apical portion definitely narrowed from stem, heavily sclerotized and almost black; mesal cavity almost entirely open; mesal plates small;

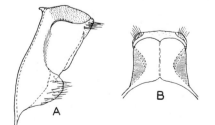

Fig. 914.—*Hydropsyche solex*, female genitalia. *A*, lateral aspect; *B*, dorsal aspect.

lateral plates wide, from lateral view hiding the meso-dorsal portion.

FEMALE.—Length 13 mm. In color and general structure similar to male. Ninth tergite, fig. 914, with clasper groove large, invaginated only slightly under dorsal cap, from dorsal view appearing to extend deeply beneath cap; lateral lobe large, with abundant setae; postero-lateral flange well developed.

Holotype, male. — Balmorhea, Texas, along stone irrigation flume: April 19, 1939, H. H. & J. A. Ross.

Allotype, female.—Same data as for holotype.

Paratypes.—Same data as for holotype, 1 ♂, 3 ♀.

Leucotrichia Mosely

(See also p. 120)

KEY TO MALES OF NEARCTIC SPECIES

1. Ninth segment with a pair of long, sclerotized spurs and long styles, fig. 915.................**notosa** n. sp.
   Ninth segment without long, projecting spurs and styles, fig. 916....... 2
2. Eighth sternite with lateral margin forming long, triangular lobes, fig. 917....................**sarita** n. sp.
   Eighth sternite without lateral lobes but with a pair of pointed lobes situated ventrad, figs. 916, 918.... 3
3. Seventh sternite with an apico-mesal, short process; aedeagus with a long, dorsal loop extending over its base, fig. 918.................**limpia** n. sp.
   Seventh sternite with no short process but instead with an apico-mesal brush of dark setae; aedeagus with a pair of short, dorsal processes not produced into a loop, fig. 916.....
   ....**pictipes** (Banks)

Leucotrichia notosa new species

The long, lateral styles of the ninth segment distinguish this species from all others in the genus, as pointed out in the preceding key.

MALE.—Length 4 mm. Color mottled light and dark shades of gray, the legs conspicuously banded, essentially similar in this characteristic to *pictipes*. General structure typical for the genus. Seventh segment without a mesal projection. Eighth segment with the tergite reduced to a narrow triangular

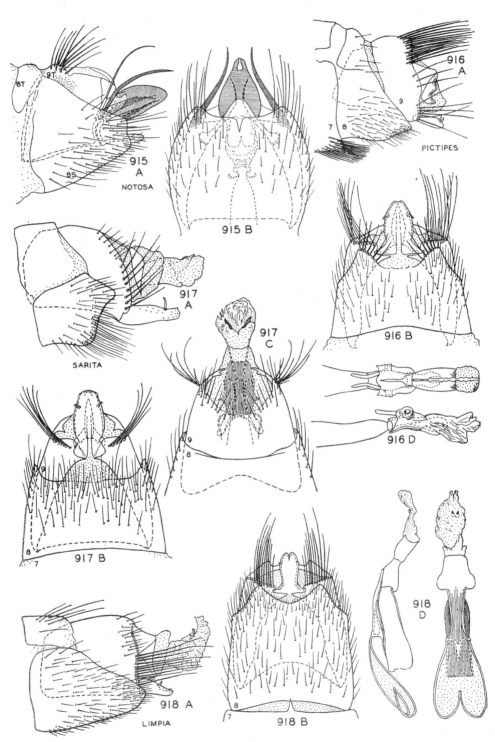

Figs. 915–918.—*Leucotrichia*, male genitalia. *A*, *B* and *C*, respectively lateral, ventral and dorsal aspects; *D*, aedeagus.

dorsal portion, the sternite large and somewhat scoop shaped, and with a broad dorso-lateral corner and a narrow sharp, V-shaped mesal incision.

Genital capsule as in fig. 915, retracted so that the ventral portion is almost entirely contained within the scoop-shaped eighth sternite. Ninth segment with a large dorsal tuft of long setae, not produced into an internal lobe, the ventral portion almost entirely cut away. Tenth tergite formed of simple strap-shaped sclerites and possibly including also the upturned sclerites at the apex of the ninth segment. Near the junction of this sclerite and the ninth segment are two long structures, a long, sinuate, heavily sclerotized spine and a long, stout seta on a long, filiform base, this seta as long as the spine. Claspers fused on meson to form a short, wide lobe. Aedeagus with a small, cylindrical base, a convoluted semimembranous neck and with the apical portion semimembranous at base, expanded into a heavily sclerotized pear-shaped apical bulb containing two internal sclerotized rods.

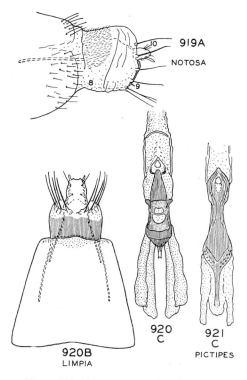

Figs. 919–921.—*Leucotrichia*, female genitalia. *A*, lateral aspect; *B*, ventral aspect; *C*, bursa copulatrix.

FEMALE.—In size, color and general structure similar to male. Eighth segment, fig. 919, narrow and cylindrical with a dorsal collar-like portion covered with short setae, the ninth and tenth segments membranous and simple.

Holotype, male.—Missouri River, Toston, Montana: June 22, 1940, H. H. & J. A. Ross.

Allotype, female.—Same data as for holotype.

Paratype.—Same data as for holotype, 1 ♀.

Leucotrichia limpia new species

This species is most closely related to *pictipes*, differing from it in the gray-green banding of the wings, the unmodified basal antennal segments in the male and the unique dorsal loop of the aedeagus.

MALE.—Length 4.5 mm. Head and body dark brown, antennae slightly paler and legs below coxae paler yet. Pubescence of head, thorax and legs chiefly gray-green; wings dark brown, the front wings with two large patches of gray-green hair, the basal one occupying most of the basal two-fifths of the wing, the apical one separated from the first by the narrow black area and covering half of the remaining length of the wing. Structure typical for genus. Ocelli present and close to mesal margin of eye. Antennae filiform. Legs with tibial spur count of 1-3-4. Hind wings with an accessory row of hamuli across the radial cell.

Male genitalia as in fig. 918. Seventh sternite with a small mesal point. Eighth segment with tergite small, bearing a scattering of long setae. Eighth sternite narrow above and widening to a broad ventral sclerite incised on the middle, so that it forms a pair of latero-apical subtriangular lobes; the entire sclerite is clothed with a scattering of fairly long setae. Ninth segment long and round dorsally and laterally but almost completely open on the venter, its apico-lateral margins bearing a row of very long, stout setae. Tenth tergite composed of a pair of sclerotized plates close to the ninth and not projecting far posterad. Claspers fused on meson, together forming a spatulate projection and each bearing a stout spine on the lateral margin. Aedeagus very complex, consisting of a basal tube articulating with the neck, which is expanded into two lateral humps; from this neck there extends anterad a sclerotized plate which terminates in a loop encircled by a thin sclerotized thread apparently supporting a connecting membrane; apical portion of aedeagus short, with a pair of thumblike, baso-lateral projections and with the posterior margin merging into a group of membranous folds embedded in which are a pair of stout sclerotized teeth.

FEMALE.—Similar in size, color and general structure to male. Genitalia as in fig. 920. Eighth segment short and cylindrical, sclerotized, the apex membranous and bearing a crown of long setae, each set in a conical membranous base. Ninth and tenth segments more or less tubular, not distinctly set off from each other, the tenth bearing a pair of apical styles. Bursa copulatrix complex, consisting of a series of membranous folds and narrow sclerotized rods at the attached end which culminate in a highly ornamented, lantern-like structure to which are attached two pairs of membranous ribbons.

Holotype, male.—Fort Davis, Texas: April 19, 1939, along Limpia Creek, H. H. & J. A. Ross.

Allotype, female.—Same data as for holotype.

Paratypes.—Same data as for holotype, 2♂, 1♀.

Leucotrichia sarita new species

This species may be distinguished from the preceding by the longer claspers and different shape of the eighth sternite.

MALE.—Length 4 mm. In color similar to preceding species but without any conspicuous gray-green patch of hair on front wings. General structure typical for preceding species. Seventh segment without a mesal projection. Eighth segment with tergite fairly wide but much narrower than sternite; sternite with postero-dorsal corner produced into a large triangular lobe, ventral margin transverse and indistinct on the meson. Genitalia as in fig. 917. Ninth segment long and round dorsally and laterally, but with the ventral margin almost completely open; postero-lateral margin bears a row of long, stout setae. Tenth tergite consisting of a pair of widely separated sclerotized lobes between which are membranous folds. Claspers fused, projecting beyond the tenth tergite, each one bearing

a long spine on its dorso-lateral margin. Aedeagus consisting of a short base, a heavily sclerotized neck which is thrown up into a series of ridges and points, with a pair of threads attached to base; apical portion widening from base to apex, the tip bearing a pair of sclerotized teeth embedded in an expanse of membranous folds.

Holotype, male. — Balmorhea, Texas: April 19, 1939, along stone irrigation flume, H. H. & J. A. Ross.

Ochrotrichia weddleae new species

This species is most closely related to the genotype, *insularis*, described from Jamaica. It differs from this species and all others in the genus in the peculiar, short claspers with their almost circular apical incision, fig. 922. The simple type of tenth tergite indicates a primitive condition similar to that found in *xena* and *unio*. It is entirely possible that this species is the most primitive yet discovered in the genus.

MALE.—Length 2.5 mm. Color very dark, almost black, the wings with a few indistinct light areas and with a slight indication of a whitish line across middle. General structure typical for genus.

Genitalia as in fig. 922. Ninth segment short and stout, the lateral portion set off from the ventral by a curved distinct fold, dorsal portion with a wide, U-shaped incision almost to base. Tenth tergite set in

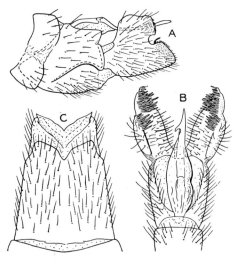

Fig. 922.—*Ochrotrichia weddleae*, genitalia. Male: *A*, lateral aspect; *B*, dorsal aspect. Female: *C*, ventral aspect.

this incision, somewhat fusiform and almost entirely membranous, with a slight constriction near base, the apex tapering to a sharp barbed point. Claspers short and wide, divided by an almost circular apical incision into two lobes; the dorsal lobe has a truncate apex, swollen dorsal margin, and a thick cluster of long, dark spines on its mesal face at apex; the ventral lobe has an oblique apex and a larger cluster of long, dark spines on its mesal face at apex. Aedeagus simple and filiform, typical for the genus.

FEMALE.—In size, color and general structure similar to male. Eighth sternite, fig. 922, set off distinctly from structures of the ninth, the apex wide and divided by a small U-shaped mesal incision into a pair of fairly large lobes which are clothed with long, scattered setae similar to those on the rest of the segment. Bursa copulatrix very long and shaped like a tuning fork, typical for the genus.

Holotype, male. — Cloudy Creek near Cloudy, Oklahoma: May 4, 1940, Mrs. Roy Weddle.

Allotype, female.—Same data as for holotype.

Paratypes.—Same data as for holotype, 1♂, 1♀.

Ochrotrichia capitana new species

This is one of the more primitive members of the genus, most closely related to *xena*. It may be separated from this, however, by the definitely marked sclerotized bands of the tenth tergite and the much different arrangement of the black spines on the inner face of the claspers.

MALE.—Length 2.5 mm. General color and structure typical for genus. Genitalia as in fig. 923. Ninth segment annular, with a triangular apical incision on the dorsum for the reception of the tenth tergite. Tenth tergite long and narrow, the dorsal portion mostly semisclerotized with some definite, heavily sclerotized bands running along the dorsum; these converge at the apex and terminate in an upturned, spinelike process. Claspers more or less boot shaped and similar in shape; the outer face is covered with scattered setae and the mesal face with a dense brush of dark spines near the middle and a linear area of long, stout spines from above that point to the apex; seen from ventral view, the claspers appear to taper even-

ly from base to the bladelike apex, the mesal face concave. Aedeagus typical for genus.

FEMALE.—Similar in size and general structure to male. Genitalia simple, fig. 923, the eighth tergite forming a single

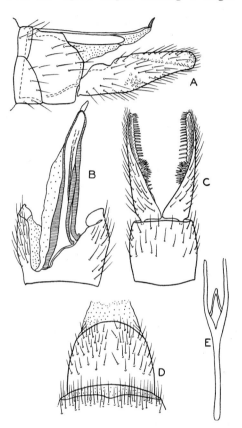

Fig. 923—*Ochrotrichia capitana*, genitalia. Male: *A*, lateral aspect; *B*, tenth tergite; *C*, ventral aspect. Female: *D*, ventral aspect; *E*, bursa copulatrix.

rounded sclerite clothed with a scattering of long setae. Bursa copulatrix with the arms of the fork slightly shorter than in other species.

Holotype, male. — McKittrick Creek, McKittrick Canyon (near Frijole) Texas: April 26, 1939, J. A. & H. H. Ross.

Allotype, female.—Same data as for holotype.

Ochrotrichia felipe new species

The closest ally of this species is *tenanga* Mosely, fig. 925, from southern Mexico. The two may be distinguished by the differ-

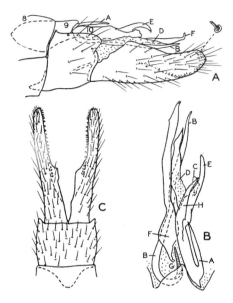

Fig. 924.—*Ochrotrichia felipe*, male genitalia. *A*, lateral aspect; *B*, tenth tergite; *C*, ventral aspect.

Fig. 925.—*Ochrotrichia tenanga*, male tenth tergite. The small capital letters in this figure and that above have been used to facilitate comparison with similar parts in figs. 468–470.

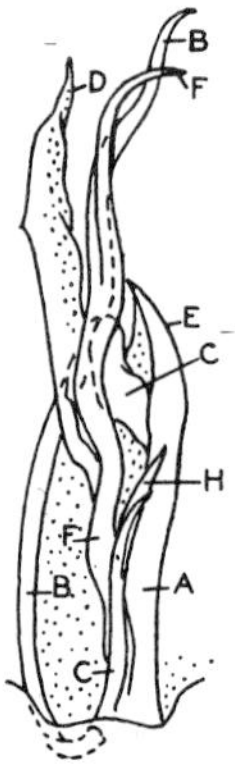

ent arrangement of the sclerotized processes making up the dorsal complex of the tenth tergite.

MALE.—Similar in size, color and general structure to the male of *capitana*. Genitalia as in fig. 924. Ninth segment annular, with the dorsal portion incised on the meson to accommodate the tenth tergite. Tenth tergite composed of a large number of sclerotized blades and processes making up the dorsal complex. These are arranged in three main groups, a right group, a left group and a dorsal, long, sinuate blade which arises between them. Claspers almost symmetrical, the lateral aspect boot shaped, the mesal face with a sinuate row of short,

stout, rounded spines. From ventral view, these appear in silhouette on the narrower apical portion and continue under the mesal angle where the clasper narrows abruptly. Aedeagus simple, tubular and filamentous, as in other species of the genus.

Holotype, male.—San Felipe Springs, Del Rio, Texas: April 19, 1939, H. H. & J. A. Ross.

Paratypes.—Same data as for holotype, 2♂.

Hydroptila waskesia new species

This species is closely related to both *delineata* and *vala*, differing from both of them in the very long lateral projections of the ninth sternite and in having the spur on the membranous appendages arising below the tenth tergite.

MALE.—Length 3.7 mm. Color various shades of dark gray and cream, the two mixing to form a salt-and-pepper pattern typical for the group. General structure typical for genus.

Genitalia as in fig. 926. Ninth segment produced into a long, triangular pair of internal projections, the posterior margin of the sides produced into a long, bladelike, tapering and sharply pointed projection which curves slightly mesad and turns slightly dorsad at apex. Tenth tergite long, composed of a pair of lateral sclerotized areas

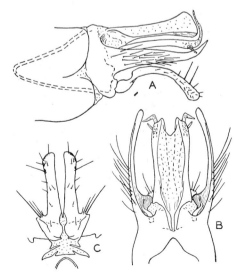

Fig. 926.—*Hydroptila waskesia*, male genitalia. *A*, lateral aspect; *B*, dorsal aspect; *C*, claspers.

separated by a high membranous fold. From below the base of the tenth tergite arise a pair of long, membranous filaments which continue beneath the full length of the tergite and then curve sharply dorsad around its tip; just before the turn these processes have a large, sharp lateral spur. Claspers with a small, triangular base and a long, slightly spatulate blade irregularly set with setae, the two blades close together at base and diverging slightly toward apex; lateral aspect curved and slightly arcuate. Aedeagus almost exactly as for *vala* (see fig. 515), having a long narrow neck, long stout spiral, the apical portion long, cylindrical and sharply angled at tip.

FEMALE.—In size, color and general stucture similar to male. Genitalia apparently identical with those of *vala*; eighth sternite with a central Y-shaped plate, the apex with an arcuate lobe bearing six long setae (see fig. 530).

Holotype, male.—Lake Waskesieu, Prince Albert National Park, Saskatchewan: Aug. 15, 1940, L. T., No. 8, Don Milne.

Allotype, female.—Same data as for holotype.

Paratypes.—Same data as for holotype, 1 ♂, 1 ♀.

Neotrichia sonora new species

This species is most closely related to *okopa*, but may be separated from it by the slender and upturned apex of the claspers, in addition to the different conformation of the tenth tergite.

MALE.—Length 2.25 mm. Color of body and appendages a uniform light shade of brown. General structure typical of the subgenus *Exitrichia*.

Genitalia as in fig. 927. Ninth segment annular, the invaginated basal portion short and subtriangular, the dorsum covered with a scattering of very short setae; the apical margin of the dorsum appears to be produced into a somewhat irregular, membranous hood covering the tenth tergite. Tenth tergite pointed at apex, seen from above, produced into a rounded mesal lobe from the base of which arise a pair of long setae. From the sides of this structure arise a pair of heavily sclerotized, long points curved slightly ventrad, and below these a pair of heavily sclerotized, triangular bodies. From the lateral margin of the ninth arise

a pair of cercus-like appendages which are slightly enlarged toward apex, clothed with a scattering of long setae and concave on the mesal face. Claspers very heavily sclerotized and black, seen from lateral view; thick at base, tapering to a flat and slightly upturned apical portion; somewhat rectangular from ventral view but with irregular margins and with apex triangular; mesal margin bearing a pair of small toothlike projections below apex, and below these there arises a stylelike appendage from the mesal face. Aedeagus practically identical with that of *okopa* except that the spiracle extends closer to the apex.

FEMALE.—Size, color and general structure as for male. Genitalia, including ornamentation and coloration of eighth sternite and bursa copulatrix, apparently identical with those of *okopa*.

Holotype, male.—Neville Spring at foot

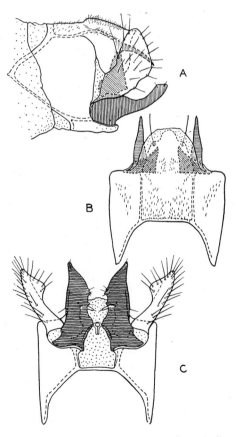

Fig. 927.—*Neotrichia sonora*, male genitalia. *A*, lateral aspect; *B*, dorsal aspect; *C*, ventral aspect.

of Chisos Mountains, Texas: April 20, 1939, J. A. & H. H. Ross.

Allotype, female.—Same data as for holotype.

Paratype.—Same data as for holotype, 1 ♂.

Neotrichia osmena new species

This species belongs with certain Mexican species of the subgenus *Exitrichia*, especially *digitata* Mosely and *eroga* Mosely. From the former, *osmena* differs in the curved and spatulate lateral processes of the ninth segment, and from the latter in the shorter, black claspers.

MALE.—Length 2.2 mm. Color dark brown. General structure, including wing venation, spur count, and other characters of head and thorax, identical with other described members of the genus.

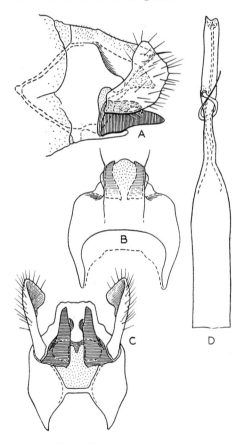

Fig. 928.—*Neotrichia osmena*, male genitalia. *A*, lateral aspect; *B*, dorsal aspect; *C*, ventral aspect; *D*, aedeagus.

Genitalia as in fig. 928. Ninth segment with invaginated portion triangular, dorsum covered with sparse short setae. Tenth tergite blunt, the medium portion of its apex produced into a rounded lobe from the base of which arise a pair of long spines. From beneath this structure arise a pair of large, heavily sclerotized, blunt structures which appear slightly forceps-like from dorsal view. From an incision on the lateral margin of the ninth segment arises a cercus-like flap which is expanded at apex, is clothed with a scattering of long setae, and is concave on the mesal face. Claspers black, with a broad base that tapers more or less regularly to the apex, and with a dorsal hook which reaches two-thirds of the distance to the apex. Aedeagus with a wide tubular base which constricts rapidly to a long narrow neck; from the apex of the neck arises a spiral process which encircles the tube slightly more than once; the apex is fairly evenly cylindrical, with the apex incised.

Holotype, male.—Blacksmith Fork Canyon, Utah: Sept. 16, 1938, at light, Knowlton.

Mayatrichia Mosely

(*See also p. 160*)

KEY TO SPECIES

Males

1. Aedeagus ending in a small, sclerotized three-pronged structure; claspers each with about 6 setae on mesal lobe, fig. 929.....**ayama** Mosely
   Aedeagus ending in a simple point, usually only lightly sclerotized; claspers each with 3 setae on mesal lobe, figs. 930, 931.............. 2
2. Claspers with mesal lobe nearly truncate, the apical setae very long and stout, fig. 930...........**ponta** n. sp.
   Claspers with mesal lobe oblique, each apical seta situated much lower than the one above, and all 3 short and slender, fig. 931......**acuna** n. sp.

Mayatrichia ponta new species

This species is most closely related to the Mexican *rualda* Mosely, from which it differs in having three instead of two large setae on each clasper and in shape of other sclerites of the genital capsule.

MALE.—Length 2.5 mm. Color brown without any conspicuous or distinctive markings. General structure typical for genus.

Male genitalia as in fig. 930. Ninth segment short, its posterior angle slightly obtuse, its posterior margin with a large, triangular, dorsal lobe bearing a line of setae near apex, and with a mitten-like projection below the triangle; this projection with its main body oval, concave on its mesal face, with a sclerotized point near apex and with a more or less thumblike postero-ventral process. Tenth tergite semimembranous and more or less hood shaped. Claspers with a broad base, a somewhat sinuate, digitate dorso-lateral lobe and a truncate, ventro-mesal lobe which bears at its apex three long, strong setae the bases of which are almost contiguous. Above the claspers is a long, sclerotized, beaklike structure which is wide at apex and bears a pair of small setae. Aedeagus long and simple, the extreme apex tapering to a very slender, filiform style.

Holotype, male.—Turner Falls State Park, Oklahoma, along Honey Creek: June 2, 1937, H. H. Ross.

Paratypes.—OKLAHOMA.—Same data as for holotype, 5 ♂. REAGAN, along Pennington Creek: June 1, 1937, H. H. Ross, 4 ♂. TURNER FALLS STATE PARK: June 7, 1938, Carl F. Grubb, 1 ♂.

This species has always been taken in company with *ayama*, and no female has been differentiated in these collections which could be associated definitely with *ponta*.

Mayatrichia acuna new species

This species is most closely related to *ponta* but may be readily distinguished from it by the very small dorso-lateral lobe of the claspers and the undulate margin of the meso-ventral lobe with its staggered and well-separated short setae.

MALE.—Length 2 mm. Color light brown, without conspicuous markings. General structure typical for genus. Male genitalia as in fig. 931. Ninth segment with the anterior projections of the lateral margin acute, the dorsal portion of this segment bearing an indefinite patch of setae, the postero-lateral margin with a long, mitten-like lobe which tapers gradually from the

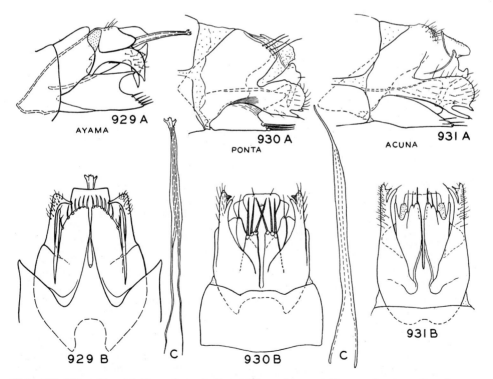

Figs. 929–931.—*Mayatrichia*, male genitalia.   *A*, lateral aspect; *B*, ventral aspect; *C*, aedeagus.

base to the middle, the ventral margin with a short apical projection and a longer digitate subapical projection, the apico-dorsal portion evenly rounded. Tenth tergite semimembranous, with a basal carina. Claspers with a small and digitate dorso-lateral lobe and with the ventro-mesal lobe subdivided into three staggered tubercles, each bearing a seta of medium length, the mesal one the stoutest. Above the claspers is a beaklike ventral projection, the central part wide and bearing a pair of sharp setae. Aedeagus similar to that of *ponta*, consisting of a small conical base, a long, tubular central portion and a threadlike apex, as in fig. 930*C*.

Holotype, male.—San Felipe Springs, Del Rio, Texas: April 19, 1939, H. H. & J. A. Ross.

Hesperophylax Banks

In this genus the ranking of various described species and varieties has varied considerably with different authors, at times all of them being considered forms of a single species. Detailed study of the genitalia of both males and females indicates that, in the material at my disposal, five species can be segregated definitely; the differences are comparative structures of the male genitalia and, where associated material is available, in the genitalia of the females, also. I have seen no material of *minutus* nor definitely associated females of *magnus* and *consimilis*. With the exception of these forms, the following key will separate the North American species.

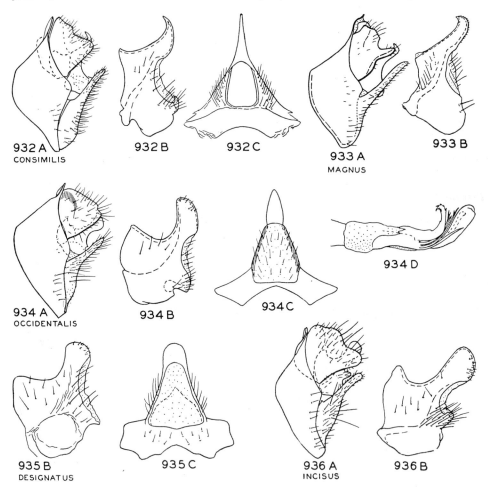

Figs. 932–936.—*Hesperophylax*, male genitalia. *A*, lateral aspect; *B* and *C*, tenth tergite, respectively lateral and caudal aspects; *D*, aedeagus.

KEY TO SPECIES

1. Apex of abdomen with a complex set of clasping organs, fig. 932 (males)   2
   Apex of abdomen with a pair of dorsal plates, fig. 937 (females).........   6
2. Apex of tenth tergite sharp and appearing pointed from both lateral and caudal view, fig. 932..........   3

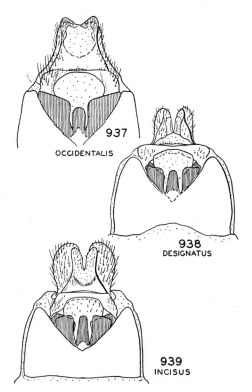

Figs. 937–939.—*Hesperophylax*, female genitalia.

Apex of tenth tergite appearing rounded from either lateral or caudal view, or both, figs. 934, 935...........   4
3. Cerci with apico-ventral corner produced into a long, narrow finger, fig. 933; silver streak of front wings conspicuous and bright.............
   ....**magnus** Banks
   Cerci with apico-ventral corner much less produced, fig. 932; silver, inconspicuous.........**consimilis** Banks
4. Ninth segment with lateral area short, anterior angle wide, fig. 936......
   ....**incisus** Banks
   Ninth segment with lateral area longer, anterior angle less obtuse, fig. 934.......................   5

5. Caudal aspect of tenth tergite wide, the lateral projections long and angulate, the membranous caudal area short, fig. 934..............
   ....**occidentalis** Banks
   Caudal aspect of tenth tergite narrower, the lateral projections shorter and trapezoidal, the membranous caudal area longer, fig. 935........
   ....**designatus**, p. 183
6. Tenth segment with lateral projections scarcely developed, fig. 937..
   ....**occidentalis** Banks
   Tenth segment with lateral projections forming definite wide flanges, figs. 938, 939..................   7
7. Tenth tergite with lateral projections occupying about a third of ventral aspect, fig. 938......**designatus**, p. 183
   Tenth tergite with lateral projections occupying nearly two-thirds of ventral aspect, fig. 939......**incisus** Banks

Limnephilus nogus new species

Most closely related to *pacificus*, this species is readily characterized by the long tenth tergite and cerci, and the curious pointed process of the claspers, fig. 940.

MALE.—Length 15 mm. Color tawny, with irregular darker brown markings on antennae, body and legs; wings tawny with a dark stigmal spot, a dark line on cord, and other irregular dark areas variable in nature. Macrochaetae of head and thorax

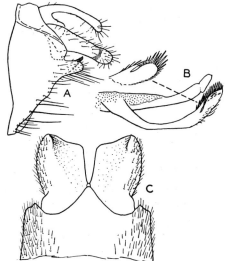

Fig. 940.—*Limnephilus nogus*, genitalia. Male: *A*, lateral aspect; *B*, aedeagus. Female: *C*, ventral aspect.

strong, tawny on head, dark brown on meso-notum. Front tibiae with basitarsus longer than succeeding segments. Eighth tergite without patch of dark spines. Genitalia as in fig. 940. Ninth segment very narrow on dorsum and venter but wide laterally. Tenth tergite forming a pair of long, curved, somewhat flattened processes with a sclero-tized ridge on meson at apex. Cerci also very long, finger-like, with a heavily scle-rotized bar across mesal face near apex. Clasper short and rounded, somewhat flat-tened, with a black, spurlike mesal projec-tion. Aedeagus with lateral arms long, end-ing in a sharp mesal process and a some-what spatulate, hairy lateral process.

FEMALE.—Similar in general color and structure to male except for five-segmented maxillary palpi. Genitalia as in fig. 940. Ninth sternite wide, with a large apico-mesal triangle and with lateral margins pro-duced into somewhat angular apical corners. Tenth segment forming a sclerotized paired structure, appearing somewhat rectangular from ventral view but with each lobe deeply excavated from dorsal view.

Holotype, male.—Near McMinnville, Oregon: Nov. 2, 1937, Kenneth Fender.

Allotype, female.—Same data as for holotype.

Paratypes.—BRITISH COLUMBIA.—VAN-COUVER: Sept. 16, 1932, H. H. Ross, 1 ♀; April 15, 1932, H. H. Ross, 1 ♀.

OREGON.—BROWNSVILLE: Aug. 19, 1907, 1 ♂. Same data as for holotype, 1 ♂, 1 ♀; same but Sept. 20–Oct. 2, 1938, 1 ♂, 2 ♀.

WASHINGTON.—CHEHALIS: Oct. 14–18, 1911, M. A. Yothers, 1 ♂. PULLMAN: 1 ♂, 6 ♀; May 29, 1897, 1 ♀; May 14, 1898, 1 ♀; Aug. 6, 1898, 1 ♀; Aug. 10, 1898, 1 ♀; Aug. 25, 1898, 1 ♀; Sept. 26, 1898, 1 ♀; May 13, 1904, 1 ♂; June 6, 1908, 1 ♂.

Paratypes are deposited with the holo-type and also in the collection of Washing-ton State College.

Limnephilus frijole new species

This species is most closely related to *aretto*, differing chiefly in the curious arcu-ate apex of the tenth tergite.

MALE.—Length 15 mm. Color tawny brown, the body, legs and wings marked with small dark brown lines and dots which give the species a salt-and-pepper mottling. Macrochaetae of head and thorax long and stout, dark brown. Front basitarsus longer

than half length of succeeding segment, front femur with a long inner patch of minute black spines. Eighth tergite with a produced area bearing a patch of dense short spines. Genitalia as in fig. 941. Ninth seg-ment straplike across dorsum, moderately

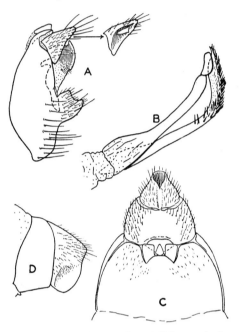

Fig. 941.—*Limnephilus frijole*, genitalia. Male: *A*, lateral aspect; *B*, aedeagus. Female: *C*, ventral aspect; *D*, lateral aspect.

wide across lateral area. Tenth tergite composed of a pair of sclerotized plates with a flanged, arcuate apex. Cerci short and triangular, with a short platelike pro-jection on meson. Claspers simple, short, wide and with apical margin concave. Aede-agus with center style and lateral arms very long, lateral arms bent sharply near apex and bearing a brush of moderately short spines.

FEMALE.—Length 18 mm. General struc-ture typical for male. Genitalia, fig. 941, with very simple parts. Ninth segment almost cylindrical, the sides somewhat flat-tened. Tenth segment tubular, the dorsal portion fairly evenly rounded, the ventral portion produced into a narrow mesal keel.

Holotype, male.—Manzaneta Spring, Frijole, Texas: April 26, 1939, J. A. & H. H. Ross.

Allotype, female.—Same data as for holotype.

Paratypes.—NEW MEXICO.—FORT WIN-GATE: Aug. 8, 1908, John Woodgate, 1 ♀ ; Aug. 24, 1 ♀ ; Sept. 1, 1 ♀ ; Sept. 21, 1 ♀ .

MEXICO.—CERRO POTOSI, elevation 8,000 feet, Municipio de Galeana: July 8, 1938, H. Hoogstraal, 1 ♂ , 1 ♀ .

TEXAS.—Same data as for holotype: 1 ♂ , 1 ♀ . McKittrick Creek, McKITTRICK CAN-YON: April 26, 1939, J. A. & H. H. Ross, 1 ♂ , 1 ♀ .

Three of the paratypes from Fort Win-gate are deposited with the Academy of Natural Sciences of Philadelphia.

Chyranda new genus

ADULTS.—General structure typical for family. Head without macrochaetae behind ocelli. Maxillary palpi very long in both

Fig. 942. — *Chyranda centralis* ♂, head.

male, fig. 942, and female. Mesonotum with warts elongate. Tibial spur count 1-3-4. Apical segment of tarsi without black spines. Wings very similar in general aspect to those of *Limnephilus*, see fig. 636.

Genotype.—*Asynarchus centralis* Banks.

The very long palpi distinguish this genus from *Limnephilus* and others to which it is related. In the North American fauna this character will separate it from all genera which do not differ from it in wing venation.

Oligophlebodes Ulmer

Additional material secured from various localities in the western mountains indicates that there are at least five species in this interesting genus. To a certain extent color characters have been found of some use in making identifications, but for the most part reliable differences are confined to the genitalia.

For the species so far differentiated, characters have been found to separate the females to species as indicated in the key.

KEY TO SPECIES

1. Eighth and ninth sternites well separated, the ninth segment annular and bearing a complicated set of parts, fig. 943 (males)............ 2
Eighth and ninth sternites merged together, the ninth platelike, fig. 948 (females)....................... 6

2. Claspers twisted so that their apex is nearly in a vertical plane and projecting almost directly back, the apex somewhat truncate in lateral view, fig. 943.................... 3
Claspers in a horizontal plane, fig. 946, sometimes sinuate, the end narrow in lateral view, fig. 945.......... 4

3. Lateral projection of ninth segment large, at least equal in area to lateral aspect of claspers; below lateral projection the segment is incised less than half its width to receive claspers; apex of ninth sternite forming a wide angle, fig. 943......**sierra** n. sp.
Lateral projection of ninth segment much smaller than lateral aspect of claspers; below lateral projection the segment is incised more than half its width to receive claspers; apex of ninth sternite acute, fig. 944 ....**minutus** Banks

4. Blade of claspers long, sometimes sinuate, narrow at tip; apex of ninth sternite long and sharp, fig. 945.... ....**ruthae** n. sp.
Blade of claspers short, stocky at tip; apex of ninth sternite shorter and with a much broader apical angle, fig. 946........................ 5

5. Blade of claspers directed almost straight back, robust, and with mesal margin armed with short teeth, fig. 946; body dark brown to black.....................**ardis** Ross
Blade of claspers angled obliquely mesad, slender, with only the curved tooth forming the apex, fig. 947; body yellow............**sigma** Milne

6. Lateral lobes of subgenital plate truncate except for a slight emargination at middle, fig. 948....**ruthae** n. sp.
Lateral lobes of subgenital plate rounded, fig. 949, or oblique, fig. 951................................ 7

7. Lateral lobes of subgenital plate rounded and projecting markedly beyond mesal lobe, fig. 949........ ....**minutus** Banks
Lateral lobes of subgenital plate not projecting beyond mesal lobe, fig. 950............................ 8

8. Mesal lobe of subgenital plate scarcely

projecting above mesal portion of lateral lobes; ventral structure of bursa copulatrix very narrow, fig. 950......................**sierra** n. sp.

Mesal lobe of subgenital plate projecting conspicuously beyond mesal portion of lateral lobes; ventral structure of bursa wider, fig. 951...
..........................**ardis** Ross

Oligophlebodes sierra new species

In color this species approaches most closely *sigma* but differs from it in the twisted apex of the claspers, large lateral lobe of the ninth segment and other characters of the genitalia. The female may be distinguished from other members of the genus by the combination of the narrow ventral lobe of the bursa copulatrix and the low and evenly sloping lateral lobes of the ninth sternite.

MALE.—Length 8 mm. Color yellowish brown, the wings without conspicuous darker markings. General structure typical for genus. Genitalia as in fig. 943. Ninth segment reduced to a line dorsally, expanded into a wide ventral portion which is produced on the meson into a short angular process; the lateral margin bears a platelike projection which is wide and high and equal to the lateral aspect of the claspers in area. Each clasper with a rounded base and a short, apical blade which is twisted into an almost vertical position and appears somewhat beaked in the lateral view. Tenth tergite entirely membranous, consisting of concave and inconspicuous membranous folds. Cerci triangular, small and bearing long setae. Aedeagus membranous and tubular and containing a pair of sclerotized rods.

FEMALE.—In size, color and general structure similar to male. Subgenital plate, fig. 950, with a low, narrow mesal lobe and wide, sloping lateral lobes; bursa copulatrix

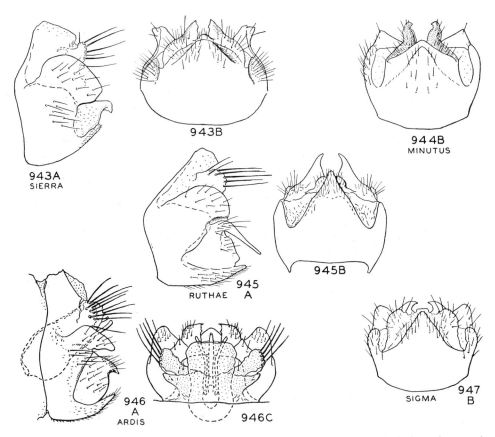

Figs. 943–947.—*Oligophlebodes*, male genitalia. *A, B* and *C*, respectively lateral, ventral and dorsal aspects.

with dorsal portion only slightly flared at apex, ventral portion fusiform, narrow and pointed at apex.

Holotype, male. — Yosemite National Park, California, along Dana Fork, Toulumne River, elevation 8,500 feet: Aug. 15, 1935, H. J. Rayner.

Allotype, female.—Same data as for holotype.

Paratypes.—Same data as for holotype, 6 ♂.

Oligophlebodes ruthae new species

The horizontal claspers place this species in the same group as *sigma* and *ardis*; it differs from both of these in the long apex of the claspers and the long and narrow mesal projection of the ninth sternite. The female may be distinguished by the scalloped lateral lobes of the ninth sternite.

MALE.—Length 8 mm. Color mostly

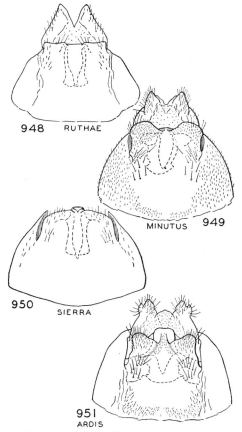

948   RUTHAE

MINUTUS   949

950   SIERRA

951
ARDIS

Figs. 948–951.—*Oligophlebodes*, female genitalia.

dark brown, the legs below coxae yellowish and the wings pale brown without conspicuous markings. In life the insect appears black with brown wings. General structure typical for genus. Genitalia as in fig. 945. Ninth segment reduced to a linelike collar on the dorsum, expanded into a broad lateral portion and a long, tonguelike and angular ventral projection; the lateral margin bears a platelike process which is large and confluent at outer margin with the posterior margin of the segment below it. Apical blade of clasper long, sharp, sometimes sinuate and with a slightly expanded base. Tenth tergite consisting of indefinite membranous folds. Cerci small with abundant, long setae. Aedeagus cylindrical and tubular, with a pair of internal sclerotized rods in addition to the central style.

FEMALE.—Similar to male in size, color and general structure. Subgenital plate, fig. 948, with a low mesal process and with lateral lobes which are nearly truncate but which have a distinct emargination in the middle of the posterior margin. Bursa copulatrix with dorsal lobe expanded at extreme tip, ventral lobe fairly wide, scarcely narrowed at base but tapering to a long, sharp point at apex. Tenth tergite with lateral lobes sclerotized dorsally.

Holotype, male.—Roe's Creek, Glacier National Park, Montana: July 12, 1940, H. H. & J. A. Ross.

Allotype, female.—Same data as for holotype.

Paratypes.—MONTANA: Same data as for holotype, 23 ♂, 10 ♀; same data but SUNRIFT CREEK, 1 ♂; same data but east of SUMMIT, Logan Pass, 1 ♂.

Psilotreta Banks

Accumulated material in this genus indicates that there are five Nearctic species readily separated by characters of the male genitalia. After the discovery of these characters I was very fortunate in being able to restudy the Banks and Hagen types in the Museum of Comparative Zoology; in addition, the redescription by Betten & Mosely (1940) of Walker's *indecisa* has cleared up the identity of that species. It is now possible to place all the names in literature except for *dissimilis* and *borealis*. Insufficient material is available to tabulate the females and immature stages. A complete list of synonymy is given in the check list.

KEY TO NEARCTIC SPECIES

Males

1. Tenth tergite forming a pair of short, broad, sclerotized plates, fig. 952... ....**rufa** (Hagen)
   Tenth tergite forming a pair of long, bladelike plates well separated on the meson, fig. 954.............. 2
2. Apical processes of tenth tergite long and sinuate, basal hook arcuate but not curled, fig. 953......**amera** (Ross)
   Apical processes of tenth tergite wide and only slightly sinuate, basal hook curled, fig. 954.................. 3
3. Apical segment of clasper with a very long, stout mesal tooth, fig. 954... ....**labida** n. sp.

Apical segment of clasper with several short teeth but without a long mesal one, fig. 955..................... 4
4. Ninth segment with a long, slender style running beneath cerci; apical segment of clasper short, fig. 955... ....**frontalis** Banks
   Ninth segment without any process of this kind; apical segment of clasper long, armed with many teeth, fig. 956................**indecisa** (Walker)

Psilotreta rufa (Hagen)

This species has been placed in various genera, but the genitalia clearly indicate its affinity with other members of the genus *Psilotreta*. The species *connexa*, described

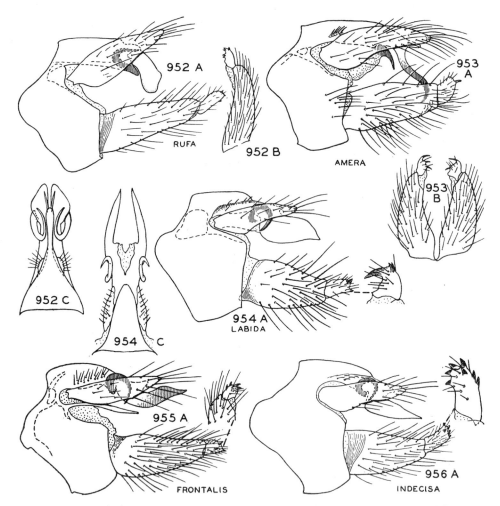

Figs. 952–956.—*Psilotreta*, male genitalia. *A*, lateral aspect; *B*, clasper, caudal aspect; *C*, tenth tergite.

by Banks in *Astoplectron* Banks, also belongs here. I have studied cleared preparations of both Banks' and Hagen's types, and they appear identical.

Psilotreta frontalis Banks

There is considerable variation in the shape of the apical blades of the tenth tergite, the holotype of *gameta* representing the narrow extreme, fig. 955, and the holotype of *frontalis* representing a wide extreme in which these blades are nearly as wide as in fig. 954. Intergrades in addition to both extremes have been taken at nearby localities in New York.

Psilotreta labida new species

The shape of cerci and tenth tergite indicates that this species is most closely related to *indecisa* but is readily separated from that and other species of the genus by characters given in the preceding key.

MALE.—Length 12 mm. Color almost entirely black, the legs and mouthparts with lighter areas of grayish brown; wings grayish brown, fairly dark, with very small and irregularly scattered lighter dots. Maxillary palpi with first two segments short, the second with a long mesal brush which usually extends the full length of, and is usually appressed to, the third segment; third segment as long as the first and second combined, fourth half the length of third, and fifth slightly longer than third; the fifth also has a basal brush of long hair which extends almost the full length of the segment and gives it a bushy appearance. Male genitalia as in fig. 954. Ninth segment deep, narrowed at the point of insertion of the cerci, and forming a long, narrow dorsal tongue which is fused with the tenth. Tenth tergite with its apex divided into a pair of long, curved, pointed wide sclerites; at the base of each of these is a curled hook. Cerci long and somewhat pointed, widest near base. Claspers with basal segment robust and fairly short, apical segment also fairly short and small, with two or three short, sclerotized lateral teeth and a long, sharp mesal tooth. Aedeagus tubular and curved, typical for genus.

FEMALE.—In size, color and general structure similar to male. Maxillary palpi of approximately the same proportion as in the male but without brushes. Genitalia

simple, without processes or conspicuous characters.

Holotype, male.—Cedar River near Indian Lake, Adirondack State Park, New York: June 20, 1941, Frison & Ross.

Allotype, female.—Same data as for holotype.

Paratypes.—MARYLAND.—GARRETT COUNTY: June 6, 1931, J. H. Roberts, 1 ♂, UM.

NEW HAMPSHIRE.—Whitcherville Brook near BENTON: June 21, 1941, Frison & Ross, 2 ♂.

NEW YORK.—Same data as for holotype, 2 ♂, 1 ♀. Small creek near TAHAWUS, Adirondack State Park: June 20, 1941, Frison & Ross, 1 ♂. McLEAN, Seaver County: June 13, 1935, M. E. Davis, 1 ♂.

PENNSYLVANIA.—Penn's Creek, UNION COUNTY: May 16, 1938, C. M. Wetzel, 1 ♂. MONROE COUNTY, near Swiftwater: 1928, F. R. Nevin (Lot 258), 2 ♂, 1 ♀.

TENNESSEE.—ELKMONT, fork of Little Pigeon River: May 27, 1934, T. H. Frison, 1 ♂.

VIRGINIA.—CURLES NECK BRIDGE: April 19, 1938, M. E. Davis & D. T. Ries, 1 ♂.

Leptocella tavara new species

The claspers, fig. 957, which have a large, truncate apical head and a moderate-sized basal flap, readily distinguish this species

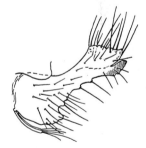

Fig. 957.—*Leptocella tavara*, claspers.

from all other Nearctic members of the genus. The well-developed basal flap will separate the species from *exquisita* and *candida*, these two having no flap; all other species of the genus have the flap much larger, as in fig. 752.

MALE.—Length 13.5 mm. Head and body light brown to straw colored, the legs below coxae almost white; head, body and legs clothed with white hair. Wing membrane transparent, the color pattern formed entirely by hair; the entire front wing white with small, yellowish linear spots situated fairly closely along every vein and with the apical fringe brownish; the contrast between the white and yellowish-brown spots small, so that the wing appears only indistinctly speckled. General structure typical for genus. Eyes small.

Male genitalia in general typical for the genus, with ninth segment with long, somewhat hoodshaped dorso-mesal portion and a long pair of finger-like processes below this. Tenth tergite long and projected, apex upturned and narrow. From near base of tenth tergite arise a pair of curved, "swan's neck" organs which are expanded at apex into a reticulate plate. Claspers, fig. 957, with the base expanded into a moderate-sized flap, above this constricted into a fairly wide neck, divided at apex into a spoonlike subapical mesal lobe and an apical, lateral area which projects some distance above subapical lobe and is fringed with very long setae; between the bases of the clasper arise a pair of medium length curved filaments, each with two or three long setae at apex. Aedeagus mostly membranous and with a spoonlike ventral plate.

FEMALE.—In size, color and general structure similar to male. Abdomen bright green. Genitalia typical for genus.

Holotype, male.—Chiefland, Florida: July 17, 1938, W. Stehr.

Allotype, female.—Same data as for holotype.

Paratypes.—FLORIDA.—Same data as for holotype, 6 ♂, 3 ♀. WINTER PARK: March 25, E. M. Davis, 1 ♂; March 26, E. M. Davis, 3 ♂; April 9, E. M. Davis, 1 ♂. TAVARES, Lake County: March 23, 1936, F. N. Young, 3 ♂.

Helicopsyche Hagen

Many collections of this genus, especially from the southwestern states, have considerably simplified the picture of the Nearctic species. It is clear that *borealis* is very widespread over most of the North American continent; Banks' species *arizonensis* proves to be the female of *mexicana*; and a third species common to both Mexico and the United States appears to be undescribed. I have examined the types of all available Antillean species, and these seem to be quite distinct from the continental species.

KEY TO NEARCTIC MALES

1. Claspers with apical corner produced into a sharp, triangular point, fig. 958................................. 2
   Claspers with apical corner rounded, figs. 960, 961.................... 3
2. Sclerotized mesal projection of sixth

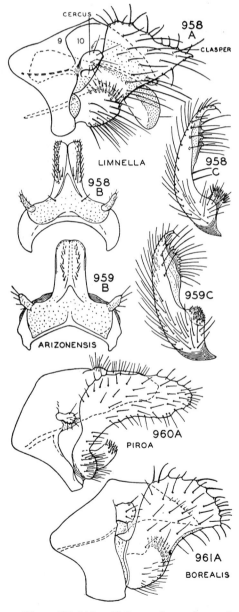

Figs. 958–961.—*Helicopsyche*, male genitalia. *A*, lateral aspect; *B*, tenth tergite; *C*, claspers, caudal aspect.

sternite black, as long as or longer than the sternite; claspers with a small, somewhat stalked cluster of spicules upon mesal face at base, fig. 958...............**limnella** Ross
Sclerotized mesal projection of sixth sternite yellowish, only about half as long as the sternite; claspers with a large, cushion-like pad of spicules upon mesal face at base, fig. 959...
...................**mexicana** Banks
3. Claspers angled and shaped like a boomerang, fig. 960.......**piroa** n. sp.
Claspers only slightly curved, broad and spatulate, fig. 961............
...................**borealis** Hagen

Helicopsyche mexicana Banks

The type of *mexicana* agrees perfectly with males taken from near the type locality of *arizonensis*. The females of this species have the first antennal segment longer than in related forms, which further identifies the type of *arizonensis*. This difference, however, is quite relative, and its use should be based on actual comparison of specimens.

In addition to various localities in Mexico, this species is now known from springs at Frijole, Texas, and from Oak Creek Canyon, Arizona, as well as Nogales, Arizona, the type locality of *arizonensis*. These United States localities are all situated in arid mountain country typical of large areas in Mexico.

Helicopsyche piroa new species

This species appears most closely related to *borealis* but may be readily separated from it by the slender, L-shaped claspers.

MALE.—Length 6.5 mm. Head, body and appendages straw color to yellowish brown,

the wings with a few irregular, colorless spots, and a short, colorless bar along the cord; rows of spines along middle legs, black. General structure, including shape of palps, wing venation, spur count, typical for genus. Sixth sternite with a long, sclerotized black spur which is about as long as the segment, slightly flattened and spatulate. Male genitalia as in fig. 960. Ninth segment with ventral half reduced to a narrow band, the dorsal portion merging with the tenth tergite. Tenth tergite about twice as long as wide, fairly deep and with a dorso-lateral ridge running its entire length and bearing a regular row of medium length setae. Claspers L-shaped, with a short, narrow vertical base and a long, wide horizontal apex which is rounded at tip; at the base of the mesal face is a short projection bearing a row of spicules along its apical margin. Aedeagus cylindrical and slightly curved, the apex subdivided into upper and lower pairs of membranous folds.

FEMALE.—Similar in size, color and general structure to male. Third and fourth sternites with a central reticulate area. Remainder of abdomen typical for genus.

Holotype, male.—San Antonio, Texas, along San Antonio River: Aug. 10, 1939, Harold Alexander.

Allotype, female.—Hacienda Vista Hermosa, Villa Santiago, Nuevo Leon, Mexico, Hoogstraal & Knight.

Paratypes.—Same data as for allotype, 6♂, 2♀.

In addition to the above records are larvae of this species taken by Mr. Hoogstraal in a spring at Sabinas Hidalgo, Nuevo Leon, Mexico. This species makes a case which is exactly like that of other species in the genus. The larva is very similar in appearance to that of *borealis*.

This list is presented chiefly as an aid in placing to genera and families, as defined in this report, those species which are not treated specifically in the preceding pages. Following is an explanation of the form used in the list. Each species line has these items in this order: the species name, the describer, the place of original description (indicated by date and page reference); in some cases, the species has, in addition, the genus in which it was originally described (if different from that under which it appears here). The item "**P. 00**" indicates that the species is treated in this report on that page. If not so treated, a brief summary of range is indicated by key letters: if the species is known from only one or two states, these are listed, standard abbreviations being used; if from more, the general section of the continent is indicated in which the species is known, abbreviations of the cardinal directions and their combinations being given; e.g., E for East, W for West, NE for Northeast. Trans. indicates transcontinental; N. Am. signifies North America, but the exact location not determined. Other abbreviations are unid. for unidentified, emend. for emendation, *N. syn.* for new synonymy, unassoc. for unassociated.

Synonyms are listed in italics under genus or species.

References are included in the bibliography.

RHYACOPHILIDAE

Rhyacophila Pictet 1834
atrata Banks 1911:351. E
valuma Milne 1936:100. B. C.
vobara Milne 1936:94. B. C.
pellisa Ross 1938d:118. W
 doddsi Ling 1938:61. *N. syn.*
minora Banks 1924:444. E
manistee Ross 1938a:104. Mich.
blarina Ross 1941b:36. Oreg.
melita Ross 1938a:104. NE
acropedes Banks 1914:201. W, N
grandis Banks 1911:350. W
 vohrna Milne 1936:94. *N. syn.*
vao Milne 1936:93. W
 vu Milne 1936:93. *N. syn.*
brunnea Banks 1911:352. W
ledra Ross 1939a:65. **P. 37**
carolina Banks 1911:353. E
 gordoni Sibley 1926a:79
fenestra Ross 1938a:102. **P. 36**
teddyi Ross 1939b:628. N. C., Tenn.
kiamichi Ross. **P. 37**
carpenteri Milne 1936:98. E
nigrita Banks 1907a:132. E
mycta Ross 1941b:38. N. C.
montana Carpenter 1933:42. N. C., Tenn.
lobifera Betten 1934:131. **P. 35**
perda Ross 1938a:105. Wash.
nevadensis Banks 1924:443. Nev.
rotunda Banks 1924:443. W
norcuta Ross 1938d:117. W
 novarotunda Ling 1938:61. *N. syn.*
vaccua Milne 1936:94. W
 complicata Ling 1938:60. *N. syn.*
 bruesi Milne & Milne 1940:154. *N. syn.*
vagrita Milne 1936:91. Alta., B. C.
unimaculata Denning 1941a:198. B. C.
verrula Milne 1936:90. W
 oregonensis Ling 1938:62. *N. syn.*
viquaea Milne 1936:92. Oreg.
visor Milne 1936:101. B. C.

vofixa Milne 1936:95. Alta.
harmstoni Ross. **P. 268**
iranda Ross 1938a:103. Wash.
alberta Banks 1918:21. NW
angelita Banks 1911:352. W
 bipartita Banks 1914:201
basalis Banks 1911:352. W
oreta Ross 1941b:39. Utah, Oreg.
glaberrima Ulmer 1907b:85. **P. 35**
 fairchildi Banks 1930a:130
 andrea Betten 1934:127
coloradensis Banks 1905b:10. W
 stigmatica Banks 1904a:108, preoccupied
 anomala Banks 1924:444
bifila Banks 1914:201. W
fuscula (Walker) 1852:10; Neuronia. **P. 36**
hyalinata Banks 1905b:10. W
vocala Milne 1936:100. B. C.
invaria (Walker) 1852:101; Polycentropus. E
 luctuosa Banks 1911:351
banksi Ross. **P. 268**
ecosa Ross 1941b:37. Oreg.
torva Hagen 1861:296. E
 terminata Banks 1907a:132.
 vinura Milne 1936:100. *N. syn.*
vaefes Milne 1936:96. B. C.
vedra Milne 1936:97. Oreg.
phryganea Ross 1941b:40. Calif., Oreg.
vemna Milne 1936:92. Wash.
vibox Milne 1936:101. **P. 36**
vepulsa Milne 1936:96. Oreg., B. C.
vetina Milne 1936:91. Wash.
vujuna Milne 1936:99. Oreg.
vuphipes Milne 1936:99. N. Y., Ont.
vuzana Milne 1936:97. Oreg.
gemona Ross 1938d:117. Wash.
betteni Ling 1938:59. Calif.
californica Ling 1938:60. Calif.
formosa Banks 1911:353. Unid. ♀; N. J.
mainensis Banks 1911:354. Unid. ♀; Maine
pacifica Banks 1895:316. Unid. ♀; Wash.
soror Provancher 1878:135. Unid.; Que.

Atopsyche Banks 1905*b*
   tripunctata Banks 1905*b*:17.   Ariz.

Palaeagapetus Ulmer 1912
   nearcticus Banks 1936*a*:265.   Wash.
   celsus (Ross) 1938*a*:111; Paragapetus.   N. H.,
       Tenn.

Glossosoma Curtis 1834
   Mystrophora Klapálek 1892
   alascense Banks 1900*b*:472.   W and NW
   pyroxum Ross 1941*b*:42.   Oreg.
   parvulum Banks 1904*a*:108.   W
   montana Ross 1941*b*:42.   Mont.
   penitum Banks 1914:202.   W
   idaho Ross 1941*b*:41.   Idaho
   traviatum Banks 1936*a*:266.   W
   ventrale Banks 1904*a*:109.   W
   velona Ross 1938*a*:109.   W
   excita Ross 1938*a*:109.   Oreg.
   oregonense Ling 1938:62.   Oreg.
   nigrior Banks 1911:355.   E
       unica (Denning) 1942:46; Eomystra.   *N.*
       syn.
   lividum (Hagen) 1861:295; Tinodes.   E
   verdona Ross 1938*a*:110.   W
   intermedium (Klapálek) 1892:19; Mystro-
       phora.   **P. 39**
   americanum Banks 1897:31.   Unid. ♀; N. H.

Anagapetus Ross 1938*a*
   debilis Ross 1938*a*:108.   W

Agapetus Curtis 1834
   malleatus Banks 1914:202.   Calif.
   marlo Milne 1936:108.   Calif.
   minutus Sibley 1926*a*:79.   N. Y.
   boulderensis Milne 1936:108.   Colo.
   artesus Ross 1938*a*:106.   **P. 40**
   vireo Ross 1941*b*:43.   Ga., Tenn.
   tomus Ross 1941*b*:44.   Ga.
   pinatus Ross 1938*a*:107.   Tenn.
   celatus McLachlan 1871:139.   Calif.
   illini Ross 1938*a*:106.   **P. 40**
   medicus Ross 1938*a*:107.   **P. 40**
   rossi Denning 1941*a*:200.   NE
   crasmus Ross 1939*a*:66.   **P. 40**
   iridis Ross.   **P. 269**.
   walkeri (Betten & Mosely) 1940:8; Syna-
       gapetus.   Unid. ♀; Ont.

Protoptila Banks 1904*d*
   ?Clymene Chambers 1873, preoccupied
   maculata (Hagen) 1861:296; Beraea?   **P. 43**
       lloydi Mosely 1934*b*:151
   palina Ross 1941*b*:46.   **P. 43**
   lega Ross 1941*b*:48.   **P. 43**
   alexanderi Ross 1941*b*:48.   Tex.
   tenebrosa (Walker) 1852:134; Hydroptila.
       P. 43
   coloma Ross 1941*b*:45.   W
   jeanae Ross 1938*a*:112.   E
   cantha Ross 1938*a*:113.   NE to W

thoracica Ross 1938*a*:114.   Wyo.
erotica Ross 1938*a*:113.   **P. 44**
balmorhea Ross 1941*b*:45.   Tex.
?aegerfasciella (Chambers) 1873:114;   Clymene.   Unid.; Ky.
?viridiventris (Say) 1823:160;   Phryganea.
   Unid.; Ohio

PHILOPOTAMIDAE

Trentonius Betten & Mosely 1940
   distinctus (Walker) 1852:104; Philopotamus.
       P. 47
       americanus (Banks) 1895:316; Philopota-
           mus
   pallidipes (Banks) 1936*a*:267; Philopotamus.
       W
   aequalis (Banks) 1924:450;   Philopotamus.
       W
   dorcus (Ross) 1938*a*:132; Philopotamus. W
       oregonensis (Ling) 1938:63; Philopotamus
   novusamericanus (Ling) 1938:63;   Philopot-
       amus.   Calif.

Dolophilus McLachlan 1868
   Paragapetus Banks 1914
   Dolophiliella Banks 1930*b*.
   moestus (Banks) 1914:202;   Paragapetus.
       P. 47
       breviatus Banks 1914:254
   major Banks 1914:254.   N. C., Tenn.
   gabriella (Banks) 1930*b*:230; Dolophiliella.
       W
   occideus Ross 1938*a*:134.   Oreg.
   shawnee Ross 1938*a*:133.   **P. 46**
   arizonensis Ling 1938:63.   SW
   cruzensis Ling 1938:64.   Calif.
   strotus Ross 1938*d*:118.   Okla.
   anillus Ross 1941*b*:50.   B. C.

Chimarra Stephens 1829
   Chimarrha Burmeister *et al.*, emend.
   aterrima Hagen 1861:297.   **P. 50**
   elia Ross.   **P. 269**
   feria Ross 1941*b*:51.   **P. 50**
   angustipennis Banks 1903*a*:242.   Tex., Ark.
   socia Hagen 1861:297.   **P. 51**
       femoralis (Banks) 1911:358; Wormaldia
   obscura (Walker) 1852:121; Beraea?   **P. 51**
       plutonis Banks 1911:358; Wormaldia
       lucia Betten 1934:175
   florida Ross.   **P. 270**
   argentella Ulmer 1906*a*:92.   Tropical Am.
   utahensis Ross 1938*a*:134.   W
       idahoensis Ling 1938:64
   texana Banks 1920:360.   Unid. ♀; Tex.

PSYCHOMYIIDAE

Phylocentropus Banks 1907*a*
   Acrocentropus Betten 1934
   lucidus (Hagen) 1861:294; Polycentropus.
       P. 56

placidus (Banks) 1905*b*:15; Holocentropus.
P. 55
maximus Vorhies 1909:711
carolinus Carpenter 1933:43. N. C.
auriceps (Banks) 1905*a*:218; Plectrocnemia.
N. C.
rabilis Milne 1936:84. *N. syn.*

Neureclipsis McLachlan 1864
bimaculatus (Linnaeus) 1758:548; Phryganea. **P. 57**
crepuscularis (Walker) 1852:87; Brachycentrus. **P. 57**
parvulus Banks 1907*b*:163
validus (Walker) 1852:100; Polycentropus.
P. 58
dubitans (Walker) 1852:113; Hydropsyche
signatus (Banks) 1897:30; Polycentropus

Polycentropus Curtis 1835*a*
cinereus Hagen 1861:293. **P. 67**
canadensis Banks 1897:31
flavicornis (Banks) 1907*b*:162; Holocentropus
pallescens (Banks) 1930*b*:231; Plectrocnemia
lutea (Betten) 1934:219; Plectrocnemia
nascotius Ross 1941*b*:73. **P. 68**
remotus Banks 1911:359. **P. 67**
albipunctus (Banks) 1930*a*:131; Plectrocnemia. NE
iculus Ross 1941*b*:74. Que.
variegatus Banks 1900*a*:259. Wash., B.C.
colei Ross 1941*b*:76. Tenn.
crassicornis Walker 1852:101. **P. 64**
adironica (Banks) 1914:256; Plectrocnemia
australis (Banks) 1907*a*:131; Plectrocnemia
aureolus (Banks) 1930*a*:130; Plectrocnemia.
P. 64
clinei (Milne) 1936:87; Plectrocnemia. NE
charlesi Ross 1941*b*:74. Tex.
halidus Milne 1936:86. N. Mex.
arizonensis Banks 1905*b*:16. Ariz.
centralis Banks 1914:258. **P. 64**
elarus Ross. **P. 65**
carolinensis Banks 1905*a*:217. **P. 66**
pixi Ross. **P. 66**
maculatus Banks 1908*a*:65. **P. 65**
pentus Ross 1941*b*:71. **P. 65**
confusus Hagen 1861:293. **P. 65**
vigilatrix Navás 1933:111; Plectrocnemia.
Unid. ♀; Mass.
interruptus (Banks) 1914:257; Holocentropus. **P. 69**
orotus (Banks) 1914:257; Holocentropus
longus (Banks) 1914:258; Holocentropus
flavus (Banks) 1908*a*:66; Holocentropus.
P. 68
grellus (Milne) 1936:87; Holocentropus. NE
glacialis (Ross) 1938*a*:135; Holocentropus.
P. 68
melanae (Ross) 1938*a*:136; Holocentropus.
Mich.

Nyctiophylax Brauer 1865
vestitus (Hagen) 1861:293; Polycentropus.
P. 70
affinis (Banks) 1897:30; Polycentropus
moestus Banks 1911:359
uncus Ross. **P. 70**

Cyrnellus Banks 1913
marginalis (Banks) 1930*b*:231; Nyctiophylax. **P. 71**
zernyi Mosely 1934*a*:142

Cernotina Ross 1938*a*
pallida (Banks) 1904*d*:214; Cyrnus. **P. 73**
calcea Ross 1938*a*:137. **P. 72**
oklahoma Ross 1938*a*:137. Okla.
spicata Ross 1938*a*:138. **P. 73**
ohio Ross 1939*b*:628. **P. 73**
astera Ross 1941*b*:76. Tex.
fraterna (Banks) 1905*b*:17; Cyrnus. Unid.
♀; D. C.

Lype McLachlan 1879
diversa (Banks) 1914:253; Psychomyia.
P. 74
griselda Betten 1934:229. *N. syn.*

Tinodes Stephens 1829
consueta McLachlan 1871:138. Calif.

Psychomyia Pictet 1834
Quissa Milne 1936
flavida Hagen 1861:294. **P. 75**
pulchella Banks 1899:217
moesta Banks 1907*a*:131
nomada (Ross) 1938*a*:138; Psychomyiella.
P. 75
lumina (Ross) 1938*a*:139; Psychomyiella.
Oreg.
?parva (Walker) 1852:134; ?Hydroptila.
Type lost. Ont.

HYDROPSYCHIDAE

Parapsyche Betten 1934
apicalis (Banks) 1908*b*:266; Arctopsyche.
P. 83
elsis Milne 1936:66. W
brevipennis (Ling) 1938:64; Arctopsyche.
N. syn.
divergens Banks 1943:368. Calif.
cardis Ross 1938*d*:119. **P. 83**
almota Ross 1938*d*:119. W
oregonensis (Ling) 1938:65; Arctopsyche

Arctopsyche McLachlan 1868
ladogensis (Kolenati) 1859*b*:201; Aphelocheira. Arctic Am.
grandis (Banks) 1900*a*:258; Hydropsyche. W
phryganoides Banks 1918:21
irrorata Banks 1905*a*:217. **P. 83**
californica Ling 1938:65. Calif.
inermis Banks 1943:368. Colo.

Diplectrona Westwood 1840
  modesta Banks 1908*b*:266.   **P. 84**
  californica Banks 1914:253.   Calif.
  doringa Milne 1936:68.   Unid.; N. C.

Aphropsyche Ross 1941*b*
  aprilis Ross 1941*b*:78.   **P. 83**

Oropsyche Ross 1941*b*
  howellae Ross 1941*b*:79.   **P. 83**

Homoplectra Ross 1938*d*
  nigripennis (Banks) 1911:358; Diplectrona.
    Calif.
  alseae Ross 1938*d*:120.   Oreg.
  oaklandensis (Ling) 1938:66; Diplectrona.
    Calif.

Potamyia Banks 1900*a*
  flava (Hagen) 1861:285; Macronema.   **P. 85**
    kansensis (Banks) 1905*b*:15; Hydropsyche

Smicridea McLachlan 1871
  fasciatella McLachlan 1871:136.   **P. 85**
    dispar (Banks) 1905*b*:16; Polycentropus
    divisa (Banks) 1903*a*:244; Hydropsyche

Rhyacophylax Müller 1879
    Pellopsyche Banks 1903*b*
  signatus (Banks) 1903*b*:243; Pellopsyche.
    SW, Mexico

Hydropsyche Pictet 1834
  slossonae Banks 1905*b*:14.   **P. 99**
  ventura Ross 1941*b*:92.   Ont.
  oslari Banks 1905*b*:13.   W
    partita Banks 1914:252
  protis Ross 1938*d*:120.   Utah
  venada Ross 1941*b*:91.   SW
  tana Ross 1938*a*:151.   Mont.
  amblis Ross 1938*d*:120.   Oreg.
  morosa Hagen 1861:287.   **P. 98**
    chlorotica Hagen 1861:290
  walkeri Betten & Mosely 1940:23.   **P. 96**
    maculicornis Walker 1852:113, preoccupied
  piatrix Ross 1938*a*:148.   **P. 97**
  vexa Ross 1938*a*:148.   **P. 97**
  recurvata Banks 1914:253.   **P. 99**
    codona Betten 1934:187
  cockerelli Banks 1905*b*:14.   W
  centra Ross 1938*a*:150.   Wash.
  bifida Banks 1905*b*:15.   **P. 97**
  cheilonis Ross 1938*a*:149.   **P. 98**
  bronta Ross 1938*a*:149.   **P. 98**
  sparna Ross 1938*a*:150.   **P. 97**
  alhedra Ross 1939*a*:67.   N. C.
  riola Denning 1942:49.   Minn.
  delrio Ross 1941*b*:85.   Tex., Mexico
  occidentalis Banks 1900*a*:258.   W
    novamexicanus Banks 1904*a*:110
  californica Banks 1899:217.   W
  solex Ross.   **P. 271**
  arinale Ross 1938*a*:143.   **P. 104**

phalerata Hagen 1861:287.   **P. 102**
aerata Ross 1938*a*:144.   **P. 101**
venularis Banks 1914:252.   E
scalaris Hagen 1861:286.   **P. 106**
placoda Ross 1941*b*:87.   **P. 103**
fattigi Ross 1941*b*:88.   Ga.
simulans Ross 1938*a*:139.   **P. 104**
bidens Ross 1938*a*:142.   **P. 107**
orris Ross 1938*d*:121.   **P. 106**
  cornuta Ross 1938*a*:141, preoccupied
frisoni Ross 1938*a*:142.   **P. 105**
demora Ross 1941*b*:86.   Ga.
valanis Ross 1938*a*:144.   **P. 105**
catawba Ross 1939*a*:67.   N. C.
hageni Banks 1905*b*:14.   **P. 103**
leonardi Ross 1938*a*:145.   Mich.
incommoda Hagen 1861:290.   **P. 106**
dicantha Ross 1938*a*:146.   **P. 102**
philo Ross 1941*b*:90.   Calif.
cuanis Ross 1938*a*:147.   **P. 100**
depravata Hagen 1861:290.   **P. 100**
betteni Ross 1938*a*:146.   **P. 99**
separata Banks 1936*b*:126.   Trans.
carolina Banks 1938:77.   N. C.
alternans (Walker) 1852:104; Philopotamus.
  Unid. ♀; Ont.
  indecisus (Walker) 1852:104; Philopotamus
dubia Walker 1852:112.   Unid. ♀; N. Am. ?
reciproca (Walker) 1852:104; Philopotamus.
  Unid. ♀; N. Am. ?
confusa (Walker) 1852:112; Philopotamus.
  Unid. ♀; Arctic Am.
marqueti Navás 1907:398.   Unid.; Mont.

Cheumatopsyche Wallengren 1891
  sordida (Hagen) 1861:290; Hydropsyche.
    P. 110
  minuscula (Banks) 1907*a*:130; Hydropsyche.
    P. 110
  enonis Ross 1938*a*:153.   Wyo.
  analis (Banks) 1903*b*:243; Hydropsyche.   **P. 112**
    pettiti (Banks) 1908*b*:265; Hydropsyche
  gracilis (Banks) 1899:216; Hydropsyche.   W
    to NE
  aphanta Ross 1938*a*:151.   **P. 111**
  gyra Ross 1938*a*:154.   N. C.
  oxa Ross 1938*a*:155.   **P. 110**
  campyla Ross 1938*a*:152.   **P. 113**
  ela Denning 1942:50.   N. C.
  lasia Ross 1938*a*:154.   **P. 114**
  speciosa (Banks) 1904*d*:214; Hydropsyche.
    P. 114
  arizonensis (Ling) 1938:66; Hydropsychodes.
    Ariz., Tex.
  helma Ross 1939*a*:68.   Ky., Tenn.
  etrona Ross 1941*b*:80.   Ga.
  mollala Ross 1941*b*:81.   Oreg.
  pinaca Ross 1941*b*:82.   Ga., Va.
  burksi Ross 1941*b*:83.   **P. 113**
  mickeli Denning 1942:50.   Calif.
  pasella Ross 1941*b*:84.   **P. 113**

robusta (Walker) 1852:114; Hydropsyche.
Unid. ♀; N. Am. ?

Macronemum Burmeister 1839
Macronema Pictet 1836
zebratum (Hagen) 1861:285; Macronema.
P. 115
carolina (Banks) 1909:342; Macronema.
P. 116
transversum (Walker) 1852:114; Hydropsyche. **P. 117**
polygrammatum (McLachlan) 1871:129; Macronema.
polygrammaticum (Betten) 1934:204; Macronema. Misspelling

HYDROPTILIDAE

Leucotrichia Mosely 1934*b*
pictipes (Banks) 1911:359; Orthotrichia.
P. 120
limpia Ross. **P. 273**
notosa Ross. **P. 271**
sarita Ross. **P. 274**

Metrichia Ross 1938*c*
nigritta (Banks) 1907*b*:163; Orthotrichia.
P. 121

Dibusa Ross 1939*a*
angata Ross 1939*a*:67. **P. 121**

Agraylea Curtis 1834
Hydrorchestria Kolenati 1848
multipunctata Curtis 1834:217. **P. 122**
signata (Banks) 1904*d*:215; Allotrichia
fraterna Banks 1907*b*:164
flavida (Banks) 1907*b*:164; Allotrichia. *N. syn.*
saltesea Ross 1938*a*:114. Mont.
costello Ross 1941*a*:15. Ont.

Ithytrichia Eaton 1873
clavata Morton 1905:67. **P. 124**
mazon Ross. **P. 124**

Tascobia Ross. **P. 124**
brustia (Ross) 1938*a*:115; Stactobia. W
delira (Ross) 1938*a*:115; Stactobia. N and E
palmata (Ross) 1938*a*:116; Stactobia. **P. 125**

Ochrotrichia Mosely 1934*b*
Polytrichia Sibley 1926*b*, preoccupied
weddleae Ross. **P. 274**
xena (Ross) 1938*a*:122; Polytrichia. **P. 130**
unio (Ross) 1941*b*:56; Polytrichia. **P. 129**
capitana Ross. **P. 275**
felipe Ross. **P. 275**
tarsalis (Hagen) 1861:275; Hydroptila. **P. 130**
shawnee (Ross) 1938*a*:120; Polytrichia. **P. 131**
anisca (Ross) 1941*b*:58; Polytrichia. **P. 131**

contorta (Ross) 1941*b*:60; Polytrichia. **P. 131**
stylata (Ross) 1938*a*:120; Polytrichia. W, Okla.
oregona (Ross) 1938*a*:121; Polytrichia. Oreg.
spinosa (Ross) 1938*a*:121; Polytrichia. **P. 132**
eliaga (Ross) 1941*b*:57; Polytrichia. **P. 132**
arva (Ross) 1941*b*:58; Polytrichia. **P. 132**
mono (Ross) 1941*b*:55; Polytrichia. Calif.
logana (Ross) 1941*b*:54; Polytrichia. Utah
lometa (Ross) 1941*b*:55; Polytrichia. N. Mex., Utah
confusa (Morton) 1905:69; Ithytrichia. **P. 133**
riesi Ross. **P. 132**

Oxyethira Eaton 1873
Loxotrichia Mosely 1937
Dampfitrichia Mosely 1937
pallida (Banks) 1904*d*:215; Orthotrichia. **P. 137**
viminalis Morton 1905:71
dualis Morton 1905:71. **P. 139**
forcipata Mosely 1934*b*:153. N. Y.
grisea Betten 1934:162. **P. 138**
novasota Ross. **P. 138**
michiganensis Mosely 1934*b*:153. N. Y.
coercens Morton 1905:70. **P. 137**
serrata Ross 1938*a*:117. **P. 136**
araya Ross 1941*a*:15. N. B.
aeola Ross 1938*a*:117. W
verna Ross 1938*a*:118. **P. 139**
zeronia Ross 1941*a*:15. **P. 139**
ulmeri (Mosely) 1937:169; Dampfitrichia. Tex., Mexico
aculea Ross 1941*b*:53. Tex.
azteca (Mosely) 1937:165; Loxotrichia. SW
glasa (Ross) 1941*b*:70; Loxotrichia. Okla.

Orthotrichia Eaton 1873
americana Banks 1904*b*:116. **P. 140**
dorsalis (Banks) 1904*d*:216; Oxyethira. *N. syn.*
brachiata Morton 1905:70. *N. syn.*
cristata Morton 1905:75. **P. 141**

Hydroptila Dalman 1819
Phrixocoma Eaton 1873
spatulata Morton 1905:66. **P. 148**
vala Ross 1938*a*:123. **P. 148**
armata Ross 1938*a*:123. **P. 147**
amoena Ross 1938*a*:124. **P. 150**
hamata Morton 1905:67. **P. 142**
ampoda Ross 1941*a*:16. N. S., Que.
tortosa Ross 1938*a*:125. Va.
virgata Ross 1938*a*:125. **P. 148**
rono Ross 1941*b*:66. W
dentata Ross 1938*a*:126. Va.
xella Ross 1941*b*:65. **P. 148**
grandiosa Ross 1938*a*:126. **P. 151**
delineata Morton 1905:66. **P. 151**

waskesia Ross. **P. 276**
gunda Milne 1936:76. Va.
albicornis Hagen 1861:275. **P. 151**
ajax Ross 1938*a*:127. **P. 153**
scolops Ross 1938*a*:128. **P. 152**
melia Ross 1938*a*:128. Okla.
berneri Ross 1941*b*:67. Fla.
strepha Ross 1941*b*:68. Pa.
perdita Morton 1905:67. **P. 153**
pecos Ross 1941*b*:64. N. Mex.
consimilis Morton 1905:65. **P. 153**
arctia Ross 1938*a*:129. Idaho
angusta Ross 1938*a*:130. **P. 152**
protera Ross 1938*a*:131. Okla.
argosa Ross 1938*a*:131. W
xera Ross 1938*a*:132. Idaho
xoncla Ross 1941*a*:16. N. S.
waubesiana Betten 1934:160. **P. 150**
nicoli Ross 1941*b*:69. N. S.
acadia Ross 1941*b*:63. N. S.
salmo Ross 1941*b*:66. Wis.
maculata (Banks) 1904*b*:116; Allotrichia. E
    transversus Banks 1907*b*:163
icona Mosely 1937:161. Okla., Mexico
perplexa Mosely 1924: 293. Unid. ♂

Neotrichia Morton 1905
    Cyllene Chambers 1873, preoccupied
    Exitrichia Mosely 1937
    Dolotrichia Mosely 1937
    Guerrotrichia Mosely 1937
    Lorotrichia Mosely 1937
collata Morton 1905:72. **P. 159**
minutisimella (Chambers) 1873:125; Cyl-
    lene. **P. 157**
falca Ross 1938*a*:119. **P. 159**
vibrans Ross 1938*a*:119. **P. 159**
caxima (Mosely) 1937:179; Guerrotrichia.
    Tex., Mexico
okopa Ross 1939*b*:629. **P. 158**
osmena Ross. **P. 278**
sonora Ross. **P. 277**
edalis Ross 1941*b*:62. **P. 158**
riegeli Ross 1941*b*:61. **P. 159**
kitae Ross 1941*b*:60. **P. 158**

Mayatrichia Mosely 1937
    ayama Mosely 1937:182. **P. 279**
    ponta Ross. **P. 278**
    acuna Ross. **P. 279**

PHRYGANEIDAE

Agrypnia Curtis 1835*b*
    Agrypnetes McLachlan 1876
    Dasystegia Wallengren 1880
    Phryganomyia Banks 1907*a*
    Prophryganea Martynov 1924
    Jyrvia Milne 1934
pagetana Curtis 1835*a*:540. Holarctic
    subsp. *nearctica* Milne 1934:3
straminea Hagen 1873:425. **P. 165**
    curvata (Banks) 1900*a*:252; Agrypnetes

obscura (Banks) 1907*a*:122; Phryganomyia
glacialis Hagen 1864:802. N and NW
    alascensis (Banks) 1900*b*:471; Asynarchus
dextra Ross 1938*a*:161. Utah
colorata Hagen 1873:424. NW and N
    bradorata (Milne) 1931:230; Prophryganea
deflata (Milne) 1931:230; Prophryganea. N
improba (Hagen) 1873:417; Phryganea. W
    and NE
    var. sackeni Banks 1943:367
macdunnoughi (Milne) 1931:230; Prophry-
    ganea. N
vestita (Walker) 1852:10; Neuronia. **P. 166**
    commixta (Walker) 1852:10; Neuronia

Fabria Milne 1934
inornata (Banks) 1907*a*:117; Neuronia. **P.
    166**
complicata (Banks) 1924:440; Ecclisomyia.
    Ont.

Oligostomis Kolenati 1848
ocelligera (Walker) 1852:8; Neuronia. **P. 167**
    stygipes (Hagen) 1873:388; Neuronia

Eubasilissa Martynov 1930
    Regina Martynov 1924, preoccupied
pardalis (Walker) 1852:7; Neuronia. **P. 168**
    var. *redmani* (Betten & Mosely) 1940:96;
    Neuronia

Banksiola Martynov 1924
concatenata (Walker) 1852:8; Neuronia.
    Fla., Ga. ˙
dossuaria (Say) 1828:44; Neuronia. NE
calva Banks 1943:366. Mass.
smithi (Banks) 1914:149; Neuronia. NE
canadensis (Banks) 1907*a*:118; Neuronia.
    Ont.
childreni (Betten & Mosely) 1940:90; Neu-
    ronia. Unid. ♀; locality unknown but may
    be N. Am.
selina Betten. **P. 169**
crotchi Banks 1944:80. B.C.

Ptilostomis Kolenati 1859*b*
angustipennis (Hagen) 1873:400; Neuronia.
    P. 174
postica (Walker) 1852:9; Neuronia. **P. 173**
ocellifera (Walker) 1852:8; Neuronia. **P. 172**
    simulans (Betten & Mosely) 1940:107;
    Neuronia. *N. syn.*
semifasciata (Say) 1828:44; Phryganea. **P.
    173**
    fusca (Walker) 1852:9; Neuronia
    dubitans (Betten & Mosely) 1940:105;
    Neuronia. *N. syn.*
kovalevskii Kolenati 1859*b*:198. Unid.;
    N. Am.

Oligotricha Rambur 1842
lapponica (Hagen) 1864:852; Neuronia.
    Alaska

Phryganea Linnaeus 1758
cinerea Walker 1852:4. **P. 175**
sayi Milne 1931:228. **P. 176**
interrupta Say 1828:44, preoccupied
californica Banks 1907a:117. Calif.

LIMNEPHILIDAE

Radema Hagen 1864
Apatidea McLachlan 1874
Apatelia Wallengren 1886
incerta (Banks) 1897:28; Enoicyla. NE
stigmatella (Zetterstedt) 1840:1066; Phry
ganea. N
pallida (Hagen) 1861:270; Apatania
frigida (McLachlan) 1867:57; Apatania
shoshone (Banks) 1924:442; Apatania. W
sorex Ross 1941b:101. Oreg.
aenicta (Ross) 1938a:162; Apatelia. Man.
nigra (Walker) 1852:83; Potamaria. NE
pictula (Banks) 1943:355; Apatania. Ariz.
hirtipes (Curtis) 1835b:64; Tinodes? Arctic
Am.
mongolica (Martynov) 1914:44; Apatania.
Alaska
arctica (Boheman) 1865:568; Goniotaulius.
Greenland
groenlandica (Kolbe) 1912:41; Apatania.
Greenland

Lepania Ross 1941b
cascada Ross 1941b:102. Oreg.

Dicosmoecus McLachlan 1875
atripes (Hagen) 1875:600; Platyphylax. W
jucundus Banks 1943:358. W
nigrescens Banks 1943:359. W
pallicornis Banks 1943:359. Calif.
gilvipes (Hagen) 1875:601; Stenophylax.
B. C.
grandis Ulmer 1905b:62. Wash.
obscuripennis Banks 1938:76. Alaska
unicolor (Banks) 1897:27; Anabolia. Wash.
occidentalis Banks 1943:362. W
alascensis Banks 1943:363. Alaska
tristis (Banks) 1900a:254; Asynarchus. Colo.
quadrinotatus (Banks) 1908a:62; Anabolia.
Newf.
coloradensis Ulmer 1905b:64. Colo.
atripennis (Banks) 1924:440. Anisogamus.
Unid. ♀; Calif.

Allocosmoecus Banks 1943
partitus Banks 1943:365. Idaho

Allomyia Banks 1916
tripunctata (Banks) 1900b:472; Apatania.
Alaska
renoa (Milne) 1935:31; Algonquina. Nev.

Parachiona Thompson 1891
pilosa Banks 1907a:121. Wash.

Platycentropus Ulmer 1905a
Hylepsyche Banks 1916
plectrus Ross 1938a:169. NE
radiatus (Say) 1824:308; Phryganea. **P. 181**
indicans (Walker) 1852:23; Limnephilus.
N. syn.
maculipennis (Kolenati) 1859b:176; Halesus. N. syn.
hostis (Hagen) 1861:266; Hallesus. N. syn.
amicus (Hagen) 1861:265; Halesus. Unassoc. ♀; La.
fraternus (Banks) 1943:349; Hylepsyche.
Mass.
indistinctus (Walker) 1852:37; Limnephilus.
NE

Glyphotaelius Stephens 1837
Glyphidotaelius Kolenati 1848
hostilis Hagen 1864:814. **P. 183**

Astenophylax Ulmer 1907b
argus (Harris) 1869:333; Phryganea. **P. 183**

Hesperophylax Banks 1916
designatus (Walker) 1852:24; Limnephilus.
P. 183
var. isolatus Banks 1943:347
magnus Banks 1918:20. Ariz.
occidentalis (Banks) 1908b:265; Platyphylax.
W
alaskensis (Banks) 1908b:265; Platyphylax
consimilis (Banks) 1900a:253; Limnephilus.
W
minutus Ling 1938:67. Calif., Oreg.
incisus Banks 1943:348. W

Ironoquia Banks 1916
parvula (Banks) 1900a:256; Chaetopterygopsis. **P. 184**

Leptophylax Banks 1900a
gracilis Banks 1900a:252. **P. 184**

Clistoronia Banks 1916
magnifica (Banks) 1899:209; Halesus. W
magnus Banks 1916:119; (misspelling)
formosa (Banks) 1900a:255; Halesus. W
maculata (Banks) 1904a:107; Dicosmoecus.
W

Grammotaulius Kolenati 1848
interrogationis (Zetterstedt) 1840:1063;
Phryganea. N
praecox Hagen 1873:451
lorettae Denning 1941b:233. Colo.
betteni Griffin 1912:18. W
sibiricus McLachlan 1874:40. Greenland

Limnephilus Leach 1815
Anabolina Banks 1903a
Apolopsyche Banks 1916
Algonquina Banks 1916
Rheophylax Sibley 1926b

gravidus Hagen 1861:257. W
  rotundatus Banks 1918:19. Calif.
vastus Hagen 1861:257. Alaska
  ?intermedius Banks 1918:20 (♀)
rillus Milne 1935:46. Nev.
oreus Milne 1935:46. Oreg.
keratus Ross 1938a:165. NE
rho Milne 1935:45. W
  bifidus (Ling) 1938:68; Clistoronia (also a
    homonym)
taronus Ross 1941b:110. Alaska
pulchellus Banks 1908a:63. Newf.
sperryi (Banks) 1943:346; Rhadicoleptus.
  Ariz.
flavicollis (Banks) 1900b:470; Asynarchus.
  Alaska
fumosus (Banks) 1900b:470; Asynarchus.
  W
caroli (Denning) 1941a:196; Anabolia. B.C.
kennicotti Banks 1920:344. N
coloradensis (Banks) 1899:208; Goniotaulius.
miser McLachlan 1875:89. Greenland
crassus Banks 1920:343. Mass.
ornatus Banks 1897:27. **P. 189**
  elegans Mosely 1929:504
morrisoni Banks 1920:343. Nev.
extractus Walker 1852:34. Ont.
hyalinus Hagen 1861:258. **P. 191**
sericeus (Say) 1824:309; Phryganea. **P. 192**
  despectus Walker 1852:31. Holarctic
  multifarius Walker 1852:32
  perforatus Walker 1852:33
  eminens Betten 1934:323
deceptus (Banks) 1899:208; Anabolia.
  Wash.
fagus Ross 1941a:18. Oreg.
abbreviatus Banks 1908b:263. Colo.
arizona Ross 1941b:108. Ariz., Wyo.
forcipatus Banks 1924:439. Alta.
modestus (Hagen) 1861:265; Anabolia. NE
nigriculus (Banks) 1908b:262; Anabolia. W
emarginatus (Banks) 1919:4; Anabolia.
  Alaska
montanus (Banks) 1907a:119; Anabolia.
  NE
curtus (Banks) 1920:345; Anabolia. NE
simplex (Banks) 1900b:469; Anabolia.
  Alaska
planifrons (Kolenati) 1848:56; Desmotaulius.
  Labr., Greenland
aldinus Ross 1941a:19. Alta.
nepus Ross 1938c:38. W
  pacificus (Banks) 1900a:254; Stenophylax,
    preoccupied
mutatus (Hagen) 1861:267; Hallesus. NE
bimaculatus Walker 1852:30. **P. 189**
sordidus (Hagen) 1861:264; Anabolia. **P. 189**
  longicercus (Denning) 1941a:195; Ana-
    bolia
ozburni (Milne) 1935:39; Arctoecia. NE
consocius Walker 1852:33. **P. 190**

medialis (Banks) 1905b:8; Colpotaulius
  ?oslari (Ling) 1938:67; Anabolia (also a
    homonym)
pacificus Banks 1899:207. W
harrimani Banks 1900b:468. W
  aequalis Banks 1914:150
moestus Banks 1908a:62. **P. 191**
  hingstoni Mosely 1929:504
cockerelli Banks 1900c:124. W
nogus Ross. **P. 281**
brevipennis (Banks) 1899:209; Stenophylax.
  W
minusculus (Banks) 1907a:120; Stenophylax. W
thorus Ross 1938a:167. Utah
externus Hagen 1861:257. Holarctic
  congener McLachlan 1875:56
  ?oslari Banks 1907a:121 (♀)
  flavostellus Banks 1918:20
  luteolus Banks 1899:207
  tersus Betten 1934:334. *N. syn.*
argenteus Banks 1914:152. NE
occidentalis Banks 1908b:264. W
ectus Ross 1941b:105. Oreg.
internalis (Banks) 1914:154; Anisogamus.
  NE
nebulosus Kirby 1837:253. N
  femoralis Kirby 1837:253
  stipatus Walker 1852:29
parvulus (Banks) 1905b:9; Stenophylax?
  NE
  pallidus (Banks) 1924:442; Apolopsyche
  roberti Banks 1930b:226. *N. syn.*
rohweri Banks 1908b:262. W
indivisus Walker 1852:34. **P. 191**
  subguttatus Walker 1852:34
rhombicus (Linnaeus) 1758:548; Phryganea.
  P. 190
  combinatus Walker 1852:28
sublunatus Provancher 1877:243. NE
  ?americanus Banks 1900a:253 (♀)
  macgillivrayi Banks 1908b:263
elongatus Banks 1920:344. W
hageni Banks 1930b:226. N
partitus Walker 1852:32. N
  adustus Banks 1920:343. *N. syn.*
sansoni Banks 1918:19. Alta.
sackeni Banks 1930b:227. N
kincaidi Banks 1900b:468. Trans.
  clausus Banks 1924:440. *N. syn.*
quaeris (Milne) 1935:41; Colpotaulius.
  Trans.
perpusillus Walker 1852:35. N and NE
  rhaeus Milne 1935:42; Colpotaulius
  merinthus Ross 1938a:166
labus Ross 1941b:105. W
lunonus Ross 1941b:107. Calif., Oreg.
acrocurvus Denning 1942:48. Minn.
acnestus Ross 1938a:164. Calif.
diversus (Banks) 1903a:244; Anabolina.
  SW
productus Banks 1914:150. Utah
lithus (Milne) 1935:40; Anabolina. SW

secludens Banks 1914:152. Trans.
tarsalis (Banks) 1920:342; Colpotaulius. W
ademus Ross 1941*a*:18. N.B.
canadensis Banks 1908*b*:264. NE
frijole Ross. **P. 282**
aretto Ross 1938*d*:121. Wash.
  tehamia (Ling) 1938:67; Colpotaulius. *N. syn.*
spinatus Banks 1914:149. W
assimilis (Banks) 1908*b*:262; Anabolia. W
janus Ross 1938*c*:37. W
  minusculus (Banks) 1924:439; Colpotaulius, preoccupied
taloga Ross 1938*a*:166. Okla., Utah
submonilifer Walker 1852:33. **P. 192**
  pudicus Hagen 1861: 262
bifidus Banks 1908*b*:263. Unassoc. ♀; W
concolor Banks 1899:207. Abdomen of type lost; Wash.
perjurus Hagen 1861:258. Abdomen of type lost; Alaska
plaga Walker 1852:35. Abdomen of type lost; Ont.
sitchensis Kolenati 1859*a*:17. Unid.; Alaska
trimaculatus Zetterstedt—a Eurasion species reported from N. Am. in error—Hagen 1861:261
subpunctulatus Zetterstedt—a Eurasion species reported from N. Am. in error—Hagen 1861:259

Chyranda Ross. **P. 283**
centralis (Banks) 1900*a*:253; Asynarchus. W
  pallidus (Banks) 1903*b*:242; Asynarchus
  signatus (Banks) 1907*a*:120; Parachiona

Stenophylax Kolenati 1848
antennatus Banks 1900*a*:254. Wash.

Clostoeca Banks 1943
sperryae Banks 1943:352. Calif.
disjunctus (Banks) 1914:156; Anisogamus. W

Philocasca Ross 1941*b*
demita Ross 1941*b*:111. Oreg.
banksi (Denning) 1941*a*:199; Anisogamus. Idaho

Halesochila Banks 1907*a*
taylori (Banks) 1904*c*:140; Halesus. B.C.

Zaporota Banks 1920
pallens Banks 1920:342. Alaska

Pycnopsyche Banks 1905*b*
  Allegophylax Banks 1916
  Eustenace Banks 1916
circularis (Provancher) 1877:260; Platyphylax. NE
divergens (Walker) 1852:30; Limnephilus. NE
  dan (Sibley) 1926*a*:81; Halesus

flavata (Banks) 1914:154; Stenophylax. N.C.
hespera (Banks) 1914:152; Stenophylax. W
  needhami (Ling) 1938:66; Astenophylax
luculenta (Betten) 1934:345; Stenophylax. **P. 196**
scabripennis (Rambur) 1842:488; Limnephilus. Mass.
antica (Walker) 1852:9; Neuronia. **P. 196**
minima Banks 1943:345. E
conspersa Banks 1943:345. NE
perplexa Betten & Mosely 1940:149. N. Am.
sonso (Milne) 1935:32; Stenophylax. N.C.
subfasciata (Say) 1828:44; Phryganea. **P. 194**
indiana (Ross) 1938*d*:121; Stenophylax. **P. 196**
lepida (Hagen) 1861:269; Enoicyla. **P. 195**
limbata (McLachlan) 1871:108; Stenophylax. NE
gentilis (McLachlan) 1871:108; Stenophylax. NE
guttifer (Walker) 1852:16; Halesus. **P. 196**
  similis Banks 1907*a*:122
aglona Ross 1941*a*:18. NE

Caborius Navás 1918
  Allophylax Banks 1907*a*, preoccupied
punctatissimus (Walker) 1852:17; Halesus. **P. 197**
lyratus Ross 1938*a*:163. **P. 198**
kaskaskia Ross. **P. 198**

Chilostigma McLachlan 1876
areolatum (Walker) 1852:35; Limnephilus. Arctic Am.

Frenesia Betten & Mosely 1940
missa (Milne) 1935:35; Chilostigma. **P. 199**
difficilis (Walker) 1852:34; Limnephilus. NE
  pallida (Banks) 1899:209; Chilostigma

Grensia Ross. **P. 201**
praeterita (Walker) 1852:32; Limnephilus. N

Glyphopsyche Banks 1904*c*
irrorata (Fabricius) 1781:389; Phryganea. B.C., Ont.
  intercisus (Walker) 1852:30; Limnephilus
  bryanti Banks 1904*c*:141
missouri Ross. **P. 200**

Psychoglypha Ross. **P. 201**
subborealis (Banks) 1924:441; Chilostigma. **P. 202**
ormiae (Ross) 1938*a*:163; Glyphopsyche. W
  atlinensis (Ling) 1938:68; Chilostigma. *N. syn.*
bella (Banks) 1903*b*:241; Glyphotaelius. B.C.
prita (Milne) 1935:25; Glyphopsyche. Alta.
ulla (Milne) 1935:24; Glyphopsyche. W
avigo (Ross) 1941*b*:113; Glyphopsyche. Oreg.

Phanocelia Banks 1943
canadensis (Banks) 1924:442; Apatania.
P. 201

Drusinus Betten 1934
uniformis Betten 1934:360. **P. 202**
virginicus (Banks) 1900a:256; Potamorites.
NE
sparsus (Banks) 1908a:63; Halesus. NE
calypso (Banks) 1911:350; Stenophylax
edwardsi (Banks) 1920:345; Anisogamus. W
frontalis Banks 1943:350. B.C.

Psychoronia Banks 1916
brevipennis (Banks) 1904a:108; Psilopteryx?
♀; N. Mex.
costalis (Banks) 1901a:286; Asynarchus. W

Ecclisomyia Banks 1907a
conspersa Banks 1907a:123. Wash.
scylla Milne 1935:37. B.C.
simulata Banks 1920:346. Nev.
maculosa Banks 1907a:123. Colo.

Homophylax Banks 1900a
crotchi Banks 1920:345. B.C.
flavipennis Banks 1900a:255. Colo.
nevadensis Banks 1903b:242. Nev.
andax Ross 1941b:112. B.C., Oreg.

Neophylax McLachlan 1871
Acronopsyche Banks 1930b
autumnus Vorhies 1909:669. **P. 203**
fuscus Banks 1903b:242. **P. 205**
mitchelli Carpenter 1933:32. N.C.
nacatus Denning 1941a:198. NE
consimilis Betten 1934:376. N.Y.
ornatus Banks 1920:346. NE
rickeri Milne 1935:22. W
pulchellus Ling 1938:68
concinnus McLachlan 1871:111. Unid.; N.Y.
stolus Ross 1938a:169. E
ayanus Ross 1938a:168. **P. 205**
oligius Ross 1938a:168. NE
sinuatus Navás 1917:10. Unid.; Mont.
occidentis Banks 1924:441. W
pilosus (Banks) 1930b:228; Acronopsyche
slossonae Banks 1943:353. N.H.
delicatus Banks 1943:354. Pa.

Oligophlebodes Ulmer 1905b
minutus (Banks) 1897:28; Halesus. W
coloradensis Ulmer 1905b:66
sigma Milne 1935:22. Utah, N. Mex.
ardis Ross 1941b:103. Colo.
sierra Ross. **P. 284**
ruthae Ross. **P. 285**

Neothremma Banks 1930b
alicia Banks 1930b:229. W

Farula Milne 1936
rainieri Milne 1936:116. Wash.

MOLANNIDAE

Molanna Curtis 1834
Apatania Kolenati 1848
uniophila Vorhies 1909:705. **P. 206**
musetta Betten 1934:248. **P. 207**
tryphena Betten 1934:248. **P. 207**
flavicornis Banks 1914:261. **P. 208**
blenda Sibley 1926b:105. **P. 208**
cinerea Hagen 1861:276. Unid. ♀; Ont.

BERAEIDAE

Beraea Stephens 1836
Thya Curtis 1834
nigritta Banks 1897:31. **P. 208**
gorteba Ross. **P. 208**

ODONTOCERIDAE

Marilia Müller 1878 (see also 1879)
flexuosa Ulmer 1905b:70. SW
fusca (Banks) 1905b:19; Anisocentropus
nobsca Milne 1936:79. Tex.

Namamyia Banks 1905b
plutonis Banks 1905b:10. Calif.

Nerophilus Banks 1899
californicus (Hagen) 1861:272; Silo. W
oregonensis Banks 1899:212

Psilotreta Banks 1899. **P. 285**
Astoplectron Banks 1914
rufa (Hagen) 1861:276; Molanna. NE
connexa (Banks) 1914:265; Astoplectron
indecisa (Walker) 1852:95; Goera. NE
frontalis Banks 1899:213. E
gameta Ross 1939a:69; Heteroplectron. *N.
syn.*
labida Ross. **P. 287**
amera (Ross) 1939a:68; Heteroplectron.
Tenn.
borealis (Provancher) 1877:263; Heteroplectron. Unid; Que.
dissimilis (Banks) 1897:30; Heteroplectron?
Unid. ♀; N.Y.

CALAMOCERATIDAE

Ganonema McLachlan 1866
americanum (Walker) 1852:85; Sericostoma.
E
nigrum Lloyd 1915b:19

Anisocentropus McLachlan 1863a
pyraloides (Walker) 1852:90; Notidobia.
Ga.
latifascia (Walker) 1852:90; Notidobia. An
Australian species, probably recorded erroneously from N. Am.
elegans (Walker) 1852:95; Goera

Notiomyia Banks 1905*b*
  mexicana (Banks) 1900*a*:257; Heteroplectron. Ariz., Mexico
  ornata Banks 1909:342. Tex.

Heteroplectron McLachlan 1871
  californicum McLachlan 1871:125. Calif.

LEPTOCERIDAE

Leptocerus Leach 1815
  Ymymia Milne 1934
  americanus (Banks) 1899:215; Setodes. **P. 212**
    grandis (Banks) 1907*a*:128; Setodes

Leptocella Banks 1899
  pavida (Hagen) 1861:282; Setodes. **P. 218**
  candida (Hagen) 1861:280; Setodes. **P. 217**
  exquisita (Walker) 1852:72; Leptocerus. **P. 217**
  piffardii (McLachlan) 1863*b*:160; Setodes. NE
  tavara Ross. **P. 287**
  albida (Walker) 1852:71; Leptocerus. **P. 220**
    nivea (Hagen) 1861:281; Setodes
  diarina Ross. **P. 218**
  texana Banks 1905*b*:19. Tex.
  intervena Banks 1914:262. Tex.
  spiloma Ross. **P. 219**
  exilis Banks 1905*b*:19. SW
    gracilis Banks 1901*b*:369, preoccupied
  coloradensis Banks 1899:215. Colo.
  minuta Banks 1900*a*:257. Wash.
  stigmatica Banks 1914:262. N.Mex.
  uwarowii (Kolenati) 1859*b*:249; Mystacides. Unid.; Alaska

Athripsodes Billberg 1820
  tarsi-punctatus (Vorhies) 1909:694; Leptocerus. **P. 229**
  nephus Ross. **P. 230**
  alagmus Ross 1938*a*:155. **P. 229**
  resurgens (Walker) 1852:70; Leptocerus. **P. 230**
    variegatus (Hagen) 1861:278; Leptocerus
    aspinosus (Betten) 1934:255; Leptocerus
  angustus (Banks) 1914:263; Leptocerus. **P. 231**
  alces Ross 1941*b*:95. Ont., Wis.
  annulicornis (Stephens) 1836:199; Leptocerus. **P. 232**
    lugens (Hagen) 1861:276; Leptocerus
    recurvatus (Banks) 1908*b*:265; Leptocerus
    futilis (Banks) 1914:264; Leptocerus
    perplexus var. *nordus* Milne 1934:15. *N. syn.*
  dilutus (Hagen) 1861:277; Leptocerus. **P. 231**
  miscus Ross 1941*b*:93. Wis., Minn.
  wetzeli Ross 1941*b*:94. NE
  arielles Denning 1942:48. Minn.
  mentieus (Walker) 1852:71; Leptocerus. **P. 232**

  vanus (Betten) 1934:262; Leptocerus
  slossonae Banks 1938:77. Fla., Pa.
  transversus (Hagen) 1861:279; Leptocerus. **P. 233**
    maculatus (Banks) 1899:214; Leptocerus
  inornatus (Banks) 1914:263; Leptocerus. Tex.
  cancellatus (Betten) 1934:256; Leptocerus. **P. 233**
  ophioderus Ross 1938*a*:157. **P. 232**
  punctatus (Banks) 1894:180; Mystacides. **P. 234**
  uvalo Ross 1938*b*:89. Pa., N.Y.
  submacula (Walker) 1852:70; Leptocerus. **P. 235**
  erraticus Milne 1936:58. **P. 235**
  saccus Ross 1938*b*:89. **P. 234**
  erullus Ross 1938*b*:90. **P. 235**
  cophus Ross 1938*a*:156. W
  ancylus (Vorhies) 1909:691; Leptocerus. **P. 227**
  flavus (Banks) 1904*d*:212; Leptocerus. **P. 228**
  albostictus (Hagen) 1861:276; Leptocerus. Unid. ♀; N. Am.
  floridanus (Banks) 1903*b*:242; Leptocerus. Unid. ♀; Fla.
  retactus (Banks) 1914:263; Leptocerus. Unid. ♀; Ont.
  stigmaticus (Navás) 1917:8; Leptocerus. Unid.; N. Mex.

Oecetis McLachlan 1877
  Oecetina Banks 1899
  Setodina Banks 1907*a*
  Oecetodes Ulmer 1909
  Friga Milne 1934
  Quaria Milne 1934
  Yrula Milne 1934
  avara (Banks) 1895:316; Setodes. **P. 240**
  disjuncta (Banks) 1920:351; Oecetina. W
  eddlestoni Ross 1938*a*:160. **P. 240**
  scala Milne 1934:17. **P. 241**
  sphyra Ross 1941*b*:99. Ga.
  ochracea (Curtis) 1825:57; Leptocerus. **P. 244**
    ssp. *carri* Milne 1934:16. *N. syn.*
  persimilis (Banks) 1907*a*:129; Oecetina. **P. 243**
  georgia Ross 1941*b*:98. Ga.
  immobilis (Hagen) 1861:283; Setodes. **P. 241**
  cinerascens (Hagen) 1861:282; Setodes. **P. 241**
    fumosa (Banks) 1899:216; Oecetina
  osteni Milne 1934:17. **P. 241**
  inconspicua (Walker) 1852:71; Leptocerus. **P. 242**
    sagitta (Hagen) 1861:284; Setodes
    micans (Hagen) 1861:283; Setodes
    flaveolata (Hagen) 1861:282; Setodes
    parvula (Banks) 1899:215; Oecetina
    flavida (Banks) 1899:216; Oecetina

floridana (Banks) 1899:216; Oecetina
apicalis (Banks) 1907*a*:129; Oecetina
inornata (Banks) 1907*a*:128; Oecetina
parva (Banks) 1907*a*:130; Setodina. Fla.

Triaenodes McLachlan 1865
  Triaenodella Mosely 1932
  Ylodes Milne 1934
helo Milne 1934:12. SE
perna Ross 1938*a*:159. **P. 250**
aba Milne 1935:20. **P. 249**
nox Ross 1941*b*:96. Ont.
ochracea (Betten & Mosely) 1940:77; Triaenodella. Ga.
tridonta Ross 1938*a*:158. Okla.
baris Ross 1938*b*:88. **P. 252**
phalacris Ross 1938*b*:88. **P. 250**
dipsia Ross 1938*b*:89. **P. 252**
flavescens Banks 1900*a*:257. **P. 251**
tarda Milne 1934:12. **P. 250**
  vorhiesi Betten 1934:286. *N. syn.*
  mephita Milne 1936:59. *N. syn.*
marginata Sibley 1926*a*:80. **P. 251**
injusta (Hagen) 1861:283; Setodes. **P. 252**
ignita (Walker) 1852:72; Leptocerus. **P. 252**
  dentata Banks 1914:261. *N. syn.*
taenia Ross 1938*a*:157. Tenn.
florida Ross 1941*b*:96. Fla.
frontalis Banks 1907*a*:127. **P. 249**
grisea Banks 1899:214. **P. 249**
borealis Banks 1900*a*:257. Unid. ♀; Minn.

Mystacides Berthold 1827
sepulchralis (Walker) 1852:70; Leptocerus.
  P. 254
alafimbriata Griffin 1912:19. W
longicornis (Linnaeus) 1758:548; Phryganea.
  P. 255
  quadrifasciata (Fabricius) 1775:308; Phry-
    ganea
  interjecta (Banks) 1914:262; Oecetina
  canadensis Banks 1924:448
nigra (Linnaeus)—a Eurasian species reported from N. Am. in error—Hagen
  1861:277

Setodes Rambur 1842
incerta (Walker) 1852:71; Leptocerus. NE
  and E
  vernalis Banks 1907*a*:127
stehri (Ross) 1941*b*:99; Leptocerus. Ga.,
  N.C.
oxapia (Ross) 1938*b*:88; Leptocerus. Okla.
guttatus (Banks) 1900*a*:257; Oecetina. NE
  autumnalis Banks 1907*a*:128
oligia (Ross) 1938*a*:160; Leptocerus. **P. 256**
floridana Banks 1905*b*:19. Unid. ♀; Fla.

GOERIDAE

Goera Curtis 1834
calcarata Banks 1899:211. E

fuscula Banks 1905*a*:216. N.C.
stylata Ross 1938*a*:172. **P. 257**

Goerita Ross 1938*a*
semata Ross 1938*a*:172. **P. 258**
genota Ross 1941*b*:116. Oreg.

Pseudogoera Carpenter 1933
singularis Carpenter 1933:38. **P. 258**

LEPIDOSTOMATIDAE

Lepidostoma Rambur 1842
  Nosopus McLachlan 1871
  Olemira Banks 1897
  Pristosilo Banks 1899
  Atomyia Banks 1905*a*
  Notiopsyche Banks 1905*a*
  Mormomyia Banks 1907*a*
  Alepomyia Banks 1908*a*
  Phanopsyche Banks 1911
  Alepomyiodes Sibley 1926*b*
  Arcadopsyche Banks 1930*a*
  Neuropsyche Carpenter 1933
  Oligopsyche Carpenter 1933
  Jenortha Milne 1936
togatum (Hagen) 1861:273; Mormonia. E,
  NE
  canadensis (Banks) 1899:212; Pristosilo
  pallidum (Banks) 1897:29; Silo
knowltoni Ross 1938*a*:175. Utah
carolina (Banks) 1911:356; Notiopsyche.
  N.C.
tibialis (Carpenter) 1933:39; Neuropsyche.
  N.C.
latipennis (Banks) 1905*a*:216; Notiopsyche.
  N.C.
podager (McLachlan) 1871:116; Nosopus.
  Calif.
quercina Ross 1938*a*:176. Oreg.
strophis Ross 1938*a*:177. N, NW
frosti (Milne) 1936:119; Atomyia. E
unicolor (Banks) 1911:357; Mormomyia.
  W, N
prominens (Banks) 1930*a*:129; Arcadopsyche. E
bryanti (Banks) 1908*a*:65; Alepomyia. NE
  wisconsinensis Vorhies 1909:685
griseum (Banks) 1911:357; Phanopsyche.
  NE
roafi (Milne) 1936:120; Atomyia. W
sackeni (Banks) 1936*a*:267; Mormomyia.
  NE
cascadensis (Milne) 1936:119; Jenortha.
  Wash.
  pleca Ross 1938*a*:175. *N. syn.*
americanum (Banks) 1897:29; Olemira. NE
  pictilis (Banks) 1899:211; Mormonia
costalis (Banks) 1914:265; Olemira. NE
pluviale (Milne) 1936:117; Olemira. W
rayneri Ross 1941*b*:117. Calif., Oreg.
ontario Ross 1941*b*:119. NE

cantha Ross 1941*b*:118. Calif.
modestum (Banks) 1905*a*:217; Alepomyia. E
swannanoa Ross 1939*a*:69. E
lydia Ross 1939*a*:70. E
vernalis (Banks) 1897:29; Mormonia. E
liba Ross 1941*b*:120. **P. 259**
cinereum (Banks) 1899:210; Silo. Unid.
♀; Calif.
deceptivum (Banks) 1907*a*:125; Thremma.
Unid. ♀; N.Mex.
stigma Banks 1907*a*:125. Unid. ♀; Colo.

Theliopsyche Banks 1911
subg. *Aopsyche* Ross 1938*a*
parva Banks 1911:356. N.Y.
epilone Ross 1938*a*:173. N.C.
corona Ross 1938*a*:174. N.C.
grisea (Hagen) 1861:273; Silo. N.Y.

BRACHYCENTRIDAE

Micrasema McLachlan 1876
rusticum (Hagen) 1868:272; Dasystoma.
P. 261
falcatum Banks 1914:265
charonis Banks 1914:266. **P. 262**
wataga Ross 1938*a*:178. **P. 262**
scissum McLachlan 1884:26. Alaska
bactro Ross 1938*d*:122. Oreg.
sprulesi Ross 1941*b*:115. NE

Brachycentrus Curtis 1834
Sphinctogaster Provancher 1877
Oligoplectrum McLachlan 1868
subg. *Amiocentrus* Ross 1938*a*
notabulus Milne 1936:112. Va.
dimicki Milne 1936:113. Oreg.
americanus (Banks) 1899:210; Oligoplectrum. **P. 266**
similis Banks 1907*a*:124
lateralis (Say) 1823:161; Phryganea. **P. 265**
numerosus (Say) 1823:160; Phryganea. **P. 264**
fuliginosus Walker 1852:88. Ont., Man.
occidentalis Banks 1911:355. W

incanus Hagen 1861:272. E
arizonicus (Ling) 1938:69; Oligoplectrum.
Ariz.
aspilus Ross 1938*a*:178. W
californicus (Ling) 1938:69; Oligoplectrum. *N. syn.*
lutescens (Provancher) 1877:262; Sphinctogaster. Unid. ♀; Que.
nigrisoma (Banks) 1905*b*:12; Sphinctogaster.
P. 265

SERICOSTOMATIDAE

Sericostoma Berthold 1827
Notidobia Stephens 1836
Schizopelex McLachlan 1876
Agarodes Banks 1899
Psiloneura Banks 1914
pele Ross 1938*a*:170. N.C.
crassicornis (Walker) 1852:113; Hydropsyche. Ga.
distinctum (Ulmer) 1905*b*:67; Agarodes. NE
lobata (Banks) 1911:356; Schizopelex
moesta (Banks) 1914:264; Psiloneura
griseolum McLachlan 1871:112. Calif.
nigriculum McLachlan 1871:113. Calif.
arizonicum (Banks) 1943:369; Notidobia.
Ariz.
assimilis Banks 1907*a*:124. Calif.
griseum (Banks) 1899:218; Agarodes. NE
americana Banks 1900*a*:256
hesperum (Banks) 1914:266; Schizopelex.
Unid. ♀; Utah

HELICOPSYCHIDAE

Helicopsyche Hagen 1866
borealis (Hagen) 1861:271; Notidobia. **P. 266**
californica Banks 1899:210. *N. syn.*
annulicornis Banks 1904*d*:212
piroa Ross. **P. 289**
mexicana Banks 1901*b*:368. SW
arizonensis Banks 1907*a*:125. *N. syn.*
limnella Ross 1938*a*:179. Ark., Okla.

LITERATURE CITED

Balduf, Walter Valentine
1939. The bionomics of entomophagus insects. Pt. 2. 384 pp., 228 figs. St. Louis.

Banks, Nathan
1894. On a collection of neuropteroid insects from Kansas. Ent. News **5**:178–80.
1895. New neuropteroid insects. Am. Ent. Soc. Trans. **22**:313–6.
1897. New North American neuropteroid insects. Am. Ent. Soc. Trans. **24**:21–31.
1899. Descriptions of new North American neuropteroid insects. Am. Ent. Soc. Trans. **25**:199–218.
1900a. New genera and species of Nearctic neuropteroid insects. Am. Ent. Soc. Trans. **26**:239–59.
1900b. Papers from the Harriman Alaska expedition. Entomological results (4). Neuropteroid insects. Wash. Acad. Sci. Proc. **2**:465–73, pls. 27–8.
1900c. Some insects of the Hudsonian zone in New Mexico: Neuroptera. Psyche **9**:124.
1901a. Some insects of the Hudsonian zone in New Mexico: neuropteroid insects. Psyche **9**:286–7.
1901b. A list of neuropteroid insects from Mexico. Am. Ent. Soc. Trans. **27**:361–71, pl. 12.
1903a. Neuropteroid insects from Arizona. Wash. Ent. Soc. Proc. **5**:237–45. 1 pl.
1903b. Some new neuropteroid insects. N. Y. Ent. Soc. Jour. **11**:236–43.
1904a. Neuropteroid insects from New Mexico. Am. Ent. Soc. Trans. **30**:97–110. 1 pl.
1904b. Two species of Hydroptilidae. Ent. News **15**:116.
1904c. Two new species of caddice-flies. Wash. Ent. Soc. Proc. **6**:140–2.
1904d. A list of neuropteroid insects, exclusive of Odonata, from the vicinity of Washington, D. C. Wash. Ent. Soc. Proc. **6**(4):201–17.
1905a. Descriptions of new species of Nearctic neuropteroid insects from the Black Mountains, N. C. Am. Mus. Nat. Hist. Bul. **21**:215–8.
1905b. Descriptions of new Nearctic neuropteroid insects. Am. Ent. Soc. Trans. **32**:1–20. 2 pls.
1907a. Descriptions of new Trichoptera. Wash. Ent. Soc. Proc. **8**(3–4):117–33, pls. 8–9.
1907b. New Trichoptera and Psocidae. N. Y. Ent. Soc. Jour. **15**:162–6. 5 figs.
1908a. Some Trichoptera, and allied insects, from Newfoundland. Psyche **15**(4):61–7, pl. 2.
1908b. Neuropteroid insects—notes and descriptions. Am. Ent. Soc. Trans. **34**:255–67, pls. 17–9.
1909. Two new caddice flies. Ent. News **20**:342.
1911. Descriptions of new species of North American neuropteroid insects. Am. Ent. Soc. Trans. **37**(4):335–60, pls. 11–3.
1913. The Stanford Expedition to Brazil: neuropteroid insects from Brazil. Psyche **20**:83–9. 1 pl.
1914. American Trichoptera—notes and descriptions. Can. Ent. **46**:149–56, 201–5, 252–8, 261–8, pls. 9, 10, 15, 20.
1916. A classification of our limnephilid caddice flies. Can. Ent. **48**:117–22.
1918. New neuropteroid insects. Harv. Univ. Mus. Comp. Zool. Bul. **62**:3–24. 26 figs.
1919. Neuropteroid insects of the Canadian Arctic Expedition 1913–8. Can. Arctic Exp. Report **3**(pt. B):3–5. 1 pl.
1920. New neuropteroid insects. Harv. Univ. Mus. Comp. Zool. Bul. **64**:297–362. 7 pls.
1924. Descriptions of new neuropteroid insects. Harv. Univ. Mus. Comp. Zool. Bul. **65**:421–55. 4 pls.
1930a. Trichoptera from Cape Breton, Nova Scotia. Brooklyn Ent. Soc. Bul. **25**(3):127–32. 10 figs.
1930b. New neuropteroid insects from the United States. Psyche **37**:223–33. 15 figs.
1936a. Four new Trichoptera from the United States. Arbeiten über Morphologische und Taxonomische Entomologie aus Berlin-Dahlem **3**(4):265–8. 9 figs. Nov. 7.
1936b. Notes on some Hydropsychidae. Psyche **43**(4):126–30. 10 figs. Dec.
1938. New native neuropteroid insects. Psyche **45**(1):72–9. 9 figs.
1943. Notes and descriptions of Nearctic Trichoptera. Harv. Univ. Mus. Comp. Zool. Bul. **92**:341–69. 6 pls.
1944. New Neuroptera and Trichoptera from the United States. Psyche **50**(3–4):74–81.

Berthold, A. A.
1827. Natürliche Familien des Thierreichs mit Anmerkungen und Zusätzen. 8+602 pp. (Translation of Latreille 1825.) Weimar.

Betten, Cornelius
1902. The larva of the caddis-fly *Molanna cinerea* Hagen. N. Y. Ent. Soc. Jour. **10**:147–54. 2 figs.
1934. The caddis flies or Trichoptera of New York state. N. Y. State Mus. Bul. **292**. 576 pp., 61 text figs., 67 pls.

Betten, Cornelius, and Martin E. Mosely
1940. The Francis Walker types of Trichoptera in the British Museum. 248 pp., 122 figs. London.

Billberg, Gustav Johann
1820. Enumeratio insectorum in Museo Billberg. 138 pp. Stockholm.

Boheman, Carl Heinrich
1865. (Title unknown.) Ofversigt af Kongl. Vetenskaps-Akademiens Förhandlingar **22**:568.

Brauer, Friedrich
1865. Zweiter Bericht über die auf der Weltfahrt der Kais. Fregatte Novara gesammelten Neuropteren. Kaiserlich-Königlichen Zoologisch-Botanischen Gesellschaft in Wien Verhandlungen **15**:415–22.

Burks, B. D., H. H. Ross and T. H. Frison
1938. An economical, portable light for collecting nocturnal insects. Jour. Econ. Ent. **31**: 317–8. 1 fig.

Burmeister, H. C. C.
1839. Handbuch der Entomologie. Neuroptera, 2(2):757–1050. Berlin.

Carpenter, F. M.
1933. Trichoptera from the mountains of North Carolina and Tennessee. Psyche **40**:32–47, figs. 1–17.

Chambers, V. T.
1873. Micro-Lepidoptera. Can. Ent. **5**:110–5, 124–8.

Curtis, John
1825. British entomology. **2**:pls. 51–98. London.
1834. Descriptions of some hitherto nondescript British species of mayflies of anglers. London and Edinburgh Philosophical Magazine and Journal of Science 4:120–5, 212–8.
1835*a*. British entomology. **12**:pls. 530–77. London.
1835*b*. Insects, *in* James Clark Ross' Appendix to John Ross' Narrative of a second voyage in search of a northwest passage. Trichoptera, p. 64.

Dalman, Johann Wilhelm
1819. Några nya insekt-genera, beskrifna. Svenska Vetenskapsakademien Handlingar **40**: 117–27. 8 pls.

DeLong, D. M., and R. H. Davidson
1937. Methods in study and preparation of leafhopper genitalia. Jour. Econ. Ent. **30**:372–4. 1 fig.

Denning, Donald G.
1937. The biology of some Minnesota Trichoptera. Am. Ent. Soc. Trans. **63**:17–43. 45 figs.
1941*a*. Descriptions and notes of new and little known species of Trichoptera. Ent. Soc. Am. Ann. **34**:195–203. 12 figs.
1941*b*. The genus *Grammotaulius* in North America, with the description of a new species (Trichoptera, Limnephilidae). Can. Ent. **73**:232–5. 1 pl.
1942. Descriptions of new Trichoptera from the United States. Can. Ent. **54**:46–51. 6 figs.
1943. The Hydropsychidae of Minnesota (Trichoptera). Ent. Am. **23**:101–71. 41 figs.

Eaton, Alfred Edwin
1873. On the Hydroptilidae, a family of the Trichoptera. London Ent. Soc. Trans. **1873** (2):125–51, pls. 2–3.

Elkins, Winston A.
1936. The immature stages of some Minnesota Trichoptera. Ent. Soc. Am. Ann. **29**:656–81. 6 pls.

Fabricius, Johann Christian
1775. Systema Entomologiae. 30+832 pp. Flensburg and Leipzig.
1781. Species Insectorum. **1**:552 pp. Hamburg.

Frison, Theodore H.
1935. The stoneflies, or Plecoptera, of Illinois. Ill. Nat. Hist. Surv. Bul. **20**:281–471. 343 figs.

Griffin, Laura Hill
1912. New Oregon Trichoptera. Ent. News **23**:17–21, pls. 3–4.

Hagen, Herman A.
1860. Die Phryganiden Pictets nach Typen bearbeitet. Stettiner Entomologische Zeitung **21**:274–90.
1861. Synopsis of the Neuroptera of North America, with a list of the South American species. Smithsn. Inst. Misc. Collect. 347 pp. Trichoptera, pp. 249–98, 328–9.
1864. Phryganidarum synopsis synonymica. Kaiserlich-Königlichen Zoologisch-Botanischen Gesellschaft in Wien Verhandlungen **14**:799–890.
1866. Description of a genus of caddis-flies, of which the larvae construct cases, known as Helicopsyche. Ent. Monthly Mag. **2**:252–5.
1868. Monographie der Gattung *Dasystoma* Rambur. Stettiner Entomologische Zeitung **29**:267–73.
1873. Beiträge zur Kenntnis der Phryganiden. Kaiserlich-Königlichen Zoologisch-Botanischen Gesellshaft in Wien Verhandlungen **23**:377–452.
1875. Report of the Pseudo-Neuroptera collected by Lieut. W. L. Carpenter in 1873 in Colorado. U. S. Geol. Survey Terr. Report for 1873, pp. 571–606.

Harris, Thaddeus William
1869. Entomological correspondence. Edited by S. H. Scudder. 375 pp., 4 pls. Boston.

Kirby, William
1837. Fauna Boreali—Americana. Pt. 4: Insects. Trichoptera, p. 253. London.

Klapálek, Franz
1892. Trichopterologický Výzkum Čech v. r. 1891. Česká akademie císaře Františka Josefa pro védy, slovesnost a umění v Praze Rozpravy **5**:1–22.

Kolbe, Herman Jul.
1912. Glazialzeitliche Reliktenfauna im Hohen Norden. Deutsche Entomologische Zeitschrift **7**:33–63.

Kolenati, Friedrich A.
1848. Genera et species Trichopterorum. Pars prior, 108 pp., 3 pls. Moscow.
1859*a*. Systematisches Verzeichniss der dem Verfasser Bekannten Phryganiden und deren Synonymik. Wiener Entomologische Monatschriften, pp. 15–23, 56–9.
1859*b*. Genera et species Trichopterorum. Pars altera, pp. 143–296, 5 pls. Moscow.

Latreille, Pierre André
1829. Les crustacées, les arachnides et les insects, *in* Le règne animal (general series by Cuvier) 5. 24+556 pp. Paris.

Leach, William Elford
1815. Article "Entomology" in Brewster's Edinburg Encyclopedia **9**(1):52–172.

Ling, Shao-win
1938. A few new caddis flies in the collection of the California Academy of Sciences. Pan-Pacific Ent. **14**(2):59–69.

Linnaeus, Carl von
1758. Systema Naturae. Tenth edition. 826 pp. Stockholm.

Lloyd, John Thomas
1915a. Notes on *Ithytrichia confusa* Morton. Can. Ent. **47**:117–21. 1 pl.
1915b. Wood-boring Trichoptera. Psyche **22**:17–21, pl. 2, figs. 1–20.
1921. The biology of North American caddis fly larvae. Lloyd Library of Botany, Pharmacy and Materia Medica Bul. **21**:1–124, figs. 1–197.

Martynov, Andreas B.
1914. Die Trichopteren Siberiens und der Angrenzenden Gebiete, III. Apataniinae (Fam. Limnophilidae). St. Pétersbourg Musée Zoologique de l'Académie Impériale des Sciences Annuaire **19**:1–87. 69+3 figs.
1924. Preliminary revision of the family Phryganeidae, its classification and evolution. Annals and Magazine of Natural History, London, series 9, **14**:209–24. 2 figs.
1930. On the trichopterous fauna of China and Tibet. Zoological Society of London Proceedings **1930**:65–112. 71 figs.

McLachlan, Robert
1863a. On *Anisocentropus*, a new genus of Trichoptera, with descriptions of five species, and of a new species of *Dipseudopsis*. Entomological Society of London Transactions, series 3, **1**:492–6. 1 pl.
1863b. Notes on North American Phryganeidae, with special reference to those contained in the collection of the British Museum. Entomologist's Annual **1863**:155–63.
1864. On the trichopterous genus *Polycentropus* and the allied genera. Entomologist's Monthly Magazine **1**:25–31.
1865. Trichoptera Britannica. A monograph of British species of caddis flies. Entomological Society of London Transactions, series 3, **5**:1–184. 14 pls.
1866. Descriptions of new or little known genera and species of exotic Trichoptera, with observations on certain species described by Mr. F. Walker. Entomological Society of London Transactions, series 3, **5**:247–75. 3 pls.
1867. Bemerkungen über europäische Phryganiden, nebst Beschreibungen einiger neuer Genera und Species. Stettiner Entomologische Zeitung **28**:50–63.
1868. Contributions to a knowledge of European Trichoptera. Entomological Society of London Transactions **1868**:289–308. 1 pl.
1871. On new forms, etc., of extra-European trichopterous insects. Journal of the Linnaean Society of London, Zoology, **11**:98–141. 3 pls.
1874–80. A monographic revision and synopsis of the Trichoptera of the European fauna. Pt. 1, 1874:1–46, pls. 1–5. Pt. 2, 1875:47–108, pls. 6–11. Pt. 3, 1875:109–44, pls. 12–15. Pt. 4, 1876:145–220, pls. 16–23. Pt. 5, 1876:221–80, pls. 24–31, w. supplement I–XII. Pt. 6, 1877:281–348, pls. 32–37. Pt. 7, 1878:349–428, pls. 38–44. Pt. 8, 1879:429–500, pls. 45–51. Pt. 9, 1880:501–23, w. supplement XIII–LXXXIV, pls. 52–59.
1884. A monographic revision and synopsis of the Trichoptera of the European fauna. First additional supplement. 76 pp., 7 pls.

Mickel, Clarence E., and Herbert E. Milliron
1939. Rearing the caddis fly, *Limnephilus indivisus* Walker, and its hymenopterous parasite, *Hemiteles biannulatus* Grav. Ent. Soc. Am. Ann. **32**(3):575–80.

Milne, Lorus J.
1931. Three new Canadian *Prophryganea*. Can. Ent. **63**:228–32. 21 figs.
1934–36. Studies in North American Trichoptera. Pt. 1, 1934:1–19. Pt. 2, 1935:20–55. Pt. 3, 1936:56–128, with 2 pls. Cambridge, Mass.

Milne, Lorus J., and Margery J. Milne
1938. The Arctopsychidae of continental America north of Mexico (Trichoptera). Brooklyn Ent. Soc. Bul. **33**(3):97–110. 3 pls.

Milne, Margery J.
1938. The "metamorphotype method" in Trichoptera. N. Y. Ent. Soc. Jour. **46**:435–7.
1939. Immature North American Trichoptera. Psyche **46**:9–19.

Milne, Margery J., and Lorus J. Milne
1939. Evolutionary trends in caddis worm case construction. Ent. Soc. Am. Ann. **32**(3): 533–42. 1 fig.
1940. A new species of *Rhyacophila*, described from metamorphotypes (Rhyacophilidae: Trichoptera). Brooklyn Ent. Soc. Bul. **35**(5):153–6. 1 pl.

Morton, Kenneth J.
1888. The larva and case of *Ithrytrichia lamellaris* Eaton, with references to other species of Hydroptilidae. Ent. Monthly Mag. **24**:171–5. 7 figs.
1905. North American Hydroptilidae. N. Y. State Mus. Bul. **86**:63–85. 1 text fig. and pls. 13–5.

Mosely, Martin E.
1924. Scent-organs in the genus *Hydroptila*. Entomological Society of London Transactions **1923**:291–4. 2 pls.
1929. Trichoptera and Ephemeroptera of Greenland. Annals and Magazine of Natural History, series 10, **4**:501–9. 6 figs.
1932. Some new African Leptoceridae (Trichoptera). Annals and Magazine of Natural History, series 10, **9**:297–313. 29 figs.
1934a. Some new exotic Trichoptera. Stylops **3**:139–42. 13 figs. June 15.
1934b. New exotic Hydroptilidae. Royal Entomological Society of London Transactions **82**(1):137–63. 58 figs. June 30.
1937. Mexican Hydroptilidae (Trichoptera). Royal Entomological Society of London Transactions **86**(10):151–90. 37 figs.
1939. The Brazilian Hydroptilidae (Trichoptera). Novitates Zoologicae **41**:217–39. 93 figs.

Müller, Fritz
1878. Sobre as casas construidas pelas larvas de insectos Trichopteros da provincia de Santa Catharina. Museu Nacional do Rio de Janeiro Archivos **3**:99–134, 209–14, pls. 8–11.
1879. Notes on the cases of some South Brazilian Trichoptera. Entomological Society of London Transactions **1879**:131–144.

Navás, Longinos
1907. Trichópteros nuevos. R. Sociedad española de historia natural Boletín **7**:397–400. 3 figs.
1917. Insecta nova. Accademia Pontificia dei Nuovi Lincei Memorie **3**:22 pp.
1918. Neurópteros nuevos o poco conocidos (Decima serie). R. Academia de Ciencias y Artes de Barcelona Memorias **14**:339–66.
1933. Neurotteri e Tricotteri del "Deutsches entomologisches Institut" di Berlin-Dahlem. Bollettino della Societá Entomologica Italiana **65**:105–13. 8 figs.

Needham, James G.
1902. A probable new type of hypermetamorphosis. Psyche **9**:375–8. 5 figs.

Pictet, François Jules
1834. Recherches pour servir à l'histoire et à l'anatomie des Phryganides. 235 pp., 20 pls. Geneva.
1836. Description de quelques nouvelles espèces de Nevroptères du Musée de Genève. Société de Physique et d'Histoire Naturelle de Genève Mémoires **7**:396–403. 1 pl.

Provancher, M. Abbé
1877. Petite faune entomologique du Canada. Trichoptères. Le Naturaliste Canadien **9**:212–7, 241–4, 257–69.
1878. Additions et corrections aux Nevroptères de la Province de Québec. Le Naturaliste Canadien **10**:124–47, 367–9.

Rambur, J. Pierre
1842. Histoire naturelle des insectes. Nevroptères. 17+534 pp., 12 pls. Paris.

Ross, Herbert H.
1938a. Descriptions of Nearctic caddis flies (Trichoptera) with special reference to the Illinois species. Ill. Nat. Hist. Surv. Bul. **21**(4):101–83. 123 figs.
1938b. Descriptions of new leptocerid Trichoptera. Ent. Soc. Am. Ann. **31**(1):88–91. 8 figs.

1938c. Lectotypes of North American caddis flies in the Museum of Comparative Zoology. Psyche **45**(1):1–61. 10 pls.
1938d. Descriptions of new North American Trichoptera. Wash. Ent. Soc. Proc. **40**(5):117–24. 2 pls.
1939a. New species of Trichoptera from the Appalachian Region. Wash. Ent. Soc. Proc. **41**(3):65–72. 11 figs.
1939b. Three new species of Nearctic Trichoptera. Ent. Soc. Am. Ann. **32**(3):628–31. 3 figs.
1941a. New species of Trichoptera from Canada and northern United States. Can. Ent. **73**(1):15–9. 1 pl.
1941b. Descriptions and records of North American Trichoptera. Am. Ent. Soc. Trans. **67**(1084):35–126. 13 pls.

Say, Thomas
1823. Descriptions of insects belonging to the order Neuroptera Linné and Latreille, collected by the expedition under the command of Major Long. West. Quart. Report **2**:160–5. Cincinnati.
1824. From the narrative of the expedition to the source of the St. Peter's River, etc., under the command of Stephen H. Long, Major U. S. T. E., **2**:268–378. Philadelphia.
1828. American entomology, or descriptions of the insects of North America. **3**, pls. 37–54. Philadelphia.

Sibley, Charles K.
1926a. New species of New York caddis flies. N. Y. Ent. Soc. Jour. **34**:79–81.
1926b. Trichoptera, *in* A preliminary biological survey of the Lloyd-Cornell Reservation. Lloyd Library of Botany, Pharmacy and Materia Medica Bul. **27** (Ent. series 5):102–8, 185–221, pls. 8–13.

Stephens, James Francis
1829. A systematic catalogue of British insects. Pt. 1. 416 pp. London.
1836–37. Illustrations of British entomology, **6**:146–234.

Thomson, C. G.
1891. Bidrag till Phryganeernas systematik och synonymi. Opuscula Entomologica **15**:1537–1600.

Tjeder, Bo
1930. *Ithytrichia lamellaris* Eat. and *clavata* Mort. in Dalecarlia. Entomologisk Tidskrift **51**:134–8. 2 pls.

Ulmer, Georg
1902. Trichopterologische Beobachtungen aus der Umgegend von Hamburg. Stettiner Entomologische Zeitung **63**:360–67, 384–7. 2 pls.
1905a. Zur Kenntnis aussereuropäischer Trichopteren. Stettiner Entomologische Zeitung **66**:1–119.
1905b. Neue und wenig bekannte aussereuropäische Tricopteren, hauptsächlich aus dem Wiener Museum. Naturhistorischen Hofmuseums Wien Annalen **20**:59–98. 75 figs.
1906a. Neuer Beitrag zur Kenntnis aussereuropäischer Trichopteren. Leyden Museum Notes **28**:1–116. 114 figs.
1906b. Uebersicht über die bisher bekannten Larven europäischer Trichopteren. Zeitschrift für Wissenschaftlichen Insekten-Biologie **2**:111–7, 162–8, 209–14, 253–8, 288–96.
1907a. Trichoptera. Catalogues de Collections Zoologiques du Baron Edm. de Selys Longchamps **6**(1):1–102. 4 pls., 132 figs.
1907b. Trichoptera. Genera Insectorum **60**. 259 pp., 41 pls.
1909. Trichoptera. Die Süsswasserfauna Deutschlands, **5–6**. 326 pp., 467 figs.
1912. Die Trichopteren des baltischen Bernsteins. Beiträge zur Naturkunde Preussens, Königsberg **10**. iv+380 pp.

Vorhies, Charles T.
1909. Studies on the Trichoptera of Wisconsin. Wis. Acad. Sci. Trans. **16**:647–738, pls. 52–61.

Walker, Francis
1852. Catalogue of the specimens of neuropterous insects in the collections of the British Museum. Pt. 1, 192 pp. London.

Wallengren, H. D. J.
1880. Om Skandinaviens arter af familjen Phryganeidae.   Entomologisk Tidskrift **1**:64–75.
1886. Skandinaviens arter af Trichopter-Familjen Apataniidae.   Entomologisk Tidskrift **7**:73–80.
1891. Skandinaviens Neuroptera.   Andra afdelningen.   Svenska Akademien Handlingar **24**(10): 173 pp.

Westwood, John Obadiah
1840. An introduction to the modern classification of insects.   Generic synopsis, **2**:49–51. London.

Zetterstedt, Johann Wilhelm
1840. Insecta Lapponica; sectio quinta.   Neuroptera, 1025–74.   Leipzig.

INDEX

The page entries in **boldface** type refer to the principal treatment of the families, genera and species in the text. Page numbers 291–303 refer to the check list. Names which are synonyms, or of changed generic assignment, are indicated by *italic* type.

A

a, Athripsodes species, 221, **235**
a, Leptocella species, 215, **221**
a, Oecetis species, 237, **244**
a, Polycentropus species, 63, **66**
a, Triaenodes species, 249, **253**
A, Hydropsychid Genus, 15, 77, **83**
A, Phryganeid Genus, 162, 163, **167**
A, Psychomyiid Genus, 53, 69, **73**, 74
aba, Triaenodes, 12, 245, 246, 247, **249**, 252, 302
abbreviatus, Limnephilus, 298
acadia, Hydroptila, 296
acnestus, Limnephilus, 298
Acrocentropus, 55, 56, 292
acrocurvus, Limnephilus, 298
Acronopsyche, 202, 300
acropedes, Rhyacophila, 291
aculea, Oxyethira, 295
acuna, Mayatrichia, 278, **279**, 296
ademus, Limnephilus, 299
adironica, Plectrocnemia, 64, 293
adustus, Limnephilus, 298
aegerfasciella, Clymene, 41, 292
aegerfasciella, Protoptila, 292
aenicta, Apatelia, 297
aenicta, Radema, 297
aeola, Oxyethira, 295
aequalis, Limnephilus, 298
aequalis, Philopotamus, 292
aequalis, Trentonius, 292
aerata, Hydropsyche, 6, 14, 87, 91, 93, **101**, 102, 294
affinis, Polycentropus, 70, 293
Agapetus, 30, 31, **39**, 292
Agarodes, 303
aglona, Pycnopsyche, 299
Agraylea, 118, 120, **122**, 295
Agrypnetes, 165, 296
Agrypnia, 164, **165**, 296
ajax, Hydroptila, 14, 141, 145, 147, **153**, 296
alafimbriata, Mystacides, 302
alagmus, Athripsodes, 223, 227, **229**, 301
alascense, Glossosoma, 292
alascensis, Asynarchus, 165, 296
alascensis, Dicosmoecus, 297
alaskensis, Platyphylax, 297
alberta, Rhyacophila, 291
albicornis, Hydroptila, 6, 141, 145, 147, **151**, 152, 296
albida, Leptocella, 11, 215, 216, 217, 219, **220**, 301
albidus, Leptocerus, 220, 301

albifrons, Phryganea, 221
albipunctus, Plectrocnemia, 293
albipunctus, Polycentropus, 293
albostictus, Athripsodes, 301
albostictus, Leptocerus, 301
alces, Athripsodes, 301
aldinus, Limnephilus, 298
Alepomyia, 258, 302
Alepomyiodes, 258, 302
alexanderi, Protoptila, 292
Algonquina, 185, 297
alhedra, Hydropsyche, 294
alicia, Neothremma, 300
Allegophylax, 193, 299
Allocosmoecus, 297
Allomyia, 297
Allophylax, 196, 299
almota, Parapsyche, 293
alseae, Homoplectra, 294
alternans, Hydropsyche, 294
alternans, Philopotamus, 294
amblis, Hydropsyche, 294
amera, Heteroplectron, 300
amera, Psilotreta, 286, 300
americana, Olemira, 258, 302
americana, Orthotrichia, **140**, 141, 295
americana, Sericostoma, 303
americana, Setodes, 212, 301
americanum, Ganonema, 209, 300
americanum, Glossosoma, 292
americanum, Lepidostoma, 302
americanum, Oligoplectrum, 266, 303
americanum, Sericostoma, 300
americanus. Brachycentrus, 263, 264, **266**, 303
americanus, Leptocerus, 11, **212**, 301
americanus, Limnephilus, 298
americanus, Philopotamus, 47, 292
amicus, Halesus, 297
amicus, Platycentropus, 297
Amiocentrus, 263, 303
amoena, Hydroptila, 7, 142, 145, **150**, 295
ampoda, Hydroptila, 295
Anabolia, 185
Anabolina, 185, 297
Anagapetus, 292
anahua, Exitrichia, 154
analis, Cheumatopsyche, 6, 13, 108, 110, **112**, 113, 294
analis, Hydropsyche, 112, 294
ancylus, Athripsodes, 221, 223, **227**, 228, 236, 301
ancylus, Leptocerus, 227, 301
andax, Homophylax, 300

andrea, Rhyacophila, 35, 291
angata, Dibusa, **121**, 295
angelita, Rhyacophila, 291
angusta, Hydroptila, 14, 141, 145, 147, **152**, 296
angustata, Molanna, 205
angustella, Hydroptila, 139
angustipennis, Chimarra, 49, 50, **51**, 292
angustipennis, Neuronia, 174, 296
angustipennis, Ptilostomis, 172, **174**, 296
angustus, Athripsodes, 223, 227, **231**, 235, 301
angustus, Leptocerus, 231, 301
anillus, Dolophilus, 292
anisca, Ochrotrichia, 7, 15, 126, 127, 129, **131**, 132, 295
anisca, Polytrichia, 131, 295
Anisocentropus, 300
annulicornis, Athripsodes, 223, 227, **232**, 301
annulicornis, Helicopsyche, 266, 303
annulicornis, Leptocerus, 232, 301
annulicornis, Psychomyia, 75
anomala, Rhyacophila, 291
antennatus, Stenophylax, 299
antica, Neuronia, 196, 299
antica, Pycnopsyche, 194, **196**, 299
Aopsyche, 260, 303
Apatania, 181, 205, 300
Apatelia, 181, 297
Apatidea, 181, 297
aphanta, Cheumatopsyche, 6, 108, 110, **111**, 113, 294
Aphropsyche, 82, **83**, 84, 294
apicalis, Arctopsyche, 83, 293
apicalis, Oecetina, 242, 302
apicalis, Parapsyche, 83, 293
Apolopsyche, 185, 297
aprilis, Aphropsyche, **83**, 84, 294
araya, Oxyethira, 295
Arcadopsyche, 259, 302
arctia, Hydroptila, 296
arctica, Goniotaulius, 297
arctica, Radema, 297
Arctoecia, 185
Arctopsyche, 78, 80, 81, **83**, 293
ardis, Oligophlebodes, 283, 284, 285, 300
areolatum, Chilostigma, 199, 299
areolatum, Limnephilus, 299
aretto, Limnephilus, 282, 299
arga, Phryganea, 183, 297
argentella, Chimarra, 292
argenteus, Limnephilus, 14, 298
argosa, Hydroptila, 296
argus, Astenophylax, 183, 297
arielles, Athripsodes, 301
arinale, Hydropsyche, 6, 87, 91, 93, **104**, 294
arizona, Limnephilus, 298
arizonensis, Cheumatopsyche, 294
arizonensis, Dolophilus, 292
arizonensis, Helicopsyche, 288, 289, 303
arizonensis, Hydropsychodes, 294
arizonensis, Polycentropus, 293
arizonica, Notidobia, 303
arizonicum, Oligoplectrum, 303
arizonicum, Sericostoma, 303

arizonicus, Brachycentrus, 303
armata, Hydroptila, 141, 142, **147**, 148, 149, 150, 151, 152, 153, 295
artesus, Agapetus, 40, 292
arva, Ochrotrichia, 128, **132**, 295
arva, Polytrichia, 132, 295
aspilus, Brachycentrus, 263, 303
aspinosus, Leptocerus, 230, 231, 301
assimilis, Anabolia, 299
assimilis, Limnephilus, 299
assimilis, Sericostoma, 303
Astenophylax, 177, 178, 179, **183**, 297
astera, Cernotina, 293
Astoplectron, 287, 300
aterrima, Chimarra, 8, 14, 49, **50**, 270, 292
Athripsodes, 6, 205, 209, 210, 211, 212, **221**, 301
atlinensis, Chilostigma, 299
Atomyia, 258, 302
Atopsyche, 30, 292
atrata, Rhyacophila, 291
atripennis, Anisogamus, 297
atripennis, Dicosmoecus, 297
atripes, Dicosmoecus, 297
atripes, Platyphylax, 297
aureolus, Plectrocnemia, 64, 293
aureolus, Polycentropus, 59, **64**, 293
auriceps, Phylocentropus, 293
auriceps, Plectrocnemia, 293
australis, Plectrocnemia, 64, 293
autumnalis, Setodes, 302
autumnus, Neophylax, 7, 8, **203**, 300
avara, Oecetis, 5, 13, 237, **240**, 301
avara, Setodes, 236, 240, 301
avigo, Glyphopsyche, 202, 299
avigo, Psychoglypha, 202, 299
ayama, Mayatrichia, 15, **160**, 278, 279, 296
ayanus, Neophylax, 203, **205**, 300
azteca, Loxotrichia, 133, 295
azteca, Oxyethira, 295

B

b, Athripsodes species, 221, **235**
b, Oecetis species, 237, **244**
b, Triaenodes species, 245, **253**
B, Psychomyiid Genus, 53, 69, **74**
bactro, Micrasema, 303
banksi, Anisogamus, 299
banksi, Philocasa, 299
banksi, Rhyacophila, **268**, 291
Banksiola, 163, 164, 165, **169**, 296
baris, Triaenodes, 12, 246, 249, **252**, 302
basalis, Rhyacophila, 291
bella, Psychoglypha, 299
bellus, Glyphotaelius, 299
Beraea, 205, **208**, 300
Beraeidae, 19, 20, 24, 25, 29, **208**, 300
berneri, Hydroptila, 296
betteni, Grammotaulius, 297
betteni, Hydropsyche, 86, 91, 93, **99**, 100, 106, 294
betteni, Rhyacophila, 291

biannulatus, Hemiteles, 5
bicolor, Leptocerus, 244
bidens, Hydropsyche, 5, 91, 95, **107**, 294
bifida, Hydropsyche, 6, 87, 91, 96, **97**, 98, 99, 100, 294
bifidus, Clistoronia, 298
bifidus, Limnephilus, 299
bifila, Rhyacophila, 291
bimaculatus, Limnephilus, 186, **189**, 298
bimaculatus, Neureclipsis, 14, 56, **57**, 293
bimaculatus, Phryganea, 56, 57, 293
bipartita, Rhyacophila, 291
blarina, Rhyacophila, 291
blenda, Molanna, 206, **208**, 300
boltoni, Glossosoma, 39
borealis, Helicopsyche, 10, **266**, 288, 289, 303
borealis, Heteroplectron, 300
borealis, Notidobia, 266, 303
borealis, Psilotreta, 285, 300
boreàlis, Triaenodes, 302
boulderensis, Agapetus, 292
brachiata, Orthotrichia, 140, 295
Brachycentridae, 2, 19, 20, 22, 26, 29, 30, **260**, 303
Brachycentrus, 261, 262, **263**, 303
bradorata, Prophryganea, 296
breviatus, Dolophilus, 47, 292
brevipennis, Arctopsyche, 293
brevipennis, Limnephilus, 298
brevipennis, Psilopteryx, 300
brevipennis, Psychoronia, 300
brevipennis, Stenophylax, 298
bronta, Hydropsyche, 6, 9, 87, 91, 95, **98**, 294
bruesi, Rhyacophila, 291
brunnea, Rhyacophila, 291
brustia, Stactobia, 124, 295
brustia, Tascobia, 124, 295
bryanti, Alepomyia, 258, 302
bryanti, Glyphopsyche, 200, 299
bryanti, Lepidostoma, 302
burksi, Cheumatopsyche, 15, 108, 112, **113**, 294

C

c, Athripsodes species, 221, **235**, 236
Caborius, 6, 178, 180, **196**, 299
Calamoceratidae, 19, 20, 22, 26, 29, **209**, 300
calcarata, Goera, 302
calcea, Cernotina, **72**, 73, 293
californica, Arctopsyche, 293
californica, Diplectrona, 84, 294
californica, Helicopsyche, 266, 303
californica, Hydropsyche, 271, 294
californica, Phryganea, 297
californica, Rhyacophila, 291
californicum, Heteroplectron, 301
californicus, Nerophilus, 300
californicus, Oligoplectrum, 303
californicus, Silo, 300
calva, Banksiola, 296
calypso, Stenophylax, 300
campyla, Cheumatopsyche, 5, 13, 108, 110, 112, **113**, 114, 294

canadensis, Apatania, 201, 300
canadensis, Banksiola, 169, 296
canadensis, Limnephilus, 299
canadensis, Mystacides, 255, 302
canadensis, Neuronia, 296
canadensis, Phanocelia, 201, 300
canadensis, Polycentropus, 67, 293
canadensis, Pristosilo, 258, 302
cancellatus, Athripsodes, 5, 222, 227, **233**, 301
cancellatus, Leptocerus, 233, 301
candida, Leptocella, 5, 215, 216, **217**, 219, 287, 301
candida, Setodes, 217, 301
canixa, Dolotrichia, 154
cantha, Lepidostoma, 303
cantha, Protoptila, 292
capitana, Ochrotrichia, **275**, 276, 295
Carborius, 196
cardis, Parapsyche, 83, 293
caroli, Anabolia, 298
caroli, Limnephilus, 298
carolina, Hydropsyche, 294
carolina, Lepidostoma, 302
carolina, Macronema, 116, 295
carolina, Macronemum, 115, **116**, 117, 295
carolina, Notiopsyche, 259, 302
carolina, Rhyacophila, 291
carolinensis, Polycentropus, 59, **66**, 293
carolinus, Phylocentropus, 293
carpenteri, Rhyacophila, 291
carri, Oecetis, 244, 301
cascada, Lepania, 297
cascadensis, Lepidostoma, 302
cascadensis, Jenortha, 259, 302
catawba, Hydropsyche, 294
caxima, Guerrotrichia, 154, 296
caxima, Neotrichia, 296
celatus, Agapetus, 292
celsus, Palaeagapetus, 38, 292
celsus, Paragapetus, 292
centra, Hydropsyche, 294
centralis, Asynarchus, 283, 299
centralis, Chyranda, 299
centralis, Polycentropus, 58, 61, 63, **64**, 67, 293
Cernotina, 52, 54, **72**, 74, 293
charlesi, Polycentropus, 293
charonis, Micrasema, 262, 303
cheilonis, Hydropsyche, 10, 87, 91, 96, **98**, 106, 294
chelifera, Triaenodella, 244
Cheumatopsyche, 7, 76, 77, 81, 82, 86, 98, **108**, 294
childreni, Banksiola, 296
childreni, Neuronia, 296
Chilostigma, 180, **199**, 299
Chimarra, 44, 45, **48**, 292
Chimarrha, 48, 292
Chironomidae, 4
chlorotica, Hydropsyche, 98, 294
Chyranda, **283**, 299
cinerascens, Oecetis, 11, 236, 237, **241**, 243, 301
cinerascens, Setodes, 241, 301
cinerea, Hydropsyche, 86
cinerea, Molanna, 205, 207, 300

cinerea, Phryganea, 11, **175**, 176, 297
cinereum, Lepidostoma, 303
cinereum, Silo, 303
cinereus, Polycentropus, 6, 58, 61, **67**, 293
circularis, Platyphylax, 299
circularis, Pycnopsyche, 299
clausus, Limnephilus, 298
clavata, Ithytrichia, 123, **124**, 295
clinei, Plectrocnemia, 293
clinei, Polycentropus, 293
Clistoronia, 297
Clostoeca, 299
Clymene, 41, 292
cockerelli, Hydropsyche, 294
cockerelli, Limnephilus, 298
codona, Hydropsyche, 99, 294
coercens, Oxyethira, 133, **137**, 295
colei, Polycentropus, 293
collata, Neotrichia, 7, 154, 157, **159**, 296
coloma, Protoptila, 292
coloradensis, Dicosmoecus, 297
coloradensis, Goniotaulius, 298
coloradensis, Leptocella, 215, 301
coloradensis, Limnephilus, 298
coloradensis, Oligophlebodes, 300
coloradensis, Rhyacophila, 291
colorata, Agrypnia, 296
Colpotaulius, 185
combinatus, Limnephilus, 190, 298
commixta, Neuronia, 166, 296
complicata, Ecclisomyia, 296
complicata, Fabria, 296
complicata, Rhyacophila, 291
concatenata, Banksiola, 170, 296
concatenata, Neuronia, 169, 296
concinnus, Neophylax, 202, 204, 300
concolor, Limnephilus, 299
confusa, Hydropsyche, 294
confusa, Ithytrichia, 121, 125, 126, 133, 295
confusa, Ochrotrichia, 127, 129, **133**, 295
confusa, Philopotamus, 294
confusa, Polytrichia, 130
confusus, Polycentropus, 59, 64, **65**, 293
congener, Limnephilus, 298
connexa, Astoplectron, 286, 300
consimilis, Hesperophylax, 280, 281, 297
consimilis, Hydroptila, 141, 145, 147, **153**, 296
consimilis, Limnephilus, 297
consimilis, Neophylax, 300
consocius, Limnephilus, 185, 186, 189, **190**, 298
conspersa, Ecclisomyia, 300
conspersa, Pycnopsyche, 299
consueta, Tinodes, 293
contorta, Ochrotrichia, 127, **131**, 295
contorta, Polytrichia, 131, 295
cophus, Athripsodes, 301
copiosa, Apatidea, 181
copiosus, Dolophilus, 45
cornuta, Hydropsyche, 106, 294
corona, Theliopsyche, 260, 303
costalis, Asynarchus, 300
costalis, Hydroptila, 133
costalis, Lepidostoma, 302

costalis, Olemira, 302
costalis, Psychoronia, 300
costello, Agraylea, 122, 295
crasmus, Agapetus, 40, 292
crassicornis, Agrypnetes, 165
crassicornis, Hydropsyche, 303
crassicornis, Polycentropus, 59, 61, **64**, 293
crassicornis, Sericostoma, 303
crassus, Limnephilus, 298
crepuscularis, Brachycentrus, 57, 293
crepuscularis, Neureclipsis, 5, 56, **57**, 293
cristata, Orthotrichia, 140, **141**, 295
crotchi, Banksiola, 296
crotchi, Homophylax, 300
cruzensis, Dolophilus, 292
cuanis, Hydropsyche, 6, 87, 91, 93, **100**, 294
curtus, Anabolia, 298
curtus, Limnephilus, 298
curvata, Agrypnetes, 165, 296
Cyllene, 154, 296
Cyrnellus, 52, 54, **71**, 74, 293

D

Dampfitrichia, 133, 295
dan, Halesus, 299
Dasystegia, 165, 166, 296
debilis, Anagapetus, 292
deceptivum, Lepidostoma, 303
deceptivum, Thremma, 303
deceptus, Anabolia, 298
deceptus, Limnephilus, 298
deflata, Agrypnia, 296
deflata, Prophryganea, 296
delicatus, Neophylax, 300
delineata, Hydroptila, 142, **151**, 276, 295
delira, Stactobia, 124, 295
delira, Tascobia, 124, 125, 295
delrio, Hydropsyche, 271, 294
demita, Philocasca, 299
demora, Hydropsyche, 294
dentata, Hydroptila, 295
dentata, Triaenodes, 252, 302
depravata, Hydropsyche, 15, 91, 93, **100**, 294
designatus, Hesperophylax, 8, **183**, 297
designatus, Limnephilus, 183, 297
despectus, Limnephilus, 192, 298
dextra, Agrypnia, 296
diarina, Leptocella, 5, 215, 216, 217, **218**, 220, 221, 301
Dibusa, 119, **121**, 295
dicantha, Hydropsyche, 91, 93, **102**, 294
Dicosmoecus, 176, 178, **181**, 297
difficilis, Frenesia, 199, 200, 299
difficilis, Limnephilus, 199, 299
digitata, Neotrichia, 278
dilutus, Athripsodes, 10, 11, 221, 223, 227, **231**, 301
dilutus, Leptocerus, 231, 301
dimicki, Brachycentrus, 303
Diplectrona, 78, 79, 81, **84**, 294
dipsia, Triaenodes, 246, **252**, 253, 302
disjuncta, Oecetina, 301
disjuncta, Oecetis, 240, 301

disjunctus, Anisogamus, 299
disjunctus, Clostoeca, 299
dispar, Polycentropus, 294
dissimilis, Heteroplectron, 300
dissimilis, Psilotreta, 285, 300
distincta, Agarodes, 303
distinctum, Sericostoma, 303
distinctus, Philopotamus, 47, 292
distinctus, Trentonius, **47**, 292
divergens, Limnephilus, 299
divergens, Parapsyche, 293
divergens, Pycnopsyche, 299
diversa, Anabolina, 185, 298
diversa, Lype, 10, **74**, 293
diversa, Psychomyia, 74, 293
diversus, Limnephilus, 298
divisa, Hydropsyche, 294
doddsi, Rhyacophila, 291
Dolophiliella, 45, 292
Dolophilus, 44, **45**, 292
Dolotrichia, 154, 296
dorcus, Philopotamus, 292
dorcus, Trentonius, 292
doringa, Diplectrona, 84, 294
dorsalis, Oxyethira, 140, 295
dossuaria, Banksiola, 296
dossuaria, Neuronia, 170, 296
Drosophila, 48
Drusinus, 181, **202**, 300
dualis, Oxyethira, 136, **139**, 295
dubia, Hydropsyche, 294
dubitans, Hydropsyche, 58, 293
dubitans, Neuronia, 173, 296

E

Ecclisomyia, 300
ecosa, Rhyacophila, 291
ectus, Limnephilus, 298
edalis, Neotrichia, 156, **158**, 296
eddlestoni, Oecetis, 237, **240**, 301
edwardsi, Anisogamus, 300
edwardsi, Drusinus, 300
ela, Cheumatopsyche, 294
elarus, Polycentropus, 59, 64, **65**, 293
elegans, Goera, 300
elegans, Limnephilus, 189, 298
elia, Chimarra, **269**, 292
eliaga, Ochrotrichia, 7, 126, 127, 129, **132**, 295
eliaga, Polytrichia, 132, 295
elongatus, Limnephilus, 298
elsis, Parapsyche, 293
emarginatus, Anabolia, 298
emarginatus, Limnephilus, 298
eminens, Limnephilus, 192, 298
enonis, Cheumatopsyche, 294
epilone, Theliopsyche, 303
eroga, Neotrichia, 278
erotica, Protoptila, 42, 43, **44**, 292
erraticus, Athripsodes, 223, 227, **235**, 301
erullus, Athripsodes, 10, 223, 227, **235**, 301
etrona, Cheumatopsyche, 294
Eubasilissa, 162, 164, **168**, 296
Eustenace, 193, **299**

excita, Glossosoma, 292
exilis, Leptocella, 301
Exitrichia, 154, 277, 278, 296
exquisita, Leptocella, 5, 11, 215, 216, **217**, 218, 287, 301
exquisita, Leptocerus, 217, 301
externus, Limnephilus, 298
extractus, Limnephilus, 298

F

Fabria, 164, **166**, 167, 296
fagus, Limnephilus, 298
fairchildi, Rhyacophila, 35, 291
falca, Neotrichia, 14, 154, 156, **159**, 296
falcatum, Micrasema, 261, 303
Farula, 176, 300
fasciatella, Smicridea, **85**, 294
fattigi, Hydropsyche, 294
felipe, Ochrotrichia, **275**, 295
felix, Diplectrona, 84
femoralis, Wormaldia, 51, 292
femoralis, Limnephilus, 298
fenestra, Rhyacophila, 7, 32, 35, **36**, 37, 291
feria, Chimarra, 7, 15, 47, 49, **50**, 292
flava, Potamyia, 5, **85**, 294
flavata, Pycnopsyche, 299
flavata, Stenophylax, 299
flaveolata, Setodes, 242, 301
flavescens, Triaenodes, 246, 249, **251**, 302
flavicollis, Asynarchus, 298
flavicollis, Limnephilus, 298
flavicornis, Holocentropus, 67, 293
flavicornis, Molanna, 205, **208**, 300
flavida, Allotrichia, 122, 295
flavida, Oecetina, 242, 301
flavida, Psychomyia, 9, **75**, 293
flavipennis, Homophylax, 300
flavo-maculata, Hydropsyche, 84
flavostellus, Limnephilus, 298
flavum, Macronema, 85, 294
flavus, Athripsodes, 7, 221, 223, 227, **228**, 301
flavus, Holocentropus, 68, 293
flavus, Leptocerus, 228, 301
flavus, Polycentropus, 59, 61, **68**, 293
flexuosa, Marilia, 300
florida, Chimarra, **270**, 292
florida, Triaenodes, 302
floridana, Oecetina, 242, 302
floridana, Setodes, 302
floridanus, Athripsodes, 301
floridanus, Leptocerus, 301
forcipata, Oxyethira, 135, **139**, 295
forcipatus, Limnephilus, 298
formosa, Clistoronia, 297
formosa, Rhyacophila, 291
formosus, Halesus, 297
fraterna, Agraylea, 122, 295
fraterna, Cernotina, 293
fraternus, Cyrnus, 293
fraternus, Hylepsyche, 297
fraternus, Platycentropus, 297
Frenesia, 177, 178, 180, **199**, 299
Friga, 236, 301

frigida, Apatania, 297
frijole, Limnephilus, **282**, 299
frisoni, Hydropsyche, 10, 87, 91, 95, **105**, 106, 294
frontalis, Drusinus, 300
frontalis, Psilotreta, 286, **287**, 300
frontalis, Triaenodes, 245, 247, **249**, 302
frosti, Atomyia, 302
frosti, Lepidostoma, 302
fuliginosus, Brachycentrus, 303
fumosa, Oecetina, 236, 241, 301
fumosus, Asynarchus, 298
fumosus, Limnephilus, 298
fusca, Anisocentropus, 300
fusca, Neuronia, 173, 296
fusca, Phryganea, 161
fuscipes, Agapetus, 39
fuscula, Goera, 302
fuscula, Neuronia, 36, 291
fuscula, Rhyacophila, 32, 34, 35, **36**, 291
fuscus, Neophylax, 203, **205**, 300
futilis, Leptocerus, 232, 301

G

gabriella, Dolophiliella, 45, 292
gabriella, Dolophilus, 292
gameta, Heteroplectron, 287, 300
Ganonema, 209, 300
gemona, Rhyacophila, 291
genota, Goerita, 302
gentilis, Pycnopsyche, 299
gentilis, Stenophylax, 299
Genus A, Hydropsychid, 15, 77, **83**
Genus A, Phryganeid, 162, 163, **167**
Genus A, Psychomyiid, 53, 69, **73**, 74
Genus B, Psychomyiid, 53, 69, **74**
georgia, Oecetis, 301
gilvipes, Dicosmoecus, 297
gilvipes, Stenophylax, 297
glaberrima, Rhyacophila, 7, 32, 34, **35**, 36, 291
glacialis, Agrypnia, 296
glacialis, Holocentropus, 68, 293
glacialis, Polycentropus, 59, 61, 63, **68**, 293
glasa, Loxotrichia, 295
glasa, Oxyethira, 295
Glossosoma, 8, 30, 31, **39**, 40, 292
Glossosomatinae, 30, **38**
Glyphidotaelius, 183, 297
Glyphopsyche, 177, 180, **200**, 202, 299
Glyphotaelius, 178, 179, **183**, 297
Goera, 256, **257**, 302
Goeridae, 2, 19, 20, 24, 26, 29, **256**, 302
Goerita, 256, 257, **258**, 302
gordoni, Rhyacophila, 291
gorteba, Beraea, **208**, 300
gracilis, Cheumatopsyche, 294
gracilis, Hydropsyche, 294
gracilis, Leptocella, 301
gracilis, Leptophylax, **184**, 297
Grammotaulius, 181, **185**, 297
grandiosa, Hydroptila, 14, 141, 142, 147, **151**, 295

grandis, Arctopsyche, 293
grandis, Dicôsmoecus, 297
grandis, Hydropsyche, 293
grandis, Phryganea, 174
grandis, Rhyacophila, 291
grandis, Setodes, 212, 301
gravidus, Limnephilus, 298
grellus, Holocentropus, 293
grellus, Polycentropus, 293
Grensia, 180, **201**, 299
grisea, Agarodes, 303
grisea, Oxyethira, 135, **138**, 295
grisea, Phanopsyche, 258, 302
grisea, Silo, 303
grisea, Theliopsyche, 303
grisea, Triaenodes, 244, 245, 247, **249**, 302
griselda, Lype, 74, 75, 293
griseolum, Sericostoma, 303
griseum, Lepidostoma, 302
griseum, Sericostoma, 303
groenlandica, Apatania, 297
groenlandica, Radema, 297
Guerrotrichia, 154, 296
gunda, Hydroptila, 296
guttatus, Oecetina, 302
guttatus, Setodes, 302
guttifer, Halesus, 196, 299
guttifer, Pycnopsyche, 194, **196**, 299
gyra, Cheumatopsyche, 294

H

hageni, Hydropsyche, 87, 91, 93, **103**, 294
hageni, Limnephilus, 298
Halesochila, 299
halidus, Polycentropus, 293
hamata, Hydroptila, 13, 141, 142, 145, **149**, 152, 295
harmstoni, Rhyacophila, **268**, 291
harrimani, Limnephilus, 298
Helicopsyche, **266**, **288**, 303
Helicopsychidae, 2, 19, 20, 22, 26, 29, **266**, 303
helma, Cheumatopsyche, 294
helo, Triaenodes, 302
Hemiteles, 5
hespera, Pycnopsyche, 299
hespera, Schizopelex, 303
hespera, Stenophylax, 299
Hesperophylax, 8, 178, 179, **183**, 280, 297
hesperum, Sericostoma, 303
Heteroplectron, 301
hiaspa, Lorotrichia, 154
hingstoni, Limnephilus, 191, 298
hirta, Phryganea, 258
hirtipes, Radema, 297
hirtipes, Tinodes, 297
Holocentropus, 52, 58
Holocentropus species 1, 69
Homophylax, 300
Homoplectra, 294
hostilis, Glyphotaelius, 183, 297
hostis, Halesus, 181, 297
howellae, Oropsyche, **83**, 294
hyalinata, Rhyacophila, 291

hyalinus, Limnephilus, 186, 189, **191**, 298
Hydrobiosinae, 30
Hydropsyche, 3, 7, 76, 77, 81, 82, 83, 85, **86**, 108, 294
Hydropsychidae, 2, 3, 4, 11, 19, 22, 25, 29, 51, **76**, 293
Hydroptila, 119, **141**, 295
Hydroptilidae, 2, 4, 6, 7, 10, 11, 14, 15, 18, 20, 22, 25, 26, 51, **117**, 295
Hydrorchestria, 122, 295
Hylepsyche, 181, 297

I

icona, Hydroptila, 154, 296
iculus, Polycentropus, 293
idaho, Glossosoma, 292
idahoensis, Chimarrha, 292
ignita, Triaenodes, 246, 249, **252**, 302
ignitus, Leptocerus, 252, 302
illini, Agapetus, 7, 14, 39, **40**, 292
immobilis, Oecetis, 11, 237, 240, **241**, 244, 301
immobilis, Setodes, 236, 241, 301
improba, Agrypnia, 296
improba, Phryganea, 296
incanus, Brachycentrus, 303
incerta, Enoicyla, 297
incerta, Leptocerus, 302
incerta, Oecetis, 236
incerta, Radema, 297
incerta, Setodes, 256, 302
incisus, Hesperophylax, 281, 297
incommoda, Hydropsyche, 15, 91, 95, 100, 105, **106**, 107, 294
inconspicua, Oecetis, 5, 8, 11, 13, 236, 237, 240, **242**, 244, 301
inconspicuus, Leptocerus, 242, 301
indecisa, Goera, 300
indecisa, Psilotreta, 285, 286, 287, 300
indecisus, Philopotamus, 294
indiana, Pycnopsyche, 194, **196**, 299
indiana, Stenophylax, 196, 299
indicans, Limnephilus, 181, 297
indistinctus, Halesus, 181
indistinctus, Limnephilus, 297
indistinctus, Platycentropus, 297
indivisus, Limnephilus, 5, 185, 186, 189, **191**, 298
inermis, Arctopsyche, 293
infernale, Radema, 181
infernalis, Anisogamus, 298
infernalis, Limnephilus, 298
injusta, Setodes, 252, 302
injusta, Triaenodes, 11, 245, 246, 247, **252**, 302
inornata, Apatania, 181
inornata, Fabria, 11, 12, **166**, 167, 296
inornata, Neuronia, 166, 296
inornata, Oecetina, 242, 302
inornatus, Athripsodes, 301
inornatus, Leptocerus, 301
instabilis, Hydropsyche, 86
insularis, Ochrotrichia, 126, 274
intercisus, Limnephilus, 299
interjecta, Oecetina, 255, 302

intermedia, Mystrophora, 39, 292
intermedium, Glossosoma, 8, **39**, 292
intermedius, Limnephilus, 298
interrogationis, Grammotaulius, 297
interrogationis, Phryganea, 185, 297
interrupta, Phryganea, 176, 212, 297
interruptus, Holocentropus, 69, 293
interruptus, Polycentropus, 12, 59, 61, 62, **69**, 293
intervena, Leptocella, 215, 219, 301
invaria, Polycentropus, 291
invaria, Rhyacophila, 268, 291
iranda, Rhyacophila, 291
iridis, Agapetus, **269**, 292
Ironoquia, 180, **184**, 297
irrorata, Arctopsyche, 83, 293
irrorata, Glyphopsyche, 200, 201, 299
irrorata, Phryganea, 299
irroratus, Polycentropus, 58
isolatus, Hesperophylax, 297
Ithytrichia, 118, 120, **123**, 295

J

janus, Limnephilus, 299
jeanae, Protoptila, 292
Jenortha, 259, 302
jucundus, Dicosmoecus, 297
Jyrvia, 165, 296

K

kansensis, Hydropsyche, 85, 294
kaskaskia, Caborius, 197, **198**, 299
kennicotti, Limnephilus, 298
keratus, Limnephilus, 298
kiamichi, Rhyacophila, 35, **37**, 291
kincaidi, Limnephilus, 298
kitae, Neotrichia, 154, 156, **158**, 296
knowltoni, Lepidostoma, 302
kovalevskii, Ptilostomis, 171, 296

L

labida, Psilotreta, 286, **287**, 300
labus, Limnephilus, 298
ladogensis, Aphelocheira, 83, 293
ladogensis, Arctopsyche, 83, 293
lamellaris, Ithytrichia, 123, 124
lapponica, Neuronia, 296
lapponica, Oligotricha, 296
lasia, Cheumatopsyche, 12, 15, 108, 110, **114**, 294
lateralis, Brachycentrus, 6, 263, **265**, 303
lateralis, Phryganea, 265, 303
latifascia, Anisocentropus, 300
latifascia, Notidobia, 300
latipennis, Lepidostoma, 302
latipennis, Notiopsyche, 258, 302
ledra, Rhyacophila, 32, 35, **37**, 291
lega, Protoptila, 42, **43**, 292
leonardi, Hydropsyche, 294
Lepania, 297
lepida, Enoicyla, 195, 299

lepida, Hydropsyche, 108
lepida, Pycnopsyche, 194, **195**, 299
Lepidostoma, **258**, 266, 302
Lepidostomatidae, 2, 20, 24, 26, 30, **258**, 302
Leptocella, 15, 17, 21, 210, 211, 212, **213**, 301
Leptoceridae, 2, 5, 6, 11, 17, 20, 22, 26, 29, **209**, 301
Leptocerus, 210, **212**, 301
Leptophylax, 179, **184**, 297
Leucotrichia, 117, **120**, **271**, 295
liba, Lepidostoma, 8, 9, **259**, 303
limbata, Pycnopsyche, 299
limbatus, Stenophylax, 193, 299
limnella, Helicopsyche, 289, 303
Limnephilidae, 2, 4, 6, 11, 20, 24, 26, 27, 28, **176**, 297
Limnephilus, 178, 181, **185**, 283, 297
limpia, Leucotrichia, 271, **273**, 295
lineatum, Macronema, 114
litha, Anabolina, 298
lithus, Limnephilus, 298
lividum, Glossosoma, 292
lividum, Tinodes, 292
lloydi, Protoptila, 43, 292
lobata, Schizopelex, 303
lobifera, Rhyacophila, 6, 32, **35**, 291
logana, Ochrotrichia, 295
logana, Polytrichia, 295
lometa, Ochrotrichia, 295
lometa, Polytrichia, 295
longicercus, Anabolia, 189, 298
longicornis, Mystacides, 11, 14, 253, 254, **255**, 302
longicornis, Phryganea, 253, 255, 302
longus, Holocentropus, 69, 293
lorettae, Grammotaulius, 297
Lorotrichia, 154, 296
Loxotrichia, 133, 295
lucia, Chimarrha, 51, 292
lucidus, Phylocentropus, 55, **56**, 292
lucidus, Polycentropus, 55, 56, 292
luctuosa, Rhyacophila, 291
luculenta, Pycnopsyche, 194, **196**, 299
luculentus, Stenophylax, 196, 299
lugens, Leptocerus, 232, 301
lumina, Psychomyia, 75, 293
lumina, Psychomyiella, 293
lunonus, Limnephilus, 298
lutea, Plectrocnemia, 67, 293
luteolus, Limnephilus, 298
lutescens, Brachycentrus, 303
lutescens, Sphinctogaster, 263, 303
lydia, Lepidostoma, 303
Lype, 51, 54, **74**, 293
lyratus, Caborius, 197, **198**, 299
lyratus, Carborius, 198

M

macdunnoughi, Agrypnia, 296
macdunnoughi, Prophryganea, 296
macgillivrayi, Limnephilus, 298
Macronema, 114, 295
Macronemum, 4, 21, 77, 79, 81, **114**, 295

maculata, Allotrichia, 296
maculata, Beraea, 41, 43, 292
maculata, Clistoronia, 297
maculata, Hydroptila, 296
maculata, Phryganea, 263
maculata, Protoptila, 41, 42, **43**, 44, 292
maculatus, Dicosmoecus, 297
maculatus, Leptocerus, 233, 301
maculatus, Polycentropus, 59, 64, **65**, 66, 293
maculicornis, Hydropsyche, 96, 294
maculipennis, Halesus, 181, 297
maculosa, Ecclisomyia, 300
magnifica, Clistoronia, 297
magnifica, Halesus, 297
magnus, Clistoronia, 297
magnus, Hesperophylax, 280, 281, 297
mainensis, Rhyacophila, 291
major, Dolophilus, 45, 292
malleatus, Agapetus, 292
manistee, Rhyacophila, 291
marginalis, Cyrnellus, 5, **71**, 293
marginalis, Nyctiophylax, 71, 293
marginata, Phryganea, 48
marginata, Triaenodes, 245, 247, 249, **251**, 302
marginata tarda, Triaenodes, 250
Marilia, 300
marlo, Agapetus, 292
marqueti, Hydropsyche, 294
marshamella, Beraea, 208
maximus, Phylocentropus, 55, 293
Mayatrichia, 117, 119, 120, **160**, **278**, 296
mazon, Ithytrichia, 123, **124**, 295
medialis, Colpotaulius, 190, 298
medicus, Agapetus, 40, 292
melanae, Holocentropus, 293
melanae, Polycentropus, 293
melia, Hydroptila, 296
melita, Rhyacophila, 291
melleopicta, Leucotrichia, 120
mentiens, Leptocerus, 232
mentieus, Athripsodes, 6, 221, 223, 227, **232**, 301
mentieus, Leptocerus, 232, 301
mephita, Triaenodes, 250, 302
merinthus, Limnephilus, 298
Metrichia, 120, **121**, 295
mexicana, Helicopsyche, 288, **289**, 303
mexicana, Heteroplectron, 301
mexicana, Notiomyia, 301
micans, Setodes, 242, 301
michiganensis, Oxyethira, 295
mickeli, Cheumatopsyche, 294
Micrasema, **261**, 303
minima, Pycnopsyche, 299
minimus, Cyrnellus, 71
minora, Rhyacophila, 291
minuscula, Cheumatopsyche, 108, **110**, 294
minuscula, Hydropsyche, 110, 294
minusculus, Colpotaulius, 299
minusculus, Limnephilus, 298
minusculus, Stenophylax, 185, 298
minuta, Leptocella, 215, 301
minutisimella, Cyllene, 154, 157, 296
minutisimella, Neotrichia, 154, 156, **157**, 296

minutus, Agapetus, 292
minutus, Halesus, 300
minutus, Hesperophylax, 280, 297
minutus, Oligophlebodes, 283, 300
miscus, Athripsodes, 301
miser, Limnephilus, 298
missa, Frenesia, 9, **199**, 299
missouri, Glyphopsyche, **200**, 299
missum, Chilostigma, 199, 299
mitchelli, Neophylax, 300
modesta, Alepomyia, 303
modesta, Atomyia, 258
modesta, Diplectrona, 8, **84**, 294
modestum, Lepidostoma, 303
modestus, Anabolia, 298
modestus, Limnephilus, 298
moesta, Psiloneura, 303
moesta, Psychomyia, 75, 293
moestus, Dolophilus, 8, 45, 46, **47**, 292
moestus, Limnephilus, 6, 14, 186, 189, **191**, 298
moestus, Nyctiophylax, 70, 293
moestus, Paragapetus, 45, 47, 292
Molanna, 181, **205**, 300
Molannidae, 2, 11, 20, 22, 26, 29, **205**, 208, 300
mollala, Cheumatopsyche, 294
mongolica, Apatania, 297
mongolica, Radema, 297
mono, Ochrotrichia, 295
mono, Polytrichia, 295
montana, Glossosoma, 292
montana, Rhyacophila, 35, 291
montanus, Anabolia, 298
montanus, Limnephilus, 298
Mormomyia, 258, 302
Mormonia, 258
morosa, Hydropsyche, 91, 96, **98**, 294
morosum, Oligoplectrum, 261
morrisoni, Limnephilus, 298
multifarius, Limnephilus, 192, 298
multipunctata, Agraylea, **122**, 295
musetta, Molanna, 206, **207**, 300
mutatus, Hallesus, 298
mutatus, Limnephilus, 298
mycta, Rhyacophila, 291
Mystacides, 210, 211, 212, **253**, 302
Mystrophora, 39, 292

N

nacatus, Neophylax, 300
Namamyia, 300
nascotius, Polycentropus, 61, **68**, 293
nearctica, Agrypnia, 296
nearcticus, Palaeagapetus, 292
nebulosus, Limnephilus, 298
needhami, Astenophylax, 299
Neophylax, 176, 178, 179, **202**, 256, 260, 300
Neothremma, 176, 300
Neotrichia, 118, 120, **154**, 160, 296
nephus, Athripsodes, 223, **230**, 301
nepus, Limnephilus, 298
Nerophilus, 300
Neureclipsis, 52, 53, 54, **56**, 293
Neuronia, 161

Neuropsyche, 259, 302
nevadensis, Homophylax, 300
nevadensis, Rhyacophila, 291
nicoli, Hydroptila, 296
nigra, Mystacides, 302
nigra, Potamaria, 297
nigra, Radema, 297
nigrescens, Dicosmoecus, 297
nigriculum, Sericostoma, 303
nigriculus, Anabolia, 298
nigriculus, Limnephilus, 298
nigrior, Glossosoma, 292
nigripennis, Diplectrona, 294
nigripennis, Homoplectra, 294
nigrisoma, Brachycentrus, 265, 303
nigrisoma, Sphinctogaster, 303
nigrita, Rhyacophila, 291
nigritta, Beraea, **208**, 209, 300
nigritta, Metrichia, **121**, 295
nigritta, Orthotrichia, 121, 295
nigrum, Ganonema, 300
nivea, Setodes, 220, 301
nobsca, Marilia, 300
nogus, Limnephilus, **281**, 298
nomada, Psychomyia, 75, 76, 293
nomada, Psychomyiella, 293
norcuta, Rhyacophila, 291
nordus, Athripsodes, 232, 301
Nosopus, 258, 302
notabulus, Brachycentrus, 303
Notidobia, 266, 303
Notiomyia, 301
Notiopsyche, 258, 302
notosa, Leucotrichia, **271**, 295
novamexicanus, Hydropsyche, 294
novarotunda, Rhyacophila, 291
novasota, Oxyethira, 135, 136, **138**, 295
novusamericanus, Philopotamus, 292
novusamericanus, Trentonius, 292
nox, Triaenodes, 302
numerosa, Phryganea, 264, 303
numerosus, Brachycentrus, 6, 263, **264**, 265, 266, 303
Nyctiophylax, 52, 54, **69**, 71, 74, 293

O

oaklandensis, Diplectrona, 294
oaklandensis, Homoplectra, 294
obscura, Beraea, 51, 292
obscura, Chimarra, 6, 7, 14, 15, 48, 49, 50, **51**, 270, 292
obscura, Phryganomyia, 165, 296
obscuripennis, Dicosmoecus, 297
obsoleta, Phryganea, 165
occidentalis, Brachycentrus, 303
occidentalis, Dicosmoecus, 297
occidentalis, Hesperophylax, 297
occidentalis, Hydropsyche, 294
occidentalis, Limnephilus, 298
occidentalis, Platyphylax, 183, 297
occidentis, Neophylax, 300
occideus, Dolophilus, 292
ocellifera, Neuronia, 172, 296

ocellifera, Ptilostomis, **172**, 173, 174, 296
ocelligera, Neuronia, 296
ocelligera, Oligostomis, **167**, 168, 296
ochracea, Oecetis, 237, 240, **244**, 301
ochracea, Triaenodella, 302
ochracea, Triaenodes, 302
ochraceus, Leptocerus, 236, 244, 301
Ochrotrichia, 117, 119, 120, **125**, 147, 295
Odontoceridae, 19, 20, 22, 26, 29, 208, **209**, 300
Oecetina, 236, 301
Oecetis, 4, 6, 209, 210, 211, 212, **236**, 301
Oecetodes, 236, 301
ohio, Cernotina, 72, **73**, 293
oklahoma, Cernotina, 293
okopa, Neotrichia, 9, 154, 157, **158**, 159, 277, 296
Olemira, 258, 302
oligia, Setodes, **256**, 302
oligius, Leptocerus, 256, 302
oligius, Neophylax, 300
Oligophlebodes, **283**, 300
Oligoplectrum, 263, 303
Oligopsyche, 259, 302
Oligostomis, 162, 164, 165, **167**, 169, 296
Oligotricha, 296
ontario, Lepidostoma, 302
ophioderus, Athripsodes, 223, **232**, 235, 301
oregona, Ochrotrichia, 295
oregona, Polytrichia, 295
oregonense, Glossosoma, 292
oregonensis, Arctopsyche, 293
oregonensis, Nerophilus, 300
oregonensis, Philopotamus, 292
oregonensis, Rhyacophila, 291
oreta, Rhyacophila, 291
oreus, Limnephilus, 298
ormiae, Glyphopsyche, 299
ormiae, Psychoglypha, 299
ornata, Notiomyia, 301
ornatus, Limnephilus, 186, **189**, 298
ornatus, Neophylax, 300
Oropsyche, 82, **83**, 294
orotus, Holocentropus, 69, 293
orris, Hydropsyche, 5, 13, 86, 93, 95, 105, **106**, 107, 294
Orthotrichia, 11, 119, **139**, 295
oslari, Anabolia, 298
oslari, Hydropsyche, 294
oslari, Limnephilus, 298
osmena, Neotrichia, **278**, 296
osteni, Oecetis, 11, 14, 237, **241**, 244, 301
oxa, Cheumatopsyche, 6, 108, **110**, 113, 294
oxapia, Leptocerus, 302
oxapia, Setodes, 302
Oxyethira, 11, 118, 120, 123, **133**, 295
ozburni, Arctoecia, 298
ozburni, Limnephilus, 298

P

pacifica, Rhyacophila, 291
pacificus, Limnephilus, 281, 298
pacificus, Stenophylax, 298
pagetana, Agrypnia, 165, 296

Palaeagapetus, 31, **38**, 292
palatus, Stenophylax, 181
palina, Protoptila, 42, **43**, 292
pallens, Zaporota, 299
pallescens, Plectrocnemia, 67, 293
pallicornis, Dicosmoecus, 297
pallida, Apatania, 297
pallida, Cernotina, 72, **73**, 293
pallida, Chilostigma, 299
pallida, Orthotrichia, 137, 295
pallida, Oxyethira, 133, 136, **137**, 295
pallidipes, Philopotamus, 292
pallidipes, Trentonius, 292
pallidum, Silo, 302
pallidus, Apolopsyche, 298
pallidus, Asynarchus, 299
pallidus, Cyrnus, 73, 293
palmata, Stactobia, 124, 125, 295
palmata, Tascobia, 124, **125**, 295
Parachiona, 297
Paragapetus, 45, 292
Parapsyche, 17, 78, 81, **83**, 293
pardalis, Eubasilissa, **168**, 296
pardalis, Neuronia, 168, 296
partita, Hydropsyche, 294
partitus, Allocosmoecus, 297
partitus, Limnephilus, 298
parva, Hydroptila, 293
parva, Oecetis, 302
parva, Psychomyia, 293
parva, Setodina, 236, 302
parva, Theliopsyche, 260, 303
parvula, Chaetopterygopsis, [1]84, 297
parvula, Ironoquia, 297
parvula, Oecetina, 242, 301
parvula, Stenophylax, 185, 298
parvulum, Glossosoma, 292
parvulus, Limnephilus, 298
parvulus, Neureclipsis, 57, 293
pasella, Cheumatopsyche, 108, 110, **113**, 295
pavida, Leptocella, 215, 216, **218**, 301
pavida, Setodes, 218, 301
pecos, Hydroptila, 296
pele, Notidobia, 303
pellisa, Rhyacophila, 291
Pellopsyche, 294
pellucidulus, Limnephilus, 183
pellucidus, Limnephilus, 183
penitum, Glossosoma, 292
pentus, Polycentropus, 8, **59**, 64, **65**, 293
perda, Rhyacophila, 291
perdita, Hydroptila, 145, 147, **153**, 296
perforatus, Limnephilus, 192, 298
perjurus, Limnephilus, 299
perna, Triaenodes, 246, 247, **250**, 253, 302
perplexa, Hydroptila, 296
perplexa, Pycnopsyche, 299
perplexus nordus, Athripsodes, 232, 301
perpusillus, Limnephilus, 298
persimilis, Oecetina, 243, 301
persimilis, Oecetis, 237, **243**, 301
pettiti, Hydropsyche, 112, 294
phaeopa, Lype, 74
phalacris, Triaenodes, 246, **250**, 253, 302

phalerata, Hydropsyche, 15, 86, 91, 93, **102**, 294
Phanocelia, 179, **201**, 300
Phanopsyche, 258, 302
philo, Hydropsyche, 294
Philocasca, 299
Philopotamidae, 2, 3, 19, 22, 25, 27, **44**, 292
Phrixocoma, 141, 295
Phryganea, 162, 164, 166, **174**, 297
phryganea, Rhyacophila, 291
Phryganeidae, 2, 11, 20, 22, 26, 27, 28, **161**, 296
phryganoides, Arctopsyche, 293
Phryganomyia, 165, 296
Phylocentropus, 3, 51, 53, **54**, 292
piatrix, Hydropsyche, 88, 96, **97**, 294
pictilis, Mormonia, 302
pictipes, Leucotrichia, 9, **120**, 133, 271, 273, 295
pictipes, Orthotrichia, 120, 295
pictula, Apatania, 297
pictula, Radema, 297
piffardii, Leptocella, 301
piffardii, Setodes, 301
pilosa, Acronopsyche, 202, 300
pilosa, Parachiona, 297
pilosa, Phryganea, 257
pinaca, Cheumatopsyche, 294
pinatus, Agapetus, 269, 292
piroa, Helicopsyche, **289**, 303
pixi, Polycentropus, 59, 63, **66**, 293
placidus, Holocentropus, 54, 55, 293
placidus, Phylocentropus, 12, **55**, 56, 293
placoda, Hydropsyche, 91, 93, **103**, 294
plaga, Limnephilus, 299
planifrons, Desmotaulius, 298
planifrons, Limnephilus, 298
Platycentropus, 178, 179, **181**, 297
pleca, Lepidostoma, 302
Plectrocnemia, 52, 58
plectrus, Platycentropus, 297
plutonis, Namamyia, 300
plutonis, Wormaldia, 51, 292
pluviale, Lepidostoma, 302
pluviale, Olemira, 302
podager, Lepidostoma, 302
podager, Nosopus, 258, 302
Polycentropidae, 51
Polycentropus, 52, 53, 54, **58**, 293
polygrammaticum, Macronema, 117, 295
polygrammatum, Macronema, 117, 295
Polytrichia, 125, 126, 295
ponta, Mayatrichia, **278**, 279, 280, 296
postica, Neuronia, 173, 296
postica, Ptilostomis, 171, 172, **173**, 296
Potamyia, 3, 78, 80, 81, 82, **85**, 294
praecox, Grammotaulius, 297
praeterita, Grensia, 201, 299
praeteritus, Limnephilus, 201, 299
principalis, Prophryganea, 165
Pristosilo, 258, 302
prita, Psychoglypha, 299
pritus, Glyphopsyche, 299
productus, Limnephilus, 298
prominens, Arcadopsyche, 259, 302

prominens, Lepidostoma, 302
Prophryganea, 165, 296
protera, Hydroptila, 296
protis, Hydropsyche, 294
Protoptila, 30, 31, 39, **41**, 292
Pseudogoera, 256, **258**, 302
Psiloneura, 303
Psilotreta, 209, **285**, 300
Psychoglypha, 180, **201**, 299
Psychomyia, 51, 52, 53, 54, **75**, 293
Psychomyiidae, 2, 3, 11, 19, 22, 26, 29, **51**, 292
Psychoronia, 300
Ptilostomis, 163, 164, 165, **171**, 296
pudicus, Limnephilus, 192, 299
pulchella, Psychomyia, 75, 293
pulchellus, Limnephilus, 298
pulchellus, Neophylax, 300
pullata, Beraea, 208
punctatissimus, Caborius, **197**, 198, 299
punctatissimus, Halesus, 196, 197, 299
punctatus, Athripsodes, 223, 227, **234**, 235, 236, 301
punctatus, Mystacides, 234, 301
punctella, Setodes, 256
Pycnopsyche, 6, 177, 178, 181, **193**, 299
pyraloides, Anisocentropus, 209, 300
pyraloides, Notidobia, 300
pyroxum, Glossosoma, 292

                    Q

quadrifasciata, Phryganea, 255, 302
quadrinotata, Anabolia, 297
quadrinotatus, Dicosmoecus, 181, 297
quaeris, Colpotaulius, 298
quaeris, Limnephilus, 298
Quaria, 236, 301
quercina, Lepidostoma, 302
Quissa, 75, 293

                    R

rabilis, Phylocentropus, 293
Radema, 179, **181**, 297
radiata, Phryganea, 181, 297
radiatus, Platycentropus, **181**, 297
rainieri, Farula, 300
rayneri, Lepidostoma, 302
reciproca, Hydropsyche, 294
reciproca, Philopotamus, 294
recurvata, Hydropsyche, 10, 14, 87, 91, 96, **99**, 294
recurvatus, Leptocerus, 232, 301
redmani, Neuronia, 296
Regina, 168, 296
regina, Neuronia, 168
remotus, Polycentropus, 12, 59, 61, 64, **67**, 293
renoa, Algonquina, 297
renoa, Allomyia, 297
resurgens, Athripsodes, 10, 223, 227, **230**, 231, 235, 236, 301
resurgens, Leptocerus, 230, 301
retactus, Athripsodes, 301

retactus, Leptocerus, 301
reticulata, Phryganea, 167
rhaeus, Colpotaulius, 298
Rheophylax, 185, 297
rho, Limnephilus, 298
rhombica, Phryganea, 190, 298
rhombicus, Limnephilus, 8, 14, 185, 186, 189, **190**, 298
Rhyacophila, 2, 4, 19, 30, 31, **32**, 38, 291
Rhyacophilidae, 2, 6, 16, 19, 20, 22, 25, 28, **30**, 291
Rhyacophilinae, 30, **31**
Rhyacophylax, 294
rickeri, Neophylax, 300
riegeli, Neotrichia, 7, 154, 156, 158, **159**, 160, 296
riesi, Ochrotrichia, 8, 126, 127, 129, **132**, 295
rillus, Limnephilus, 298
riola, Hydropsyche, 294
roafi, Atomyia, 302
roafi, Lepidostoma, 302
roberti, Limnephilus, 298
robusta, Cheumatopsyche, 295
robusta, Hydropsyche, 295
rohweri, Limnephilus, 298
rono, Hydroptila, 295
rossi, Agapetus, 292
rotunda, Rhyacophila, 291
rotundatus, Limnephilus, 298
rotundatus, Palaeagapetus, 38
rualda, Mayatrichia, 278
rufa, Molanna, 300
rufa, Psilotreta, **286**, 300
rusticum, Dasystoma, 261, 303
rusticum, Micrasema, **261**, 303
ruthae, Oligophlebodes, 283, **285**, 300

S

saccus, Athripsodes, 223, 227, **234**, 235, 301
sackeni, Agrypnia, 296
sackeni, Lepidostoma, 302
sackeni, Limnephilus, 298
sackeni, Mormomyia, 302
sagitta, Setodes, 242, 301
salmo, Hydroptila, 296
saltesea, Agraylea, 295
sansoni, Limnephilus, 298
sarita, Leucotrichia, 271, **274**, 295
sayi, Phryganea, 11, 12, 174, 175, **176**, 297
scabripennis, Limnephilus, 193, 196, 299
scabripennis, Pycnopsyche, 196, 299
scala, Oecetis, 236, 237, **241**, 301
scalaris, Hydropsyche, 91, 95, **106**, 294
Schizopelex, 266, 303
scissum, Micrasema, 303
scolops, Hydroptila, 145, **152**, 296
scylla, Ecclisomyia, 300
secludens, Limnephilus, 299
selina, Banksiola, 11, 162, 165, **169**, 170, 296
semata, Goerita, 258, 302
semifasciata, Phryganea, 173, 296
semifasciata, Ptilostomis, 171, 172, **173**, 296
separata, Hydropsyche, 294

sepulchralis, Leptocerus, 254, 302
sepulchralis, Mystacides, 11, 253, **254**, 255, 302
sericeus, Limnephilus, 186, 189, **192**, 298
sericeus, Phryganea, 192, 298
Sericostoma, 266, 303
Sericostomatidae, 2, 19, 20, 22, 26, 29, 176, **266**, 303
serrata, Oxyethira, 133, **136**, 295
Setodes, 210, 212, **256**, 302
Setodina, 236, 301
shawnee, Dolophilus, 7, 15, 45, **46**, 47, 292
shawnee, Ochrotrichia, 7, 126, 129, **131**, 295
shawnee, Polytrichia, 131, 295
shoshone, Apatania, 297
shoshone, Radema, 297
sibiricus, Grammotaulius, 297
sieboldi, Chilostigma, 199
sierra, Oligophlebodes, 283, **284**, 300
sigma, Oligophlebodes, 283, 284, 285, 300
signata, Allotrichia, 122, 295
signatus, Parachiona, 299
signatus, Pellopsyche, 294
signatus, Polycentropus, 58, 293
signatus, Rhyacophylax, 294
similis, Brachycentrus, 266, 303
similis, Pycnopsyche, 196, 299
simplex, Anabolia, 298
simplex, Limnephilus, 298
simulans, Hydropsyche, 5, 13, 87, 91, 95, **104**, 105, 106, 107, 294
simulans, Neuronia, 172, 174, 296
simulata, Ecclisomyia, 300
sinensis, Nyctiophylax, 69
singularis, Pseudogoera, 258, 302
sinuatus, Neophylax, 300
sitchensis, Limnephilus, 299
slossonae, Athripsodes, 301
slossonae, Hydropsyche, 8, 14, 87, 88, 96, **99**, 294
slossonae, Neophylax, 300
Smicridea, 78, 79, 81, **85**, 294
smithi, Banksiola, 296
smithi, Neuronia, 296
socia, Chimarra, 49, 50, **51**, 292
solex, Hydropsyche, **271**, 294
sonora, Neotrichia, **277**, 296
sonso, Pycnopsyche, 299
sonso, Stenophylax, 299
sordida, Anabolia, 189, 298
sordida, Cheumatopsyche, 14, 108, **110**, 294
sordida, Hydropsyche, 110, 294
sordidus, Limnephilus, 186, **189**, 298
sorex, Radema, 297
soror, Rhyacophila, 291
sparna, Hydropsyche, 88, 96, **97**, 102, 294
sparsa, Hydroptila, 141
sparsus, Drusinus, 300
sparsus, Halesus, 300
spatulata, Hydroptila, 141, 142, 147, **148**, 295
species 1, Holocentropus, 69
species 3, Hydropsyche, 102
species a, Athripsodes, 221, **235**
species a, Leptocella, 215, **221**

species a, Oecetis, 237, **244**
species a, Polycentropus, 63, **66**
species a, Triaenodes, 249, **253**
species b, Athripsodes, 221, **235**
species b, Oecetis, 237, **244**
species b, Triaenodes, 245, **253**
species c, Athripsodes 221, **235**, 236
speciosa, Cheumatopsyche, 108, 110, **114**, 294
speciosa, Hydropsyche, 114, 294
sperryae, Clostoeca, 299
sperryi, Limnephilus, 298
sperryi, Rhadicoleptus, 298
Sphinctogaster, 263, 303
sphyra, Oecetis, 301
spicata, Cernotina 72. **73**, 293
spiloma, Leptocella, 216, 217, **219**, 301
spinatus, Limnephilus, 299
spinosa, Ochrotrichia, 8, 126, 127, 129, **132**, 133, 295
spinosa, Polytrichia, 132, 295
sprulesi, Micrasema, 303
squamulosum, Lepidostoma, 258
Stactobia, 124
stehri, Leptocerus, 302
stehri, Setodes, 302
Stenophylax, 299
stigma, Lepidostoma, 303
stigmatella, Phryganea, 297
stigmatella, Radema, 297
stigmatica, Leptocella, 220, 301
stigmatica, Rhyacophila, 291
stigmaticus, Athripsodes, 301
stigmaticus, Leptocerus, 301
stipatus, Limnephilus, 299
stolus, Neophylax, 205, 300
straminea, Agrypnia, 162, **165**, 166, 296
strepha, Hydroptila, 296
strophis, Lepidostoma, 302
strotus, Dolophilus, 292
stygipes, Neuronia, 168, 296
stylata, Goera, 257, 302
stylata, Ochrotrichia, 131, 295
stylata, Polytrichia, 295
subborealis, Chilostigma, 299
subborealis, Psychoglypha, 202, 299
subfasciata, Phryganea, 193, 194, 299
subfasciata, Pycnopsyche, **194**, 195, 196, 299
subguttatus, Limnephilus, 191, 298
sublunatus, Limnephilus, 298
submacula, Athripsodes, 223, 227, **235**, 301
submaculus, Leptocerus, 235, 301
submonilifer, Limnephilus, 185, 186, **192**, 299
subnubilus, Brachycentrus, 263
subpunctulatus, Limnephilus, 299
swannanoa, Lepidostoma, 303

T

taenia, Triaenodes, 302
taloga, Limnephilus, 299
tana, Hydropsyche, 294
tarda, Triaenodes, 11, 245, 247, 249, **250**, 251, 252, 253, 302
taronus, Limnephilus, 298

tarsalis, Colpotaulius, 299
tarsalis, Hydroptila, 130, 295
tarsalis, Limnephilus, 299
tarsalis, Ochrotrichia, 126, 128, **130**, 131, 295
tarsi-punctatus, Athripsodes, 11, 223, 227, 229, 230, 301
tarsi-punctatus, Leptocerus, 229, 301
Tascobia, 119, **124**, 295
tavara, Leptocella, **287**, 301
taylori, Halesochila, 299
taylori, Halesus, 299
teddyi, Rhyacophila, 291
tehamia, Colpotaulius, 299
tenanga, Ochrotrichia, 275
tenebrosa, Hydroptila, 43, 292
tenebrosa, Protoptila, 42, **43**, 292
terminata, Rhyacophila, 291
tersus, Limnephilus, 298
texana, Chimarra, 292
texana, Leptocella, 219, 301
Theliopsyche, 258, **260**, 303
thoracica, Protoptila, 292
thorus, Limnephilus, 298
Thya, 208, 300
tibialis, Lepidostoma, 302
tibialis, Neuropsyche, 259, 302
tineoides, Hydroptila, 141
Tinodes, 51, 293
togatum, Lepidostoma, 302
togatum, Mormonia. 258 302
tomus, Agapetus. 292
tortosa. Hydroptila, 295
torva, Rhyacophila, 291
transversa, Hydropsyche, 117, 295
transversum, Macronemum, 15, 115, **117**, 295
transversus, Athripsodes, 5, 223, 227, **233**, 234, 301
transversus, Hydroptila, 296
transversus, Leptocerus, 233, 301
traviatum, Glossosoma, 292
Trentonius, 44, 45, **47**, 292
Triaenodella, 244, 302
Triaenodes, 2, 6, 210, 211, **244**, 302
tridonta, Triaenodes, 302
trimaculatus, Limnephilus, 299
tripunctata, Allomyia, 297
tripunctata, Apatania, 297
tripunctata, Atopsyche, 292
tristis, Asynarchus, 297
tristis, Dicosmoecus, 297
tryphena, Molanna, 8, 206, **207**, 300

U

ulla, Psychoglypha, 299
ullus, Glyphopsyche, 299
ulmeri, Dampfitrichia, 133, 295
ulmeri, Oxyethira, 295
uncus, Nyctiophylax, **70**, 293
unica, Eomystra, 292
unicolor, Anabolia, 297
unicolor, Dicosmoecus, 297
unicolor, Lepidostoma, 302
unicolor, Mormomyia, 302

uniformis, Drusinus, 8, **202**, 300
unimaculata, Rhyacophila, 291
unio, Ochrotrichia, 7, 126, 128, **129**, 130, 131, 132, 133, 274, 295
unio, Polytrichia, 129, 295
uniophila, Molanna, 11, **206**, 207, 208, 300
utahensis, Chimarra, 269, 292
uvalo, Athripsodes, 234, 301
uwarowii, Leptocella, 221, 301
uwarowii, Mystacides, 213, 220, 301

V

vaccua, Rhyacophila, 291
vaefes, Rhyacophila, 291
vagrita, Rhyacophila, 291
vala, Hydroptila, 7, 142, 147, **148**, 276, 277, 295
valanis, Hydropsyche, 6, 91, 95, **105**, 294
validus, Neureclipsis, 56, 57, **58**, 293
validus, Polycentropus, 58, 293
valuma, Rhyacophila, 291
vanus, Leptocerus, 232, 301
vao, Rhyacophila, 291
variegatus, Leptocerus, 230, 231, 301
variegatus, Polycentropus, 293
vastus, Limnephilus, 298
vedra, Rhyacophila, 291
velona, Glossosoma, 292
vemna, Rhyacophila, 291
venada, Hydropsyche, 294
ventrale, Glossosoma, 292
ventura, Hydropsyche, 294
venularis, Hydropsyche, 294
vepulsa, Rhyacophila, 291
verdona, Glossosoma, 292
verna, Oxyethira, 135, **139**, 295
vernalis, Lepidostoma, 303
vernalis, Mormonia, 258, 303
vernalis, Setodes, 302
verrula, Rhyacophila, 291
vestita, Agrypnia, 11, 162, 165, **166**, 296
vestita, Neuronia, 165, 166, 296
vestita, Phryganea, 205
vestitus, Nyctiophylax, 6, **70**, 293
vestitus, Polycentropus, 70, 293
vetina, Rhyacophila, 291
vexa, Hydropsyche, 88, 96, **97**, 294
vibox, Rhyacophila, 8, 32, 34, 35, **36**, 291
vibrans, Neotrichia, 156, 157, **159**, 296
vigilatrix, Polycentropus, 293
viminalis, Oxyethira, 137, 295
vinura, Rhyacophila, 291

viquaea, Rhyacophila, 291
vireo, Agapetus, 292
virgata, Hydroptila, 7, 142, 147, **148**, 295
virginicus, Drusinus, 202, 300
virginicus, Potamorites, 300
viridiventris, Phryganea, 292
viridiventris, Protoptila, 292
visor, Rhyacophila, 291
vobara, Rhyacophila, 291
vocala, Rhyacophila, 291
vofixa, Rhyacophila, 268, 291
vohrna, Rhyacophila, 291
vorhiesi, Triaenodes, 250, 302
vu, Rhyacophila, 291
vujuna, Rhyacophila, 291
vulgaris, Rhyacophila, 32
vulgata, Rhyacophila, 32
vuphipes, Rhyacophila, 291
vuzana, Rhyacophila, 291

W

walkeri, Hydropsyche, 87, 93, **96**, 97, 294
walkeri, Agapetus, 292
walkeri, Synagapetus, 292
waskesia, Hydroptila, **276**, 296
wataga, Micrasema, 262, 303
waubesiana, Hydroptila, 142, 147, **150**, 296
weddleae, Ochrotrichia, **274**, 295
wetzeli, Athripsodes, 301
wisconsinensis, Lepidostoma, 258, 302

X

xella, Hydroptila, 142, 145, **148**, 295
xena, Ochrotrichia, 126, 128, **130**, 274, 275, 295
xena, Polytrichia, 130, 295
xera, Hydroptila, 296
xoncla, Hydroptila, 296

Y

Ylodes, 244, 302
Ymymia, 212, 301
Yrula, 236, 301

Z

Zaporota, 299
zebratum, Macronema, 115, 295
zebratum, Macronemum, **115**, 116, 295
zernyi, Cyrnellus, 71, 293
zeronia, Oxyethira, 135, **139**, 295